C# 4.0:
The Complete Reference

About the Author

Herbert Schildt is a leading authority on C#, C++, C, and Java. His programming books have sold millions of copies worldwide and have been translated into all major foreign languages. He is the author of numerous bestsellers, including *Java: The Complete Reference, C++: The Complete Reference,* and *C: The Complete Reference,* among many others. Although interested in all facets of computing, his primary focus is computer languages, including compilers, interpreters, and robotic control languages. He also has an active interest in the standardization of languages. Schildt holds both graduate and undergraduate degrees from the University of Illinois. He can be reached at his consulting office at (217) 586-4683. His web site is **www.HerbSchildt.com**.

About the Technical Editor

Michael Howard is a principal security program manager on the Trustworthy Computing (TwC) Group's Security Engineering team at Microsoft, where he is responsible for managing secure design, programming, and testing techniques across the company. Howard is an architect of the Security Development Lifecycle (SDL), a process for improving the security of Microsoft's software.

Howard began his career with Microsoft in 1992 at the company's New Zealand office, working for the first two years with Windows and compilers on the Product Support Services team and then with Microsoft Consulting Services, where he provided security infrastructure support to customers and assisted in the design of custom solutions and development of software. In 1997, Howard moved to the United States to work for the Windows division on Internet Information Services, Microsoft's next-generation web server, before moving to his current role in 2000.

Howard is an editor of *IEEE Security & Privacy,* a frequent speaker at security-related conferences, and he regularly publishes articles on secure coding and design. Howard is the co-author of six security books, including the award-winning *Writing Secure Code, 24 Deadly Sins of Software Security, The Security Development Lifecycle,* and his most recent release, *Writing Secure Code for Windows Vista.*

C# 4.0:
The Complete Reference

Herbert Schildt

New York   Chicago   San Francisco
Athens   London   Madrid
Mexico City   Milan   New Delhi
Singapore   Sydney   Toronto

Library of Congress Cataloging-in-Publication Data

Schildt, Herbert.
   C# 4.0 : the complete reference / Herbert Schildt.
      p. cm.
   ISBN 978-0-07-174116-3 (alk. paper)
  1. C# (Computer program language)   I. Title.
   QA76.73.C154S337   2010
   005.13'3--dc22

                  2010014885

McGraw-Hill Education books are available at special quantity discounts to use as premiums and sales promotions, or for use in corporate training programs. To contact a representative, please visit the Contact Us pages at www.mhprofessional.com.

C# 4.0: The Complete Reference

1234567890 DOC DOC 109876543210

ISBN   978-0-07-174116-3
MHID   0-07-174116-X

Sponsoring Editor	**Proofreader**
Jane K. Brownlow	Paul Tyler
Editorial Supervisor	**Indexer**
Patty Mon	Sheryl Schildt
Project Editor	**Production Supervisor**
LeeAnn Pickrell	Jean Bodeaux
Acquisitions Coordinator	**Composition**
Joya Anthony	Apollo Publishing
Technical Editor	**Illustration**
Michael Howard	Apollo Publishing
Copy Editor	**Art Director, Cover Designer**
LeeAnn Pickrell	Jeff Weeks

Contents at a Glance

Contents

Special Thanks

Special thanks go to Michael Howard for his excellent technical edit of this book. His insights, suggestions, and advice were of great value.

Preface

We programmers are a demanding bunch, always looking for ways to improve the performance, efficiency, and portability of our programs. We also demand much from the tools we use, especially when it comes to programming languages. There are many programming languages, but only a few are great. A great programming language must be powerful, yet flexible. Its syntax must be terse, yet clear. It must facilitate the creation of correct code while not getting in our way. It must support state-of-the-art features, but not trendy dead ends. Finally, a great programming language must have one more, almost intangible quality: It must feel right when we use it. C# is such a language.

Created by Microsoft to support its .NET Framework, C# builds on a rich programming heritage. Its chief architect was long-time programming guru Anders Hejlsberg. C# is directly descended from two of the world's most successful computer languages: C and C++. From C, it derives its syntax, many of its keywords, and most of its operators. It builds upon and improves the object model defined by C++. C# is also closely related to another very successful language: Java.

Sharing a common ancestry, but differing in many important ways, C# and Java are more like cousins. Both support distributed programming and both use intermediate code to achieve safety and portability, but the details differ. They both also provide a significant amount of runtime error checking, security, and managed execution, but again, the details differ. However, unlike Java, C# also gives you access to pointers—a feature supported by C++. Thus, C# combines the raw power of C++ with the type safety of Java. Furthermore, the trade-offs between power and safety are carefully balanced and are nearly transparent.

Throughout the history of computing, programming languages have evolved to accommodate changes in the computing environment, advances in computer language theory, and new ways of thinking about and approaching the job of programming. C# is no exception. In the ongoing process of refinement, adaptation, and innovation, C# has demonstrated its ability to respond rapidly to the changing needs of the programmer. This fact is testified to by the many new features added to C# since its initial 1.0 release in 2000. Consider the following.

The first major revision of C# was version 2.0. It added several features that made it easier for programmers to write more resilient, reliable, and nimble code. Without question, the most important 2.0 addition was generics. Through the use of generics, it became possible to create type-safe, reusable code in C#. Thus, the addition of generics fundamentally expanded the power and scope of the language.

The second major revision was version 3.0. It is not an exaggeration to say that 3.0 added features that redefined the very core of C#, raising the bar in computer language development in the process. Of its many innovative features, two stand out: LINQ and lambda expressions. LINQ, which stands for Language Integrated Query, enables you to create database-style queries by using elements of the C# language. Lambda expressions implement a functional-style syntax that uses the => lambda operator, and lambda expressions are frequently used in LINQ expressions.

The third major revision is C# 4.0, and this is the version described in this book. It builds upon the previous releases by providing a number of new features that streamline common programming tasks. For example, it adds named and optional arguments. These make some types of method calls more convenient. It adds the **dynamic** keyword, which facilitates the use of C# in situations in which a data type is obtained at runtime, such as when interfacing to COM or when using reflection. The covariance and contravariance features already supported by C# have been expanded for use with type parameters. Through enhancements to the .NET Framework (which is C#'s library), support for parallel programming is provided by the Task Parallel Library (TPL) and by Parallel LINQ (PLINQ). These subsystems make it easy to create code that automatically scales to better utilize multicore computers. Thus, with the release of 4.0, C# is ready to take advantage of high-performance computing platforms.

Because of its ability to adapt rapidly to the changing demands of the programming landscape, C# has remained a vibrant and innovative language. As a result, it defines one of the most powerful, feature-rich languages in modern computing. It is also a language that no programmer can afford to ignore. This book is designed to help you master it.

What's Inside

This book describes C# 4.0. It is divided into two parts. Part I provides a comprehensive discussion of the C# language, including the new features added by version 4.0. This is the largest part in the book, and it describes the keywords, syntax, and features that define the language. I/O, file handling, reflection, and the preprocessor are also discussed in Part I.

Part II explores the C# class library, which is the .NET Framework class library. This library is huge! Because of space limitations, it is not possible to cover the entire .NET Framework class library in one book. Instead, Part II focuses on the core library, which is contained in the **System** namespace. Also covered are collections, multithreading, the Task Parallel Library and PLINQ, and networking. These are the parts of the library that nearly every C# programmer will use.

A Book for All Programmers

This book does not require any previous programming experience. If you already know C++ or Java, you will be able to advance quite rapidly because C# has much in common with those languages. If you don't have any previous programming experience, you will still be able learn C# from this book, but you will need to work carefully through the examples in each chapter.

Required Software

To compile and run C# 4.0 programs, you must use Visual Studio 2010 or later.

Don't Forget: Code on the Web

Remember, the source code for all of the programs in this book is available free-of-charge on the Web at **www.mhprofessional.com**.

For Further Study

C# 4.0: The Complete Reference is your gateway to the Herb Schildt series of programming books. Here are some others that you will find of interest.

To learn about Java programming, we recommend the following:

Java: The Complete Reference

Java: A Beginner's Guide

Swing: A Beginner's Guide

The Art of Java

Herb Schildt's Java Programming Cookbook

To learn about C++, you will find these books especially helpful:

C++: The Complete Reference

C++: A Beginner's Guide

C++ From the Ground Up

STL Programming From the Ground Up

The Art of C++

Herb Schildt's C++ Programming Cookbook

If you want to learn more about the C language, the foundation of all modern programming, the following title will be of interest:

C: The Complete Reference

When you need solid answers, fast, turn to Herbert Schildt, the recognized authority on programming.

The C# Language

Part 1 discusses the elements of the C# language, including its keywords, syntax, and operators. Also described are several foundational C# techniques, such as using I/O and reflection, which are tightly linked with the C# language.

The Creation of C#

C# is Microsoft's premier language for .NET development. It leverages time-tested features with cutting-edge innovations and provides a highly usable, efficient way to write programs for the modern enterprise computing environment. It is, by any measure, one of the most important languages of the twenty-first century.

The purpose of this chapter is to place C# into its historical context, including the forces that drove its creation, its design philosophy, and how it was influenced by other computer languages. This chapter also explains how C# relates to the .NET Framework. As you will see, C# and the .NET Framework work together to create a highly refined programming environment.

C#'s Family Tree

Computer languages do not exist in a void. Rather, they relate to one another, with each new language influenced in one form or another by the ones that came before. In a process akin to cross-pollination, features from one language are adapted by another, a new innovation is integrated into an existing context, or an older construct is removed. In this way, languages evolve and the art of programming advances. C# is no exception.

C# inherits a rich programming legacy. It is directly descended from two of the world's most successful computer languages: C and C++. It is closely related to another: Java. Understanding the nature of these relationships is crucial to understanding C#. Thus, we begin our examination of C# by placing it in the historical context of these three languages.

C: The Beginning of the Modern Age of Programming

The creation of C marks the beginning of the modern age of programming. C was invented by Dennis Ritchie in the 1970s on a DEC PDP-11 that used the UNIX operating system. While some earlier languages, most notably Pascal, had achieved significant success, it was C that established the paradigm that still charts the course of programming today.

C grew out of the *structured programming* revolution of the 1960s. Prior to structured programming, large programs were difficult to write because the program logic tended to degenerate into what is known as "spaghetti code," a tangled mass of jumps, calls, and returns that is difficult to follow. Structured languages addressed this problem by adding well-defined control statements, subroutines with local variables, and other improvements. Through the use of structured techniques programs became better organized, more reliable, and easier to manage.

3

Although there were other structured languages at the time, C was the first to successfully combine power, elegance, and expressiveness. Its terse, yet easy-to-use syntax coupled with its philosophy that the programmer (not the language) was in charge quickly won many converts. It can be a bit hard to understand from today's perspective, but C was a breath of fresh air that programmers had long awaited. As a result, C became the most widely used structured programming language of the 1980s.

However, even the venerable C language had its limits. One of the most troublesome was its inability to handle large programs. The C language hits a barrier once a project reaches a certain size, and after that point, C programs are difficult to understand and maintain. Precisely where this limit is reached depends upon the program, the programmer, and the tools at hand, but there is always a threshold beyond which a C program becomes unmanageable.

The Creation of OOP and C++

By the late 1970s, the size of many projects was near or at the limits of what structured programming methodologies and the C language could handle. To solve this problem, a new way to program began to emerge. This method is called *object-oriented programming* (OOP). Using OOP, a programmer could handle much larger programs. The trouble was that C, the most popular language at the time, did not support object-oriented programming. The desire for an object-oriented version of C ultimately led to the creation of C++.

C++ was invented by Bjarne Stroustrup beginning in 1979 at Bell Laboratories in Murray Hill, New Jersey. He initially called the new language "C with Classes." However, in 1983 the name was changed to C++. C++ contains the entire C language. Thus, C is the foundation upon which C++ is built. Most of the additions that Stroustrup made to C were designed to support object-oriented programming. In essence, C++ is the object-oriented version of C. By building upon the foundation of C, Stroustrup provided a smooth migration path to OOP. Instead of having to learn an entirely new language, a C programmer needed to learn only a few new features before reaping the benefits of the object-oriented methodology.

C++ simmered in the background during much of the 1980s, undergoing extensive development. By the beginning of the 1990s, C++ was ready for mainstream use, and its popularity exploded. By the end of the decade, it had become the most widely used programming language. Today, C++ is still the preeminent language for the development of high-performance system code.

It is critical to understand that the invention of C++ was not an attempt to create an entirely new programming language. Instead, it was an enhancement to an already highly successful language. This approach to language development—beginning with an existing language and moving it forward—established a trend that continues today.

The Internet and Java Emerge

The next major advance in programming languages is Java. Work on Java, which was originally called Oak, began in 1991 at Sun Microsystems. The main driving force behind Java's design was James Gosling. Patrick Naughton, Chris Warth, Ed Frank, and Mike Sheridan also played a role.

Java is a structured, object-oriented language with a syntax and philosophy derived from C++. The innovative aspects of Java were driven not so much by advances in the art of programming (although some certainly were), but rather by changes in the computing environment. Prior to the mainstreaming of the Internet, most programs were written, compiled, and targeted for a specific CPU and a specific operating system. While it has always been true that programmers like to reuse their code, the ability to port a program easily from one environment to another took a backseat to more pressing problems. However, with the rise of the Internet, in which many different types of CPUs and operating systems are connected, the old problem of portability reemerged with a vengeance. To solve the problem of portability, a new language was needed, and this new language was Java.

Although the single most important aspect of Java (and the reason for its rapid acceptance) is its ability to create cross-platform, portable code, it is interesting to note that the original impetus for Java was not the Internet, but rather the need for a platform-independent language that could be used to create software for embedded controllers. In 1993, it became clear that the issues of cross-platform portability found when creating code for embedded controllers are also encountered when attempting to create code for the Internet. Remember: the Internet is a vast, distributed computing universe in which many different types of computers live. The same techniques that solved the portability problem on a small scale could be applied to the Internet on a large scale.

Java achieved portability by translating a program's source code into an intermediate language called *bytecode*. This bytecode was then executed by the Java Virtual Machine (JVM). Therefore, a Java program could run in any environment for which a JVM was available. Also, since the JVM is relatively easy to implement, it was readily available for a large number of environments.

Java's use of bytecode differed radically from both C and C++, which were nearly always compiled to executable machine code. Machine code is tied to a specific CPU and operating system. Thus, if you wanted to run a C/C++ program on a different system, it needed to be recompiled to machine code specifically for that environment. Therefore, to create a C/C++ program that would run in a variety of environments, several different executable versions of the program would be needed. Not only was this impractical, it was expensive. Java's use of an intermediate language was an elegant, cost-effective solution. It is also a solution that C# would adapt for its own purposes.

As mentioned, Java is descended from C and C++. Its syntax is based on C, and its object model is evolved from C++. Although Java code is neither upwardly nor downwardly compatible with C or C++, its syntax is sufficiently similar that the large pool of existing C/C++ programmers could move to Java with very little effort. Furthermore, because Java built upon and improved an existing paradigm, Gosling, et al., were free to focus their attentions on the new and innovative features. Just as Stroustrup did not need to "reinvent the wheel" when creating C++, Gosling did not need to create an entirely new language when developing Java. Moreover, with the creation of Java, C and C++ became an accepted substrata upon which to base a new computer language.

The Creation of C#

While Java successfully addresses many of the issues surrounding portability in the Internet environment, there are still features that it lacks. One is *cross-language interoperability*, also called *mixed-language programming*. This is the ability for the code produced by one language to work easily with the code produced by another. Cross-language interoperability is needed for the creation of large, distributed software systems. It is also desirable for programming software components because the most valuable component is one that can be used by the widest variety of computer languages, in the greatest number of operating environments.

Another feature lacking in Java is full integration with the Windows platform. Although Java programs can be executed in a Windows environment (assuming that the Java Virtual Machine has been installed), Java and Windows are not closely coupled. Since Windows is the mostly widely used operating system in the world, lack of direct support for Windows is a drawback to Java.

To answer these and other needs, Microsoft developed C#. C# was created at Microsoft late in the 1990s and was part of Microsoft's overall .NET strategy. It was first released in its alpha version in the middle of 2000. C#'s chief architect was Anders Hejlsberg. Hejlsberg is one of the world's leading language experts, with several notable accomplishments to his credit. For example, in the 1980s he was the original author of the highly successful and influential Turbo Pascal, whose streamlined implementation set the standard for all future compilers.

C# is directly related to C, C++, and Java. This is not by accident. These are three of the most widely used—and most widely liked—programming languages in the world. Furthermore, at the time of C#'s creation, nearly all professional programmers knew C, C++, and/or Java. By building C# upon a solid, well-understood foundation, C# offered an easy migration path from these languages. Since it was neither necessary nor desirable for Hejlsberg to "reinvent the wheel," he was free to focus on specific improvements and innovations.

The family tree for C# is shown in Figure 1-1. The grandfather of C# is C. From C, C# derives its syntax, many of its keywords, and its operators. C# builds upon and improves the object model defined by C++. If you know C or C++, then you will feel at home with C#.

C# and Java have a bit more complicated relationship. As explained, Java is also descended from C and C++. It too shares the C/C++ syntax and object model. Like Java, C# is designed to produce portable code. However, C# is not descended from Java. Instead, C# and Java are more like cousins, sharing a common ancestry, but differing in many important ways. The good news, though, is that if you know Java, then many C# concepts will be familiar. Conversely, if in the future you need to learn Java, then many of the things you learn about C# will carry over.

FIGURE 1-1
The C# family tree

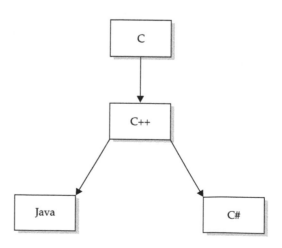

C# contains many innovative features that we will examine at length throughout the course of this book, but some of its most important relate to its built-in support for software components. In fact, C# has been characterized as being a component-oriented language because it contains integral support for the writing of software components. For example, C# includes features that directly support the constituents of components, such as properties, methods, and events. However, C#'s ability to work in a secure, mixed-language environment is perhaps its most important component-oriented feature.

The Evolution of C#

Since its original 1.0 release, C# has been evolving at a rapid pace. Not long after C# 1.0, Microsoft released version 1.1. It contained many minor tweaks but added no major features. However, the situation was much different with the release of C# 2.0.

C# 2.0 was a watershed event in the lifecycle of C# because it added many new features, such as generics, partial types, and anonymous methods, that fundamentally expanded the scope, power, and range of the language. Version 2.0 firmly put C# at the forefront of computer language development. It also demonstrated Microsoft's long-term commitment to the language.

The next major release of C# was 3.0. Because of the many new features added by C# 2.0, one might have expected the development of C# to slow a bit, just to let programmers catch up, but this was not the case. With the release of C# 3.0, Microsoft once again put C# on the cutting edge of language design, this time adding a set of innovative features that redefined the programming landscape. These include lambda expressions, language-integrated query (LINQ), extension methods, and implicitly typed variables, among others. Although all of the new 3.0 features were important, the two that had the most high-profile impact on the language were LINQ and lambda expressions. They added a completely new dimension to C# and further emphasized its lead in the ongoing evolution of computer languages.

The current release is C# 4.0, and that is the version of C# described by this book. C# 4.0 builds on the strong foundation established by the previous three major releases, adding several new features. Perhaps the most important are named and optional arguments. Named arguments let you link an argument with a parameter by name. Optional arguments give you a way to specify a default argument for a parameter. Another important new feature is the **dynamic** type, which is used to declare objects that are type-checked at runtime, rather than compile time. Covariance and contravariance support is also provided for type parameters, which are supported by new uses of the **in** and **out** keywords. For those programmers using the Office Automation APIs (and COM in general), access has been simplified. (Office Automation and COM are outside the scope of this book). In general, the new 4.0 features further streamline coding and improve the usability of C#.

There is another major feature that relates directly to C# 4.0 programming, but which is provided by the .NET Framework 4.0. This is support for parallel programming through two major new features. The first is the Task Parallel Library (TPL) and the second is Parallel LINQ (PLINQ). Both of these dramatically enhance and simplify the process of creating programs that use concurrency. Both also make it easier to create multithreaded code that automatically scales to utilize the number of processors available in the computer. Put directly, multicore computers are becoming commonplace, and the ability to parallelize your code to take advantage of them is an increasingly important part of nearly every C# programmer's job description. Because of the significant impact the TPL and PLINQ are having on programming, both are covered in this book.

How C# Relates to the .NET Framework

Although C# is a computer language that can be studied on its own, it has a special relationship to its runtime environment, the .NET Framework. The reason for this is twofold. First, C# was initially designed by Microsoft to create code for the .NET Framework. Second, the libraries used by C# are the ones defined by the .NET Framework. Thus, even though it is theoretically possible to separate C# the language from the .NET environment, the two are closely linked. Because of this, it is important to have a general understanding of the .NET Framework and why it is important to C#.

What Is the .NET Framework?

The .NET Framework defines an environment that supports the development and execution of highly distributed, component-based applications. It enables differing computer languages to work together and provides for security, program portability, and a common programming model for the Windows platform. As it relates to C#, the .NET Framework defines two very important entities. The first is the *Common Language Runtime* (CLR). This is the system that manages the execution of your program. Along with other benefits, the Common Language Runtime is the part of the .NET Framework that enables programs to be portable, supports mixed-language programming, and provides for secure execution.

The second entity is the .NET *class library*. This library gives your program access to the runtime environment. For example, if you want to perform I/O, such as displaying something on the screen, you will use the .NET class library to do it. If you are new to programming, then the term *class* may be new. Although it is explained in detail later in this book, for now a brief definition will suffice: a class is an object-oriented construct that helps organize programs. As long as your program restricts itself to the features defined by the .NET class library, your programs can run anywhere that the .NET runtime system is supported. Since C# automatically uses the .NET Framework class library, C# programs are automatically portable to all .NET environments.

How the Common Language Runtime Works

The Common Language Runtime manages the execution of .NET code. Here is how it works: When you compile a C# program, the output of the compiler is not executable code. Instead, it is a file that contains a special type of pseudocode called *Microsoft Intermediate Language* (MSIL). MSIL defines a set of portable instructions that are independent of any specific CPU. In essence, MSIL defines a portable assembly language. One other point: although MSIL is similar in concept to Java's bytecode, the two are not the same.

It is the job of the CLR to translate the intermediate code into executable code when a program is run. Thus, any program compiled to MSIL can be run in any environment for which the CLR is implemented. This is part of how the .NET Framework achieves portability.

Microsoft Intermediate Language is turned into executable code using a *JIT compiler.* "JIT" stands for "Just-In-Time." The process works like this: When a .NET program is executed, the CLR activates the JIT compiler. The JIT compiler converts MSIL into native code on demand as each part of your program is needed. Thus, your C# program actually executes as native code even though it is initially compiled into MSIL. This means that your program runs nearly as fast as it would if it had been compiled to native code in the first place, but it gains the portability benefits of MSIL. Also, during compilation, code verification takes place to ensure type safety (unless a security policy has been established that avoids this step).

In addition to MSIL, one other thing is output when you compile a C# program: *metadata*. Metadata describes the data used by your program and enables your code to interact easily with other code. The metadata is contained in the same file as the MSIL.

Managed vs. Unmanaged Code

In general, when you write a C# program, you are creating what is called *managed code*. Managed code is executed under the control of the Common Language Runtime, as just described. Because it is running under the control of the CLR, managed code is subject to certain constraints—and derives several benefits. The constraints are easily described and met: the compiler must produce an MSIL file targeted for the CLR (which C# does) and use the .NET class library (which C# does). The benefits of managed code are many, including modern memory management, the ability to mix languages, better security, support for version control, and a clean way for software components to interact.

The opposite of managed code is unmanaged code. Unmanaged code does not execute under the Common Language Runtime. Thus, Windows programs prior to the creation of the .NET Framework use unmanaged code. It is possible for managed code and unmanaged code to work together, so the fact that C# generates managed code does not restrict its ability to operate in conjunction with preexisting programs.

The Common Language Specification

Although all managed code gains the benefits provided by the CLR, if your code will be used by other programs written in different languages, then, for maximum usability, it should adhere to the *Common Language Specification* (CLS). The CLS describes a set of features that different .NET-compatible languages have in common. CLS compliance is especially important when creating software components that will be used by other languages. The CLS includes a subset of the *Common Type System* (CTS). The CTS defines the rules concerning data types. Of course, C# supports both the CLS and the CTS.

An Overview of C#

By far, the hardest thing about learning a programming language is the fact that no element exists in isolation. Instead, the components of the language work together. This interrelatedness makes it difficult to discuss one aspect of C# without involving another. To help overcome this problem, this chapter provides a brief overview of several C# features, including the general form of a C# program, some basic control statements, and operators. It does not go into too many details, but rather concentrates on the general concepts common to any C# program. Most of the topics discussed here are examined in greater detail in the remaining chapters of Part I.

Object-Oriented Programming

At the center of C# is *object-oriented programming* (OOP). The object-oriented methodology is inseparable from C#, and all C# programs are to at least some extent object oriented. Because of its importance to C#, it is useful to understand OOP's basic principles before you write even a simple C# program.

OOP is a powerful way to approach the job of programming. Programming methodologies have changed dramatically since the invention of the computer, primarily to accommodate the increasing complexity of programs. For example, when computers were first invented, programming was done by toggling in the binary machine instructions using the computer's front panel. As long as programs were just a few hundred instructions long, this approach worked. As programs grew, assembly language was invented so that a programmer could deal with larger, increasingly complex programs, using symbolic representations of the machine instructions. As programs continued to grow, high-level languages such as FORTRAN and COBOL were introduced that gave the programmer more tools with which to handle complexity. When these early languages began to reach their breaking point, structured programming languages, such as C, were invented.

At each milestone in the history of programming, techniques and tools were created to allow the programmer to deal with increasingly greater complexity. Each step of the way, the new approach took the best elements of the previous methods and moved forward. The same is true of object-oriented programming. Prior to OOP, many projects were nearing (or exceeding) the point where the structured approach no longer worked. A better way to handle complexity was needed, and object-oriented programming was the solution.

Object-oriented programming took the best ideas of structured programming and combined them with several new concepts. The result was a different and better way of organizing a program. In the most general sense, a program can be organized in one of two ways: around its code (what is happening) or around its data (what is being affected). Using only structured programming techniques, programs are typically organized around code. This approach can be thought of as "code acting on data."

Object-oriented programs work the other way around. They are organized around data, with the key principle being "data controlling access to code." In an object-oriented language, you define the data and the code that is permitted to act on that data. Thus, a data type defines precisely the operations that can be applied to that data.

To support the principles of object-oriented programming, all OOP languages, including C#, have three traits in common: encapsulation, polymorphism, and inheritance. Let's examine each.

Encapsulation

Encapsulation is a programming mechanism that binds together code and the data it manipulates, and that keeps both safe from outside interference and misuse. In an object-oriented language, code and data can be bound together in such a way that a self-contained *black box* is created. Within the box are all necessary data and code. When code and data are linked together in this fashion, an *object* is created. In other words, an object is the device that supports encapsulation.

Within an object, the code, data, or both may be *private* to that object or *public*. Private code or data is known to and accessible by only another part of the object. That is, private code or data cannot be accessed by a piece of the program that exists outside the object. When code or data is public, other parts of your program can access it even though it is defined within an object. Typically, the public parts of an object are used to provide a controlled interface to the private elements.

C#'s basic unit of encapsulation is the *class*. A class defines the form of an object. It specifies both the data and the code that will operate on that data. C# uses a class specification to construct *objects*. Objects are instances of a class. Thus, a class is essentially a set of plans that specify how to build an object.

Collectively, the code and data that constitute a class are called its *members*. The data defined by the class is referred to as *fields*. The terms *member variables* and *instance variables* also are used. The code that operates on that data is contained within *function members*, of which the most common is the *method*. Method is C#'s term for a subroutine. (Other function members include properties, events, and constructors.) Thus, the methods of a class contain code that acts on the fields defined by that class.

Polymorphism

Polymorphism (from Greek, meaning "many forms") is the quality that allows one interface to access a general class of actions. A simple example of polymorphism is found in the steering wheel of an automobile. The steering wheel (the interface) is the same no matter what type of actual steering mechanism is used. That is, the steering wheel works the same whether your car has manual steering, power steering, or rack-and-pinion steering. Thus, turning the steering wheel left causes the car to go left no matter what type of steering is used. The benefit of the uniform interface is, of course, that once you know how to operate the steering wheel, you can drive any type of car.

The same principle can also apply to programming. For example, consider a *stack* (which is a first-in, last-out list). You might have a program that requires three different types of stacks. One stack is used for integer values, one for floating-point values, and one for characters. In this case, the algorithm that implements each stack is the same, even though the data being stored differs. In a non-object-oriented language, you would be required to create three different sets of stack routines, with each set using different names. However, because of polymorphism, in C# you can create one general set of stack routines that works for all three specific situations. This way, once you know how to use one stack, you can use them all.

More generally, the concept of polymorphism is often expressed by the phrase "one interface, multiple methods." This means that it is possible to design a generic interface to a group of related activities. Polymorphism helps reduce complexity by allowing the same interface to be used to specify a *general class of action*. It is the compiler's job to select the *specific action* (that is, method) as it applies to each situation. You, the programmer, don't need to do this selection manually. You need only remember and utilize the general interface.

Inheritance

Inheritance is the process by which one object can acquire the properties of another object. This is important because it supports the concept of hierarchical classification. If you think about it, most knowledge is made manageable by hierarchical (that is, top-down) classifications. For example, a Red Delicious apple is part of the classification *apple,* which in turn is part of the *fruit* class, which is under the larger class *food.* That is, the *food* class possesses certain qualities (edible, nutritious, and so on) which also, logically, apply to its subclass, *fruit.* In addition to these qualities, the *fruit* class has specific characteristics (juicy, sweet, and so on) that distinguish it from other food. The *apple* class defines those qualities specific to an apple (grows on trees, not tropical, and so on). A Red Delicious apple would, in turn, inherit all the qualities of all preceding classes and would define only those qualities that make it unique.

Without the use of hierarchies, each object would have to explicitly define all of its characteristics. Using inheritance, an object need only define those qualities that make it unique within its class. It can inherit its general attributes from its parent. Thus, the inheritance mechanism makes it possible for one object to be a specific instance of a more general case.

A First Simple Program

It is now time to look at an actual C# program. We will begin by compiling and running the short program shown next.

```
/*
   This is a simple C# program.

   Call this program Example.cs.
*/

using System;

class Example {

  // A C# program begins with a call to Main().
  static void Main() {
    Console.WriteLine("A simple C# program.");
  }
}
```

The primary development environment for C# is Microsoft's Visual Studio. To compile all of the programs in this book, including those that use the new C# 4.0 features, you will need to use a version of Visual Studio 2010 (or later) that supports C#.

Using Visual Studio, there are two general approaches that you can take to creating, compiling, and running a C# program. First, you can use the Visual Studio IDE. Second, you can use the command-line compiler, **csc.exe**. Both methods are described here.

Using csc.exe, the C# Command-Line Compiler

Although the Visual Studio IDE is what you will probably be using for your commercial projects, some readers will find the C# command-line compiler more convenient, especially for compiling and running the sample programs shown in this book. The reason is that you don't have to create a project for the program. You can simply create the program and then compile it and run it—all from the command line. Therefore, if you know how to use the Command Prompt window and its command-line interface, using the command-line compiler will be faster and easier than using the IDE.

CAUTION *If you are not familiar with the Command Prompt window, then it is probably better to use the Visual Studio IDE. Although the Command Prompt is not difficult to master, trying to learn both the Command Prompt and C# at the same time will be a challenging experience.*

To create and run programs using the C# command-line compiler, follow these three steps:

1. Enter the program using a text editor.
2. Compile the program using **csc.exe**.
3. Run the program.

Entering the Program

The source code for programs shown in this book is available at **www.mhprofessional.com**. However, if you want to enter the programs by hand, you are free to do so. In this case, you must enter the program into your computer using a text editor, such as Notepad. Remember, you must create text-only files, not formatted word-processor files, because the format information in a word processor file will confuse the C# compiler. When entering the program, call the file **Example.cs**.

Compiling the Program

To compile the program, execute the C# compiler, **csc.exe**, specifying the name of the source file on the command line, as shown here:

```
C:\>csc Example.cs
```

The **csc** compiler creates a file called **Example.exe** that contains the MSIL version of the program. Although MSIL is not executable code, it is still contained in an **exe** file. The Common Language Runtime automatically invokes the JIT compiler when you attempt to execute **Example.exe**. Be aware, however, that if you try to execute **Example.exe** (or any other **exe** file that contains MSIL) on a computer for which the .NET Framework is not installed, the program will not execute because the CLR will be missing.

NOTE *Prior to running* **csc.exe** *you will need to open a Command Prompt window that is configured for Visual Studio. The easiest way to do this is to select Visual Studio Command Prompt under Visual Studio Tools in the Start menu. Alternatively, you can start an unconfigured Command Prompt window and then run the batch file* **vsvars32.bat**, *which is provided by Visual Studio.*

Running the Program

To actually run the program, just type its name on the command line, as shown here:

```
C:\>Example
```

When the program is run, the following output is displayed:

```
A simple C# program.
```

Using the Visual Studio IDE

Visual Studio is Microsoft's *integrated programming environment* (IDE). It lets you edit, compile, run, and debug a C# program, all without leaving its well-thought-out environment. Visual Studio offers convenience and helps manage your programs. It is most effective for larger projects, but it can be used to great success with smaller programs, such as those that constitute the examples in this book.

The steps required to edit, compile, and run a C# program using the Visual Studio 2010 IDE are shown here. These steps assume the IDE provided by Visual Studio 2010 Professional. Slight differences may exist with other versions of Visual Studio.

1. Create a new, empty C# project by selecting File | New | Project. Then, select Windows in the Installed Templates list. Next, select Empty Project:

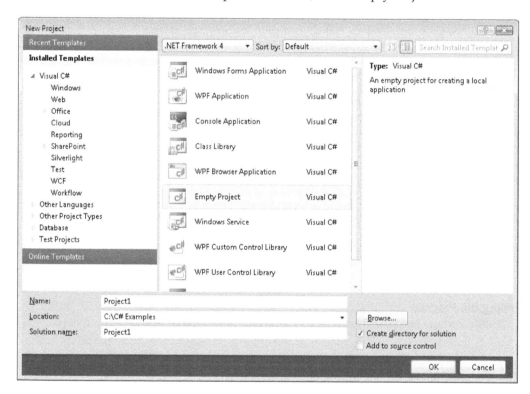

Then, press OK to create the project.

NOTE *The name of your project and its location may differ from that shown here.*

2. Once the new project is created, the Visual Studio IDE will look like this:

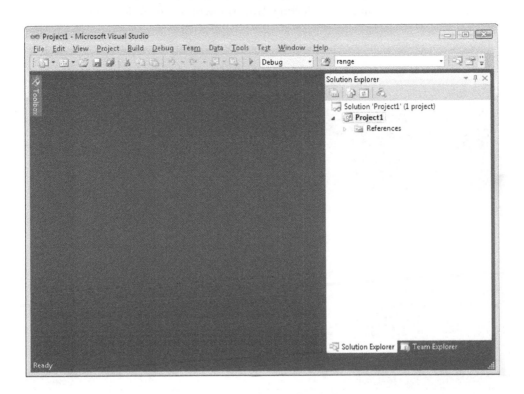

If for some reason you do not see the Solution Explorer window, activate it by selecting Solution Explorer from the View menu.

3. At this point, the project is empty and you will need to add a C# source file to it. Do this by right-clicking on the project's name (which is Project1 in this example) in the Solution Explorer and then selecting Add. You will see the following:

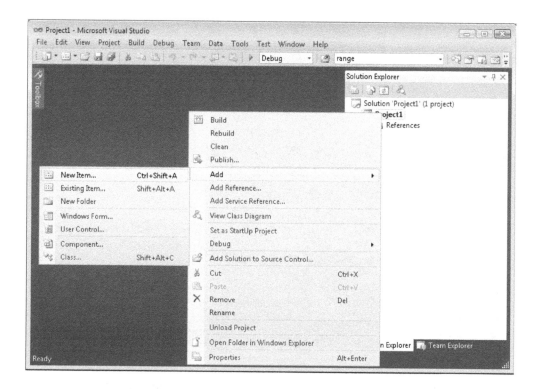

4. Next, select New Item. This causes the Add New Item dialog to be displayed. Select Code in the Installed Templates list. Next, select Code File and then change the name to **Example.cs**, as shown here:

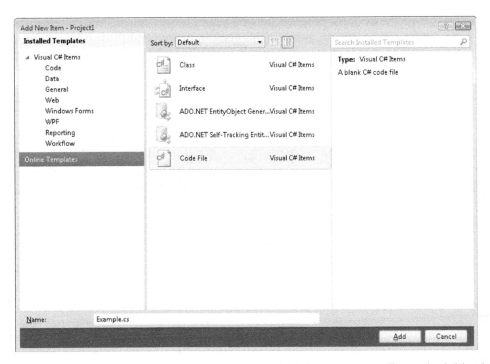

5. Next, add the file to the project by pressing Add. Your screen will now look like this:

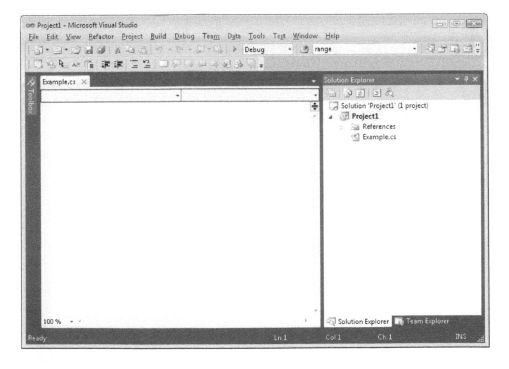

6. Next, type the example program into the Example.cs window. (You can download the source code to the programs in this book from **www.mhprofessional.com** so you won't have to type in each example manually.) When done, your screen will look like this:

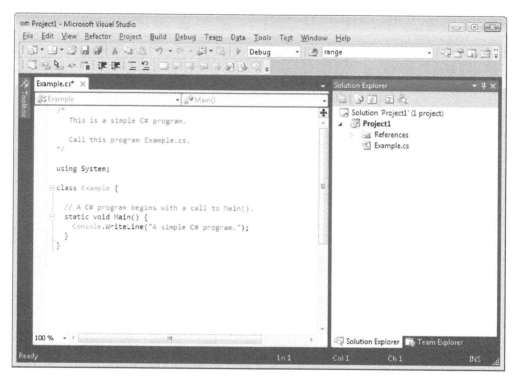

7. Compile the program by selecting Build Solution from the Build menu.

8. Run the program by selecting Start Without Debugging from the Debug menu. When you run the program, you will see the window shown here.

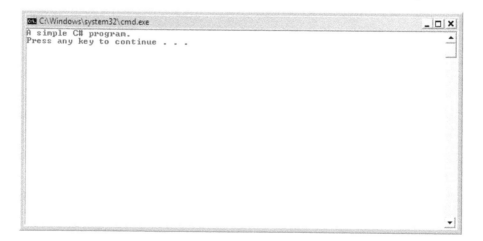

As the preceding instructions show, compiling short sample programs using the IDE involves a number of steps. However, you don't need to create a new project for each example program in this book. Instead, you can use the same C# project. Just delete the current source file and add the new file. Then recompile and run. This approach greatly simplifies the process. Understand, however, that for real-world applications, each program will use its own project.

NOTE *Although the preceding instructions are sufficient to compile and run the programs in this book, if you will be using the Visual Studio IDE for your main work environment, you should become familiar with all of its capabilities and features. It is a very powerful development environment that helps make large projects manageable. The IDE also provides a way of organizing the files and resources associated with a project. It is worth the time and effort that you spend to become proficient at running Visual Studio.*

The First Sample Program, Line by Line

Although **Example.cs** is quite short, it includes several key features that are common to all C# programs. Let's closely examine each part of the program, beginning with its name.

The name of a C# program is arbitrary. Unlike some computer languages (most notably, Java) in which the name of a program file is very important, this is not the case for C#. You were told to call the sample program **Example.cs** so that the instructions for compiling and running the program would apply, but as far as C# is concerned, you could have called the file by another name. For example, the preceding sample program could have been called **Sample.cs**, **Test.cs**, or even **X.cs**.

By convention, C# programs use the **.cs** file extension, and this is a convention that you should follow. Also, many programmers call a file by the name of the principal class defined within the file. This is why the filename **Example.cs** was chosen. Since the names of C# programs are arbitrary, names won't be specified for most of the sample programs in this book. Just use names of your own choosing.

The program begins with the following lines:

```
/*
   This is a simple C# program.

   Call this program Example.cs.
*/
```

This is a *comment*. Like most other programming languages, C# lets you enter a remark into a program's source file. The contents of a comment are ignored by the compiler. Instead, a comment describes or explains the operation of the program to anyone who is reading its source code. In this case, the comment describes the program and reminds you to call the source file **Example.cs**. Of course, in real applications, comments generally explain how some part of the program works or what a specific feature does.

C# supports three styles of comments. The one shown at the top of the program is called a *multiline comment*. This type of comment must begin with /* and end with */. Anything between these two comment symbols is ignored by the compiler. As the name suggests, a multiline comment can be several lines long.

The next line in the program is

```
using System;
```

This line indicates that the program is using the **System** namespace. In C#, a *namespace* defines a declarative region. Although we will examine namespaces in detail later in this book, a brief description is useful now. Through the use of namespaces, it is possible to keep one set of names separate from another. In essence, names declared in one namespace will not conflict with names declared in a different namespace. The namespace used by the program is **System**, which is the namespace reserved for items associated with the .NET Framework class library, which is the library used by C#. The **using** keyword simply states that the program is using the names in the given namespace. (As a point of interest, it is also possible to create your own namespaces, which is especially helpful for large projects.)

The next line of code in the program is shown here:

```
class Example {
```

This line uses the keyword **class** to declare that a new class is being defined. As mentioned, the class is C#'s basic unit of encapsulation. **Example** is the name of the class. The class definition begins with the opening curly brace ({) and ends with the closing curly brace (}). The elements between the two braces are members of the class. For the moment, don't worry too much about the details of a class except to note that in C#, most program activity occurs within one.

The next line in the program is the *single-line comment,* shown here:

```
// A C# program begins with a call to Main().
```

This is the second type of comment supported by C#. A single-line comment begins with a // and ends at the end of the line. Although styles vary, it is not uncommon for programmers to use multiline comments for longer remarks and single-line comments for brief, line-by-line descriptions. (The third type of comment supported by C# aids in the creation of documentation and is described in the Appendix.)

The next line of code is shown here:

```
static void Main() {
```

This line begins the **Main()** method. As mentioned earlier, in C#, a subroutine is called a method. As the comment preceding it suggests, this is the line at which the program will begin executing. All C# applications begin execution by calling **Main()**. The complete meaning of each part of this line cannot be given now, since it involves a detailed understanding of several other C# features. However, since many of the examples in this book will use this line of code, we will take a brief look at it here.

The line begins with the keyword **static**. A method that is modified by **static** can be called before an object of its class has been created. This is necessary because **Main()** is called at program startup. The keyword **void** indicates that **Main()** does not return a value. As you will see, methods can also return values. The empty parentheses that follow **Main** indicate that no information is passed to **Main()**. Although it is possible to pass information into **Main()**, none is passed in this example. The last character on the line is the {. This signals the start of **Main()**'s body. All of the code that comprises a method will occur between the method's opening curly brace and its closing curly brace.

The next line of code is shown here. Notice that it occurs inside **Main()**.

```
Console.WriteLine("A simple C# program.");
```

This line outputs the string "A simple C# program." followed by a new line on the screen. Output is actually accomplished by the built-in method **WriteLine()**. In this case, **WriteLine()** displays the string that is passed to it. Information that is passed to a method is called an *argument*. In addition to strings, **WriteLine()** can be used to display other types of information. The line begins with **Console**, which is the name of a predefined class that supports console I/O. By connecting **Console** with **WriteLine()**, you are telling the compiler that **WriteLine()** is a member of the **Console** class. The fact that C# uses an object to define console output is further evidence of its object-oriented nature.

Notice that the **WriteLine()** statement ends with a semicolon, as does the **using System** statement earlier in the program. In general, statements in C# end with a semicolon. The exception to this rule are *blocks*, which begin with a { and end with a }. This is why those lines in the program don't end with a semicolon. Blocks provide a mechanism for grouping statements and are discussed later in this chapter.

The first } in the program ends **Main()**, and the last } ends the **Example** class definition.

One last point: C# is case-sensitive. Forgetting this can cause serious problems. For example, if you accidentally type **main** instead of **Main**, or **writeline** instead of **WriteLine**, the preceding program will be incorrect. Furthermore, although the C# compiler *will* compile classes that do not contain a **Main()** method, it has no way to execute them. So, had you mistyped **Main**, you would see an error message that states that **Example.exe** does not have an entry point defined.

Handling Syntax Errors

If you are new to programming, it is important to learn how to interpret and respond to errors that may occur when you try to compile a program. Most compilation errors are caused by typing mistakes. As all programmers soon find out, accidentally typing something incorrectly is quite easy. Fortunately, if you type something wrong, the compiler will report a *syntax error* message when it tries to compile your program. This message gives you the line number at which the error is found and a description of the error itself.

Although the syntax errors reported by the compiler are, obviously, helpful, they sometimes can also be misleading. The C# compiler attempts to make sense out of your source code no matter what you have written. For this reason, the error that is reported may not always reflect the actual cause of the problem. In the preceding program, for example, an accidental omission of the opening curly brace after the **Main()** method generates the following sequence of errors when compiled by the **csc** command-line compiler. (Similar errors are generated when compiling using the IDE.)

```
Example.CS(12,21): error CS1002: ; expected
Example.CS(13,22): error CS1519: Invalid token '(' in class, struct, or
interface member declaration
Example.CS(15,1): error CS1022: Type or namespace definition, or
end-of-file expected
```

Clearly, the first error message is completely wrong, because what is missing is not a semicolon, but a curly brace. The second two messages are equally confusing.

The point of this discussion is that when your program contains a syntax error, don't necessarily take the compiler's messages at face value. They may be misleading. You may need to "second guess" an error message in order to find the problem. Also, look at the last few lines of code immediately preceding the one in which the error was reported. Sometimes an error will not be reported until several lines after the point at which the error really occurred.

A Small Variation

Although all of the programs in this book will use it, the line

```
using System;
```

at the start of the first example program is not technically needed. It is, however, a valuable convenience. The reason it's not necessary is that in C# you can always *fully qualify* a name with the namespace to which it belongs. For example, the line

```
Console.WriteLine("A simple C# program.");
```

can be rewritten as

```
System.Console.WriteLine("A simple C# program.");
```

Thus, the first example could be recoded as shown here:

```
// This version does not include "using System;".

class Example {

  // A C# program begins with a call to Main().
  static void Main() {

    // Here, Console.WriteLine is fully qualified.
    System.Console.WriteLine("A simple C# program.");
  }
}
```

Since it is quite tedious to always specify the **System** namespace whenever a member of that namespace is used, most C# programmers include **using System** at the top of their programs, as will all of the programs in this book. It is important to understand, however, that you can explicitly qualify a name with its namespace if needed.

A Second Simple Program

Perhaps no other construct is as important to a programming language as the variable. A *variable* is a named memory location that can be assigned a value. It is called a variable because its value can be changed during the execution of a program. In other words, the content of a variable is changeable, not fixed.

The following program creates two variables called **x** and **y**.

```
// This program demonstrates variables.

using System;

class Example2 {
  static void Main() {
    int x; // this declares a variable
    int y; // this declares another variable

    x = 100; // this assigns 100 to x

    Console.WriteLine("x contains " + x);
```

```
    y = x / 2;

    Console.Write("y contains x / 2: ");
    Console.WriteLine(y);
  }
}
```

When you run this program, you will see the following output:

```
x contains 100
y contains x / 2: 50
```

This program introduces several new concepts. First, the statement

```
int x; // this declares a variable
```

declares a variable called **x** of type integer. In C#, all variables must be declared before they are used. Further, the kind of values that the variable can hold must also be specified. This is called the *type* of the variable. In this case, **x** can hold integer values. These are whole numbers. In C#, to declare a variable to be of type integer, precede its name with the keyword **int**. Thus, the preceding statement declares a variable called **x** of type **int**.

The next line declares a second variable called **y**.

```
int y; // this declares another variable
```

Notice that it uses the same format as the first except that the name of the variable is different.

In general, to declare a variable, you will use a statement like this:

type var-name;

Here, *type* specifies the type of variable being declared, and *var-name* is the name of the variable. In addition to **int**, C# supports several other data types.

The following line of code assigns **x** the value **100**:

```
x = 100; // this assigns 100 to x
```

In C#, the assignment operator is the single equal sign. It copies the value on its right side into the variable on its left.

The next line of code outputs the value of **x** preceded by the string "x contains ".

```
Console.WriteLine("x contains " + x);
```

In this statement, the plus sign causes the value of **x** to be displayed after the string that precedes it. This approach can be generalized. Using the + operator, you can chain together as many items as you want within a single **WriteLine( )** statement.

The next line of code assigns **y** the value of **x** divided by **2**:

```
y = x / 2;
```

This line divides the value in **x** by 2 and then stores that result in **y**. Thus, after the line executes, **y** will contain the value 50. The value of **x** will be unchanged. Like most other computer languages, C# supports a full range of arithmetic operators, including those shown here:

+	Addition
–	Subtraction
*	Multiplication
/	Division

Here are the next two lines in the program:

```
Console.Write("y contains x / 2: ");
Console.WriteLine(y);
```

Two new things are occurring here. First, the built-in method **Write()** is used to display the string "y contains x / 2: ". This string is *not* followed by a new line. This means that when the next output is generated, it will start on the same line. The **Write()** method is just like **WriteLine()**, except that it does not output a new line after each call. Second, in the call to **WriteLine()**, notice that **y** is used by itself. Both **Write()** and **WriteLine()** can be used to output values of any of C#'s built-in types.

One more point about declaring variables before we move on: It is possible to declare two or more variables using the same declaration statement. Just separate their names by commas. For example, **x** and **y** could have been declared like this:

```
int x, y; // both declared using one statement
```

NOTE *C# includes a feature called an* implicitly typed variable. *Implicitly typed variables are variables whose type is automatically determined by the compiler. Implicitly typed variables are discussed in Chapter 3.*

Another Data Type

In the preceding program, a variable of type **int** was used. However, an **int** variable can hold only whole numbers. It cannot be used when a fractional component is required. For example, an **int** variable can hold the value 18, but not the value 18.3. Fortunately, **int** is only one of several data types defined by C#. To allow numbers with fractional components, C# defines two floating-point types: **float** and **double**, which represent single- and double-precision values, respectively. Of the two, **double** is the most commonly used.

To declare a variable of type **double**, use a statement similar to that shown here:

```
double result;
```

Here, **result** is the name of the variable, which is of type **double**. Because **result** has a floating-point type, it can hold values such as 122.23, 0.034, or –19.0.

To better understand the difference between **int** and **double**, try the following program:

```
/*
   This program illustrates the differences
   between int and double.
*/
```

```
using System;

class Example3 {
  static void Main() {
    int ivar;      // this declares an int variable
    double dvar;   // this declares a floating-point variable

    ivar = 100;    // assign ivar the value 100

    dvar = 100.0;  // assign dvar the value 100.0

    Console.WriteLine("Original value of ivar: " + ivar);
    Console.WriteLine("Original value of dvar: " + dvar);

    Console.WriteLine(); // print a blank line

    // Now, divide both by 3.
    ivar = ivar / 3;
    dvar = dvar / 3.0;

    Console.WriteLine("ivar after division: " + ivar);
    Console.WriteLine("dvar after division: " + dvar);
  }
}
```

The output from this program is shown here:

```
Original value of ivar: 100
Original value of dvar: 100

ivar after division: 33
dvar after division: 33.3333333333333
```

As you can see, when **ivar** (an **int** variable) is divided by 3, a whole-number division is performed, and the outcome is 33—the fractional component is lost. However, when **dvar** (a **double** variable) is divided by 3, the fractional component is preserved.

As the program shows, when you want to specify a floating-point value in a program, you must include a decimal point. If you don't, it will be interpreted as an integer. For example, in C#, the value 100 is an integer, but the value 100.0 is a floating-point value.

There is one other new thing to notice in the program. To print a blank line, simply call **WriteLine()** without any arguments.

The floating-point data types are often used when working with real-world quantities where fractional components are commonly needed. For example, this program computes the area of a circle. It uses the value 3.1416 for pi.

```
// Compute the area of a circle.

using System;

class Circle {
  static void Main() {
    double radius;
    double area;
```

```
    radius = 10.0;
    area = radius * radius * 3.1416;

    Console.WriteLine("Area is " + area);
  }
}
```

The output from the program is shown here:

```
Area is 314.16
```

Clearly, the computation of a circle's area could not be achieved satisfactorily without the use of floating-point data.

Two Control Statements

Inside a method, execution proceeds from one statement to the next, top to bottom. It is possible to alter this flow through the use of the various program control statements supported by C#. Although we will look closely at control statements later, two are briefly introduced here because we will be using them to write sample programs.

The if Statement

You can selectively execute part of a program through the use of C#'s conditional statement: the **if**. The **if** statement works in C# much like the IF statement in any other language. For example, it is syntactically identical to the **if** statements in C, C++, and Java. Its simplest form is shown here:

if(*condition*) *statement*;

Here, *condition* is a Boolean (that is, true or false) expression. If *condition* is true, then the statement is executed. If *condition* is false, then the statement is bypassed. Here is an example:

```
if(10 < 11) Console.WriteLine("10 is less than 11");
```

In this case, since 10 is less than 11, the conditional expression is true, and **WriteLine()** will execute. However, consider the following:

```
if(10 < 9) Console.WriteLine("this won't be displayed");
```

In this case, 10 is not less than 9. Thus, the call to **WriteLine()** will not take place.

C# defines a full complement of relational operators that can be used in a conditional expression. They are shown here:

Operator	Meaning
<	Less than
<=	Less than or equal to
>	Greater than
>=	Greater than or equal to
= =	Equal to
!=	Not equal

Here is a program that illustrates the **if** statement:

```
// Demonstrate the if.

using System;

class IfDemo {
  static void Main() {
    int a, b, c;

    a = 2;
    b = 3;

    if(a < b) Console.WriteLine("a is less than b");

    // This won't display anything.
    if(a == b) Console.WriteLine("you won't see this");

    Console.WriteLine();

    c = a - b; // c contains -1

    Console.WriteLine("c contains -1");
    if(c >= 0) Console.WriteLine("c is non-negative");
    if(c < 0) Console.WriteLine("c is negative");

    Console.WriteLine();

    c = b - a; // c now contains 1
    Console.WriteLine("c contains 1");
    if(c >= 0) Console.WriteLine("c is non-negative");
    if(c < 0) Console.WriteLine("c is negative");
  }
}
```

The output generated by this program is shown here:

```
a is less than b

c contains -1
c is negative

c contains 1
c is non-negative
```

Notice one other thing in this program. The line

```
int a, b, c;
```

declares three variables, **a**, **b**, and **c**, by use of a comma-separated list. As mentioned earlier, when you need two or more variables of the same type, they can be declared in one statement. Just separate the variable names with commas.

The for Loop

You can repeatedly execute a sequence of code by creating a *loop*. C# supplies a powerful assortment of loop constructs. The one we will look at here is the **for** loop. Like the **if** statement, the C# **for** loop is similar to its counterpart in C, C++, and Java. The simplest form of the **for** loop is shown here:

for(*initialization*; *condition*; *iteration*) *statement*;

In its most common form, the *initialization* portion of the loop sets a loop control variable to an initial value. The *condition* is a Boolean expression that tests the loop control variable. If the outcome of that test is true, the **for** loop continues to iterate. If it is false, the loop terminates. The *iteration* expression determines how the loop control variable is changed each time the loop iterates. Here is a short program that illustrates the **for** loop:

```
// Demonstrate the for loop.

using System;

class ForDemo {
  static void Main() {
    int count;

    for(count = 0; count < 5; count = count+1)
      Console.WriteLine("This is count: " + count);

    Console.WriteLine("Done!");
  }
}
```

The output generated by the program is shown here:

```
This is count: 0
This is count: 1
This is count: 2
This is count: 3
This is count: 4
Done!
```

In this example, **count** is the loop control variable. It is set to zero in the initialization portion of the **for**. At the start of each iteration (including the first one), the conditional test **count < 5** is performed. If the outcome of this test is true, the **WriteLine()** statement is executed. Next, the iteration portion of the loop is executed, which adds 1 to **count**. This process continues until **count** reaches 5. At this point, the conditional test becomes false, causing the loop to terminate. Execution picks up at the bottom of the loop.

As a point of interest, in professionally written C# programs you will almost never see the iteration portion of the loop written as shown in the preceding program. That is, you will seldom see statements like this:

```
count = count + 1;
```

The reason is that C# includes a special increment operator that performs this operation. The increment operator is **++** (that is, two consecutive plus signs). The increment operator increases its operand by one. By use of the increment operator, the preceding statement can be written like this:

```
count++;
```

Thus, the **for** in the preceding program will usually be written like this:

```
for(count = 0; count < 5; count++)
```

You might want to try this. As you will see, the loop still runs exactly the same as it did before.

C# also provides a decrement operator, which is specified as – –. This operator decreases its operand by one.

Using Code Blocks

Another key element of C# is the *code block*. A code block is a grouping of statements. This is done by enclosing the statements between opening and closing curly braces. Once a block of code has been created, it becomes a logical unit that can be used any place a single statement can. For example, a block can be a target for **if** and **for** statements. Consider this **if** statement:

```
if(w < h) {
  v = w * h;
  w = 0;
}
```

Here, if **w** is less than **h**, then both statements inside the block will be executed. Thus, the two statements inside the block form a logical unit, and one statement cannot execute without the other also executing. The key point here is that whenever you need to logically link two or more statements, you do so by creating a block. Code blocks allow many algorithms to be implemented with greater clarity and efficiency.

Here is a program that uses a code block to prevent a division by zero:

```
// Demonstrate a block of code.

using System;

class BlockDemo {
  static void Main() {
    int i, j, d;

    i = 5;
    j = 10;

    // The target of this if is a block.
    if(i != 0) {
      Console.WriteLine("i does not equal zero");
      d = j / i;
      Console.WriteLine("j / i is " + d);
    }
  }
}
```

The output generated by this program is shown here:

```
i does not equal zero
j / i is 2
```

In this case, the target of the **if** statement is a block of code and not just a single statement. If the condition controlling the **if** is true (as it is in this case), the three statements inside the block will be executed. Try setting **i** to zero and observe the result.

Here is another example. It uses a code block to compute the sum and the product of the numbers from 1 to 10.

```
// Compute the sum and product of the numbers from 1 to 10.

using System;

class ProdSum {
  static void Main() {
    int prod;
    int sum;
    int i;

    sum = 0;
    prod = 1;

    for(i=1; i <= 10; i++) {
      sum = sum + i;
      prod = prod * i;
    }
    Console.WriteLine("Sum is " + sum);
    Console.WriteLine("Product is " + prod);

  }
}
```

The output is shown here:

```
Sum is 55
Product is 3628800
```

Here, the block enables one loop to compute both the sum and the product. Without the use of the block, two separate **for** loops would have been required.

One last point: Code blocks do not introduce any runtime inefficiencies. In other words, the { and } do not consume any extra time during the execution of a program. In fact, because of their ability to simplify (and clarify) the coding of certain algorithms, the use of code blocks generally results in increased speed and efficiency.

Semicolons, Positioning, and Indentation

In C#, the semicolon signals the end of a statement. That is, each individual statement must end with a semicolon.

As you know, a block is a set of logically connected statements that are surrounded by opening and closing braces. A block is *not* terminated with a semicolon. Since a block is a group of statements, it makes sense that a block is not terminated by a semicolon; instead, the end of the block is indicated by the closing brace.

C# does not recognize the end of the line as the end of a statement—only a semicolon terminates a statement. For this reason, it does not matter where on a line you put a statement. For example, to C#,

```
x = y;
y = y + 1;
Console.WriteLine(x + " " + y);
```

is the same as

```
x = y;   y = y + 1;   Console.WriteLine(x + " " + y);
```

Furthermore, the individual elements of a statement can also be put on separate lines. For example, the following is perfectly acceptable:

```
Console.WriteLine("This is a long line of output" +
                  x + y + z +
                  "more output");
```

Breaking long lines in this fashion is often used to make programs more readable. It can also help prevent excessively long lines from wrapping.

You may have noticed in the previous examples that certain statements were indented. C# is a free-form language, meaning that it does not matter where you place statements relative to each other on a line. However, over the years, a common and accepted indentation style has developed that allows for very readable programs. This book follows that style, and it is recommended that you do so as well. Using this style, you indent one level after each opening brace and move back out one level after each closing brace. There are certain statements that encourage some additional indenting; these will be covered later.

The C# Keywords

At its foundation, a computer language is defined by its keywords because they determine the features built into the language. C# defines two general types of keywords: *reserved* and *contextual.* The reserved keywords cannot be used as names for variables, classes, or methods. They can be used only as keywords. This is why they are called *reserved.* The terms *reserved words* or *reserved identifiers* are also sometimes used. There are currently 77 reserved keywords defined by version 4.0 of the C# language. They are shown in Table 2-1.

C# 4.0 defines 18 contextual keywords that have a special meaning in certain contexts. In those contexts, they act as keywords. Outside those contexts, they can be used as names for other program elements, such as variable names. Thus, they are not technically reserved. As a general rule, however, you should consider the contextual keywords reserved and avoid using them for any other purpose. Using a contextual keyword as a name for some other program element can be confusing and is considered bad practice by many programmers. The contextual keywords are shown in Table 2-2.

abstract	as	base	bool	break
byte	case	catch	char	checked
class	const	continue	decimal	default
delegate	do	double	else	enum
event	explicit	extern	false	finally
fixed	float	for	foreach	goto
if	implicit	in	int	interface
internal	is	lock	long	namespace
new	null	object	operator	out
override	params	private	protected	public
readonly	ref	return	sbyte	sealed
short	sizeof	stackalloc	static	string
struct	switch	this	throw	true
try	typeof	uint	ulong	unchecked
unsafe	ushort	using	virtual	volatile
void	while			

TABLE 2-1   The C# Reserved Keywords

add	dynamic	from	get	global
group	into	join	let	orderby
partial	remove	select	set	value
var	where	yield		

TABLE 2-2   The C# Contextual Keywords

Identifiers

In C#, an identifier is a name assigned to a method, a variable, or any other user-defined item. Identifiers can be one or more characters long. Identifiers may start with any letter of the alphabet or an underscore. Next may be a letter, a digit, or an underscore. The underscore can be used to enhance the readability of a variable name, as in **line_count**. However, identifers containing two consecutive underscores, such as **max_ _value**, are reserved for use by the compiler. Uppercase and lowercase are different; that is, to C#, **myvar** and **MyVar** are separate names. Here are some examples of acceptable identifiers:

Test	x	y2	MaxLoad
up	_top	my_var	sample23

Remember, you can't start an identifier with a digit. Thus, **12x** is invalid, for example. Good programming practice dictates that you choose identifiers that reflect the meaning or usage of the items being named.

Although you cannot use any of the reserved C# keywords as identifiers, C# does allow you to precede a keyword with an @, allowing it to be a legal identifier. For example, **@for** is a valid identifier. In this case, the identifier is actually **for** and the @ is ignored. Here is a program that illustrates the use of an @ identifier:

```
// Demonstrate an @ identifier.

using System;

class IdTest {
  static void Main() {
    int @if; // use if as an identifier

    for(@if = 0; @if < 10; @if++)
      Console.WriteLine("@if is " + @if);
  }
}
```

The output shown here proves the **@if** is properly interpreted as an identifier:

```
@if is 0
@if is 1
@if is 2
@if is 3
@if is 4
@if is 5
@if is 6
@if is 7
@if is 8
@if is 9
```

Frankly, using @-qualified keywords for identifiers is not recommended, except for special purposes. Also, the @ can precede any identifier, but this is considered bad practice.

The .NET Framework Class Library

The sample programs shown in this chapter make use of two built-in methods: **WriteLine()** and **Write()**. As mentioned, these methods are members of the **Console** class, which is part of the **System** namespace, which is defined by the .NET Framework's class library. As explained earlier in this chapter, the C# environment relies on the .NET Framework class library to provide support for such things as I/O, string handling, networking, and GUIs. Thus, the C# environment as a totality is a combination of the C# language itself, plus the .NET standard classes. As you will see, the class library provides much of the functionality that is part of any C# program. Indeed, part of becoming a C# programmer is learning to use these standard classes. Throughout Part I, various elements of the .NET library classes and methods are described. Part II examines portions of the .NET library in detail.

Data Types, Literals, and Variables

This chapter examines three fundamental elements of C#: data types, literals, and variables. In general, the types of data that a language provides define the kinds of problems to which the language can be applied. As you might expect, C# offers a rich set of built-in data types, which makes C# suitable for a wide range of applications. You can create variables of any of these types, and you can specify constants of each type, which in the language of C# are called *literals*.

Why Data Types Are Important

Data types are especially important in C# because it is a strongly typed language. This means that, as a general rule, all operations are type-checked by the compiler for type compatibility. Illegal operations will not be compiled. Thus, strong type-checking helps prevent errors and enhances reliability. To enable strong type-checking, all variables, expressions, and values have a type. There is no concept of a "typeless" variable, for example. Furthermore, a value's type determines what operations are allowed on it. An operation allowed on one type might not be allowed on another.

NOTE *C# 4.0 adds a new data type called* **dynamic**, *which causes type checking to be deferred until runtime, rather than occurring at compile time. Thus, the* **dynamic** *type is an exception to C#'s normal compile-time type checking. The* **dynamic** *type is discussed in Chapter 17.*

C#'s Value Types

C# contains two general categories of built-in data types: *value types* and *reference types*. The difference between the two types is what a variable contains. For a value type, a variable holds an actual value, such 3.1416 or 212. For a reference type, a variable holds a reference to the value. The most commonly used reference type is the class, and a discussion of classes and reference types is deferred until later in this book. The value types are described here.

At the core of C# are the 13 value types shown in Table 3-1. Collectively, these are referred to as the *simple types*. They are called simple types because they consist of a single value. (In other words, they are not a composite of two or more values.) They form the foundation of C#'s type system, providing the basic, low-level data elements upon which a program operates. The simple types are also sometimes referred to as *primitive types*.

Type	Meaning
bool	Represents true/false values
byte	8-bit unsigned integer
char	Character
decimal	Numeric type for financial calculations
double	Double-precision floating point
float	Single-precision floating point
int	Integer
long	Long integer
sbyte	8-bit signed integer
short	Short integer
uint	An unsigned integer
ulong	An unsigned long integer
ushort	An unsigned short integer

TABLE 3-1   The C# Value Types

C# strictly specifies a range and behavior for each value type. Because of portability requirements, C# is uncompromising on this account. For example, an **int** is the same in all execution environments. There is no need to rewrite code to fit a specific platform. Although strictly specifying the size of the value types may cause a small loss of performance in some environments, it is necessary in order to achieve portability.

NOTE   *In addition to the simple types, C# defines three other categories of value types. These are enumerations, structures, and nullable types, all of which are described later in this book.*

Integers

C# defines nine integer types: **char**, **byte**, **sbyte**, **short**, **ushort**, **int**, **uint**, **long**, and **ulong**. However, the **char** type is primarily used for representing characters, and it is discussed later in this chapter. The remaining eight integer types are used for numeric calculations. Their bit-width and ranges are shown here:

Type	Width in Bits	Range
byte	8	0 to 255
sbyte	8	−128 to 127
short	16	−32,768 to 32,767
ushort	16	0 to 65,535
int	32	−2,147,483,648 to 2,147,483,647
uint	32	0 to 4,294,967,295
long	64	−9,223,372,036,854,775,808 to 9,223,372,036,854,775,807
ulong	64	0 to 18,446,744,073,709,551,615

As the table shows, C# defines both signed and unsigned versions of the various integer types. The difference between signed and unsigned integers is in the way the high-order bit of the integer is interpreted. If a signed integer is specified, then the C# compiler will generate code that assumes the high-order bit of an integer is to be used as a *sign flag*. If the sign flag is 0, then the number is positive; if it is 1, then the number is negative. Negative numbers are almost always represented using the *two's complement* approach. In this method, all bits in the negative number are reversed, and then 1 is added to this number.

Signed integers are important for a great many algorithms, but they have only half the absolute magnitude of their unsigned relatives. For example, as a **short**, here is 32,767:

01111111 11111111

For a signed value, if the high-order bit were set to 1, the number would then be interpreted as –1 (assuming the two's complement format). However, if you declared this to be a **ushort**, then when the high-order bit was set to 1, the number would become 65,535.

Probably the most commonly used integer type is **int**. Variables of type **int** are often employed to control loops, to index arrays, and for general-purpose integer math. When you need an integer that has a range greater than **int**, you have many options. If the value you want to store is unsigned, you can use **uint**. For large signed values, use **long**. For large unsigned values, use **ulong**. For example, here is a program that computes the distance from the Earth to the sun, in inches. Because this value is so large, the program uses a **long** variable to hold it.

```
// Compute the distance from the Earth to the sun, in inches.

using System;

class Inches {
  static void Main() {
    long inches;
    long miles;

    miles = 93000000; // 93,000,000 miles to the sun

    // 5,280 feet in a mile, 12 inches in a foot.
    inches = miles * 5280 * 12;

    Console.WriteLine("Distance to the sun: " +
                      inches + " inches.");

  }
}
```

Here is the output from the program:

```
Distance to the sun: 5892480000000 inches.
```

Clearly, the result could not have been held in an **int** or **uint** variable.

The smallest integer types are **byte** and **sbyte**. The **byte** type is an unsigned value between 0 and 255. Variables of type **byte** are especially useful when working with raw binary data, such as a byte stream produced by some device. For small signed integers, use **sbyte**. Here is an example that uses a variable of type **byte** to control a **for** loop that produces the summation of the number 100.

```
// Use byte.

using System;

class Use_byte {
  static void Main() {
    byte x;
    int sum;

    sum = 0;
    for(x = 1; x <= 100; x++)
      sum = sum + x;

    Console.WriteLine("Summation of 100 is " + sum);
  }
}
```

The output from the program is shown here:

```
Summation of 100 is 5050
```

Since the **for** loop runs only from 0 to 100, which is well within the range of a **byte**, there is no need to use a larger type variable to control it.

When you need an integer that is larger than a **byte** or **sbyte**, but smaller than an **int** or **uint**, use **short** or **ushort**.

Floating-Point Types

The floating-point types can represent numbers that have fractional components. There are two kinds of floating-point types, **float** and **double**, which represent single- and double-precision numbers, respectively. The type **float** is 32 bits wide and has an approximate range of 1.5E–45 to 3.4E+38. The **double** type is 64 bits wide and has an approximate range of 5E–324 to 1.7E+308.

Of the two, **double** is the most commonly used. One reason for this is that many of the math functions in C#'s class library (which is the .NET Framework library) use **double** values. For example, the **Sqrt()** method (which is defined by the library class **System.Math**) returns a **double** value that is the square root of its **double** argument. Here, **Sqrt()** is used to compute the radius of a circle given the circle's area:

```
// Find the radius of a circle given its area.

using System;

class FindRadius {
  static void Main() {
    Double r;
    Double area;

    area = 10.0;

    r = Math.Sqrt(area / 3.1416);
```

```
      Console.WriteLine("Radius is " + r);
   }
}
```

The output from the program is shown here:

```
Radius is 1.78412203012729
```

One other point about the preceding example. As mentioned, **Sqrt( )** is a member of the **Math** class. Notice how **Sqrt( )** is called; it is preceded by the name **Math**. This is similar to the way **Console** precedes **WriteLine( )**. Although not all standard methods are called by specifying their class name first, several are, as the next example shows.

The following program demonstrates several of C#'s trigonometric functions, which are also part of C#'s math library. They also operate on **double** data. The program displays the sine, cosine, and tangent for the angles (measured in radians) from 0.1 to 1.0.

```
// Demonstrate Math.Sin(), Math.Cos(), and Math.Tan().

using System;

class Trigonometry {
  static void Main() {
    Double theta; // angle in radians

    for(theta = 0.1; theta <= 1.0; theta = theta + 0.1) {
      Console.WriteLine("Sine of " + theta + "  is " +
                          Math.Sin(theta));
      Console.WriteLine("Cosine of " + theta + "  is " +
                          Math.Cos(theta));
      Console.WriteLine("Tangent of " + theta + "  is " +
                          Math.Tan(theta));
      Console.WriteLine();
    }
  }
}
```

Here is a portion of the program's output:

```
Sine of 0.1  is 0.0998334166468282
Cosine of 0.1  is 0.995004165278026
Tangent of 0.1  is 0.100334672085451

Sine of 0.2  is 0.198669330795061
Cosine of 0.2  is 0.980066577841242
Tangent of 0.2  is 0.202710035508673

Sine of 0.3  is 0.29552020666134
Cosine of 0.3  is 0.955336489125606
Tangent of 0.3  is 0.309336249609623
```

To compute the sine, cosine, and tangent, the standard library methods **Math.Sin( )**, **Math.Cos( )**, and **Math.Tan( )** are used. Like **Math.Sqrt( )**, the trigonometric methods are called with a **double** argument, and they return a **double** result. The angles must be specified in radians.

The decimal Type

Perhaps the most interesting C# numeric type is **decimal**, which is intended for use in monetary calculations. The **decimal** type utilizes 128 bits to represent values within the range 1E–28 to 7.9E+28. As you may know, normal floating-point arithmetic is subject to a variety of rounding errors when it is applied to decimal values. The **decimal** type eliminates these errors and can accurately represent up to 28 decimal places (or 29 places in some cases). This ability to represent decimal values without rounding errors makes it especially useful for computations that involve money.

Here is a program that uses a **decimal** type in a financial calculation. The program computes the discounted price given the original price and a discount percentage.

```
// Use the decimal type to compute a discount.

using System;

class UseDecimal {
  static void Main() {
    decimal price;
    decimal discount;
    decimal discounted_price;

    // Compute discounted price.
    price = 19.95m;
    discount = 0.15m; // discount rate is 15%

    discounted_price = price - ( price * discount);

    Console.WriteLine("Discounted price: $" + discounted_price);
  }
}
```

The output from this program is shown here:

```
Discounted price: $16.9575
```

In the program, notice that the decimal constants are followed by the *m* suffix. This is necessary because without the suffix, these values would be interpreted as standard floating-point constants, which are not compatible with the **decimal** data type. You can assign an integer value, such as 10, to a **decimal** variable without the use of the *m* suffix, though. (A detailed discussion of numeric constants is found later in this chapter.)

Here is another example that uses the **decimal** type. It computes the future value of an investment that has a fixed rate of return over a period of years.

```
/*
   Use the decimal type to compute the future value
   of an investment.
*/

using System;

class FutVal {
```

```
static void Main() {
  decimal amount;
  decimal rate_of_return;
  int years, i;

  amount = 1000.0M;
  rate_of_return = 0.07M;
  years = 10;

  Console.WriteLine("Original investment: $" + amount);
  Console.WriteLine("Rate of return: " + rate_of_return);
  Console.WriteLine("Over " + years + " years");

  for(i = 0; i < years; i++)
    amount = amount + (amount * rate_of_return);

  Console.WriteLine("Future value is $" + amount);
  }
}
```

Here is the output:

```
Original investment: $1000
Rate of return: 0.07
Over 10 years
Future value is $1967.15135728956532249000
```

Notice that the result is accurate to several decimal places—more than you would probably want! Later in this chapter you will see how to format such output in a more appealing fashion.

Characters

In C#, characters are not 8-bit quantities like they are in many other computer languages, such as C++. Instead, C# uses a 16-bit character type called *Unicode.* Unicode defines a character set that is large enough to represent all of the characters found in all human languages. Although many languages, such as English, French, and German, use relatively small alphabets, some languages, such as Chinese, use very large character sets that cannot be represented using just 8 bits. To address this situation, in C#, **char** is an unsigned 16-bit type having a range of 0 to 65,535. The standard 8-bit ASCII character set is a subset of Unicode and ranges from 0 to 127. Thus, the ASCII characters are still valid C# characters.

A character variable can be assigned a value by enclosing the character inside single quotes. For example, this assigns X to the variable **ch**:

```
char ch;
ch = 'X';
```

You can output a **char** value using a **WriteLine( )** statement. For example, this line outputs the value in **ch**:

```
Console.WriteLine("This is ch: " + ch);
```

Although **char** is defined by C# as an integer type, it cannot be freely mixed with integers in all cases. This is because there are no automatic type conversions from integer to **char**. For example, the following fragment is invalid:

```
char ch;

ch = 88; // error, won't work
```

The reason the preceding code will not work is that 10 is an integer value, and it won't automatically convert to a **char**. If you attempt to compile this code, you will see an error message. To make the assignment legal, you would need to employ a cast, which is described later in this chapter.

The bool Type

The **bool** type represents true/false values. C# defines the values true and false using the reserved words **true** and **false**. Thus, a variable or expression of type **bool** will be one of these two values. Furthermore, there is no conversion defined between **bool** and integer values. For example, 1 does not convert to true, and 0 does not convert to false.

Here is a program that demonstrates the **bool** type:

```
// Demonstrate bool values.

using System;

class BoolDemo {
  static void Main() {
    bool b;

    b = false;
    Console.WriteLine("b is " + b);
    b = true;
    Console.WriteLine("b is " + b);

    // A bool value can control the if statement.
    if(b) Console.WriteLine("This is executed.");

    b = false;
    if(b) Console.WriteLine("This is not executed.");

    // Outcome of a relational operator is a bool value.
    Console.WriteLine("10 > 9 is " + (10 > 9));
  }
}
```

The output generated by this program is shown here:

```
b is False
b is True
This is executed.
10 > 9 is True
```

There are three interesting things to notice about this program. First, as you can see, when a **bool** value is output by **WriteLine( )**, "True" or "False" is displayed. Second, the value of a **bool** variable is sufficient, by itself, to control the **if** statement. There is no need to write an **if** statement like this:

```
if(b == true) ...
```

Third, the outcome of a relational operator, such as <, is a **bool** value. This is why the expression **10 > 9** displays the value "True." Further, the extra set of parentheses around **10 > 9** is necessary because the **+** operator has a higher precedence than the **>**.

Some Output Options

Up to this point, when data has been output using a **WriteLine( )** statement, it has been displayed using the default format. However, the .NET Framework defines a sophisticated formatting mechanism that gives you detailed control over how data is displayed. Although formatted I/O is covered in detail later in this book, it is useful to introduce some formatting options at this time. Using these options, you will be able to specify the way values look when output via a **WriteLine( )** statement. Doing so enables you to produce more appealing output. Keep in mind that the formatting mechanism supports many more features than described here.

When outputting lists of data, you have been separating each part of the list with a plus sign, as shown here:

```
Console.WriteLine("You ordered " + 2 + " items at $" + 3 + " each.");
```

While very convenient, outputting numeric information in this way does not give you any control over how that information appears. For example, for a floating-point value, you can't control the number of decimal places displayed. Consider the following statement:

```
Console.WriteLine("Here is 10/3: " + 10.0/3.0);
```

It generates this output:

```
Here is 10/3: 3.33333333333333
```

Although this might be fine for some purposes, displaying so many decimal places could be inappropriate for others. For example, in financial calculations, you will usually want to display two decimal places.

To control how numeric data is formatted, you will need to use a second form of **WriteLine( )**, shown here, which allows you to embed formatting information:

WriteLine(*"format string"*, *arg0, arg1, ... , argN*);

In this version, the arguments to **WriteLine( )** are separated by commas and not **+** signs. The *format string* contains two items: regular, printing characters that are displayed as-is, and format specifiers. Format specifiers take this general form:

{*argnum, width: fmt*}

Here, *argnum* specifies the number of the argument (starting from zero) to display. The minimum width of the field is specified by *width,* and the format is specified by *fmt.* The *width* and *fmt* are optional.

During execution, when a format specifier is encountered in the format string, the corresponding argument, as specified by *argnum,* is substituted and displayed. Thus, the position of a format specification within the format string determines where its matching data will be displayed. Both *width* and *fmt* are optional. Therefore, in its simplest form, a format specifier simply indicates which argument to display. For example, {0} indicates *arg0,* {1} specifies *arg1,* and so on.

Let's begin with a simple example. The statement

```
Console.WriteLine("February has {0} or {1} days.", 28, 29);
```

produces the following output:

```
February has 28 or 29 days.
```

As you can see, the value 28 is substituted for {0}, and 29 is substituted for {1}. Thus, the format specifiers identify the location at which the subsequent arguments, in this case 28 and 29, are displayed within the string. Furthermore, notice that the additional values are separated by commas, not + signs.

Here is a variation of the preceding statement that specifies minimum field widths:

```
Console.WriteLine("February has {0,10} or {1,5} days.", 28, 29);
```

It produces the following output:

```
February has         28 or    29 days.
```

As you can see, spaces have been added to fill out the unused portions of the fields. Remember, a minimum field width is just that: the *minimum* width. Output can exceed that width if needed.

Of course, the arguments associated with a format command need not be constants. For example, this program displays a table of squares and cubes. It uses format commands to output the values.

```
// Use format commands.

using System;

class DisplayOptions {
  static void Main() {
    int i;

    Console.WriteLine("Value\tSquared\tCubed");

    for(i = 1; i < 10; i++)
      Console.WriteLine("{0}\t{1}\t{2}", i, i*i, i*i*i);
  }
}
```

The output is shown here:

```
Value   Squared Cubed
1       1       1
2       4       8
3       9       27
4       16      64
5       25      125
6       36      216
7       49      343
8       64      512
9       81      729
```

In the preceding examples, no formatting was applied to the values themselves. Of course, the purpose of using format specifiers is to control the way the data looks. The types of data most commonly formatted are floating-point and decimal values. One of the easiest ways to specify a format is to describe a template that **WriteLine( )** will use. To do this, show an example of the format that you want, using #s to mark the digit positions. You can also specify the decimal point and commas. For example, here is a better way to display 10 divided by 3:

```
Console.WriteLine("Here is 10/3: {0:#.##}", 10.0/3.0);
```

The output from this statement is shown here:

```
Here is 10/3: 3.33
```

In this example, the template is **#.##**, which tells **WriteLine( )** to display two decimal places. It is important to understand, however, that **WriteLine( )** will display more than one digit to the left of the decimal point, if necessary, so as not to misrepresent the value.

Here is another example. This statement

```
Console.WriteLine("{0:###,###.##}", 123456.56);
```

generates this output:

```
123,456.56
```

If you want to display monetary values, use the **C** format specifier. For example:

```
decimal balance;

balance = 12323.09m;
Console.WriteLine("Current balance is {0:C}", balance);
```

The output from this sequence is shown here (in U.S. dollar format):

```
Current balance is $12,323.09
```

The **C** format can be used to improve the output from the price discount program shown earlier:

```
// Use the C format specifier to output dollars and cents.

using System;
```

```
class UseDecimal {
  static void Main() {
    decimal price;
    decimal discount;
    decimal discounted_price;

    // Compute discounted price.
    price = 19.95m;
    discount = 0.15m; // discount rate is 15%

    discounted_price = price - ( price * discount);

    Console.WriteLine("Discounted price: {0:C}", discounted_price);
  }
}
```

Here is the way the output now looks:

```
Discounted price: $16.96
```

Literals

In C#, *literals* refer to fixed values that are represented in their human-readable form. For example, the number 100 is a literal. For the most part, literals and their usage are so intuitive that they have been used in one form or another by all the preceding sample programs. Now the time has come to explain them formally.

C# literals can be of any simple type. The way each literal is represented depends upon its type. As explained earlier, character literals are enclosed between single quotes. For example, 'a' and '%' are both character literals.

Integer literals are specified as numbers without fractional components. For example, 10 and –100 are integer literals. Floating-point literals require the use of the decimal point followed by the number's fractional component. For example, 11.123 is a floating-point literal. C# also allows you to use scientific notation for floating-point numbers.

Since C# is a strongly typed language, literals, too, have a type. Naturally, this raises the following question: What is the type of a numeric literal? For example, what is the type of 12, 123987, or 0.23? Fortunately, C# specifies some easy-to-follow rules that answer these questions.

First, for integer literals, the type of the literal is the smallest integer type that will hold it, beginning with **int**. Thus, an integer literal is either of type **int**, **uint**, **long**, or **ulong**, depending upon its value. Second, floating-point literals are of type **double**.

If C#'s default type is not what you want for a literal, you can explicitly specify its type by including a suffix. To specify a **long** literal, append an *l* or an *L*. For example, 12 is an **int**, but 12L is a **long**. To specify an unsigned integer value, append a *u* or *U*. Thus, 100 is an **int**, but 100U is a **uint**. To specify an unsigned, long integer, use *ul* or *UL*. For example, 984375UL is of type **ulong**.

To specify a **float** literal, append an *F* or *f* to the constant. For example, 10.19F is of type **float**. Although redundant, you can specify a **double** literal by appending a *D* or *d*. (As just mentioned, floating-point literals are **double** by default.)

To specify a **decimal** literal, follow its value with an *m* or *M*. For example, 9.95M is a **decimal** literal.

Although integer literals create an **int**, **uint**, **long**, or **ulong** value by default, they can still be assigned to variables of type **byte**, **sbyte**, **short**, or **ushort** as long as the value being assigned can be represented by the target type.

Hexadecimal Literals

As you probably know, in programming it is sometimes easier to use a number system based on 16 instead of 10. The base 16 number system is called *hexadecimal* and uses the digits 0 through 9 plus the letters A through F, which stand for 10, 11, 12, 13, 14, and 15. For example, the hexadecimal number 10 is 16 in decimal. Because of the frequency with which hexadecimal numbers are used, C# allows you to specify integer literals in hexadecimal format. A hexadecimal literal must begin with **0x** (a 0 followed by an *x*). Here are some examples:

```
count = 0xFF; // 255 in decimal
incr = 0x1a;  // 26 in decimal
```

Character Escape Sequences

Enclosing character literals in single quotes works for most printing characters, but a few characters, such as the carriage return, pose a special problem when a text editor is used. In addition, certain other characters, such as the single and double quotes, have special meaning in C#, so you cannot use them directly. For these reasons, C# provides special *escape sequences*, sometimes referred to as *backslash character constants*, shown in Table 3-2. These sequences are used in place of the characters they represent.

For example, this assigns **ch** the tab character:

```
ch = '\t';
```

The next example assigns a single quote to **ch**:

```
ch = '\'';
```

Escape Sequence	Description
\a	Alert (bell)
\b	Backspace
\f	Form feed
\n	New line (linefeed)
\r	Carriage return
\t	Horizontal tab
\v	Vertical tab
\0	Null
\'	Single quote
\"	Double quote
\\	Backslash

TABLE 3-2   Character Escape Sequences

String Literals

C# supports one other type of literal: the *string*. A string literal is a set of characters enclosed by double quotes. For example,

```
"this is a test"
```

is a string. You have seen examples of strings in many of the **WriteLine( )** statements in the preceding sample programs.

In addition to normal characters, a string literal can also contain one or more of the escape sequences just described. For example, consider the following program. It uses the **\n** and **\t** escape sequences.

```
// Demonstrate escape sequences in strings.

using System;

class StrDemo {
  static void Main() {
    Console.WriteLine("Line One\nLine Two\nLine Three");
    Console.WriteLine("One\tTwo\tThree");
    Console.WriteLine("Four\tFive\tSix");

    // Embed quotes.
    Console.WriteLine("\"Why?\", he asked.");
  }
}
```

The output is shown here:

```
Line One
Line Two
Line Three
One     Two     Three
Four    Five    Six
"Why?", he asked.
```

Notice how the **\n** escape sequence is used to generate a new line. You don't need to use multiple **WriteLine( )** statements to get multiline output. Just embed **\n** within a longer string at the points where you want the new lines to occur. Also note how a quotation mark is generated inside a string.

In addition to the form of string literal just described, you can also specify a *verbatim string literal*. A verbatim string literal begins with an @, which is followed by a quoted string. The contents of the quoted string are accepted without modification and can span two or more lines. Thus, you can include newlines, tabs, and so on, but you don't need to use the escape sequences. The only exception is that to obtain a double quote ("), you must use two double quotes in a row (""). Here is a program that demonstrates verbatim string literals:

```
// Demonstrate verbatim string literals.

using System;

class Verbatim {
  static void Main() {
```

```
      Console.WriteLine(@"This is a verbatim
string literal
that spans several lines.
");
      Console.WriteLine(@"Here is some tabbed output:
1       2       3       4
5       6       7       8
");
      Console.WriteLine(@"Programmers say, ""I like C#.""");
  }
}
```

The output from this program is shown here:

```
This is a verbatim
string literal
that spans several lines.

Here is some tabbed output:
1       2       3       4
5       6       7       8

Programmers say, "I like C#."
```

The important point to notice about the preceding program is that the verbatim string literals are displayed precisely as they are entered into the program.

The advantage of verbatim string literals is that you can specify output in your program exactly as it will appear on the screen. However, in the case of multiline strings, the wrapping will obscure the indentation of your program. For this reason, the programs in this book will make only limited use of verbatim string literals. That said, they are still a wonderful benefit for many formatting situations.

One last point: Don't confuse strings with characters. A character literal, such as 'X', represents a single letter of type **char**. A string containing only one letter, such as "X", is still a string.

A Closer Look at Variables

Variables are declared using this form of statement:

type var-name;

where *type* is the data type of the variable and *var-name* is its name. You can declare a variable of any valid type, including the value types just described. It is important to understand that a variable's capabilities are determined by its type. For example, a variable of type **bool** cannot be used to store floating-point values. Furthermore, the type of a variable cannot change during its lifetime. An **int** variable cannot turn into a **char** variable, for example.

All variables in C# must be declared prior to their use. As a general rule, this is necessary because the compiler must know what type of data a variable contains before it can properly compile any statement that uses the variable. It also enables the compiler to perform strict type-checking.

C# defines several different kinds of variables. The kind that we have been using are called *local variables* because they are declared within a method.

Initializing a Variable

One way to give a variable a value is through an assignment statement, as you have already seen. Another way is by giving it an initial value when it is declared. To do this, follow the variable's name with an equal sign and the value being assigned. The general form of initialization is shown here:

   type var-name = value;

Here, *value* is the value that is given to the variable when it is created. The value must be compatible with the specified type.

   Here are some examples:

```
int count = 10; // give count an initial value of 10
char ch = 'X';  // initialize ch with the letter X
float f = 1.2F; // f is initialized with 1.2
```

   When declaring two or more variables of the same type using a comma-separated list, you can give one or more of those variables an initial value. For example:

```
int a, b = 8, c = 19, d; // b and c have initializations
```

In this case, only **b** and **c** are initialized.

Dynamic Initialization

Although the preceding examples have used only constants as initializers, C# allows variables to be initialized dynamically, using any expression valid at the point at which the variable is declared. For example, here is a short program that computes the hypotenuse of a right triangle given the lengths of its two opposing sides.

```
// Demonstrate dynamic initialization.

using System;

class DynInit {
  static void Main() {
    // Length of sides.
    double s1 = 4.0;
    double s2 = 5.0;

    // Dynamically initialize hypot.
    double hypot = Math.Sqrt( (s1 * s1) + (s2 * s2) );

    Console.Write("Hypotenuse of triangle with sides " +
                  s1 + " by " + s2 + " is ");

    Console.WriteLine("{0:#.###}.", hypot);

  }
}
```

   Here is the output:

```
Hypotenuse of triangle with sides 4 by 5 is 6.403.
```

Here, three local variables—**s1**, **s2**, and **hypot**—are declared. The first two, **s1** and **s2**, are initialized by constants. However, **hypot** is initialized dynamically to the length of the hypotenuse. Notice that the initialization involves calling **Math.Sqrt( )**. As explained, you can use any expression that is valid at the point of the initialization. Since a call to **Math.Sqrt( )** (or any other library method) is valid at this point, it can be used in the initialization of **hypot**. The key point here is that the initialization expression can use any element valid at the time of the initialization, including calls to methods, other variables, or literals.

Implicitly Typed Variables

As explained, in C# all variables must be declared. Normally, a declaration includes the type of the variable, such as **int** or **bool**, followed by the name of the variable. However, beginning with C# 3.0, it became possible to let the compiler determine the type of a local variable based on the value used to initialize it. This is called an *implicitly typed variable.*

An implicitly typed variable is declared using the keyword **var**, and it must be initialized. The compiler uses the type of the initializer to determine the type of the variable. Here is an example:

```
var e = 2.7183;
```

Because **e** is initialized with a floating-point literal (whose type is **double** by default), the type of **e** is **double**. Had **e** been declared like this:

```
var e = 2.7183F;
```

then **e** would have the type **float**, instead.

The following program demonstrates implicitly typed variables. It reworks the program shown in the preceding section so that all variables are implicitly typed.

```
// Demonstrate implicitly typed variables.

using System;

class ImplicitlyTypedVar {
  static void Main() {

    // These are now implicitly typed variables. They
    // are of type double because their initializing
    // expressions are of type double.
    var s1 = 4.0;
    var s2 = 5.0;

    // Now, hypot is implicitly typed.  Its type is double
    // because the return type of Sqrt() is double.
    var hypot = Math.Sqrt( (s1 * s1) + (s2 * s2) );

    Console.Write("Hypotenuse of triangle with sides " +
                 s1 + " by " + s2 + " is ");

    Console.WriteLine("{0:#.###}.", hypot);

    // The following statement will not compile because
    // s1 is a double and cannot be assigned a decimal value.
```

```
//    s1 = 12.2M;  // Error!
  }
}
```

The output is the same as before.

It is important to emphasize that an implicitly typed variable is still a strongly typed variable. Notice this commented-out line in the program:

```
//    s1 = 12.2M;  // Error!
```

This assignment is invalid because **s1** is of type **double**. Thus, it cannot be assigned a **decimal** value. The only difference between an implicitly typed variable and a "normal" explicitly typed variable is how the type is determined. Once that type has been determined, the variable has a type, and this type is fixed throughout the lifetime of the variable. Thus, the type of **s1** cannot be changed during execution of the program.

Implicitly typed variables were not added to C# to replace "normal" variable declarations. Instead, implicitly typed variables are designed to handle some special-case situations, the most important of which relate to Language-Integrated Query (LINQ), which is described in Chapter 19. Therefore, for most variable declarations, you should continue to use explicitly typed variables because they make your code easier to read and easier to understand.

One last point: Only one implicitly typed variable can be declared at any one time. Therefore, the following declaration,

```
var s1 = 4.0, s2 = 5.0; // Error!
```

is wrong and won't compile because it attempts to declare both **s1** and **s2** at the same time.

The Scope and Lifetime of Variables

So far, all of the variables that we have been using are declared at the start of the **Main()** method. However, C# allows a local variable to be declared within any block. As explained in Chapter 1, a block begins with an opening curly brace and ends with a closing curly brace. A block defines a *scope*. Thus, each time you start a new block, you are creating a new scope. A scope determines what names are visible to other parts of your program without qualification. It also determines the lifetime of local variables.

The most important scopes in C# are those defined by a class and those defined by a method. A discussion of class scope (and variables declared within it) is deferred until later in this book, when classes are described. For now, we will examine only the scopes defined by or within a method.

The scope defined by a method begins with its opening curly brace and ends with its closing curly brace. However, if that method has parameters, they too are included within the scope defined by the method.

As a general rule, local variables declared inside a scope are not visible to code that is defined outside that scope. Thus, when you declare a variable within a scope, you are protecting it from access or modification from outside the scope. Indeed, the scope rules provide the foundation for encapsulation.

Scopes can be nested. For example, each time you create a block of code, you are creating a new, nested scope. When this occurs, the outer scope encloses the inner scope. This means that local variables declared in the outer scope will be visible to code within the inner scope.

However, the reverse is not true. Local variables declared within the inner scope will not be visible outside it.

To understand the effect of nested scopes, consider the following program:

```
// Demonstrate block scope.

using System;

class ScopeDemo {
  static void Main() {
    int x; // known to all code within Main()

    x = 10;
    if(x == 10) { // start new scope
      int y = 20; // known only to this block

      // x and y both known here.
      Console.WriteLine("x and y: " + x + " " + y);
      x = y * 2;
    }
    // y = 100; // Error! y not known here.

    // x is still known here.
    Console.WriteLine("x is " + x);
  }
}
```

As the comments indicate, the variable **x** is declared at the start of **Main( )**'s scope and is accessible to all subsequent code within **Main( )**. Within the **if** block, **y** is declared. Since a block defines a scope, **y** is visible only to other code within its block. This is why outside of its block, the line **y = 100;** is commented out. If you remove the leading comment symbol, a compile-time error will occur because **y** is not visible outside of its block. Within the **if** block, **x** can be used because code within a block (that is, a nested scope) has access to variables declared by an enclosing scope.

Within a block, variables can be declared at any point, but are valid only after they are declared. Thus, if you define a variable at the start of a method, it is available to all of the code within that method. Conversely, if you declare a variable at the end of a block, it is effectively useless, because no code will have access to it.

If a variable declaration includes an initializer, then that variable will be reinitialized each time the block in which it is declared is entered. For example, consider this program:

```
// Demonstrate lifetime of a variable.

using System;

class VarInitDemo {
  static void Main() {
    int x;

    for(x = 0; x < 3; x++) {
      int y = -1; // y is initialized each time block is entered
      Console.WriteLine("y is: " + y); // this always prints -1
```

```
      y = 100;
      Console.WriteLine("y is now: " + y);
    }
  }
 }
}
```

The output generated by this program is shown here:

```
y is: -1
y is now: 100
y is: -1
y is now: 100
y is: -1
y is now: 100
```

As you can see, **y** is always reinitialized to –1 each time the inner **for** loop is entered. Even though it is subsequently assigned the value 100, this value is lost.

There is one quirk to C#'s scope rules that may surprise you: Although blocks can be nested, no variable declared within an inner scope can have the same name as a variable declared by an enclosing scope. For example, the following program, which tries to declare two separate variables with the same name, will not compile.

```
/*
   This program attempts to declare a variable
   in an inner scope with the same name as one
   defined in an outer scope.

   *** This program will not compile. ***
*/

using System;

class NestVar {
  static void Main() {
    int count;

    for(count = 0; count < 10; count = count+1) {
      Console.WriteLine("This is count: " + count);

      int count; // illegal!!!
      for(count = 0; count < 2; count++)
        Console.WriteLine("This program is in error!");
    }
  }
}
```

If you come from a C/C++ background, then you know that there is no restriction on the names you give variables declared in an inner scope. Thus, in C/C++ the declaration of **count** within the block of the outer **for** loop is completely valid. However, in C/C++, such a declaration hides the outer variable. The designers of C# felt that this type of *name hiding* could easily lead to programming errors and disallowed it.

Type Conversion and Casting

In programming, it is common to assign one type of variable to another. For example, you might want to assign an **int** value to a **float** variable, as shown here:

```
int i;
float f;

i = 10;
f = i; // assign an int to a float
```

When compatible types are mixed in an assignment, the value of the right side is automatically converted to the type of the left side. Thus, in the preceding fragment, the value in **i** is converted into a **float** and then assigned to **f**. However, because of C#'s strict type-checking, not all types are compatible, and thus, not all type conversions are implicitly allowed. For example, **bool** and **int** are not compatible. Fortunately, it is still possible to obtain a conversion between incompatible types by using a *cast*. A cast performs an explicit type conversion. Both automatic type conversion and casting are examined here.

Automatic Conversions

When one type of data is assigned to another type of variable, an *implicit* type conversion will take place automatically if

- The two types are compatible.
- The destination type has a range that is greater than the source type.

When these two conditions are met, a *widening conversion* takes place. For example, the **int** type is always large enough to hold all valid **byte** values, and both **int** and **byte** are compatible integer types, so an implicit conversion can be applied.

For widening conversions, the numeric types, including integer and floating-point types, are compatible with each other. For example, the following program is perfectly valid since **long** to **double** is a widening conversion that is automatically performed.

```
// Demonstrate implicit conversion from long to double.

using System;

class LtoD {
  static void Main() {
    long L;
    double D;

    L = 100123285L;
    D = L;

    Console.WriteLine("L and D: " + L + " " + D);
  }
}
```

Although there is an implicit conversion from **long** to **double**, there is no implicit conversion from **double** to **long** since this is not a widening conversion. Thus, the following version of the preceding program is invalid:

```
// *** This program will not compile. ***

using System;

class LtoD {
  static void Main() {
    long L;
    double D;

    D = 100123285.0;
    L = D; // Illegal!!!

    Console.WriteLine("L and D: " + L + " " + D);

  }
}
```

In addition to the restrictions just described, there are no implicit conversions between **decimal** and **float** or **double**, or from the numeric types to **char** or **bool**. Also, **char** and **bool** are not compatible with each other.

Casting Incompatible Types

Although the implicit type conversions are helpful, they will not fulfill all programming needs because they apply only to widening conversions between compatible types. For all other cases you must employ a cast. A *cast* is an instruction to the compiler to convert the outcome of an expression into a specified type. Thus, it requests an explicit type conversion. A cast has this general form:

> (*target-type*) *expression*

Here, *target-type* specifies the desired type to convert the specified expression to. For example, given

```
double x, y;
```

if you want the type of the expression **x/y** to be **int**, you can write

```
(int) (x / y)
```

Here, even though **x** and **y** are of type **double**, the cast converts the outcome of the expression to **int**. The parentheses surrounding **x / y** are necessary. Otherwise, the cast to **int** would apply only to the **x** and not to the outcome of the division. The cast is necessary here because there is no implicit conversion from **double** to **int**.

When a cast involves a *narrowing conversion*, information might be lost. For example, when casting a **long** into an **int**, information will be lost if the **long**'s value is greater than the range of an **int** because its high-order bits are removed. When a floating-point value is cast to an integer type, the fractional component will also be lost due to truncation. For example, if the value 1.23 is assigned to an integer, the resulting value will simply be 1. The 0.23 is lost.

The following program demonstrates some type conversions that require casts. It also shows some situations in which the casts cause data to be lost.

```
// Demonstrate casting.

using System;

class CastDemo {
  static void Main() {
    double x, y;
    byte b;
    int i;
    char ch;
    uint u;
    short s;
    long l;

    x = 10.0;
    y = 3.0;

    // Cast double to int, fractional component lost.
    i = (int) (x / y);
    Console.WriteLine("Integer outcome of x / y: " + i);
    Console.WriteLine();

    // Cast an int into a byte, no data lost.
    i = 255;
    b = (byte) i;
    Console.WriteLine("b after assigning 255: " + b +
                      " -- no data lost.");

    // Cast an int into a byte, data lost.
    i = 257;
    b = (byte) i;
    Console.WriteLine("b after assigning 257: " + b +
                      " -- data lost.");
    Console.WriteLine();

    // Cast a uint into a short, no data lost.
    u = 32000;
    s = (short) u;
    Console.WriteLine("s after assigning 32000: " + s +
                      " -- no data lost.");

    // Cast a uint into a short, data lost.
    u = 64000;
    s = (short) u;
    Console.WriteLine("s after assigning 64000: " + s +
                      " -- data lost.");
    Console.WriteLine();
```

```
      // Cast a long into a uint, no data lost.
      l = 64000;
      u = (uint) l;
      Console.WriteLine("u after assigning 64000: " + u +
                          " -- no data lost.");

      // Cast a long into a uint, data lost.
      l = -12;
      u = (uint) l;
      Console.WriteLine("u after assigning -12: " + u +
                          " -- data lost.");
      Console.WriteLine();

      // Cast an int into a char.
      b = 88; // ASCII code for X
      ch = (char) b;
      Console.WriteLine("ch after assigning 88: " + ch);
   }
}
```

The output from the program is shown here:

```
Integer outcome of x / y: 3

b after assigning 255: 255 -- no data lost.
b after assigning 257: 1 -- data lost.

s after assigning 32000: 32000 -- no data lost.
s after assigning 64000: -1536 -- data lost.

u after assigning 64000: 64000 -- no data lost.
u after assigning -12: 4294967284 -- data lost.

ch after assigning 88: X
```

Let's look at each assignment. The cast of **(x / y)** to **int** results in the truncation of the fractional component, and information is lost.

No loss of information occurs when **b** is assigned the value 255 because a **byte** can hold the value 255. However, when the attempt is made to assign **b** the value 257, information loss occurs because 257 exceeds a **byte**'s range. In both cases the casts are needed because there is no implicit conversion from **int** to **byte**.

When the **short** variable **s** is assigned the value 32,000 through the **uint** variable **u**, no data is lost because a **short** can hold the value 32,000. However, in the next assignment, **u** has the value 64,000, which is outside the range of a **short**, and data is lost. In both cases the casts are needed because there is no implicit conversion from **uint** to **short**.

Next, **u** is assigned the value 64,000 through the **long** variable **l**. In this case, no data is lost because 64,000 is within the range of a **uint**. However, when the value –12 is assigned to **u**, data is lost because a **uint** cannot hold negative numbers. In both cases the casts are needed because there is no implicit conversion from **long** to **uint**.

Finally, no information is lost, but a cast is needed when assigning a **byte** value to a **char**.

Type Conversion in Expressions

In addition to occurring within an assignment, type conversions also take place within an expression. In an expression, you can freely mix two or more different types of data as long as they are compatible with each other. For example, you can mix **short** and **long** within an expression because they are both numeric types. When different types of data are mixed within an expression, they are converted to the same type, on an operation-by-operation basis.

The conversions are accomplished through the use of C#'s *type promotion rules.* Here is the algorithm that they define for binary operations:

IF one operand is a **decimal**, THEN the other operand is promoted to **decimal** (unless it is of type **float** or **double**, in which case an error results).

ELSE IF one operand is a **double**, the second is promoted to **double**.

ELSE IF one operand is a **float**, the second is promoted to **float**.

ELSE IF one operand is a **ulong**, the second is promoted to **ulong** (unless it is of type **sbyte**, **short**, **int**, or **long**, in which case an error results).

ELSE IF one operand is a **long**, the second is promoted to **long**.

ELSE IF one operand is a **uint** and the second is of type **sbyte**, **short**, or **int**, both are promoted to **long**.

ELSE IF one operand is a **uint**, the second is promoted to **uint**.

ELSE both operands are promoted to **int**.

There are a couple of important points to be made about the type promotion rules. First, not all types can be mixed in an expression. Specifically, there is no implicit conversion from **float** or **double** to **decimal**, and it is not possible to mix **ulong** with any signed integer type. To mix these types requires the use of an explicit cast.

Second, pay special attention to the last rule. It states that if none of the preceding rules applies, then all other operands are promoted to **int**. Therefore, in an expression, all **char**, **sbyte**, **byte**, **ushort**, and **short** values are promoted to **int** for the purposes of calculation. This is called *integer promotion.* It also means that the outcome of all arithmetic operations will be no smaller than **int**.

It is important to understand that type promotions only apply to the values operated upon when an expression is evaluated. For example, if the value of a **byte** variable is promoted to **int** inside an expression, outside the expression, the variable is still a **byte**. Type promotion only affects the evaluation of an expression.

Type promotion can, however, lead to somewhat unexpected results. For example, when an arithmetic operation involves two **byte** values, the following sequence occurs. First, the **byte** operands are promoted to **int**. Then the operation takes place, yielding an **int** result. Thus, the outcome of an operation involving two **byte** values will be an **int**. This is not what you might intuitively expect. Consider the following program.

```
// A promotion surprise!

using System;

class PromDemo {
  static void Main() {
    byte b;

    b = 10;
    b = (byte) (b * b); // cast needed!!

    Console.WriteLine("b: "+ b);
  }
}
```

Somewhat counterintuitively, a cast to **byte** is needed when assigning **b * b** back to **b**! The reason is because in **b * b**, the value of **b** is promoted to **int** when the expression is evaluated. Thus, **b * b** results in an **int** value, which cannot be assigned to a **byte** variable without a cast. Keep this in mind if you get unexpected type-incompatibility error messages on expressions that would otherwise seem perfectly correct.

This same sort of situation also occurs when performing operations on **char**s. For example, in the following fragment, the cast back to **char** is needed because of the promotion of **ch1** and **ch2** to **int** within the expression

```
char ch1 = 'a', ch2 = 'b';

ch1 = (char) (ch1 + ch2);
```

Without the cast, the result of adding **ch1** to **ch2** would be **int**, which can't be assigned to a **char**.

Type promotions also occur when a unary operation, such as the unary –, takes place. For the unary operations, operands smaller than **int** (**byte**, **sbyte**, **short**, and **ushort**) are promoted to **int**. Also, a **char** operand is converted to **int**. Furthermore, if a **uint** value is negated, it is promoted to **long**.

Using Casts in Expressions

A cast can be applied to a specific portion of a larger expression. This gives you fine-grained control over the way type conversions occur when an expression is evaluated. For example, consider the following program. It displays the square roots of the numbers from 1 to 10. It also displays the whole number portion and the fractional part of each result, separately. To do so, it uses a cast to convert the result of **Math.Sqrt( )** to **int**.

```
// Using casts in an expression.

using System;

class CastExpr {
  static void Main() {
    double n;

    for(n = 1.0; n <= 10; n++) {
```

```
        Console.WriteLine("The square root of {0} is {1}",
                        n, Math.Sqrt(n));

        Console.WriteLine("Whole number part: {0}" ,
                        (int) Math.Sqrt(n));

        Console.WriteLine("Fractional part: {0}",
                        Math.Sqrt(n) - (int) Math.Sqrt(n) );
        Console.WriteLine();
    }
  }
}
```

Here is the output from the program:

```
The square root of 1 is 1
Whole number part: 1
Fractional part: 0

The square root of 2 is 1.4142135623731
Whole number part: 1
Fractional part: 0.414213562373095

The square root of 3 is 1.73205080756888
Whole number part: 1
Fractional part: 0.732050807568877

The square root of 4 is 2
Whole number part: 2
Fractional part: 0

The square root of 5 is 2.23606797749979
Whole number part: 2
Fractional part: 0.23606797749979

The square root of 6 is 2.44948974278318
Whole number part: 2
Fractional part: 0.449489742783178

The square root of 7 is 2.64575131106459
Whole number part: 2
Fractional part: 0.645751311064591

The square root of 8 is 2.82842712474619
Whole number part: 2
Fractional part: 0.82842712474619

The square root of 9 is 3
Whole number part: 3
Fractional part: 0

The square root of 10 is 3.16227766016838
Whole number part: 3
Fractional part: 0.16227766016838
```

As the output shows, the cast of **Math.Sqrt( )** to **int** results in the whole number component of the value. In this expression

```
Math.Sqrt(n) - (int) Math.Sqrt(n)
```

the cast to **int** obtains the whole number component, which is then subtracted from the complete value, yielding the fractional component. Thus, the outcome of the expression is **double**. Only the value of the second call to **Math.Sqrt( )** is cast to **int**.

Operators

C# provides an extensive set of operators that give the programmer detailed control over the construction and evaluation of expressions. Most of C#'s operators fall into the following categories: *arithmetic, bitwise, relational,* and *logical.* These operators are examined in this chapter. Also discussed are the assignment operator and the ? operator. C# also defines several other operators that handle specialized situations, such as array indexing, member access, and the lambda operator. These special operators are examined later in this book, when the features to which they apply are described.

Arithmetic Operators

C# defines the following arithmetic operators:

Operator	Meaning
+	Addition
–	Subtraction (also unary minus)
*	Multiplication
/	Division
%	Modulus
++	Increment
– –	Decrement

The operators +, –, *, and / all work in the expected way. These can be applied to any built-in numeric data type.

Although the actions of arithmetic operators are well known to all readers, a few special situations warrant some explanation. First, remember that when / is applied to an integer, any remainder will be truncated; for example, 10/3 will equal 3 in integer division. You can obtain the remainder of this division by using the modulus operator, %. The % is also referred to as the *remainder operator.* It yields the remainder of an integer division. For example, 10 % 3 is 1. In C#, the % can be applied to both integer and floating-point types. Thus, 10.0 % 3.0 is also 1. (This differs from C/C++, which allow modulus operations only on integer types.) The following program demonstrates the modulus operator.

```
// Demonstrate the % operator.

using System;

class ModDemo {
  static void Main() {
    int iresult, irem;
    double dresult, drem;

    iresult = 10 / 3;
    irem = 10 % 3;

    dresult = 10.0 / 3.0;
    drem = 10.0 % 3.0;

    Console.WriteLine("Result and remainder of 10 / 3: " +
                      iresult + " " + irem);
    Console.WriteLine("Result and remainder of 10.0 / 3.0: " +
                      dresult + " " + drem);
  }
}
```

The output from the program is shown here:

```
Result and remainder of 10 / 3: 3 1
Result and remainder of 10.0 / 3.0: 3.33333333333333 1
```

As you can see, the % yields a remainder of 1 for both integer and floating-point operations.

Increment and Decrement

Introduced in Chapter 2, the **++** and the **– –** are the increment and decrement operators. As you will see, they have some special properties that make them quite interesting. Let's begin by reviewing precisely what the increment and decrement operators do.

The increment operator adds 1 to its operand, and the decrement operator subtracts 1. Therefore,

```
x = x + 1;
```

is the same as

```
x++;
```

and

```
x = x - 1;
```

is the same as

```
x--;
```

Understand, however, that in the increment or decrement forms, x is evaluated only once, not twice. This can improve efficiency in some cases.

Both the increment and decrement operators can either precede (prefix) or follow (postfix) the operand. For example

```
x = x + 1;
```

can be written as

```
++x; // prefix form
```

or as

```
x++; // postfix form
```

In the foregoing example, there is no difference whether the increment is applied as a prefix or a postfix. However, when an increment or decrement is used as part of a larger expression, there is an important difference. When an increment or decrement operator *precedes* its operand, the result of the operation is the value of the operand *after* the increment. If the operator *follows* its operand, the result of the operation is the value of the operand *before* the increment. Consider the following:

```
x = 10;
y = ++x;
```

In this case, **y** will be set to 11. This is because **x** is first incremented and then its value is returned. However, if the code is written as

```
x = 10;
y = x++;
```

then **y** will be set to 10. In this case, the value of **x** is first obtained, **x** is incremented, and then the original value of **x** is returned. In both cases, **x** is still set to 11. The difference is what is returned by the operation.

There are significant advantages in being able to control when the increment or decrement operation takes place. Consider the following program, which generates a series of numbers:

```
// Demonstrate the difference between prefix and
// postfix forms of ++.

using System;

class PrePostDemo {
  static void Main() {
    int x, y;
    int i;

    x = 1;
    y = 0;
    Console.WriteLine("Series generated using y = y + x++;");
    for(i = 0; i < 10; i++) {
      y = y + x++; // postfix ++

      Console.WriteLine(y + " ");
    }
```

```
    Console.WriteLine();

    x = 1;
    y = 0;
    Console.WriteLine("Series generated using y = y + ++x;");
    for(i = 0; i < 10; i++) {

      y = y + ++x; // prefix ++

      Console.WriteLine(y + " ");
    }
    Console.WriteLine();
  }
}
```

The output is shown here:

```
Series generated using y = y + x++;
1
3
6
10
15
21
28
36
45
55

Series generated using y = y + ++x;
2
5
9
14
20
27
35
44
54
65
```

As the output confirms, the statement

```
y = y + x++;
```

adds the current values of x and y, and assigns this result back to y. The value of x is incremented after its value has been obtained. However, the statement

```
y = y + ++x;
```

obtains the value of x, increments x, and then adds that value to the current value of y. This result is assigned to y. As the output shows, simply changing ++x to x++ changes the number series quite substantially.

One other point about the preceding example: Don't let expressions like

```
y + ++x
```

intimidate you. Although having two operators back-to-back is a bit unsettling at first glance, the compiler keeps it all straight. Just remember, this expression simply adds the value of **y** to the value of **x** incremented.

Relational and Logical Operators

In the terms *relational operator* and *logical operator*, *relational* refers to the relationships that values can have with one another, and *logical* refers to the ways in which true and false values can be connected together. Since the relational operators produce true or false results, they often work with the logical operators. For this reason they will be discussed together here.

The relational operators are as follows:

Operator	Meaning
==	Equal to
!=	Not equal to
>	Greater than
<	Less than
>=	Greater than or equal to
<=	Less than or equal to

The logical operators are shown next:

Operator	Meaning
&	AND
|	OR
^	XOR (exclusive OR)
||	Short-circuit OR
&&	Short-circuit AND
!	NOT

The outcome of the relational and logical operators is a **bool** value.

In general, objects can be compared for equality or inequality using == and !=. However, the comparison operators, <, >, <=, or >=, can be applied only to those types that support an ordering relationship. Therefore, all of the relational operators can be applied to all numeric types. However, values of type **bool** can only be compared for equality or inequality since the **true** and **false** values are not ordered. For example, **true > false** has no meaning in C#.

For the logical operators, the operands must be of type **bool**, and the result of a logical operation is of type **bool**. The logical operators, **&**, |, ^, and !, support the basic logical operations AND, OR, XOR, and NOT, according to the following truth table:

p	q	p & q	p	q	p ^ q	!p
False	False	False	False	False	True
True	False	False	True	True	False
False	True	False	True	True	True
True	True	True	True	False	False

As the table shows, the outcome of an exclusive OR operation is true when one and only one operand is true.

Here is a program that demonstrates several of the relational and logical operators:

```
// Demonstrate the relational and logical operators.

using System;

class RelLogOps {
  static void Main() {
    int i, j;
    bool b1, b2;

    i = 10;
    j = 11;
    if(i < j) Console.WriteLine("i < j");
    if(i <= j) Console.WriteLine("i <= j");
    if(i != j) Console.WriteLine("i != j");
    if(i == j) Console.WriteLine("this won't execute");
    if(i >= j) Console.WriteLine("this won't execute");
    if(i > j) Console.WriteLine("this won't execute");

    b1 = true;
    b2 = false;
    if(b1 & b2) Console.WriteLine("this won't execute");
    if(!(b1 & b2)) Console.WriteLine("!(b1 & b2) is true");
    if(b1 | b2) Console.WriteLine("b1 | b2 is true");
    if(b1 ^ b2) Console.WriteLine("b1 ^ b2 is true");
  }
}
```

The output from the program is shown here:

```
i < j
i <= j
i != j
!(b1 & b2) is true
b1 | b2 is true
b1 ^ b2 is true
```

The logical operators provided by C# perform the most commonly used logical operations. However, several other operations are defined by the rules for formal logic. These other logical operations can be constructed using the logical operators supported by C#. Thus, C# supplies a set of logical operators sufficient to construct any other logical operation. For example, another logical operation is *implication*. Implication is a binary operation in which the outcome is false only when the left operand is true and the right operand is false. (The implication operation reflects the idea that true cannot imply false.) Thus, the truth table for the implication operator is shown here:

p	q	p implies q
True	True	True
True	False	False
False	False	True
False	True	True

The implication operation can be constructed using a combination of the ! and the | operator, as shown here:

!p | q

The following program demonstrates this implementation:

```
// Create an implication operator in C#.

using System;

class Implication {
  static void Main() {
    bool p=false, q=false;
    int i, j;

    for(i = 0; i < 2; i++) {
      for(j = 0; j < 2; j++) {
        if(i==0) p = true;
        if(i==1) p = false;
        if(j==0) q = true;
        if(j==1) q = false;

        Console.WriteLine("p is " + p + ", q is " + q);
        if(!p | q) Console.WriteLine(p + " implies " + q +
                     " is " + true);
        Console.WriteLine();
      }
    }
  }
}
```

The output is shown here:

```
p is True, q is True
True implies True is True

p is True, q is False
```

```
p is False, q is True
False implies True is True

p is False, q is False
False implies False is True
```

Short-Circuit Logical Operators

C# supplies special *short-circuit* versions of its AND and OR logical operators that can be used to produce more efficient code. To understand why, consider the following. In an AND operation, if the first operand is false, then the outcome is false no matter what value the second operand has. In an OR operation, if the first operand is true, then the outcome of the operation is true no matter what the value of the second operand. Thus, in these two cases there is no need to evaluate the second operand. By not evaluating the second operand, time is saved and more efficient code is produced.

The short-circuit AND operator is **&&** and the short-circuit OR operator is **||**. As described earlier, their normal counterparts are **&** and **|**. The only difference between the normal and short-circuit versions is that the normal operands will always evaluate each operand, but short-circuit versions will evaluate the second operand only when necessary.

Here is a program that demonstrates the short-circuit AND operator. The program determines if the value in **d** is a factor of **n**. It does this by performing a modulus operation. If the remainder of **n / d** is zero, then **d** is a factor. However, since the modulus operation involves a division, the short-circuit form of the AND is used to prevent a divide-by-zero error.

```
// Demonstrate the short-circuit operators.

using System;

class SCops {
  static void Main() {
    int n, d;

    n = 10;
    d = 2;
    if(d != 0 && (n % d) == 0)
      Console.WriteLine(d + " is a factor of " + n);

    d = 0; // now, set d to zero

    // Since d is zero, the second operand is not evaluated.
    if(d != 0 && (n % d) == 0)
      Console.WriteLine(d + " is a factor of " + n);

    // Now, try the same thing without the short-circuit operator.
    // This will cause a divide-by-zero error.
    if(d != 0 & (n % d) == 0)
      Console.WriteLine(d + " is a factor of " + n);
  }
}
```

To prevent a divide-by-zero error, the **if** statement first checks to see if **d** is equal to zero. If it is, then the short-circuit AND stops at that point and does not perform the modulus division. Thus, in the first test, **d** is 2 and the modulus operation is performed. The second test fails because **d** is set to zero, and the modulus operation is skipped, avoiding a divide-by-zero error. Finally, the normal AND operator is tried. This causes both operands to be evaluated, which leads to a runtime error when the division-by-zero occurs.

Since the short-circuit operators are, in some cases, more efficient than their normal counterparts, you might be wondering why C# still offers the normal AND and OR operators. The answer is that in some cases you will want both operands of an AND or OR operation to be evaluated because of the side effects produced. Consider the following:

```
// Side effects can be important.

using System;

class SideEffects {
  static void Main() {
    int i;
    bool someCondition = false;

    i = 0;

    // Here, i is still incremented even though the if statement fails.
    if(someCondition & (++i < 100))
       Console.WriteLine("this won't be displayed");
    Console.WriteLine("if statement executed: " + i); // displays 1

    // In this case, i is not incremented because the short-circuit
    // operator skips the increment.
    if(someCondition && (++i < 100))
      Console.WriteLine("this won't be displayed");
    Console.WriteLine("if statement executed: " + i); // still 1 !!
  }
}
```

First, notice that the **bool** variable **someCondition** is initialized to **false**. Next, examine each **if** statement. As the comments indicate, in the first **if** statement, **i** is incremented despite the fact that **someCondition** is false. When the **&** is used, as it is in the first **if** statement, the expression on the right side of the **&** is evaluated no matter what value the expression on the left has. However, in the second **if** statement, the short-circuit operator is used. In this case, the variable **i** is not incremented because the left operand, **someCondition**, is false, which causes the expression on the right to be skipped. The lesson here is that if your code expects the right-hand operand of an AND or OR operation to be evaluated, then you must use C#'s non-short-circuit forms for these operations.

One other point: The short-circuit AND is also known as the *conditional AND*, and the short-circuit OR is also called the *conditional OR*.

The Assignment Operator

The *assignment operator* is the single equal sign, =. The assignment operator works in C# much as it does in other computer languages. It has this general form:

    var-name = *expression*;

Here, the type of *var-name* must be compatible with the type of *expression*.

The assignment operator does have one interesting attribute that you may not be familiar with: It allows you to create a chain of assignments. For example, consider this fragment:

```
int x, y, z;

x = y = z = 100; // set x, y, and z to 100
```

This fragment sets the variables **x**, **y**, and **z** to 100 using a single statement. This works because the **=** is an operator that yields the assigned value. Thus, the value of **z = 100** is 100, which is then assigned to **y**, which in turn is assigned to **x**. Using a "chain of assignment" is an easy way to set a group of variables to a common value.

Compound Assignments

C# provides special compound assignment operators that simplify the coding of certain assignment statements. Let's begin with an example. The assignment statement shown here:

```
x = x + 10;
```

can be written using a compound assignment as

```
x += 10;
```

The operator pair **+=** tells the compiler to assign to **x** the value of **x** plus 10.
    Here is another example. The statement

```
x = x - 100;
```

is the same as

```
x -= 100;
```

Both statements assign to **x** the value of **x** minus 100.
    There are compound assignment operators for many of the binary operators (that is, those that require two operands). The general form of the shorthand is

var-name op = expression;

Thus, the arithmetic and logical assignment operators are

+=	-=	*=	/=
%=	&=	| =	^=

Because the compound assignment statements are shorter than their noncompound equivalents, the compound assignment operators are also sometimes called the *shorthand assignment* operators.
    The compound assignment operators provide two benefits. First, they are more compact than their "longhand" equivalents. Second, they can result in more efficient executable code (because the left-hand operand is evaluated only once). For these reasons, you will often see the compound assignment operators used in professionally written C# programs.

The Bitwise Operators

C# provides a set of *bitwise* operators that expand the types of problems to which C# can be applied. The bitwise operators act directly upon the bits of their operands. They are defined only for integer operands. They cannot be used on **bool**, **float**, or **double**.

They are called the *bitwise* operators because they are used to test, set, or shift the bits that comprise an integer value. Among other uses, bitwise operations are important to a wide variety of systems-level programming tasks, such as analyzing status information from a device. Table 4-1 lists the bitwise operators.

The Bitwise AND, OR, XOR, and NOT Operators

The bitwise operators AND, OR, XOR, and NOT are &, |, ^, and ~. They perform the same operations as their Boolean logic equivalents described earlier. The difference is that the bitwise operators work on a bit-by-bit basis. The following table shows the outcome of each operation using 1s and 0s:

p	q	p & q	p | q	p ^ q	~p
0	0	0	0	0	1
1	0	0	1	1	0
0	1	0	1	1	1
1	1	1	1	0	0

In terms of its most common usage, you can think of the bitwise AND as a way to turn bits off. That is, any bit that is 0 in either operand will cause the corresponding bit in the outcome to be set to 0. For example

```
    1101 0011
&   1010 1010
    ---------------------
    1000 0010
```

Operator	Result
&	Bitwise AND
|	Bitwise OR
^	Bitwise exclusive OR (XOR)
>>	Shift right
<<	Shift left
~	One's complement (unary NOT)

TABLE 4-1   The Bitwise Operators

The following program demonstrates the **&** by using it to convert odd numbers into even numbers. It does this by turning off bit zero. For example, the low-order byte of the number 9 in binary is 0000 1001. When bit zero is turned off, this number becomes 8, or 0000 1000 in binary.

```
// Use bitwise AND to make a number even.

using System;

class MakeEven {
  static void Main() {
    ushort num;
    ushort i;

    for(i = 1; i <= 10; i++) {
      num = i;

      Console.WriteLine("num: " + num);

      num = (ushort) (num & 0xFFFE);

      Console.WriteLine("num after turning off bit zero: "
                        +  num + "\n");
    }
  }
}
```

The output from this program is shown here:

```
num: 1
num after turning off bit zero: 0

num: 2
num after turning off bit zero: 2

num: 3
num after turning off bit zero: 2

num: 4
num after turning off bit zero: 4

num: 5
num after turning off bit zero: 4

num: 6
num after turning off bit zero: 6

num: 7
num after turning off bit zero: 6

num: 8
num after turning off bit zero: 8

num: 9
num after turning off bit zero: 8
```

```
num: 10
num after turning off bit zero: 10
```

The value **0xFFFE** used in the AND statement is the hexadecimal representation of 1111 1111 1111 1110. Therefore, the AND operation leaves all bits in **num** unchanged except for bit zero, which is set to zero. Thus, even numbers are unchanged, but odd numbers are made even by reducing their value by 1.

The AND operator is also useful when you want to determine whether a bit is on or off. For example, this program determines if a number is odd:

```
// Use bitwise AND to determine if a number is odd.

using System;

class IsOdd {
  static void Main() {
    ushort num;

    num = 10;

    if((num & 1) == 1)
      Console.WriteLine("This won't display.");

    num = 11;

    if((num & 1) == 1)
      Console.WriteLine(num + " is odd.");

  }
}
```

The output is shown here:

```
11 is odd.
```

In the **if** statements, the value of **num** is ANDed with 1. If bit zero in **num** is set, the result of **num & 1** is 1; otherwise, the result is zero. Therefore, the **if** statement can succeed only when the number is odd.

You can use the bit-testing capability of the bitwise **&** to create a program that uses the bitwise **&** to show the bits of a **byte** value in binary format. Here is one approach:

```
// Display the bits within a byte.

using System;

class ShowBits {
  static void Main() {
    int t;
    byte val;

    val = 123;
    for(t=128; t > 0; t = t/2) {
      if((val & t) != 0) Console.Write("1 ");
```

```
    if((val & t) == 0) Console.Write("0 ");
    }
  }
}
```

The output is shown here:

```
0 1 1 1 1 0 1 1
```

The **for** loop successively tests each bit in **val**, using the bitwise AND, to determine if it is on or off. If the bit is on, the digit **1** is displayed; otherwise, **0** is displayed.

The bitwise OR can be used to turn bits on. Any bit that is set to 1 in either operand will cause the corresponding bit in the variable to be set to 1. For example

```
    1101 0011
|   1010 1010
    --------------------
    1111 1011
```

You can make use of the OR to change the make-even program shown earlier into a make-odd program, as shown here:

```
//  Use bitwise OR to make a number odd.

using System;

class MakeOdd {
  static void Main() {
    ushort num;
    ushort i;

    for(i = 1; i <= 10; i++) {
      num = i;

      Console.WriteLine("num: " + num);

      num = (ushort) (num | 1);

      Console.WriteLine("num after turning on bit zero: "
                        +  num + "\n");
    }
  }
}
```

The output from this program is shown here:

```
num: 1
num after turning on bit zero: 1

num: 2
num after turning on bit zero: 3

num: 3
num after turning on bit zero: 3
```

```
num: 4
num after turning on bit zero: 5

num: 5
num after turning on bit zero: 5

num: 6
num after turning on bit zero: 7

num: 7
num after turning on bit zero: 7

num: 8
num after turning on bit zero: 9

num: 9
num after turning on bit zero: 9

num: 10
num after turning on bit zero: 11
```

The program works by ORing each number with the value 1, because 1 is the value that produces a value in binary in which only bit zero is set. When this value is ORed with any other value, it produces a result in which the low-order bit is set and all other bits remain unchanged. Thus, a value that is even will be increased by 1, becoming odd.

An exclusive OR, usually abbreviated XOR, will set a bit on if, and only if, the bits being compared are different, as illustrated here:

```
  0 1 1 1 1 1 1 1
^ 1 0 1 1 1 0 0 1
  -------------------------
  1 1 0 0 0 1 1 0
```

The XOR operator has an interesting property that is useful in a variety of situations. When some value X is XORed with another value Y, and then that result is XORed with Y again, X is produced. That is, given the sequence

R1 = X ^ Y;
R2 = R1 ^ Y;

R2 is the same value as X. Thus, the outcome of a sequence of two XORs using the same value produces the original value. This feature of the XOR can be put into action to create a simple cipher in which some integer is the key that is used to both encode and decode a message by XORing the characters in that message. To encode, the XOR operation is applied the first time, yielding the ciphertext. To decode, the XOR is applied a second time, yielding the plaintext. Of course, such a cipher has no practical value, being trivially easy to break. It does, however, provide an interesting way to demonstrate the effects of the XOR, as the following program shows:

```
// Demonstrate the XOR.

using System;
```

```
class Encode {
  static void Main() {
    char ch1 = 'H';
    char ch2 = 'i';
    char ch3 = '!';
    int key = 88;

    Console.WriteLine("Original message: " + ch1 + ch2 + ch3);

    // Encode the message.
    ch1 = (char) (ch1 ^ key);
    ch2 = (char) (ch2 ^ key);
    ch3 = (char) (ch3 ^ key);

    Console.WriteLine("Encoded message: " + ch1 + ch2 + ch3);

    // Decode the message.
    ch1 = (char) (ch1 ^ key);
    ch2 = (char) (ch2 ^ key);
    ch3 = (char) (ch3 ^ key);

    Console.WriteLine("Decoded message: " + ch1 + ch2 + ch3);
  }
}
```

Here is the output:

```
Original message: Hi!
Encoded message: □1y
Decoded message: Hi!
```

As you can see, the result of two XORs using the same key produces the decoded message. (Remember, this simple XOR cipher is not suitable for any real-world, practical use because it is inherently insecure.)

The unary one's complement (NOT) operator reverses the state of all the bits of the operand. For example, if some integer called **A** has the bit pattern 1001 0110, then ~**A** produces a result with the bit pattern 0110 1001.

The following program demonstrates the NOT operator by displaying a number and its complement in binary:

```
// Demonstrate the bitwise NOT.

using System;

class NotDemo {
  static void Main() {
    sbyte b = -34;

    for(int t=128; t > 0; t = t/2) {
      if((b & t) != 0) Console.Write("1 ");
      if((b & t) == 0) Console.Write("0 ");
    }
    Console.WriteLine();
```

```
    // reverse all bits
    b = (sbyte) ~b;

    for(int t=128; t > 0; t = t/2) {
      if((b & t) != 0) Console.Write("1 ");
      if((b & t) == 0) Console.Write("0 ");
    }
  }
}
```

Here is the output:

```
1 1 0 1 1 1 1 0
0 0 1 0 0 0 0 1
```

The Shift Operators

In C# it is possible to shift the bits that comprise an integer value to the left or to the right by a specified amount. C# defines the two bit-shift operators shown here:

<<	Left shift
>>	Right shift

The general forms for these operators are shown here:

value << num-bits
value >> num-bits

Here, *value* is the value being shifted by the number of bit positions specified by *num-bits*.

A left shift causes all bits within the specified value to be shifted left one position and a zero bit to be brought in on the right. A right shift causes all bits to be shifted right one position. In the case of a right shift on an unsigned value, a 0 is brought in on the left. In the case of a right shift on a signed value, the sign bit is preserved. Recall that negative numbers are represented by setting the high-order bit of an integer value to 1. Thus, if the value being shifted is negative, each right shift brings in a 1 on the left. If the value is positive, each right shift brings in a 0 on the left.

For both left and right shifts, the bits shifted out are lost. Thus, a shift is not a rotate and there is no way to retrieve a bit that has been shifted out.

Here is a program that graphically illustrates the effect of a left and right shift. Here, an integer is given an initial value of 1, which means that its low-order bit is set. Then, eight shifts are performed on the integer. After each shift, the lower eight bits of the value are shown. The process is then repeated, except that a 1 is put in the eighth bit position, and right shifts are performed.

```
// Demonstrate the shift << and >> operators.

using System;

class ShiftDemo {
  static void Main() {
    int val = 1;
```

```
    for(int i = 0; i < 8; i++) {
      for(int t=128; t > 0; t = t/2) {
        if((val & t) != 0) Console.Write("1 ");
        if((val & t) == 0) Console.Write("0 ");
      }
      Console.WriteLine();
      val = val << 1; // left shift
    }
    Console.WriteLine();

    val = 128;
    for(int i = 0; i < 8; i++) {
      for(int t=128; t > 0; t = t/2) {
        if((val & t) != 0) Console.Write("1 ");
        if((val & t) == 0) Console.Write("0 ");
      }
      Console.WriteLine();
      val = val >> 1; // right shift
    }
  }
}
```

The output from the program is shown here:

```
0 0 0 0 0 0 0 1
0 0 0 0 0 0 1 0
0 0 0 0 0 1 0 0
0 0 0 0 1 0 0 0
0 0 0 1 0 0 0 0
0 0 1 0 0 0 0 0
0 1 0 0 0 0 0 0
1 0 0 0 0 0 0 0

1 0 0 0 0 0 0 0
0 1 0 0 0 0 0 0
0 0 1 0 0 0 0 0
0 0 0 1 0 0 0 0
0 0 0 0 1 0 0 0
0 0 0 0 0 1 0 0
0 0 0 0 0 0 1 0
0 0 0 0 0 0 0 1
```

Since binary is based on powers of 2, the shift operators can be used as a way to multiply or divide an integer by 2. A shift left doubles a value. A shift right halves it. Of course, this works only as long as you are not shifting bits off one end or the other. Here is an example:

```
// Use the shift operators to multiply and divide by 2.

using System;

class MultDiv {
  static void Main() {
    int n;

    n = 10;
```

```
    Console.WriteLine("Value of n: " + n);

    // Multiply by 2.
    n = n << 1;
    Console.WriteLine("Value of n after n = n * 2: " + n);

    // Multiply by 4.
    n = n << 2;
    Console.WriteLine("Value of n after n = n * 4: " + n);

    // Divide by 2.
    n = n >> 1;
    Console.WriteLine("Value of n after n = n / 2: " + n);

    // Divide by 4.
    n = n >> 2;
    Console.WriteLine("Value of n after n = n / 4: " + n);
    Console.WriteLine();

    // Reset n.
    n = 10;
    Console.WriteLine("Value of n: " + n);

    // Multiply by 2, 30 times.
    n = n << 30; // data is lost
    Console.WriteLine("Value of n after left-shifting 30 places: " + n);
  }
}
```

The output is shown here:

```
Value of n: 10
Value of n after n = n * 2: 20
Value of n after n = n * 4: 80
Value of n after n = n / 2: 40
Value of n after n = n / 4: 10

Value of n: 10
Value of n after left-shifting 30 places: -2147483648
```

Notice the last line in the output. When the value 10 is left-shifted 30 times, information is lost because bits are shifted out of the range of an **int**. In this case, the garbage value produced is negative because a 1 bit is shifted into the high-order bit, which is used as a sign bit, causing the number to be interpreted as negative. This illustrates why you must be careful when using the shift operators to multiply or divide a value by 2. (See Chapter 3 for an explanation of signed vs. unsigned data types.)

Bitwise Compound Assignments

All of the binary bitwise operators can be used in compound assignments. For example, the following two statements both assign to **x** the outcome of an XOR of **x** with the value 127:

```
x = x ^ 127;
x ^= 127;
```

The ? Operator

One of C#'s most fascinating operators is the **?**, which is C#'s conditional operator. The **?** operator is often used to replace certain types of if-then-else constructions. The **?** is called a *ternary operator* because it requires three operands. It takes the general form

Exp1 ? *Exp2* : *Exp3*;

where *Exp1* is a **bool** expression, and *Exp2* and *Exp3* are expressions. The type of *Exp2* and *Exp3* must be the same (or, an implicit conversion between them must exist). Notice the use and placement of the colon.

The value of a **?** expression is determined like this: *Exp1* is evaluated. If it is true, then *Exp2* is evaluated and becomes the value of the entire **?** expression. If *Exp1* is false, then *Exp3* is evaluated, and its value becomes the value of the expression. Consider this example, which assigns **absval** the absolute value of **val**:

```
absval = val < 0 ? -val : val; // get absolute value of val
```

Here, **absval** will be assigned the value of **val** if **val** is zero or greater. If **val** is negative, then **absval** will be assigned the negative of that value (which yields a positive value).

Here is another example of the **?** operator. This program divides two numbers, but will not allow a division by zero.

```
// Prevent a division by zero using the ?.

using System;

class NoZeroDiv {
  static void Main() {
    int result;

    for(int i = -5; i < 6; i++) {
      result = i != 0 ? 100 / i : 0;
      if(i != 0)
        Console.WriteLine("100 / " + i + " is " + result);
    }
  }
}
```

The output from the program is shown here:

```
100 / -5 is -20
100 / -4 is -25
100 / -3 is -33
100 / -2 is -50
100 / -1 is -100
100 / 1 is 100
100 / 2 is 50
100 / 3 is 33
100 / 4 is 25
100 / 5 is 20
```

Pay special attention to this line from the program:

```
result = i != 0 ? 100 / i : 0;
```

Here, **result** is assigned the outcome of the division of 100 by **i**. However, this division takes place only if **i** is not 0. When **i** is 0, a placeholder value of 0 is assigned to **result**.

You don't actually have to assign the value produced by the **?** to some variable. For example, you could use the value as an argument in a call to a method. Or, if the expressions are all of type **bool**, the **?** can be used as the conditional expression in a loop or **if** statement. For example, the following program displays the results of dividing 100 by only even, non-zero values:

```
// Divide by only even, non-zero values.

using System;

class NoZeroDiv2 {
  static void Main() {

    for(int i = -5; i < 6; i++)
      if(i != 0 ? (i%2 == 0) : false)
        Console.WriteLine("100 / " + i + " is " + 100 / i);
  }
}
```

Notice the **if** statement. If **i** is zero, then the outcome of the **if** is false. Otherwise, if **i** is non-zero, then the outcome of the **if** is true if **i** is even and false if **i** is odd. Thus, only even, non-zero divisors are allowed. Although this example is somewhat contrived for the sake of illustration, such constructs are occasionally very useful.

Spacing and Parentheses

An expression in C# can have tabs and spaces in it to make it more readable. For example, the following two expressions are the same, but the second is easier to read:

```
x=10/y*(127+x);

x = 10 / y * (127 + x);
```

Parentheses can be used to group subexpressions, thereby effectively increasing the precedence of the operations contained within them, just like in algebra. Use of redundant or additional parentheses will not cause errors or slow down execution of the expression. You are encouraged to use parentheses to make clear the exact order of evaluation, both for yourself and for others who may have to figure out your program later. For example, which of the following two expressions is easier to read?

```
x = y/3-34*temp+127;

x = (y/3) - (34*temp) + 127;
```

Operator Precedence

Table 4-2 shows the order of precedence for all C# operators, from highest to lowest. This table includes several operators that will be discussed later in this book.

Highest									
()	[]	.	++ (postfix)	- - (postfix)	checked	new	->	typeof	unchecked
!	~	(cast)	+ (unary)	- (unary)	++ (prefix)	- - (prefix)	sizeof	& (address of)	
*	/	%							
+	-								
<<	>>								
<	>	<=	>=	is	as				
==	!=								
&									
^									
|									
&&									
||									
??									
?:									
=	op=	=>							
Lowest									

TABLE 4-2 The Precedence of the C# Operators

Program Control Statements

This chapter discusses C#'s program control statements. There are three categories of program control statements: *selection* statements, which are the **if** and the **switch**; *iteration* statements, which consist of the **for**, **while**, **do-while**, and **foreach** loops; and *jump* statements, which include **break**, **continue**, **goto**, **return**, and **throw**. Except for **throw**, which is part of C#'s exception-handling mechanism and is discussed in Chapter 13, the others are examined here.

The if Statement

Chapter 2 introduced the **if** statement. It is examined in detail here. The complete form of the **if** statement is

```
if(condition) statement;
else statement;
```

where the targets of the **if** and **else** are single statements. The **else** clause is optional. The targets of both the **if** and **else** can be blocks of statements. The general form of the **if** using blocks of statements is

```
if(condition)
{
  statement sequence
}
else
{
  statement sequence
}
```

If the conditional expression is true, the target of the **if** will be executed; otherwise, if it exists, the target of the **else** will be executed. At no time will both of them be executed. The conditional expression controlling the **if** must produce a **bool** result.

Here is a simple example that uses an **if** and **else** to report if a number is positive or negative:

```
// Determine if a value is positive or negative.

using System;
```

```
class PosNeg {
  static void Main() {
    int i;

    for(i=-5; i <= 5; i++) {
      Console.Write("Testing " + i + ": ");

      if(i < 0) Console.WriteLine("negative");
      else Console.WriteLine("positive");
    }
  }
}
```

The output is shown here:

```
Testing -5: negative
Testing -4: negative
Testing -3: negative
Testing -2: negative
Testing -1: negative
Testing 0: positive
Testing 1: positive
Testing 2: positive
Testing 3: positive
Testing 4: positive
Testing 5: positive
```

In this example, if **i** is less than zero, then the target of the **if** is executed. Otherwise, the target of the **else** is executed. In no case are both executed.

Nested ifs

A *nested if* is an **if** statement that is the target of another **if** or **else**. Nested **if**s are very common in programming. The main thing to remember about nested **if**s in C# is that an **else** clause always refers to the nearest **if** statement that is within the same block as the **else** and not already associated with an **else**. Here is an example:

```
if(i == 10) {
  if(j < 20) a = b;
  if(k > 100) c = d;
  else a = c; // this else refers to if(k > 100)
}
else a = d; // this else refers to if(i == 10)
```

As the comments indicate, the final **else** is not associated with **if(j < 20)** because it is not in the same block (even though it is the nearest **if** without an **else**). Rather, the final **else** is associated with **if(i == 10)**. The inner **else** refers to **if(k > 100)** because it is the closest **if** within the same block.

The following program demonstrates a nested **if**. In the positive/negative program shown earlier, zero is reported as positive. However, as a general rule, zero is considered signless. The following version of the program reports zero as being neither positive nor negative.

```
// Determine if a value is positive, negative, or zero.

using System;

class PosNegZero {
  static void Main() {
    int i;

    for(i=-5; i <= 5; i++) {

      Console.Write("Testing " + i + ": ");

      if(i < 0) Console.WriteLine("negative");
      else if(i == 0) Console.WriteLine("no sign");
        else Console.WriteLine("positive");
    }
  }
}
```

Here is the output:

```
Testing -5: negative
Testing -4: negative
Testing -3: negative
Testing -2: negative
Testing -1: negative
Testing 0: no sign
Testing 1: positive
Testing 2: positive
Testing 3: positive
Testing 4: positive
Testing 5: positive
```

The if-else-if Ladder

A common programming construct that is based upon the nested **if** is the *if-else-if ladder*. It looks like this:

> if(*condition*)
>   *statement*;
> else if(*condition*)
>   *statement*;
> else if(*condition*)
>   *statement*;
>
>   .
>
>   .
>
>   .
>
> else
>   *statement*;

The conditional expressions are evaluated from the top downward. As soon as a true condition is found, the statement associated with it is executed, and the rest of the ladder is bypassed.

If none of the conditions is true, then the final **else** clause will be executed. The final **else** often acts as a default condition. That is, if all other conditional tests fail, then the last **else** clause is executed. If there is no final **else** and all other conditions are false, then no action will take place.

The following program demonstrates the **if-else-if** ladder. It finds the smallest single-digit factor (other than 1) for a given value.

```
// Determine smallest single-digit factor.

using System;

class Ladder {
  static void Main() {
    int num;

    for(num = 2; num < 12; num++) {
      if((num % 2) == 0)
        Console.WriteLine("Smallest factor of " + num + " is 2.");
      else if((num % 3) == 0)
        Console.WriteLine("Smallest factor of " + num + " is 3.");
      else if((num % 5) == 0)
        Console.WriteLine("Smallest factor of " + num + " is 5.");
      else if((num % 7) == 0)
        Console.WriteLine("Smallest factor of " + num + " is 7.");
      else
        Console.WriteLine(num + " is not divisible by 2, 3, 5, or 7.");
    }
  }
}
```

The program produces the following output:

```
Smallest factor of 2 is 2.
Smallest factor of 3 is 3.
Smallest factor of 4 is 2.
Smallest factor of 5 is 5.
Smallest factor of 6 is 2.
Smallest factor of 7 is 7.
Smallest factor of 8 is 2.
Smallest factor of 9 is 3.
Smallest factor of 10 is 2.
11 is not divisible by 2, 3, 5, or 7.
```

As you can see, the **else** is executed only if none of the preceding **if** statements succeeds.

The switch Statement

The second of C#'s selection statements is **switch**. The **switch** provides for a multiway branch. Thus, it enables a program to select among several alternatives. Although a series of nested **if** statements can perform multiway tests, for many situations the **switch** is a more efficient approach. It works like this: The value of an expression is successively tested against a list of constants. When a match is found, the statement sequence associated with that match is executed. The general form of the **switch** statement is

```
switch(expression) {
  case constant1:
    statement sequence
    break;
  case constant2:
    statement sequence
    break;
  case constant3:
    statement sequence
    break;

    .
    .
    .

  default:
    statement sequence
    break;
}
```

The **switch** expression must be of an integer type, such as **char**, **byte**, **short**, or **int**, of an enumeration type, or of type **string**. (Enumerations and the **string** type are described later in this book.) Thus, floating-point expressions, for example, are not allowed. Frequently, the expression controlling the **switch** is simply a variable. The **case** constants must be of a type compatible with the expression. No two **case** constants in the same **switch** can have identical values.

The **default** sequence is executed if no **case** constant matches the expression. The **default** is optional; if it is not present, no action takes place if all matches fail. When a match is found, the statements associated with that **case** are executed until the **break** is encountered.

The following program demonstrates the **switch**:

```
// Demonstrate the switch.

using System;

class SwitchDemo {
  static void Main() {
    int i;

    for(i=0; i<10; i++)
      switch(i) {
        case 0:
          Console.WriteLine("i is zero");
          break;
        case 1:
          Console.WriteLine("i is one");
          break;
        case 2:
          Console.WriteLine("i is two");
          break;
        case 3:
          Console.WriteLine("i is three");
          break;
```

```
        case 4:
          Console.WriteLine("i is four");
          break;
        default:
          Console.WriteLine("i is five or more");
          break;
      }
    }
}
```

The output produced by this program is shown here:

```
i is zero
i is one
i is two
i is three
i is four
i is five or more
i is five or more
i is five or more
i is five or more
i is five or more
```

As you can see, each time through the loop, the statements associated with the **case** constant that matches **i** are executed. All others are bypassed. When **i** is five or greater, no **case** constants match, so the **default** is executed.

In the preceding example, the **switch** was controlled by an **int** variable. As explained, you can control a **switch** with any integer type, including **char**. Here is an example that uses a **char** expression and **char case** constants:

```
// Use a char to control the switch.

using System;

class SwitchDemo2 {
  static void Main() {
    char ch;

    for(ch='A'; ch<= 'E'; ch++)
      switch(ch) {
        case 'A':
          Console.WriteLine("ch is A");
          break;
        case 'B':
          Console.WriteLine("ch is B");
          break;
        case 'C':
          Console.WriteLine("ch is C");
          break;
        case 'D':
          Console.WriteLine("ch is D");
          break;
        case 'E':
          Console.WriteLine("ch is E");
```

```
        break;
      }
   }
}
```

The output from this program is shown here:

```
ch is A
ch is B
ch is C
ch is D
ch is E
```

Notice that this example does not include a **default** case. Remember, the **default** is optional. When not needed, it can be left out.

In C#, it is an error for the statement sequence associated with one **case** to continue on into the next **case**. This is called the "no fall-through" rule. This is why **case** sequences end with a **break** statement. (You can avoid fall-through in other ways, such as by using the **goto** discussed later in this chapter, but **break** is by far the most commonly used approach.) When encountered within the statement sequence of a **case**, the **break** statement causes program flow to exit from the entire **switch** statement and resume at the next statement outside the **switch**. The **default** sequence also must not "fall through," and it too usually ends with **break**.

The no fall-through rule is one point on which C# differs from C, C++, and Java. In those languages, one **case** may continue on (that is, fall through) into the next **case**. There are two reasons that C# instituted the no fall-through rule for **case**s: First, it allows the compiler to freely rearrange the order of the **case** sequences, perhaps for purposes of optimization. Such a rearrangement would not be possible if one **case** could flow into the next. Second, requiring each **case** to explicitly end prevents a programmer from accidentally allowing one **case** to flow into the next.

Although you cannot allow one **case** sequence to fall through into another, you can have two or more **case** labels refer to the same code sequence, as shown in this example:

```
// Empty cases can fall through.

using System;

class EmptyCasesCanFall {
  static void Main() {
    int i;

    for(i=1; i < 5; i++)
      switch(i) {
        case 1:
        case 2:
        case 3: Console.WriteLine("i is 1, 2 or 3");
          break;
        case 4: Console.WriteLine("i is 4");
          break;
      }

  }
}
```

The output is shown here:

```
i is 1, 2 or 3
i is 1, 2 or 3
i is 1, 2 or 3
i is 4
```

In this example, if **i** has the value 1, 2, or 3, then the first **WriteLine( )** statement executes. If **i** is 4, then the second **WriteLine( )** statement executes. The stacking of **cases** does not violate the no fall-through rule, because the **case** statements all use the same statement sequence.

Stacking **case** labels is a commonly employed technique when several **cases** share common code. This technique prevents the unnecessary duplication of code sequences.

Nested switch Statements

It is possible to have a **switch** as part of the statement sequence of an outer **switch**. This is called a *nested switch*. The **case** constants of the inner and outer **switch** can contain common values and no conflicts will arise. For example, the following code fragment is perfectly acceptable:

```
switch(ch1) {
  case 'A': Console.WriteLine("This A is part of outer switch.");
    switch(ch2) {
      case 'A':
        Console.WriteLine("This A is part of inner switch");
        break;
      case 'B': // ...
    } // end of inner switch
    break;
  case 'B': // ...
```

The for Loop

The **for** loop was introduced in Chapter 2. Here, it is examined in detail. You might be surprised at just how powerful and flexible the **for** loop is. Let's begin by reviewing the basics, starting with the most traditional forms of the **for**.

The general form of the **for** loop for repeating a single statement is

for(*initialization; condition; iteration*) *statement;*

For repeating a block, the general form is

for(*initialization; condition; iteration*)
{
    statement sequence
}

The *initialization* is usually an assignment statement that sets the initial value of the *loop control variable*, which acts as the counter that controls the loop. The *condition* is a Boolean expression that determines whether the loop will repeat. The *iteration* expression defines the amount by which the loop control variable will change each time the loop is repeated. Notice that these three major sections of the loop must be separated by semicolons. The **for** loop will continue to execute as long as the condition tests true. Once the condition becomes false, the loop will exit, and program execution will resume on the statement following the **for**.

The **for** loop can proceed in a positive or negative fashion, and it can change the loop control variable by any amount. For example, the following program prints the numbers 100 to –100, in decrements of 5:

```
// A negatively running for loop.

using System;

class DecrFor {
  static void Main() {
    int x;

    for(x = 100; x > -100; x -= 5)
      Console.WriteLine(x);
  }
}
```

An important point about **for** loops is that the conditional expression is always tested at the top of the loop. This means that the code inside the loop may not be executed at all if the condition is false to begin with. Here is an example:

```
for(count=10; count < 5; count++)
  x += count; // this statement will not execute
```

This loop will never execute because its control variable, **count**, is greater than 5 when the loop is first entered. This makes the conditional expression, **count < 5**, false from the outset; thus, not even one iteration of the loop will occur.

The **for** loop is most useful when you will be iterating a known number of times. For example, the following program uses two **for** loops to find the prime numbers between 2 and 20. If the number is not prime, then its largest factor is displayed.

```
// Determine if a number is prime. If it is not, then
// display its largest factor.

using System;

class FindPrimes {
  static void Main() {
    int num;
    int i;
    int factor;
    bool isprime;

    for(num = 2; num < 20; num++) {
      isprime = true;
      factor = 0;

      // See if num is evenly divisible.
      for(i=2; i <= num/2; i++) {
        if((num % i) == 0) {
```

```
             // num is evenly divisible. Thus, it is not prime.
             isprime = false;
             factor = i;
           }
         }

         if(isprime)
           Console.WriteLine(num + " is prime.");
         else
           Console.WriteLine("Largest factor of " + num +
                            " is " + factor);
       }
     }
   }
```

The output from the program is shown here:

```
2 is prime.
3 is prime.
Largest factor of 4 is 2
5 is prime.
Largest factor of 6 is 3
7 is prime.
Largest factor of 8 is 4
Largest factor of 9 is 3
Largest factor of 10 is 5
11 is prime.
Largest factor of 12 is 6
13 is prime.
Largest factor of 14 is 7
Largest factor of 15 is 5
Largest factor of 16 is 8
17 is prime.
Largest factor of 18 is 9
19 is prime.
```

Some Variations on the for Loop

The **for** is one of the most versatile statements in the C# language because it allows a wide range of variations. They are examined here.

Using Multiple Loop Control Variables

The **for** loop allows you to use two or more variables to control the loop. When using multiple loop control variables, the initialization and increment statements for each variable are separated by commas. Here is an example:

```
// Use commas in a for statement.

using System;

class Comma {
  static void Main() {
    int i, j;
```

```
      for(i=0, j=10; i < j; i++, j--)
        Console.WriteLine("i and j: " + i + " " + j);
  }
}
```

The output from the program is shown here:

```
i and j: 0 10
i and j: 1 9
i and j: 2 8
i and j: 3 7
i and j: 4 6
```

Here, commas separate the two initialization statements and the two iteration expressions. When the loop begins, both **i** and **j** are initialized. Each time the loop repeats, **i** is incremented and **j** is decremented. Multiple loop control variables are often convenient and can simplify certain algorithms. You can have any number of initialization and iteration statements, but in practice, more than two make the **for** loop unwieldy.

Here is a practical use of multiple loop control variables in a **for** statement. This program uses two loop control variables within a single **for** loop to find the largest and smallest factor of a number, in this case 100. Pay special attention to the termination condition. It relies on both loop control variables.

```
// Use commas in a for statement to find the largest and
// smallest factor of a number.

using System;

class Comma {
  static void Main() {
    int i, j;
    int smallest, largest;
    int num;

    num = 100;

    smallest = largest = 1;

    for(i=2, j=num/2; (i <= num/2) & (j >= 2); i++, j--) {

      if((smallest == 1) & ((num % i) == 0))
        smallest = i;

      if((largest == 1) & ((num % j) == 0))
        largest = j;

    }

    Console.WriteLine("Largest factor: " + largest);
    Console.WriteLine("Smallest factor: " + smallest);
  }
}
```

Here is the output from the program:

```
Largest factor: 50
Smallest factor: 2
```

Through the use of two loop control variables, a single **for** loop can find both the smallest and the largest factor of a number. The control variable **i** is used to search for the smallest factor. It is initially set to 2 and incremented until its value exceeds one half of **num**. The control variable **j** is used to search for the largest factor. Its value is initially set to one half the **num** and decremented until it is less than 2. The loop runs until both **i** and **j** are at their termination values. When the loop ends, both factors will have been found.

The Conditional Expression

The conditional expression controlling a **for** loop can be any valid expression that produces a **bool** result. It does not need to involve the loop control variable. For example, in the next program, the **for** loop is controlled by the value of **done**.

```csharp
// Loop condition can be any bool expression.

using System;

class forDemo {
  static void Main() {
    int i, j;
    bool done = false;

    for(i=0, j=100; !done; i++, j--) {

      if(i*i >= j) done = true;

      Console.WriteLine("i, j: " + i + " " + j);
    }
  }
}
```

The output is shown here:

```
i, j: 0 100
i, j: 1 99
i, j: 2 98
i, j: 3 97
i, j: 4 96
i, j: 5 95
i, j: 6 94
i, j: 7 93
i, j: 8 92
i, j: 9 91
i, j: 10 90
```

In this example, the **for** loop iterates until the **bool** variable **done** is true. This variable is set to true inside the loop when **i** squared is greater than or equal to **j**.

Missing Pieces

Some interesting **for** loop variations are created by leaving pieces of the loop definition empty. In C#, it is possible for any or all of the initialization, condition, or iteration portions of the **for** loop to be empty. For example, consider the following program:

```
// Parts of the for can be empty.

using System;

class Empty {
  static void Main() {
    int i;

    for(i = 0; i < 10; ) {
      Console.WriteLine("Pass #" + i);
      i++; // increment loop control var
    }

  }
}
```

Here, the iteration expression of the **for** is empty. Instead, the loop control variable **i** is incremented inside the body of the loop. This means that each time the loop repeats, **i** is tested to see whether it equals 10, but no further action takes place. Of course, since **i** is incremented within the body of the loop, the loop runs normally, displaying the following output:

```
Pass #0
Pass #1
Pass #2
Pass #3
Pass #4
Pass #5
Pass #6
Pass #7
Pass #8
Pass #9
```

In the next example, the initialization portion is also moved out of the **for**:

```
// Move more out of the for loop.

using System;

class Empty2 {
  static void Main() {
    int i;

    i = 0; // move initialization out of loop
    for(; i < 10; ) {
      Console.WriteLine("Pass #" + i);
      i++; // increment loop control var
    }
  }
}
```

In this version, **i** is initialized before the loop begins, rather than as part of the **for**. Normally, you will want to initialize the loop control variable inside the **for**. Placing the initialization outside of the loop is generally done only when the initial value is derived through a complex process that does not lend itself to containment inside the **for** statement.

The Infinite Loop

You can create an *infinite loop* (a loop that never terminates) using the **for** by leaving the conditional expression empty. For example, the following fragment shows the way many C# programmers create an infinite loop:

```
for(;;) // intentionally infinite loop
{
  //...
}
```

This loop will run forever. Although there are some programming tasks, such as operating system command processors, that require an infinite loop, most "infinite loops" are really just loops with special termination requirements. (See "Using **break** to Exit a Loop," later in this chapter.)

Loops with No Body

In C#, the body associated with a **for** loop (or any other loop) can be empty. This is because an *empty statement* is syntactically valid. Bodyless loops are often useful. For example, the following program uses a bodyless loop to sum the numbers 1 through 5:

```
// The body of a loop can be empty.

using System;

class Empty3 {
  static void Main() {
    int i;
    int sum = 0;

    // Sum the numbers through 5.
    for(i = 1; i <= 5; sum += i++) ;

    Console.WriteLine("Sum is " + sum);
  }
}
```

The output from the program is shown here:

```
Sum is 15
```

Notice that the summation process is handled entirely within the **for** statement, and no body is needed. Pay special attention to the iteration expression:

```
sum += i++
```

Don't be intimidated by statements like this. They are common in professionally written C# programs and are easy to understand if you break them down into their parts. In words, this statement says "add to **sum** the value of **sum** plus **i**, then increment **i**." Thus, it is the same as this sequence of statements:

```
sum = sum + i;
i++;
```

Declaring Loop Control Variables Inside the for Loop

Often the variable that controls a **for** loop is needed only for the purposes of the loop and is not used elsewhere. When this is the case, it is possible to declare the variable inside the initialization portion of the **for**. For example, the following program computes both the summation and the factorial of the numbers 1 through 5. It declares its loop control variable **i** inside the **for**:

```
// Declare loop control variable inside the for.

using System;

class ForVar {
  static void Main() {
    int sum = 0;
    int fact = 1;

    // Compute the factorial of the numbers 1 through 5.
    for(int i = 1; i <= 5; i++) {
      sum += i;  // i is known throughout the loop.
      fact *= i;
    }

    // But, i is not known here.

    Console.WriteLine("Sum is " + sum);
    Console.WriteLine("Factorial is " + fact);
  }
}
```

When you declare a variable inside a **for** loop, there is one important point to remember: The scope of that variable ends when the **for** statement does. (That is, the scope of the variable is limited to the **for** loop.) Outside the **for** loop, the variable will cease to exist. Thus, in the preceding example, **i** is not accessible outside the **for** loop. If you need to use the loop control variable elsewhere in your program, you will not be able to declare it inside the **for** loop.

Before moving on, you might want to experiment with your own variations on the **for** loop. As you will find, it is a fascinating loop.

The while Loop

Another of C#'s loops is the **while**. The general form of the **while** loop is

while(*condition*) *statement*;

where *statement* can be a single statement or a block of statements, and *condition* defines the condition that controls the loop and may be any valid Boolean expression. The statement is performed while the condition is true. When the condition becomes false, program control passes to the line immediately following the loop.

Here is a simple example in which a **while** is used to compute the order of magnitude of an integer:

```
// Compute the order of magnitude of an integer.

using System;

class WhileDemo {
  static void Main() {
    int num;
    int mag;

    num = 435679;
    mag = 0;

    Console.WriteLine("Number: " + num);

    while(num > 0) {
      mag++;
      num = num / 10;
    };

    Console.WriteLine("Magnitude: " + mag);
  }
}
```

The output is shown here:

```
Number: 435679
Magnitude: 6
```

The **while** loop works like this: The value of **num** is tested. If **num** is greater than 0, the **mag** counter is incremented, and **num** is divided by 10. As long as the value in **num** is greater than 0, the loop repeats. When **num** is 0, the loop terminates and **mag** contains the order of magnitude of the original value.

As with the **for** loop, the **while** checks the conditional expression at the top of the loop, which means that the loop code may not execute at all. This eliminates the need for performing a separate test before the loop. The following program illustrates this characteristic of the **while** loop. It computes the integer powers of 2 from 0 to 9.

```
// Compute integer powers of 2.

using System;

class Power {
  static void Main() {
    int e;
    int result;

    for(int i=0; i < 10; i++) {
      result = 1;
      e = i;
```

```
      while(e > 0) {
        result *= 2;
        e--;
      }

      Console.WriteLine("2 to the " + i + " power is " + result);
    }
  }
}
```

The output from the program is shown here:

```
2 to the 0 power is 1
2 to the 1 power is 2
2 to the 2 power is 4
2 to the 3 power is 8
2 to the 4 power is 16
2 to the 5 power is 32
2 to the 6 power is 64
2 to the 7 power is 128
2 to the 8 power is 256
2 to the 9 power is 512
```

Notice that the **while** loop executes only when **e** is greater than 0. Thus, when **e** is 0, as it is in the first iteration of the **for** loop, the **while** loop is skipped.

The do-while Loop

The third C# loop is the **do-while**. Unlike the **for** and the **while** loops, in which the condition is tested at the top of the loop, the **do-while** loop checks its condition at the bottom of the loop. This means that a **do-while** loop will always execute at least once. The general form of the **do-while** loop is

do {
    statements;
} while(*condition*);

Although the braces are not necessary when only one statement is present, they are often used to improve readability of the **do-while** construct, thus preventing confusion with the **while**. The **do-while** loop executes as long as the conditional expression is true.

The following program uses a **do-while** loop to display the digits of an integer in reverse order:

```
// Display the digits of an integer in reverse order.

using System;

class DoWhileDemo {
  static void Main() {
    int num;
    int nextdigit;

    num = 198;
```

```
    Console.WriteLine("Number: " + num);

    Console.Write("Number in reverse order: ");

    do {
      nextdigit = num % 10;
      Console.Write(nextdigit);
      num = num / 10;
    } while(num > 0);

    Console.WriteLine();
  }
}
```

The output is shown here:

```
Number: 198
Number in reverse order: 891
```

Here is how the loop works: With each iteration, the leftmost digit is obtained by computing the remainder of an integer division by 10. This digit is then displayed. Next, the value in **num** is divided by 10. Since this is an integer division, this results in the leftmost digit being removed. This process repeats until **num** is 0.

The foreach Loop

The **foreach** loop cycles through the elements of a *collection*. A collection is a group of objects. C# defines several types of collections, of which one is an array. The **foreach** loop is examined in Chapter 7, when arrays are discussed.

Using break to Exit a Loop

It is possible to force an immediate exit from a loop, bypassing any code remaining in the body of the loop and the loop's conditional test, by using the **break** statement. When a **break** statement is encountered inside a loop, the loop is terminated, and program control resumes at the next statement following the loop. Here is a simple example:

```
// Using break to exit a loop.

using System;

class BreakDemo {
  static void Main() {

    // Use break to exit this loop.
    for(int i=-10; i <= 10; i++) {
      if(i > 0) break; // terminate loop when i is positive
      Console.Write(i + " ");
    }
    Console.WriteLine("Done");
  }
}
```

This program generates the following output:

```
-10 -9 -8 -7 -6 -5 -4 -3 -2 -1 0 Done
```

As you can see, although the **for** loop is designed to run from –10 to 10, the **break** statement causes it to terminate early, when **i** becomes positive.

The **break** statement can be used with any of C#'s loops. For example, here is the previous program recoded to use a **do-while** loop:

```
// Using break to exit a do-while loop.

using System;

class BreakDemo2 {
  static void Main() {
    int i;

    i = -10;
    do {
      if(i > 0) break;
      Console.Write(i + " ");
      i++;
    } while(i <= 10);

    Console.WriteLine("Done");
  }
}
```

Here is a more practical example of **break**. This program finds the smallest factor of a number.

```
// Find the smallest factor of a value.

using System;

class FindSmallestFactor {
  static void Main() {
    int factor = 1;
    int num = 1000;

    for(int i=2; i <= num/i; i++) {
      if((num%i) == 0) {
        factor = i;
        break; // stop loop when factor is found
      }
    }
    Console.WriteLine("Smallest factor is " + factor);
  }
}
```

The output is shown here:

```
Smallest factor is 2
```

The **break** stops the **for** loop as soon as a factor is found. The use of **break** in this situation prevents the loop from trying any other values once a factor has been found, thus preventing inefficiency.

When used inside a set of nested loops, the **break** statement will break out of only the innermost loop. For example:

```
// Using break with nested loops.

using System;

class BreakNested {
  static void Main() {

    for(int i=0; i<3; i++) {
      Console.WriteLine("Outer loop count: " + i);
      Console.Write("    Inner loop count: ");

      int t = 0;
      while(t < 100) {
        if(t == 10) break; // terminate loop if t is 10
        Console.Write(t + " ");
        t++;
      }
      Console.WriteLine();
    }
    Console.WriteLine("Loops complete.");
  }
}
```

This program generates the following output:

```
Outer loop count: 0
    Inner loop count: 0 1 2 3 4 5 6 7 8 9
Outer loop count: 1
    Inner loop count: 0 1 2 3 4 5 6 7 8 9
Outer loop count: 2
    Inner loop count: 0 1 2 3 4 5 6 7 8 9
Loops complete.
```

As you can see, the **break** statement in the inner loop causes only the termination of that loop. The outer loop is unaffected.

Here are two other points to remember about **break**: First, more than one **break** statement may appear in a loop. However, be careful. Too many **break** statements have the tendency to destructure your code. Second, the **break** that exits a **switch** statement affects only that **switch** statement and not any enclosing loops.

Using continue

It is possible to force an early iteration of a loop, bypassing the loop's normal control structure. This is accomplished using **continue**. The **continue** statement forces the next iteration of the loop to take place, skipping any code in between. Thus, **continue** is essentially the complement of **break**. For example, the following program uses **continue** to help print the even numbers between 0 and 100.

```
// Use continue.

using System;

class ContDemo {
  static void Main() {

    // Print even numbers between 0 and 100.
    for(int i = 0; i <= 100; i++) {
      if((i%2) != 0) continue; // iterate
      Console.WriteLine(i);
    }
  }
}
```

Only even numbers are printed, because an odd number will cause the loop to iterate early, bypassing the call to **WriteLine( )**.

In **while** and **do-while** loops, a **continue** statement will cause control to go directly to the conditional expression and then continue the looping process. In the case of the **for**, the iteration expression of the loop is evaluated, then the conditional expression is executed, and then the loop continues.

Good uses of **continue** are rare. One reason is that C# provides a rich set of loop statements that fit most applications. However, for those special circumstances in which early iteration is needed, the **continue** statement provides a structured way to accomplish it.

return

The **return** statement causes a method to return. It can also be used to return a value. It is examined in Chapter 6.

The goto

The **goto** is C#'s unconditional jump statement. When encountered, program flow jumps to the location specified by the **goto**. The statement fell out of favor with programmers many years ago because it encouraged the creation of "spaghetti code." However, the **goto** is still occasionally—and sometimes effectively—used. This book will not make a judgment regarding its validity as a form of program control. It should be stated, however, that there are no programming situations that require the use of the **goto** statement—it is not necessary for making the language complete. Rather, **goto** is a convenience that, if used wisely, can be a benefit in certain programming situations. As such, the **goto** is not used in this book outside of this section. The chief concern most programmers have about the **goto** is its tendency to clutter a program and render it nearly unreadable. However, there are times when the use of the **goto** can clarify program flow rather than confuse it.

The **goto** requires a label for operation. A *label* is a valid C# identifier followed by a colon. The label must be in the same method as the **goto** that uses it and within scope. For example, a loop from 1 to 100 could be written using a **goto** and a label, as shown here:

```
x = 1;
loop1:
  x++;
  if(x < 100) goto loop1;
```

The **goto** can also be used to jump to a **case** or **default** statement within a **switch**. Technically, the **case** and **default** statements of a **switch** are labels. Thus, they can be targets of a **goto**. However, the **goto** statement must be executed from within the **switch**. That is, you cannot use the **goto** to jump into a **switch** statement. Here is an example that illustrates **goto** with a **switch**:

```
// Use goto with a switch.

using System;

class SwitchGoto {
  static void Main() {

    for(int i=1; i < 5; i++) {
      switch(i) {
        case 1:
          Console.WriteLine("In case 1");
          goto case 3;
        case 2:
          Console.WriteLine("In case 2");
          goto case 1;
        case 3:
          Console.WriteLine("In case 3");
          goto default;
        default:
          Console.WriteLine("In default");
          break;
      }

      Console.WriteLine();
    }

//    goto case 1; // Error! Can't jump into a switch.
  }
}
```

The output from the program is shown here:

```
In case 1
In case 3
In default

In case 2
In case 1
In case 3
In default

In case 3
In default

In default
```

Inside the **switch**, notice how the **goto** is used to jump to other **case** statements or the **default** statement. Furthermore, notice that the **case** statements do not end with a **break**. Since the **goto** prevents one **case** from falling through to the next, the no fall-through rule is not violated, and there is no need for a **break** statement. As explained, it is not possible to use the **goto** to jump into a **switch**. If you remove the comment symbols from the start of this line

```
//    goto case 1; // Error! Can't jump into a switch.
```

the program will not compile. Frankly, using a **goto** with a **switch** can be useful in some special-case situations, but it is not recommended style in general.

One good use for the **goto** is to exit from a deeply nested routine. Here is a simple example:

```
// Demonstrate the goto.

using System;

class Use_goto {
  static void Main() {
    int i=0, j=0, k=0;

    for(i=0; i < 10; i++) {
      for(j=0; j < 10; j++ ) {
        for(k=0; k < 10; k++) {
          Console.WriteLine("i, j, k: " + i + " " + j + " " + k);
          if(k == 3) goto stop;
        }
      }
    }

stop:
    Console.WriteLine("Stopped! i, j, k: " + i + ", " + j + " " + k);

  }
}
```

The output from the program is shown here:

```
i, j, k: 0 0 0
i, j, k: 0 0 1
i, j, k: 0 0 2
i, j, k: 0 0 3
Stopped! i, j, k: 0, 0 3
```

Eliminating the **goto** would force the use of three **if** and **break** statements. In this case, the **goto** simplifies the code. While this is a contrived example used for illustration, you can probably imagine situations in which a **goto** might be beneficial.

One last point: Although you can jump out of a block (as the preceding example shows), you can't use the **goto** to jump into a block.

CHAPTER

Introducing Classes and Objects

This chapter introduces the class. The class is the foundation of C# because it defines the nature of an object. Furthermore, the class forms the basis for object-oriented programming. Within a class are defined both code and data. Because classes and objects are fundamental to C#, they constitute a large topic, which spans several chapters. This chapter begins the discussion by covering their main features.

Class Fundamentals

We have been using classes since the start of this book. Of course, only extremely simple classes have been used, and we have not taken advantage of the majority of their features. Classes are substantially more powerful than the limited ones presented so far.

Let's begin by reviewing the basics. A *class* is a template that defines the form of an object. It specifies both the data and the code that will operate on that data. C# uses a class specification to construct *objects*. Objects are *instances* of a class. Thus, a class is essentially a set of plans that specify how to build an object. It is important to be clear on one issue: A class is a logical abstraction. It is not until an object of that class has been created that a physical representation of that class exists in memory.

The General Form of a Class

When you define a class, you declare the data that it contains and the code that operates on it. While very simple classes might contain only code or only data, most real-world classes contain both.

In general terms, data is contained in *data members* defined by the class, and code is contained in *function members*. It is important to state at the outset that C# defines several specific flavors of data and function members. For example, data members (also called *fields*) include instance variables and static variables. Function members include methods, constructors, destructors, indexers, events, operators, and properties. For now, we will limit our discussion of the class to its essential elements: instance variables and methods. Later in this chapter constructors and destructors are discussed. The other types of members are described in later chapters.

A class is created by use of the keyword **class**. Here is the general form of a simple **class** definition that contains only instance variables and methods:

```
class classname {
    // declare instance variables
    access type var1;
    access type var2;
    // ...
    access type varN;

    // declare methods
    access ret-type method1(parameters) {
        // body of method
    }
    access ret-type method2(parameters) {
        // body of method
    }
    // ...
    access ret-type methodN(parameters) {
        // body of method
    }
}
```

Notice that each variable and method declaration is preceded with *access*. Here, *access* is an access specifier, such as **public**, which specifies how the member can be accessed. As mentioned in Chapter 2, class members can be private to a class or more accessible. The access specifier determines what type of access is allowed. The access specifier is optional, and if absent, then the member is private to the class. Members with private access can be used only by other members of their class. For the examples in this chapter, all members (except for the **Main( )** method) will be specified as **public**, which means that they can be used by all other code—even code defined outside the class. We will return to the topic of access specifiers in Chapter 8.

NOTE *In addition to an access specifier, the declaration of a class member can also contain one or more type modifiers. These modifiers are discussed later in this book.*

Although there is no syntactic rule that enforces it, a well-designed class should define one and only one logical entity. For example, a class that stores names and telephone numbers will not normally also store information about the stock market, average rainfall, sunspot cycles, or other unrelated information. The point here is that a well-designed class groups logically connected information. Putting unrelated information into the same class will quickly destructure your code.

Up to this point, the classes that we have been using have had only one method: **Main( )**. However, notice that the general form of a class does not specify a **Main( )** method. A **Main( )** method is required only if that class is the starting point for your program.

Define a Class

To illustrate classes, we will be evolving a class that encapsulates information about buildings, such as houses, stores, offices, and so on. This class is called **Building**, and it will store three items of information about a building: the number of floors, the total area, and the number of occupants.

The first version of **Building** is shown here. It defines three instance variables: **Floors**, **Area**, and **Occupants**. Notice that **Building** does not contain any methods. Thus, it is currently a data-only class. (Subsequent sections will add methods to it.)

```
class Building {
  public int Floors;     // number of floors
  public int Area;       // total square footage of building
  public int Occupants;  // number of occupants
}
```

The instance variables defined by **Building** illustrate the way that instance variables are declared in general. The general form for declaring an instance variable is shown here:

access type var-name;

Here, *access* specifies the access; *type* specifies the type of variable; and *var-name* is the variable's name. Thus, aside from the access specifier, you declare an instance variable in the same way that you declare local variables. For **Building**, the variables are preceded by the **public** access modifier. As explained, this allows them to be accessed by code outside of **Building**.

A **class** definition creates a new data type. In this case, the new data type is called **Building**. You will use this name to declare objects of type **Building**. Remember that a **class** declaration is only a type description; it does not create an actual object. Thus, the preceding code does not cause any objects of type **Building** to come into existence.

To actually create a **Building** object, you will use a statement like the following:

```
Building house = new Building(); // create an object of type building
```

After this statement executes, **house** will be an instance of **Building**. Thus, it will have "physical" reality. For the moment, don't worry about the details of this statement.

Each time you create an instance of a class, you are creating an object that contains its own copy of each instance variable defined by the class. Thus, every **Building** object will contain its own copies of the instance variables **Floors**, **Area**, and **Occupants**. To access these variables, you will use the member access operator, which is a period. It is commonly referred to as the *dot operator*. The dot operator links the name of an object with the name of a member. The general form of the dot operator is shown here:

object.member

Thus, the *object* is specified on the left, and the *member* is put on the right. For example, to assign the **Floors** variable of **house** the value 2, use the following statement:

```
house.Floors = 2;
```

In general, you can use the dot operator to access both instance variables and methods.

Here is a complete program that uses the **Building** class:

```
// A program that uses the Building class.

using System;
```

```
class Building {
  public int Floors;    // number of floors
  public int Area;      // total square footage of building
  public int Occupants; // number of occupants
}

// This class declares an object of type Building.
class BuildingDemo {
  static void Main() {
    Building house = new Building(); // create a Building object
    int areaPP; // area per person

    // Assign values to fields in house.
    house.Occupants = 4;
    house.Area = 2500;
    house.Floors = 2;

    // Compute the area per person.
    areaPP = house.Area / house.Occupants;

    Console.WriteLine("house has:\n   " +
                    house.Floors + " floors\n   " +
                    house.Occupants + " occupants\n   " +
                    house.Area + " total area\n   " +
                    areaPP + " area per person");
  }
}
```

This program consists of two classes: **Building** and **BuildingDemo**. Inside **BuildingDemo**, the **Main( )** method creates an instance of **Building** called **house**. Then the code within **Main( )** accesses the instance variables associated with **house**, assigning them values and using those values. It is important to understand that **Building** and **BuildingDemo** are two separate classes. The only relationship they have to each other is that one class creates an instance of the other. Although they are separate classes, code inside **BuildingDemo** can access the members of **Building** because they are declared **public**. If they had not been given the **public** access specifier, their access would have been limited to the **Building** class, and **BuildingDemo** would not have been able to use them.

Assume that you call the preceding file **UseBuilding.cs**. Compiling this program creates a file called **UseBuilding.exe**. Both the **Building** and **BuildingDemo** classes are automatically part of the executable file. The program displays the following output:

```
house has:
  2 floors
  4 occupants
  2500 total area
  625 area per person
```

It is not necessary for the **Building** and the **BuildingDemo** classes to actually be in the same source file. You could put each class in its own file, called **Building.cs** and **BuildingDemo.cs**, for example. Just tell the C# compiler to compile both files and link them together. For example, you could use this command line to compile the program if you split it into two pieces as just described:

```
csc Building.cs BuildingDemo.cs
```

If you are using the Visual Studio IDE, you will need to add both files to your project and then build.

Before moving on, let's review a fundamental principle: Each object has its own copies of the instance variables defined by its class. Thus, the contents of the variables in one object can differ from the contents of the variables in another. There is no connection between the two objects except for the fact that they are both objects of the same type. For example, if you have two **Building** objects, each has its own copy of **Floors**, **Area**, and **Occupants**, and the contents of these can (and often will) differ between the two objects. The following program demonstrates this fact:

```
// This program creates two Building objects.

using System;

class Building {
  public int Floors;     // number of floors
  public int Area;       // total square footage of building
  public int Occupants;  // number of occupants
}

// This class declares two objects of type Building.
class BuildingDemo {
  static void Main() {
    Building house = new Building();
    Building office = new Building();

    int areaPP; // area per person

    // Assign values to fields in house.
    house.Occupants = 4;
    house.Area = 2500;
    house.Floors = 2;

    // Assign values to fields in office.
    office.Occupants = 25;
    office.Area = 4200;
    office.Floors = 3;

    // Compute the area per person in house.
    areaPP = house.Area / house.Occupants;

    Console.WriteLine("house has:\n  " +
                      house.Floors + " floors\n  " +
                      house.Occupants + " occupants\n  " +
                      house.Area + " total area\n  " +
                      areaPP + " area per person");
```

```
    Console.WriteLine();

    // Compute the area per person in office.
    areaPP = office.Area / office.Occupants;

    Console.WriteLine("office has:\n  " +
                office.Floors + " floors\n  " +
                office.Occupants + " occupants\n  " +
                office.Area + " total area\n  " +
                areaPP + " area per person");
  }
}
```

The output produced by this program is shown here:

```
house has:
  2 floors
  4 occupants
  2500 total area
  625 area per person

office has:
  3 floors
  25 occupants
  4200 total area
  168 area per person
```

As you can see, **house**'s data is completely separate from the data contained in **office**. Figure 6-1 depicts this situation.

How Objects Are Created

In the preceding programs, the following line was used to declare an object of type **Building**:

```
Building house = new Building();
```

This declaration performs three functions. First, it declares a variable called **house** of the class type **Building**. This variable is not, itself, an object. Instead, it is simply a variable that can *refer to* an object. Second, the declaration creates an actual, physical copy of the object.

FIGURE 6-1
One object's instance variables are separate from another's.

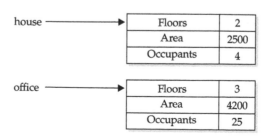

house	→	Floors	2
		Area	2500
		Occupants	4

office	→	Floors	3
		Area	4200
		Occupants	25

This is done by using the **new** operator. Finally, it assigns to **house** a reference to that object. Thus, after the line executes, **house** refers to an object of type **Building**.

The **new** operator dynamically allocates (that is, allocates at runtime) memory for an object and returns a reference to it. This reference is then stored in a variable. Thus, in C#, all class objects must be dynamically allocated.

As you might expect, it is possible to separate the declaration of **house** from the creation of the object to which it will refer, as shown here:

```
Building house; // declare reference to object
house = new Building(); // allocate a Building object
```

The first line declares **house** as a reference to an object of type **Building**. Thus, **house** is a variable that can refer to an object, but it is not an object, itself. The next line creates a new **Building** object and assigns a reference to it to **house**. Now, **house** is linked with an object.

The fact that class objects are accessed through a reference explains why classes are called *reference types*. The key difference between value types and reference types is what a variable of each type means. For a value type variable, the variable, itself, contains the value. For example, given

```
int x;
x = 10;
```

x contains the value 10 because **x** is a variable of type **int**, which is a value type. However, in the case of

```
Building house = new Building();
```

house does not, itself, contain the object. Instead, it contains a reference to the object.

Reference Variables and Assignment

In an assignment operation, reference variables act differently than do variables of a value type, such as **int**. When you assign one value type variable to another, the situation is straightforward. The variable on the left receives a *copy* of the *value* of the variable on the right. When you assign one object reference variable to another, the situation is a bit more complicated because the assignment causes the reference variable on the left to refer to the same object to which the reference variable on the right refers. The object, itself, is not copied. The effect of this difference can cause some counterintuitive results. For example, consider the following fragment:

```
Building house1 = new Building();
Building house2 = house1;
```

At first glance, it is easy to think that **house1** and **house2** refer to separate and distinct objects, but this is not the case. Instead, **house1** and **house2** will both refer to the *same* object. The assignment of **house1** to **house2** simply makes **house2** refer to the same object that **house1** does. Thus, the object can be acted upon by either **house1** or **house2**. For example, after the assignment

```
house1.Area = 2600;
```

executes, both of these **WriteLine( )** statements

```
Console.WriteLine(house1.Area);
Console.WriteLine(house2.Area);
```

display the same value: 2600.

Although **house1** and **house2** both refer to the same object, they are not linked in any other way. For example, a subsequent assignment to **house2** simply changes what object **house2** refers to. For example:

```
Building house1 = new Building();
Building house2 = house1;
Building house3 = new Building();

house2 = house3; // now house2 and house3 refer to the same object.
```

After this sequence executes, **house2** refers to the same object as **house3**. The object referred to by **house1** is unchanged.

Methods

As explained, instance variables and methods are two of the primary constituents of classes. So far, the **Building** class contains data, but no methods. Although data-only classes are perfectly valid, most classes will have methods. *Methods* are subroutines that manipulate the data defined by the class and, in many cases, provide access to that data. Typically, other parts of your program will interact with a class through its methods.

A method contains one or more statements. In well-written C# code, each method performs only one task. Each method has a name, and it is this name that is used to call the method. In general, you can name a method using any valid identifier that you please. However, remember that **Main( )** is reserved for the method that begins execution of your program. Also, don't use C#'s keywords for method names.

When denoting methods in text, this book has used and will continue to use a convention that has become common when writing about C#. A method will have parentheses after its name. For example, if a method's name is **GetVal**, then it will be written **GetVal( )** when its name is used in a sentence. This notation will help you distinguish variable names from method names in this book.

The general form of a method is shown here:

access ret-type name(parameter-list) {
   // body of method
}

Here, *access* is an access modifier that governs what other parts of your program can call the method. As explained earlier, the access modifier is optional. If not present, then the method is private to the class in which it is declared. For now, we will declare methods as **public** so that they can be called by any other code in the program. The *ret-type* specifies the type of data returned by the method. This can be any valid type, including class types that you create. If the method does not return a value, its return type must be **void**. The name of the method is specified by *name*. This can be any legal identifier other than those that would cause conflicts within the current declaration space. The *parameter-list* is a sequence of type and identifier pairs separated by commas. Parameters are variables that receive the value of the *arguments* passed to the method when it is called. If the method has no parameters, then the parameter list will be empty.

Add a Method to the Building Class

As just explained, the methods of a class typically manipulate and provide access to the data of the class. With this in mind, recall that **Main( )** in the preceding examples computed the area-per-person by dividing the total area by the number of occupants. Although technically correct, this is not the best way to handle this computation. The calculation of area-per-person is something that is best handled by the **Building** class, itself. The reason for this conclusion is easy to understand: The area-per-person of a building is dependent upon the values in the **Area** and **Occupants** fields, which are encapsulated by **Building**. Thus, it is possible for the **Building** class to perform this calculation on its own. Furthermore, by adding this calculation to **Building**, you prevent each program that uses **Building** from having to perform this calculation manually. This prevents the unnecessary duplication of code. Finally, by adding a method to **Building** that computes the area-per-person, you are enhancing its object-oriented structure by encapsulating the quantities that relate directly to a building inside **Building**.

To add a method to **Building**, specify it within **Building**'s declaration. For example, the following version of **Building** contains a method called **AreaPerPerson( )** that displays the area-per-person for a building:

```
// Add a method to Building.

using System;

class Building {
  public int Floors;    // number of floors
  public int Area;      // total square footage of building
  public int Occupants; // number of occupants

  // Display the area per person.
  public void AreaPerPerson() {
    Console.WriteLine("  " + Area / Occupants + " area per person");
  }
}

// Use the AreaPerPerson() method.
class BuildingDemo {
  static void Main() {
    Building house = new Building();
    Building office = new Building();

    // Assign values to fields in house.
    house.Occupants = 4;
    house.Area = 2500;
    house.Floors = 2;

    // Assign values to fields in office.
    office.Occupants = 25;
```

```
        office.Area = 4200;
        office.Floors = 3;


        Console.WriteLine("house has:\n   " +
                      house.Floors + " floors\n   " +
                      house.Occupants + " occupants\n   " +
                      house.Area + " total area");
        house.AreaPerPerson();

        Console.WriteLine();

        Console.WriteLine("office has:\n   " +
                      office.Floors + " floors\n   " +
                      office.Occupants + " occupants\n   " +
                      office.Area + " total area");
        office.AreaPerPerson();
    }
}
```

This program generates the following output, which is the same as before:

```
house has:
  2 floors
  4 occupants
  2500 total area
  625 area per person

office has:
  3 floors
  25 occupants
  4200 total area
  168 area per person
```

Let's look at the key elements of this program, beginning with the **AreaPerPerson( )** method, itself. The first line of **AreaPerPerson( )** is

```
public void AreaPerPerson() {
```

This line declares a method called **AreaPerPerson( )** that has no parameters. It is specified as **public**, so it can be used by all other parts of the program. Its return type is **void**. Thus, **AreaPerPerson( )** does not return a value to the caller. The line ends with the opening curly brace of the method body.

The body of **AreaPerPerson( )** consists solely of this statement:

```
Console.WriteLine("   " + Area / Occupants + " area per person");
```

This statement displays the area-per-person of a building by dividing **Area** by **Occupants**. Since each object of type **Building** has its own copy of **Area** and **Occupants**, when **AreaPerPerson( )** is called, the computation uses the calling object's copies of those variables.

The **AreaPerPerson( )** method ends when its closing curly brace is encountered. This causes program control to transfer back to the caller.

Next, look closely at this line of code from inside **Main( )**:

```
house.AreaPerPerson();
```

This statement invokes the **AreaPerPerson( )** method on **house**. That is, it calls **AreaPerPerson( )** relative to the object referred to by **house**, by use of the dot operator. When a method is called, program control is transferred to the method. When the method terminates, control is transferred back to the caller, and execution resumes with the line of code following the call.

In this case, the call to **house.AreaPerPerson( )** displays the area-per-person of the building defined by **house**. In similar fashion, the call to **office.AreaPerPerson( )** displays the area-per-person of the building defined by **office**. Each time **AreaPerPerson( )** is invoked, it displays the area-per-person for the specified object.

There is something very important to notice inside the **AreaPerPerson( )** method: The instance variables **Area** and **Occupants** are referred to directly, without use of the dot operator. When a method uses an instance variable that is defined by its class, it does so directly, without explicit reference to an object and without use of the dot operator. This is easy to understand if you think about it. A method is always invoked relative to some object of its class. Once this invocation has occurred, the object is known. Thus, within a method, there is no need to specify the object a second time. This means that **Area** and **Occupants** inside **AreaPerPerson( )** implicitly refer to the copies of those variables found in the object that invokes **AreaPerPerson( )**.

NOTE *As a point of interest, in the AreaPerPerson( ) method, Occupants must not equal zero (which it won't for all of the examples in this chapter). If Occupants were zero, then a division-by-zero error would occur. In Chapter 13, you will learn about exceptions, which are C#'s approach to handling errors, and see how to watch for errors that can occur at runtime.*

Return from a Method

In general, there are two conditions that cause a method to return. The first, as the **AreaPerPerson( )** method in the preceding example shows, is when the method's closing curly brace is encountered. The second is when a **return** statement is executed. There are two forms of **return**: one for use in **void** methods (those that do not return a value) and one for returning values. The first form is examined here. The next section explains how to return values.

In a **void** method, you can cause the immediate termination of a method by using this form of **return**:

```
return ;
```

When this statement executes, program control returns to the caller, skipping any remaining code in the method. For example, consider this method:

```
public void MyMeth() {
  int i;

  for(i=0; i<10; i++) {
    if(i == 5) return; // stop at 5
    Console.WriteLine();
  }
}
```

Here, the **for** loop will only run from 0 to 5, because once **i** equals 5, the method returns.

It is permissible to have multiple **return** statements in a method, especially when there are two or more routes out of it. For example,

```
public void MyMeth() {
  // ...
  if(done) return;
  // ...
  if(error) return;
}
```

Here, the method returns if it is done or if an error occurs. Be careful, however. Having too many exit points in a method can destructure your code, so avoid using them casually.

To review: A **void** method can return in one of two ways—its closing curly brace is reached, or a **return** statement is executed.

Return a Value

Although methods with a return type of **void** are not rare, most methods will return a value. In fact, the ability to return a value is one of a method's most useful features. You have already seen an example of a return value when we used the **Math.Sqrt( )** function in Chapter 3 to obtain a square root.

Return values are used for a variety of purposes in programming. In some cases, such as with **Math.Sqrt( )**, the return value contains the outcome of some calculation. In other cases, the return value may simply indicate success or failure. In still others, it may contain a status code. Whatever the purpose, using method return values is an integral part of C# programming.

Methods return a value to the calling routine using this form of **return**:

return *value*;

Here, *value* is the value returned.

You can use a return value to improve the implementation of **AreaPerPerson( )**. Instead of displaying the area-per-person, a better approach is to have **AreaPerPerson( )** return this value. Among the advantages to this approach is that you can use the value for other calculations. The following example modifies **AreaPerPerson( )** to return the area-per-person rather than displaying it:

```
// Return a value from AreaPerPerson().

using System;

class Building {
  public int Floors;    // number of floors
  public int Area;      // total square footage of building
  public int Occupants; // number of occupants

  // Return the area per person.
  public int AreaPerPerson() {
    return Area / Occupants;
  }
}
```

```
// Use the return value from AreaPerPerson().
class BuildingDemo {
  static void Main() {
    Building house = new Building();
    Building office = new Building();
    int areaPP; // area per person

    // Assign values to fields in house.
    house.Occupants = 4;
    house.Area = 2500;
    house.Floors = 2;

    // Assign values to fields in office.
    office.Occupants = 25;
    office.Area = 4200;
    office.Floors = 3;

    // Obtain area per person for house.
    areaPP = house.AreaPerPerson();

    Console.WriteLine("house has:\n  " +
                      house.Floors + " floors\n  " +
                      house.Occupants + " occupants\n  " +
                      house.Area + " total area\n  " +
                      areaPP + " area per person");


    Console.WriteLine();

    // Obtain area per person for office.
    areaPP = office.AreaPerPerson();

    Console.WriteLine("office has:\n  " +
                      office.Floors + " floors\n  " +
                      office.Occupants + " occupants\n  " +
                      office.Area + " total area\n  " +
                      areaPP + " area per person");
  }
}
```

The output is the same as shown earlier.

In the program, notice that when **AreaPerPerson( )** is called, it is put on the right side of an assignment statement. On the left is a variable that will receive the value returned by **AreaPerPerson( )**. Thus, after

```
areaPP = house.AreaPerPerson();
```

executes, the area-per-person of the **house** object is stored in **areaPP**.

Notice that **AreaPerPerson( )** now has a return type of **int**. This means that it will return an integer value to the caller. The return type of a method is important because the type of data returned by a method must be compatible with the return type specified by the method. Thus, if you want a method to return data of type **double**, then its return type must be type **double**.

Although the preceding program is correct, it is not written as efficiently as it could be. Specifically, there is no need for the **areaPP** variable. A call to **AreaPerPerson( )** can be used in the **WriteLine( )** statement directly, as shown here:

```
Console.WriteLine("house has:\n  " +
                  house.Floors + " floors\n  " +
                  house.Occupants + " occupants\n  " +
                  house.Area + " total area\n  " +
                  house.AreaPerPerson() + " area per person");
```

In this case, when **WriteLine( )** is executed, **house.AreaPerPerson( )** is called automatically, and its value will be passed to **WriteLine( )**. Furthermore, you can use a call to **AreaPerPerson( )** whenever the area-per-person of a **Building** object is needed. For example, this statement compares the per-person areas of two buildings:

```
if(b1.AreaPerPerson() > b2.AreaPerPerson())
  Console.WriteLine("b1 has more space for each person");
```

Use Parameters

It is possible to pass one or more values to a method when the method is called. A value passed to a method is called an *argument*. Inside the method, the variable that receives the argument is called a *formal parameter*, or just *parameter*, for short. Parameters are declared inside the parentheses that follow the method's name. The parameter declaration syntax is the same as that used for variables. The scope of a parameter is the body of its method. Aside from its special task of receiving an argument, it acts like any other local variable.

Here is a simple example that uses a parameter. Inside the **ChkNum** class, the method **IsPrime( )** returns **true** if the value that it is passed is prime. It returns **false** otherwise. Therefore, **IsPrime( )** has a return type of **bool**.

```
// A simple example that uses a parameter.

using System;

class ChkNum {
  // Return true if x is prime.
  public bool IsPrime(int x) {
    if(x <= 1) return false;

    for(int i=2; i <= x/i; i++)
      if((x %i) == 0) return false;

    return true;
  }
}

class ParmDemo {
  static void Main() {
    ChkNum ob = new ChkNum();

    for(int i=2; i < 10; i++)
      if(ob.IsPrime(i)) Console.WriteLine(i + " is prime.");
```

```
    else Console.WriteLine(i + " is not prime.");
  }
}
```

Here is the output produced by the program:

```
2 is prime.
3 is prime.
4 is not prime.
5 is prime.
6 is not prime.
7 is prime.
8 is not prime.
9 is not prime.
```

In the program, **IsPrime( )** is called eight times, and each time a different value is passed. Let's look at this process closely. First, notice how **IsPrime( )** is called. The argument is specified between the parentheses. When **IsPrime( )** is called the first time, it is passed the value 2. Thus, when **IsPrime( )** begins executing, the parameter **x** receives the value 2. In the second call, 3 is the argument, and **x** then has the value 3. In the third call, the argument is 4, which is the value that **x** receives, and so on. The point is that the value passed as an argument when **IsPrime( )** is called is the value received by its parameter, **x**.

A method can have more than one parameter. Simply declare each parameter, separating one from the next with a comma. For example, here the **ChkNum** class is expanded by adding a method called **LeastComFactor( )**, which returns the smallest factor that its two arguments have in common. In other words, it returns the smallest whole number value that can evenly divide both arguments.

```
// Add a method that takes two arguments.

using System;

class ChkNum {
  // Return true if x is prime.
  public bool IsPrime(int x) {
    if(x <= 1) return false;

    for(int i=2; i <= x/i; i++)
      if((x %i) == 0) return false;

    return true;
  }

  // Return the least common factor.
  public int LeastComFactor(int a, int b) {
    int max;

    if(IsPrime(a) || IsPrime(b)) return 1;

    max = a < b ? a : b;

    for(int i=2; i <= max/2; i++)
      if(((a%i) == 0) && ((b%i) == 0)) return i;
```

```
          return 1;
      }
}

class ParmDemo {
  static void Main() {
    ChkNum ob = new ChkNum();
    int a, b;

    for(int i=2; i < 10; i++)
      if(ob.IsPrime(i)) Console.WriteLine(i + " is prime.");
      else Console.WriteLine(i + " is not prime.");

    a = 7;
    b = 8;
    Console.WriteLine("Least common factor for " +
                      a + " and " + b + " is " +
                      ob.LeastComFactor(a, b));

    a = 100;
    b = 8;
    Console.WriteLine("Least common factor for " +
                      a + " and " + b + " is " +
                      ob.LeastComFactor(a, b));

    a = 100;
    b = 75;
    Console.WriteLine("Least common factor for " +
                      a + " and " + b + " is " +
                      ob.LeastComFactor(a, b));

  }
}
```

Notice that when **LeastComFactor( )** is called, the arguments are also separated by commas. The output from the program is shown here:

```
2 is prime.
3 is prime.
4 is not prime.
5 is prime.
6 is not prime.
7 is prime.
8 is not prime.
9 is not prime.
Least common factor for 7 and 8 is 1
Least common factor for 100 and 8 is 2
Least common factor for 100 and 75 is 5
```

When using multiple parameters, each parameter specifies its own type, which can differ from the others. For example, this is perfectly valid:

```
int MyMeth(int a, double b, float c) {
  // ...
```

Add a Parameterized Method to Building

You can use a parameterized method to add a new feature to the **Building** class: the ability to compute the maximum number of occupants for a building assuming that each occupant must have a certain minimal space. This new method is called **MaxOccupant( )**. It is shown here:

```
// Return the maximum number of occupants if each
// is to have at least the specified minimum area.
public int MaxOccupant(int minArea) {
  return Area / minArea;
}
```

When **MaxOccupant( )** is called, the parameter **minArea** receives the minimum space needed for each occupant. The method divides the total area of the building by this value and returns the result.

The entire **Building** class that includes **MaxOccupant( )** is shown here:

```
/*
   Add a parameterized method that computes the
   maximum number of people that can occupy a
   building assuming each needs a specified
   minimum space.
*/

using System;

class Building {
  public int Floors;    // number of floors
  public int Area;      // total square footage of building
  public int Occupants; // number of occupants

  // Return the area per person.
  public int AreaPerPerson() {
    return Area / Occupants;
  }

  // Return the maximum number of occupants if each
  // is to have at least the specified minimum area.
  public int MaxOccupant(int minArea) {
    return Area / minArea;
  }
}

// Use MaxOccupant().
class BuildingDemo {
  static void Main() {
    Building house = new Building();
    Building office = new Building();

    // Assign values to fields in house.
    house.Occupants = 4;
    house.Area = 2500;
    house.Floors = 2;
```

```
     // Assign values to fields in office.
     office.Occupants = 25;
     office.Area = 4200;
     office.Floors = 3;

     Console.WriteLine("Maximum occupants for house if each has " +
                       300 + " square feet: " +
                       house.MaxOccupant(300));

     Console.WriteLine("Maximum occupants for office if each has " +
                       300 + " square feet: " +
                       office.MaxOccupant(300));
  }
}
```

The output from the program is shown here:

```
Maximum occupants for house if each has 300 square feet: 8
Maximum occupants for office if each has 300 square feet: 14
```

Avoiding Unreachable Code

When creating methods, you should avoid causing a situation in which a portion of code cannot, under any circumstances, be executed. This is called *unreachable code,* and it is considered incorrect in C#. The compiler will issue a warning message if you create a method that contains unreachable code. For example:

```
public void MyMeth() {
  char a, b;

  // ...

  if(a==b) {
    Console.WriteLine("equal");
    return;
  } else {
    Console.WriteLine("not equal");
    return;
  }
  Console.WriteLine("this is unreachable");
}
```

Here, the method **MyMeth( )** will always return before the final **WriteLine( )** statement is executed. If you try to compile this method, you will receive a warning. In general, unreachable code constitutes a mistake on your part, so it is a good idea to take unreachable code warnings seriously.

Constructors

In the preceding examples, the instance variables of each **Building** object had to be set manually using a sequence of statements, such as

```
house.Occupants = 4;
house.Area = 2500;
house.Floors = 2;
```

An approach like this would never be used in professionally written C# code. Aside from this approach being error prone (you might forget to set one of the fields), there is simply a better way to accomplish this task: the constructor.

A *constructor* initializes an object when it is created. It has the same name as its class and is syntactically similar to a method. However, constructors have no explicit return type. The general form of a constructor is shown here:

> *access class-name(param-list)* {
> // constructor code
> }

Typically, you will use a constructor to give initial values to the instance variables defined by the class or to perform any other startup procedures required to create a fully formed object. Also, usually, *access* is **public** because constructors are normally called from outside their class. The *param-list* can be empty, or it can specify one or more parameters.

All classes have constructors, whether you define one or not, because C# automatically provides a default constructor that causes all member variables to be initialized to their default values. For most value types, the default value is zero. For **bool**, the default is **false**. For reference types, the default is null. However, once you define your own constructor, the default constructor is no longer used.

Here is a simple example that uses a constructor:

```
// A simple constructor.

using System;

class MyClass {
  public int x;

  public MyClass() {
    x = 10;
  }
}

class ConsDemo {
  static void Main() {
    MyClass t1 = new MyClass();
    MyClass t2 = new MyClass();

    Console.WriteLine(t1.x + " " + t2.x);
  }
}
```

In this example, the constructor for **MyClass** is

```
public MyClass() {
  x = 10;
}
```

Notice that the constructor is specified as **public**. This is because the constructor will be called from code defined outside of its class. This constructor assigns the instance variable **x** of **MyClass** the value 10. This constructor is called by **new** when an object is created. For example, in the line

```
MyClass t1 = new MyClass();
```

the constructor **MyClass( )** is called on the **t1** object, giving **t1.x** the value 10. The same is true for **t2**. After construction, **t2.x** has the value 10. Thus, the output from the program is

```
10 10
```

Parameterized Constructors

In the preceding example, a parameterless constructor was used. While this is fine for some situations, most often you will need a constructor that has one or more parameters. Parameters are added to a constructor in the same way they are added to a method: just declare them inside the parentheses after the constructor's name. For example, here **MyClass** is given a parameterized constructor:

```
// A parameterized constructor.

using System;

class MyClass {
  public int x;

  public MyClass(int i) {
    x = i;
  }
}

class ParmConsDemo {
  static void Main() {
    MyClass t1 = new MyClass(10);
    MyClass t2 = new MyClass(88);

    Console.WriteLine(t1.x + " " + t2.x);
  }
}
```

The output from this program is shown here:

```
10 88
```

In this version of the program, the **MyClass( )** constructor defines one parameter called **i**, which is used to initialize the instance variable, **x**. Thus, when the line

```
MyClass t1 = new MyClass(10);
```

executes, the value 10 is passed to **i**, which is then assigned to **x**.

Add a Constructor to the Building Class

We can improve the **Building** class by adding a constructor that automatically initializes the **Floors**, **Area**, and **Occupants** fields when an object is constructed. Pay special attention to how **Building** objects are created.

```
// Add a constructor to Building.

using System;

class Building {
  public int Floors;    // number of floors
  public int Area;      // total square footage of building
  public int Occupants; // number of occupants

  // A parameterized constructor for Building.
  public Building(int f, int a, int o) {
    Floors = f;
    Area = a;
    Occupants = o;
  }

  // Display the area per person.
  public int AreaPerPerson() {
    return Area / Occupants;
  }

  // Return the maximum number of occupants if each
  // is to have at least the specified minimum area.
  public int MaxOccupant(int minArea) {
    return Area / minArea;
  }
}

// Use the parameterized Building constructor.
class BuildingDemo {
  static void Main() {
    Building house = new Building(2, 2500, 4);
    Building office = new Building(3, 4200, 25);

    Console.WriteLine("Maximum occupants for house if each has " +
                      300 + " square feet: " +
                      house.MaxOccupant(300));

    Console.WriteLine("Maximum occupants for office if each has " +
                      300 + " square feet: " +
                      office.MaxOccupant(300));
  }
}
```

The output from this program is the same as for the previous version.

Both **house** and **office** were initialized by the **Building( )** constructor when they were created. Each object is initialized as specified in the parameters to its constructor. For example, in the following line,

```
Building house = new Building(2, 2500, 4);
```

the values 2, 2500, and 4 are passed to the **Building( )** constructor when **new** creates the object. Thus, **house**'s copy of **Floors**, **Area**, and **Occupants** will contain the values 2, 2500, and 4, respectively.

The new Operator Revisited

Now that you know more about classes and their constructors, let's take a closer look at the **new** operator. As it relates to classes, the **new** operator has this general form:

new *class-name(arg-list)*

Here, *class-name* is the name of the class that is being instantiated. The class name followed by parentheses specifies the constructor for the class. If a class does not define its own constructor, **new** will use the default constructor supplied by C#. Thus, **new** can be used to create an object of any class type.

Since memory is finite, it is possible that **new** will not be able to allocate memory for an object because insufficient memory exists. If this happens, a runtime exception will occur. (You will learn how to handle exceptions in Chapter 13.) For the sample programs in this book, you won't need to worry about running out of memory, but you may need to consider this possibility in real-world programs that you write.

Using new with Value Types

At this point, you might be asking why you don't need to use **new** for variables of the value types, such as **int** or **float**? In C#, a variable of a value type contains its own value. Memory to hold this value is automatically provided when the program is run. Thus, there is no need to explicitly allocate this memory using **new**. Conversely, a reference variable stores a reference to an object. The memory to hold this object must be allocated dynamically, during execution.

Not making the fundamental types, such **int** or **char**, into reference types greatly improves your program's performance. When using a reference type, there is a layer of indirection that adds overhead to each object access. This layer of indirection is avoided by a value type.

As a point of interest, it is permitted to use **new** with the value types, as shown here:

```
int i = new int();
```

Doing so invokes the default constructor for type **int**, which initializes **i** to zero. For example:

```
// Use new with a value type.

using System;

class newValue {
  static void Main() {
    int i = new int(); // initialize i to zero
```

```
    Console.WriteLine("The value of i is: " + i);
  }
}
```

The output from this program is

```
The value of i is: 0
```

As the output verifies, **i** is initialized to zero. Remember, without the use of **new**, **i** would be uninitialized, and it would cause an error to attempt to use it in the **WriteLine( )** statement without explicitly giving it a value first.

In general, invoking **new** for a value type invokes the default constructor for that type. It does not, however, dynamically allocate memory. Frankly, most programmers do not use **new** with the value types.

Garbage Collection and Destructors

As you have seen, objects are dynamically allocated from a pool of free memory by using the **new** operator. Of course, memory is not infinite, and the free memory can be exhausted. Thus, it is possible for **new** to fail because there is insufficient free memory to create the desired object. For this reason, one of the key components of any dynamic allocation scheme is the recovery of free memory from unused objects, making that memory available for subsequent reallocation. In many programming languages, the release of previously allocated memory is handled manually. For example, in C++, the **delete** operator is used to free memory that was allocated. However, C# uses a different, more trouble-free approach: *garbage collection.*

C#'s garbage collection system reclaims objects automatically—occurring transparently, behind the scenes, without any programmer intervention. It works like this: When no references to an object exist, that object is assumed to be no longer needed, and the memory occupied by the object is eventually released and collected. This recycled memory can then be used for a subsequent allocation.

Garbage collection occurs only sporadically during the execution of your program. It will not occur simply because one or more objects exist that are no longer used. Thus, you can't know, or make assumptions about, precisely when garbage collection will take place.

Destructors

It is possible to define a method that will be called just prior to an object's final destruction by the garbage collector. This method is called a *destructor,* and it can be used in some highly specialized situations to ensure that an object terminates cleanly. For example, you might use a destructor to ensure that a system resource owned by an object is released. It must be stated at the outset that destructors are a very advanced feature that are applicable only to certain rare cases. They are not normally needed. They are briefly described here for completeness.

Destructors have this general form:

```
~class-name( ) {
  // destruction code
}
```

Here, *class-name* is the name of the class. Thus, a destructor is declared like a constructor except that it is preceded with a ~ (tilde). Notice it has no return type and takes no arguments.

To add a destructor to a class, you simply include it as a member. It is called whenever an object of its class is about to be recycled. Inside the destructor, you will specify those actions that must be performed before an object is destroyed.

It is important to understand that the destructor is called just prior to garbage collection. It is not called when a variable containing a reference to an object goes out of scope, for example. (This differs from destructors in C++, which *are* called when an object goes out of scope.) This means that you cannot know precisely when a destructor will be executed. Furthermore, it is possible for your program to end before garbage collection occurs, so a destructor might not get called at all.

The following program demonstrates a destructor. It works by creating and destroying a large number of objects. During this process, at some point the garbage collector will be activated, and the destructors for the objects will be called.

```csharp
// Demonstrate a destructor.

using System;

class Destruct {
  public int x;

  public Destruct(int i) {
    x = i;
  }

  // Called when object is recycled.
  ~Destruct() {
    Console.WriteLine("Destructing " + x);
  }

  // Generates an object that is immediately destroyed.
  public void Generator(int i) {
    Destruct o = new Destruct(i);
  }

}

class DestructDemo {
  static void Main() {
    int count;

    Destruct ob = new Destruct(0);

    /* Now, generate a large number of objects. At
       some point, garbage collection will occur.
       Note: You might need to increase the number
       of objects generated in order to force
       garbage collection. */

    for(count=1; count < 100000; count++)
```

```
    ob.Generator(count);

  Console.WriteLine("Done");
  }
}
```

Here is how the program works. The constructor sets the instance variable **x** to a known value. In this example, **x** is used as an object ID. The destructor displays the value of **x** when an object is recycled. Of special interest is **Generator( )**. This method creates and then promptly destroys a **Destruct** object. The **DestructDemo** class creates an initial **Destruct** object called **ob**. Then using **ob**, it creates 100,000 objects by calling **Generator( )** on **ob**. This has the net effect of creating and destroying 100,000 objects. At various points in the middle of this process, garbage collection will take place. Precisely how often or when is dependent upon several factors, such as the initial amount of free memory, the operating system, and so on. However, at some point, you will start to see the messages generated by the destructor. If you don't see the messages prior to program termination (that is, before you see the "Done" message), try increasing the number of objects being generated by upping the count in the **for** loop.

One important point: The call to **WriteLine( )** inside **~Destruct( )** is purely for the sake of illustration in this rather contrived example. Normally, a destructor should act only on the instance variables defined by its class.

Because of the nondeterministic way in which destructors are called, they should not be used to perform actions that must occur at a specific point in your program. One other point: It is possible to request garbage collection. This is described in Part II, when C#'s class library is discussed. However, manually initiating garbage collection is not recommended for most circumstances, because it can lead to inefficiencies. Also, because of the way the garbage collector works, even if you explicitly request garbage collection, there is no way to know precisely when a specific object will be recycled.

The this Keyword

Before concluding this chapter, it is necessary to introduce **this**. When a method is called, it is automatically passed a reference to the invoking object (that is, the object on which the method is called). This reference is called **this**. Therefore, **this** refers to the object on which the method is acting. To understand **this**, first consider a program that creates a class called **Rect** that encapsulates the width and height of a rectangle and that includes a method called **Area( )** that returns its area.

```
using System;

class Rect {
  public int Width;
  public int Height;

  public Rect(int w, int h) {
    Width = w;
    Height = h;
  }

  public int Area() {
```

```
      return Width * Height;
  }
}

class UseRect {
  static void Main() {
    Rect r1 = new Rect(4, 5);
    Rect r2 = new Rect(7, 9);

    Console.WriteLine("Area of r1: " + r1.Area());

    Console.WriteLine("Area of r2: " + r2.Area());
  }
}
```

As you know, within a method, the other members of a class can be accessed directly, without any object or class qualification. Thus, inside **Area( )**, the statement

```
return Width * Height;
```

means that the copies of **Width** and **Height** associated with the invoking object will be multiplied together and the result returned. However, the same statement can also be written like this:

```
return this.Width * this.Height;
```

Here, **this** refers to the object on which **Area( )** was called. Thus, **this.Width** refers to that object's copy of **Width**, and **this.Height** refers to that object's copy of **Height**. For example, if **Area( )** had been invoked on an object called **x**, then **this** in the preceding statement would have been referring to **x**. Writing the statement without using **this** is really just shorthand.

It is also possible to use **this** inside a constructor. In this case, **this** refers to the object that is being constructed. For example, inside **Rect( )**, the statements

```
Width = w;
Height = h;
```

can be written like this:

```
this.Width = w;
this.Height = h;
```

Of course, there is no benefit in doing so in this case.

For the sake of illustration, here is the entire **Rect** class written using the **this** reference:

```
using System;

class Rect {
  public int Width;
  public int Height;

  public Rect(int w, int h) {
```

```
      this.Width = w;
      this.Height = h;
    }

    public int Area() {
      return this.Width * this.Height;
    }
}

class UseRect {
  static void Main() {
    Rect r1 = new Rect(4, 5);
    Rect r2 = new Rect(7, 9);

    Console.WriteLine("Area of r1: " + r1.Area());

    Console.WriteLine("Area of r2: " + r2.Area());

  }
}
```

Actually, no C# programmer would use **this** as just shown because nothing is gained and the standard form is easier. However, **this** has some important uses. For example, the C# syntax permits the name of a parameter or a local variable to be the same as the name of an instance variable. When this happens, the local name *hides* the instance variable. You can gain access to the hidden instance variable by referring to it through **this**. For example, the following is a syntactically valid way to write the **Rect( )** constructor:

```
public Rect(int Width, int Height) {
  this.Width = Width;
  this.Height = Height;
}
```

In this version, the names of the parameters are the same as the names of the instance variables, thus hiding them. However, **this** is used to "uncover" the instance variables.

Arrays and Strings

This chapter returns to the subject of C#'s data types. It discusses arrays and the **string** type. The **foreach** loop is also examined.

Arrays

An *array* is a collection of variables of the same type that are referred to by a common name. In C#, arrays can have one or more dimensions, although the one-dimensional array is the most common. Arrays are used for a variety of purposes because they offer a convenient means of grouping together related variables. For example, you might use an array to hold a record of the daily high temperature for a month, a list of stock prices, or your collection of programming books.

The principal advantage of an array is that it organizes data in such a way that it can be easily manipulated. For example, if you have an array containing the dividends for a selected group of stocks, it is easy to compute the average income by cycling through the array. Also, arrays organize data in such a way that it can be easily sorted.

Although arrays in C# can be used just like arrays in many other programming languages, they have one special attribute: They are implemented as objects. This fact is one reason that a discussion of arrays was deferred until objects had been introduced. By implementing arrays as objects, several important advantages are gained, not the least of which is that unused arrays can be garbage-collected.

One-Dimensional Arrays

A *one-dimensional array* is a list of related variables. Such lists are common in programming. For example, you might use a one-dimensional array to store the account numbers of the active users on a network. Another array might store the current batting averages for a baseball team.

Because arrays in C# are implemented as objects, two steps are needed to obtain an array for use in your program. First, you must declare a variable that can refer to an array. Second, you must create an instance of the array by use of **new**. Therefore, to declare a one-dimensional array, you will typically use this general form:

type[ ] *array-name* = new *type*[*size*];

Here, *type* declares the *element type* of the array. The element type determines the data type of each element that comprises the array. Notice the square brackets that follow *type*. They indicate that a one-dimensional array is being declared. The number of elements that the array will hold is determined by *size*.

NOTE *If you come from a C or C++ background, pay special attention to the way arrays are declared. Specifically, the square brackets follow the type name, not the array name.*

Here is an example. The following creates an **int** array of ten elements and links it to an array reference variable named **sample**.

```
int[] sample = new int[10];
```

The **sample** variable holds a reference to the memory allocated by **new**. This memory is large enough to hold ten elements of type **int**.

As is the case when creating an instance of a class, it is possible to break the preceding declaration in two. For example:

```
int[] sample;
sample = new int[10];
```

In this case, when **sample** is first created, it refers to no physical object. It is only after the second statement executes that **sample** refers to an array.

An individual element within an array is accessed by use of an index. An *index* describes the position of an element within an array. In C#, all arrays have 0 as the index of their first element. Because **sample** has 10 elements, it has index values of 0 through 9. To index an array, specify the number of the element you want, surrounded by square brackets. Thus, the first element in **sample** is **sample[0]**, and the last element is **sample[9]**. For example, the following program loads **sample** with the numbers 0 through 9:

```
// Demonstrate a one-dimensional array.

using System;

class ArrayDemo {
  static void Main() {
    int[] sample = new int[10];
    int i;

    for(i = 0; i < 10; i = i+1)
      sample[i] = i;

    for(i = 0; i < 10; i = i+1)
      Console.WriteLine("sample[" + i + "]: " + sample[i]);
  }
}
```

The output from the program is shown here:

```
sample[0]: 0
sample[1]: 1
sample[2]: 2
```

```
sample[3]: 3
sample[4]: 4
sample[5]: 5
sample[6]: 6
sample[7]: 7
sample[8]: 8
sample[9]: 9
```

Conceptually, the **sample** array looks like this:

0	1	2	3	4	5	6	7	8	9
sample [0]	sample [1]	sample [2]	sample [3]	sample [4]	sample [5]	sample [6]	sample [7]	sample [8]	sample [9]

Arrays are common in programming because they let you deal easily with large numbers of related variables. For example, the following program finds the average of the set of values stored in the **nums** array by cycling through the array using a **for** loop:

```
// Compute the average of a set of values.

using System;

class Average {
  static void Main() {
    int[] nums = new int[10];
    int avg = 0;

    nums[0] = 99;
    nums[1] = 10;
    nums[2] = 100;
    nums[3] = 18;
    nums[4] = 78;
    nums[5] = 23;
    nums[6] = 63;
    nums[7] = 9;
    nums[8] = 87;
    nums[9] = 49;

    for(int i=0; i < 10; i++)
      avg = avg + nums[i];

    avg = avg / 10;

    Console.WriteLine("Average: " + avg);
  }
}
```

The output from the program is shown here:

```
Average: 53
```

Initializing an Array

In the preceding program, the **nums** array was given values by hand, using ten separate assignment statements. While that is perfectly correct, there is an easier way to accomplish this. Arrays can be initialized when they are created. The general form for initializing a one-dimensional array is shown here:

   type[ ] *array-name* = { *val1, val2, val3, ..., valN* };

Here, the initial values are specified by *val1* through *valN*. They are assigned in sequence, left to right, in index order. C# automatically allocates an array large enough to hold the initializers that you specify. There is no need to use the **new** operator explicitly. For example, here is a better way to write the **Average** program:

```
// Compute the average of a set of values.

using System;

class Average {
  static void Main() {
    int[] nums = { 99, 10, 100, 18, 78, 23,
                   63, 9, 87, 49 };
    int avg = 0;

    for(int i=0; i < 10; i++)
      avg = avg + nums[i];

    avg = avg / 10;

    Console.WriteLine("Average: " + avg);
  }
}
```

As a point of interest, although not needed, you can use **new** when initializing an array. For example, this is a proper, but redundant, way to initialize **nums** in the foregoing program:

```
int[] nums = new int[] { 99, 10, 100, 18, 78, 23,
                         63, 9, 87, 49 };
```

Although redundant here, the **new** form of array initialization is useful when you are assigning a new array to an already-existent array reference variable. For example:

```
int[] nums;
nums = new int[] { 99, 10, 100, 18, 78, 23,
                   63, 9, 87, 49 };
```

In this case, **nums** is declared in the first statement and initialized by the second.

One last point: It is permissible to specify the array size explicitly when initializing an array, but the size must agree with the number of initializers. For example, here is another way to initialize **nums**:

```
int[] nums = new int[10] { 99, 10, 100, 18, 78, 23,
                           63, 9, 87, 49 };
```

In this declaration, the size of **nums** is explicitly stated as 10.

Boundaries Are Enforced

Array boundaries are strictly enforced in C#; it is a runtime error to overrun or underrun the ends of an array. If you want to confirm this for yourself, try the following program that purposely overruns an array:

```
// Demonstrate an array overrun.

using System;

class ArrayErr {
  static void Main() {
    int[] sample = new int[10];
    int i;

    // Generate an array overrun.
    for(i = 0; i < 100; i = i+1)
      sample[i] = i;
  }
}
```

As soon as **i** reaches 10, an **IndexOutOfRangeException** is generated and the program is terminated. (See Chapter 13 for a discussion of exceptions and exception handling.)

Multidimensional Arrays

Although the one-dimensional array is the most commonly used array in programming, multidimensional arrays are certainly not rare. A *multidimensional array* is an array that has two or more dimensions, and an individual element is accessed through the combination of two or more indices.

Two-Dimensional Arrays

The simplest form of the multidimensional array is the two-dimensional array. In a two-dimensional array, the location of any specific element is specified by two indices. If you think of a two-dimensional array as a table of information, one index indicates the row, the other indicates the column.

To declare a two-dimensional integer array **table** of size 10, 20, you would write

```
int[,] table = new int[10, 20];
```

Pay careful attention to the declaration. Notice that the two dimensions are separated from each other by a comma. In the first part of the declaration, the syntax

```
[,]
```

indicates that a two-dimensional array reference variable is being created. When memory is actually allocated for the array using **new**, this syntax is used:

```
int[10, 20]
```

This creates a 10×20 array, and again, the comma separates the dimensions.

To access an element in a two-dimensional array, you must specify both indices, separating the two with a comma. For example, to assign the value 10 to location 3, 5 of array **table**, you would use

```
table[3, 5] = 10;
```

Here is a complete example. It loads a two-dimensional array with the numbers 1 through 12 and then displays the contents of the array.

```
// Demonstrate a two-dimensional array.

using System;

class TwoD {
  static void Main() {
    int t, i;
    int[,] table = new int[3, 4];

    for(t=0; t < 3; ++t) {
      for(i=0; i < 4; ++i) {
        table[t,i] = (t*4)+i+1;
        Console.Write(table[t,i] + " ");
      }
      Console.WriteLine();
    }
  }
}
```

In this example, **table[0, 0]** will have the value 1, **table[0, 1]** the value 2, **table[0, 2]** the value 3, and so on. The value of **table[2, 3]** will be 12. Conceptually, the array will look like the one shown in Figure 7-1.

NOTE *If you have previously programmed in C, C++, or Java, be careful when declaring or accessing multidimensional arrays in C#. In these other languages, array dimensions and indices are specified within their own set of brackets. C# separates dimensions using commas.*

Arrays of Three or More Dimensions

C# allows arrays with more than two dimensions. Here is the general form of a multidimensional array declaration:

type[, ...] *name* = new *type*[*size1*, *size2*, ..., *sizeN*];

FIGURE 7-1
A conceptual view of the **table** array created by the **TwoD** program

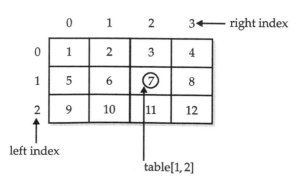

For example, the following declaration creates a 4×10×3 three-dimensional integer array:

```
int[,,] multidim = new int[4, 10, 3];
```

To assign element 2, 4, 1 of **multidim** the value 100, use this statement:

```
multidim[2, 4, 1] = 100;
```

Here is a program that uses a three-dimensional array that holds a 3×3×3 matrix of values. It then sums the value on one of the diagonals through the cube.

```
// Sum the values on a diagonal of a 3x3x3 matrix.

using System;

class ThreeDMatrix {
  static void Main() {
    int[,,] m = new int[3, 3, 3];
    int sum = 0;
    int n = 1;

    for(int x=0; x < 3; x++)
      for(int y=0; y < 3; y++)
        for(int z=0; z < 3; z++)
          m[x, y, z] = n++;

    sum = m[0, 0, 0] + m[1, 1, 1] + m[2, 2, 2];

    Console.WriteLine("Sum of first diagonal: " + sum);
  }
}
```

The output is shown here:

```
Sum of first diagonal: 42
```

Initializing Multidimensional Arrays

A multidimensional array can be initialized by enclosing each dimension's initializer list within its own set of curly braces. For example, the general form of array initialization for a two-dimensional array is shown here:

> *type[,] array_name* = {
>   { *val, val, val, ..., val* },
>   { *val, val, val, ..., val* },
>
>   .
>
>   .
>
>   .
>
>   { *val, val, val, ..., val* }
> };

Here, *val* indicates an initialization value. Each inner block designates a row. Within each row, the first value will be stored in the first position, the second value in the second position, and so on. Notice that commas separate the initializer blocks and that a semicolon follows the closing }.

For example, the following program initializes an array called **sqrs** with the numbers 1 through 10 and their squares.

```
// Initialize a two-dimensional array.

using System;

class Squares {
  static void Main() {
    int[,] sqrs = {
      { 1, 1 },
      { 2, 4 },
      { 3, 9 },
      { 4, 16 },
      { 5, 25 },
      { 6, 36 },
      { 7, 49 },
      { 8, 64 },
      { 9, 81 },
      { 10, 100 }
    };
    int i, j;

    for(i=0; i < 10; i++) {
      for(j=0; j < 2; j++)
        Console.Write(sqrs[i,j] + " ");
      Console.WriteLine();
    }
  }
}
```

Here is the output from the program:

```
1 1
2 4
3 9
4 16
5 25
6 36
7 49
8 64
9 81
10 100
```

Jagged Arrays

In the preceding examples, when you created a two-dimensional array, you were creating what is called a *rectangular array*. Thinking of two-dimensional arrays as tables, a rectangular array is a two-dimensional array in which the length of each row is the same for the entire array. However, C# also allows you to create a special type of two-dimensional array called a *jagged array*. A jagged array is an *array of arrays* in which the length of each array can differ. Thus, a jagged array can be used to create a table in which the lengths of the rows are not the same.

Jagged arrays are declared by using sets of square brackets to indicate each dimension. For example, to declare a two-dimensional jagged array, you will use this general form:

type[ ] [ ] *array-name* = new *type*[*size*][ ];

Here, *size* indicates the number of rows in the array. The rows, themselves, have not been allocated. Instead, the rows are allocated individually. This allows for the length of each row to vary. For example, the following code allocates memory for the first dimension of **jagged** when it is declared. It then allocates the second dimensions manually.

```
int[][] jagged = new int[3][];
jagged[0] = new int[4];
jagged[1] = new int[3];
jagged[2] = new int[5];
```

After this sequence executes, **jagged** looks like this:

It is easy to see how jagged arrays got their name!

Once a jagged array has been created, an element is accessed by specifying each index within its own set of brackets. For example, to assign the value 10 to element 2, 1 of **jagged**, you would use this statement:

```
jagged[2][1] = 10;
```

Note that this differs from the syntax that is used to access an element of a rectangular array.

The following program demonstrates the creation of a jagged two-dimensional array:

```
// Demonstrate jagged arrays.

using System;

class Jagged {
  static void Main() {
    int[][] jagged = new int[3][];
    jagged[0] = new int[4];
    jagged[1] = new int[3];
    jagged[2] = new int[5];

    int i;

    // Store values in first array.
    for(i=0; i < 4; i++)
      jagged[0][i] = i;

    // Store values in second array.
    for(i=0; i < 3; i++)
      jagged[1][i] = i;
```

```
    // Store values in third array.
    for(i=0; i < 5; i++)
      jagged[2][i] = i;

    // Display values in first array.
    for(i=0; i < 4; i++)
      Console.Write(jagged[0][i] + " ");

    Console.WriteLine();

    // Display values in second array.
    for(i=0; i < 3; i++)
      Console.Write(jagged[1][i] + " ");

    Console.WriteLine();

    // Display values in third array.
    for(i=0; i < 5; i++)
      Console.Write(jagged[2][i] + " ");

    Console.WriteLine();
  }
}
```

The output is shown here:

```
0 1 2 3
0 1 2
0 1 2 3 4
```

Jagged arrays are not used by all applications, but they can be effective in some situations. For example, if you need a very large two-dimensional array that is sparsely populated (that is, one in which not all of the elements will be used), then a jagged array might be a perfect solution.

One last point: Because jagged arrays are arrays of arrays, there is no restriction that requires that the arrays be one-dimensional. For example, the following creates an array of two-dimensional arrays:

```
int[][,] jagged = new int[3][,];
```

The next statement assigns **jagged[0]** a reference to a 4×2 array:

```
jagged[0] = new int[4, 2];
```

The following statement assigns a value to **jagged[0][1,0]**:

```
jagged[0][1,0] = i;
```

Assigning Array References

As with other objects, when you assign one array reference variable to another, you are simply making both variables refer to the same array. You are neither causing a copy of the array to be created, nor are you causing the contents of one array to be copied to the other. For example, consider this program:

```
// Assigning array reference variables.

using System;

class AssignARef {
  static void Main() {
    int i;

    int[] nums1 = new int[10];
    int[] nums2 = new int[10];

    for(i=0; i < 10; i++) nums1[i] = i;

    for(i=0; i < 10; i++) nums2[i] = -i;

    Console.Write("Here is nums1: ");
    for(i=0; i < 10; i++)
      Console.Write(nums1[i] + " ");
    Console.WriteLine();

    Console.Write("Here is nums2: ");
    for(i=0; i < 10; i++)
      Console.Write(nums2[i] + " ");
    Console.WriteLine();

    nums2 = nums1; // now nums2 refers to nums1

    Console.Write("Here is nums2 after assignment: ");
    for(i=0; i < 10; i++)
      Console.Write(nums2[i] + " ");
    Console.WriteLine();

    // Next, operate on nums1 array through nums2.
    nums2[3] = 99;

    Console.Write("Here is nums1 after change through nums2: ");
    for(i=0; i < 10; i++)
      Console.Write(nums1[i] + " ");
    Console.WriteLine();
  }
}
```

The output from the program is shown here:

```
Here is nums1: 0 1 2 3 4 5 6 7 8 9
Here is nums2: 0 -1 -2 -3 -4 -5 -6 -7 -8 -9
Here is nums2 after assignment: 0 1 2 3 4 5 6 7 8 9
Here is nums1 after change through nums2: 0 1 2 99 4 5 6 7 8 9
```

As the output shows, after the assignment of **nums1** to **nums2**, both array reference variables refer to the same object.

Using the Length Property

A number of benefits result because C# implements arrays as objects. One comes from the fact that each array has associated with it a **Length** property that contains the number of elements that an array can hold. Thus, each array provides a means by which its length can be determined. Here is a program that demonstrates this property:

```
// Use the Length array property.

using System;

class LengthDemo {
  static void Main() {
    int[] nums = new int[10];

    Console.WriteLine("Length of nums is " + nums.Length);

    // Use Length to initialize nums.
    for(int i=0; i < nums.Length; i++)
      nums[i] = i * i;

    // Now use Length to display nums.
    Console.Write("Here is nums: ");
    for(int i=0; i < nums.Length; i++)
      Console.Write(nums[i] + " ");

    Console.WriteLine();
  }
}
```

This program displays the following output:

```
Length of nums is 10
Here is nums: 0 1 4 9 16 25 36 49 64 81
```

In **LengthDemo** notice the way that **nums.Length** is used by the **for** loops to govern the number of iterations that take place. Since each array carries with it its own length, you can use this information rather than manually keeping track of an array's size. Keep in mind that the value of **Length** has nothing to do with the number of elements that are actually in use. **Length** contains the number of elements that the array is capable of holding.

When the length of a multidimensional array is obtained, the total number of elements that can be held by the array is returned. For example:

```
// Use the Length array property on a 3D array.

using System;

class LengthDemo3D {
  static void Main() {
    int[,,] nums = new int[10, 5, 6];

    Console.WriteLine("Length of nums is " + nums.Length);
  }
}
```

The output is shown here:

```
Length of nums is 300
```

As the output verifies, **Length** obtains the number of elements that **nums** can hold, which is 300 (10×5×6) in this case. It is not possible to use **Length** to obtain the length of a specific dimension.

The inclusion of the **Length** property simplifies many algorithms by making certain types of array operations easier—and safer—to perform. For example, the following program uses **Length** to reverse the contents of an array by copying it back-to-front into another array:

```
// Reverse an array.

using System;

class RevCopy {
  static void Main() {
    int i,j;
    int[] nums1 = new int[10];
    int[] nums2 = new int[10];

    for(i=0; i < nums1.Length; i++) nums1[i] = i;

    Console.Write("Original contents: ");
    for(i=0; i < nums2.Length; i++)
      Console.Write(nums1[i] + " ");

    Console.WriteLine();

    // Reverse copy nums1 to nums2.
    if(nums2.Length >= nums1.Length) // make sure nums2 is long enough
      for(i=0, j=nums1.Length-1; i < nums1.Length; i++, j--)
        nums2[j] = nums1[i];

    Console.Write("Reversed contents: ");
    for(i=0; i < nums2.Length; i++)
      Console.Write(nums2[i] + " ");

    Console.WriteLine();
  }
}
```

Here is the output:

```
Original contents: 0 1 2 3 4 5 6 7 8 9
Reversed contents: 9 8 7 6 5 4 3 2 1 0
```

Here, **Length** helps perform two important functions. First, it is used to confirm that the target array is large enough to hold the contents of the source array. Second, it provides the termination condition of the **for** loop that performs the reverse copy. Of course, in this simple example, the size of the arrays is easily known, but this same approach can be applied to a wide range of more challenging situations.

Using Length with Jagged Arrays

A special case occurs when **Length** is used with jagged arrays. In this situation, it is possible to obtain the length of each individual array. For example, consider the following program, which simulates the CPU activity on a network with four nodes:

```
// Demonstrate Length with jagged arrays.

using System;

class Jagged {
  static void Main() {
    int[][] network_nodes = new int[4][];
    network_nodes[0] = new int[3];
    network_nodes[1] = new int[7];
    network_nodes[2] = new int[2];
    network_nodes[3] = new int[5];


    int i, j;

    // Fabricate some fake CPU usage data.
    for(i=0; i < network_nodes.Length; i++)
      for(j=0; j < network_nodes[i].Length; j++)
        network_nodes[i][j] = i * j + 70;


    Console.WriteLine("Total number of network nodes: " +
                      network_nodes.Length + "\n");

    for(i=0; i < network_nodes.Length; i++) {
      for(j=0; j < network_nodes[i].Length; j++) {
        Console.Write("CPU usage at node " + i +
                      " CPU " + j + ": ");
        Console.Write(network_nodes[i][j] + "% ");
        Console.WriteLine();
      }
      Console.WriteLine();
    }
  }
}
```

The output is shown here:

```
Total number of network nodes: 4

CPU usage at node 0 CPU 0: 70%
CPU usage at node 0 CPU 1: 70%
CPU usage at node 0 CPU 2: 70%

CPU usage at node 1 CPU 0: 70%
CPU usage at node 1 CPU 1: 71%
CPU usage at node 1 CPU 2: 72%
CPU usage at node 1 CPU 3: 73%
CPU usage at node 1 CPU 4: 74%
```

```
CPU usage at node 1 CPU 5: 75%
CPU usage at node 1 CPU 6: 76%

CPU usage at node 2 CPU 0: 70%
CPU usage at node 2 CPU 1: 72%

CPU usage at node 3 CPU 0: 70%
CPU usage at node 3 CPU 1: 73%
CPU usage at node 3 CPU 2: 76%
CPU usage at node 3 CPU 3: 79%
CPU usage at node 3 CPU 4: 82%
```

Pay special attention to the way **Length** is used on the jagged array **network_nodes**. Recall, a two-dimensional jagged array is an array of arrays. Thus, when the expression

```
network_nodes.Length
```

is used, it obtains the number of *arrays* stored in **network_nodes**, which is four in this case. To obtain the length of any individual array in the jagged array, you will use an expression such as this:

```
network_nodes[0].Length
```

which, in this case, obtains the length of the first array.

Implicitly Typed Arrays

As explained in Chapter 3, C# 3.0 added the ability to declare implicitly typed variables by using the **var** keyword. These are variables whose type is determined by the compiler, based on the type of the initializing expression. Thus, all implicitly typed variables must be initialized. Using the same mechanism, it is also possible to create an implicitly typed array. As a general rule, implicitly typed arrays are for use in certain types of queries involving LINQ, which is described in Chapter 19. In most other cases, you will use the "normal" array declaration approach. Implicitly typed arrays are introduced here for completeness.

An implicitly typed array is declared using the keyword **var**, but you *do not* follow **var** with [ ]. Furthermore, the array must be initialized because it is the type of the initializers that determine the element type of the array. All of the initializers must be of the same or compatible type. Here is an example of an implicitly typed array:

```
var vals = new[] { 1, 2, 3, 4, 5 };
```

This creates an array of **int** that is five elements long. A reference to that array is assigned to **vals**. Thus, the type of **vals** is "array of **int**" and it has five elements. Again, notice that **var** is not followed by [ ]. Also, even though the array is being initialized, you must include **new**[ ]. It's not optional in this context.

Here is another example. It creates a two-dimensional array of **double**:

```
var vals = new[,] { {1.1, 2.2}, {3.3, 4.4},{ 5.5, 6.6} };
```

In this case, **vals** has the dimensions 2×3.

You can also declare implicitly typed jagged arrays. For example, consider the following program:

```
// Demonstrate an implicitly typed jagged array.

using System;

class Jagged {
  static void Main() {

    var jagged = new[] {
      new[] { 1, 2, 3, 4 },
      new[] { 9, 8, 7 },
      new[] { 11, 12, 13, 14, 15 }
    };

    for(int j = 0; j < jagged.Length; j++) {
      for(int i=0; i < jagged[j].Length; i++)
        Console.Write(jagged[j][i] + " ");

      Console.WriteLine();
    }
  }
}
```

The program produces the following output:

```
1 2 3 4
9 8 7
11 12 13 14 15
```

Pay special attention to the declaration of **jagged**:

```
var jagged = new[] {
  new[] { 1, 2, 3, 4 },
  new[] { 9, 8, 7 },
  new[] { 11, 12, 13, 14, 15 }
};
```

Notice how **new[ ]** is used in two ways. First, it creates the array of arrays. Second, it creates each individual array, based on the number and type of initializers. As you would expect, all of the initializers in the individual arrays must be of the same type. The same general approach used to declare **jagged** can be used to declare any implicitly typed jagged array.

As mentioned, implicitly typed arrays are most applicable to LINQ-based queries. They are not meant for general use. In most cases, you should use explicitly typed arrays.

The foreach Loop

In Chapter 5, it was mentioned that C# defines a loop called **foreach**, but a discussion of that statement was deferred until later. The time for that discussion has now come.

The **foreach** loop is used to cycle through the elements of a *collection*. A collection is a group of objects. C# defines several types of collections, of which one is an array. The general form of **foreach** is shown here:

foreach(*type loopvar* in *collection*) *statement*;

Here, *type loopvar* specifies the type and name of an *iteration variable*. The iteration variable receives the value of the next element in the collection each time the **foreach** loop iterates. The collection being cycled through is specified by *collection,* which, for the rest of this discussion, is an array. Thus, *type* must be the same as (or compatible with) the element type of the array. The *type* can also be **var**, in which case the compiler determines the type based on the element type of the array. This can be useful when working with certain queries, as described later in this book. Normally, you will explicitly specify the type.

Here is how **foreach** works. When the loop begins, the first element in the array is obtained and assigned to *loopvar*. Each subsequent iteration obtains the next element from the array and stores it in *loopvar*. The loop ends when there are no more elements to obtain. Thus, the **foreach** cycles through the array one element at a time, from start to finish.

One important point to remember about **foreach** is that the iteration variable *loopvar* is read-only. This means you can't change the contents of an array by assigning the iteration variable a new value.

Here is a simple example that uses **foreach**. It creates an array of integers and gives it some initial values. It then displays those values, computing the summation in the process.

```
// Use the foreach loop.

using System;

class ForeachDemo {
  static void Main() {
    int sum = 0;
    int[] nums = new int[10];

    // Give nums some values.
    for(int i = 0; i < 10; i++)
      nums[i] = i;

    // Use foreach to display and sum the values.
    foreach(int x in nums) {
      Console.WriteLine("Value is: " + x);
      sum += x;
    }
    Console.WriteLine("Summation: " + sum);
  }
}
```

The output from the program is shown here:

```
Value is: 0
Value is: 1
Value is: 2
Value is: 3
Value is: 4
Value is: 5
Value is: 6
Value is: 7
```

```
Value is: 8
Value is: 9
Summation: 45
```

As this output shows, **foreach** cycles through an array in sequence from the lowest index to the highest.

Although the **foreach** loop iterates until all elements in an array have been examined, it is possible to terminate a **foreach** loop early by using a **break** statement. For example, this program sums only the first five elements of **nums**:

```csharp
// Use break with a foreach.

using System;

class ForeachDemo {
  static void Main() {
    int sum = 0;
    int[] nums = new int[10];

    // Give nums some values.
    for(int i = 0; i < 10; i++)
      nums[i] = i;

    // Use foreach to display and sum the values.
    foreach(int x in nums) {
      Console.WriteLine("Value is: " + x);
      sum += x;
      if(x == 4) break; // stop the loop when 4 is obtained
    }
    Console.WriteLine("Summation of first 5 elements: " + sum);
  }
}
```

This is the output produced:

```
Value is: 0
Value is: 1
Value is: 2
Value is: 3
Value is: 4
Summation of first 5 elements: 10
```

As is evident, the **foreach** loop stops after the fifth element has been obtained.

The **foreach** loop also works on multidimensional arrays. It returns those elements in row order, from first to last.

```csharp
// Use foreach on a two-dimensional array.

using System;

class ForeachDemo2 {
  static void Main() {
    int sum = 0;
    int[,] nums = new int[3,5];
```

```
    // Give nums some values.
    for(int i = 0; i < 3; i++)
      for(int j=0; j < 5; j++)
        nums[i,j] = (i+1)*(j+1);

    // Use foreach to display and sum the values.
    foreach(int x in nums) {
      Console.WriteLine("Value is: " + x);
      sum += x;
    }
    Console.WriteLine("Summation: " + sum);
  }
}
```

The output from this program is shown here:

```
Value is: 1
Value is: 2
Value is: 3
Value is: 4
Value is: 5
Value is: 2
Value is: 4
Value is: 6
Value is: 8
Value is: 10
Value is: 3
Value is: 6
Value is: 9
Value is: 12
Value is: 15
Summation: 90
```

Since the **foreach** loop can only cycle through an array sequentially, from start to finish, you might think that its use is limited. However, this is not true. A large number of algorithms require exactly this mechanism, of which one of the most common is searching. For example, the following program uses a **foreach** loop to search an array for a value. It stops if the value is found.

```
// Search an array using foreach.

using System;

class Search {
  static void Main() {
    int[] nums = new int[10];
    int val;
    bool found = false;

    // Give nums some values.
    for(int i = 0; i < 10; i++)
      nums[i] = i;

    val = 5;
```

```
// Use foreach to search nums for key.
foreach(int x in nums) {
  if(x == val) {
    found = true;
    break;
  }
}

if(found)
  Console.WriteLine("Value found!");
  }
}
```

The output is shown here:

```
Value found!
```

The **foreach** loop is an excellent choice in this application because searching an array involves examining each element. Other types of **foreach** applications include such things as computing an average, finding the minimum or maximum of a set, looking for duplicates, and so on. As you will see later in this book, **foreach** is especially useful when operating on other types of collections.

Strings

From a day-to-day programming standpoint, **string** is one of C#'s most important data types because it defines and supports character strings. In many other programming languages, a string is an array of characters. This is not the case with C#. In C#, strings are objects. Thus, **string** is a reference type. Although **string** is a built-in data type in C#, a discussion of **string** needed to wait until classes and objects had been introduced.

Actually, you have been using the **string** class since Chapter 2, but you did not know it. When you create a string literal, you are actually creating a **string** object. For example, in the statement

```
Console.WriteLine("In C#, strings are objects.");
```

the string "In C#, strings are objects." is automatically made into a **string** object by C#. Thus, the use of the **string** class has been "below the surface" in the preceding programs. In this section, you will learn to handle them explicitly.

Constructing Strings

The easiest way to construct a **string** is to use a string literal. For example, here **str** is a **string** reference variable that is assigned a reference to a string literal:

```
string str = "C# strings are powerful.";
```

In this case, **str** is initialized to the character sequence "C# strings are powerful."
You can also create a **string** from a **char** array. For example:

```
char[] charray = {'t', 'e', 's', 't'};
string str = new string(charray);
```

Once you have created a **string** object, you can use it nearly anywhere that a quoted string is allowed. For example, you can use a **string** object as an argument to **WriteLine( )**, as shown in this example:

```
// Introduce string.

using System;

class StringDemo {
  static void Main() {

    char[] charray = {'A', ' ', 's', 't', 'r', 'i', 'n', 'g', '.' };
    string str1 = new string(charray);
    string str2 = "Another string.";

    Console.WriteLine(str1);
    Console.WriteLine(str2);
  }
}
```

The output from the program is shown here:

```
A string.
Another string.
```

Operating on Strings

The **string** class contains several methods that operate on strings. Table 7-1 shows a few. Notice that several of the methods take a parameter of type **StringComparison**. This is an enumeration type that defines various values that determine how a comparison involving strings will be conducted. (Enumerations are described in Chapter 12, and the use of **StringComparison** here does not require an understanding of enumerations.) As you might guess, there are various ways in which two strings can be compared. For example, they can be compared based on the binary values of the characters that comprise them. This is called an *ordinal* comparison. Strings can also be compared in a way that takes into account various cultural metrics, such as dictionary order. This type of comparison is called *culture-sensitive.* (Culture sensitivity is especially important in applications that are being internationalized.) Furthermore, comparisons can either be case-sensitive or ignore case differences. Although overloads of methods such as **Compare( )**, **Equals( )**, **IndexOf( )**, and **LastIndexOf( )** do exist that provide a default string comparison approach, it is now considered best to explicitly specify what type of comparison you want. Doing so helps avoid ambiguity in this regard. (It also helps with internationalizing an application.) This is why these forms are shown here.

In general, and with some exceptions, if you want to compare two strings for sorting relative to the cultural norms, you will use **StringComparison.CurrentCulture** as the comparison approach. If you want to compare two strings based solely on the value of their characters, it is usually best to use **StringComparison.Ordinal**. To ignore case differences, specify either **StringComparison.CurrentCultureIgnoreCase** or **StringComparison.OrdinalIgnoreCase**. You can also specify an invariant culture. (See Chapter 22.)

Notice that in Table 7-1, **Compare()** is declared as **static**. The **static** modifier is described in Chapter 8, but briefly, as it is used here, it means that **Compare()** is called on its class name, not an instance of its class. Thus, to call **Compare()**, you will use this general form:

result = string.Compare(*str1*, *str2*, *how*);

where *how* specifies the string comparison approach.

> **NOTE** *Additional information about approaches to string comparisons and searches, including the importance of choosing the right technique, is found in Chapter 22, where string handling is discussed in detail.*

Also notice the two methods **ToUpper()** and **ToLower()**, which uppercase or lowercase a string, respectively. The forms shown here both have a **CultureInfo** parameter. This is a class that describes the cultural attributes to use for the conversion. The examples in this book use the current culture settings. These settings are specified by passing **CultureInfo.CurrentCulture**. The **CultureInfo** class is in **System.Globalization**. As a point of interest, there are versions of these methods that use the current culture by default, but to avoid ambiguity on this point, this book will explicitly specify this argument.

The **string** type also includes the **Length** property, which contains the length of the string.

Method	Description
static int Compare(string *strA*, string *strB*, StringComparison *comparisonType*)	Returns less than zero if *strA* is less than *strB*, greater than zero if *strA* is greater than *strB*, and zero if the strings are equal. How the comparison is conducted is specified by *comparisonType*.
bool Equals(string *value*, StringComparison *comparisonType*)	Returns true if the invoking string is the same as *value*. How the comparison is conducted is specified by *comparisonType*.
int IndexOf(char *value*)	Searches the invoking string for the first occurrence of the character specified by *value*. An ordinal search is used. Returns the index of the first match, or –1 on failure.
int IndexOf(string *value*, StringComparison *comparisonType*)	Searches the invoking string for the first occurrence of the substring specified by *value*. How the search is conducted is specified by *comparisonType*. Returns the index of the first match, or –1 on failure.
int LastIndexOf(char *value*)	Searches the invoking string for the last occurrence of the character specified by *value*. An ordinal search is used. Returns the index of the first match, or –1 on failure.
int LastIndexOf(string *value*, StringComparison *comparisonType*)	Searches the invoking string for the last occurrence of the substring specified by *value*. How the search is conducted is specified by *comparisonType*. Returns the index of the last match, or –1 on failure.
string ToLower(CultureInfo.CurrentCulture *culture*)	Returns a lowercase version of the invoking string. How the conversion is performed is specified by *culture*.
string ToUpper(CultureInfo.CurrentCulture *culture*)	Returns an uppercase version of the invoking string. How the conversion is performed is specified by *culture*.

TABLE 7-1   A Sampling of Common String Handling Methods

To obtain the value of an individual character of a string, you simply use an index. For example:

```
string str = "test";
Console.WriteLine(str[0]);
```

This displays "t", the first character of "test". Like arrays, string indexes begin at zero. One important point, however, is that you cannot assign a new value to a character within a string using an index. An index can only be used to obtain a character.

You can use the = = operator to test two strings for equality. Normally, when the = = operator is applied to object references, it determines if both references refer to the same object. This differs for objects of type **string**. When the = = is applied to two **string** references, the contents of the strings themselves are compared for equality. The same is true for the != operator: when comparing **string** objects, the contents of the strings are compared. In both cases, an ordinal comparison is performed. To test two strings for equality using cultural information, use **Equals()** and specify the comparison approach, such as **StringComparison.CurrentCulture**. One other point: the **Compare()** method is intended to compare strings to determine an ordering relationship, such as for sorting. To test for equality, use **Equals()** or the string operators.

Here is a program that demonstrates several string operations:

```
// Some string operations.

using System;
using System.Globalization;

class StrOps {
  static void Main() {
    string str1 = "When it comes to .NET programming, C# is #1.";
    string str2 = "When it comes to .NET programming, C# is #1.";
    string str3 = "C# strings are powerful.";
    string strUp, strLow;
    int result, idx;

    Console.WriteLine("str1: " + str1);

    Console.WriteLine("Length of str1: " + str1.Length);

    // Create upper- and lowercase versions of str1.
    strLow = str1.ToLower(CultureInfo.CurrentCulture);
    strUp =  str1.ToUpper(CultureInfo.CurrentCulture);
    Console.WriteLine("Lowercase version of str1:\n     " +
                      strLow);
    Console.WriteLine("Uppercase version of str1:\n     " +
                      strUp);

    Console.WriteLine();

    // Display str1, one char at a time.
    Console.WriteLine("Display str1, one char at a time.");
    for(int i=0; i < str1.Length; i++)
      Console.Write(str1[i]);
    Console.WriteLine("\n");
```

```
    // Compare strings using == and !=. These comparisons are ordinal.
    if(str1 == str2)
      Console.WriteLine("str1 == str2");
    else
      Console.WriteLine("str1 != str2");

    if(str1 == str3)
      Console.WriteLine("str1 == str3");
    else
      Console.WriteLine("str1 != str3");

    // This comparison is culture-sensitive.
    result = string.Compare(str1, str3, StringComparison.CurrentCulture);
    if(result == 0)
      Console.WriteLine("str1 and str3 are equal");
    else if(result < 0)
      Console.WriteLine("str1 is less than str3");
    else
      Console.WriteLine("str1 is greater than str3");

    Console.WriteLine();

    // Assign a new string to str2.
    str2 = "One Two Three One";

    // Search a string.
    idx = str2.IndexOf("One", StringComparison.Ordinal);
    Console.WriteLine("Index of first occurrence of One: " + idx);
    idx = str2.LastIndexOf("One", StringComparison.Ordinal);
    Console.WriteLine("Index of last occurrence of One: " + idx);

  }
}
```

This program generates the following output:

```
str1: When it comes to .NET programming, C# is #1.
Length of str1: 44
Lowercase version of str1:
    when it comes to .net programming, c# is #1.
Uppercase version of str1:
    WHEN IT COMES TO .NET PROGRAMMING, C# IS #1.

Display str1, one char at a time.
When it comes to .NET programming, C# is #1.

str1 == str2
str1 != str3
str1 is greater than str3

Index of first occurrence of One: 0
Index of last occurrence of One: 14
```

Before moving on, in the program notice that **Compare()** is called as shown here:

```
result = string.Compare(str1, str3, StringComparison.CurrentCulture);
```

As explained, because **Compare()** is declared as **static**, it is called on its class name, not an instance of its class.

You can *concatenate* (join together) two strings using the + operator. For example, this statement:

```
string str1 = "One";
string str2 = "Two";
string str3 = "Three";
string str4 = str1 + str2 + str3;
```

initializes **str4** with the string "OneTwoThree".

One other point: The **string** keyword is an *alias* for (that is, maps directly to) the **System.String** class defined by the .NET Framework class library. Thus, the fields and methods defined by **string** are those of the **System.String** class, which includes more than the sampling described here. **System.String** is examined in detail in Part II.

Arrays of Strings

Like any other data type, strings can be assembled into arrays. For example:

```
// Demonstrate string arrays.

using System;

class StringArrays {
  static void Main() {
    string[] str = { "This", "is", "a", "test." };

    Console.WriteLine("Original array: ");
    for(int i=0; i < str.Length; i++)
      Console.Write(str[i] + " ");
    Console.WriteLine("\n");

    // Change a string.
    str[1] = "was";
    str[3] = "test, too!";

    Console.WriteLine("Modified array: ");
    for(int i=0; i < str.Length; i++)
      Console.Write(str[i] + " ");
  }
}
```

Here is the output from this program:

```
Original array:
This is a test.

Modified array:
This was a test, too!
```

Here is a more interesting example. The following program displays an integer value using words. For example, the value 19 will display as "one nine".

```
// Display the digits of an integer using words.

using System;

class ConvertDigitsToWords {
  static void Main() {
    int num;
    int nextdigit;
    int numdigits;
    int[] n = new int[20];

    string[] digits = { "zero", "one", "two",
                        "three", "four", "five",
                        "six", "seven", "eight",
                        "nine" };

    num = 1908;

    Console.WriteLine("Number: " + num);

    Console.Write("Number in words: ");

    nextdigit = 0;
    numdigits = 0;

    // Get individual digits and store in n.
    // These digits are stored in reverse order.
    do {
      nextdigit = num % 10;
      n[numdigits] = nextdigit;
      numdigits++;
      num = num / 10;
    } while(num > 0);
    numdigits--;

    // Display the words.
    for( ; numdigits >= 0; numdigits--)
      Console.Write(digits[n[numdigits]] + " ");

    Console.WriteLine();
  }
}
```

The output is shown here:

```
Number: 1908
Number in words: one nine zero eight
```

In the program, the **string** array **digits** holds in order the word equivalents of the digits from zero to nine. The program converts an integer into words by first obtaining each digit of the value and storing those digits, in reverse order, in the **int** array called **n**. Then, this array is cycled through from back to front. In the process, each integer value in **n** is used as an index into **digits**, with the corresponding string being displayed.

Strings Are Immutable

Here is something that might surprise you: The contents of a **string** object are immutable. That is, once created, the character sequence comprising that string cannot be altered. This restriction allows strings to be implemented more efficiently. Even though this probably sounds like a serious drawback, it isn't. When you need a string that is a variation on one that already exists, simply create a new string that contains the desired changes. Because unused string objects are automatically garbage-collected, you don't even need to worry about what happens to the discarded strings.

It must be made clear, however, that **string** reference variables may, of course, change which object they refer to. It is just that the contents of a specific **string** object cannot be changed after it is created.

To fully understand why immutable strings are not a hindrance, we will use another of **string**'s methods: **Substring( )**. The **Substring( )** method returns a new string that contains a specified portion of the invoking string. Because a new **string** object is manufactured that contains the substring, the original string is unaltered, and the rule of immutability is still intact. The form of **Substring( )** that we will be using is shown here:

string Substring(int *startIndex*, int *length*)

Here, *startIndex* specifies the beginning index, and *length* specifies the length of the substring.

Here is a program that demonstrates **Substring( )** and the principle of immutable strings:

```
// Use Substring().

using System;

class SubStr {
  static void Main() {
    string orgstr = "C# makes strings easy.";

    // Construct a substring.
    string substr = orgstr.Substring(5, 12);

    Console.WriteLine("orgstr: " + orgstr);
    Console.WriteLine("substr: " + substr);
  }
}
```

Here is the output from the program:

```
orgstr: C# makes strings easy.
substr: kes strings
```

As you can see, the original string **orgstr** is unchanged, and **substr** contains the substring.

One more point: Although the immutability of **string** objects is not usually a restriction or hindrance, there may be times when it would be beneficial to be able to modify a string. To allow this, C# offers a class called **StringBuilder**, which is in the **System.Text** namespace. It creates string objects that can be changed. For most purposes, however, you will want to use **string**, not **StringBuilder**.

Strings Can Be Used in switch Statements

A **string** can be used to control a **switch** statement. It is the only non-integer type that can be used in the **switch**. The fact that strings can be used in **switch** statements makes it possible to handle some otherwise difficult situations quite easily. For example, the following program displays the digit equivalent of the words "one," "two," and "three":

```
// A string can control a switch statement.

using System;

class StringSwitch {
  static void Main() {
    string[] strs = { "one", "two", "three", "two", "one" };

    foreach(string s in strs) {
      switch(s) {
        case "one":
          Console.Write(1);
          break;
        case "two":
          Console.Write(2);
          break;
        case "three":
          Console.Write(3);
          break;
      }
    }
    Console.WriteLine();
  }
}
```

The output is shown here:

```
12321
```

A Closer Look at Methods and Classes

This chapter resumes the examination of classes and methods. It begins by explaining how to control access to the members of a class. It then discusses the passing and returning of objects, method overloading, the various forms of **Main()**, recursion, and the use of the keyword **static**.

Controlling Access to Class Members

In its support for encapsulation, the class provides two major benefits. First, it links data with code. You have been taking advantage of this aspect of the class since Chapter 6. Second, it provides the means by which access to members can be controlled. It is this second feature that is examined here.

Although C#'s approach is a bit more sophisticated, in essence, there are two basic types of class members: public and private. A public member can be freely accessed by code defined outside of its class. This is the type of class member that we have been using up to this point. A private member can be accessed only by methods defined by its class. It is through the use of private members that access is controlled.

Restricting access to a class' members is a fundamental part of object-oriented programming because it helps prevent the misuse of an object. By allowing access to private data only through a well-defined set of methods, you can prevent improper values from being assigned to that data—by performing a range check, for example. It is not possible for code outside the class to set the value of a private member directly. You can also control precisely how and when the data within an object is used. Thus, when correctly implemented, a class creates a "black box" that can be used, but the inner workings of which are not open to tampering.

C#'s Access Modifiers

Member access control is achieved through the use of four *access modifiers*: **public**, **private**, **protected**, and **internal**. In this chapter, we will be concerned with **public** and **private**. The **protected** modifier applies only when inheritance is involved and is described in Chapter 11.

The **internal** modifier applies mostly to the use of an *assembly,* which for C# loosely means a deployable program or library. The **internal** modifier is examined in Chapter 16.

When a member of a class is modified by the **public** specifier, that member can be accessed by any other code in your program. This includes methods defined inside other classes.

When a member of a class is specified as **private**, then that member can be accessed only by other members of its class. Thus, methods in other classes are not able to access a **private** member of another class. As explained in Chapter 6, if no access specifier is used, a class member is private to its class by default. Thus, the **private** specifier is optional when creating private class members.

An access specifier precedes the rest of a member's type specification. That is, it must begin a member's declaration statement. Here are some examples:

```
public string errMsg;
private double bal;
private bool isError(byte status) { // ...
```

To understand the difference between **public** and **private**, consider the following program:

```
// Public vs. private access.

using System;

class MyClass {
  private int alpha; // private access explicitly specified
  int beta;          // private access by default
  public int gamma;  // public access

  // Methods to access alpha and beta. It is OK for a member
  // of a class to access a private member of the same class.

  public void SetAlpha(int a) {
    alpha = a;
  }

  public int GetAlpha() {
    return alpha;
  }

  public void SetBeta(int a) {
    beta = a;
  }

  public int GetBeta() {
    return beta;
  }
}

class AccessDemo {
  static void Main() {
    MyClass ob = new MyClass();
```

```
    // Access to alpha and beta is allowed only through methods.
    ob.SetAlpha(-99);
    ob.SetBeta(19);
    Console.WriteLine("ob.alpha is " + ob.GetAlpha());
    Console.WriteLine("ob.beta is " + ob.GetBeta());

    // You cannot access alpha or beta like this:
//  ob.alpha = 10; // Wrong! alpha is private!
//  ob.beta = 9;   // Wrong! beta is private!

    // It is OK to directly access gamma because it is public.
    ob.gamma = 99;
  }
}
```

As you can see, inside the **MyClass** class, **alpha** is specified as **private**, **beta** is private by default, and **gamma** is specified as **public**. Because **alpha** and **beta** are private, they cannot be accessed by code outside of their class. Therefore, inside the **AccessDemo** class, neither can be used directly. Each must be accessed through public methods, such as **SetAlpha()** and **GetAlpha()**. For example, if you were to remove the comment symbol from the beginning of the following line

```
//  ob.alpha = 10; // Wrong! alpha is private!
```

you would not be able to compile this program because of the access violation. Although access to **alpha** by code outside of **MyClass** is not allowed, methods defined within **MyClass** can freely access it, as the **SetAlpha()** and **GetAlpha()** methods show. The same is true for **beta**.

The key point is this: A private member can be used freely by other members of its class, but it cannot be accessed by code outside its class.

Applying Public and Private Access

The proper use of public and private access is a key component of successful object-oriented programming. Although there are no hard and fast rules, here are some general principles that serve as guidelines:

- Members of a class that are used only within the class itself should be private.
- Instance data that must be within a specific range should be private, with access provided through public methods that can perform range checks.
- If changing a member can cause an effect that extends beyond the member itself (that is, affects other aspects of the object), that member should be private, and access to it should be controlled.
- Members that can cause harm to an object when improperly used should be private. Access to these members should be through public methods that prevent improper usage.
- Methods that get and set the values of private data must be public.
- Public instance variables are permissible when there is no reason for them to be private.

Of course, there are many nuances that the preceding rules do not address, and special cases cause one or more rules to be violated. But, in general, if you follow these rules, you will be creating resilient objects that are not easily misused.

Controlling Access: A Case Study

To better understand the "how and why" behind access control, a case study is useful. One of the quintessential examples of object-oriented programming is a class that implements a stack. As you probably know, a *stack* is a data structure that implements a last-in, first-out list. Its name comes from the analogy of a stack of plates on a table. The first plate on the table is the last one to be used.

A stack is a classic example of object-oriented programming because it combines storage for information along with the methods that access that information. Thus, a stack is a *data engine* that enforces the last-in, first-out usage. Such a combination is an excellent choice for a class in which the members that provide storage for the stack are private, and public methods provide access. By encapsulating the underlying storage, it is not possible for code that uses the stack to access the elements out of order.

A stack defines two basic operations: *push* and *pop*. A push puts a value onto the top of the stack. A pop removes a value from the top of the stack. Thus, a pop is consumptive; once a value has been popped off the stack, it has been removed and cannot be accessed again.

The example shown here creates a class called **Stack** that implements a stack. The underlying storage for the stack is provided by a private array. The push and pop operations are available through the public methods of the **Stack** class. Thus, the public methods enforce the last-in, first-out mechanism. As shown here, the **Stack** class stores characters, but the same mechanism could be used to store any type of data:

```
// A stack class for characters.

using System;

class Stack {
  // These members are private.
  char[] stck; // holds the stack
  int tos;     // index of the top of the stack

  // Construct an empty Stack given its size.
  public Stack(int size) {
    stck = new char[size]; // allocate memory for stack
    tos = 0;
  }

  // Push characters onto the stack.
  public void Push(char ch) {
    if(tos==stck.Length) {
      Console.WriteLine(" -- Stack is full.");
      return;
    }

    stck[tos] = ch;
    tos++;
  }

  // Pop a character from the stack.
```

```
  public char Pop() {
    if(tos==0) {
      Console.WriteLine(" -- Stack is empty.");
      return (char) 0;
    }

    tos--;
    return stck[tos];
  }

  // Return true if the stack is full.
  public bool IsFull() {
    return tos==stck.Length;
  }

  // Return true if the stack is empty.
  public bool IsEmpty() {
    return tos==0;
  }

  // Return total capacity of the stack.
  public int Capacity() {
    return stck.Length;
  }

  // Return number of objects currently on the stack.
  public int GetNum() {
    return tos;
  }
}
```

Let's examine this class closely. The **Stack** class begins by declaring these two instance variables:

```
// These members are private.
char[] stck; // holds the stack
int tos;     // index of the top of the stack
```

The **stck** array provides the underlying storage for the stack, which in this case holds characters. Notice that no array is allocated. The allocation of the actual array is handled by the **Stack** constructor. The **tos** member holds the index of the top of the stack.

Both the **tos** and **stck** members are private. This enforces the last-in, first-out stack mechanism. If public access to **stck** were allowed, then the elements on the stack could be accessed out of order. Also, since **tos** holds the index of the top element in the stack, manipulations of **tos** by code outside the **Stack** class must be prevented in order to avoid corruption of the stack. Access to **stck** and **tos** is available, indirectly, to the user of **Stack** through the various public methods described shortly.

The stack constructor is shown next:

```
// Construct an empty Stack given its size.
public Stack(int size) {
  stck = new char[size]; // allocate memory for stack
  tos = 0;
}
```

The constructor is passed the desired size of the stack. It allocates the underlying array and sets **tos** to zero. Thus, a zero value in **tos** indicates that the stack is empty.

The public **Push()** method puts an element onto the stack. It is shown here:

```
// Push characters onto the stack.
public void Push(char ch) {
  if(tos==stck.Length) {
    Console.WriteLine(" -- Stack is full.");
    return;
  }

  stck[tos] = ch;
  tos++;
}
```

The element to be pushed onto the stack is passed in **ch**. Before the element is added to the stack, a check is made to ensure that there is still room in the underlying array. This is done by making sure that **tos** does not exceed the length of **stck**. If there is still room, the element is stored in **stck** at the index specified by **tos**, and then **tos** is incremented. Thus, **tos** always contains the index of the next free element in **stck**.

To remove an element from the stack, call the public method **Pop()**. It is shown here:

```
// Pop a character from the stack.
public char Pop() {
  if(tos==0) {
    Console.WriteLine(" -- Stack is empty.");
    return (char) 0;
  }

  tos--;
  return stck[tos];
}
```

Here, the value of **tos** is checked. If it is zero, the stack is empty. Otherwise, **tos** is decremented, and the element at that index is returned.

Although **Push()** and **Pop()** are the only methods needed to implement a stack, some others are quite useful, and the **Stack** class defines four more. These are **IsFull()**, **IsEmpty()**, **Capacity()**, and **GetNum()**, and they provide information about the state of the stack. They are shown here:

```
// Return true if the stack is full.
public bool IsFull() {
  return tos==stck.Length;
}

// Return true if the stack is empty.
public bool IsEmpty() {
  return tos==0;
}

// Return total capacity of the stack.
```

```
public int Capacity() {
  return stck.Length;
}

// Return number of objects currently on the stack.
public int GetNum() {
  return tos;
}
```

The **IsFull()** method returns **true** when the stack is full and **false** otherwise. The **IsEmpty()** method returns **true** when the stack is empty and **false** otherwise. To obtain the total capacity of the stack (that is, the total number of elements it can hold), call **Capacity()**. To obtain the number of elements currently stored on the stack, call **GetNum()**. These methods are useful because the information they provide requires access to **tos**, which is private. They are also examples of how public methods can provide safe access to private members.

The following program demonstrates the stack:

```
// Demonstrate the Stack class.

using System;

class StackDemo {
  static void Main() {
    Stack stk1 = new Stack(10);
    Stack stk2 = new Stack(10);
    Stack stk3 = new Stack(10);
    char ch;
    int i;

    // Put some characters into stk1.
    Console.WriteLine("Push A through J onto stk1.");
    for(i=0; !stk1.IsFull(); i++)
      stk1.Push((char) ('A' + i));

    if(stk1.IsFull()) Console.WriteLine("stk1 is full.");

    // Display the contents of stk1.
    Console.Write("Contents of stk1: ");
    while( !stk1.IsEmpty() ) {
      ch = stk1.Pop();
      Console.Write(ch);
    }

    Console.WriteLine();

    if(stk1.IsEmpty()) Console.WriteLine("stk1 is empty.\n");

    // Put more characters into stk1.
    Console.WriteLine("Again push A through J onto stk1.");
    for(i=0; !stk1.IsFull(); i++)
      stk1.Push((char) ('A' + i));

    // Now, pop from stk1 and push the element in stk2.
```

```
      // This causes stk2 to hold the elements in reverse order.
      Console.WriteLine("Now, pop chars from stk1 and push " +
                        "them onto stk2.");
      while( !stk1.IsEmpty() ) {
        ch = stk1.Pop();
        stk2.Push(ch);
      }

      Console.Write("Contents of stk2: ");
      while( !stk2.IsEmpty() ) {
        ch = stk2.Pop();
        Console.Write(ch);
      }

      Console.WriteLine("\n");

      // Put 5 characters into stack.
      Console.WriteLine("Put 5 characters on stk3.");
      for(i=0; i < 5; i++)
        stk3.Push((char) ('A' + i));

      Console.WriteLine("Capacity of stk3: " + stk3.Capacity());
      Console.WriteLine("Number of objects in stk3: " +
                        stk3.GetNum());
  }
}
```

The output from the program is shown here:

```
Push A through J onto stk1.
stk1 is full.
Contents of stk1: JIHGFEDCBA
stk1 is empty.

Again push A through J onto stk1.
Now, pop chars from stk1 and push them onto stk2.
Contents of stk2: ABCDEFGHIJ

Put 5 characters on stk3.
Capacity of stk3: 10
Number of objects in stk3: 5
```

Pass References to Methods

Up to this point, the examples in this book have been using value types, such as **int** or **double**, as parameters to methods. However, it is both correct and common to use a reference type as a parameter. Doing so allows an object to be passed to a method. For example, consider the following program:

```
// References can be passed to methods.

using System;

class MyClass {
  int alpha, beta;
```

```
  public MyClass(int i, int j) {
    alpha = i;
    beta = j;
  }

  // Return true if ob contains the same values as the invoking object.
  public bool SameAs(MyClass ob) {
    if((ob.alpha == alpha) & (ob.beta == beta))
        return true;
    else return false;
  }

  // Make a copy of ob.
  public void Copy(MyClass ob) {
    alpha = ob.alpha;
    beta  = ob.beta;
  }

  public void Show() {
    Console.WriteLine("alpha: {0}, beta: {1}",
                      alpha, beta);
  }
}

class PassOb {
  static void Main() {
    MyClass ob1 = new MyClass(4, 5);
    MyClass ob2 = new MyClass(6, 7);

    Console.Write("ob1: ");
    ob1.Show();

    Console.Write("ob2: ");
    ob2.Show();

    if(ob1.SameAs(ob2))
      Console.WriteLine("ob1 and ob2 have the same values.");
    else
      Console.WriteLine("ob1 and ob2 have different values.");

    Console.WriteLine();

    // Now, make ob1 a copy of ob2.
    ob1.Copy(ob2);

    Console.Write("ob1 after copy: ");
    ob1.Show();

    if(ob1.SameAs(ob2))
      Console.WriteLine("ob1 and ob2 have the same values.");
    else
      Console.WriteLine("ob1 and ob2 have different values.");
  }
}
```

This program generates the following output:

```
ob1: alpha: 4, beta: 5
ob2: alpha: 6, beta: 7
ob1 and ob2 have different values.

ob1 after copy: alpha: 6, beta: 7
ob1 and ob2 have the same values.
```

The **SameAs()** and **Copy()** methods each take a reference of type **MyClass** as an argument. The **SameAs()** method compares the values of **alpha** and **beta** in the invoking object with the values of **alpha** and **beta** in the object passed via **ob**. The method returns **true** only if the two objects contain the same values for these instance variables. The **Copy()** method assigns the values of **alpha** and **beta** in the object referred to by **ob** to **alpha** and **beta** in the invoking object. As this example shows, syntactically, reference types are passed to methods in the same way as are value types.

How Arguments Are Passed

As the preceding example demonstrated, passing an object reference to a method is a straightforward task. However, there are some nuances that the example did not show. In certain cases, the effects of passing a reference type will be different than those experienced when passing a value type. To see why, let's review the two ways in which an argument can be passed to a subroutine.

The first way is *call-by-value*. This method *copies* the *value* of an argument into the formal parameter of the subroutine. Therefore, changes made to the parameter of the subroutine have no effect on the argument used in the call. The second way an argument can be passed is *call-by-reference*. In this method, a *reference* to an argument (not the value of the argument) is passed to the parameter. Inside the subroutine, this reference is used to access the actual argument specified in the call. This means that changes made to the parameter will affect the argument used to call the subroutine.

By default, C# uses call-by-value, which means that a copy of the argument is made and given to the receiving parameter. Thus, when you pass a value type, such as **int** or **double**, what occurs to the parameter that receives the argument has no effect outside the method. For example, consider the following program:

```
// Value types are passed by value.

using System;

class Test {
  /* This method causes no change to the arguments
     used in the call. */
  public void NoChange(int i, int j) {
    i = i + j;
    j = -j;
  }
}

class CallByValue {
  static void Main() {
    Test ob = new Test();
```

```
    int a = 15, b = 20;

    Console.WriteLine("a and b before call: " +
                       a + " " + b);

    ob.NoChange(a, b);

    Console.WriteLine("a and b after call: " +
                       a + " " + b);
  }
}
```

The output from this program is shown here:

```
a and b before call: 15 20
a and b after call: 15 20
```

As you can see, the operations that occur inside **NoChange( )** have no effect on the values of **a** and **b** used in the call. Again, this is because *copies* of the *value* of **a** and **b** have been given to parameters **i** and **j**, but **a** and **b** are otherwise completely independent of **i** and **j**. Thus, assigning **i** a new value will not affect **a**.

When you pass a reference to a method, the situation is a bit more complicated. In this case, the reference, itself, is still passed by value. Thus, a copy of the reference is made and changes to the parameter will not affect the argument. (For example, making the parameter refer to a new object will not change the object to which the argument refers.) However— and this is a big however—changes *made to the object* being referred to by the parameter *will* affect the object referred to by the argument. Let's see why.

Recall that when you create a variable of a class type, you are only creating a reference to an object. Thus, when you pass this reference to a method, the parameter that receives it will refer to the same object as that referred to by the argument. Therefore, the argument and the parameter will both refer to the same object. This means that objects are passed to methods by what is effectively call-by-reference. Thus, changes to the object inside the method *do* affect the object used as an argument. For example, consider the following program:

```
// Objects are passed by reference.

using System;

class Test {
  public int a, b;

  public Test(int i, int j) {
    a = i;
    b = j;
  }

  /* Pass an object. Now, ob.a and ob.b in object
     used in the call will be changed. */
  public void Change(Test ob) {
    ob.a = ob.a + ob.b;
    ob.b = -ob.b;
  }
}
```

```
class CallByRef {
  static void Main() {
    Test ob = new Test(15, 20);

    Console.WriteLine("ob.a and ob.b before call: " +
                      ob.a + " " + ob.b);

    ob.Change(ob);

    Console.WriteLine("ob.a and ob.b after call: " +
                      ob.a + " " + ob.b);
  }
}
```

This program generates the following output:

```
ob.a and ob.b before call: 15 20
ob.a and ob.b after call: 35 -20
```

As you can see, in this case, the actions inside **Change()** have affected the object used as an argument.

To review: When a reference is passed to a method, the reference itself is passed by use of call-by-value. Thus, a copy of that reference is made. However, the copy of that reference will still refer to the same object as its corresponding argument. This means that objects are implicitly passed using call-by-reference.

Use ref and out Parameters

As just explained, value types, such as **int** or **char**, are passed by value to a method. This means that changes to the parameter that receives a value type will not affect the actual argument used in the call. You can, however, alter this behavior. Through the use of the **ref** and **out** keywords, it is possible to pass any of the value types by reference. Doing so allows a method to alter the argument used in the call.

Before going into the mechanics of using **ref** and **out**, it is useful to understand why you might want to pass a value type by reference. In general, there are two reasons: to allow a method to alter the contents of its arguments or to allow a method to return more than one value. Let's look at each reason in detail.

Often you will want a method to be able to operate on the actual arguments that are passed to it. The quintessential example of this is a **Swap()** method that exchanges the values of its two arguments. Since value types are passed by value, it is not possible to write a method that swaps the value of two **int**s, for example, using C#'s default call-by-value parameter passing mechanism. The **ref** modifier solves this problem.

As you know, a **return** statement enables a method to return a value to its caller. However, a method can return *only one* value each time it is called. What if you need to return two or more pieces of information? For example, what if you want to create a method that decomposes a floating-point number into its integer and fractional parts? To do this requires that two pieces of information be returned: the integer portion and the fractional component. This method cannot be written using only a single return value. The **out** modifier solves this problem.

Use ref

The **ref** parameter modifier causes C# to create a call-by-reference, rather than a call-by-value. The **ref** modifier is specified when the method is declared and when it is called. Let's begin with a simple example. The following program creates a method called **Sqr()** that returns in-place the square of its integer argument. Notice the use and placement of **ref**.

```
// Use ref to pass a value type by reference.

using System;

class RefTest {
  // This method changes its argument. Notice the use of ref.
  public void Sqr(ref int i) {
    i = i * i;
  }
}

class RefDemo {
  static void Main() {
    RefTest ob = new RefTest();

    int a = 10;

    Console.WriteLine("a before call: " + a);

    ob.Sqr(ref a); // notice the use of ref

    Console.WriteLine("a after call: " + a);
  }
}
```

Notice that **ref** precedes the entire parameter declaration in the method and that it precedes the argument when the method is called. The output from this program, shown here, confirms that the value of the argument, **a**, was indeed modified by **Sqr()**:

```
a before call: 10
a after call: 100
```

Using **ref**, it is now possible to write a method that exchanges the values of its two value-type arguments. For example, here is a program that contains a method called **Swap()** that exchanges the values of the two integer arguments with which it is called:

```
// Swap two values.

using System;

class ValueSwap {
  // This method now changes its arguments.
  public void Swap(ref int a, ref int b) {
    int t;
```

```
      t = a;
      a = b;
      b = t;
  }
}

class ValueSwapDemo {
  static void Main() {
    ValueSwap ob = new ValueSwap();

    int x = 10, y = 20;

    Console.WriteLine("x and y before call: " + x + " " + y);

    ob.Swap(ref x, ref y);

    Console.WriteLine("x and y after call: " + x + " " + y);
  }
}
```

The output from this program is shown here:

```
x and y before call: 10 20
x and y after call: 20 10
```

Here is one important point to understand about **ref**: An argument passed by **ref** must be assigned a value prior to the call. The reason is that the method that receives such an argument assumes that the parameter refers to a valid value. Thus, using **ref**, you cannot use a method to give an argument an initial value.

Use out

Sometimes you will want to use a reference parameter to receive a value from a method, but not pass in a value. For example, you might have a method that performs some function, such as opening a network socket, that returns a success/fail code in a reference parameter. In this case, there is no information to pass into the method, but there is information to pass back out. The problem with this scenario is that a **ref** parameter must be initialized to a value prior to the call. Thus, to use a **ref** parameter would require giving the argument a dummy value just to satisfy this constraint. Fortunately, C# provides a better alternative: the **out** parameter.

An **out** parameter is similar to a **ref** parameter with this one exception: It can only be used to pass a value out of a method. It is not necessary (or useful) to give the variable used as an **out** parameter an initial value prior to calling the method. The method will give the variable a value. Furthermore, inside the method, an **out** parameter is considered *unassigned*; that is, it is assumed to have no initial value. This implies that the method *must* assign the parameter a value prior to the method's termination. Thus, after the call to the method, an **out** parameter will contain a value.

Here is an example that uses an **out** parameter. In the class **Decompose**, the **GetParts()** method decomposes a floating-point number into its integer and fractional parts. Notice how each component is returned to the caller.

```
// Use out.

using System;

class Decompose {

  /* Decompose a floating-point value into its
     integer and fractional parts. */
  public int GetParts(double n, out double frac) {
    int whole;

    whole = (int) n;
    frac = n - whole; // pass fractional part back through frac
    return whole; // return integer portion
  }
}

class UseOut {
  static void Main() {
   Decompose ob = new Decompose();
    int i;
    double f;

    i = ob.GetParts(10.125, out f);

    Console.WriteLine("Integer portion is " + i);
    Console.WriteLine("Fractional part is " + f);
  }
}
```

The output from the program is shown here:

```
Integer portion is 10
Fractional part is 0.125
```

The **GetParts()** method returns two pieces of information. First, the integer portion of **n** is returned as **GetParts()**'s return value. Second, the fractional portion of **n** is passed back to the caller through the **out** parameter **frac**. As this example shows, by using **out**, it is possible for one method to return two values.

Of course, you are not limited to only one **out** parameter. A method can return as many pieces of information as necessary through **out** parameters. Here is an example that uses two **out** parameters. The method **HasComFactor()** performs two functions. First, it determines if two integers have a common factor (other than 1). It returns **true** if they do and **false** otherwise. Second, if they do have a common factor, **HasComFactor()** returns the least and greatest common factors in **out** parameters.

```
// Use two out parameters.

using System;

class Num {
  /* Determine if x and v have a common divisor.
```

```
        If so, return least and greatest common factors in
        the out parameters. */
    public bool HasComFactor(int x, int y,
                              out int least, out int greatest) {
      int i;
      int max = x < y ? x : y;
      bool first = true;

      least = 1;
      greatest = 1;

      // Find least and greatest common factors.
      for(i=2; i <= max/2 + 1; i++) {
        if( ((y%i)==0) & ((x%i)==0) ) {
          if(first) {
            least = i;
            first = false;
          }
          greatest = i;
        }
      }

      if(least != 1) return true;
      else return false;
    }
  }

  class DemoOut {
    static void Main() {
      Num ob = new Num();
      int lcf, gcf;

      if(ob.HasComFactor(231, 105, out lcf, out gcf)) {
        Console.WriteLine("Lcf of 231 and 105 is " + lcf);
        Console.WriteLine("Gcf of 231 and 105 is " + gcf);
      }
      else
        Console.WriteLine("No common factor for 35 and 49.");

      if(ob.HasComFactor(35, 51, out lcf, out gcf)) {
        Console.WriteLine("Lcf of 35 and 51 " + lcf);
        Console.WriteLine("Gcf of 35 and 51 is " + gcf);
      }
      else
        Console.WriteLine("No common factor for 35 and 51.");
    }
  }
```

In **Main()**, notice that **lcf** and **gcf** are not assigned values prior to the call to **HasComFactor()**. This would be an error if the parameters had been **ref** rather than **out**. The method returns either **true** or **false**, depending upon whether the two integers have a common factor. If they do, the least and greatest common factors are returned in the **out** parameters. The output from this program is shown here:

```
Lcf of 231 and 105 is 3
Gcf of 231 and 105 is 21
No common factor for 35 and 51.
```

Use ref and out on References

The use of **ref** and **out** is not limited to the passing of value types. They can also be used when a reference is passed. When **ref** or **out** modifies a reference, it causes the reference, itself, to be passed by reference. This allows a method to change what object the reference refers to. Consider the following program, which uses **ref** reference parameters to exchange the objects to which two references are referring:

```
// Swap two references.

using System;

class RefSwap {
  int a, b;

  public RefSwap(int i, int j) {
    a = i;
    b = j;
  }

  public void Show() {
    Console.WriteLine("a: {0}, b: {1}", a, b);
  }

  // This method changes its arguments.
  public void Swap(ref RefSwap ob1, ref RefSwap ob2) {
    RefSwap t;

    t = ob1;
    ob1 = ob2;
    ob2 = t;
  }
}

class RefSwapDemo {
  static void Main() {
    RefSwap x = new RefSwap(1, 2);
    RefSwap y = new RefSwap(3, 4);

    Console.Write("x before call: ");
    x.Show();

    Console.Write("y before call: ");
    y.Show();

    Console.WriteLine();

    // Exchange the objects to which x and y refer.
    x.Swap(ref x, ref y);
```

```
      Console.Write("x after call: ");
      x.Show();

      Console.Write("y after call: ");
      y.Show();

   }
}
```

The output from this program is shown here:

```
x before call: a: 1, b: 2
y before call: a: 3, b: 4

x after call: a: 3, b: 4
y after call: a: 1, b: 2
```

In this example, the method **Swap()** exchanges the objects to which the two arguments to **Swap( )** refer. Before calling **Swap()**, x refers to an object that contains the values 1 and 2, and **y** refers to an object that contains the values 3 and 4. After the call to **Swap()**, x refers to the object that contains the values 3 and 4, and **y** refers to the object that contains the values 1 and 2. If **ref** parameters had not been used, then the exchange inside **Swap()** would have had no effect outside **Swap()**. You might want to prove this by removing **ref** from **Swap()**.

Use a Variable Number of Arguments

When you create a method, you usually know in advance the number of arguments that you will be passing to it, but this is not always the case. Sometimes you will want to create a method that can be passed an arbitrary number of arguments. For example, consider a method that finds the smallest of a set of values. Such a method might be passed as few as two values, or three, or four, and so on. In all cases, you want that method to return the smallest value. Such a method cannot be created using normal parameters. Instead, you must use a special type of parameter that stands for an arbitrary number of parameters. This is done by creating a **params** parameter.

The **params** modifier is used to declare an array parameter that will be able to receive zero or more arguments. The number of elements in the array will be equal to the number of arguments passed to the method. Your program then accesses the array to obtain the arguments.

Here is an example that uses **params** to create a method called **MinVal()**, which returns the minimum value from a set of values:

```
// Demonstrate params.

using System;

class Min {
  public int MinVal(params int[] nums) {
    int m;

    if(nums.Length == 0) {
```

```
      Console.WriteLine("Error: no arguments.");
      return 0;
    }

    m = nums[0];
    for(int i=1; i < nums.Length; i++)
      if(nums[i] < m) m = nums[i];

    return m;
  }
}

class ParamsDemo {
  static void Main() {
    Min ob = new Min();
    int min;
    int a = 10, b = 20;

    // Call with 2 values.
    min = ob.MinVal(a, b);
    Console.WriteLine("Minimum is " + min);

    // Call with 3 values.
    min = ob.MinVal(a, b, -1);
    Console.WriteLine("Minimum is " + min);

    // Call with 5 values.
    min = ob.MinVal(18, 23, 3, 14, 25);
    Console.WriteLine("Minimum is " + min);

    // Can call with an int array, too.
    int[] args = { 45, 67, 34, 9, 112, 8 };
    min = ob.MinVal(args);
    Console.WriteLine("Minimum is " + min);
  }
}
```

The output from the program is shown here:

```
Minimum is 10
Minimum is -1
Minimum is 3
Minimum is 8
```

Each time **MinVal()** is called, the arguments are passed to it via the **nums** array. The length of the array equals the number of elements. Thus, you can use **MinVal()** to find the minimum of any number of values.

Notice the last call to **MinVal()**. Rather than being passed the values individually, it is passed an array containing the values. This is perfectly legal. When a **params** parameter is created, it will accept either a variable-length list of arguments or an array containing the arguments.

Although you can pass a **params** parameter any number of arguments, they all must be of a type compatible with the array type specified by the parameter. For example, calling **MinVal()** like this:

```
min = ob.MinVal(1, 2.2); // Wrong!
```

is illegal because there is no automatic conversion from **double** (2.2) to **int**, which is the type of **nums** in **MinVal()**.

When using **params**, you need to be careful about boundary conditions because a **params** parameter can accept any number of arguments—*even zero!* For example, it is syntactically valid to call **MinVal()** as shown here:

```
min = ob.MinVal();  // no arguments
min = ob.MinVal(3); // 1 argument
```

This is why there is a check in **MinVal()** to confirm that at least one element is in the **nums** array before there is an attempt to access that element. If the check were not there, then a runtime exception would result if **MinVal()** were called with no arguments. (Exceptions are described in Chapter 13.) Furthermore, the code in **MinVal()** was written in such a way as to permit calling **MinVal()** with one argument. In that situation, the lone argument is returned.

A method can have normal parameters and a variable-length parameter. For example, in the following program, the method **ShowArgs()** takes one **string** parameter and then a **params** integer array:

```
// Use regular parameter with a params parameter.

using System;

class MyClass {
  public void ShowArgs(string msg, params int[] nums) {
    Console.Write(msg + ": ");

    foreach(int i in nums)
      Console.Write(i + " ");

    Console.WriteLine();
  }
}

class ParamsDemo2 {
  static void Main() {
    MyClass ob = new MyClass();

    ob.ShowArgs("Here are some integers",
                1, 2, 3, 4, 5);

    ob.ShowArgs("Here are two more",
                17, 20);
  }
}
```

This program displays the following output:

```
Here are some integers: 1 2 3 4 5
Here are two more: 17 20
```

In cases where a method has regular parameters and a **params** parameter, the **params** parameter must be the last one in the parameter list. Furthermore, in all situations, there must be only one **params** parameter.

Return Objects

A method can return any type of data, including class types. For example, the following version of the **Rect** class includes a method called **Enlarge()** that creates a rectangle that is proportionally the same as the invoking rectangle, but larger by a specified factor:

```
// Return an object.

using System;

class Rect {
  int width;
  int height;

  public Rect(int w, int h) {
    width = w;
    height = h;
  }

  public int Area() {
    return width * height;
  }

  public void Show() {
    Console.WriteLine(width + " " + height);
  }

  /* Return a rectangle that is a specified
     factor larger than the invoking rectangle. */
  public Rect Enlarge(int factor) {
    return new Rect(width * factor, height * factor);
  }
}

class RetObj {
  static void Main() {
    Rect r1 = new Rect(4, 5);

    Console.Write("Dimensions of r1: ");
    r1.Show();
    Console.WriteLine("Area of r1: " + r1.Area());

    Console.WriteLine();

    // Create a rectangle that is twice as big as r1.
    Rect r2 = r1.Enlarge(2);
```

```
      Console.Write("Dimensions of r2: ");
      r2.Show();
      Console.WriteLine("Area of r2: " + r2.Area());
  }
}
```

The output is shown here:

```
Dimensions of r1: 4 5
Area of r1: 20

Dimensions of r2: 8 10
Area of r2: 80
```

When an object is returned by a method, it remains in existence until there are no more references to it. At that point, it is subject to garbage collection. Thus, an object won't be destroyed just because the method that created it terminates.

One application of object return types is the *class factory*. A class factory is a method that is used to construct objects of its class. In some situations, you may not want to give users of a class access to the class' constructor because of security concerns or because object construction depends upon certain external factors. In such cases, a class factory is used to construct objects. Here is a simple example:

```
// Use a class factory.

using System;

class MyClass {
  int a, b; // private

  // Create a class factory for MyClass.
  public MyClass Factory(int i, int j) {
    MyClass t = new MyClass();

    t.a = i;
    t.b = j;

    return t; // return an object
  }

  public void Show() {
    Console.WriteLine("a and b: " + a + " " + b);
  }

}

class MakeObjects {
  static void Main() {
    MyClass ob = new MyClass();
    int i, j;

    // Generate objects using the factory.
    for(i=0, j=10; i < 10; i++, j--) {
```

```
      MyClass anotherOb = ob.Factory(i, j); // make an object
      anotherOb.Show();
    }

    Console.WriteLine();
  }
}
```

The output is shown here:

```
a and b: 0 10
a and b: 1 9
a and b: 2 8
a and b: 3 7
a and b: 4 6
a and b: 5 5
a and b: 6 4
a and b: 7 3
a and b: 8 2
a and b: 9 1
```

Let's look closely at this example. **MyClass** does not define a constructor, so only the default constructor is available. Thus, it is not possible to set the values of **a** and **b** using a constructor. However, the class factory **Factory()** can create objects in which **a** and **b** are given values. Moreover, since **a** and **b** are private, using **Factory()** is the only way to set these values.

In **Main()**, a **MyClass** object is instantiated, and its factory method is used inside the **for** loop to create ten other objects. The line of code that creates objects is shown here:

```
MyClass anotherOb = ob.Factory(i, j); // get an object
```

With each iteration, an object reference called **anotherOb** is created, and it is assigned a reference to the object constructed by the factory. At the end of each iteration of the loop, **anotherOb** goes out of scope, and the object to which it refers is recycled.

Return an Array

Since in C# arrays are implemented as objects, a method can also return an array. (This differs from C++ in which arrays are not valid as return types.) For example, in the following program, the method **FindFactors()** returns an array that holds the factors of the argument that it is passed:

```
// Return an array.

using System;

class Factor {
  /* Return an array containing the factors of num.
     On return, numfactors will contain the number of
     factors found. */
  public int[] FindFactors(int num, out int numfactors) {
    int[] facts = new int[80]; // size of 80 is arbitrary
    int i, j;
```

```
    // Find factors and put them in the facts array.
    for(i=2, j=0; i < num/2 + 1; i++)
      if( (num%i)==0 ) {
        facts[j] = i;
        j++;
      }

    numfactors = j;
    return facts;
  }
}

class FindFactors {
  static void Main() {
    Factor f = new Factor();
    int numfactors;
    int[] factors;

    factors = f.FindFactors(1000, out numfactors);

    Console.WriteLine("Factors for 1000 are: ");
    for(int i=0; i < numfactors; i++)
      Console.Write(factors[i] + " ");

    Console.WriteLine();
  }
}
```

The output is shown here:

```
Factors for 1000 are:
2 4 5 8 10 20 25 40 50 100 125 200 250 500
```

In **Factor, FindFactors()** is declared like this:

```
public int[] FindFactors(int num, out int numfactors) {
```

Notice how the **int** array return type is specified. This syntax can be generalized. Whenever a method returns an array, specify it in a similar fashion, adjusting the type and dimensions as needed. For example, the following declares a method called **someMeth()** that returns a two-dimensional array of **double**:

```
public double[,] someMeth() { // ...
```

Method Overloading

In C#, two or more methods within the same class can share the same name, as long as their parameter declarations are different. When this is the case, the methods are said to be *overloaded*, and the process is referred to as *method overloading*. Method overloading is one of the ways that C# implements polymorphism.

In general, to overload a method, simply declare different versions of it. The compiler takes care of the rest. You must observe one important restriction: The type and/or number of the parameters of each overloaded method must differ. It is not sufficient for two methods to differ only in their return types. They must differ in the types or number of their parameters.

(Return types do not provide sufficient information in all cases for C# to decide which method to use.) Of course, overloaded methods *may* differ in their return types, too. When an overloaded method is called, the version of the method executed is the one whose parameters match the arguments.

Here is a simple example that illustrates method overloading:

```
// Demonstrate method overloading.

using System;

class Overload {
  public void OvlDemo() {
    Console.WriteLine("No parameters");
  }

  // Overload OvlDemo for one integer parameter.
  public void OvlDemo(int a) {
    Console.WriteLine("One parameter: " + a);
  }

  // Overload OvlDemo for two integer parameters.
  public int OvlDemo(int a, int b) {
    Console.WriteLine("Two parameters: " + a + " " + b);
    return a + b;
  }

  // Overload OvlDemo for two double parameters.
  public double OvlDemo(double a, double b) {
    Console.WriteLine("Two double parameters: " +
                          a + " "+ b);
    return a + b;
  }
}

class OverloadDemo {
  static void Main() {
    Overload ob = new Overload();
    int resI;
    double resD;

    // Call all versions of OvlDemo().
    ob.OvlDemo();
    Console.WriteLine();

    ob.OvlDemo(2);
    Console.WriteLine();

    resI = ob.OvlDemo(4, 6);
    Console.WriteLine("Result of ob.OvlDemo(4, 6): " + resI);
    Console.WriteLine();

    resD = ob.OvlDemo(1.1, 2.32);
    Console.WriteLine("Result of ob.OvlDemo(1.1, 2.32): " + resD);
  }
}
```

This program generates the following output:

```
No parameters

One parameter: 2

Two parameters: 4 6
Result of ob.OvlDemo(4, 6): 10

Two double parameters: 1.1 2.32
Result of ob.OvlDemo(1.1, 2.32): 3.42
```

As you can see, **OvlDemo()** is overloaded four times. The first version takes no parameters; the second takes one integer parameter; the third takes two integer parameters; and the fourth takes two **double** parameters. Notice that the first two versions of **OvlDemo()** return **void** and the second two return a value. This is perfectly valid, but as explained, overloading is not affected one way or the other by the return type of a method. Thus, attempting to use these two versions of **OvlDemo()** will cause an error:

```
// One OvlDemo(int) is OK.
public void OvlDemo(int a) {
  Console.WriteLine("One parameter: " + a);
}

/* Error! Two OvlDemo(int)s are not OK even though
   return types differ. */
public int OvlDemo(int a) {
  Console.WriteLine("One parameter: " + a);
  return a * a;
}
```

As the comments suggest, the difference in their return types is an insufficient difference for the purposes of overloading.

As you will recall from Chapter 3, C# provides certain implicit (i.e., automatic) type conversions. These conversions also apply to parameters of overloaded methods. For example, consider the following:

```
// Implicit type conversions can affect overloaded method resolution.

using System;

class Overload2 {
  public void MyMeth(int x) {
    Console.WriteLine("Inside MyMeth(int): " + x);
  }

  public void MyMeth(double x) {
    Console.WriteLine("Inside MyMeth(double): " + x);
  }
}

class TypeConv {
  static void Main() {
```

```
    Overload2 ob = new Overload2();

    int i = 10;
    double d = 10.1;

    byte b = 99;
    short s = 10;
    float f = 11.5F;


    ob.MyMeth(i); // calls ob.MyMeth(int)
    ob.MyMeth(d); // calls ob.MyMeth(double)

    ob.MyMeth(b); // calls ob.MyMeth(int) -- type conversion
    ob.MyMeth(s); // calls ob.MyMeth(int) -- type conversion
    ob.MyMeth(f); // calls ob.MyMeth(double) -- type conversion
  }
}
```

The output from the program is shown here:

```
Inside MyMeth(int): 10
Inside MyMeth(double): 10.1
Inside MyMeth(int): 99
Inside MyMeth(int): 10
Inside MyMeth(double): 11.5
```

In this example, only two versions of **MyMeth()** are defined: one that has an **int** parameter and one that has a **double** parameter. However, it is possible to pass **MyMeth()** a **byte**, **short**, or **float** value. In the case of **byte** and **short**, C# automatically converts them to **int**. Thus, **MyMeth(int)** is invoked. In the case of **float**, the value is converted to **double** and **MyMeth(double)** is called.

It is important to understand, however, that the implicit conversions apply only if there is no exact type match between a parameter and an argument. For example, here is the preceding program with the addition of a version of **MyMeth()** that specifies a **byte** parameter:

```
// Add MyMeth(byte).

using System;

class Overload2 {
  public void MyMeth(byte x) {
    Console.WriteLine("Inside MyMeth(byte): " + x);
  }

  public void MyMeth(int x) {
    Console.WriteLine("Inside MyMeth(int): " + x);
  }

  public void MyMeth(double x) {
    Console.WriteLine("Inside MyMeth(double): " + x);
  }
}
```

```
class TypeConv {
  static void Main() {
    Overload2 ob = new Overload2();

    int i = 10;
    double d = 10.1;

    byte b = 99;
    short s = 10;
    float f = 11.5F;


    ob.MyMeth(i); // calls ob.MyMeth(int)
    ob.MyMeth(d); // calls ob.MyMeth(double)

    ob.MyMeth(b); // calls ob.MyMeth(byte) -- now, no type conversion

    ob.MyMeth(s); // calls ob.MyMeth(int) -- type conversion
    ob.MyMeth(f); // calls ob.MyMeth(double) -- type conversion
  }
}
```

Now when the program is run, the following output is produced:

```
Inside MyMeth(int): 10
Inside MyMeth(double): 10.1
Inside MyMeth(byte): 99
Inside MyMeth(int): 10
Inside MyMeth(double): 11.5
```

In this version, since there is a version of **MyMeth()** that takes a **byte** argument, when **MyMeth()** is called with a **byte** argument, **MyMeth(byte)** is invoked and the automatic conversion to **int** does not occur.

Both **ref** and **out** participate in overload resolution. For example, the following defines two distinct and separate methods:

```
public void MyMeth(int x) {
  Console.WriteLine("Inside MyMeth(int): " + x);
}

public void MyMeth(ref int x) {
  Console.WriteLine("Inside MyMeth(ref int): " + x);
}
```

Thus,

```
ob.MyMeth(i)
```

invokes **MyMeth(int x)**, but

```
ob.MyMeth(ref i)
```

invokes **MyMeth(ref int x)**.

Although **ref** and **out** participate in overload resolution, the difference between the two alone is not sufficient. For example, these two versions of **MyMeth()** are invalid:

```
// Wrong!
public void MyMeth(out int x) { // ...
public void MyMeth(ref int x) { // ...
```

In this case, the compiler cannot differentiate between the two versions of **MyMeth()** simply because one uses an **out int** parameter and the other uses a **ref int** parameter.

Method overloading supports polymorphism because it is one way that C# implements the "one interface, multiple methods" paradigm. To understand how, consider the following. In languages that do not support method overloading, each method must be given a unique name. However, frequently you will want to implement essentially the same method for different types of data. Consider the absolute value function. In languages that do not support overloading, there are usually three or more versions of this function, each with a slightly different name. For instance, in C, the function **abs()** returns the absolute value of an integer, **labs()** returns the absolute value of a long integer, and **fabs()** returns the absolute value of a floating-point value.

Since C does not support overloading, each function must have its own unique name, even though all three functions do essentially the same thing. This makes the situation more complex, conceptually, than it actually is. Although the underlying concept of each function is the same, you still have three names to remember. This situation does not occur in C# because each absolute value method can use the same name. Indeed, the .NET Framework class library includes an absolute value method called **Abs()**. This method is overloaded by the **System.Math** class to handle the numeric types. C# determines which version of **Abs()** to call based upon the type of argument.

A principal value of overloading is that it allows related methods to be accessed by use of a common name. Thus, the name **Abs** represents the *general action* that is being performed. It is left to the compiler to choose the right *specific* version for a particular circumstance. You, the programmer, need only remember the general operation being performed. Through the application of polymorphism, several names have been reduced to one. Although this example is fairly simple, if you expand the concept, you can see how overloading can help manage greater complexity.

When you overload a method, each version of that method can perform any activity you desire. There is no rule stating that overloaded methods must relate to one another. However, from a stylistic point of view, method overloading implies a relationship. Thus, while you can use the same name to overload unrelated methods, you should not. For example, you could use the name **Sqr** to create methods that return the *square* of an integer and the *square root* of a floating-point value. But these two operations are fundamentally different. Applying method overloading in this manner defeats its original purpose. In practice, you should only overload closely related operations.

C# defines the term *signature*, which includes the name of a method plus its parameter list. Thus, for the purposes of overloading, no two methods within the same class can have the same signature. Notice that a signature does not include the return type since it is not used by C# for overload resolution. Also, the **params** modifier is not part of the signature.

Overload Constructors

Like methods, constructors can also be overloaded. Doing so allows you to construct objects in a variety of ways. For example, consider the following program:

```
// Demonstrate an overloaded constructor.

using System;

class MyClass {
  public int x;

  public MyClass() {
    Console.WriteLine("Inside MyClass().");
    x = 0;
  }

  public MyClass(int i) {
    Console.WriteLine("Inside MyClass(int).");
    x = i;
  }

  public MyClass(double d) {
    Console.WriteLine("Inside MyClass(double).");
    x = (int) d;
  }

  public MyClass(int i, int j) {
    Console.WriteLine("Inside MyClass(int, int).");
    x = i * j;
  }
}

class OverloadConsDemo {
  static void Main() {
    MyClass t1 = new MyClass();
    MyClass t2 = new MyClass(88);
    MyClass t3 = new MyClass(17.23);
    MyClass t4 = new MyClass(2, 4);

    Console.WriteLine("t1.x: " + t1.x);
    Console.WriteLine("t2.x: " + t2.x);
    Console.WriteLine("t3.x: " + t3.x);
    Console.WriteLine("t4.x: " + t4.x);
  }
}
```

The output from the program is shown here:

```
Inside MyClass().
Inside MyClass(int).
Inside MyClass(double).
Inside MyClass(int, int).
```

```
t1.x: 0
t2.x: 88
t3.x: 17
t4.x: 8
```

MyClass() is overloaded four ways, each constructing an object differently. The proper constructor is called based upon the arguments specified when **new** is executed. By overloading a class' constructor, you give the user of your class flexibility in the way objects are constructed.

One of the most common reasons that constructors are overloaded is to allow one object to initialize another. For example, here is an enhanced version of the **Stack** class developed earlier that allows one stack to be constructed from another:

```
// A stack class for characters.

using System;

class Stack {
  // These members are private.
  char[] stck; // holds the stack
  int tos;     // index of the top of the stack

  // Construct an empty Stack given its size.
  public Stack(int size) {
    stck = new char[size]; // allocate memory for stack
    tos = 0;
  }

  // Construct a Stack from a stack.
  public Stack(Stack ob) {
    // Allocate memory for stack.
    stck = new char[ob.stck.Length];

    // Copy elements to new stack.
    for(int i=0; i < ob.tos; i++)
      stck[i] = ob.stck[i];

    // Set tos for new stack.
    tos = ob.tos;
  }

  // Push characters onto the stack.
  public void Push(char ch) {
    if(tos==stck.Length) {
      Console.WriteLine(" -- Stack is full.");
      return;
    }

    stck[tos] = ch;
    tos++;
  }

  // Pop a character from the stack.
```

```csharp
  public char Pop() {
    if(tos==0) {
      Console.WriteLine(" -- Stack is empty.");
      return (char) 0;
    }

    tos--;
    return stck[tos];
  }

  // Return true if the stack is full.
  public bool IsFull() {
    return tos==stck.Length;
  }

  // Return true if the stack is empty.
  public bool IsEmpty() {
    return tos==0;
  }

  // Return total capacity of the stack.
  public int Capacity() {
    return stck.Length;
  }

  // Return number of objects currently on the stack.
  public int GetNum() {
    return tos;
  }
}

// Demonstrate the Stack class.
class StackDemo {
  static void Main() {
    Stack stk1 = new Stack(10);
    char ch;
    int i;

    // Put some characters into stk1.
    Console.WriteLine("Push A through J onto stk1.");
    for(i=0; !stk1.IsFull(); i++)
      stk1.Push((char) ('A' + i));

    // Create a copy of stck1.
    Stack stk2 = new Stack(stk1);

    // Display the contents of stk1.
    Console.Write("Contents of stk1: ");
    while( !stk1.IsEmpty() ) {
      ch = stk1.Pop();
      Console.Write(ch);
    }
```

```
    Console.WriteLine();

    Console.Write("Contents of stk2: ");
    while ( !stk2.IsEmpty() ) {
      ch = stk2.Pop();
      Console.Write(ch);
    }

    Console.WriteLine("\n");

  }
}
```

The output is shown here:

```
Push A through J onto stk1.
Contents of stk1: JIHGFEDCBA
Contents of stk2: JIHGFEDCBA
```

In **StackDemo**, the first stack, **stk1**, is constructed and filled with characters. This stack is then used to construct the second stack, **stk2**. This causes the following **Stack** constructor to be executed:

```
// Construct a Stack from a stack.
public Stack(Stack ob) {
  // Allocate memory for stack.
  stck = new char[ob.stck.Length];

  // Copy elements to new stack.
  for(int i=0; i < ob.tos; i++)
    stck[i] = ob.stck[i];

  // Set tos for new stack.
  tos = ob.tos;
}
```

Inside this constructor, an array is allocated that is long enough to hold the elements contained in the stack passed in **ob**. Then, the contents of **ob**'s array are copied to the new array, and **tos** is set appropriately. After the constructor finishes, the new stack and the original stack are separate, but identical.

Invoke an Overloaded Constructor Through this

When working with overloaded constructors, it is sometimes useful for one constructor to invoke another. In C#, this is accomplished by using another form of the **this** keyword. The general form is shown here:

constructor-name(*parameter-list1*) : this(*parameter-list2*) {
    // ... body of constructor, which may be empty
}

When the constructor is executed, the overloaded constructor that matches the parameter list specified by *parameter-list2* is first executed. Then, if there are any statements inside the original constructor, they are executed. Here is an example:

```
// Demonstrate invoking a constructor through this.

using System;

class XYCoord {
  public int x, y;

  public XYCoord() : this(0, 0) {
    Console.WriteLine("Inside XYCoord()");
  }

  public XYCoord(XYCoord obj) : this(obj.x, obj.y) {
    Console.WriteLine("Inside XYCoord(obj)");
  }

  public XYCoord(int i, int j) {
    Console.WriteLine("Inside XYCoord(int, int)");
    x = i;
    y = j;
  }
}

class OverloadConsDemo {
  static void Main() {
    XYCoord t1 = new XYCoord();
    XYCoord t2 = new XYCoord(8, 9);
    XYCoord t3 = new XYCoord(t2);

    Console.WriteLine("t1.x, t1.y: " + t1.x + ", " + t1.y);
    Console.WriteLine("t2.x, t2.y: " + t2.x + ", " + t2.y);
    Console.WriteLine("t3.x, t3.y: " + t3.x + ", " + t3.y);
  }
}
```

The output from the program is shown here:

```
Inside XYCoord(int, int)
Inside XYCoord()
Inside XYCoord(int, int)
Inside XYCoord(int, int)
Inside XYCoord(obj)
t1.x, t1.y: 0, 0
t2.x, t2.y: 8, 9
t3.x, t3.y: 8, 9
```

Here is how the program works. In the **XYCoord** class, the only constructor that actually initializes the x and y fields is **XYCoord(int, int)**. The other two constructors simply invoke **XYCoord(int, int)** through **this**. For example, when object **t1** is created, its constructor, **XYCoord()**, is called. This causes **this(0, 0)** to be executed, which in this case translates into a call to **XYCoord(0, 0)**. The creation of **t2** works in similar fashion.

One reason why invoking overloaded constructors through **this** can be useful is that it can prevent the unnecessary duplication of code. In the foregoing example, there is no reason for all three constructors to duplicate the same initialization sequence, which the use of **this** avoids. Another advantage is that you can create constructors with implied "default arguments" that are used when these arguments are not explicitly specified. For example, you could create another **XYCoord** constructor as shown here:

```
public XYCoord(int x) : this(x, x) { }
```

This constructor automatically defaults the **y** coordinate to the same value as the **x** coordinate. Of course, it is wise to use such "default arguments" carefully because their misuse could easily confuse users of your classes.

Object Initializers

Object initializers provide another way to create an object and initialize its fields and properties. (See Chapter 10 for a discussion of properties.) Using object initializers, you do not call a class' constructor in the normal way. Rather, you specify the names of the fields and/or properties to be initialized, giving each an initial value. Thus, the object initializer syntax provides an alternative to explicitly invoking a class' constructor. The primary use of the object initializer syntax is with anonymous types created in a LINQ expression. (Anonymous types and LINQ are described in Chapter 19.) However, because the object initializers can be used (and occasionally are used) with a named class, the fundamentals of object initialization are introduced here.

Let's begin with a simple example:

```
// A simple demonstration that uses object initializers.

using System;

class MyClass {
  public int Count;
  public string Str;
}

class ObjInitDemo {
  static void Main() {
    // Construct a MyClass object by using object initializers.
    MyClass obj = new MyClass { Count = 100, Str = "Testing" };

    Console.WriteLine(obj.Count + " " + obj.Str);
  }
}
```

This produces the following output:

```
100 Testing
```

As the output shows, the value of **obj.Count** has been initialized to 100 and the value of **obj.Str** has been initialized to "Testing". Notice, however, that **MyClass** does not define any explicit constructors, and that the normal constructor syntax has not been used. Rather, **obj** is created using the following line:

```
MyClass obj = new MyClass { Count = 100, Str = "Testing" };
```

Here, the names of the fields are explicitly specified along with their initial values. This results in a default instance of **MyClass** being constructed (by use of the implicit default constructor) and then **Count** and **Str** are given the specified initial values.

It is important to understand that the order of the initializers is not important. For example, **obj** could have been initialized as shown here:

```
MyClass obj = new MyClass { Str = "Testing", Count = 100 };
```

In this statement, the initialization of **Str** precedes the initialization of **Count**. In the program, it was the other way around. However, in either case, the end result is the same.

Here is the general form of object initialization syntax:

new *class-name* { *name* = *expr*, *name* = *expr*, *name* = *expr*, ... }

Here, *name* specifies the name of a field or property that is an accessible member of *class-name*. Of course, the type of the initializing expression specified by *expr* must be compatible with the type of field or property.

Although you can use object initializers with a named class (such as **MyClass** in the example), you usually won't. In general, you will use the normal constructor call syntax when working with named classes. As mentioned, object initializers are most applicable to anonymous types generated by a LINQ expression.

Optional Arguments

C# 4.0 has a new feature that adds flexibility to the way that arguments are specified when a method is called. Called *optional arguments,* this feature lets you define a default value for a method's parameter. This default value will be used if an argument that corresponds to that parameter is not specified when the method is called. Thus, specifying an argument for such a parameter is optional. Optional arguments can simplify the calling of methods in which default arguments apply to some of the parameters. They can also be used as a "shorthand" form of method overloading.

An optional argument is enabled by creating an *optional parameter.* To do this, simply specify a default value for the parameter, using a syntax similar to a variable initialization. The default value must be a constant expression. For example, consider this method declaration:

```
static void OptArgMeth(int alpha, int beta=10, int gamma = 20) {
```

Here, two optional parameters are declared. They are **beta** and **gamma**. In this case, **beta** has a default value of 10, and **gamma** has a default value of 20. These defaults are used if no arguments are specified for these parameters when the method is called. Notice that **alpha** is not an optional parameter. Rather, it is a normal parameter, and an argument for it is always required.

Assuming the preceding declaration of **OptArgMeth()**, it can be called in the following ways:

```
// Pass all arguments explicitly.
OptArgMeth(1, 2, 3);

// Let gamma default.
OptArgMeth(1, 2);
```

```
// Let both beta and gamma default.
OptArgMeth(1);
```

The first call passes the value 1 to **alpha**, 2 to **beta**, and 3 to **gamma**. Thus, all three arguments are specified explicitly, and no default values are used. The second call passes the value 1 to **alpha** and 2 to **beta**, but lets **gamma** default to 20. The third call passes 1 to **alpha**, and lets both **beta** and **gamma** default. It is important to understand that at no time can **beta** default without **gamma** also defaulting. Once the first argument defaults, all remaining arguments must also default.

The following program shows the entire process just described.:

```
// Demonstrate optional arguments.

using System;

class OptionArgDemo {
  static void OptArgMeth(int alpha, int beta=10, int gamma = 20) {
    Console.WriteLine("Here is alpha, beta, and gamma: " +
                      alpha + " " + beta + " " + gamma);
  }

  static void Main() {
    // Pass all arguments explicitly.
    OptArgMeth(1, 2, 3);

    // Let gamma default.
    OptArgMeth(1, 2);

    // Let both beta and gamma default.
    OptArgMeth(1);
  }
}
```

The output shown here confirms the use of the default arguments:

```
Here is alpha, beta, and gamma: 1 2 3
Here is alpha, beta, and gamma: 1 2 20
Here is alpha, beta, and gamma: 1 10 20
```

As the output shows, when an argument is not specified, its default value is used.

It is important to understand that all optional parameters must appear to the right of those that are required. For example, the following declaration is invalid:

```
int Sample(string name = "user", int userId) { // Error!
```

To fix this declaration, you must declare **userId** before **name**. Once you begin declaring optional parameters, you cannot specify a required one. For example, this declaration is also incorrect:

```
int Sample(int accountId, string name = "user", int userId) { // Error!
```

Because **name** is optional, **userId** must come before **name** (or **userId** must also be optional).

In addition to methods, optional arguments can be also used in a constructor, indexer, or delegate. (Indexers and delegates are described later in this book.)

One benefit of optional arguments is that they enable the programmer to more easily manage complex method calls and constructor invocations. Quite frequently, a method will specify more parameters than are required for its most common usage. In many cases, through the careful use of optional arguments, some of those parameters can be made optional. This means that you need pass only those arguments that are meaningful to your situation, rather than all of them, as would otherwise be required. Such an approach streamlines the method and makes it easier for the programmer.

Optional Arguments vs. Overloading

In some cases, optional arguments can provide an alternative to method overloading. To understand why, again consider the **OptArgMeth()** method just shown. Prior to the addition of optional arguments to C#, you would need to create three different versions of **OptArgMeth()** to achieve the same functionality as the one version shown earlier. These versions would have the following declarations:

```
static void OptArgMeth(int alpha)
static void OptArgMeth(int alpha, int beta)
static void OptArgMeth(int alpha, int beta, int gamma)
```

These overloads enable the method to be called with one, two, or three arguments. (The bodies of the methods would have to provide the values of **beta** and **gamma** when they are not passed.) While it is certainly not wrong to implement **OptArgMeth()**'s functionality using overloading, the use of optional arguments is a better approach. Of course, not all overloading situations lend themselves to such an approach.

Optional Arguments and Ambiguity

One problem that can result when using optional arguments is ambiguity. This can occur when a method that has optional parameters is overloaded. In some cases, the compiler may not be able to determine which version to call when the optional arguments are not specified. For example, consider the following two versions of **OptArgMeth()**:

```
static void OptArgMeth(int alpha, int beta=10, int gamma = 20) {
  Console.WriteLine("Here is alpha, beta, and gamma: " +
                    alpha + " " + beta + " " + gamma);
}

static void OptArgMeth(int alpha, double beta=10.0, double gamma = 20.0) {
  Console.WriteLine("Here is alpha, beta, and gamma: " +
                    alpha + " " + beta + " " + gamma);
}
```

Notice that the only difference between the two versions is the types of **beta** and **gamma**, which are the optional parameters. In the first version, their type is **int**. In the second version, it is **double**. Given these two overloads, the following call to **OptArgMeth()** is ambiguous:

```
OptArgMeth(1); // Error! Ambiguous
```

This call is ambiguous because the compiler doesn't know if it should use the version in which **beta** and **gamma** are **int**, or the version in which they are **double**. The key point is that even though the overloading of **OptArgMeth()** is not inherently ambiguous, a specific call might be.

In general, since ambiguity may be a factor when overloading methods that allow optional arguments, it is important that you consider the implications of such overloading. In some cases, you may need to avoid the use of an optional parameter in order to avoid ambiguity that prevents your method from being used in the way that you intend.

A Practical Example of Optional Arguments

For a more practical illustration of how an optional argument can simplify calls to some types of methods, consider the following program. It declares a method called **Display()**, which displays a string. The string can be displayed in its entirety or only a portion of the string can be displayed.

```
// Use an optional argument to simplify a call to a method.

using System;

class UseOptArgs {

  // Display part or all of string.
  static void Display(string str, int start = 0, int stop = -1) {

    if(stop < 0)
      stop = str.Length;

    // Check for out-of-range condition.
    if(stop > str.Length | start > stop | start < 0)
      return;

    for(int i=start; i < stop; i++)
      Console.Write(str[i]);

    Console.WriteLine();
  }

  static void Main() {
    Display("this is a test");
    Display("this is a test", 10);
    Display("this is a test", 5, 12);
  }
}
```

The output is shown here:

```
this is a test
test
is a te
```

Look carefully at the **Display()** method. The string to be displayed is passed in the first argument. This argument is required. The second and third arguments are optional. The optional arguments specify the starting and stopping indexes of the portion of the string to display. If **stop** is not passed a value, then it defaults to –1, which indicates that the stopping point is the end of the string. If **start** is not passed a value, then it defaults to 0. Therefore, if neither optional argument is present, the string is displayed in its entirety. Otherwise, the indicated portion of the string is displayed. This means that if you call **Display()** with one argument (the string to display), the string is shown in its entirety. If you call **Display()** with two arguments, then the characters beginning at **start** through the end of the string are shown. If all three arguments are passed, then the portion of the string from **start** to **stop** is shown.

Although this example is quite simple, it does demonstrate the essential benefit that optional arguments offer. It lets you specify only those arguments that are needed by your usage. Default values don't need to be explicitly passed.

Before moving on, an important point must be made. Although optional arguments are a powerful tool when used correctly, they can also be misused. The point of optional arguments is to allow a method to perform its job in an efficient, easy-to-use manner while still allowing considerable flexibility. Toward this end, the default values of all optional arguments should facilitate the normal use of a method. When this is not the case, the use of optional arguments can destructure your code and mislead others. Finally, the default value of an optional parameter should cause no harm. In other words, the accidental use of an optional argument should not have irreversible, negative consequences. For example, forgetting to specify an argument should not cause an important data file to be erased!

Named Arguments

Another feature related to passing arguments to a method is the *named argument*. Named arguments were added by C# 4.0. As you know, normally, when you pass arguments to a method, the order of the arguments must match the order of the parameters defined by the method. In other words, an argument's position in the argument list determines to which parameter it is assigned. Named arguments remove this restriction. With a named argument, you specify the name of the parameter to which an argument applies. Using this approach, the order of the arguments is not important. Thus, named arguments are a bit like object initializers described earlier, although the syntax differs.

To specify an argument by name, use this syntax:

param-name : *value*

Here, *param-name* specifies the name of the parameter to which *value* is passed. Of course, *param-name* must specify a valid parameter name for the method being called.

Here is a simple example that demonstrates named arguments. It creates a method called **IsFactor()** that returns true if the first parameter can be evenly divided by the second.

```
// Use named arguments.

using System;

class NamedArgsDemo {

  // Determine if one value is evenly divisible by another.
  static bool IsFactor(int val, int divisor) {
    if((val % divisor) == 0) return true;
    return false;
  }
```

```
static void Main() {
  // The following show various ways in which IsFactor() can be called.

  // Call by use of positional arguments.
  if(IsFactor(10, 2))
    Console.WriteLine("2 is factor of 10.");

  // Call by use of named arguments.
  if(IsFactor(val: 10, divisor: 2))
    Console.WriteLine("2 is factor of 10.");

  // Order doesn't matter with a named argument.
  if(IsFactor(divisor: 2, val: 10))
    Console.WriteLine("2 is factor of 10.");

  // Use both a positional argument and a named argument.
  if(IsFactor(10, divisor: 2))
    Console.WriteLine("2 is factor of 10.");
  }
}
```

The output is shown here:

```
2 is factor of 10.
2 is factor of 10.
2 is factor of 10.
2 is factor of 10.
```

As the output shows, each method of calling **IsFactor()** produces the same result.

Beyond showing the named argument syntax in action, the program demonstrates two important aspects of named arguments. First, the order of specifying the arguments doesn't matter. For example, these two calls are equivalent:

```
IsFactor(val :10, divisor: 2)
IsFactor(divisor: 2, val: 10)
```

Being order-independent is a primary benefit of named arguments. It means that you don't need to remember (or even know) the order of the parameters in the method being called. This can be a benefit when working with COM interfaces, for example. Second, notice that you can specify a positional argument and a named argument in the same call, as this call to **IsFactor()** does:

```
IsFactor(10, divisor: 2)
```

Be aware, however, that when mixing both named and positional arguments, all positional arguments must come before any named arguments.

Named arguments can also be used in conjunction with optional arguments. For example, assuming the **Display()** method shown in the previous section, here are some ways it can be called with named arguments:

```
// Specify all arguments by name.
Display(stop: 10, str: "this is a test", start: 0);
```

```
// Let start default.
Display(stop: 10, str: "this is a test");

// Specify the string by position, stop by name, and
// let start default.
Display("this is a test", stop: 10);
```

In general, the combination of named and optional arguments can make it easier to call large, complicated methods that have many parameters.

Because the named argument syntax is more verbose than the normal positional syntax, most of the time you will want to use positional arguments to call a method. However, in those cases in which named arguments are appropriate, they can be used quite effectively.

NOTE *In addition to methods, named and optional arguments can be used with constructors, indexers, and delegates. (Indexers and delegates are described later in this book.)*

The Main( ) Method

Up to this point, you have been using one form of **Main()**. However, it has several overloaded forms. Some can be used to return a value, and some can receive arguments. Each is examined here.

Return Values from Main( )

When a program ends, you can return a value to the calling process (often the operating system) by returning a value from **Main()**. To do so, you can use this form of **Main()**:

    static int Main( )

Notice that instead of being declared **void**, this version of **Main()** has a return type of **int**.

Usually, the return value from **Main()** indicates whether the program ended normally or due to some abnormal condition. By convention, a return value of zero usually indicates normal termination. All other values indicate some type of error occurred.

Pass Arguments to Main( )

Many programs accept what are called *command-line* arguments. A command-line argument is the information that directly follows the program's name on the command line when it is executed. For C# programs, these arguments are then passed to the **Main()** method. To receive the arguments, you must use one of these forms of **Main()**:

    static void Main(string[ ] args)
    static int Main(string[ ] args)

The first form returns **void**; the second can be used to return an integer value, as described in the preceding section. For both, the command-line arguments are stored as strings in the **string** array passed to **Main()**. The length of the *args* array will be equal to the number of command-line arguments, which might be zero.

For example, the following program displays all of the command-line arguments that it is called with:

```
// Display all command-line information.

using System;
```

```
class CLDemo {
  static void Main(string[] args) {
    Console.WriteLine("There are " + args.Length +
                      " command-line arguments.");

    Console.WriteLine("They are: ");
    for(int i=0; i < args.Length; i++)
      Console.WriteLine(args[i]);
  }
}
```

If **CLDemo** is executed like this:

```
CLDemo one two three
```

you will see the following output:

```
There are 3 command-line arguments.
They are:
one
two
three
```

To understand the way that command-line arguments can be used, consider the next program. It uses a simple substitution cipher to encode or decode messages. The message to be encoded or decoded is specified on the command line. The cipher is very simple: To encode a word, each letter is incremented by 1. Thus, A becomes B, and so on. To decode, each letter is decremented. Of course, such a cipher is of no practical value, being trivially easy to break. But it does provide an enjoyable pastime for children.

```
// Encode or decode a message using a simple substitution cipher.

using System;

class Cipher {
  static int Main(string[] args) {

    // See if arguments are present.
    if(args.Length < 2) {
      Console.WriteLine("Usage: encode/decode word1 [word2...wordN]");
      return 1; // return failure code
    }

    // If args present, first arg must be encode or decode.
    if(args[0] != "encode" & args[0] != "decode") {
      Console.WriteLine("First arg must be encode or decode.");
      return 1; // return failure code
    }

    // Encode or decode message.
    for(int n=1; n < args.Length; n++) {
      for(int i=0; i < args[n].Length; i++) {
```

```
      if(args[0] == "encode")
        Console.Write((char) (args[n][i] + 1) );
      else
        Console.Write((char) (args[n][i] - 1) );
    }
    Console.Write(" ");
  }

  Console.WriteLine();

  return 0;
  }
}
```

To use the program, specify either the "encode" or "decode" command followed by the phrase that you want to encrypt or decrypt. Assuming the program is called Cipher, here are two sample runs:

```
C:>Cipher encode one two
pof uxp

C:>Cipher decode pof uxp
one two
```

There are two interesting things in this program. First, notice how the program checks that a command-line argument is present before it continues executing. This is very important and can be generalized. When a program relies on there being one or more command-line arguments, it must always confirm that the proper arguments have been supplied. Failure to do this can lead to program malfunctions. Also, since the first command-line argument must be either "encode" or "decode," the program also checks this before proceeding.

Second, notice how the program returns a termination code. If the required command line is not present, then 1 is returned, indicating abnormal termination. Otherwise, 0 is returned when the program ends.

Recursion

In C#, a method can call itself. This process is called *recursion,* and a method that calls itself is said to be *recursive.* In general, recursion is the process of defining something in terms of itself and is somewhat similar to a circular definition. The key component of a recursive method is that it contains a statement that executes a call to itself. Recursion is a powerful control mechanism.

The classic example of recursion is the computation of the factorial of a number. The factorial of a number *N* is the product of all the whole numbers between 1 and *N*. For example, 3 factorial is 1×2×3, or 6. The following program shows a recursive way to compute the factorial of a number. For comparison purposes, a nonrecursive equivalent is also included.

```
// A simple example of recursion.

using System;

class Factorial {
```

```
  // This is a recursive method.
  public int FactR(int n) {
    int result;

    if(n==1) return 1;
    result = FactR(n-1) * n;
    return result;
  }

  // This is an iterative equivalent.
  public int FactI(int n) {
    int t, result;

    result = 1;
    for(t=1; t <= n; t++) result *= t;
    return result;
  }
}

class Recursion {
  static void Main() {
    Factorial f = new Factorial();

    Console.WriteLine("Factorials using recursive method.");
    Console.WriteLine("Factorial of 3 is " + f.FactR(3));
    Console.WriteLine("Factorial of 4 is " + f.FactR(4));
    Console.WriteLine("Factorial of 5 is " + f.FactR(5));
    Console.WriteLine();

    Console.WriteLine("Factorials using iterative method.");
    Console.WriteLine("Factorial of 3 is " + f.FactI(3));
    Console.WriteLine("Factorial of 4 is " + f.FactI(4));
    Console.WriteLine("Factorial of 5 is " + f.FactI(5));
  }
}
```

The output from this program is shown here:

```
Factorials using recursive method.
Factorial of 3 is 6
Factorial of 4 is 24
Factorial of 5 is 120

Factorials using iterative method.
Factorial of 3 is 6
Factorial of 4 is 24
Factorial of 5 is 120
```

The operation of the nonrecursive method **FactI()** should be clear. It uses a loop starting at 1 and progressively multiplies each number by the moving product.

The operation of the recursive **FactR()** is a bit more complex. When **FactR()** is called with an argument of 1, the method returns 1; otherwise, it returns the product of **FactR(n–1)*n**. To evaluate this expression, **FactR()** is called with **n–1**. This process repeats until **n** equals 1 and the calls to the method begin returning. For example, when the factorial of 2 is calculated, the first call to **FactR()** will cause a second call to be made with an argument of 1. This call will return 1, which is then multiplied by 2 (the original value of **n**). The answer is then 2. You might find it interesting to insert **WriteLine()** statements into **FactR()** that show the level of recursion of each call and what the intermediate results are.

When a method calls itself, new local variables and parameters are allocated storage on the stack, and the method code is executed with these new variables from the start. A recursive call does not make a new copy of the method. Only the arguments are new. As each recursive call returns, the old local variables and parameters are removed from the stack, and execution resumes at the point of the call inside the method. Recursive methods could be said to "telescope" out and back.

Here is another example of recursion. The **DisplayRev()** method uses recursion to display its string argument backward.

```
// Display a string in reverse by using recursion.

using System;

class RevStr {

  // Display a string backward.
  public void DisplayRev(string str) {
    if(str.Length > 0)
      DisplayRev(str.Substring(1, str.Length-1));
    else
      return;

    Console.Write(str[0]);
  }
}

class RevStrDemo {
  static void Main() {
    string s = "this is a test";
    RevStr rsOb = new RevStr();

    Console.WriteLine("Original string: " + s);

    Console.Write("Reversed string: ");
    rsOb.DisplayRev(s);

    Console.WriteLine();
  }
}
```

Here is the output:

```
Original string: this is a test
Reversed string: tset a si siht
```

Each time **DisplayRev()** is called, it first checks to see if **str** has a length greater than zero. If it does, it recursively calls **DisplayRev()** with a new string that consists of **str** minus its first character. This process repeats until a zero-length string is passed. This causes the recursive calls to start unraveling. As they do, the first character of **str** in each call is displayed. This results in the string being displayed in reverse order.

Recursive versions of many routines may execute a bit more slowly than the iterative equivalent because of the added overhead of the additional method calls. Too many recursive calls to a method could cause a stack overrun. Because storage for parameters and local variables is on the stack, and each new call creates a new copy of these variables, it is possible that the stack could be exhausted. If this occurs, the CLR will throw an exception. However, you probably will not have to worry about this unless a recursive routine runs wild.

The main advantage to recursion is that some types of algorithms can be more clearly and simply implemented recursively than iteratively. For example, the quicksort sorting algorithm is quite difficult to implement in an iterative way. Also, some problems, especially AI-related ones, seem to lend themselves to recursive solutions.

When writing recursive methods, you must have a conditional statement, such as an **if**, somewhere to force the method to return without the recursive call being executed. If you don't do this, once you call the method, it will never return. This type of error is very common when developing recursive methods. Use **WriteLine()** statements liberally so that you can watch what is going on and abort execution if you see that you have made a mistake.

Understanding static

There will be times when you will want to define a class member that will be used independently of any object of that class. Normally, a class member must be accessed through an object of its class, but it is possible to create a member that can be used by itself, without reference to a specific instance. To create such a member, precede its declaration with the keyword **static**. When a member is declared **static**, it can be accessed before any objects of its class are created and without reference to any object. You can declare both methods and variables to be **static**. The most common example of a **static** member is **Main()**, which is declared **static** because it must be called by the operating system when your program begins.

Outside the class, to use a **static** member, you must specify the name of its class followed by the dot operator. No object needs to be created. In fact, a **static** member cannot be accessed through an object reference. It must be accessed through its class name. For example, if you want to assign the value 10 to a **static** variable called **count** that is part of a class called **Timer**, use this line:

```
Timer.count = 10;
```

This format is similar to that used to access normal instance variables through an object, except that the class name is used. A **static** method can be called in the same way—by use of the dot operator on the name of the class.

Variables declared as **static** are, essentially, global variables. When objects of its class are declared, no copy of a **static** variable is made. Instead, all instances of the class share the same **static** variable. A **static** variable is initialized before its class is used. If no explicit initializer is specified, it is initialized to zero for numeric types, null in the case of reference types, or **false** for variables of type **bool**. Thus, a **static** variable always has a value.

The difference between a **static** method and a normal method is that the **static** method can be called through its class name, without any instance of that class being created. You have seen an example of this already: the **Sqrt()** method, which is a **static** method within C#'s **System.Math** class.

Here is an example that declares a **static** variable and a **static** method:

```
// Use static.

using System;

class StaticDemo {
  // A static variable.
  public static int Val = 100;

  // A static method.
  public static int ValDiv2() {
    return Val/2;
  }
}

class SDemo {
  static void Main() {

    Console.WriteLine("Initial value of StaticDemo.Val is "
                      + StaticDemo.Val);

    StaticDemo.Val = 8;
    Console.WriteLine("StaticDemo.Val is " + StaticDemo.Val);
    Console.WriteLine("StaticDemo.ValDiv2(): " +
                      StaticDemo.ValDiv2());
  }
}
```

The output is shown here:

```
Initial value of StaticDemo.Val is 100
StaticDemo.Val is 8
StaticDemo.ValDiv2(): 4
```

As the output shows, a **static** variable is initialized before any object of its class is created. There are several restrictions that apply to **static** methods:

- A **static** method does not have a **this** reference. This is because a **static** method does not execute relative to any object.

- A **static** method can directly call only other **static** methods of its class. It cannot directly call an instance method of its class. The reason is that instance methods operate on specific objects, but a **static** method is not called on an object. Thus, on what object would the instance method operate?

- A similar restriction applies to **static** data. A **static** method can directly access only other **static** data defined by its class. It cannot operate on an instance variable of its class because there is no object to operate on.

For example, in the following class, the **static** method **ValDivDenom()** is illegal:

```
class StaticError {
  public int Denom = 3; // a normal instance variable
  public static int Val = 1024; // a static variable
```

```
  /* Error! Can't directly access a non-static variable
     from within a static method. */
  static int ValDivDenom() {
    return Val/Denom; // won't compile!
  }
}
```

Here, **Denom** is a normal instance variable that cannot be accessed within a **static** method. However, the use of **Val** is okay since it is a **static** variable.

The same problem occurs when trying to call a non-**static** method from within a **static** method of the same class. For example:

```
using System;

class AnotherStaticError {
  // A non-static method.
  void NonStaticMeth() {
    Console.WriteLine("Inside NonStaticMeth().");
  }

  /* Error! Can't directly call a non-static method
     from within a static method. */
  static void staticMeth() {
    NonStaticMeth(); // won't compile
  }
}
```

In this case, the attempt to call a non-**static** (that is, instance method) from a **static** method causes a compile-time error.

It is important to understand that a **static** method *can* call instance methods and access instance variables of its class if it does so through an object of that class. It is just that it cannot use an instance variable or method without an object qualification. For example, this fragment is perfectly valid:

```
class MyClass {
  // A non-static method.
  void NonStaticMeth() {
    Console.WriteLine("Inside NonStaticMeth().");
  }

  /* Can call a non-static method through an
     object reference from within a static method. */
  public static void staticMeth(MyClass ob) {
    ob.NonStaticMeth(); // this is OK
  }
}
```

Here, **NonStaticMeth()** is called by **staticMeth()** through **ob**, which is an object of type **MyClass**.

Because **static** fields are independent of any specific object, they are useful when you need to maintain information that is applicable to an entire class. Here is an example of such a situation. It uses a **static** field to maintain a count of the number of objects that are in existence.

```
// Use a static field to count instances.

using System;

class CountInst {
  static int count = 0;

  // Increment count when object is created.
  public CountInst() {
    count++;
  }

  // Decrement count when object is destroyed.
  ~CountInst() {
    count--;
  }

  public static int GetCount() {
    return count;
  }
}

class CountDemo {
  static void Main() {
    CountInst ob;

    for(int i=0; i < 10; i++) {
      ob = new CountInst();
      Console.WriteLine("Current count: " + CountInst.GetCount());
    }
  }
}
```

The output is shown here:

```
Current count: 1
Current count: 2
Current count: 3
Current count: 4
Current count: 5
Current count: 6
Current count: 7
Current count: 8
Current count: 9
Current count: 10
```

Each time that an object of type **CountInst** is created, the **static** field **count** is incremented. Each time an object is recycled, **count** is decremented. Thus, **count** always contains a count of the number of objects currently in existence. This is possible only through the use of a **static** field. There is no way for an instance variable to maintain the count because the count relates to the class as a whole, not to a specific instance.

Here is one more example that uses **static**. Earlier in this chapter, you saw how a class factory could be used to create objects. In that example, the class factory was a non-**static** method, which meant that it could be called only through an object reference. This meant that a default object of the class needed to be created so that the factory method could be called. However, a better way to implement a class factory is as a **static** method, which allows the class factory to be called without creating an unnecessary object. Here is the class factory example rewritten to reflect this improvement:

```
// Use a static class factory.

using System;

class MyClass {
  int a, b;

  // Create a class factory for MyClass.
  static public MyClass Factory(int i, int j) {
    MyClass t = new MyClass();

    t.a = i;
    t.b = j;

    return t; // return an object
  }

  public void Show() {
    Console.WriteLine("a and b: " + a + " " + b);
  }
}

class MakeObjects {
  static void Main() {
    int i, j;

    // Generate objects using the factory.
    for(i=0, j=10; i < 10; i++, j--) {
      MyClass ob = MyClass.Factory(i, j); // get an object
      ob.Show();
    }

    Console.WriteLine();
  }
}
```

In this version, **Factory()** is invoked through its class name in this line of code:

```
MyClass ob = MyClass.Factory(i, j); // get an object
```

There is no need to create a **MyClass** object prior to using the factory.

Static Constructors

A constructor can also be specified as **static**. A **static** constructor is typically used to initialize features that apply to a class rather than an instance. Thus, it is used to initialize aspects of a class before any objects of the class are created. Here is a simple example:

```
// Use a static constructor.

using System;

class Cons {
  public static int alpha;
  public int beta;

  // A static constructor.
  static Cons() {
    alpha = 99;
    Console.WriteLine("Inside static constructor.");
  }

  // An instance constructor.
  public Cons() {
    beta = 100;
    Console.WriteLine("Inside instance constructor.");
  }
}

class ConsDemo {
  static void Main() {
    Cons ob = new Cons();

    Console.WriteLine("Cons.alpha: " + Cons.alpha);
    Console.WriteLine("ob.beta: " + ob.beta);
  }
}
```

Here is the output:

```
Inside static constructor.
Inside instance constructor.
Cons.alpha: 99
ob.beta: 100
```

Notice that the **static** constructor is called automatically (when the class is first loaded) and before the instance constructor. This can be generalized. In all cases, the **static** constructor will be executed before any instance constructor. Furthermore, **static** constructors cannot have access modifiers (thus, they use default access) and cannot be called by your program.

Static Classes

A class can be declared **static**. There are two key features of a **static** class. First, no object of a **static** class can be created. Second, a **static** class must contain only **static** members. A **static** class is created by modifying a class declaration with the keyword **static**, shown here:

static class *class-name* { // ...

Within the class, all members must be explicitly specified as **static**. Making a class **static** does not automatically make its members **static**.

static classes have two primary uses. First, a **static** class is required when creating an *extension method*. Extension methods relate mostly to LINQ, and a discussion of extension methods is found in Chapter 19. Second, a **static** class is used to contain a collection of related **static** methods. This second use is demonstrated here.

The following example uses a **static** class called **NumericFn** to hold a set of **static** methods that operate on a numeric value. Because all of the members of **NumericFn** are declared **static**, the class can also be declared **static**, which prevents it from being instantiated. Thus, **NumericFn** serves an organizational role, providing a good way to logically group related methods.

```
// Demonstrate a static class.

using System;

static class NumericFn {
  // Return the reciprocal of a value.
  static public double Reciprocal(double num) {
    return 1/num;
  }

  // Return the fractional part of a value.
  static public double FracPart(double num) {
    return num - (int) num;
  }

  // Return true if num is even.
  static public bool IsEven(double num) {
    return (num % 2) == 0 ? true : false;
  }

  // Return true if num is odd.
  static public bool IsOdd(double num) {
    return !IsEven(num);
  }

}

class StaticClassDemo {
  static void Main() {
    Console.WriteLine("Reciprocal of 5 is " +
                      NumericFn.Reciprocal(5.0));

    Console.WriteLine("Fractional part of 4.234 is " +
                      NumericFn.FracPart(4.234));

    if(NumericFn.IsEven(10))
      Console.WriteLine("10 is even.");

    if(NumericFn.IsOdd(5))
      Console.WriteLine("5 is odd.");

    // The following attempt to create an instance of
    // NumericFn will cause an error.
```

```
//  NumericFn ob = new NumericFn(); // Wrong!
  }
}
```

The output from the program is shown here.

```
Reciprocal of 5 is 0.2
Fractional part of 4.234 is 0.234
10 is even.
5 is odd.
```

Notice that the last line in the program is commented-out. Because **NumericFn** is a **static** class, any attempt to create an object will result in a compile-time error. It would also be an error to attempt to give **NumericFn** a non-**static** member.

One last point: Although a **static** class cannot have an instance constructor, it can have a **static** constructor.

CHAPTER

9

Operator Overloading

C# allows you to define the meaning of an operator relative to a class that you create. This process is called *operator overloading.* By overloading an operator, you expand its usage to your class. The effects of the operator are completely under your control and may differ from class to class. For example, a class that defines a linked list might use the + operator to add an object to the list. A class that implements a stack might use the + to push an object onto the stack. Another class might use the + operator in an entirely different way.

When an operator is overloaded, none of its original meaning is lost. It is simply that a new operation, relative to a specific class, is added. Therefore, overloading the + to handle a linked list, for example, does not cause its meaning relative to integers (that is, addition) to be changed.

A principal advantage of operator overloading is that it allows you to seamlessly integrate a new class type into your programming environment. This *type extensibility* is an important part of the power of an object-oriented language such as C#. Once operators are defined for a class, you can operate on objects of that class using the normal C# expression syntax. You can even use an object in expressions involving other types of data. Operator overloading is one of C#'s most powerful features.

Operator Overloading Fundamentals

Operator overloading is closely related to method overloading. To overload an operator, use the **operator** keyword to define an *operator method,* which defines the action of the operator relative to its class.

There are two forms of **operator** methods: one for unary operators and one for binary operators. The general form for each is shown here:

```
// General form for overloading a unary operator
public static ret-type operator op(param-type operand)
{
  // operations
}


// General form for overloading a binary operator
public static ret-type operator op(param-type1 operand1, param-type1 operand2)
{
  // operations
}
```

Here, the operator that you are overloading, such as + or /, is substituted for *op*. The *ret-type* specifies the type of value returned by the specified operation. Although it can be any type you choose, the return value is often of the same type as the class for which the operator is being overloaded. This correlation facilitates the use of the overloaded operator in expressions. For unary operators, the operand is passed in *operand*. For binary operators, the operands are passed in *operand1* and *operand2*. Notice that **operator** methods must be both **public** and **static**.

For unary operators, the operand must be of the same type as the class for which the operator is being defined. For binary operators, at least one of the operands must be of the same type as its class. Thus, you cannot overload any C# operators for objects that you have not created. For example, you can't redefine + for **int** or **string**.

One other point: Operator parameters must not use the **ref** or **out** modifier.

Overloading Binary Operators

To see how operator overloading works, let's start with an example that overloads two binary operators, the + and the −. The following program creates a class called **ThreeD**, which maintains the coordinates of an object in three-dimensional space. The overloaded + adds the individual coordinates of one **ThreeD** object to another. The overloaded − subtracts the coordinates of one object from the other.

```
// An example of operator overloading.

using System;

// A three-dimensional coordinate class.
class ThreeD {
  int x, y, z; // 3-D coordinates

  public ThreeD() { x = y = z = 0; }
  public ThreeD(int i, int j, int k) { x = i; y = j; z = k; }

  // Overload binary +.
  public static ThreeD operator +(ThreeD op1, ThreeD op2)
  {
    ThreeD result = new ThreeD();

    /* This adds together the coordinates of the two points
       and returns the result. */
    result.x = op1.x + op2.x; // These are integer additions
    result.y = op1.y + op2.y; // and the + retains its original
    result.z = op1.z + op2.z; // meaning relative to them.

    return result;
  }

  // Overload binary -.
  public static ThreeD operator -(ThreeD op1, ThreeD op2)
  {
    ThreeD result = new ThreeD();

    /* Notice the order of the operands. op1 is the left
       operand and op2 is the right. */
```

```
      result.x = op1.x - op2.x; // these are integer subtractions
      result.y = op1.y - op2.y;
      result.z = op1.z - op2.z;

      return result;
    }

    // Show X, Y, Z coordinates.
    public void Show()
    {
      Console.WriteLine(x + ", " + y + ", " + z);
    }
}

class ThreeDDemo {
    static void Main() {
      ThreeD a = new ThreeD(1, 2, 3);
      ThreeD b = new ThreeD(10, 10, 10);
      ThreeD c;

      Console.Write("Here is a: ");
      a.Show();
      Console.WriteLine();
      Console.Write("Here is b: ");
      b.Show();
      Console.WriteLine();

      c = a + b; // add a and b together
      Console.Write("Result of a + b: ");
      c.Show();
      Console.WriteLine();

      c = a + b + c; // add a, b, and c together
      Console.Write("Result of a + b + c: ");
      c.Show();
      Console.WriteLine();

      c = c - a; // subtract a
      Console.Write("Result of c - a: ");
      c.Show();
      Console.WriteLine();

      c = c - b; // subtract b
      Console.Write("Result of c - b: ");
      c.Show();
      Console.WriteLine();
    }
}
```

This program produces the following output:

```
Here is a: 1, 2, 3

Here is b: 10, 10, 10
```

```
Result of a + b: 11, 12, 13

Result of a + b + c: 22, 24, 26

Result of c - a: 21, 22, 23

Result of c - b: 11, 12, 13
```

Let's examine the preceding program carefully, beginning with the overloaded operator +. When two objects of type **ThreeD** are operated on by the + operator, the magnitudes of their respective coordinates are added together, as shown in **operator+( )**. Notice, however, that this method does not modify the value of either operand. Instead, a new object of type **ThreeD**, which contains the result of the operation, is returned by the method. To understand why the + operation does not change the contents of either object, think about the standard arithmetic + operation as applied like this: 10 + 12. The outcome of this operation is 22, but neither 10 nor 12 is changed by it. Although no rule prevents an overloaded operator from altering the value of one of its operands, it is best for the actions of an overloaded operator to be consistent with its usual meaning.

Notice that **operator+( )** returns an object of type **ThreeD**. Although the method could have returned any valid C# type, the fact that it returns a **ThreeD** object allows the + operator to be used in compound expressions, such as **a+b+c**. Here, **a+b** generates a result that is of type **ThreeD**. This value can then be added to **c**. Had any other type of value been generated by **a+b**, such an expression would not work.

Here is another important point: When the coordinates are added together inside **operator+( )**, the addition of the individual coordinates results in an integer addition. This is because the individual coordinates, **x**, **y**, and **z**, are integer quantities. The fact that the + operator is overloaded for objects of type **ThreeD** has no effect on the + as it is applied to integer values.

Now, look at **operator–( )**. The – operator works just like the + operator except that the order of the parameters is important. Recall that addition is commutative, but subtraction is not. (That is, A – B is not the same as B – A!) For all binary operators, the first parameter to an operator method will contain the left operand. The second parameter will contain the one on the right. When implementing overloaded versions of the noncommutative operators, you must remember which operand is on the left and which is on the right.

Overloading Unary Operators

The unary operators are overloaded just like the binary operators. The main difference, of course, is that there is only one operand. For example, here is a method that overloads the unary minus for the **ThreeD** class:

```
// Overload unary -.
public static ThreeD operator -(ThreeD op)
{
  ThreeD result = new ThreeD();

  result.x = -op.x;
  result.y = -op.y;
  result.z = -op.z;

  return result;
}
```

Here, a new object is created that contains the negated fields of the operand. This object is then returned. Notice that the operand is unchanged. Again, this is in keeping with the usual meaning of the unary minus. For example, in an expression such as this,

```
a = -b
```

a receives the negation of **b**, but **b** is not changed.

In C#, overloading **++** and **− −** is quite easy; simply return the incremented or decremented value, but don't change the invoking object. C# will automatically handle that for you, taking into account the difference between the prefix and postfix forms. For example, here is an **operator++()** method for the **ThreeD** class:

```
// Overload unary ++.
public static ThreeD operator ++(ThreeD op)
{
  ThreeD result = new ThreeD();

  // Return the incremented result.
  result.x = op.x + 1;
  result.y = op.y + 1;
  result.z = op.z + 1;

  return result;
}
```

Here is an expanded version of the previous example program that demonstrates the unary **−** and the **++** operator:

```
// More operator overloading.

using System;

// A three-dimensional coordinate class.
class ThreeD {
  int x, y, z; // 3-D coordinates

  public ThreeD() { x = y = z = 0; }
  public ThreeD(int i, int j, int k) { x = i; y = j; z = k; }

  // Overload binary +.
  public static ThreeD operator +(ThreeD op1, ThreeD op2)
  {
    ThreeD result = new ThreeD();

    /* This adds together the coordinates of the two points
       and returns the result. */
    result.x = op1.x + op2.x;
    result.y = op1.y + op2.y;
    result.z = op1.z + op2.z;

    return result;
  }

  // Overload binary -.
```

```
    public static ThreeD operator -(ThreeD op1, ThreeD op2)
    {
      ThreeD result = new ThreeD();

      /* Notice the order of the operands. op1 is the left
         operand and op2 is the right. */
      result.x = op1.x - op2.x;
      result.y = op1.y - op2.y;
      result.z = op1.z - op2.z;

      return result;
    }

    // Overload unary -.
    public static ThreeD operator -(ThreeD op)
    {
      ThreeD result = new ThreeD();

      result.x = -op.x;
      result.y = -op.y;
      result.z = -op.z;

      return result;
    }

    // Overload unary ++.
    public static ThreeD operator ++(ThreeD op)
    {
      ThreeD result = new ThreeD();

      // Return the incremented result.
      result.x = op.x + 1;
      result.y = op.y + 1;
      result.z = op.z + 1;

      return result;
    }
    // Show X, Y, Z coordinates.
    public void Show()
    {
      Console.WriteLine(x + ", " + y + ", " + z);
    }
  }

class ThreeDDemo {
  static void Main() {
    ThreeD a = new ThreeD(1, 2, 3);
    ThreeD b = new ThreeD(10, 10, 10);
    ThreeD c = new ThreeD();

    Console.Write("Here is a: ");
    a.Show();
    Console.WriteLine();
```

```
    Console.Write("Here is b: ");
    b.Show();
    Console.WriteLine();

    c = a + b; // add a and b together
    Console.Write("Result of a + b: ");
    c.Show();
    Console.WriteLine();

    c = a + b + c; // add a, b, and c together
    Console.Write("Result of a + b + c: ");
    c.Show();
    Console.WriteLine();

    c = c - a; // subtract a
    Console.Write("Result of c - a: ");
    c.Show();
    Console.WriteLine();

    c = c - b; // subtract b
    Console.Write("Result of c - b: ");
    c.Show();
    Console.WriteLine();

    c = -a; // assign -a to c
    Console.Write("Result of -a: ");
    c.Show();
    Console.WriteLine();

    c = a++; // post-increment a
    Console.WriteLine("Given c = a++");
    Console.Write("c is ");
    c.Show();
    Console.Write("a is ");
    a.Show();

    // Reset a to 1, 2, 3
    a = new ThreeD(1, 2, 3);
    Console.Write("\nResetting a to ");
    a.Show();

    c = ++a; // pre-increment a
    Console.WriteLine("\nGiven c = ++a");
    Console.Write("c is ");
    c.Show();
    Console.Write("a is ");
    a.Show();
  }
}
```

The output from the program is shown here:

```
Here is a: 1, 2, 3
```

```
Here is b: 10, 10, 10

Result of a + b: 11, 12, 13

Result of a + b + c: 22, 24, 26

Result of c - a: 21, 22, 23

Result of c - b: 11, 12, 13

Result of -a: -1, -2, -3

Given c = a++
c is 1, 2, 3
a is 2, 3, 4

Resetting a to 1, 2, 3

Given c = ++a
c is 2, 3, 4
a is 2, 3, 4
```

Handling Operations on C# Built-in Types

For any given class and operator, an **operator** method can, itself, be overloaded. One of the most common reasons for this is to allow operations between a class type and other types of data, such as a built-in type. For example, once again consider the **ThreeD** class. To this point, you have seen how to overload the **+** so that it adds the coordinates of one **ThreeD** object to another. However, this is not the only way in which you might want to define addition for **ThreeD**. For example, it might be useful to add an integer value to each coordinate of a **ThreeD** object. Such an operation could be used to translate axes. To perform such an operation, you will need to overload **+** a second time, as shown here:

```
// Overload binary + for ThreeD + int.
public static ThreeD operator +(ThreeD op1, int op2)
{
  ThreeD result = new ThreeD();

  result.x = op1.x + op2;
  result.y = op1.y + op2;
  result.z = op1.z + op2;

  return result;
}
```

Notice that the second parameter is of type **int**. Thus, the preceding method allows an integer value to be added to each field of a **ThreeD** object. This is permissible because, as explained earlier, when overloading a binary operator, one of the operands must be of the same type as the class for which the operator is being overloaded. However, the other operand can be of any other type.

Here is a version of **ThreeD** that has two overloaded **+** methods:

```csharp
// Overload addition for ThreeD + ThreeD, and for ThreeD + int.

using System;

// A three-dimensional coordinate class.
class ThreeD {
  int x, y, z; // 3-D coordinates

  public ThreeD() { x = y = z = 0; }
  public ThreeD(int i, int j, int k) { x = i; y = j; z = k; }

  // Overload binary + for ThreeD + ThreeD.
  public static ThreeD operator +(ThreeD op1, ThreeD op2)
  {
    ThreeD result = new ThreeD();

    /* This adds together the coordinates of the two points
       and returns the result. */
    result.x = op1.x + op2.x;
    result.y = op1.y + op2.y;
    result.z = op1.z + op2.z;

    return result;
  }

  // Overload binary + for object + int.
  public static ThreeD operator +(ThreeD op1, int op2)
  {
    ThreeD result = new ThreeD();

    result.x = op1.x + op2;
    result.y = op1.y + op2;
    result.z = op1.z + op2;

    return result;
  }

  // Show X, Y, Z coordinates.
  public void Show()
  {
    Console.WriteLine(x + ", " + y + ", " + z);
  }
}

class ThreeDDemo {
  static void Main() {
    ThreeD a = new ThreeD(1, 2, 3);
    ThreeD b = new ThreeD(10, 10, 10);
    ThreeD c = new ThreeD();

    Console.Write("Here is a: ");
    a.Show();
    Console.WriteLine();
    Console.Write("Here is b: ");
```

```
      b.Show();
      Console.WriteLine();

      c = a + b; // ThreeD + ThreeD
      Console.Write("Result of a + b: ");
      c.Show();
      Console.WriteLine();

      c = b + 10; // ThreeD + int
      Console.Write("Result of b + 10: ");
      c.Show();
   }
}
```

The output from this program is shown here:

```
Here is a: 1, 2, 3

Here is b: 10, 10, 10

Result of a + b: 11, 12, 13

Result of b + 10: 20, 20, 20
```

As the output confirms, when the + is applied to two **ThreeD** objects, their coordinates are added together. When the + is applied to a **ThreeD** object and an integer, the coordinates are increased by the integer value.

While the overloading of + just shown certainly adds a useful capability to the **ThreeD** class, it does not quite finish the job. Here is why. The **operator+(ThreeD, int)** method allows statements like this:

   ob1 = ob2 + 10;

It does not, unfortunately, allow ones like this:

   ob1 = 10 + ob2;

The reason is that the integer argument is the second argument, which is the right-hand operand, but the preceding statement puts the integer argument on the left. To allow both forms of statements, you will need to overload the + yet another time. This version must have its first parameter as type **int** and its second parameter as type **ThreeD**. One version of the **operator+( )** method handles **ThreeD** + integer, and the other handles integer + **ThreeD**. Overloading the + (or any other binary operator) this way allows a built-in type to occur on the left or right side of the operator. Here is a version **ThreeD** that overloads the + operator as just described:

```
// Overload the + for ThreeD + ThreeD, ThreeD + int, and int + ThreeD.

using System;

// A three-dimensional coordinate class.
class ThreeD {
  int x, y, z; // 3-D coordinates
```

```
   public ThreeD() { x = y = z = 0; }
   public ThreeD(int i, int j, int k) { x = i; y = j; z = k; }

   // Overload binary + for ThreeD + ThreeD.
   public static ThreeD operator +(ThreeD op1, ThreeD op2)
   {
     ThreeD result = new ThreeD();

     /* This adds together the coordinates of the two points
        and returns the result. */
     result.x = op1.x + op2.x;
     result.y = op1.y + op2.y;
     result.z = op1.z + op2.z;

     return result;
   }

   // Overload binary + for ThreeD + int.
   public static ThreeD operator +(ThreeD op1, int op2)
   {
     ThreeD result = new ThreeD();

     result.x = op1.x + op2;
     result.y = op1.y + op2;
     result.z = op1.z + op2;

     return result;
   }

   // Overload binary + for int + ThreeD.
   public static ThreeD operator +(int op1, ThreeD op2)
   {
     ThreeD result = new ThreeD();

     result.x = op2.x + op1;
     result.y = op2.y + op1;
     result.z = op2.z + op1;

     return result;
   }

   // Show X, Y, Z coordinates.
   public void Show()
   {
     Console.WriteLine(x + ", " + y + ", " + z);
   }
}

class ThreeDDemo {
   static void Main() {
     ThreeD a = new ThreeD(1, 2, 3);
     ThreeD b = new ThreeD(10, 10, 10);
     ThreeD c = new ThreeD();
```

```
      Console.Write("Here is a: ");
      a.Show();
      Console.WriteLine();
      Console.Write("Here is b: ");
      b.Show();
      Console.WriteLine();

      c = a + b; // ThreeD + ThreeD
      Console.Write("Result of a + b: ");
      c.Show();
      Console.WriteLine();

      c = b + 10; // ThreeD + int
      Console.Write("Result of b + 10: ");
      c.Show();
      Console.WriteLine();

      c = 15 + b; // int + ThreeD
      Console.Write("Result of 15 + b: ");
      c.Show();
    }
}
```

The output from this program is shown here:

```
Here is a: 1, 2, 3

Here is b: 10, 10, 10

Result of a + b: 11, 12, 13

Result of b + 10: 20, 20, 20

Result of 15 + b: 25, 25, 25
```

Overloading the Relational Operators

The relational operators, such as = = or <, can also be overloaded and the process is straightforward. Usually, an overloaded relational operator returns a **true** or **false** value. This is in keeping with the normal usage of these operators and allows the overloaded relational operators to be used in conditional expressions. If you return a different type result, then you are greatly restricting the operator's utility.

Here is a version of the **ThreeD** class that overloads the < and > operators. In this example, these operators compare **ThreeD** objects based on their distance from the origin. One object is greater than another if its distance from the origin is greater. One object is less than another if its distance from the origin is less than the other. Given two points, such an implementation could be used to determine which point lies on the larger sphere. If neither operator returns true, then the two points lie on the same sphere. Of course, other ordering schemes are possible.

```
// Overload < and >.

using System;

// A three-dimensional coordinate class.
class ThreeD {
  int x, y, z; // 3-D coordinates

  public ThreeD() { x = y = z = 0; }
  public ThreeD(int i, int j, int k) { x = i; y = j; z = k; }

  // Overload <.
  public static bool operator <(ThreeD op1, ThreeD op2)
  {
    if(Math.Sqrt(op1.x * op1.x + op1.y * op1.y + op1.z * op1.z) <
       Math.Sqrt(op2.x * op2.x + op2.y * op2.y + op2.z * op2.z))
      return true;
    else
      return false;
  }

  // Overload >.
  public static bool operator >(ThreeD op1, ThreeD op2)
  {
    if(Math.Sqrt(op1.x * op1.x + op1.y * op1.y + op1.z * op1.z) >
       Math.Sqrt(op2.x * op2.x + op2.y * op2.y + op2.z * op2.z))
      return true;
    else
      return false;
  }

  // Show X, Y, Z coordinates.
  public void Show()
  {
    Console.WriteLine(x + ", " + y + ", " + z);
  }
}

class ThreeDDemo {
  static void Main() {
    ThreeD a = new ThreeD(5, 6, 7);
    ThreeD b = new ThreeD(10, 10, 10);
    ThreeD c = new ThreeD(1, 2, 3);
    ThreeD d = new ThreeD(6, 7, 5);

    Console.Write("Here is a: ");
    a.Show();
    Console.Write("Here is b: ");
    b.Show();
    Console.Write("Here is c: ");
    c.Show();
    Console.Write("Here is d: ");
    d.Show();
```

```
          Console.WriteLine();

        if(a > c) Console.WriteLine("a > c is true");
        if(a < c) Console.WriteLine("a < c is true");
        if(a > b) Console.WriteLine("a > b is true");
        if(a < b) Console.WriteLine("a < b is true");

        if(a > d) Console.WriteLine("a > d is true");
        else if(a < d) Console.WriteLine("a < d is true");
        else Console.WriteLine("a and d are same distance from origin");
    }
}
```

The output from this program is shown here:

```
Here is a: 5, 6, 7
Here is b: 10, 10, 10
Here is c: 1, 2, 3
Here is d: 6, 7, 5

a > c is true
a < b is true
a and d are same distance from origin
```

An important restriction applies to overloading the relational operators: You must overload them in pairs. For example, if you overload <, you must also overload >, and vice versa. The operator pairs are

==	!=
<	>
<=	>=

One other point: If you overload the == and != operators, then you will usually need to override **Object.Equals( )** and **Object.GetHashCode( )**. These methods and the technique of overriding are discussed in Chapter 11.

Overloading true and false

The keywords **true** and **false** can also be used as unary operators for the purposes of overloading. Overloaded versions of these operators provide custom determinations of true and false relative to classes that you create. Once true and false are overloaded for a class, you can use objects of that class to control the **if, while, for,** and **do-while** statements, or in a **?** expression.

The **true** and **false** operators must be overloaded as a pair. You cannot overload just one. Both are unary operators and they have this general form:

public static bool operator true(*param-type operand*)
{
    // return true or false
}

```
public static bool operator false(param-type operand)
{
    // return true or false
}
```

Notice that each returns a **bool** result.

The following example shows how **true** and **false** can be implemented for the **ThreeD** class. Each assumes that a **ThreeD** object is true if at least one coordinate is non-zero. If all three coordinates are zero, then the object is false. The decrement operator is also implemented for the purpose of illustration.

```
// Overload true and false for ThreeD.

using System;

// A three-dimensional coordinate class.
class ThreeD {
  int x, y, z; // 3-D coordinates

  public ThreeD() { x = y = z = 0; }
  public ThreeD(int i, int j, int k) { x = i; y = j; z = k; }

  // Overload true.
  public static bool operator true(ThreeD op) {
    if((op.x != 0) || (op.y != 0) || (op.z != 0))
      return true; // at least one coordinate is non-zero
    else
      return false;
  }

  // Overload false.
  public static bool operator false(ThreeD op) {
    if((op.x == 0) && (op.y == 0) && (op.z == 0))
      return true; // all coordinates are zero
    else
      return false;
  }

  // Overload unary --.
  public static ThreeD operator --(ThreeD op)
  {
    ThreeD result = new ThreeD();

    // Return the decremented result.
    result.x = op.x - 1;
    result.y = op.y - 1;
    result.z = op.z - 1;

    return result;
  }

  // Show X, Y, Z coordinates.
  public void Show()
  {
```

```
      Console.WriteLine(x + ", " + y + ", " + z);
    }
  }

class TrueFalseDemo {
  static void Main() {
    ThreeD a = new ThreeD(5, 6, 7);
    ThreeD b = new ThreeD(10, 10, 10);
    ThreeD c = new ThreeD(0, 0, 0);

    Console.Write("Here is a: ");
    a.Show();
    Console.Write("Here is b: ");
    b.Show();
    Console.Write("Here is c: ");
    c.Show();
    Console.WriteLine();

    if(a) Console.WriteLine("a is true.");
    else Console.WriteLine("a is false.");

    if(b) Console.WriteLine("b is true.");
    else Console.WriteLine("b is false.");

    if(c) Console.WriteLine("c is true.");
    else Console.WriteLine("c is false.");

    Console.WriteLine();

    Console.WriteLine("Control a loop using a ThreeD object.");
    do {
      b.Show();
      b--;
    } while(b);
  }
}
```

The output is shown here:

```
Here is a: 5, 6, 7
Here is b: 10, 10, 10
Here is c: 0, 0, 0

a is true.
b is true.
c is false.

Control a loop using a ThreeD object.
10, 10, 10
9, 9, 9
8, 8, 8
7, 7, 7
6, 6, 6
5, 5, 5
```

```
4, 4, 4
3, 3, 3
2, 2, 2
1, 1, 1
```

Notice how the **ThreeD** objects are used to control **if** statements and a **do-while** loop. In the case of the **if** statements, the **ThreeD** object is evaluated using **true**. If the result of this operation is true, then the **if** statement succeeds. In the case of the **do-while** loop, each iteration of the loop decrements **b**. The loop repeats as long as **b** evaluates as true (that is, it contains at least one non-zero coordinate). When **b** contains all zero coordinates, it evaluates as false when the **true** operator is applied and the loop stops.

Overloading the Logical Operators

As you know, C# defines the following logical operators: **&**, **|**, **!**, **&&**, and **||**. Of these, only the **&**, **|**, and **!** can be overloaded. By following certain rules, however, the benefits of the short-circuit **&&** and **||** can still be obtained. Each situation is examined here.

A Simple Approach to Overloading the Logical Operators

Let's begin with the simplest situation. If you will not be making use of the short-circuit logical operators, then you can overload **&** and **|** as you would intuitively think, with each returning a **bool** result. An overloaded **!** will also usually return a **bool** result.

Here is an example that overloads the **!**, **&**, and **|** logical operators for objects of type **ThreeD**. As before, each assumes that a **ThreeD** object is true if at least one coordinate is non-zero. If all three coordinates are zero, then the object is false.

```
// A simple way to overload !, |, and & for ThreeD.

using System;

// A three-dimensional coordinate class.
class ThreeD {
  int x, y, z; // 3-D coordinates

  public ThreeD() { x = y = z = 0; }
  public ThreeD(int i, int j, int k) { x = i; y = j; z = k; }


  // Overload |.
  public static bool operator |(ThreeD op1, ThreeD op2)
  {
    if( ((op1.x != 0) || (op1.y != 0) || (op1.z != 0)) |
        ((op2.x != 0) || (op2.y != 0) || (op2.z != 0)) )
      return true;
    else
      return false;
  }

  // Overload &.
  public static bool operator &(ThreeD op1, ThreeD op2)
  {
```

```
    if( ((op1.x != 0) && (op1.y != 0) && (op1.z != 0)) &
        ((op2.x != 0) && (op2.y != 0) && (op2.z != 0)) )
      return true;
    else
      return false;
  }

  // Overload !.
  public static bool operator !(ThreeD op)
  {
    if((op.x != 0) || (op.y != 0) || (op.z != 0))
      return false;
    else return true;
  }

  // Show X, Y, Z coordinates.
  public void Show()
  {
    Console.WriteLine(x + ", " + y + ", " + z);
  }
}

class LogicalOpDemo {
  static void Main() {
    ThreeD a = new ThreeD(5, 6, 7);
    ThreeD b = new ThreeD(10, 10, 10);
    ThreeD c = new ThreeD(0, 0, 0);

    Console.Write("Here is a: ");
    a.Show();
    Console.Write("Here is b: ");
    b.Show();
    Console.Write("Here is c: ");
    c.Show();
    Console.WriteLine();

    if(!a) Console.WriteLine("a is false.");
    if(!b) Console.WriteLine("b is false.");
    if(!c) Console.WriteLine("c is false.");

    Console.WriteLine();

    if(a & b) Console.WriteLine("a & b is true.");
    else Console.WriteLine("a & b is false.");

    if(a & c) Console.WriteLine("a & c is true.");
    else Console.WriteLine("a & c is false.");

    if(a | b) Console.WriteLine("a | b is true.");
    else Console.WriteLine("a | b is false.");

    if(a | c) Console.WriteLine("a | c is true.");
    else Console.WriteLine("a | c is false.");
  }
}
```

The output from the program is shown here:

```
Here is a: 5, 6, 7
Here is b: 10, 10, 10
Here is c: 0, 0, 0

c is false.

a & b is true.
a & c is false.
a | b is true.
a | c is true.
```

In this approach, the &, |, and ! operator methods each return a **bool** result. This is necessary if the operators are to be used in their normal manner (that is, in places that expect a **bool** result). Recall that for all built-in types, the outcome of a logical operation is a value of type **bool**. Thus, having the overloaded versions of these operators return type **bool** is a rational approach. Unfortunately, this approach works only if you will not be needing the short-circuit operators.

Enabling the Short-Circuit Operators

To enable the use of the && and | | short-circuit operators, you must follow four rules. First, the class must overload & and |. Second, the return type of the overloaded & and | methods must be the same as the class for which the operators are being overloaded. Third, each parameter must be a reference to an object of the class for which the operator is being overloaded. Fourth, the **true** and **false** operators must be overloaded for the class. When these conditions have been met, the short-circuit operators automatically become available for use.

The following program shows how to properly implement the & and | for the **ThreeD** class so that the short-circuit operators && and | | are available.

```
/* A better way to overload !, |, and & for ThreeD.
   This version automatically enables the && and || operators. */

using System;

// A three-dimensional coordinate class.
class ThreeD {
  int x, y, z; // 3-D coordinates

  public ThreeD() { x = y = z = 0; }
  public ThreeD(int i, int j, int k) { x = i; y = j; z = k; }

  // Overload | for short-circuit evaluation.
  public static ThreeD operator |(ThreeD op1, ThreeD op2)
  {
    if( ((op1.x != 0) || (op1.y != 0) || (op1.z != 0)) |
        ((op2.x != 0) || (op2.y != 0) || (op2.z != 0)) )
      return new ThreeD(1, 1, 1);
    else
      return new ThreeD(0, 0, 0);
  }
```

```
    // Overload & for short-circuit evaluation.
    public static ThreeD operator &(ThreeD op1, ThreeD op2)
    {
      if( ((op1.x != 0) && (op1.y != 0) && (op1.z != 0)) &
          ((op2.x != 0) && (op2.y != 0) && (op2.z != 0)) )
        return new ThreeD(1, 1, 1);
      else
        return new ThreeD(0, 0, 0);
    }

    // Overload !.
    public static bool operator !(ThreeD op)
    {
      if(op) return false;
      else return true;
    }

    // Overload true.
    public static bool operator true(ThreeD op) {
      if((op.x != 0) || (op.y != 0) || (op.z != 0))
        return true; // at least one coordinate is non-zero
      else
        return false;
    }

    // Overload false.
    public static bool operator false(ThreeD op) {
      if((op.x == 0) && (op.y == 0) && (op.z == 0))
        return true; // all coordinates are zero
      else
        return false;
    }

    // Show X, Y, Z coordinates.
    public void Show()
    {
      Console.WriteLine(x + ", " + y + ", " + z);
    }
}

class LogicalOpDemo {
  static void Main() {
    ThreeD a = new ThreeD(5, 6, 7);
    ThreeD b = new ThreeD(10, 10, 10);
    ThreeD c = new ThreeD(0, 0, 0);

    Console.Write("Here is a: ");
    a.Show();
    Console.Write("Here is b: ");
    b.Show();
    Console.Write("Here is c: ");
    c.Show();
    Console.WriteLine();
```

```
      if(a) Console.WriteLine("a is true.");
      if(b) Console.WriteLine("b is true.");
      if(c) Console.WriteLine("c is true.");

      if(!a) Console.WriteLine("a is false.");
      if(!b) Console.WriteLine("b is false.");
      if(!c) Console.WriteLine("c is false.");

      Console.WriteLine();

      Console.WriteLine("Use & and |");
      if(a & b) Console.WriteLine("a & b is true.");
      else Console.WriteLine("a & b is false.");

      if(a & c) Console.WriteLine("a & c is true.");
      else Console.WriteLine("a & c is false.");

      if(a | b) Console.WriteLine("a | b is true.");
      else Console.WriteLine("a | b is false.");

      if(a | c) Console.WriteLine("a | c is true.");
      else Console.WriteLine("a | c is false.");

      Console.WriteLine();

      // Now use short-circuit ops.
      Console.WriteLine("Use short-circuit && and ||");
      if(a && b) Console.WriteLine("a && b is true.");
      else Console.WriteLine("a && b is false.");

      if(a && c) Console.WriteLine("a && c is true.");
      else Console.WriteLine("a && c is false.");

      if(a || b) Console.WriteLine("a || b is true.");
      else Console.WriteLine("a || b is false.");

      if(a || c) Console.WriteLine("a || c is true.");
      else Console.WriteLine("a || c is false.");
  }
}
```

The output from the program is shown here:

```
Here is a: 5, 6, 7
Here is b: 10, 10, 10
Here is c: 0, 0, 0

a is true.
b is true.
c is false.

Use & and |
a & b is true.
```

```
a & c is false.
a | b is true.
a | c is true.

Use short-circuit && and ||
a && b is true.
a && c is false.
a || b is true.
a || c is true.
```

Let's look closely at how the **&** and **|** are implemented. They are shown here:

```
// Overload | for short-circuit evaluation.
public static ThreeD operator |(ThreeD op1, ThreeD op2)
{
  if( ((op1.x != 0) || (op1.y != 0) || (op1.z != 0)) |
      ((op2.x != 0) || (op2.y != 0) || (op2.z != 0)) )
    return new ThreeD(1, 1, 1);
  else
    return new ThreeD(0, 0, 0);
}

// Overload & for short-circuit evaluation.
public static ThreeD operator &(ThreeD op1, ThreeD op2)
{
  if( ((op1.x != 0) && (op1.y != 0) && (op1.z != 0)) &
      ((op2.x != 0) && (op2.y != 0) && (op2.z != 0)) )
    return new ThreeD(1, 1, 1);
  else
    return new ThreeD(0, 0, 0);
}
```

Notice first that both now return an object of type **ThreeD**. Pay attention to how this object is generated. If the outcome of the operation is true, then a true **ThreeD** object (one in which at least one coordinate is non-zero) is created and returned. If the outcome is false, then a false object is created and returned. Thus, in a statement like this

```
if(a & b) Console.WriteLine("a & b is true.");
else Console.WriteLine("a & b is false.");
```

the outcome of **a & b** is a **ThreeD** object, which in this case is a true object. Since the operators **true** and **false** are defined, this resulting object is subjected to the **true** operator, and a **bool** result is returned. In this case, the result is **true** and the **if** succeeds.

Because the necessary rules have been followed, the short-circuit operators are now available for use on **ThreeD** objects. They work like this. The first operand is tested by using **operator true** (for **||**) or **operator false** (for **&&**). If it can determine the outcome of the operation, then the corresponding **&** or **|** is not evaluated. Otherwise, the corresponding overloaded **&** or **|** is used to determine the result. Thus, using a **&&** or **||** causes the corresponding **&** or **|** to be invoked only when the first operand cannot determine the outcome of the expression. For example, consider this statement from the program:

```
if(a || c) Console.WriteLine("a || c is true.");
```

The **true** operator is first applied to **a**. Since **a** is true in this situation, there is no need to use the I **operator** method. However, if the statement were rewritten like this:

```
if(c || a) Console.WriteLine("c || a is true.");
```

then the **true** operator would first be applied to **c**, which in this case is false. Thus, the I **operator** method would be invoked to determine if **a** was true (which it is in this case).

Although you might at first think that the technique used to enable the short-circuit operators is a bit convoluted, it makes sense if you think about it a bit. By overloading **true** and **false** for a class, you enable the compiler to utilize the short-circuit operators without having to explicitly overload either. Furthermore, you gain the ability to use objects in conditional expressions. In general, unless you need a very narrow implementation of **&** and I, you are better off creating a full implementation.

Conversion Operators

In some situations, you will want to use an object of a class in an expression involving other types of data. Sometimes, overloading one or more operators can provide the means of doing this. However, in other cases, what you want is a simple type conversion from the class type to the target type. To handle these cases, C# allows you to create a special type of **operator** method called a *conversion operator*. A conversion operator converts an object of your class into another type. Conversion operators help fully integrate class types into the C# programming environment by allowing objects of a class to be freely mixed with other data types as long as a conversion to those other types is defined.

There are two forms of conversion operators, implicit and explicit. The general form for each is shown here:

public static operator implicit *target-type*(*source-type v*) { **return** *value*; }
public static operator explicit *target-type*(*source-type v*) { return *value*; }

Here, *target-type* is the target type that you are converting to; *source-type* is the type you are converting from; and *value* is the value of the class after conversion. The conversion operators return data of type *target-type,* and no other return type specifier is allowed.

If the conversion operator specifies **implicit**, then the conversion is invoked automatically, such as when an object is used in an expression with the target type. When the conversion operator specifies **explicit**, the conversion is invoked when a cast is used. You cannot define both an implicit and explicit conversion operator for the same target and source types.

To illustrate a conversion operator, we will create one for the **ThreeD** class. Suppose you want to convert an object of type **ThreeD** into an integer so it can be used in an integer expression. Further, the conversion will take place by using the product of the three dimensions. To accomplish this, you will use an implicit conversion operator that looks like this:

```
public static implicit operator int(ThreeD op1)
{
  return op1.x * op1.y * op1.z;
}
```

Here is a program that illustrates this conversion operator:

```
// An example that uses an implicit conversion operator.

using System;

// A three-dimensional coordinate class.
class ThreeD {
  int x, y, z; // 3-D coordinates

  public ThreeD() { x = y = z = 0; }
  public ThreeD(int i, int j, int k) { x = i; y = j; z = k; }

  // Overload binary +.
  public static ThreeD operator +(ThreeD op1, ThreeD op2)
  {
    ThreeD result = new ThreeD();

    result.x = op1.x + op2.x;
    result.y = op1.y + op2.y;
    result.z = op1.z + op2.z;

    return result;
  }

  // An implicit conversion from ThreeD to int.
  public static implicit operator int(ThreeD op1)
  {
    return op1.x * op1.y * op1.z;
  }

  // Show X, Y, Z coordinates.
  public void Show()
  {
    Console.WriteLine(x + ", " + y + ", " + z);
  }
}

class ThreeDDemo {
  static void Main() {
    ThreeD a = new ThreeD(1, 2, 3);
    ThreeD b = new ThreeD(10, 10, 10);
    ThreeD c = new ThreeD();
    int i;

    Console.Write("Here is a: ");
    a.Show();
    Console.WriteLine();
    Console.Write("Here is b: ");
    b.Show();
    Console.WriteLine();

    c = a + b; // add a and b together
    Console.Write("Result of a + b: ");
    c.Show();
```

```
      Console.WriteLine();

      i = a; // convert to int
      Console.WriteLine("Result of i = a: " + i);
      Console.WriteLine();

      i = a * 2 - b; // convert to int
      Console.WriteLine("result of a * 2 - b: " + i);
  }
}
```

This program displays the output:

```
Here is a: 1, 2, 3

Here is b: 10, 10, 10

Result of a + b: 11, 12, 13

Result of i = a: 6

result of a * 2 - b: -988
```

As the program illustrates, when a **ThreeD** object is used in an integer expression, such as **i = a**, the conversion is applied to the object. In this specific case, the conversion returns the value 6, which is the product of coordinates stored in **a**. However, when an expression does not require a conversion to **int**, the conversion operator is not called. This is why **c = a + b** *does not* invoke **operator int( )**.

Remember that you can create different conversion operators to meet different needs. You could define a second conversion operator that converts **ThreeD** to **double**, for example. Each conversion is applied automatically and independently.

An implicit conversion operator is applied automatically when a conversion is required in an expression, when passing an object to a method, in an assignment, and also when an explicit cast to the target type is used. Alternatively, you can create an explicit conversion operator, which is invoked only when an explicit cast is used. An explicit conversion operator is not invoked automatically. For example, here is the previous program reworked to use an explicit conversion to **int**:

```
// Use an explicit conversion.

using System;

// A three-dimensional coordinate class.
class ThreeD {
  int x, y, z; // 3-D coordinates

  public ThreeD() { x = y = z = 0; }
  public ThreeD(int i, int j, int k) { x = i; y = j; z = k; }

  // Overload binary +.
  public static ThreeD operator +(ThreeD op1, ThreeD op2)
  {
    ThreeD result = new ThreeD();
```

```
      result.x = op1.x + op2.x;
      result.y = op1.y + op2.y;
      result.z = op1.z + op2.z;

      return result;
    }

    // This is now explicit.
    public static explicit operator int(ThreeD op1)
    {
      return op1.x * op1.y * op1.z;
    }

    // Show X, Y, Z coordinates.
    public void Show()
    {
      Console.WriteLine(x + ", " + y + ", " + z);
    }
  }

class ThreeDDemo {
  static void Main() {
    ThreeD a = new ThreeD(1, 2, 3);
    ThreeD b = new ThreeD(10, 10, 10);
    ThreeD c = new ThreeD();
    int i;

    Console.Write("Here is a: ");
    a.Show();
    Console.WriteLine();
    Console.Write("Here is b: ");
    b.Show();
    Console.WriteLine();

    c = a + b; // add a and b together
    Console.Write("Result of a + b: ");
    c.Show();
    Console.WriteLine();

    i = (int) a; // explicitly convert to int -- cast required
    Console.WriteLine("Result of i = a: " + i);
    Console.WriteLine();

    i = (int)a * 2 - (int)b; // casts required
    Console.WriteLine("result of a * 2 - b: " + i);

  }
}
```

Because the conversion operator is now marked as explicit, conversion to **int** must be explicitly cast. For example, in this line:

```
i = (int) a; // explicitly convert to int -- cast required
```

if you remove the cast, the program will not compile.

There are a few restrictions to conversion operators:

- Either the target type or the source type of the conversion must be the class in which the conversion is declared. You cannot, for example, redefine the conversion from **double** to **int**.

- You cannot define a conversion to or from **object**.

- You cannot define both an implicit and an explicit conversion for the same source and target types.

- You cannot define a conversion from a base class to a derived class. (See Chapter 11 for a discussion of base and derived classes.)

- You cannot define a conversion from or to an interface. (See Chapter 12 for a discussion of interfaces.)

In addition to these rules, there are suggestions that you should normally follow when choosing between implicit and explicit conversion operators. Although convenient, implicit conversions should be used only in situations in which the conversion is inherently error-free. To ensure this, implicit conversions should be created only when these two conditions are met: First, that no loss of information, such as truncation, overflow, or loss of sign, occurs, or that such loss of information is acceptable based on the circumstances. Second, that the conversion does not cause an exception. If the conversion cannot meet these two requirements, then you should use an explicit conversion.

Operator Overloading Tips and Restrictions

The action of an overloaded operator as applied to the class for which it is defined need not bear any relationship to that operator's default usage, as applied to C#'s built-in types. However, for the purposes of the structure and readability of your code, an overloaded operator should reflect, when possible, the spirit of the operator's original use. For example, the + relative to **ThreeD** is conceptually similar to the + relative to integer types. There would be little benefit in defining the + operator relative to some class in such a way that it acts more the way you would expect the / operator to perform, for instance. The central concept is that while you can give an overloaded operator any meaning you like, for clarity it is best when its new meaning is related to its original meaning.

There are some restrictions to overloading operators. You cannot alter the precedence of any operator. You cannot alter the number of operands required by the operator, although your **operator** method could choose to ignore an operand. There are several operators that you cannot overload. Perhaps most significantly, you cannot overload any assignment operator, including the compound assignments, such as +=. Here are the other operators that cannot be overloaded. (This list includes several operators that are discussed later in this book.)

&&	()	.	?
??	[ ]	||	=
=>	->	as	checked
default	is	new	sizeof
typeof	unchecked		

Although you cannot overload the cast operator ( ) explicitly, you can create conversion operators, as shown earlier, that perform this function.

It may seem like a serious restriction that operators such as += can't be overloaded, but it isn't. In general, if you have defined an operator, then if that operator is used in a compound assignment, your overloaded operator method is invoked. Thus, += automatically uses your version of **operator+( )**. For example, assuming the **ThreeD** class, if you use a sequence like this:

```
ThreeD a = new ThreeD(1, 2, 3);
ThreeD b = new ThreeD(10, 10, 10);

b += a; // add a and b together
```

ThreeD's **operator+( )** is automatically invoked, and **b** will contain the coordinate 11, 12, 13.

One last point: Although you cannot overload the [ ] array indexing operator using an **operator** method, you can create indexers, which are described in the next chapter.

Another Example of Operator Overloading

Throughout this chapter we have been using the **ThreeD** class to demonstrate operator overloading, and in this regard it has served us well. Before concluding this chapter, however, it is useful to work through another example. Although the general principles of operator overloading are the same no matter what class is used, the following example helps show the power of operator overloading—especially where type extensibility is concerned.

This example develops a four-bit integer type and defines several operations for it. As you might know, in the early days of computing, the four-bit quantity was common because it represented half a byte. It is also large enough to hold one hexadecimal digit. Since four bits are half a byte, a four-bit quantity is sometimes referred to as a *nybble*. In the days of front-panel machines in which programmers entered code one nybble at a time, thinking in terms of nybbles was an everyday affair! Although not as common now, a four-bit type still makes an interesting addition to the other C# integers. Traditionally, a nybble is an unsigned value.

The following example uses the **Nybble** class to implement a nybble data type. It uses an **int** for its underlying storage, but it restricts the values that can be held to 0 through 15. It defines the following operators:

- Addition of a **Nybble** to a **Nybble**
- Addition of an **int** to a **Nybble**
- Addition of a **Nybble** to an **int**
- Greater than and less than
- The increment operator
- Conversion to **Nybble** from **int**
- Conversion to **int** from **Nybble**

These operations are sufficient to show how a class type can be fully integrated into the C# type system. However, for complete **Nybble** implementation, you will need to define all of the other operators. You might want to try adding these on your own.

The complete **Nybble** class is shown here along with a **NybbleDemo**, which demonstrates its use:

```
// Create a 4-bit type called Nybble.

using System;

// A 4-bit type.
class Nybble {
  int val; // underlying storage

  public Nybble() { val = 0; }

  public Nybble(int i) {
    val = i;
    val = val & 0xF; // retain lower 4 bits
  }

  // Overload binary + for Nybble + Nybble.
  public static Nybble operator +(Nybble op1, Nybble op2)
  {
    Nybble result = new Nybble();

    result.val = op1.val + op2.val;

    result.val = result.val & 0xF; // retain lower 4 bits

    return result;
  }

  // Overload binary + for Nybble + int.
  public static Nybble operator +(Nybble op1, int op2)
  {
    Nybble result = new Nybble();

    result.val = op1.val + op2;

    result.val = result.val & 0xF; // retain lower 4 bits

    return result;
  }

  // Overload binary + for int + Nybble.
  public static Nybble operator +(int op1, Nybble op2)
  {
    Nybble result = new Nybble();

    result.val = op1 + op2.val;

    result.val = result.val & 0xF; // retain lower 4 bits

    return result;
  }

  // Overload ++.
```

```
  public static Nybble operator ++(Nybble op)
  {
    Nybble result = new Nybble();
    result.val = op.val + 1;

    result.val = result.val & 0xF; // retain lower 4 bits

    return result;
  }

  // Overload >.
  public static bool operator >(Nybble op1, Nybble op2)
  {
    if(op1.val > op2.val) return true;
    else return false;
  }

  // Overload <.
  public static bool operator <(Nybble op1, Nybble op2)
  {
    if(op1.val < op2.val) return true;
    else return false;
  }

  // Convert a Nybble into an int.
  public static implicit operator int (Nybble op)
  {
    return op.val;
  }

  // Convert an int into a Nybble.
  public static implicit operator Nybble (int op)
  {
    return new Nybble(op);
  }
}

class NybbleDemo {
  static void Main() {
    Nybble a = new Nybble(1);
    Nybble b = new Nybble(10);
    Nybble c = new Nybble();
    int t;

    Console.WriteLine("a: " + (int) a);
    Console.WriteLine("b: " + (int) b);

    // Use a Nybble in an if statement.
    if(a < b) Console.WriteLine("a is less than b\n");

    // Add two Nybbles together.
    c = a + b;
    Console.WriteLine("c after c = a + b: " + (int) c);
```

```
// Add an int to a Nybble.
a += 5;
Console.WriteLine("a after a += 5: " + (int) a);

Console.WriteLine();

// Use a Nybble in an int expression.
t = a * 2 + 3;
Console.WriteLine("Result of a * 2 + 3: " + t);

Console.WriteLine();

// Illustrate int assignment and overflow.
a = 19;
Console.WriteLine("Result of a = 19: " + (int) a);

Console.WriteLine();

// Use a Nybble to control a loop.
Console.WriteLine("Control a for loop with a Nybble.");
for(a = 0; a < 10; a++)
  Console.Write((int) a + " ");

Console.WriteLine();
  }
}
```

The output from the program is shown here:

```
a: 1
b: 10
a is less than b

c after c = a + b: 11
a after a += 5: 6

Result of a * 2 + 3: 15

Result of a = 19: 3

Control a for loop with a Nybble.
0 1 2 3 4 5 6 7 8 9
```

Although most of the operation of **Nybble** should be easy to understand, there is one important point to make: The conversion operators play a large role in the integration of **Nybble** into the C# type system. Because conversions are defined from **Nybble** to **int** and from **int** to **Nybble**, a **Nybble** object can be freely mixed in arithmetic expressions. For example, consider this expression from the program:

```
t = a * 2 + 3;
```

Here, **t** is an **int**, as are 2 and 3, but **a** is a **Nybble**. These two types are compatible in the expression because of the implicit conversion of **Nybble** to **int**. In this case, since the rest of the expression is of type **int**, **a** is converted to **int** by its conversion method.

The conversion from **int** to **Nybble** allows a **Nybble** object to be assigned an **int** value. For example, in the program, the statement

```
a = 19;
```

works like this. The conversion operator from **int** to **Nybble** is executed. This causes a new **Nybble** object to be created that contains the low-order 4 bits of the value 19, which is 3 because 19 overflows the range of a **Nybble**. (In this example, such overflow is acceptable.) This object is then assigned to **a**. Without the conversion operators, such expressions would not be allowed.

The conversion of **Nybble** to **int** is also used by the **for** loop. Without this conversion, it would not be possible to write the **for** loop in such a straightforward way.

NOTE *As an exercise, you might want to try creating a version of **Nybble** that prevents overflow when an out-of-range value is assigned. The best way to do this is by thowing an exception. See Chapter 13 for a discussion of exceptions.*

Indexers and Properties

This chapter examines two special types of class members that have a close relationship to each other: indexers and properties. Each expands the power of a class by enhancing its integration into C#'s type system and improving its resiliency. Indexers provide the mechanism by which an object can be indexed like an array. Properties offer a streamlined way to manage access to a class' instance data. They relate to each other because both rely upon another feature of C#: the accessor.

Indexers

As you know, array indexing is performed using the [ ] operator. It is possible to define the [ ] operator for classes that you create, but you don't use an **operator** method. Instead, you create an *indexer*. An indexer allows an object to be indexed like an array. The main use of indexers is to support the creation of specialized arrays that are subject to one or more constraints. However, you can use an indexer for any purpose for which an array-like syntax is beneficial. Indexers can have one or more dimensions. We will begin with one-dimensional indexers.

Creating One-Dimensional Indexers

A simple one-dimensional indexer has this general form:

```
element-type this[int index] {
  // The get accessor
  get {
    // return the value specified by index
  }

  // The set accessor
  set {
    // set the value specified by index
  }
}
```

Here, *element-type* is the element type of the indexer. Thus, each element accessed by the indexer will be of type *element-type*. This type corresponds to the element type of an array. The parameter *index* receives the index of the element being accessed. Technically, this parameter does not have to be of type **int**, but since indexers are typically used to provide array indexing, using an integer type is quite common.

Inside the body of the indexer two *accessors* are defined that are called **get** and **set**. An accessor is similar to a method except that it does not declare a return type or parameters. The accessors are automatically called when the indexer is used, and both accessors receive *index* as a parameter. If the indexer is on the left side of an assignment statement, then the **set** accessor is called and the element specified by *index* must be set. Otherwise, the **get** accessor is called and the value associated with *index* must be returned. The **set** method also receives an implicit parameter called **value**, which contains the value being assigned to the specified index.

One of the benefits of an indexer is that you can control precisely how an array is accessed, heading off improper access. Here is an example. In the following program, the **FailSoftArray** class implements an array that traps boundary errors, thus preventing runtime exceptions if the array is indexed out-of-bounds. This is accomplished by encapsulating the array as a private member of a class, allowing access to the array only through the indexer. With this approach, any attempt to access the array beyond its boundaries can be prevented, with such an attempt failing gracefully (resulting in a "soft landing" rather than a "crash"). Since **FailSoftArray** uses an indexer, the array can be accessed using the normal array notation.

```
// Use an indexer to create a fail-soft array.

using System;

class FailSoftArray {
  int[] a;     // reference to underlying array

  public int Length; // Length is public

  public bool ErrFlag; // indicates outcome of last operation

  // Construct array given its size.
  public FailSoftArray(int size) {
    a = new int[size];
    Length = size;
  }

  // This is the indexer for FailSoftArray.
  public int this[int index] {
    // This is the get accessor.
    get {
      if(ok(index)) {
        ErrFlag = false;
        return a[index];
      } else {
        ErrFlag = true;
        return 0;
      }
    }
```

```
      // This is the set accessor.
      set {
        if(ok(index)) {
          a[index] = value;
          ErrFlag = false;
        }
        else ErrFlag = true;
      }
    }

    // Return true if index is within bounds.
    private bool ok(int index) {
      if(index >= 0 & index < Length) return true;
      return false;
    }
  }

// Demonstrate the fail-soft array.
class FSDemo {
  static void Main() {
    FailSoftArray fs = new FailSoftArray(5);
    int x;

    // Show quiet failures.
    Console.WriteLine("Fail quietly.");
    for(int i=0; i < (fs.Length * 2); i++)
      fs[i] = i*10;

    for(int i=0; i < (fs.Length * 2); i++) {
      x = fs[i];
      if(x != -1) Console.Write(x + " ");
    }
    Console.WriteLine();

    // Now, display failures.
    Console.WriteLine("\nFail with error reports.");
    for(int i=0; i < (fs.Length * 2); i++) {
      fs[i] = i*10;
      if(fs.ErrFlag)
        Console.WriteLine("fs[" + i + "] out-of-bounds");
    }

    for(int i=0; i < (fs.Length * 2); i++) {
      x = fs[i];
      if(!fs.ErrFlag) Console.Write(x + " ");
      else
        Console.WriteLine("fs[" + i + "] out-of-bounds");
    }
  }
}
```

The output from the program is shown here:

```
Fail quietly.
0 10 20 30 40 0 0 0 0 0
```

```
Fail with error reports.
fs[5] out-of-bounds
fs[6] out-of-bounds
fs[7] out-of-bounds
fs[8] out-of-bounds
fs[9] out-of-bounds
0 10 20 30 40 fs[5] out-of-bounds
fs[6] out-of-bounds
fs[7] out-of-bounds
fs[8] out-of-bounds
fs[9] out-of-bounds
```

The indexer prevents the array boundaries from being overrun. Let's look closely at each part of the indexer. It begins with this line:

```
public int this[int index] {
```

This declares an indexer that operates on **int** elements. The index is passed in **index**. The indexer is public, allowing it to be used by code outside of its class.

The **get** accessor is shown here:

```
get {
  if(ok(index)) {
    ErrFlag = false;
    return a[index];
  } else {
    ErrFlag = true;
    return 0;
  }
}
```

The **get** accessor prevents array boundary errors by first confirming that the index is not out-of-bounds. This range check is performed by the **ok()** method, which returns true if the index is valid and false otherwise. If the specified index is within bounds, the element corresponding to the index is returned. If it is out of bounds, no operation takes place and no overrun occurs. In this version of **FailSoftArray**, a variable called **ErrFlag** contains the outcome of each operation. This field can be examined after each operation to assess the success or failure of the operation. (In Chapter 13, you will see a better way to handle errors by using C#'s exception subsystem, but for now, using an error flag is an acceptable approach.)

The **set** accessor is shown here. It too prevents a boundary error.

```
set {
  if(ok(index)) {
    a[index] = value;
    ErrFlag = false;
  }
  else ErrFlag = true;
}
```

Here, if **index** is within bounds, the value passed in **value** is assigned to the corresponding element. Otherwise, **ErrFlag** is set to **true**. Recall that in an accessor method, **value** is an implicit parameter that contains the value being assigned. You do not need to (nor can you) declare it.

It is not necessary for an indexer to support both **get** and **set**. You can create a read-only indexer by implementing only the **get** accessor. You can create a write-only indexer by implementing only **set**.

Indexers Can Be Overloaded

An indexer can be overloaded. The version executed will be the one that has the closest type-match between its parameter and the argument used as an index. Here is an example that overloads the **FailSoftArray** indexer for indexes of type **double**. The **double** indexer rounds its index to the nearest integer value.

```
// Overload the FailSoftArray indexer.

using System;

class FailSoftArray {
  int[] a;    // reference to underlying array

  public int Length; // Length is public

  public bool ErrFlag; // indicates outcome of last operation

  // Construct array given its size.
  public FailSoftArray(int size) {
    a = new int[size];
    Length = size;
  }

  // This is the int indexer for FailSoftArray.
  public int this[int index] {
    // This is the get accessor.
    get {
      if(ok(index)) {
        ErrFlag = false;
        return a[index];
      } else {
        ErrFlag = true;
        return 0;
      }
    }

    // This is the set accessor.
    set {
      if(ok(index)) {
        a[index] = value;
        ErrFlag = false;
      }
      else ErrFlag = true;
    }
  }
}
```

```
    /* This is another indexer for FailSoftArray.
       This index takes a double argument. It then
       rounds that argument to the nearest integer index. */
    public int this[double idx] {
      // This is the get accessor.
      get {
        int index;

        // Round to nearest int.
        if( (idx - (int) idx) < 0.5) index = (int) idx;
        else index = (int) idx + 1;

        if(ok(index)) {
          ErrFlag = false;
          return a[index];
        } else {
          ErrFlag = true;
          return 0;
        }
      }

      // This is the set accessor.
      set {
        int index;

        // Round to nearest int.
        if( (idx - (int) idx) < 0.5) index = (int) idx;
        else index = (int) idx + 1;

        if(ok(index)) {
          a[index] = value;
          ErrFlag = false;
        }
        else ErrFlag = true;
      }
    }

  // Return true if index is within bounds.
  private bool ok(int index) {
   if(index >= 0 & index < Length) return true;
   return false;
  }
}

// Demonstrate the fail-soft array.
class FSDemo {
  static void Main() {
    FailSoftArray fs = new FailSoftArray(5);

    // Put some values in fs.
    for(int i=0; i < fs.Length; i++)
      fs[i] = i;

    // Now index with ints and doubles.
    Console.WriteLine("fs[1]: " + fs[1]);
```

```
    Console.WriteLine("fs[2]: " + fs[2]);

    Console.WriteLine("fs[1.1]: " + fs[1.1]);
    Console.WriteLine("fs[1.6]: " + fs[1.6]);
  }
}
```

This program produces the following output:

```
fs[1]: 1
fs[2]: 2
fs[1.1]: 1
fs[1.6]: 2
```

As the output shows, the **double** indexes are rounded to their nearest integer value. Specifically, 1.1 is rounded to 1, and 1.6 is rounded to 2.

Although overloading an indexer as shown in this program is valid, it is not common. Most often, an indexer is overloaded to enable an object of a class to be used as an index, with the index computed in some special way.

Indexers Do Not Require an Underlying Array

It is important to understand that there is no requirement that an indexer actually operate on an array. It simply must provide functionality that appears "array-like" to the user of the indexer. For example, the following program has an indexer that acts like a read-only array that contains the powers of 2 from 0 to 15. Notice, however, that no actual array exists. Instead, the indexer simply computes the proper value for a given index.

```
// Indexers don't have to operate on actual arrays.

using System;

class PwrOfTwo {

  /* Access a logical array that contains
     the powers of 2 from 0 to 15. */
  public int this[int index] {
    // Compute and return power of 2.
    get {
      if((index >= 0) && (index < 16)) return pwr(index);
      else return -1;
    }

    // There is no set accessor.
  }

  int pwr(int p) {
    int result = 1;

    for(int i=0; i < p; i++)
      result *= 2;

    return result;
  }
}
```

```
class UsePwrOfTwo {
  static void Main() {
    PwrOfTwo pwr = new PwrOfTwo();

    Console.Write("First 8 powers of 2: ");
    for(int i=0; i < 8; i++)
      Console.Write(pwr[i] + " ");
    Console.WriteLine();

    Console.Write("Here are some errors: ");
    Console.Write(pwr[-1] + " " + pwr[17]);

    Console.WriteLine();
  }
}
```

The output from the program is shown here:

```
First 8 powers of 2: 1 2 4 8 16 32 64 128
Here are some errors: -1 -1
```

Notice that the indexer for **PwrOfTwo** includes a **get** accessor, but no **set** accessor. As explained, this means that the indexer is read-only. Thus, a **PwrOfTwo** object can be used on the right side of an assignment statement, but not on the left. For example, attempting to add this statement to the preceding program won't work:

```
pwr[0] = 11; // won't compile
```

This statement will cause a compilation error because no **set** accessor is defined for the indexer.

There are two important restrictions to using indexers. First, because an indexer does not define a storage location, a value produced by an indexer cannot be passed as a **ref** or **out** parameter to a method. Second, an indexer must be an instance member of its class; it cannot be declared **static**.

Multidimensional Indexers

You can create indexers for multidimensional arrays, too. For example, here is a two-dimensional fail-soft array. Pay close attention to the way that the indexer is declared.

```
// A two-dimensional fail-soft array.

using System;

class FailSoftArray2D {
  int[,] a; // reference to underlying 2D array
  int rows, cols; // dimensions
  public int Length; // Length is public

  public bool ErrFlag; // indicates outcome of last operation

  // Construct array given its dimensions.
  public FailSoftArray2D(int r, int c) {
```

```
      rows = r;
      cols = c;
      a = new int[rows, cols];
      Length = rows * cols;
    }

  // This is the indexer for FailSoftArray2D.
  public int this[int index1, int index2] {
    // This is the get accessor.
    get {
      if(ok(index1, index2)) {
        ErrFlag = false;
        return a[index1, index2];
      } else {
        ErrFlag = true;
        return 0;
      }
    }

    // This is the set accessor.
    set {
      if(ok(index1, index2)) {
        a[index1, index2] = value;
        ErrFlag = false;
      }
      else ErrFlag = true;
    }
  }

  // Return true if indexes are within bounds.
  private bool ok(int index1, int index2) {
   if(index1 >= 0 & index1 < rows &
      index2 >= 0 & index2 < cols)
        return true;

   return false;
  }
}

// Demonstrate a 2D indexer.
class TwoDIndexerDemo {
  static void Main() {
    FailSoftArray2D fs = new FailSoftArray2D(3, 5);
    int x;

    // Show quiet failures.
    Console.WriteLine("Fail quietly.");
    for(int i=0; i < 6; i++)
      fs[i, i] = i*10;

    for(int i=0; i < 6; i++) {
      x = fs[i,i];
      if(x != -1) Console.Write(x + " ");
    }
```

```
      Console.WriteLine();

      // Now, display failures.
      Console.WriteLine("\nFail with error reports.");
      for(int i=0; i < 6; i++) {
        fs[i,i] = i*10;
        if(fs.ErrFlag)
          Console.WriteLine("fs[" + i + ", " + i + "] out-of-bounds");
      }

      for(int i=0; i < 6; i++) {
        x = fs[i,i];
        if(!fs.ErrFlag) Console.Write(x + " ");
        else
          Console.WriteLine("fs[" + i + ", " + i + "] out-of-bounds");
      }
    }
  }
}
```

The output from this program is shown here:

```
Fail quietly.
0 10 20 0 0 0

Fail with error reports.
fs[3, 3] out-of-bounds
fs[4, 4] out-of-bounds
fs[5, 5] out-of-bounds
0 10 20 fs[3, 3] out-of-bounds
fs[4, 4] out-of-bounds
fs[5, 5] out-of-bounds
```

Properties

Another type of class member is the *property*. As a general rule, a property combines a field with the methods that access it. As some examples earlier in this book have shown, you will often want to create a field that is available to users of an object, but you want to maintain control over the operations allowed on that field. For instance, you might want to limit the range of values that can be assigned to that field. While it is possible to accomplish this goal through the use of a private variable along with methods to access its value, a property offers a better, more streamlined approach.

Properties are similar to indexers. A property consists of a name along with **get** and **set** accessors. The accessors are used to get and set the value of a variable. The key benefit of a property is that its name can be used in expressions and assignments like a normal variable, but in actuality the **get** and **set** accessors are automatically invoked. This is similar to the way that an indexer's **get** and **set** accessors are automatically used.

The general form of a property is shown here:

type name {
  get {
    // get accessor code
  }

```
    set {
       // set accessor code
    }
  }
```

Here, *type* specifies the type of the property, such as **int**, and *name* is the name of the property. Once the property has been defined, any use of *name* results in a call to its appropriate accessor. The **set** accessor automatically receives a parameter called **value** that contains the value being assigned to the property.

It is important to understand that properties do not define storage locations. Instead, a property typically manages access to a field. It does not, itself, provide that field. The field must be specified independently of the property. (The exception is the *auto-implemented* property, which is described shortly.)

Here is a simple example that defines a property called **MyProp**, which is used to access the field **prop**. In this case, the property allows only positive values to be assigned.

```
// A simple property example.

using System;

class SimpProp {
  int prop; // field being managed by MyProp

  public SimpProp() { prop = 0; }

  /* This is the property that supports access to
     the private instance variable prop. It
     allows only positive values. */
  public int MyProp {
    get {
      return prop;
    }
    set {
      if(value >= 0) prop = value;
    }
  }
}

// Demonstrate a property.
class PropertyDemo {
  static void Main() {
    SimpProp ob = new SimpProp();

    Console.WriteLine("Original value of ob.MyProp: " + ob.MyProp);

    ob.MyProp = 100; // assign value
    Console.WriteLine("Value of ob.MyProp: " + ob.MyProp);

    // Can't assign negative value to prop.
    Console.WriteLine("Attempting to assign -10 to ob.MyProp");
    ob.MyProp = -10;
    Console.WriteLine("Value of ob.MyProp: " + ob.MyProp);
  }
}
```

Output from this program is shown here:

```
Original value of ob.MyProp: 0
Value of ob.MyProp: 100
Attempting to assign -10 to ob.MyProp
Value of ob.MyProp: 100
```

Let's examine this program carefully. The program defines one private field, called **prop**, and a property called **MyProp** that manages access to **prop**. As explained, a property by itself does not define a storage location. Instead, most properties simply manage access to a field. Furthermore, because **prop** is private, it can be accessed *only* through **MyProp**.

The property **MyProp** is specified as **public** so it can be accessed by code outside of its class. This makes sense because it provides access to **prop**, which is private. The **get** accessor simply returns the value of **prop**. The **set** accessor sets the value of **prop** if and only if that value is positive. Thus, the **MyProp** property controls what values **prop** can have. This is the essence of why properties are important.

The type of property defined by **MyProp** is called a read-write property because it allows its underlying field to be read and written. It is possible, however, to create read-only and write-only properties. To create a read-only property, define only a **get** accessor. To define a write-only property, define only a **set** accessor.

You can use a property to further improve the fail-soft array class. As you know, all arrays have a **Length** property associated with them. Up to now, the **FailSoftArray** class simply used a public integer field called **Length** for this purpose. This is not good practice, though, because it allows **Length** to be set to some value other than the length of the fail-soft array. (For example, a malicious programmer could intentionally corrupt its value.) We can remedy this situation by transforming **Length** into a read-only property, as shown in the following version of **FailSoftArray**:

```
// Add Length property to FailSoftArray.

using System;

class FailSoftArray {
  int[] a; // reference to underlying array
  int len; // length of array -- underlies Length property

  public bool ErrFlag; // indicates outcome of last operation

  // Construct array given its size.
  public FailSoftArray(int size) {
    a = new int[size];
    len = size;
  }

  // Read-only Length property.
  public int Length {
    get {
      return len;
    }
  }
```

```
  // This is the indexer for FailSoftArray.
  public int this[int index] {
    // This is the get accessor.
    get {
      if(ok(index)) {
        ErrFlag = false;
        return a[index];
      } else {
        ErrFlag = true;
        return 0;
      }
    }

    // This is the set accessor.
    set {
      if(ok(index)) {
        a[index] = value;
        ErrFlag = false;
      }
      else ErrFlag = true;
    }
  }

  // Return true if index is within bounds.
  private bool ok(int index) {
   if(index >= 0 & index < Length) return true;
   return false;
  }
}

// Demonstrate the improved fail-soft array.
class ImprovedFSDemo {
  static void Main() {
    FailSoftArray fs = new FailSoftArray(5);
    int x;

    // Can read Length.
    for(int i=0; i < fs.Length; i++)
      fs[i] = i*10;

    for(int i=0; i < fs.Length; i++) {
      x = fs[i];
      if(x != -1) Console.Write(x + " ");
    }
    Console.WriteLine();

    // fs.Length = 10; // Error, illegal!
  }
}
```

Length is now a property that uses the private variable **len** for its storage. **Length** defines only a **get** accessor, which means that it is read-only. Thus, **Length** can be read, but not changed. To prove this to yourself, try removing the comment symbol preceding this line in the program:

```
// fs.Length = 10; // Error, illegal!
```

When you try to compile, you will receive an error message stating that **Length** is read-only.

Although the addition of the **Length** property improves **FailSoftArray**, it is not the only improvement that properties can make. The **ErrFlag** member is also a prime candidate for conversion into a property since access to it should also be limited to read-only. Here is the final improvement of **FailSafeArray**. It creates a property called **Error** that uses the original **ErrFlag** variable as its storage, and **ErrFlag** is made private to **FailSoftArray**.

```
// Convert ErrFlag into a property.

using System;

class FailSoftArray {
  int[] a; // reference to underlying array
  int len; // length of array

  bool ErrFlag; // now private

  // Construct array given its size.
  public FailSoftArray(int size) {
    a = new int[size];
    len = size;
  }

  // Read-only Length property.
  public int Length {
    get {
      return len;
    }
  }

  // Read-only Error property.
  public bool Error {
    get {
      return ErrFlag;
    }
  }

  // This is the indexer for FailSoftArray.
  public int this[int index] {
    // This is the get accessor.
    get {
      if(ok(index)) {
        ErrFlag = false;
        return a[index];
      } else {
        ErrFlag = true;
        return 0;
      }
    }
```

```
    // This is the set accessor.
    set {
      if(ok(index)) {
        a[index] = value;
        ErrFlag = false;
      }
      else ErrFlag = true;
    }
  }

  // Return true if index is within bounds.
  private bool ok(int index) {
    if(index >= 0 & index < Length) return true;
    return false;
  }
}

// Demonstrate the improved fail-soft array.
class FinalFSDemo {
  static void Main() {
    FailSoftArray fs = new FailSoftArray(5);

    // Use Error property.
    for(int i=0; i < fs.Length + 1; i++) {
      fs[i] = i*10;
      if(fs.Error)
        Console.WriteLine("Error with index " + i);
    }
  }
}
```

The creation of the **Error** property has caused two changes to be made to **FailSoftArray**.
First, **ErrFlag** has been made private because it is now used as the underlying storage for
the **Error** property. Thus, it won't be available directly. Second, the read-only **Error** property
has been added. Now, programs that need to detect errors will interrogate **Error**. This is
demonstrated in **Main( )**, where a boundary error is intentionally generated, and the **Error**
property is used to detect it.

Auto-Implemented Properties

Beginning with C# 3.0, it became possible to implement very simple properties without
having to explicitly define the variable managed by the property. Instead, you can let the
compiler automatically supply the underlying variable. This is called an *auto-implemented
property*. It has the following general form:

> *type name* { get; set; }

Here, *type* specifies the type of the property and *name* specifies the name. Notice that **get**
and **set** are immediately followed by a semicolon. The accessors for an auto-implemented
property have no bodies. This syntax tells the compiler to automatically create a storage
location (sometimes referred to as a *backing field*) that holds the value. This variable is not
named and is not directly available to you. Instead, it can be accessed only through the
property.

Here is how a property called **UserCount** is declared using an auto-implemented property:

```
public int UserCount { get; set; }
```

Notice that no variable is explicitly declared. As explained, the compiler automatically generates an anonymous field that holds the value. Otherwise, **UserCount** acts like and is used like any other property.

Unlike normal properties, an auto-implemented property cannot be read-only or write-only. Both the **get** and **set** must be specified in all cases. However, you can approximate the same effect by declaring either **get** or **set** as **private**, as explained in "Use Access Modifiers with Accessors" later in this chapter.

Although auto-implemented properties offer convenience, their use is limited to those cases in which you do not need control over the getting or setting of the backing field. Remember, you cannot access the backing field directly. This means that there is no way to constrain the value an auto-implemented property can have. Thus, auto-implemented properties simply let the name of the property act as a proxy for the field, itself. However, sometimes this is exactly what you want. Also, they can be very useful in cases in which properties are used to expose functionality to a third party, possibly through a design tool.

Use Object Initializers with Properties

As discussed in Chapter 8, an *object initializer* provides an alternative to explicitly calling a constructor when creating an object. When using object initializers, you specify initial values for the fields and/or properties that you want to initialize. Furthermore, the object initializer syntax is the same for both properties or fields. For example, here is the object initializer demonstration program from Chapter 8, reworked to show the use of object initializers with properties. Recall that the version shown in Chapter 8 used fields. The only difference between this version of the program and the one shown in Chapter 8 is that **Count** and **Str** have been converted from fields into properties. The object initializer syntax is unchanged.

```
// Use object initializers with properties.

using System;

class MyClass {
  // These are now properties.
  public int Count { get; set; }
  public string Str { get; set; }
}

class ObjInitDemo {
  static void Main() {
    // Construct a MyClass object by using object initializers.
    MyClass obj = new MyClass { Count = 100, Str = "Testing" };

    Console.WriteLine(obj.Count + " " + obj.Str);
  }
}
```

As you can see, the properties **Count** and **Str** are set via object initializer expressions. The output is the same as that produced by the program in Chapter 8 and is shown here:

```
100 Testing
```

As explained in Chapter 8, the object initializer syntax is most useful when working with anonymous types generated by a LINQ expression. In most other cases, you will use the normal constructor syntax.

Property Restrictions

Properties have some important restrictions. First, because a property does not define a storage location, it cannot be passed as a **ref** or **out** parameter to a method. Second, you cannot overload a property. (You *can* have two different properties that both access the same variable, but this would be unusual.) Finally, a property should not alter the state of the underlying variable when the **get** accessor is called. Although this rule is not enforced by the compiler, violating it is semantically wrong. A **get** operation should be nonintrusive.

Use Access Modifiers with Accessors

By default, the **set** and **get** accessors have the same accessibility as the indexer or property of which they are a part. For example, if the property is declared **public**, then by default the **get** and **set** accessors are also public. It is possible, however, to give **set** or **get** its own access modifier, such as **private**. In all cases, the access modifier for an accessor must be more restrictive than the access specification of its property or indexer.

There are a number of reasons why you may want to restrict the accessibility of an accessor. For example, you might want to let anyone obtain the value of a property, but allow only members of its class to set the property. To do this, declare the **set** accessor as **private**. For example, here is a property called **MyProp** that has its **set** accessor specified as **private**.

```
// Use an access modifier with an accessor.

using System;

class PropAccess {
  int prop; // field being managed by MyProp

  public PropAccess() { prop = 0; }

  /* This is the property that supports access to
     the private instance variable prop. It allows
     any code to obtain the value of prop, but only
     other class members can set the value of prop. */
  public int MyProp {
    get {
      return prop;
    }
    private set { // now, private
      prop = value;
    }
  }
```

```
    // This class member increments the value of MyProp.
    public void IncrProp() {
      MyProp++; // OK, in same class.
    }
}

// Demonstrate accessor access modifier.
class PropAccessDemo {
  static void Main() {
    PropAccess ob = new PropAccess();

    Console.WriteLine("Original value of ob.MyProp: " + ob.MyProp);

//    ob.MyProp = 100; // can't access set

    ob.IncrProp();
    Console.WriteLine("Value of ob.MyProp after increment: "
                      + ob.MyProp);
  }
}
```

In the **PropAccess** class, the **set** accessor is specified **private**. This means that it can be accessed by other class members, such as **IncrProp()**, but it cannot be accessed by code outside of **PropAccess**. This is why the attempt to assign **ob.MyProp** a value inside **PropAccessDemo** is commented out.

Perhaps the most important use of restricting an accessor's access is found when working with auto-implemented properties. As explained, it is not possible to create a read-only or write-only auto-implemented property because both the **get** and **set** accessors must be specified when the auto-implemented property is declared. However, you can gain much the same effect by declaring either **get** or **set** as **private**. For example, this declares what is effectively a read-only, auto-implemented **Length** property for the **FailSoftArray** class shown earlier.

```
public int Length { get; private set; }
```

Because **set** is **private**, **Length** can be set only by code within its class. Outside its class, an attempt to change **Length** is illegal. Thus, outside its class, **Length** is effectively read-only. The same technique can also be applied to the **Error** property, like this:

```
public bool Error { get; private set; }
```

This allows **Error** to be read, but not set, by code outside **FailSoftArray**.

To try the auto-implemented version of **Length** and **Error** with **FailSoftArray**, first remove the **len** and **ErrFlag** variables. They are no longer needed. Then, replace each use of **len** inside **FailSoftArray** with **Length** and each use of **ErrFlag** with **Error**. Here is the updated version of **FailSoftArray** along with a **Main()** method to demonstrate it:

```
// Use read-only, auto-implemented properties for Length and Error.

using System;
```

```
class FailSoftArray {
  int[] a; // reference to underlying array

  // Construct array given its size.
  public FailSoftArray(int size) {
    a = new int[size];
    Length = size;
  }

  // An auto-implemented, read-only Length property.
  public int Length { get; private set; }

  // An auto-implemented, read-only Error property.
  public bool Error { get; private set; }

  // This is the indexer for FailSoftArray.
  public int this[int index] {
    // This is the get accessor.
    get {
      if(ok(index)) {
        Error = false;
        return a[index];
      } else {
        Error = true;
        return 0;
      }
    }

    // This is the set accessor.
    set {
      if(ok(index)) {
        a[index] = value;
        Error = false;
      }
      else Error = true;
    }
  }

  // Return true if index is within bounds.
  private bool ok(int index) {
   if(index >= 0 & index < Length) return true;
   return false;
  }
}

// Demonstrate the improved fail-soft array.
class FinalFSDemo {
  static void Main() {
    FailSoftArray fs = new FailSoftArray(5);

    // Use Error property.
    for(int i=0; i < fs.Length + 1; i++) {
      fs[i] = i*10;
```

```
    if(fs.Error)
      Console.WriteLine("Error with index " + i);
   }
 }
}
```

This version of **FailSoftArray** works the same as the previous version, but it does not contain the explicitly declared backing fields.

Here are some restrictions that apply to using access modifiers with accessors. First, only the **set** or **get** accessor can be modified, not both. Furthermore, the access modifier must be more restrictive than the access level of the property or indexer. Finally, an access modifier cannot be used when declaring an accessor within an interface or when implementing an accessor specified by an interface. (Interfaces are described in Chapter 12.)

Using Indexers and Properties

Although the preceding examples have demonstrated the basic mechanism of indexers and properties, they haven't displayed their full power. To conclude this chapter, a class called **RangeArray** is developed that uses indexers and properties to create an array type in which the index range of the array is determined by the programmer.

As you know, in C# all arrays begin indexing at zero. However, some applications would benefit from an array that allows indexes to begin at any arbitrary point. For example, in some situations it might be more convenient for an array to begin indexing with 1. In another situation, it might be beneficial to allow negative indexes, such as an array that runs from –5 to 5. The **RangeArray** class developed here allows these and other types of indexing.

Using **RangeArray**, you can write code like this:

```
RangeArray ra = new RangeArray(-5, 10); // array with indexes from -5 to 10

for(int i=-5; i <= 10; i++) ra[i] = i; // index from -5 to 10
```

As you can guess, the first line constructs a **RangeArray** that runs from –5 to 10, inclusive. The first argument specifies the beginning index. The second argument specifies the ending index. Once **ra** has been constructed, it can be indexed from –5 to 10.

The entire **RangeArray** class is shown here, along with **RangeArrayDemo**, which demonstrates the array. As implemented here, **RangeArray** supports arrays of **int**, but you can change the data type, if desired.

```
/* Create a specifiable range array class.
   The RangeArray class allows indexing to begin at
   some value other than 0. When you create a RangeArray,
   you specify the beginning and ending index. Negative
   indexes are also allowed. For example, you can create
   arrays that index from -5 to 5, 1 to 10, or 50 to 56.
*/

using System;

class RangeArray {
  // Private data.
  int[] a; // reference to underlying array
```

```
    int lowerBound; // smallest index
    int upperBound; // largest index

    // An auto-implemented, read-only Length property.
    public int Length { get; private set; }

    // An auto-implemented, read-only Error property.
    public bool Error { get; private set; }

    // Construct array given its size.
    public RangeArray(int low, int high) {
      high++;
      if(high <= low) {
        Console.WriteLine("Invalid Indices");
        high = 1; // create a minimal array for safety
        low = 0;
      }
      a = new int[high - low];
      Length = high - low;

      lowerBound = low;
      upperBound = --high;
    }

    // This is the indexer for RangeArray.
    public int this[int index] {
      // This is the get accessor.
      get {
        if(ok(index)) {
          Error = false;
          return a[index - lowerBound];
        } else {
          Error = true;
          return 0;
        }
      }

      // This is the set accessor.
      set {
        if(ok(index)) {
          a[index - lowerBound] = value;
          Error = false;
        }
        else Error = true;
      }
    }

    // Return true if index is within bounds.
    private bool ok(int index) {
      if(index >= lowerBound & index <= upperBound) return true;
      return false;
    }
}
```

```
// Demonstrate the index-range array.
class RangeArrayDemo {
  static void Main() {
    RangeArray ra = new RangeArray(-5, 5);
    RangeArray ra2 = new RangeArray(1, 10);
    RangeArray ra3 = new RangeArray(-20, -12);

    // Demonstrate ra.
    Console.WriteLine("Length of ra: " + ra.Length);

    for(int i = -5; i <= 5; i++)
      ra[i] = i;

    Console.Write("Contents of ra: ");
    for(int i = -5; i <= 5; i++)
      Console.Write(ra[i] + " ");

    Console.WriteLine("\n");

    // Demonstrate ra2.
    Console.WriteLine("Length of ra2: " + ra2.Length);

    for(int i = 1; i <= 10; i++)
      ra2[i] = i;

    Console.Write("Contents of ra2: ");
    for(int i = 1; i <= 10; i++)
      Console.Write(ra2[i] + " ");

    Console.WriteLine("\n");

    // Demonstrate ra3.
    Console.WriteLine("Length of ra3: " + ra3.Length);

    for(int i = -20; i <= -12; i++)
      ra3[i] = i;

    Console.Write("Contents of ra3: ");
    for(int i = -20; i <= -12; i++)
      Console.Write(ra3[i] + " ");

    Console.WriteLine("\n");
  }
}
```

The output from the program is shown here:

```
Length of ra: 11
Contents of ra: -5 -4 -3 -2 -1 0 1 2 3 4 5

Length of ra2: 10
Contents of ra2: 1 2 3 4 5 6 7 8 9 10

Length of ra3: 9
Contents of ra3: -20 -19 -18 -17 -16 -15 -14 -13 -12
```

As the output verifies, objects of type **RangeArray** can be indexed in ways other than starting at zero. Let's look more closely at how **RangeArray** is implemented.

RangeArray begins by defining the following private instance variables:

```
// Private data.
int[] a; // reference to underlying array
int lowerBound; // smallest index
int upperBound; // largest index
```

The underlying array is referred to by **a**. This array is allocated by the **RangeArray** constructor. The index of the lower bound of the array is stored in **lowerBound**, and the index of the upper bound is stored in **upperBound**.

Next, the auto-implemented, read-only properties **Length** and **Error** are declared:

```
// An auto-implemented, read-only Length property.
public int Length { get; private set; }

// An auto-implemented, read-only Error property.
public bool Error { get; private set; }
```

Notice that for both properties, the **set** accessor is private. As explained earlier in this chapter, this results in what is effectively a read-only, auto-implemented property.

The **RangeArray** constructor is shown here:

```
// Construct array given its size.
public RangeArray(int low, int high) {
  high++;
  if(high <= low) {
    Console.WriteLine("Invalid Indices");
    high = 1; // create a minimal array for safety
    low = 0;
  }
  a = new int[high - low];
  Length = high - low;

  lowerBound = low;
  upperBound = --high;
}
```

A **RangeArray** is constructed by passing the lower bound index in **low** and the upper bound index in **high**. The value of **high** is then incremented because the indexes specified are inclusive. Next, a check is made to ensure that the upper index is greater than the lower index. If not, an error is reported and a one-element array is created. Next, storage for the array is allocated and assigned to **a**. Then the **Length** property is set equal to the number of elements in the array. Finally, **lowerBound** and **upperBound** are set.

Next, **RangeArray** implements its indexer, as shown here:

```
// This is the indexer for RangeArray.
public int this[int index] {
  // This is the get accessor.
  get {
    if(ok(index)) {
```

```
      Error = false;
      return a[index - lowerBound];
    } else {
      Error = true;
      return 0;
    }
  }

  // This is the set accessor.
  set {
    if(ok(index)) {
      a[index - lowerBound] = value;
      Error = false;
    }
    else Error = true;
  }
}
```

This indexer is similar to the one used by **FailSoftArray**, with one important exception. Notice the expression that indexes **a**. It is

```
index - lowerBound
```

This expression transforms the index passed in **index** into a zero-based index suitable for use on **a**. This expression works whether **lowerBound** is positive, negative, or zero.

The **ok( )** method is shown here:

```
// Return true if index is within bounds.
private bool ok(int index) {
  if(index >= lowerBound & index <= upperBound) return true;
  return false;
}
```

It is similar to the one used by **FailSoftArray** except that the range is checked by testing it against the values in **lowerBound** and **upperBound**.

RangeArray illustrates just one kind of custom array that you can create through the use of indexers and properties. There are, of course, several others. For example, you can create dynamic arrays, which expand and contract as needed, associative arrays, and sparse arrays. You might want to try creating one of these types of arrays as an exercise.

Inheritance

Inheritance is one of the three foundational principles of object-oriented programming because it allows the creation of hierarchical classifications. Using inheritance, you can create a general class that defines traits common to a set of related items. This class can then be inherited by other, more specific classes, each adding those things that are unique to it.

In the language of C#, a class that is inherited is called a *base class*. The class that does the inheriting is called a *derived class*. Therefore, a derived class is a specialized version of a base class. It inherits all of the variables, methods, properties, and indexers defined by the base class and adds its own unique elements.

Inheritance Basics

C# supports inheritance by allowing one class to incorporate another class into its declaration. This is done by specifying a base class when a derived class is declared. Let's begin with an example. The following class called **TwoDShape** stores the width and height of a two-dimensional object, such as a square, rectangle, triangle, and so on.

```
// A class for two-dimensional objects.
class TwoDShape {
  public double Width;
  public double Height;

  public void ShowDim() {
    Console.WriteLine("Width and height are " +
                      Width + " and " + Height);
  }
}
```

TwoDShape can be used as a base class (that is, as a starting point) for classes that describe specific types of two-dimensional objects. For example, the following program uses **TwoDShape** to derive a class called **Triangle**. Pay close attention to the way that **Triangle** is declared.

```
// A simple class hierarchy.

using System;

// A class for two-dimensional objects.
class TwoDShape {
  public double Width;
  public double Height;

  public void ShowDim() {
    Console.WriteLine("Width and height are " +
                      Width + " and " + Height);
  }
}

// Triangle is derived from TwoDShape.
class Triangle : TwoDShape {
  public string Style; // style of triangle

  // Return area of triangle.
  public double Area() {
    return Width * Height / 2;
  }

  // Display a triangle's style.
  public void ShowStyle() {
    Console.WriteLine("Triangle is " + Style);
  }
}

class Shapes {
  static void Main() {
    Triangle t1 = new Triangle();
    Triangle t2 = new Triangle();

    t1.Width = 4.0;
    t1.Height = 4.0;
    t1.Style = "isosceles";

    t2.Width = 8.0;
    t2.Height = 12.0;
    t2.Style = "right";

    Console.WriteLine("Info for t1: ");
    t1.ShowStyle();
    t1.ShowDim();
    Console.WriteLine("Area is " + t1.Area());

    Console.WriteLine();

    Console.WriteLine("Info for t2: ");
    t2.ShowStyle();
    t2.ShowDim();
```

```
      Console.WriteLine("Area is " + t2.Area());
   }
}
```

The output from this program is shown here:

```
Info for t1:
Triangle is isosceles
Width and height are 4 and 4
Area is 8

Info for t2:
Triangle is right
Width and height are 8 and 12
Area is 48
```

The **Triangle** class creates a specific type of **TwoDShape**, in this case, a triangle. The **Triangle** class includes all of **TwoDShape** and adds the field **Style**, the method **Area( )**, and the method **ShowStyle( )**. A description of the type of triangle is stored in **Style**; **Area( )** computes and returns the area of the triangle; and **ShowStyle( )** displays the triangle style.

Notice the syntax that **Triangle** uses to inherit **TwoDShape**:

```
class Triangle : TwoDShape {
```

This syntax can be generalized. Whenever one class inherits another, the base class name follows the name of the derived class, separated by a colon. In C#, the syntax for inheriting a class is remarkably simple and easy to use.

Because **Triangle** includes all of the members of its base class, **TwoDShape**, it can access **Width** and **Height** inside **Area( )**. Also, inside **Main( )**, objects **t1** and **t2** can refer to **Width** and **Height** directly, as if they were part of **Triangle**. Figure 11-1 depicts conceptually how **TwoDShape** is incorporated into **Triangle**.

Even though **TwoDShape** is a base for **Triangle**, it is also a completely independent, stand-alone class. Being a base class for a derived class does not mean that the base class cannot be used by itself. For example, the following is perfectly valid:

```
TwoDShape shape = new TwoDShape();

shape.Width = 10;
shape.Height = 20;

shape.ShowDim();
```

Of course, an object of **TwoDShape** has no knowledge of or access to any classes derived from **TwoDShape**.

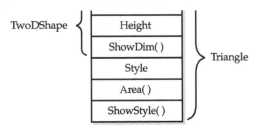

FIGURE 11-1   A conceptual depiction of the **Triangle** class

The general form of a **class** declaration that inherits a base class is shown here:

class *derived-class-name* : *base-class-name* {
    // body of class
}

You can specify only one base class for any derived class that you create. C# does not support the inheritance of multiple base classes into a single derived class. (This differs from C++, in which you can inherit multiple base classes. Be aware of this when converting C++ code to C#.) You can, however, create a hierarchy of inheritance in which a derived class becomes a base class of another derived class. (Of course, no class can be a base class of itself, either directly or indirectly.) In all cases, a derived class inherits all of the members of its base class. This includes instance variables, methods, properties, and indexers.

A major advantage of inheritance is that once you have created a base class that defines the attributes common to a set of objects, it can be used to create any number of more specific derived classes. Each derived class can precisely tailor its own classification. For example, here is another class derived from **TwoDShape** that encapsulates rectangles:

```
// A derived class of TwoDShape for rectangles.
class Rectangle : TwoDShape {
  // Return true if the rectangle is square.
  public bool IsSquare() {
    if(Width == Height) return true;
    return false;
  }

  // Return area of the rectangle.
  public double Area() {
    return Width * Height;
  }
}
```

The **Rectangle** class includes **TwoDShape** and adds the methods **IsSquare( )**, which determines if the rectangle is square, and **Area( )**, which computes the area of a rectangle.

Member Access and Inheritance

As explained in Chapter 8, members of a class are often declared private to prevent their unauthorized use or tampering. Inheriting a class *does not* overrule the private access restriction. Thus, even though a derived class includes all of the members of its base class, it cannot access those members of the base class that are private. For example, if, as shown here, **Width** and **Height** are made private in **TwoDShape**, then **Triangle** will not be able to access them:

```
// Access to private members is not inherited.

// This example will not compile.
using System;

// A class for two-dimensional objects.
class TwoDShape {
```

```
    double Width;  // now private
    double Height; // now private

  public void ShowDim() {
    Console.WriteLine("Width and height are " +
                      Width + " and " + Height);
  }
}

// Triangle is derived from TwoDShape.
class Triangle : TwoDShape {
  public string Style; // style of triangle

  // Return area of triangle.
  public double Area() {
    return Width * Height / 2; // Error, can't access private member
  }

  // Display a triangle's style.
  public void ShowStyle() {
    Console.WriteLine("Triangle is " + Style);
  }
}
```

The **Triangle** class will not compile because the use of **Width** and **Height** inside the **Area( )** method is illegal. Since **Width** and **Height** are now private, they are accessible only to other members of their own class. Derived classes have no access to them.

REMEMBER   *A private class member will remain private to its class. It is not accessible to any code outside its class, including derived classes.*

At first, you might think that it is a serious restriction that derived classes do not have access to the private members of base classes because it would prevent the use of private members in many situations. However, this is not true; C# provides various solutions. One is to use **protected** members, which is described in the next section. A second is to use public properties to provide access to private data.

As explained in the previous chapter, a property allows you to manage access to an instance variable. For example, you can enforce constraints on its values, or you can make the variable read-only. By making a property public, but declaring its underlying variable private, a derived class can still use the property, but it cannot directly access the underlying private variable.

Here is a rewrite of the **TwoDShape** class that makes **Width** and **Height** into properties. In the process, it ensures that the values of **Width** and **Height** will be positive. This would allow you, for example, to specify the **Width** and **Height** using the coordinates of the shape in any quadrant of the Cartesian plane without having to first obtain their absolute values.

```
// Use public properties to set and get private members.

using System;

// A class for two-dimensional objects.
```

```csharp
class TwoDShape {
  double pri_width;  // now private
  double pri_height; // now private

  // Properties for width and height.
  public double Width {
     get { return pri_width; }
     set { pri_width = value < 0 ? -value : value; }
  }

  public double Height {
     get { return pri_height; }
     set { pri_height = value < 0 ? -value : value; }
  }

  public void ShowDim() {
    Console.WriteLine("Width and height are " +
                       Width + " and " + Height);
  }
}

// A derived class of TwoDShape for triangles.
class Triangle : TwoDShape {
  public string Style; // style of triangle

  // Return area of triangle.
  public double Area() {
    return Width * Height / 2;
  }

  // Display a triangle's style.
  public void ShowStyle() {
    Console.WriteLine("Triangle is " + Style);
  }
}

class Shapes2 {
  static void Main() {
    Triangle t1 = new Triangle();
    Triangle t2 = new Triangle();

    t1.Width = 4.0;
    t1.Height = 4.0;
    t1.Style = "isosceles";

    t2.Width = 8.0;
    t2.Height = 12.0;
    t2.Style = "right";

    Console.WriteLine("Info for t1: ");
    t1.ShowStyle();
    t1.ShowDim();
    Console.WriteLine("Area is " + t1.Area());
```

```
    Console.WriteLine();

    Console.WriteLine("Info for t2: ");
    t2.ShowStyle();
    t2.ShowDim();
    Console.WriteLine("Area is " + t2.Area());
  }
}
```

In this version, the properties **Width** and **Height** provide access to the private members, **pri_width** and **pri_height**, which actually store the values. Therefore, even though **pri_width** and **pri_height** are private to **TwoDShape**, their values can still be set and obtained through their corresponding public properties.

When referring to base and derived classes, sometimes the terms *superclass* and *subclass* are used. These terms come from Java programming. What Java calls a superclass, C# calls a base class. What Java calls a subclass, C# calls a derived class. You will commonly hear both sets of terms applied to a class of either language, but this book will continue to use the standard C# terms. C++ also uses the base-class/derived-class terminology.

Using Protected Access

As just explained, a private member of a base class is not accessible to a derived class. This would seem to imply that if you wanted a derived class to have access to some member in the base class, it would need to be public. Of course, making the member public also makes it available to all other code, which may not be desirable. Fortunately, this implication is untrue because C# allows you to create a *protected member*. A protected member is public within a class hierarchy, but private outside that hierarchy.

A protected member is created by using the **protected** access modifier. When a member of a class is declared as **protected**, that member is, with one important exception, private. The exception occurs when a protected member is inherited. In this case, a protected member of the base class becomes a protected member of the derived class and is, therefore, accessible to the derived class. Therefore, by using **protected**, you can create class members that are private to their class but that can still be inherited and accessed by a derived class.

Here is a simple example that uses **protected**:

```
// Demonstrate protected.

using System;

class B {
  protected int i, j; // private to B, but accessible by D

  public void Set(int a, int b) {
    i = a;
    j = b;
  }

  public void Show() {
    Console.WriteLine(i + " " + j);
  }
}
```

```
class D : B {
  int k; // private

  // D can access B's i and j
  public void Setk() {
    k = i * j;
  }

  public void Showk() {
    Console.WriteLine(k);
  }
}

class ProtectedDemo {
  static void Main() {
    D ob = new D();

    ob.Set(2, 3); // OK, known to D
    ob.Show();    // OK, known to D

    ob.Setk();  // OK, part of D
    ob.Showk(); // OK, part of D
  }
}
```

In this example, because **B** is inherited by **D** and because **i** and **j** are declared as **protected** in **B**, the **Setk( )** method can access them. If **i** and **j** had been declared as private by **B**, then **D** would not have access to them, and the program would not compile.

Like **public** and **private**, **protected** status stays with a member no matter how many layers of inheritance are involved. Therefore, when a derived class is used as a base class for another derived class, any protected member of the initial base class that is inherited by the first derived class is also inherited as protected by a second derived class.

Although **protected** access is quite useful, it doesn't apply in all situations. For example, in the case of **TwoDShape** shown in the preceding section, we specifically want the **Width** and **Height** values to be publicly accessible. It's just that we want to manage the values they are assigned. Therefore, declaring them **protected** is not an option. In this case, the use of properties supplies the proper solution by controlling, rather than preventing, access. Remember, use **protected** when you want to create a member that is accessible throughout a class hierarchy, but otherwise private. To manage access to a value, use a property.

Constructors and Inheritance

In a hierarchy, it is possible for both base classes and derived classes to have their own constructors. This raises an important question: What constructor is responsible for building an object of the derived class? The one in the base class, the one in the derived class, or both? Here is the answer: The constructor for the base class constructs the base class portion of the object, and the constructor for the derived class constructs the derived class part. This makes sense because the base class has no knowledge of or access to any element in a derived class. Thus, their construction must be separate. The preceding examples have relied upon the default constructors created automatically by C#, so this was not an issue. However, in practice, most classes will define constructors. Here you will see how to handle this situation.

When only the derived class defines a constructor, the process is straightforward: Simply construct the derived class object. The base class portion of the object is constructed automatically using its default constructor. For example, here is a reworked version of **Triangle** that defines a constructor. It also makes **Style** private since it is now set by the constructor.

```
// Add a constructor to Triangle.

using System;

// A class for two-dimensional objects.
class TwoDShape {
  double pri_width;
  double pri_height;

  // Properties for Width and Height.
  public double Width {
     get { return pri_width; }
     set { pri_width = value < 0 ? -value : value; }
  }

  public double Height {
     get { return pri_height; }
     set { pri_height = value < 0 ? -value : value; }
  }

  public void ShowDim() {
    Console.WriteLine("Width and height are " +
                      Width + " and " + Height);
  }
}

// A derived class of TwoDShape for triangles.
class Triangle : TwoDShape {
  string Style;

  // Constructor.
  public Triangle(string s, double w, double h) {
    Width = w;  // init the base class
    Height = h; // init the base class

    Style = s;  // init the derived class
  }

  // Return area of triangle.
  public double Area() {
    return Width * Height / 2;
  }

  // Display a triangle's style.
  public void ShowStyle() {
    Console.WriteLine("Triangle is " + Style);
  }
}
```

```
class Shapes3 {
  static void Main() {
    Triangle t1 = new Triangle("isosceles", 4.0, 4.0);
    Triangle t2 = new Triangle("right", 8.0, 12.0);

    Console.WriteLine("Info for t1: ");
    t1.ShowStyle();
    t1.ShowDim();
    Console.WriteLine("Area is " + t1.Area());

    Console.WriteLine();

    Console.WriteLine("Info for t2: ");
    t2.ShowStyle();
    t2.ShowDim();
    Console.WriteLine("Area is " + t2.Area());
  }
}
```

Here, **Triangle**'s constructor initializes the members of **TwoDShape** that it inherits along with its own **Style** field.

When both the base class and the derived class define constructors, the process is a bit more complicated because both the base class and derived class constructors must be executed. In this case, you must use another of C#'s keywords, **base**, which has two uses. The first use is to call a base class constructor. The second is to access a member of the base class that has been hidden by a member of a derived class. Here, we will look at its first use.

Calling Base Class Constructors

A derived class can call a constructor defined in its base class by using an expanded form of the derived class' constructor declaration and the **base** keyword. The general form of this expanded declaration is shown here:

derived-constructor(*parameter-list*) : base(*arg-list*) {
    // body of constructor
}

Here, *arg-list* specifies any arguments needed by the constructor in the base class. Notice the placement of the colon.

To see how **base** is used, consider the version of **TwoDShape** in the following program. It defines a constructor that initializes the **Width** and **Height** properties. This constructor is then called by the **Triangle** constructor.

```
// Add constructor to TwoDShape.

using System;

// A class for two-dimensional objects.
class TwoDShape {
  double pri_width;
  double pri_height;
```

```csharp
  // Constructor for TwoDShape.
  public TwoDShape(double w, double h) {
    Width = w;
    Height = h;
  }

  // Properties for Width and Height.
  public double Width {
    get { return pri_width; }
    set { pri_width = value < 0 ? -value : value; }
  }

  public double Height {
    get { return pri_height; }
    set { pri_height = value < 0 ? -value : value; }
  }

  public void ShowDim() {
    Console.WriteLine("Width and height are " +
                      Width + " and " + Height);
  }
}

 // A derived class of TwoDShape for triangles.
class Triangle : TwoDShape {
  string Style;

  // Call the base class constructor.
  public Triangle(string s, double w, double h) : base(w, h) {
    Style = s;
  }

  // Return area of triangle.
  public double Area() {
    return Width * Height / 2;
  }

  // Display a triangle's style.
  public void ShowStyle() {
    Console.WriteLine("Triangle is " + Style);
  }
}

class Shapes4 {
  static void Main() {
    Triangle t1 = new Triangle("isosceles", 4.0, 4.0);
    Triangle t2 = new Triangle("right", 8.0, 12.0);

    Console.WriteLine("Info for t1: ");
    t1.ShowStyle();
    t1.ShowDim();
    Console.WriteLine("Area is " + t1.Area());
```

```
    Console.WriteLine();

    Console.WriteLine("Info for t2: ");
    t2.ShowStyle();
    t2.ShowDim();
    Console.WriteLine("Area is " + t2.Area());
  }
}
```

Notice that the **Triangle** constructor is now declared as shown here.

```
public Triangle(string s, double w, double h) : base(w, h) {
```

In this version, **Triangle( )** calls **base** with the parameters **w** and **h**. This causes the **TwoDShape( )** constructor to be called, which initializes **Width** and **Height** using these values. **Triangle** no longer initializes these values itself. It need only initialize the value unique to it: **Style**. This leaves **TwoDShape** free to construct its subobject in any manner that it chooses. Furthermore, **TwoDShape** can add functionality about which existing derived classes have no knowledge, thus preventing existing code from breaking.

Any form of constructor defined by the base class can be called by **base**. The constructor executed will be the one that matches the arguments. For example, here are expanded versions of both **TwoDShape** and **Triangle** that include default constructors and constructors that take one argument.

```
// Add more constructors to TwoDShape.

using System;

class TwoDShape {
  double pri_width;
  double pri_height;

  // Default constructor.
  public TwoDShape() {
    Width = Height = 0.0;
  }

  // Constructor for TwoDShape.
  public TwoDShape(double w, double h) {
    Width = w;
    Height = h;
  }

  // Construct object with equal width and height.
  public TwoDShape(double x) {
    Width = Height = x;
  }

  // Properties for Width and Height.
  public double Width {
    get { return pri_width; }
    set { pri_width = value < 0 ? -value : value; }
  }
```

```
  public double Height {
     get { return pri_height; }
     set { pri_height = value < 0 ? -value : value; }
  }

  public void ShowDim() {
    Console.WriteLine("Width and height are " +
                      Width + " and " + Height);
  }
}

// A derived class of TwoDShape for triangles.
class Triangle : TwoDShape {
  string Style;

  /* A default constructor. This automatically invokes
     the default constructor of TwoDShape. */
  public Triangle() {
    Style = "null";
  }

  // Constructor that takes three arguments.
  public Triangle(string s, double w, double h) : base(w, h) {
    Style = s;
  }

  // Construct an isosceles triangle.
  public Triangle(double x) : base(x) {
    Style = "isosceles";
  }

  // Return area of triangle.
  public double Area() {
    return Width * Height / 2;
  }

  // Display a triangle's style.
  public void ShowStyle() {
    Console.WriteLine("Triangle is " + Style);
  }
}

class Shapes5 {
  static void Main() {
    Triangle t1 = new Triangle();
    Triangle t2 = new Triangle("right", 8.0, 12.0);
    Triangle t3 = new Triangle(4.0);

    t1 = t2;

    Console.WriteLine("Info for t1: ");
    t1.ShowStyle();
    t1.ShowDim();
    Console.WriteLine("Area is " + t1.Area());
```

```
    Console.WriteLine();

    Console.WriteLine("Info for t2: ");
    t2.ShowStyle();
    t2.ShowDim();
    Console.WriteLine("Area is " + t2.Area());

    Console.WriteLine();

    Console.WriteLine("Info for t3: ");
    t3.ShowStyle();
    t3.ShowDim();
    Console.WriteLine("Area is " + t3.Area());

    Console.WriteLine();
  }
}
```

Here is the output from this version:

```
Info for t1:
Triangle is right
Width and height are 8 and 12
Area is 48

Info for t2:
Triangle is right
Width and height are 8 and 12
Area is 48

Info for t3:
Triangle is isosceles
Width and height are 4 and 4
Area is 8
```

Let's review the key concepts behind **base**. When a derived class specifies a **base** clause, it is calling the constructor of its immediate base class. Thus, **base** always refers to the base class immediately above the calling class. This is true even in a multileveled hierarchy. You pass arguments to the base constructor by specifying them as arguments to **base**. If no **base** clause is present, then the base class' default constructor is called automatically.

Inheritance and Name Hiding

It is possible for a derived class to define a member that has the same name as a member in its base class. When this happens, the member in the base class is hidden within the derived class. While this is not technically an error in C#, the compiler will issue a warning message. This warning alerts you to the fact that a name is being hidden. If your intent is to hide a base class member, then to prevent this warning, the derived class member must be preceded by the **new** keyword. Understand that this use of **new** is separate and distinct from its use when creating an object instance.

Here is an example of name hiding:

```
// An example of inheritance-related name hiding.

using System;

class A {
  public int i = 0;
}

// Create a derived class.
class B : A {
  new int i; // this i hides the i in A

  public B(int b) {
    i = b; // i in B
  }

  public void Show() {
    Console.WriteLine("i in derived class: " + i);
  }
}

class NameHiding {
  static void Main() {
    B ob = new B(2);

    ob.Show();
  }
}
```

First, notice the use of **new** in this line.

```
new int i; // this i hides the i in A
```

In essence, it tells the compiler that you know a new variable called **i** is being created that hides the **i** in the base class **A**. If you leave **new** out, a warning is generated.

The output produced by this program is shown here:

```
i in derived class: 2
```

Since **B** defines its own instance variable called **i**, it hides the **i** in **A**. Therefore, when **Show( )** is invoked on an object of type **B**, the value of **i** as defined by **B** is displayed—not the one defined in **A**.

Using base to Access a Hidden Name

There is a second form of **base** that acts somewhat like **this**, except that it always refers to the base class of the derived class in which it is used. This usage has the following general form:

base.*member*

Here, *member* can be either a method or an instance variable. This form of **base** is most applicable to situations in which member names of a derived class hide members by the same name in the base class. Consider this version of the class hierarchy from the preceding example:

```
// Using base to overcome name hiding.

using System;

class A {
  public int i = 0;
}

// Create a derived class.
class B : A {
  new int i; // this i hides the i in A

  public B(int a, int b) {
    base.i = a; // this uncovers the i in A
    i = b; // i in B
  }

  public void Show() {
    // This displays the i in A.
    Console.WriteLine("i in base class: " + base.i);

    // This displays the i in B.
    Console.WriteLine("i in derived class: " + i);
  }
}

class UncoverName {
  static void Main() {
    B ob = new B(1, 2);

    ob.Show();
  }
}
```

This program displays the following:

```
i in base class: 1
i in derived class: 2
```

Although the instance variable **i** in **B** hides the **i** in **A**, **base** allows access to the **i** defined in the base class.

Hidden methods can also be called through the use of **base**. For example, in the following code, class **B** inherits class **A**, and both **A** and **B** declare a method called **Show()**. Inside, **B**'s **Show()**, the version of **Show()** defined by **A** is called through the use of **base**.

```
// Call a hidden method.

using System;

class A {
```

```
  public int i = 0;

  // Show() in A
  public void Show() {
    Console.WriteLine("i in base class: " + i);
  }
}

// Create a derived class.
class B : A {
  new int i; // this i hides the i in A

  public B(int a, int b) {
    base.i = a; // this uncovers the i in A
    i = b; // i in B
  }

  // This hides Show() in A. Notice the use of new.
  new public void Show() {
    base.Show(); // this calls Show() in A

    // this displays the i in B
    Console.WriteLine("i in derived class: " + i);
  }
}

class UncoverName {
  static void Main() {
    B ob = new B(1, 2);

    ob.Show();
  }
}
```

The output from the program is shown here:

```
i in base class: 1
i in derived class: 2
```

As you can see, **base.Show( )** calls the base class version of **Show( )**.

One other point: Notice that **new** is used in this program to tell the compiler that you know a new method called **Show( )** is being declared that hides the **Show( )** in **A**.

Creating a Multilevel Hierarchy

Up to this point, we have been using simple class hierarchies consisting of only a base class and a derived class. However, you can build hierarchies that contain as many layers of inheritance as you like. As mentioned, it is perfectly acceptable to use a derived class as a base class of another. For example, given three classes called **A**, **B**, and **C**, **C** can be derived from **B**, which can be derived from **A**. When this type of situation occurs, each derived class inherits all of the traits found in all of its base classes. In this case, **C** inherits all aspects of **B** and **A**.

To see how a multilevel hierarchy can be useful, consider the following program. In it, the derived class **Triangle** is used as a base class to create the derived class called **ColorTriangle**. **ColorTriangle** inherits all of the traits of **Triangle** and **TwoDShape** and adds a field called **color**, which holds the color of the triangle.

```csharp
// A multilevel hierarchy.

using System;

class TwoDShape {
  double pri_width;
  double pri_height;

  // Default constructor.
  public TwoDShape() {
    Width = Height = 0.0;
  }

  // Constructor for TwoDShape.
  public TwoDShape(double w, double h) {
    Width = w;
    Height = h;
  }

  // Construct object with equal width and height.
  public TwoDShape(double x) {
    Width = Height = x;
  }

  // Properties for Width and Height.
  public double Width {
     get { return pri_width; }
     set { pri_width = value < 0 ? -value : value; }
  }

  public double Height {
     get { return pri_height; }
     set { pri_height = value < 0 ? -value : value; }
  }

  public void ShowDim() {
    Console.WriteLine("Width and height are " +
                      Width + " and " + Height);
  }
}

// A derived class of TwoDShape for triangles.
class Triangle : TwoDShape {
  string Style; // private

  /* A default constructor. This invokes the default
     constructor of TwoDShape. */
  public Triangle() {
    Style = "null";
  }
```

```
    // Constructor.
    public Triangle(string s, double w, double h) : base(w, h) {
      Style = s;
    }

    // Construct an isosceles triangle.
    public Triangle(double x) : base(x) {
      Style = "isosceles";
    }

    // Return area of triangle.
    public double Area() {
      return Width * Height / 2;
    }

    // Display a triangle's style.
    public void ShowStyle() {
      Console.WriteLine("Triangle is " + Style);
    }
}

// Extend Triangle.
class ColorTriangle : Triangle {
  string color;

  public ColorTriangle(string c, string s,
                       double w, double h) : base(s, w, h) {
    color = c;
  }

  // Display the color.
  public void ShowColor() {
    Console.WriteLine("Color is " + color);
  }
}

class Shapes6 {
  static void Main() {
    ColorTriangle t1 =
        new ColorTriangle("Blue", "right", 8.0, 12.0);
    ColorTriangle t2 =
        new ColorTriangle("Red", "isosceles", 2.0, 2.0);

    Console.WriteLine("Info for t1: ");
    t1.ShowStyle();
    t1.ShowDim();
    t1.ShowColor();
    Console.WriteLine("Area is " + t1.Area());

    Console.WriteLine();

    Console.WriteLine("Info for t2: ");
    t2.ShowStyle();
    t2.ShowDim();
    t2.ShowColor();
```

```
      Console.WriteLine("Area is " + t2.Area());
  }
}
```

The output of this program is shown here:

```
Info for t1:
Triangle is right
Width and height are 8 and 12
Color is Blue
Area is 48

Info for t2:
Triangle is isosceles
Width and height are 2 and 2
Color is Red
Area is 2
```

Because of inheritance, **ColorTriangle** can make use of the previously defined classes of **Triangle** and **TwoDShape**, adding only the extra information it needs for its own, specific application. This is part of the value of inheritance; it allows the reuse of code.

This example illustrates one other important point: **base** always refers to the constructor in the closest base class. The **base** in **ColorTriangle** calls the constructor in **Triangle**. The **base** in **Triangle** calls the constructor in **TwoDShape**. In a class hierarchy, if a base class constructor requires parameters, then all derived classes must pass those parameters "up the line." This is true whether or not a derived class needs parameters of its own.

When Are Constructors Called?

In the foregoing discussion of inheritance and class hierarchies, an important question may have occurred to you: When a derived class object is created, whose constructor is executed first? The one in the derived class or the one defined by the base class? For example, given a derived class called **B** and a base class called **A**, is **A**'s constructor called before **B**'s, or vice versa? The answer is that in a class hierarchy, constructors are called in order of derivation, from base class to derived class. Furthermore, this order is the same whether or not **base** is used. If **base** is not used, then the default (parameterless) constructor of each base class will be executed. The following program illustrates the order of constructor execution:

```
// Demonstrate when constructors are called.

using System;

// Create a base class.
class A {
  public A() {
    Console.WriteLine("Constructing A.");
  }
}

// Create a class derived from A.
class B : A {
  public B() {
```

```
      Console.WriteLine("Constructing B.");
  }
}

// Create a class derived from B.
class C : B {
  public C() {
    Console.WriteLine("Constructing C.");
  }
}

class OrderOfConstruction {
  static void Main() {
    C c = new C();
  }
}
```

The output from this program is shown here:

```
Constructing A.
Constructing B.
Constructing C.
```

As you can see, the constructors are called in order of derivation.

If you think about it, it makes sense that constructors are executed in order of derivation. Because a base class has no knowledge of any derived class, any initialization it needs to perform is separate from and possibly prerequisite to any initialization performed by the derived class. Therefore, it must be executed first.

Base Class References and Derived Objects

As you know, C# is a strongly typed language. Aside from the standard conversions and automatic promotions that apply to its value types, type compatibility is strictly enforced. Therefore, a reference variable for one class type cannot normally refer to an object of another class type. For example, consider the following program that declares two classes that are identical in their composition:

```
// This program will not compile.

class X {
  int a;

  public X(int i) { a = i; }
}

class Y {
  int a;

  public Y(int i) { a = i; }
}

class IncompatibleRef {
  static void Main() {
```

```
    X x = new X(10);
    X x2;
    Y y = new Y(5);

    x2 = x; // OK, both of same type

    x2 = y; // Error, not of same type
  }
}
```

Here, even though class **X** and class **Y** are physically the same, it is not possible to assign a reference of type **Y** to a variable of type **X** because they have different types. Therefore, this line is incorrect because it causes a compile-time type mismatch:

```
x2 = y; // Error, not of same type
```

In general, an object reference variable can refer only to objects of its type.

There is, however, an important exception to C#'s strict type enforcement. A reference variable of a base class can be assigned a reference to an object of any class derived from that base class. This is legal because an instance of a derived type encapsulates an instance of the base type. Thus, a base class reference can refer to it. Here is an example:

```
// A base class reference can refer to a derived class object.

using System;

class X {
  public int a;

  public X(int i) {
    a = i;
  }
}

class Y : X {
  public int b;

  public Y(int i, int j) : base(j) {
    b = i;
  }
}

class BaseRef {
  static void Main() {
    X x = new X(10);
    X x2;
    Y y = new Y(5, 6);

    x2 = x; // OK, both of same type
    Console.WriteLine("x2.a: " + x2.a);

    x2 = y; // OK because Y is derived from X
    Console.WriteLine("x2.a: " + x2.a);
```

```
    // X references know only about X members
    x2.a = 19; // OK
//    x2.b = 27; // Error, X doesn't have a b member
  }
}
```

In this program, **Y** is derived from **X**. Now, the assignment

```
x2 = y; // OK because Y is derived from X
```

is permissible because a base class reference, **x2** in this case, can refer to a derived class object (which is the object referred to by **y**).

It is important to understand that it is the type of the reference variable—not the type of the object that it refers to—that determines what members can be accessed. That is, when a reference to a derived class object is assigned to a base class reference variable, you will have access only to those parts of the object defined by the base class. This is why **x2** can't access **b** even when it refers to a **Y** object. This makes sense because the base class has no knowledge of what a derived class adds to it. This is why the last line of code in the program is commented out.

Although the preceding discussion may seem a bit esoteric, it has some important practical applications. One is described here. The other is discussed later in this chapter, when virtual methods are covered.

An important place where derived class references are assigned to base class variables is when constructors are called in a class hierarchy. As you know, it is common for a class to define a constructor that takes an object of its class as a parameter. This allows the class to construct a copy of an object. Classes derived from such a class can take advantage of this feature. For example, consider the following versions of **TwoDShape** and **Triangle**. Both add constructors that take an object as a parameter.

```
// Pass a derived class reference to a base class reference.

using System;

class TwoDShape {
  double pri_width;
  double pri_height;

  // Default constructor.
  public TwoDShape() {
    Width = Height = 0.0;
  }

  // Constructor for TwoDShape.
  public TwoDShape(double w, double h) {
    Width = w;
    Height = h;
  }

  // Construct object with equal width and height.
  public TwoDShape(double x) {
    Width = Height = x;
  }
```

```csharp
    // Construct a copy of a TwoDShape object.
    public TwoDShape(TwoDShape ob) {
      Width = ob.Width;
      Height = ob.Height;
    }

    // Properties for Width and Height.
    public double Width {
       get { return pri_width; }
       set { pri_width = value < 0 ? -value : value; }
    }

    public double Height {
       get { return pri_height; }
       set { pri_height = value < 0 ? -value : value; }
    }

    public void ShowDim() {
      Console.WriteLine("Width and height are " +
                        Width + " and " + Height);
    }
}

// A derived class of TwoDShape for triangles.
class Triangle : TwoDShape {
  string Style;

  // A default constructor.
  public Triangle() {
    Style = "null";
  }

  // Constructor for Triangle.
  public Triangle(string s, double w, double h) : base(w, h) {
    Style = s;
  }

  // Construct an isosceles triangle.
  public Triangle(double x) : base(x) {
    Style = "isosceles";
  }

  // Construct a copy of a Triangle object.
  public Triangle(Triangle ob) : base(ob) {
    Style = ob.Style;
  }

  // Return area of triangle.
  public double Area() {
    return Width * Height / 2;
  }
```

```
  // Display a triangle's style.
  public void ShowStyle() {
    Console.WriteLine("Triangle is " + Style);
  }
}

class Shapes7 {
  static void Main() {
    Triangle t1 = new Triangle("right", 8.0, 12.0);

    // Make a copy of t1.
    Triangle t2 = new Triangle(t1);

    Console.WriteLine("Info for t1: ");
    t1.ShowStyle();
    t1.ShowDim();
    Console.WriteLine("Area is " + t1.Area());

    Console.WriteLine();

    Console.WriteLine("Info for t2: ");
    t2.ShowStyle();
    t2.ShowDim();
    Console.WriteLine("Area is " + t2.Area());
  }
}
```

In this program, **t2** is constructed from **t1** and is, thus, identical. The output is shown here:

```
Info for t1:
Triangle is right
Width and height are 8 and 12
Area is 48

Info for t2:
Triangle is right
Width and height are 8 and 12
Area is 48
```

Pay special attention to this **Triangle** constructor:

```
public Triangle(Triangle ob) : base(ob) {
  Style = ob.Style;
}
```

It receives an object of type **Triangle**, and it passes that object (through **base**) to this **TwoDShape** constructor:

```
public TwoDShape(TwoDShape ob) {
  Width = ob.Width;
  Height = ob.Height;
}
```

The key point is that **TwoDShape( )** is expecting a **TwoDShape** object. However, **Triangle( )** passes it a **Triangle** object. As explained, the reason this works is because a base class reference can refer to a derived class object. Thus, it is perfectly acceptable to pass **TwoDShape( )** a reference to an object of a class derived from **TwoDShape**. Because the **TwoDShape( )** constructor is initializing only those portions of the derived class object that are members of **TwoDShape**, it doesn't matter that the object might also contain other members added by derived classes.

Virtual Methods and Overriding

A *virtual method* is a method that is declared as **virtual** in a base class. The defining characteristic of a virtual method is that it can be redefined in one or more derived classes. Thus, each derived class can have its own version of a virtual method. Virtual methods are interesting because of what happens when one is called through a base class reference. In this situation, C# determines which version of the method to call based upon the *type* of the object *referred to* by the reference—and this determination is made *at runtime*. Thus, when different objects are referred to, different versions of the virtual method are executed. In other words, it is the type of the object being referred to (not the type of the reference) that determines which version of the virtual method will be executed. Therefore, if a base class contains a virtual method and classes are derived from that base class, then when different types of objects are referred to through a base class reference, different versions of the virtual method can be executed.

You declare a method as virtual inside a base class by preceding its declaration with the keyword **virtual**. When a virtual method is redefined by a derived class, the **override** modifier is used. Thus, the process of redefining a virtual method inside a derived class is called *method overriding*. When overriding a method, the name, return type, and signature of the overriding method must be the same as the virtual method that is being overridden. Also, a virtual method cannot be specified as **static** or **abstract** (discussed later in this chapter).

Method overriding forms the basis for one of C#'s most powerful concepts: *dynamic method dispatch*. Dynamic method dispatch is the mechanism by which a call to an overridden method is resolved at runtime, rather than compile time. Dynamic method dispatch is important because this is how C# implements runtime polymorphism.

Here is an example that illustrates virtual methods and overriding:

```
// Demonstrate a virtual method.

using System;

class Base {
  // Create virtual method in the base class.
  public virtual void Who() {
    Console.WriteLine("Who() in Base");
  }
}

class Derived1 : Base {
  // Override Who() in a derived class.
  public override void Who() {
    Console.WriteLine("Who() in Derived1");
  }
}
```

```
class Derived2 : Base {
  // Override Who() again in another derived class.
  public override void Who() {
    Console.WriteLine("Who() in Derived2");
  }
}

class OverrideDemo {
  static void Main() {
    Base baseOb = new Base();
    Derived1 dOb1 = new Derived1();
    Derived2 dOb2 = new Derived2();

    Base baseRef; // a base class reference

    baseRef = baseOb;
    baseRef.Who();

    baseRef = dOb1;
    baseRef.Who();

    baseRef = dOb2;
    baseRef.Who();
  }
}
```

The output from the program is shown here:

```
Who() in Base
Who() in Derived1
Who() in Derived2
```

This program creates a base class called **Base** and two derived classes, called **Derived1** and **Derived2**. **Base** declares a method called **Who( )**, and the derived classes override it. Inside the **Main( )** method, objects of type **Base**, **Derived1**, and **Derived2** are declared. Also, a reference of type **Base**, called **baseRef**, is declared. The program then assigns a reference to each type of object to **baseRef** and uses that reference to call **Who( )**. As the output shows, the version of **Who( )** executed is determined by the type of object being referred to at the time of the call, not by the class type of **baseRef**.

It is not necessary to override a virtual method. If a derived class does not provide its own version of a virtual method, then the one in the base class is used. For example:

```
/* When a virtual method is not overridden,
   the base class method is used. */

using System;

class Base {
  // Create virtual method in the base class.
  public virtual void Who() {
    Console.WriteLine("Who() in Base");
  }
}
```

```
class Derived1 : Base {
  // Override Who() in a derived class.
  public override void Who() {
    Console.WriteLine("Who() in Derived1");
  }
}

class Derived2 : Base {
  // This class does not override Who().
}

class NoOverrideDemo {
  static void Main() {
    Base baseOb = new Base();
    Derived1 dOb1 = new Derived1();
    Derived2 dOb2 = new Derived2();

    Base baseRef; // a base class reference

    baseRef = baseOb;
    baseRef.Who();

    baseRef = dOb1;
    baseRef.Who();

    baseRef = dOb2;
    baseRef.Who(); // calls Base's Who()
  }
}
```

The output from this program is shown here:

```
Who() in Base
Who() in Derived1
Who() in Base
```

Here, **Derived2** does not override **Who( )**. Thus, when **Who( )** is called on a **Derived2** object, the **Who( )** in **Base** is executed.

In the case of a multilevel hierarchy, if a derived class does not override a virtual method, then, while moving up the hierarchy, the first override of the method that is encountered is the one executed. For example:

```
/*  In a multilevel hierarchy, the first override of a virtual
    method that is found while moving up the hierarchy is the
    one executed. */

using System;

class Base {
  // Create virtual method in the base class.
  public virtual void Who() {
    Console.WriteLine("Who() in Base");
```

```
  }
}

class Derived1 : Base {
  // Override Who() in a derived class.
  public override void Who() {
    Console.WriteLine("Who() in Derived1");
  }
}

class Derived2 : Derived1 {
  // This class also does not override Who().
}

class Derived3 : Derived2 {
  // This class does not override Who().
}

class NoOverrideDemo2 {
  static void Main() {
    Derived3 dOb = new Derived3();
    Base baseRef; // a base class reference

    baseRef = dOb;
    baseRef.Who(); // calls Derived1's Who()
  }
}
```

The output is shown here:

```
Who() in Derived1
```

Here, **Derived3** inherits **Derived2**, which inherits **Derived1**, which inherits **Base**. As the output verifies, since **Who( )** is not overridden by either **Derived3** or **Derived2**, it is the override of **Who( )** in **Derived1** that is executed, since it is the first version of **Who( )** that is found.

One other point: Properties can also be modified by the **virtual** keyword and overridden using **override**. The same is true for indexers.

Why Overridden Methods?

Overridden methods allow C# to support runtime polymorphism. Polymorphism is essential to object-oriented programming for one reason: It allows a general class to specify methods that will be common to all of its derivatives, while allowing derived classes to define the specific implementation of some or all of those methods. Overridden methods are another way that C# implements the "one interface, multiple methods" aspect of polymorphism.

Part of the key to applying polymorphism successfully is understanding that the base classes and derived classes form a hierarchy that moves from lesser to greater specialization. Used correctly, the base class provides all elements that a derived class can use directly. Through virtual methods, it also defines those methods that the derived class can implement on its own. This allows the derived class flexibility, yet still enforces a consistent interface. Thus, by combining inheritance with overridden methods, a base class can define the general form of the methods that will be used by all of its derived classes.

Applying Virtual Methods

To better understand the power of virtual methods, we will apply them to the **TwoDShape** class. In the preceding examples, each class derived from **TwoDShape** defines a method called **Area( )**. This suggests that it might be better to make **Area( )** a virtual method of the **TwoDShape** class, allowing each derived class to override it, defining how the area is calculated for the type of shape that the class encapsulates. The following program does this. For convenience, it also adds a name property to **TwoDShape**. (This makes it easier to demonstrate the classes.)

```
// Use virtual methods and polymorphism.

using System;

class TwoDShape {
  double pri_width;
  double pri_height;

  // A default constructor.
  public TwoDShape() {
    Width = Height = 0.0;
    name = "null";
  }

  // Parameterized constructor.
  public TwoDShape(double w, double h, string n) {
    Width = w;
    Height = h;
    name = n;
  }

  // Construct object with equal width and height.
  public TwoDShape(double x, string n) {
    Width = Height = x;
    name = n;
  }

  // Construct a copy of a TwoDShape object.
  public TwoDShape(TwoDShape ob) {
    Width = ob.Width;
    Height = ob.Height;
    name = ob.name;
  }

  // Properties for Width and Height.
  public double Width {
    get { return pri_width; }
    set { pri_width = value < 0 ? -value : value; }
  }

  public double Height {
    get { return pri_height; }
    set { pri_height = value < 0 ? -value : value; }
  }
```

```
  public string name { get; set; }

  public void ShowDim() {
    Console.WriteLine("Width and height are " +
                       Width + " and " + Height);
  }

  public virtual double Area() {
    Console.WriteLine("Area() must be overridden");
    return 0.0;
  }
}

// A derived class of TwoDShape for triangles.
class Triangle : TwoDShape {
  string Style;

  // A default constructor.
  public Triangle() {
    Style = "null";
  }

  // Constructor for Triangle.
  public Triangle(string s, double w, double h) :
    base(w, h, "triangle") {
      Style = s;
  }

  // Construct an isosceles triangle.
  public Triangle(double x) : base(x, "triangle") {
    Style = "isosceles";
  }

  // Construct a copy of a Triangle object.
  public Triangle(Triangle ob) : base(ob) {
    Style = ob.Style;
  }

  // Override Area() for Triangle.
  public override double Area() {
    return Width * Height / 2;
  }

  // Display a triangle's style.
  public void ShowStyle() {
    Console.WriteLine("Triangle is " + Style);
  }
}

// A derived class of TwoDShape for rectangles.
class Rectangle : TwoDShape {

  // Constructor for Rectangle.
  public Rectangle(double w, double h) :
    base(w, h, "rectangle"){ }
```

```
  // Construct a square.
  public Rectangle(double x) :
    base(x, "rectangle") { }

  // Construct a copy of a Rectangle object.
  public Rectangle(Rectangle ob) : base(ob) { }

  // Return true if the rectangle is square.
  public bool IsSquare() {
    if(Width == Height) return true;
    return false;
  }

  // Override Area() for Rectangle.
  public override double Area() {
    return Width * Height;
  }
}

class DynShapes {
  static void Main() {
    TwoDShape[] shapes = new TwoDShape[5];

    shapes[0] = new Triangle("right", 8.0, 12.0);
    shapes[1] = new Rectangle(10);
    shapes[2] = new Rectangle(10, 4);
    shapes[3] = new Triangle(7.0);
    shapes[4] = new TwoDShape(10, 20, "generic");

    for(int i=0; i < shapes.Length; i++) {
      Console.WriteLine("object is " + shapes[i].name);
      Console.WriteLine("Area is " + shapes[i].Area());

      Console.WriteLine();
    }
  }
}
```

The output from the program is shown here:

```
object is triangle
Area is 48

object is rectangle
Area is 100

object is rectangle
Area is 40

object is triangle
Area is 24.5

object is generic
Area() must be overridden
Area is 0
```

Let's examine this program closely. First, as explained, **Area( )** is declared as **virtual** in the **TwoDShape** class and is overridden by **Triangle** and **Rectangle**. Inside **TwoDShape**, **Area( )** is given a placeholder implementation that simply informs the user that this method must be overridden by a derived class. Each override of **Area( )** supplies an implementation that is suitable for the type of object encapsulated by the derived class. Thus, if you were to implement an ellipse class, for example, then **Area( )** would need to compute the area of an ellipse.

There is one other important feature in the preceding program. Notice in **Main( )** that **shapes** is declared as an array of **TwoDShape** objects. However, the elements of this array are assigned **Triangle**, **Rectangle**, and **TwoDShape** references. This is valid because a base class reference can refer to a derived class object. The program then cycles through the array, displaying information about each object. Although quite simple, this illustrates the power of both inheritance and method overriding. The type of object stored in a base class reference variable is determined at runtime and acted on accordingly. If an object is derived from **TwoDShape**, then its area can be obtained by calling **Area( )**. The interface to this operation is the same no matter what type of shape is being used.

Using Abstract Classes

Sometimes you will want to create a base class that defines only a generalized form that will be shared by all of its derived classes, leaving it to each derived class to fill in the details. Such a class determines the nature of the methods that the derived classes must implement, but does not, itself, provide an implementation of one or more of these methods. One way this situation can occur is when a base class is unable to create a meaningful implementation for a method. This is the case with the version of **TwoDShape** used in the preceding example. The definition of **Area( )** is simply a placeholder. It will not compute and display the area of any type of object.

You will see as you create your own class libraries that it is not uncommon for a method to have no meaningful definition in the context of its base class. You can handle this situation two ways. One way, as shown in the previous example, is to simply have it report a warning message. Although this approach can be useful in certain situations—such as debugging—it is not usually appropriate. You may have methods that must be overridden by the derived class in order for the derived class to have any meaning. Consider the class **Triangle**. It is incomplete if **Area( )** is not defined. In such a case, you want some way to ensure that a derived class does, indeed, override all necessary methods. C#'s solution to this problem is the *abstract method.*

An abstract method is created by specifying the **abstract** type modifier. An abstract method contains no body and is, therefore, not implemented by the base class. Thus, a derived class must override it—it cannot simply use the version defined in the base class. As you can probably guess, an abstract method is automatically virtual, and there is no need to use the **virtual** modifier. In fact, it is an error to use **virtual** and **abstract** together.

To declare an abstract method, use this general form:

abstract *type name(parameter-list)*;

As you can see, no method body is present. The **abstract** modifier can be used only on instance methods. It cannot be applied to **static** methods. Properties and indexers can also be abstract.

A class that contains one or more abstract methods must also be declared as abstract by preceding its **class** declaration with the **abstract** specifier. Since an abstract class does not define a complete implementation, there can be no objects of an abstract class. Thus, attempting to create an object of an abstract class by using **new** will result in a compile-time error.

When a derived class inherits an abstract class, it must implement all of the abstract methods in the base class. If it doesn't, then the derived class must also be specified as **abstract**. Thus, the **abstract** attribute is inherited until such time as a complete implementation is achieved.

Using an abstract class, you can improve the **TwoDShape** class. Since there is no meaningful concept of area for an undefined two-dimensional figure, the following version of the preceding program declares **Area( )** as **abstract** inside **TwoDShape** and **TwoDShape** as **abstract**. This, of course, means that all classes derived from **TwoDShape** must override **Area( )**.

```
// Create an abstract class.

using System;

abstract class TwoDShape {
  double pri_width;
  double pri_height;

  // A default constructor.
  public TwoDShape() {
    Width = Height = 0.0;
    name = "null";
  }

  // Parameterized constructor.
  public TwoDShape(double w, double h, string n) {
    Width = w;
    Height = h;
    name = n;
  }

  // Construct object with equal width and height.
  public TwoDShape(double x, string n) {
    Width = Height = x;
    name = n;
  }

  // Construct a copy of a TwoDShape object.
  public TwoDShape(TwoDShape ob) {
    Width = ob.Width;
    Height = ob.Height;
    name = ob.name;
  }

  // Properties for Width and Height.
  public double Width {
    get { return pri_width; }
    set { pri_width = value < 0 ? -value : value; }
  }
```

```
  public double Height {
     get { return pri_height; }
     set { pri_height = value < 0 ? -value : value; }
  }

  public string name { get; set; }

  public void ShowDim() {
    Console.WriteLine("Width and height are " +
                      Width + " and " + Height);
  }

  // Now, Area() is abstract.
  public abstract double Area();
}

// A derived class of TwoDShape for triangles.
class Triangle : TwoDShape {
  string Style;

  // A default constructor.
  public Triangle() {
    Style = "null";
  }

  // Constructor for Triangle.
  public Triangle(string s, double w, double h) :
    base(w, h, "triangle") {
      Style = s;
  }

  // Construct an isosceles triangle.
  public Triangle(double x) : base(x, "triangle") {
    Style = "isosceles";
  }

  // Construct a copy of a Triangle object.
  public Triangle(Triangle ob) : base(ob) {
    Style = ob.Style;
  }

  // Override Area() for Triangle.
  public override double Area() {
    return Width * Height / 2;
  }

  // Display a triangle's style.
  public void ShowStyle() {
    Console.WriteLine("Triangle is " + Style);
  }
}

// A derived class of TwoDShape for rectangles.
class Rectangle : TwoDShape {
```

```
    // Constructor for Rectangle.
    public Rectangle(double w, double h) :
      base(w, h, "rectangle"){ }

    // Construct a square.
    public Rectangle(double x) :
      base(x, "rectangle") { }

    // Construct a copy of a Rectangle object.
    public Rectangle(Rectangle ob) : base(ob) { }

    // Return true if the rectangle is square.
    public bool IsSquare() {
      if(Width == Height) return true;
      return false;
    }

    // Override Area() for Rectangle.
    public override double Area() {
      return Width * Height;
    }
}

class AbsShape {
  static void Main() {
    TwoDShape[] shapes = new TwoDShape[4];

    shapes[0] = new Triangle("right", 8.0, 12.0);
    shapes[1] = new Rectangle(10);
    shapes[2] = new Rectangle(10, 4);
    shapes[3] = new Triangle(7.0);

    for(int i=0; i < shapes.Length; i++) {
      Console.WriteLine("object is " + shapes[i].name);
      Console.WriteLine("Area is " + shapes[i].Area());

      Console.WriteLine();
    }
  }
}
```

As the program illustrates, all derived classes *must* override **Area( )** (or also be declared **abstract**). To prove this to yourself, try creating a derived class that does not override **Area( )**. You will receive a compile-time error. Of course, it is still possible to create an object reference of type **TwoDShape**, which the program does. However, it is no longer possible to declare objects of type **TwoDShape**. Because of this, in **Main( )** the **shapes** array has been shortened to 4, and a generic **TwoDShape** object is no longer created.

One other point: Notice that **TwoDShape** still includes the **ShowDim( )** method and that it is not modified by **abstract**. It is perfectly acceptable—indeed, quite common—for an abstract class to contain concrete methods that a derived class is free to use as-is. Only those methods declared as **abstract** must be overridden by derived classes.

Using sealed to Prevent Inheritance

As powerful and useful as inheritance is, sometimes you will want to prevent it. For example, you might have a class that encapsulates the initialization sequence of some specialized hardware device, such as a medical monitor. In this case, you don't want users of your class to be able to change the way the monitor is initialized, possibly setting the device incorrectly. Whatever the reason, in C# it is easy to prevent a class from being inherited by using the keyword **sealed**.

To prevent a class from being inherited, precede its declaration with **sealed**. As you might expect, it is illegal to declare a class as both **abstract** and **sealed** because an abstract class is incomplete by itself and relies upon its derived classes to provide complete implementations.

Here is an example of a **sealed** class:

```
sealed class A {
  // ...
}

// The following class is illegal.
class B : A { // ERROR! Can't derive from class A
  // ...
}
```

As the comments imply, it is illegal for **B** to inherit **A** because **A** is declared as **sealed**.

One other point: **sealed** can also be used on virtual methods to prevent further overrrides. For example, assume a base class called **B** and a derived class called **D**. A method declared **virtual** in **B** can be declared **sealed** by **D**. This would prevent any class that inherits **D** from overriding the method. This situation is illustrated by the following:

```
class B {
  public virtual void MyMethod() { /* ... */ }
}

class D : B {
  // This seals MyMethod() and prevents further overrides.
  sealed public override void MyMethod() { /* ... */ }
}

class X : D {
  // Error! MyMethod() is sealed!
  public override void MyMethod() { /* ... */ }
}
```

Because **MyMethod()** is sealed by **D**, it can't be overridden by **X**.

The object Class

C# defines one special class called **object** that is an implicit base class of all other classes and for all other types (including the value types). In other words, all other types are derived from **object**. This means that a reference variable of type **object** can refer to an object of any other type. Also, since arrays are implemented as objects, a variable of type **object** can also refer to any array. Technically, the C# name **object** is just another name for **System.Object**, which is part of the .NET Framework class library.

The **object** class defines the methods shown in Table 11-1, which means that they are available in every object.

A few of these methods warrant some additional explanation. By default, the **Equals(object)** method determines if the invoking object refers to the same object as the one referred to by the argument. (That is, it determines if the two references are the same.) It returns true if the objects are the same, and false otherwise. You can override this method in classes that you create. Doing so allows you to define what equality means relative to a class. For example, you could define **Equals(object)** so that it compares the contents of two objects for equality.

The **GetHashCode( )** method returns a hash code associated with the invoking object. A hash code is needed by any algorithm that employs hashing as a means of accessing stored objects. It is important to understand that the default implementation of **GetHashCode( )** will not be adequate for all uses.

As mentioned in Chapter 9, if you overload the = = operator, then you will usually need to override **Equals(object)** and **GetHashCode( )** because most of the time you will want the = = operator and the **Equals(object)** methods to function the same. When **Equals( )** is overridden, you often need to override **GetHashCode( )**, so that the two methods are compatible.

The **ToString( )** method returns a string that contains a description of the object on which it is called. Also, this method is automatically called when an object is output using

Method	Purpose
public virtual bool Equals(object *obj*)	Determines whether the invoking object is the same as the one referred to by *obj*.
public static bool Equals(object *objA*, object *objB*)	Determines whether *objA* is the same as *objB*.
protected virtual Finalize( )	Performs shutdown actions prior to garbage collection. In C#, **Finalize( )** is accessed through a destructor.
public virtual int GetHashCode( )	Returns the hash code associated with the invoking object.
public Type GetType( )	Obtains the type of an object at runtime.
protected object MemberwiseClone( )	Makes a "shallow copy" of the object. This is one in which the members are copied, but objects referred to by members are not.
public static bool ReferenceEquals(object *objA*, object *objB*)	Determines whether *objA* and *objB* refer to the same object.
public virtual string ToString( )	Returns a string that describes the object.

TABLE 11-1 Methods of the **object** Class

WriteLine( ). Many classes override this method. Doing so allows them to tailor a description specifically for the types of objects that they create. For example:

```
// Demonstrate ToString()

using System;

class MyClass {
  static int count = 0;
  int id;

  public MyClass() {
    id = count;
    count++;
  }

  public override string ToString() {
    return "MyClass object #" + id;
  }
}

class Test {
  static void Main() {
    MyClass ob1 = new MyClass();
    MyClass ob2 = new MyClass();
    MyClass ob3 = new MyClass();

    Console.WriteLine(ob1);
    Console.WriteLine(ob2);
    Console.WriteLine(ob3);
  }
}
```

The output from the program is shown here:

```
MyClass object #0
MyClass object #1
MyClass object #2
```

Boxing and Unboxing

As explained, all C# types, including the value types, are derived from **object**. Thus, a reference of type **object** can be used to refer to any other type, including value types. When an **object** reference refers to a value type, a process known as *boxing* occurs. Boxing causes the value of a value type to be stored in an object instance. Thus, a value type is "boxed" inside an object. This object can then be used like any other object. In all cases, boxing occurs automatically. You simply assign a value to an **object** reference. C# handles the rest.

Unboxing is the process of retrieving a value from a boxed object. This action is performed using an explicit cast from the **object** reference to its corresponding value type. Attempting to unbox an object into a different type will result in a runtime error.

Here is a simple example that illustrates boxing and unboxing:

```
// A simple boxing/unboxing example.

using System;

class BoxingDemo {
  static void Main() {
    int x;
    object obj;

    x = 10;
    obj = x; // box x into an object

    int y = (int)obj; // unbox obj into an int
    Console.WriteLine(y);
  }
}
```

This program displays the value 10. Notice that the value in **x** is boxed simply by assigning it to **obj**, which is an **object** reference. The integer value in **obj** is retrieved by casting **obj** to **int**.

Here is another, more interesting example of boxing. In this case, an **int** is passed as an argument to the **Sqr( )** method, which uses an **object** parameter.

```
// Boxing also occurs when passing values.

using System;

class BoxingDemo {
  static void Main() {
    int x;

    x = 10;
    Console.WriteLine("Here is x: " + x);

    // x is automatically boxed when passed to Sqr().
    x = BoxingDemo.Sqr(x);
    Console.WriteLine("Here is x squared: " + x);
  }

  static int Sqr(object o) {
    return (int)o * (int)o;
  }
}
```

The output from the program is shown here:

```
Here is x: 10
Here is x squared: 100
```

Here, the value of **x** is automatically boxed when it is passed to **Sqr( )**.

Boxing and unboxing allow C#'s type system to be fully unified. All types derive from **object**. A reference to any type can be assigned to a variable of type **object**. Boxing and unboxing automatically handle the details for the value types. Furthermore, because all types are derived from **object**, they all have access to **object**'s methods. For example, consider the following rather surprising program:

```
// Boxing makes it possible to call methods on a value!

using System;

class MethOnValue {
  static void Main() {

    Console.WriteLine(10.ToString());

  }
}
```

This program displays 10. The reason is that the **ToString( )** method returns a string representation of the object on which it is called. In this case, the string representation of 10 is 10!

Is object a Universal Data Type?

Given that **object** is a base class for all other types and that boxing of the value types takes place automatically, it is possible to use **object** as a "universal" data type. For example, consider the following program that creates an array of **object** and then assigns various other types of data to its elements:

```
// Use object to create a "generic" array.

using System;

class GenericDemo {
  static void Main() {
    object[] ga = new object[10];

    // Store ints.
    for(int i=0; i < 3; i++)
      ga[i] = i;

    // Store doubles.
    for(int i=3; i < 6; i++)
      ga[i] = (double) i / 2;


    // Store two strings, a bool, and a char.
    ga[6] = "Hello";
    ga[7] = true;
    ga[8] = 'X';
    ga[9] = "end";

    for(int i = 0; i < ga.Length; i++)
      Console.WriteLine("ga[" + i + "]: " + ga[i] + " ");
  }
}
```

The output is shown here:

```
ga[0]: 0
ga[1]: 1
ga[2]: 2
ga[3]: 1.5
ga[4]: 2
ga[5]: 2.5
ga[6]: Hello
ga[7]: True
ga[8]: X
ga[9]: end
```

As this program illustrates, because an **object** reference can hold a reference to any other type of data, it is possible to use an **object** reference to refer to any type of data. Thus, an array of **object** as used by the program can store any type of data. Expanding on this concept, it is easy to see how you could construct a stack class, for example, that stored **object** references. This would enable the stack to store any type of data.

Although the universal-type feature of **object** is powerful and can be used quite effectively in some situations, it is a mistake to think that you should use **object** as a way around C#'s otherwise strong type checking. In general, when you need to store an **int**, use an **int** variable; when you need to store a **string**, use a **string** reference; and so on.

More importantly, since version 2.0, true generic types are available to the C# programmer. (Generics are described in Chapter 18.) Generics enable you to easily define classes and algorithms that automatically work with different types of data in a type-safe manner. Because of generics, you will normally not need to use **object** as a universal type when creating new code. Today, it's best to reserve **object**'s universal nature for specialized situations.

Interfaces, Structures, and Enumerations

T his chapter discusses one of C#'s most important features: the interface. An *interface* defines a set of methods that will be implemented by a class. An interface does not, itself, implement any method. Thus, an interface is a purely logical construct that describes functionality without specifying implementation.

Also discussed in this chapter are two more C# data types: structures and enumerations. *Structures* are similar to classes except that they are handled as value types rather than reference types. *Enumerations* are lists of named integer constants. Structures and enumerations contribute to the richness of the C# programming environment.

Interfaces

In object-oriented programming it is sometimes helpful to define what a class must do, but not how it will do it. You have already seen an example of this: the abstract method. An abstract method declares the return type and signature for a method, but provides no implementation. A derived class must provide its own implementation of each abstract method defined by its base class. Thus, an abstract method specifies the *interface* to the method, but not the *implementation*. Although abstract classes and methods are useful, it is possible to take this concept a step further. In C#, you can fully separate a class' interface from its implementation by using the keyword **interface**.

Interfaces are syntactically similar to abstract classes. However, in an interface, no method can include a body. That is, an interface provides no implementation whatsoever. It specifies what must be done, but not how. Once an interface is defined, any number of classes can implement it. Also, one class can implement any number of interfaces.

To implement an interface, a class must provide bodies (implementations) for the methods described by the interface. Each class is free to determine the details of its own implementation. Thus, two classes might implement the same interface in different ways, but each class still supports the same set of methods. Therefore, code that has knowledge of the interface can use objects of either class since the interface to those objects is the same. By providing the interface, C# allows you to fully utilize the "one interface, multiple methods" aspect of polymorphism.

Interfaces are declared by using the **interface** keyword. Here is a simplified form of an interface declaration:

interface *name* {
  ret-type method-name1(param-list);
  ret-type method-name2(param-list);
  // ...
  ret-type method-nameN(param-list);
}

The name of the interface is specified by *name*. Methods are declared using only their return type and signature. They are, essentially, abstract methods. As explained, in an interface, no method can have an implementation. Thus, each class that includes an interface must implement all of the methods. In an interface, methods are implicitly **public**, and no explicit access specifier is allowed.

Here is an example of an interface. It specifies the interface to a class that generates a series of numbers.

```
public interface ISeries {
  int GetNext(); // return next number in series
  void Reset(); // restart
  void SetStart(int x); // set starting value
}
```

The name of this interface is **ISeries**. Although the prefix **I** is not necessary, many programmers prefix interfaces with **I** to differentiate them from classes. **ISeries** is declared **public** so that it can be implemented by any class in any program.

In addition to methods, interfaces can specify properties, indexers, and events. Events are described in Chapter 15, and we will be concerned with only methods, properties, and indexers here. Interfaces cannot have data members. They cannot define constructors, destructors, or operator methods. Also, no member can be declared as **static**.

Implementing Interfaces

Once an interface has been defined, one or more classes can implement that interface. To implement an interface, the name of the interface is specified after the class name in just the same way that a base class is specified. The general form of a class that implements an interface is shown here:

class *class-name* : *interface-name* {
  // class-body
}

The name of the interface being implemented is specified in *interface-name*. When a class implements an interface, the class must implement the entire interface. It cannot pick and choose which parts to implement, for example.

A class can implement more than one interface. When a class implements more than one interface, specify each interface in a comma-separated list. A class can inherit a base class and also implement one or more interfaces. In this case, the name of the base class must come first in the comma-separated list.

The methods that implement an interface must be declared **public**. The reason for this is that methods are implicitly public within an interface, so their implementation must also be public. Also, the return type and signature of the implementing method must match exactly the return type and signature specified in the **interface** definition.

Here is an example that implements the **ISeries** interface shown earlier. It creates a class called **ByTwos**, which generates a series of numbers, each two greater than the previous one.

```
// Implement ISeries.
class ByTwos : ISeries {
  int start;
  int val;

  public ByTwos() {
    start = 0;
    val = 0;
  }

  public int GetNext() {
    val += 2;
    return val;
  }

  public void Reset() {
    val = start;
  }

  public void SetStart(int x) {
    start = x;
    val = start;
  }
}
```

As you can see, **ByTwos** implements all three methods defined by **ISeries**. As explained, this is necessary since a class cannot create a partial implementation of an interface.

Here is a class that demonstrates **ByTwos**:

```
// Demonstrate the ISeries interface.

using System;

class SeriesDemo {
  static void Main() {
    ByTwos ob = new ByTwos();

    for(int i=0; i < 5; i++)
      Console.WriteLine("Next value is " +
                         ob.GetNext());

    Console.WriteLine("\nResetting");
    ob.Reset();
    for(int i=0; i < 5; i++)
      Console.WriteLine("Next value is " +
                         ob.GetNext());
```

```
      Console.WriteLine("\nStarting at 100");
      ob.SetStart(100);
      for(int i=0; i < 5; i++)
        Console.WriteLine("Next value is " +
                              ob.GetNext());
    }
  }
```

To compile **SeriesDemo**, you must include the files that contain **ISeries**, **ByTwos**, and **SeriesDemo** in the compilation. The compiler will automatically compile all three files to create the final executable. For example, if you called these files **ISeries.cs**, **ByTwos.cs**, and **SeriesDemo.cs**, then the following command line will compile the program:

```
>csc SeriesDemo.cs ISeries.cs ByTwos.cs
```

If you are using the Visual Studio IDE, simply add all three files to your C# project. One other point: It is perfectly valid to put all three of these classes in the same file, too.

The output from this program is shown here:

```
Next value is 2
Next value is 4
Next value is 6
Next value is 8
Next value is 10

Resetting
Next value is 2
Next value is 4
Next value is 6
Next value is 8
Next value is 10

Starting at 100
Next value is 102
Next value is 104
Next value is 106
Next value is 108
Next value is 110
```

It is both permissible and common for classes that implement interfaces to define additional members of their own. For example, the following version of **ByTwos** adds the method **GetPrevious( )**, which returns the previous value:

```
// Implement ISeries and add GetPrevious().
 class ByTwos : ISeries {
   int start;
   int val;
   int prev;

   public ByTwos() {
     start = 0;
     val = 0;
     prev = -2;
   }
```

```
public int GetNext() {
  prev = val;
  val += 2;
  return val;
}

public void Reset() {
  val = start;
  prev = start - 2;
}

public void SetStart(int x) {
  start = x;
  val = start;
  prev = val - 2;
}

// A method not specified by ISeries.
public int GetPrevious() {
  return prev;
}
}
```

Notice that the addition of **GetPrevious( )** required a change to the implementations of the methods defined by **ISeries**. However, since the interface to those methods stays the same, the change is seamless and does not break preexisting code. This is one of the advantages of interfaces.

As explained, any number of classes can implement an **interface**. For example, here is a class called **Primes** that generates a series of prime numbers. Notice that its implementation of **ISeries** is fundamentally different than the one provided by **ByTwos**.

```
// Use ISeries to implement a series of prime numbers.
class Primes : ISeries {
  int start;
  int val;

  public Primes() {
    start = 2;
    val = 2;
  }

  public int GetNext() {
    int i, j;
    bool isprime;

    val++;
    for(i = val; i < 1000000; i++) {
      isprime = true;
      for(j = 2; j <= i/j; j++) {
        if((i%j)==0) {
          isprime = false;
          break;
        }
      }
```

```
      if(isprime) {
        val = i;
        break;
      }
    }
    return val;
  }

  public void Reset() {
    val = start;
  }

  public void SetStart(int x) {
    start = x;
    val = start;
  }
}
```

The key point is that even though **ByTwos** and **Primes** generate completely unrelated series of numbers, both implement **ISeries**. As explained, an interface says nothing about the implementation, so each class is free to implement the interface as it sees fit.

Using Interface References

You might be somewhat surprised to learn that you can declare a reference variable of an interface type. In other words, you can create an interface reference variable. Such a variable can refer to any object that implements its interface. When you call a method on an object through an interface reference, it is the version of the method implemented by the object that is executed. This process is similar to using a base class reference to access a derived class object, as described in Chapter 11.

The following example illustrates the use of an interface reference. It uses the same interface reference variable to call methods on objects of both **ByTwos** and **Primes**. For clarity, it shows all pieces of the program, assembled into a single file.

```
// Demonstrate interface references.

using System;

// Define the interface.
public interface ISeries {
  int GetNext(); // return next number in series
  void Reset(); // restart
  void SetStart(int x); // set starting value
}

// Use ISeries to implement a series in which each
// value is two greater than the previous one.
class ByTwos : ISeries {
  int start;
  int val;
```

```
  public ByTwos() {
    start = 0;
    val = 0;
  }

  public int GetNext() {
    val += 2;
    return val;
  }

  public void Reset() {
    val = start;
  }

  public void SetStart(int x) {
    start = x;
    val = start;
  }
}

// Use ISeries to implement a series of prime numbers.
class Primes : ISeries {
  int start;
  int val;

  public Primes() {
    start = 2;
    val = 2;
  }

  public int GetNext() {
    int i, j;
    bool isprime;

    val++;
    for(i = val; i < 1000000; i++) {
      isprime = true;
      for(j = 2; j <= i/j; j++) {
        if((i%j)==0) {
          isprime = false;
          break;
        }
      }
      if(isprime) {
        val = i;
        break;
      }
    }
    return val;
  }

  public void Reset() {
    val = start;
  }
```

```
      public void SetStart(int x) {
        start = x;
        val = start;
      }
    }

    class SeriesDemo2 {
      static void Main() {
        ByTwos twoOb = new ByTwos();
        Primes primeOb = new Primes();
        ISeries ob;

        for(int i=0; i < 5; i++) {
          ob = twoOb;
          Console.WriteLine("Next ByTwos value is " +
                              ob.GetNext());
          ob = primeOb;
          Console.WriteLine("Next prime number is " +
                              ob.GetNext());
        }
      }
    }
```

The output from the program is shown here:

```
Next ByTwos value is 2
Next prime number is 3
Next ByTwos value is 4
Next prime number is 5
Next ByTwos value is 6
Next prime number is 7
Next ByTwos value is 8
Next prime number is 11
Next ByTwos value is 10
Next prime number is 13
```

In **Main( )**, **ob** is declared to be a reference to an **ISeries** interface. This means that it can be used to store references to any object that implements **ISeries**. In this case, it is used to refer to **twoOb** and **primeOb**, which are objects of type **ByTwos** and **Primes**, respectively, which both implement **ISeries**.

One other point: An interface reference variable has knowledge only of the methods declared by its **interface** declaration. Thus, an interface reference cannot be used to access any other variables or methods that might be supported by the object.

Interface Properties

Like methods, properties are specified in an interface without any body. Here is the general form of a property specification:

```
// interface property
type name {
  get;
  set;
}
```

Of course, only **get** or **set** will be present for read-only or write-only properties, respectively.

Although the declaration of a property in an interface looks similar to how an auto-implemented property is declared in a class, the two are not the same. The interface declaration does not cause the property to be auto-implemented. It only specifies the name and type of the property. Implementation is left to each implementing class. Also, no access modifiers are allowed on the accessors when a property is declared in an **interface**. Thus, the **set** accessor, for example, cannot be specified as private in an **interface**.

Here is a rewrite of the **ISeries** interface and the **ByTwos** class that uses a property called **Next** to obtain and set the next element in the series:

```
// Use a property in an interface.

using System;

public interface ISeries {
  // An interface property.
  int Next {
    get; // return the next number in series
    set; // set next number
  }
}

// Implement ISeries.
class ByTwos : ISeries {
  int val;

  public ByTwos() {
    val = 0;
  }

  // Get or set value.
  public int Next {
    get {
      val += 2;
      return val;
    }
    set {
      val = value;
    }
  }
}

// Demonstrate an interface property.
class SeriesDemo3 {
  static void Main() {
    ByTwos ob = new ByTwos();

    // Access series through a property.
    for(int i=0; i < 5; i++)
      Console.WriteLine("Next value is " + ob.Next);

    Console.WriteLine("\nStarting at 21");
    ob.Next = 21;
```

```
      for(int i=0; i < 5; i++)
        Console.WriteLine("Next value is " + ob.Next);
    }
  }
```

The output from this program is shown here:

```
Next value is 2
Next value is 4
Next value is 6
Next value is 8
Next value is 10

Starting at 21
Next value is 23
Next value is 25
Next value is 27
Next value is 29
Next value is 31
```

Interface Indexers

An interface can specify an indexer. A simple one-dimensional indexer declared in an interface has this general form:

> // interface indexer
> *element-type* this[int *index*] {
>   get;
>   set;
> }

As before, only **get** or **set** will be present for read-only or write-only indexers, respectively. Also, no access modifiers are allowed on the accessors when an indexer is declared in an **interface**.

Here is another version of **ISeries** that adds a read-only indexer that returns the *i*-th element in the series.

```
// Add an indexer in an interface.

using System;

public interface ISeries {
  // An interface property.
  int Next {
    get; // return the next number in series
    set; // set next number
  }

  // An interface indexer.
  int this[int index] {
    get; // return the specified number in series
  }
}
```

```
// Implement ISeries.
class ByTwos : ISeries {
  int val;

  public ByTwos() {
    val = 0;
  }

  // Get or set value using a property.
  public int Next {
    get {
      val += 2;
      return val;
    }
    set {
      val = value;
    }
  }

  // Get a value using an index.
  public int this[int index] {
    get {
      val = 0;
      for(int i=0; i < index; i++)
        val += 2;
      return val;
    }
  }
}

// Demonstrate an interface indexer.
class SeriesDemo4 {
  static void Main() {
    ByTwos ob = new ByTwos();

    // Access series through a property.
    for(int i=0; i < 5; i++)
      Console.WriteLine("Next value is " + ob.Next);

    Console.WriteLine("\nStarting at 21");
    ob.Next = 21;
    for(int i=0; i < 5; i++)
      Console.WriteLine("Next value is " +
                          ob.Next);

    Console.WriteLine("\nResetting to 0");
    ob.Next = 0;

    // Access series through an indexer.
    for(int i=0; i < 5; i++)
      Console.WriteLine("Next value is " + ob[i]);
  }
}
```

The output from this program is shown here:

```
Next value is 2
Next value is 4
Next value is 6
Next value is 8
Next value is 10

Starting at 21
Next value is 23
Next value is 25
Next value is 27
Next value is 29
Next value is 31

Resetting to 0
Next value is 0
Next value is 2
Next value is 4
Next value is 6
Next value is 8
```

Interfaces Can Be Inherited

One interface can inherit another. The syntax is the same as for inheriting classes. When a class implements an interface that inherits another interface, it must provide implementations for all the members defined within the interface inheritance chain. Here is an example:

```
// One interface can inherit another.

using System;

public interface IA {
  void Meth1();
  void Meth2();
}

// IB now includes Meth1() and Meth2() -- it adds Meth3().
public interface IB : IA {
  void Meth3();
}

// This class must implement all of IA and IB.
class MyClass : IB {
  public void Meth1() {
    Console.WriteLine("Implement Meth1().");
  }

  public void Meth2() {
    Console.WriteLine("Implement Meth2().");
  }

  public void Meth3() {
    Console.WriteLine("Implement Meth3().");
```

```
    }
  }

class IFExtend {
  static void Main() {
    MyClass ob = new MyClass();

    ob.Meth1();
    ob.Meth2();
    ob.Meth3();
  }
}
```

As an experiment, you might try removing the implementation for **Meth1( )** in **MyClass**. This will cause a compile-time error. As stated earlier, any class that implements an interface must implement all methods defined by that interface, including any that are inherited from other interfaces.

Name Hiding with Interface Inheritance

When one interface inherits another, it is possible to declare a member in the derived interface that hides one defined by the base interface. This happens when a member in a derived interface has the same declaration as one in the base interface. In this case, the base interface name is hidden. This will cause a warning message unless you specify the derived interface member with **new**.

Explicit Implementations

When implementing a member of an interface, it is possible to *fully qualify* its name with its interface name. Doing this creates an *explicit interface member implementation,* or *explicit implementation,* for short. For example, given

```
interface IMyIF {
  int MyMeth(int x);
}
```

then it is legal to implement **IMyIF** as shown here:

```
class MyClass : IMyIF {
  int IMyIF.MyMeth(int x) {
    return x / 3;
  }
}
```

As you can see, when the **MyMeth( )** member of **IMyIF** is implemented, its complete name, including its interface name, is specified.

There are two reasons that you might need to create an explicit implementation of an interface method. First, when you implement an interface method using its fully qualified name, you are providing an implementation that *cannot* be accessed through an object of the class. Instead, it must be accessed via an interface reference. Thus, an explicit implementation gives you a way to implement an interface method so that it is not a public member of the class that provides the implementation. Second, it is possible for a class to implement two interfaces, both of which declare methods by the same name and type signature. Qualifying the names with their interfaces removes the ambiguity from this situation. Let's look at an example of each.

The following program contains an interface called **IEven**, which defines two methods, **IsEven( )** and **IsOdd( )**, which determine if a number is even or odd. **MyClass** then implements **IEven**. When it does so, it implements **IsOdd( )** explicitly.

```
// Explicitly implement an interface member.

using System;

interface IEven {
  bool IsOdd(int x);
  bool IsEven(int x);
}

class MyClass : IEven {

  // Explicit implementation. Notice that this member is private
  // by default.
  bool IEven.IsOdd(int x) {
    if((x%2) != 0) return true;
    else return false;
  }

  // Normal implementation.
  public bool IsEven(int x) {
    IEven o = this; // Interface reference to the invoking object.

    return !o.IsOdd(x);
  }
}

class Demo {
  static void Main() {
    MyClass ob = new MyClass();
    bool result;

    result = ob.IsEven(4);
    if(result) Console.WriteLine("4 is even.");

    // result = ob.IsOdd(4); // Error, IsOdd not exposed.

    // But, this is OK. It creates an IEven reference to a MyClass object
    // and then calls IsOdd() through that reference.
    IEven iRef = (IEven) ob;
    result = iRef.IsOdd(3);
    if(result) Console.WriteLine("3 is odd.");

  }
}
```

Since **IsOdd()** is implemented explicitly, it is not exposed as a public member of **MyClass**. Instead, **IsOdd()** can be accessed only through an interface reference. This is why it is invoked through **o** (which is a reference variable of type **IEven**) in the implementation for **IsEven()**.

Here is an example in which two interfaces are implemented and both interfaces declare a method called **Meth( )**. Explicit implementation is used to eliminate the ambiguity inherent in this situation.

```
// Use explicit implementation to remove ambiguity.

using System;

interface IMyIF_A {
  int Meth(int x);
}

interface IMyIF_B {
  int Meth(int x);
}

// MyClass implements both interfaces.
class MyClass : IMyIF_A, IMyIF_B {

  // Explicitly implement the two Meth()s.
  int IMyIF_A.Meth(int x) {
    return x + x;
  }
  int IMyIF_B.Meth(int x) {
    return x * x;
  }

  // Call Meth() through an interface reference.
  public int MethA(int x){
    IMyIF_A a_ob;
    a_ob = this;
    return a_ob.Meth(x); // calls IMyIF_A
  }

  public int MethB(int x){
    IMyIF_B b_ob;
    b_ob = this;
    return b_ob.Meth(x); // calls IMyIF_B
  }
}

class FQIFNames {
  static void Main() {
    MyClass ob = new MyClass();

    Console.Write("Calling IMyIF_A.Meth(): ");
    Console.WriteLine(ob.MethA(3));
```

```
    Console.Write("Calling IMyIF_B.Meth(): ");
    Console.WriteLine(ob.MethB(3));
  }
}
```

The output from this program is shown here:

```
Calling IMyIF_A.Meth(): 6
Calling IMyIF_B.Meth(): 9
```

Looking at the program, first notice that **Meth()** has the same signature in both **IMyIF_A** and **IMyIF_B**. Thus, when **MyClass** implements both of these interfaces, it explicitly implements each one separately, fully qualifying its name in the process. Since the only way that an explicitly implemented method can be called is on an interface reference, **MyClass** creates two such references, one for **IMyIF_A** and one for **IMyIF_B**, inside **MethA()** and **MethB()**, respectively. It then calls these methods, which call the interface methods, thereby removing the ambiguity.

Choosing Between an Interface and an Abstract Class

One of the more challenging parts of C# programming is knowing when to create an interface and when to use an abstract class in cases in which you want to describe functionality but not implementation. The general rule is this: When you can fully describe the concept in terms of "what it does" without needing to specify any "how it does it," then you should use an interface. If you need to include some implementation details, then you will need to represent your concept in an abstract class.

The .NET Standard Interfaces

The .NET Framework defines a large number of interfaces that a C# program can use. For example, **System.IComparable** defines the **CompareTo()** method, which allows objects to be compared when an ordering relationship is required. Interfaces also form an important part of the Collections classes, which provide various types of storage (such as stacks and queues) for groups of objects. For example, **System.Collections.ICollection** defines the functionality of a collection. **System.Collections.IEnumerator** offers a way to sequence through the elements in a collection. These and many other interfaces are described in Part II.

Structures

As you know, classes are reference types. This means that class objects are accessed through a reference. This differs from the value types, which are accessed directly. However, sometimes it would be useful to be able to access an object directly, in the way that value types are. One reason for this is efficiency. Accessing class objects through a reference adds overhead onto every access. It also consumes space. For very small objects, this extra space might be significant. To address these concerns, C# offers the structure. A *structure* is similar to a class, but is a value type, rather than a reference type.

Structures are declared using the keyword **struct** and are syntactically similar to classes. Here is the general form of a **struct**:

```
struct name : interfaces {
  // member declarations
}
```

The name of the structure is specified by *name*.

Structures cannot inherit other structures or classes or be used as a base for other structures or classes. (All structures do, however, implicitly inherit **System.ValueType**, which inherits **object**.) However, a structure can implement one or more interfaces. These are specified after the structure name using a comma-separated list. Like classes, structure members include methods, fields, indexers, properties, operator methods, and events. Structures can also define constructors, but not destructors. However, you cannot define a default (parameterless) constructor for a structure. The reason for this is that a default constructor is automatically defined for all structures, and this default constructor can't be changed. The default constructor initializes the fields of a structure to their default value. Since structures do not support inheritance, structure members cannot be specified as **abstract**, **virtual**, or **protected**.

A structure object can be created using **new** in the same way as a class object, but it is not required. When **new** is used, the specified constructor is called. When **new** is not used, the object is still created, but it is not initialized. Thus, you will need to perform any initialization manually.

Here is an example that uses a structure to hold information about a book:

```
// Demonstrate a structure.

using System;

// Define a structure.
struct Book {
  public string Author;
  public string Title;
  public int Copyright;

  public Book(string a, string t, int c) {
    Author = a;
    Title = t;
    Copyright = c;
  }
}

// Demonstrate Book structure.
class StructDemo {
  static void Main() {
    Book book1 = new Book("Herb Schildt",
                          "C# 4.0: The Complete Reference",
                          2010); // explicit constructor

    Book book2 = new Book(); // default constructor
    Book book3; // no constructor

    Console.WriteLine(book1.Title + " by " + book1.Author +
                      ", (c) " + book1.Copyright);
    Console.WriteLine();
```

```
      if(book2.Title == null)
        Console.WriteLine("book2.Title is null.");

      // Now, give book2 some info.
      book2.Title = "Brave New World";
      book2.Author = "Aldous Huxley";
      book2.Copyright = 1932;
      Console.Write("book2 now contains: ");
      Console.WriteLine(book2.Title + " by " + book2.Author +
                       ", (c) " + book2.Copyright);

      Console.WriteLine();

// Console.WriteLine(book3.Title); // error, must initialize first
      book3.Title = "Red Storm Rising";

      Console.WriteLine(book3.Title); // now OK
    }
  }
```

The output from this program is shown here:

```
C# 4.0: The Complete Reference by Herb Schildt, (c) 2010

book2.Title is null.
book2 now contains: Brave New World by Aldous Huxley, (c) 1932

Red Storm Rising
```

As the program shows, a structure can be created either by using **new** to invoke a constructor or by simply declaring an object. If **new** is used, then the fields of the structure will be initialized either by the default constructor, which initializes all fields to their default value, or by a user-defined constructor. If **new** is not used, as is the case with **book3**, then the object is not initialized, and its fields must be set prior to using the object.

When you assign one structure to another, a copy of the object is made. This is an important way in which **struct** differs from **class**. As explained earlier in this book, when you assign one class reference to another, you are simply making the reference on the left side of the assignment refer to the same object as that referred to by the reference on the right. When you assign one **struct** variable to another, you are making a *copy* of the object on the right. For example, consider the following program:

```
// Copy a struct.

using System;

// Define a structure.
struct MyStruct {
  public int x;
}

// Demonstrate structure assignment.
class StructAssignment {
```

```
static void Main() {
  MyStruct a;
  MyStruct b;

  a.x = 10;
  b.x = 20;

  Console.WriteLine("a.x {0}, b.x {1}", a.x, b.x);

  a = b;
  b.x = 30;

  Console.WriteLine("a.x {0}, b.x {1}", a.x, b.x);
  }
}
```

The output is shown here:

```
a.x 10, b.x 20
a.x 20, b.x 30
```

As the output shows, after the assignment

```
a = b;
```

the structure variables **a** and **b** are still separate and distinct. That is, **a** does not refer to or relate to **b** in any way other than containing a copy of **b**'s value. This would not be the case if **a** and **b** were class references. For example, here is the **class** version of the preceding program:

```
// Use a class.

using System;

// Now a class.
class MyClass {
  public int x;
}

// Now show a class object assignment.
class ClassAssignment {
  static void Main() {
    MyClass a = new MyClass();
    MyClass b = new MyClass();

    a.x = 10;
    b.x = 20;

    Console.WriteLine("a.x {0}, b.x {1}", a.x, b.x);

    a = b;
    b.x = 30;
```

```
    Console.WriteLine("a.x {0}, b.x {1}", a.x, b.x);
  }
}
```

The output from this version is shown here:

```
a.x 10, b.x 20
a.x 30, b.x 30
```

As you can see, after the assignment of **b** to **a**, both variables refer to the same object—the one originally referred to by **b**.

Why Structures?

At this point, you might be wondering why C# includes the **struct** since it seems to be a less-capable version of a **class**. The answer lies in efficiency and performance. Because structures are value types, they are operated on directly rather than through a reference. Thus, a **struct** does not require a separate reference variable. This means that less memory is used in some cases. Furthermore, because a **struct** is accessed directly, it does not suffer from the performance loss that is inherent in accessing a class object. Because classes are reference types, all access to class objects is through a reference. This indirection adds overhead to every access. Structures do not incur this overhead. In general, if you need to simply store a group of related data, but don't need inheritance and don't need to operate on that data through a reference, then a **struct** can be a more efficient choice.

Here is another example that shows how a structure might be used in practice. It simulates an e-commerce transaction record. Each transaction includes a packet header that contains the packet number and the length of the packet. This is followed by the account number and the amount of the transaction. Because the packet header is a self-contained unit of information, it is organized as a structure. This structure can then be used to create a transaction record, or any other type of information packet.

```
// Structures are good when grouping small amounts of data.

using System;

// Define a packet structure.
struct PacketHeader {
  public uint PackNum; // packet number
  public ushort PackLen; // length of packet
}

// Use PacketHeader to create an e-commerce transaction record.
class Transaction {
  static uint transacNum = 0;

  PacketHeader ph;  // incorporate PacketHeader into Transaction
  string accountNum;
  double amount;
```

```
  public Transaction(string acc, double val) {
   // create packet header
    ph.PackNum = transacNum++;
    ph.PackLen = 512;  // arbitrary length

    accountNum = acc;
    amount = val;
  }

  // Simulate a transaction.
  public void sendTransaction() {
    Console.WriteLine("Packet #: " + ph.PackNum +
                      ", Length: " + ph.PackLen +
                      ",\n     Account #: " + accountNum +
                      ", Amount: {0:C}\n", amount);
  }
}

// Demonstrate Packet.
class PacketDemo {
  static void Main() {
    Transaction t = new Transaction("31243", -100.12);
    Transaction t2 = new Transaction("AB4655", 345.25);
    Transaction t3 = new Transaction("8475-09", 9800.00);

    t.sendTransaction();
    t2.sendTransaction();
    t3.sendTransaction();
  }
}
```

The output from the program is shown here:

```
Packet #: 0, Length: 512,
    Account #: 31243, Amount: ($100.12)

Packet #: 1, Length: 512,
    Account #: AB4655, Amount: $345.25

Packet #: 2, Length: 512,
    Account #: 8475-09, Amount: $9,800.00
```

PacketHeader is a good choice for a **struct** because it contains only a small amount of data and does not use inheritance or even contain methods. As a structure, **PacketHeader** does not incur the additional overhead of a reference, as a class would. Thus, any type of transaction record can use **PacketHeader** without affecting its efficiency.

As a point of interest, C++ also has structures and uses the **struct** keyword. However, C# and C++ structures are not the same. In C++, **struct** defines a class type. Thus, in C++, **struct** and **class** are nearly equivalent. (The difference has to do with the default access of their members, which is private for **class** and public for **struct**.) In C#, a **struct** defines a value type, and a **class** defines a reference type.

Enumerations

An *enumeration* is a set of named integer constants. The keyword **enum** declares an enumerated type. The general form for an enumeration is

> enum *name* { *enumeration list* };

Here, the type name of the enumeration is specified by *name*. The *enumeration list* is a comma-separated list of identifiers.

Here is an example. It defines an enumeration called **Apple** that enumerates various types of apples:

```
enum Apple { Jonathan, GoldenDel, RedDel, Winesap,
             Cortland, McIntosh };
```

A key point to understand about an enumeration is that each of the symbols stands for an integer value. However, no implicit conversions are defined between an **enum** type and the built-in integer types, so an explicit cast must be used. Also, a cast is required when converting between two enumeration types. Since enumerations represent integer values, you can use an enumeration to control a **switch** statement or as the control variable in a **for** loop, for example.

Each enumeration symbol is given a value one greater than the symbol that precedes it. By default, the value of the first enumeration symbol is 0. Therefore, in the **Apple** enumeration, **Jonathan** is 0, **GoldenDel** is 1, **RedDel** is 2, and so on.

The members of an enumeration are accessed through their type name via the dot operator. For example

```
Console.WriteLine(Apple.RedDel + " has the value " +
                  (int)Apple.RedDel);
```

displays

```
RedDel has the value 2
```

As the output shows, when an enumerated value is displayed, its name is used. To obtain its integer value, a cast to **int** must be employed.

Here is a program that illustrates the **Apple** enumeration:

```
// Demonstrate an enumeration.

using System;

class EnumDemo {
  enum Apple { Jonathan, GoldenDel, RedDel, Winesap,
               Cortland, McIntosh };

  static void Main() {
    string[] color = {
      "Red",
      "Yellow",
      "Red",
      "Red",
```

```
      "Red",
      "Reddish Green"
    };

    Apple i; // declare an enum variable

    // Use i to cycle through the enum.
    for(i = Apple.Jonathan; i <= Apple.McIntosh; i++)
      Console.WriteLine(i + " has value of " + (int)i);

    Console.WriteLine();

    // Use an enumeration to index an array.
    for(i = Apple.Jonathan; i <= Apple.McIntosh; i++)
      Console.WriteLine("Color of " + i + " is " +
                        color[(int)i]);
  }
}
```

The output from the program is shown here:

```
Jonathan has value of 0
GoldenDel has value of 1
RedDel has value of 2
Winesap has value of 3
Cortland has value of 4
McIntosh has value of 5

Color of Jonathan is Red
Color of GoldenDel is Yellow
Color of RedDel is Red
Color of Winesap is Red
Color of Cortland is Red
Color of McIntosh is Reddish Green
```

Notice how the **for** loops are controlled by a variable of type **Apple**. Because the enumerated values in **Apple** start at zero, these values can be used to index **color** to obtain the color of the apple. Notice that a cast is required when the enumeration value is used to index the **color** array. As mentioned, there are no implicit conversions defined between integers and enumeration types. An explicit cast is required.

One other point: all enumerations implicitly inherit **System.Enum**, which inherits **System.ValueType**, which inherits **object**.

Initialize an Enumeration

You can specify the value of one or more of the symbols by using an initializer. Do this by following the symbol with an equal sign and an integer constant expression. Symbols that appear after initializers are assigned values greater than the previous initialization value. For example, the following code assigns the value of 10 to **RedDel**:

```
enum Apple { Jonathan, GoldenDel, RedDel = 10, Winesap,
             Cortland, McIntosh };
```

Now the values of these symbols are

Jonathan	0
GoldenDel	1
RedDel	10
Winesap	11
Cortland	12
McIntosh	13

Specify the Underlying Type of an Enumeration

By default, enumerations are based on type **int**, but you can create an enumeration of any integral type, except for type **char**. To specify a type other than **int**, put the desired type after the enumeration name, separated by a colon. For example, this statement makes **Apple** an enumeration based on **byte**:

```
enum Apple : byte { Jonathan, GoldenDel, RedDel, Winesap,
                    Cortland, McIntosh };
```

Now **Apple.Winesap**, for example, is a **byte** quantity.

Use Enumerations

At first glance you might think that enumerations are an interesting but relatively unimportant part of C#, yet this is not the case. Enumerations are very useful when your program requires one or more specialized symbols. For example, imagine that you are writing a program that controls a conveyor belt in a factory. You might create a method called **Conveyor( )** that accepts the following commands as parameters: start, stop, forward, and reverse. Instead of passing **Conveyor( )** integers, such as 1 for start, 2 for stop, and so on, which is error-prone, you can create an enumeration that assigns words to these values. Here is an example of this approach:

```
// Simulate a conveyor belt.

using System;

class ConveyorControl {
  // Enumerate the conveyor commands.
  public enum Action { Start, Stop, Forward, Reverse };

  public void Conveyor(Action com) {
    switch(com) {
      case Action.Start:
        Console.WriteLine("Starting conveyor.");
        break;
      case Action.Stop:
        Console.WriteLine("Stopping conveyor.");
        break;
```

```
      case Action.Forward:
        Console.WriteLine("Moving forward.");
        break;
      case Action.Reverse:
        Console.WriteLine("Moving backward.");
        break;
    }
  }
}

class ConveyorDemo {
  static void Main() {
    ConveyorControl c = new ConveyorControl();

    c.Conveyor(ConveyorControl.Action.Start);
    c.Conveyor(ConveyorControl.Action.Forward);
    c.Conveyor(ConveyorControl.Action.Reverse);
    c.Conveyor(ConveyorControl.Action.Stop);

  }
}
```

The output from the program is shown here:

```
Starting conveyor.
Moving forward.
Moving backward.
Stopping conveyor.
```

Because **Conveyor( )** takes an argument of type **Action**, only the values defined by **Action** can be passed to the method. For example, here an attempt is made to pass the value 22 to **Conveyor( )**:

```
c.Conveyor(22); // Error!
```

This won't compile because there is no predefined conversion from **int** to **Action**. This prevents the passing of invalid commands to **Conveyor( )**. Of course, you could use a cast to force a conversion, but this would require a premeditated act, not an accidental misuse. Also, because commands are specified by name rather than by number, it is less likely that a user of **Conveyor( )** will inadvertently pass the wrong value.

There is one other interesting thing in this example: Notice that an enumeration type is used to control the **switch** statement. Because enumerations are integral types, they are perfectly valid for use in a **switch**.

Exception Handling

An *exception* is an error that occurs at runtime. Using C#'s exception-handling subsystem, you can, in a structured and controlled manner, handle runtime errors. A principal advantage of exception handling is that it automates much of the error-handling code that previously had to be entered "by hand" into any large program. For example, in a computer language without exception handling, error codes must be returned when a method fails, and these values must be checked manually each time the method is called. This approach is both tedious and error-prone. Exception handling streamlines error-handling by allowing your program to define a block of code, called an *exception handler*, that is executed automatically when an error occurs. It is not necessary to manually check the success or failure of each specific operation or method call. If an error occurs, it will be processed by the exception handler.

Exception handling is also important because C# defines standard exceptions for common program errors, such as divide-by-zero or index-out-of-range. To respond to these errors, your program must watch for and handle these exceptions. In the final analysis, to be a successful C# programmer means that you are fully capable of navigating C#'s exception-handling subsystem.

The System.Exception Class

In C#, exceptions are represented by classes. All exception classes must be derived from the built-in exception class **Exception**, which is part of the **System** namespace. Thus, all exceptions are subclasses of **Exception**.

One very important subclass of **Exception** is **SystemException**. This is the exception class from which all exceptions generated by the C# runtime system (that is, the CLR) are derived. **SystemException** does not add anything to **Exception**. It simply defines the top of the standard exceptions hierarchy.

The .NET Framework defines several built-in exceptions that are derived from **SystemException**. For example, when a division-by-zero is attempted, a **DivideByZeroException** exception is generated. As you will see later in this chapter, you can create your own exception classes by deriving them from **Exception**.

Exception-Handling Fundamentals

C# exception handling is managed via four keywords: **try**, **catch**, **throw**, and **finally**. They form an interrelated subsystem in which the use of one implies the use of another. Throughout the course of this chapter, each keyword is examined in detail. However, it is useful at the outset to have a general understanding of the role each plays in exception handling. Briefly, here is how they work.

Program statements that you want to monitor for exceptions are contained within a **try** block. If an exception occurs within the **try** block, it is *thrown*. Your code can catch this exception using **catch** and handle it in some rational manner. System-generated exceptions are automatically thrown by the runtime system. To manually throw an exception, use the keyword **throw**. Any code that absolutely must be executed upon exiting from a **try** block is put in a **finally** block.

Using try and catch

At the core of exception handling are **try** and **catch**. These keywords work together, and you can't have a **catch** without a **try**. Here is the general form of the **try**/**catch** exception-handling blocks:

```
try {
  // block of code to monitor for errors
}

catch (ExcepType1 exOb) {
  // handler for ExcepType1
}

catch (ExcepType2 exOb) {
  // handler for ExcepType2
}
.
.
.
```

Here, *ExcepType* is the type of exception that has occurred. When an exception is thrown, it is caught by its corresponding **catch** clause, which then processes the exception. As the general form shows, more than one **catch** clause can be associated with a **try**. The type of the exception determines which **catch** is executed. That is, if the exception type specified by a **catch** matches that of the exception, then that **catch** is executed (and all others are bypassed). When an exception is caught, the exception variable *exOb* will receive its value.

Actually, specifying *exOb* is optional. If the exception handler does not need access to the exception object (as is often the case), there is no need to specify *exOb*. The exception type alone is sufficient. For this reason, many of the examples in this chapter will not specify *exOb*.

Here is an important point: If no exception is thrown, then a **try** block ends normally, and all of its **catch** clauses are bypassed. Execution resumes with the first statement following the last **catch**. Thus, a **catch** is executed only if an exception is thrown.

A Simple Exception Example

Here is a simple example that illustrates how to watch for and catch an exception. As you know, it is an error to attempt to index an array beyond its boundaries. When this error occurs, the CLR throws an **IndexOutOfRangeException**, which is a standard exception defined by the .NET Framework. The following program purposely generates such an exception and then catches it:

```
// Demonstrate exception handling.

using System;

class ExcDemo1 {
  static void Main() {
    int[] nums = new int[4];

    try {
      Console.WriteLine("Before exception is generated.");

      // Generate an index out-of-bounds exception.
      for(int i=0; i < 10; i++) {
        nums[i] = i;
        Console.WriteLine("nums[{0}]: {1}", i, nums[i]);
      }

      Console.WriteLine("this won't be displayed");
    }
    catch (IndexOutOfRangeException) {
      // Catch the exception.
      Console.WriteLine("Index out-of-bounds!");
    }
    Console.WriteLine("After catch block.");
  }
}
```

This program displays the following output:

```
Before exception is generated.
nums[0]: 0
nums[1]: 1
nums[2]: 2
nums[3]: 3
Index out-of-bounds!
After catch block.
```

Notice that **nums** is an **int** array of four elements. However, the **for** loop tries to index **nums** from 0 to 9, which causes an **IndexOutOfRangeException** to occur when an index value of 4 is tried.

Although quite short, the preceding program illustrates several key points about exception handling. First, the code that you want to monitor for errors is contained within a **try** block. Second, when an exception occurs (in this case, because of the attempt to index **nums** beyond its bounds inside the **for** loop), the exception is thrown out of the **try** block and caught by the **catch**. At this point, control passes to the **catch** block, and the **try** block is terminated. That is, **catch** is *not* called. Rather, program execution is transferred to it. Thus, the **WriteLine()** statement following the out-of-bounds index will never execute. After the **catch** block executes, program control continues with the statements following the **catch**. Thus, it is the job of your exception handler to remedy the problem that caused the exception so program execution can continue normally.

Notice that no exception variable is specified in the **catch** clause. Instead, only the type of the exception (**IndexOutOfRangeException** in this case) is required. As mentioned, an exception variable is needed only when access to the exception object is required. In some cases, the value of the exception object can be used by the exception handler to obtain additional information about the error, but in many cases, it is sufficient to simply know that an exception occurred. Thus, it is not unusual for the **catch** variable to be absent in the exception handler, as is the case in the preceding program.

As explained, if no exception is thrown by a **try** block, no **catch** will be executed and program control resumes after the **catch**. To confirm this, in the preceding program, change the **for** loop from

```
for(int i=0; i < 10; i++) {
```

to

```
for(int i=0; i < nums.Length; i++) {
```

Now, the loop does not overrun **nums'** boundary. Thus, no exception is generated, and the **catch** block is not executed.

A Second Exception Example

It is important to understand that all code executed within a **try** block is monitored for exceptions. This includes exceptions that might be generated by a method called from within the **try** block. An exception thrown by a method called from within a **try** block can be caught by that **try** block, assuming, of course, that the method itself did not catch the exception.

For example, consider the following program. **Main()** establishes a **try** block from which the method **GenException()** is called. Inside **GenException()**, an **IndexOutOfRangeException** is generated. This exception is not caught by **GenException()**. However, since **GenException()** was called from within a **try** block in **Main()**, the exception is caught by the **catch** statement associated with that **try**.

```
/* An exception can be generated by one
   method and caught by another. */

using System;

class ExcTest {
  // Generate an exception.
  public static void GenException() {
    int[] nums = new int[4];

    Console.WriteLine("Before exception is generated.");

    // Generate an index out-of-bounds exception.
    for(int i=0; i < 10; i++) {
      nums[i] = i;
      Console.WriteLine("nums[{0}]: {1}", i, nums[i]);
    }
```

```
      Console.WriteLine("this won't be displayed");
  }
}

class ExcDemo2 {
  static void Main() {

    try {
      ExcTest.GenException();
    }
    catch (IndexOutOfRangeException) {
      // Catch the exception.
      Console.WriteLine("Index out-of-bounds!");
    }
    Console.WriteLine("After catch block.");
  }
}
```

This program produces the following output, which is the same as that produced by the first version of the program shown earlier:

```
Before exception is generated.
nums[0]: 0
nums[1]: 1
nums[2]: 2
nums[3]: 3
Index out-of-bounds!
After catch block.
```

As explained, because **GenException( )** is called from within a **try** block, the exception that it generates (and does not catch) is caught by the **catch** in **Main( )**. Understand, however, that if **GenException( )** had caught the exception, then it never would have been passed back to **Main( )**.

The Consequences of an Uncaught Exception

Catching one of the standard exceptions, as the preceding program does, has a side benefit: It prevents abnormal program termination. When an exception is thrown, it must be caught by some piece of code, somewhere. In general, if your program does not catch an exception, it will be caught by the runtime system. The trouble is that the runtime system will report an error and terminate the program. For instance, in this example, the index out-of-bounds exception is not caught by the program:

```
// Let the C# runtime system handle the error.

using System;

class NotHandled {
  static void Main() {
    int[] nums = new int[4];
```

```
    Console.WriteLine("Before exception is generated.");

    // Generate an index out-of-bounds exception.
    for(int i=0; i < 10; i++) {
      nums[i] = i;
      Console.WriteLine("nums[{0}]: {1}", i, nums[i]);
    }

  }
}
```

When the array index error occurs, execution is halted and the following error message is displayed:

```
Unhandled Exception: System.IndexOutOfRangeException:
        Index was outside the bounds of the array.
   at NotHandled.Main()
```

Although such a message is useful while debugging, you would not want others to see it, to say the least! This is why it is important for your program to handle exceptions itself.

As mentioned earlier, the type of the exception must match the type specified in a **catch**. If it doesn't, the exception won't be caught. For example, the following program tries to catch an array boundary error with a **catch** for a **DivideByZeroException** (another built-in exception). When the array boundary is overrun, an **IndexOutOfRangeException** is generated, but it won't be caught by the **catch**. This results in abnormal program termination.

```
// This won't work!

using System;

class ExcTypeMismatch {
  static void Main() {
    int[] nums = new int[4];

    try {
      Console.WriteLine("Before exception is generated.");

      // Generate an index out-of-bounds exception.
      for(int i=0; i < 10; i++) {
        nums[i] = i;
        Console.WriteLine("nums[{0}]: {1}", i, nums[i]);
      }

      Console.WriteLine("this won't be displayed");
    }

    /* Can't catch an array boundary error with a
       DivideByZeroException. */
    catch (DivideByZeroException) {
      // Catch the exception.
      Console.WriteLine("Index out-of-bounds!");
    }
```

```
      Console.WriteLine("After catch block.");
   }
}
```

The output is shown here:

```
Before exception is generated.
nums[0]: 0
nums[1]: 1
nums[2]: 2
nums[3]: 3

Unhandled Exception: System.IndexOutOfRangeException:
        Index was outside the bounds of the array.
   at ExcTypeMismatch.Main()
```

As the output demonstrates, a **catch** for **DivideByZeroException** won't catch an **IndexOutOfRangeException**.

Exceptions Let You Handle Errors Gracefully

One of the key benefits of exception handling is that it enables your program to respond to an error and then continue running. For example, consider the following example that divides the elements of one array by the elements of another. If a division-by-zero occurs, a **DivideByZeroException** is generated. In the program, this exception is handled by reporting the error and then continuing with execution. Thus, attempting to divide by zero does not cause an abrupt runtime error resulting in the termination of the program. Instead, it is handled gracefully, allowing program execution to continue.

```
// Handle error gracefully and continue.

using System;

class ExcDemo3 {
  static void Main() {
    int[] numer = { 4, 8, 16, 32, 64, 128 };
    int[] denom = { 2, 0, 4, 4, 0, 8 };

    for(int i=0; i < numer.Length; i++) {
      try {
        Console.WriteLine(numer[i] + " / " +
                          denom[i] + " is " +
                          numer[i]/denom[i]);
      }
      catch (DivideByZeroException) {
        // Catch the exception.
        Console.WriteLine("Can't divide by Zero!");
      }
    }
  }
}
```

The output from the program is shown here:

```
4 / 2 is 2
Can't divide by Zero!
16 / 4 is 4
32 / 4 is 8
Can't divide by Zero!
128 / 8 is 16
```

This example makes another important point: Once an exception has been handled, it is removed from the system. Therefore, in the program, each pass through the loop enters the **try** block anew—any prior exceptions have been handled. This enables your program to handle repeated errors.

Using Multiple catch Clauses

You can associate more than one **catch** clause with a **try**. In fact, it is common to do so. However, each **catch** must catch a different type of exception. For example, the program shown here catches both array boundary and divide-by-zero errors:

```
// Use multiple catch clauses.

using System;

class ExcDemo4 {
  static void Main() {
    // Here, numer is longer than denom.
    int[] numer = { 4, 8, 16, 32, 64, 128, 256, 512 };
    int[] denom = { 2, 0, 4, 4, 0, 8 };

    for(int i=0; i < numer.Length; i++) {
      try {
        Console.WriteLine(numer[i] + " / " +
                          denom[i] + " is " +
                          numer[i]/denom[i]);
      }
      catch (DivideByZeroException) {
        Console.WriteLine("Can't divide by Zero!");
      }
      catch (IndexOutOfRangeException) {
        Console.WriteLine("No matching element found.");
      }
    }
  }
}
```

This program produces the following output:

```
4 / 2 is 2
Can't divide by Zero!
16 / 4 is 4
32 / 4 is 8
Can't divide by Zero!
128 / 8 is 16
```

```
No matching element found.
No matching element found.
```

As the output confirms, each **catch** clause responds only to its own type of exception.

In general, **catch** clauses are checked in the order in which they occur in a program. Only the first matching clause is executed. All other **catch** blocks are ignored.

Catching All Exceptions

Occasionally, you might want to catch all exceptions, no matter the type. To do this, use a **catch** clause that specifies no exception type or variable. It has this general form:

```
catch {
   // handle exceptions
}
```

This creates a "catch all" handler that ensures that all exceptions are caught by your program.

Here is an example of a "catch all" exception handler. Notice that it catches both the **IndexOutOfRangeException** and the **DivideByZeroException** generated by the program:

```
// Use the "catch all" catch.

using System;

class ExcDemo5 {
  static void Main() {
    // Here, numer is longer than denom.
    int[] numer = { 4, 8, 16, 32, 64, 128, 256, 512 };
    int[] denom = { 2, 0, 4, 4, 0, 8 };

    for(int i=0; i < numer.Length; i++) {
      try {
        Console.WriteLine(numer[i] + " / " +
                          denom[i] + " is " +
                          numer[i]/denom[i]);
      }
      catch { // A "catch-all" catch.
        Console.WriteLine("Some exception occurred.");
      }
    }
  }
}
```

The output is shown here:

```
4 / 2 is 2
Some exception occurred.
16 / 4 is 4
32 / 4 is 8
Some exception occurred.
128 / 8 is 16
Some exception occurred.
Some exception occurred.
```

There is one point to remember about using a catch-all **catch**: It must be the last **catch** clause in the **catch** sequence.

NOTE *In the vast majority of cases you should not use the "catch all" handler as a means of dealing with exceptions. It is normally better to deal individually with the exceptions that your code can generate. The inappropriate use of the "catch all" handler can lead to situations in which errors that would otherwise be noticed during testing are masked. It is also difficult to correctly handle all types of exceptions with a single handler. That said, a "catch all" handler might be appropriate in certain specialized circumstances, such as in a runtime code analysis tool.*

Nesting try Blocks

One **try** block can be nested within another. An exception generated within the inner **try** block that is not caught by a **catch** associated with that **try** is propagated to the outer **try** block. For example, here the **IndexOutOfRangeException** is not caught by the inner **try** block, but by the outer **try**:

```
// Use a nested try block.

using System;

class NestTrys {
  static void Main() {
    // Here, numer is longer than denom.
    int[] numer = { 4, 8, 16, 32, 64, 128, 256, 512 };
    int[] denom = { 2, 0, 4, 4, 0, 8 };

    try { // outer try
      for(int i=0; i < numer.Length; i++) {
        try { // nested try
          Console.WriteLine(numer[i] + " / " +
                            denom[i] + " is " +
                            numer[i]/denom[i]);
        }
        catch (DivideByZeroException) {
          Console.WriteLine("Can't divide by Zero!");
        }
      }
    }
    catch (IndexOutOfRangeException) {
      Console.WriteLine("No matching element found.");
      Console.WriteLine("Fatal error -- program terminated.");
    }
  }
}
```

The output from the program is shown here:

```
4 / 2 is 2
Can't divide by Zero!
16 / 4 is 4
```

```
32 / 4 is 8
Can't divide by Zero!
128 / 8 is 16
No matching element found.
Fatal error -- program terminated.
```

In this example, an exception that can be handled by the inner **try**—in this case a divide-by-zero error—allows the program to continue. However, an array boundary error is caught by the outer **try**, which causes the program to terminate.

Although certainly not the only reason for nested **try** statements, the preceding program makes an important point that can be generalized. Often, nested **try** blocks are used to allow different categories of errors to be handled in different ways. Some types of errors are catastrophic and cannot be fixed. Some are minor and can be handled immediately. Many programmers use an outer **try** block to catch the most severe errors, allowing inner **try** blocks to handle less serious ones. You can also use an outer **try** block as a "catch all" block for those errors that are not handled by the inner block.

Throwing an Exception

The preceding examples have been catching exceptions generated automatically by the runtime system. However, it is possible to throw an exception manually by using the **throw** statement. Its general form is shown here:

throw *exceptOb*;

The *exceptOb* must be an object of an exception class derived from **Exception**.

Here is an example that illustrates the **throw** statement by manually throwing a **DivideByZeroException**:

```
// Manually throw an exception.

using System;

class ThrowDemo {
  static void Main() {
    try {
      Console.WriteLine("Before throw.");
      throw new DivideByZeroException();
    }
    catch (DivideByZeroException) {
      Console.WriteLine("Exception caught.");
    }
    Console.WriteLine("After try/catch statement.");
  }
}
```

The output from the program is shown here:

```
Before throw.
Exception caught.
After try/catch statement.
```

Notice how the **DivideByZeroException** was created using **new** in the **throw** statement. Remember, **throw** throws an object. Thus, you must create an object for it to throw. That is, you can't just throw a type. In this case, the default constructor is used to create a **DivideByZeroException** object, but other constructors are available for exceptions.

Most often, exceptions that you throw will be instances of exception classes that you created. As you will see later in this chapter, creating your own exception classes allows you to handle errors in your code as part of your program's overall exception-handling strategy.

Rethrowing an Exception

An exception caught by one **catch** can be rethrown so that it can be caught by an outer **catch**. The most likely reason for rethrowing an exception is to allow multiple handlers access to the exception. For example, perhaps one exception handler manages one aspect of an exception, and a second handler copes with another aspect. To rethrow an exception, you simply specify **throw**, without specifying an expression. That is, you use this form of **throw**:

throw ;

Remember, when you rethrow an exception, it will not be recaught by the same **catch** clause. Instead, it will propagate to an outer **catch**.

The following program illustrates rethrowing an exception. In this case, it rethrows an **IndexOutOfRangeException**.

```
// Rethrow an exception.

using System;

class Rethrow {
  public static void GenException() {
    // Here, numer is longer than denom.
    int[] numer = { 4, 8, 16, 32, 64, 128, 256, 512 };
    int[] denom = { 2, 0, 4, 4, 0, 8 };

    for(int i=0; i<numer.Length; i++) {
      try {
        Console.WriteLine(numer[i] + " / " +
                          denom[i] + " is " +
                          numer[i]/denom[i]);
      }
      catch (DivideByZeroException) {
        Console.WriteLine("Can't divide by Zero!");
      }
      catch (IndexOutOfRangeException) {
        Console.WriteLine("No matching element found.");
        throw; // rethrow the exception
      }
    }
  }
}

class RethrowDemo {
  static void Main() {
    try {
```

```
      Rethrow.GenException();
    }
    catch(IndexOutOfRangeException) {
      // recatch exception
      Console.WriteLine("Fatal error -- " + "program terminated.");
    }
  }
}
```

In this program, divide-by-zero errors are handled locally, by **GenException( )**, but an array boundary error is rethrown. In this case, the **IndexOutOfRangeException** is handled by **Main( )**.

Using finally

Sometimes you will want to define a block of code that will execute when a **try/catch** block is left. For example, an exception might cause an error that terminates the current method, causing its premature return. However, that method may have opened a file or a network connection that needs to be closed. Such types of circumstances are common in programming, and C# provides a convenient way to handle them: **finally**.

To specify a block of code to execute when a **try/catch** block is exited, include a **finally** block at the end of a **try/catch** sequence. The general form of a **try/catch** that includes **finally** is shown here:

```
try {
  // block of code to monitor for errors
}
catch (ExcepType1 exOb) {
  // handler for ExcepType1
}
catch (ExcepType2 exOb) {
  // handler for ExcepType2
}
  .
  .
  .
finally {
  // finally code
}
```

The **finally** block will be executed whenever execution leaves a **try/catch** block, no matter what conditions cause it. That is, whether the **try** block ends normally, or because of an exception, the last code executed is that defined by **finally**. The **finally** block is also executed if any code within the **try** block or any of its **catch** blocks returns from the method.

Here is an example of **finally**:

```
// Use finally.

using System;

class UseFinally {
  public static void GenException(int what) {
```

```
      int t;
      int[] nums = new int[2];

      Console.WriteLine("Receiving " + what);
      try {
        switch(what) {
          case 0:
            t = 10 / what; // generate div-by-zero error
            break;
          case 1:
            nums[4] = 4; // generate array index error
            break;
          case 2:
            return; // return from try block
        }
      }
      catch (DivideByZeroException) {
        Console.WriteLine("Can't divide by Zero!");
        return; // return from catch
      }
      catch (IndexOutOfRangeException) {
        Console.WriteLine("No matching element found.");
      }
      finally {
        Console.WriteLine("Leaving try.");
      }
    }
}

class FinallyDemo {
  static void Main() {

    for(int i=0; i < 3; i++) {
      UseFinally.GenException(i);
      Console.WriteLine();
    }
  }
}
```

Here is the output produced by the program:

```
Receiving 0
Can't divide by Zero!
Leaving try.

Receiving 1
No matching element found.
Leaving try.

Receiving 2
Leaving try.
```

As the output shows, no matter how the **try** block is exited, the **finally** block is executed.

One other point: Syntactically, when a **finally** block follows a **try** block, no **catch** clauses are technically required. Thus, you can have a **try** followed by a **finally** with no **catch** clauses. In this case, the **finally** block is executed when the **try** exits, but no exceptions are handled.

A Closer Look at the Exception Class

Up to this point, we have been catching exceptions, but we haven't been doing anything with the exception object itself. As explained earlier, a **catch** clause allows you to specify an exception type *and* a variable. The variable receives a reference to the exception object. Since all exceptions are derived from **Exception**, all exceptions support the members defined by **Exception**. Here we will examine several of its most useful members and constructors, and put the exception variable to use.

Exception defines several properties. Three of the most interesting are **Message**, **StackTrace**, and **TargetSite**. All are read-only. **Message** contains a string that describes the nature of the error. **StackTrace** contains a string that contains the stack of calls that lead to the exception. **TargetSite** obtains an object that specifies the method that generated the exception.

Exception also defines several methods. One that you will often use is **ToString( )**, which returns a string that describes the exception. **ToString( )** is automatically called when an exception is displayed via **WriteLine( )**, for example.

The following program demonstrates these properties and this method:

```
// Using Exception members.

using System;

class ExcTest {
  public static void GenException() {
    int[] nums = new int[4];

    Console.WriteLine("Before exception is generated.");

    // Generate an index out-of-bounds exception.
      for(int i=0; i < 10; i++) {
        nums[i] = i;
        Console.WriteLine("nums[{0}]: {1}", i, nums[i]);
      }

    Console.WriteLine("this won't be displayed");
  }
}

class UseExcept {
  static void Main() {

    try {
      ExcTest.GenException();
    }
    catch (IndexOutOfRangeException exc) {
```

```
      Console.WriteLine("Standard message is: ");
      Console.WriteLine(exc); // calls ToString()
      Console.WriteLine("Stack trace: " + exc.StackTrace);
      Console.WriteLine("Message: " + exc.Message);
      Console.WriteLine("TargetSite: " + exc.TargetSite);
    }
    Console.WriteLine("After catch block.");
  }
}
```

The output from this program is shown here:

```
Before exception is generated.
nums[0]: 0
nums[1]: 1
nums[2]: 2
nums[3]: 3
Standard message is:
System.IndexOutOfRangeException: Index was outside the bounds of the array.
   at ExcTest.GenException()
   at UseExcept.Main()
Stack trace:    at ExcTest.GenException()
   at UseExcept.Main()
Message: Index was outside the bounds of the array.
TargetSite: Void GenException()
After catch block.
```

Exception defines the following four constructors:

public Exception( )

public Exception(string *message*)

public Exception(string *message*, Exception *innerException*)

protected Exception(System.Runtime.Serialization.SerializationInfo *info*,
            System.Runtime.Serialization.StreamingContext *context*)

The first is the default constructor. The second specifies the string associated with the
Message property associated with the exception. The third specifies what is called an *inner
exception*. It is used when one exception gives rise to another. In this case, *innerException*
specifies the first exception, which will be null if no inner exception exists. (The inner exception,
if it exists, can be obtained from the **InnerException** property defined by **Exception**.) The
last constructor handles exceptions that occur remotely and require deserialization.

One other point: In the fourth **Exception** constructor shown above, notice that the types
SerializationInfo and **StreamingContext** are contained in the **System.Runtime.Serialization**
namespace.

Commonly Used Exceptions

The **System** namespace defines several standard, built-in exceptions. All are derived (either
directly or indirectly) from **SystemException** since they are generated by the CLR when
runtime errors occur. Several of the more commonly used standard exceptions are shown
in Table 13-1.

Exception	Meaning
ArrayTypeMismatchException	Type of value being stored is incompatible with the type of the array.
DivideByZeroException	Division by zero attempted.
IndexOutOfRangeException	Array index is out-of-bounds.
InvalidCastException	A runtime cast is invalid.
OutOfMemoryException	Insufficient free memory exists to continue program execution. For example, this exception will be thrown if there is not sufficient free memory to create an object via **new**.
OverflowException	An arithmetic overflow occurred.
NullReferenceException	An attempt was made to operate on a null reference—that is, a reference that does not refer to an object.

TABLE 13-1   Commonly Used Exceptions Defined Within the **System** Namespace

Most of the exceptions in Table 13-1 are self-explanatory, with the possible exception of **NullReferenceException**. This exception is thrown when there is an attempt to use a null reference as if it referred to an object—for example, if you attempt to call a method on a null reference. A *null reference* is a reference that does not point to any object. One way to create a null reference is to explicitly assign it the value null by using the keyword **null**. Null references can also occur in other ways that are less obvious. Here is a program that demonstrates the **NullReferenceException**:

```
// Use the NullReferenceException.

using System;

class X {
  int x;
  public X(int a) {
    x = a;
  }

  public int Add(X o) {
    return x + o.x;
  }
}

// Demonstrate NullReferenceException.
class NREDemo {
  static void Main() {
    X p = new X(10);
    X q = null; // q is explicitly assigned null
    int val;
```

```
    try {
      val = p.Add(q); // this will lead to an exception
    } catch (NullReferenceException) {
      Console.WriteLine("NullReferenceException!");
      Console.WriteLine("fixing...\n");

      // Now, fix it.
      q = new X(9);
      val = p.Add(q);
    }

    Console.WriteLine("val is {0}", val);
  }
}
```

The output from the program is shown here:

```
NullReferenceException!
fixing...

val is 19
```

The program creates a class called **X** that defines a member called **x** and the **Add( )** method, which adds the invoking object's **x** to the **x** in the object passed as a parameter. In **Main( )**, two **X** objects are created. The first, **p**, is initialized. The second, **q**, is not. Instead, it is explicitly assigned **null**. Then **p.Add( )** is called with **q** as an argument. Because **q** does not refer to any object, a **NullReferenceException** is generated when the attempt is made to obtain the value of **q.x**.

Deriving Exception Classes

Although C#'s built-in exceptions handle most common errors, C#'s exception-handling mechanism is not limited to these errors. In fact, part of the power of C#'s approach to exceptions is its ability to handle exception types that you create. You can use custom exceptions to handle errors in your own code. Creating an exception is easy. Just define a class derived from **Exception**. Your derived classes don't need to actually implement anything—it is their existence in the type system that allows you to use them as exceptions.

NOTE *In the past, custom exceptions were derived from **ApplicationException** since this is the hierarchy that was originally reserved for application-related exceptions. However, Microsoft no longer recommends this. Instead, at the time of this writing, Microsoft recommends deriving custom exceptions from **Exception**. For this reason, this approach is used here.*

The exception classes that you create will automatically have the properties and methods defined by **Exception** available to them. Of course, you can override one or more of these members in exception classes that you create.

When creating your own exception class, you will generally want your class to support all of the constructors defined by **Exception**. For simple custom exception classes, this is easy to do because you can simply pass along the constructor's arguments to the corresponding **Exception** constructor via **base**. Of course, technically, you need to provide only those constructors actually used by your program.

Here is an example that makes use of a custom exception type. At the end of Chapter 10 an array class called **RangeArray** was developed. As you may recall, **RangeArray** supports single-dimensional **int** arrays in which the starting and ending index is specified by the user. For example, an array that ranges from –5 to 27 is perfectly legal for a **RangeArray**. In Chapter 10, if an index was out of range, a special error variable defined by **RangeArray** was set. This meant that the error variable had to be checked after each operation by the code that used **RangeArray**. Of course, such an approach is error-prone and clumsy. A far better design is to have **RangeArray** throw a custom exception when a range error occurs. This is precisely what the following version of **RangeArray** does:

```
// Use a custom Exception for RangeArray errors.

using System;

// Create a RangeArray exception.
class RangeArrayException : Exception {
  /* Implement all of the Exception constructors. Notice that
     the constructors simply execute the base class constructor.
     Because RangeArrayException adds nothing to Exception,
     there is no need for any further actions. */
  public RangeArrayException() : base() { }
  public RangeArrayException(string message) : base(message) { }
  public RangeArrayException(string message, Exception innerException) :
    base(message, innerException) { }
  protected RangeArrayException(
    System.Runtime.Serialization.SerializationInfo info,
    System.Runtime.Serialization.StreamingContext context) :
      base(info, context) { }

  // Override ToString for RangeArrayException.
  public override string ToString() {
    return Message;
  }
}

// An improved version of RangeArray.
class RangeArray {
  // Private data.
  int[] a; // reference to underlying array
  int lowerBound; // smallest index
  int upperBound; // largest index

  // An auto-implemented, read-only Length property.
  public int Length { get; private set; }
```

```csharp
    // Construct array given its size.
    public RangeArray(int low, int high) {
      high++;
      if(high <= low) {
        throw new RangeArrayException("Low index not less than high.");
      }
      a = new int[high - low];
      Length = high - low;

      lowerBound = low;
      upperBound = --high;
    }

    // This is the indexer for RangeArray.
    public int this[int index] {
      // This is the get accessor.
      get {
        if(ok(index)) {
          return a[index - lowerBound];
        } else {
          throw new RangeArrayException("Range Error.");
        }
      }

      // This is the set accessor.
      set {
        if(ok(index)) {
          a[index - lowerBound] = value;
        }
        else throw new RangeArrayException("Range Error.");
      }
    }

    // Return true if index is within bounds.
    private bool ok(int index) {
      if(index >= lowerBound & index <= upperBound) return true;
      return false;
    }
  }

  // Demonstrate the index-range array.
  class RangeArrayDemo {
    static void Main() {
      try {
        RangeArray ra = new RangeArray(-5, 5);
        RangeArray ra2 = new RangeArray(1, 10);

        // Demonstrate ra.
        Console.WriteLine("Length of ra: " + ra.Length);

        for(int i = -5; i <= 5; i++)
          ra[i] = i;
```

```
    Console.Write("Contents of ra: ");
    for(int i = -5; i <= 5; i++)
      Console.Write(ra[i] + " ");

    Console.WriteLine("\n");

    // Demonstrate ra2.
    Console.WriteLine("Length of ra2: " + ra2.Length);

    for(int i = 1; i <= 10; i++)
      ra2[i] = i;

    Console.Write("Contents of ra2: ");
    for(int i = 1; i <= 10; i++)
      Console.Write(ra2[i] + " ");

    Console.WriteLine("\n");

  } catch (RangeArrayException exc) {
    Console.WriteLine(exc);
  }

  // Now, demonstrate some errors.
  Console.WriteLine("Now generate some range errors.");

  // Use an invalid constructor.
  try {
    RangeArray ra3 = new RangeArray(100, -10); // Error
  } catch (RangeArrayException exc) {
    Console.WriteLine(exc);
  }

  // Use an invalid index.
  try {
    RangeArray ra3 = new RangeArray(-2, 2);

    for(int i = -2; i <= 2; i++)
      ra3[i] = i;

    Console.Write("Contents of ra3: ");
    for(int i = -2; i <= 10; i++) // generate range error
      Console.Write(ra3[i] + " ");

  } catch (RangeArrayException exc) {
    Console.WriteLine(exc);
  }
  }
}
```

The output from the program is shown here:

```
Length of ra: 11
Contents of ra: -5 -4 -3 -2 -1 0 1 2 3 4 5
```

```
Length of ra2: 10
Contents of ra2: 1 2 3 4 5 6 7 8 9 10

Now generate some range errors.
Low index not less than high.
Contents of ra3: -2 -1 0 1 2 Range Error.
```

When a range error occurs, **RangeArray** throws an object of type **RangeArrayException**. Notice there are three places in **RangeArray** that this might occur: in the **get** indexer accessor, in the **set** indexer accessor, and by the **RangeArray** constructor. To catch these exceptions implies that **RangeArray** objects must be constructed and accessed from within a **try** block, as the program illustrates. By using an exception to report errors, **RangeArray** now acts like one of C#'s built-in types and can be fully integrated into a program's exception-handling mechanism.

Notice that none of the **RangeArrayException** constructors provide any statements in their body. Instead, they simply pass their arguments along to **Exception** via **base**. As explained, in cases in which your exception class does not add any functionality, you can simply let the **Exception** constructors handle the process. There is no requirement that your derived class add anything to what is inherited from **Exception**.

Before moving on, you might want to experiment with this program a bit. For example, try commenting-out the override of **ToString( )** and observe the results. Also, try creating an exception using the default constructor, and observe what C# generates as its default message.

Catching Derived Class Exceptions

You need to be careful how you order **catch** clauses when trying to catch exception types that involve base and derived classes, because a **catch** for a base class will also match any of its derived classes. For example, because the base class of all exceptions is **Exception**, catching **Exception** catches all possible exceptions. Of course, using **catch** without an exception type provides a cleaner way to catch all exceptions, as described earlier. However, the issue of catching derived class exceptions is very important in other contexts, especially when you create exceptions of your own.

If you want to catch exceptions of both a base class type and a derived class type, put the derived class first in the **catch** sequence. This is necessary because a base class **catch** will also catch all derived classes. Fortunately, this rule is self-enforcing because putting the base class first causes a compile-time error.

The following program creates two exception classes called **ExceptA** and **ExceptB**. **ExceptA** is derived from **Exception**. **ExceptB** is derived from **ExceptA**. The program then throws an exception of each type. For brevity, the custom exceptions supply only one constructor (which takes a string that describes the exception). But remember, in commercial code, your custom exception classes will normally provide all four of the constructors defined by **Exception**.

```
// Derived exceptions must appear before base class exceptions.

using System;

// Create an exception.
class ExceptA : Exception {
  public ExceptA(string message) : base(message) { }
```

```
    public override string ToString() {
      return Message;
    }
}

// Create an exception derived from ExceptA.
class ExceptB : ExceptA {
  public ExceptB(string message) : base(message) { }

  public override string ToString() {
    return Message;
  }
}

class OrderMatters {
  static void Main() {
    for(int x = 0; x < 3; x++) {
      try {
        if(x==0) throw new ExceptA("Caught an ExceptA exception");
        else if(x==1) throw new ExceptB("Caught an ExceptB exception");
        else throw new Exception();
      }
      catch (ExceptB exc) {
        Console.WriteLine(exc);
      }
      catch (ExceptA exc) {
        Console.WriteLine(exc);
      }
      catch (Exception exc) {
        Console.WriteLine(exc);
      }
    }
  }
}
```

The output from the program is shown here:

```
Caught an ExceptA exception
Caught an ExceptB exception
System.Exception: Exception of type 'System.Exception' was thrown.
   at OrderMatters.Main()
```

Notice the type and order of the **catch** clauses. This is the only order in which they can occur. Since **ExceptB** is derived from **ExceptA**, the **catch** for **ExceptB** must be before the one for **ExceptA**. Similarly, the **catch** for **Exception** (which is the base class for all exceptions) must appear last. To prove this point for yourself, try rearranging the **catch** clauses. Doing so will result in a compile-time error.

One good use of a base class **catch** clause is to catch an entire category of exceptions. For example, imagine you are creating a set of exceptions for some device. If you derive all of the exceptions from a common base class, then applications that don't need to know precisely what problem occurred could simply catch the base class exception, avoiding the unnecessary duplication of code.

Using checked and unchecked

A special feature in C# relates to the generation of overflow exceptions in arithmetic computations. As you know, it is possible for some types of arithmetic computations to produce a result that exceeds the range of the data type involved in the computation. When this occurs, the result is said to *overflow*. For example, consider the following sequence:

```
byte a, b, result;
a = 127;
b = 127;

result = (byte) (a * b);
```

Here, the product of **a** and **b** exceeds the range of a **byte** value. Thus, the result overflows the type of the result.

C# allows you to specify whether your code will raise an exception when overflow occurs by using the keywords **checked** and **unchecked**. To specify that an expression be checked for overflow, use **checked**. To specify that overflow be ignored, use **unchecked**. In this case, the result is truncated to fit into the target type of the expression.

The **checked** keyword has these two general forms. One checks a specific expression and is called the *operator form* of **checked**. The other checks a block of statements and is called the *statement form*.

checked (*expr*)

checked {
   // statements to be checked
}

Here, *expr* is the expression being checked. If a checked expression overflows, then an **OverflowException** is thrown.

The **unchecked** keyword also has two general forms. The first is the operator form, which ignores overflow for a specific expression. The second ignores overflow for a block of statements.

unchecked (*expr*)

unchecked {
   // statements for which overflow is ignored
}

Here, *expr* is the expression that is not being checked for overflow. If an unchecked expression overflows, then truncation will occur.

Here is a program that demonstrates both **checked** and **unchecked**:

```
// Using checked and unchecked.

using System;

class CheckedDemo {
  static void Main() {
    byte a, b;
```

```
    byte result;

    a = 127;
    b = 127;

    try {
      result = unchecked((byte)(a * b));
      Console.WriteLine("Unchecked result: " + result);

      result = checked((byte)(a * b)); // this causes exception
      Console.WriteLine("Checked result: " + result); // won't execute
    }
    catch (OverflowException exc) {
      Console.WriteLine(exc);
    }
  }
}
```

The output from the program is shown here:

```
Unchecked result: 1
System.OverflowException: Arithmetic operation resulted in an overflow.
   at CheckedDemo.Main()
```

As is evident, the unchecked expression resulted in a truncation. The checked expression caused an exception.

The preceding program demonstrated the use of **checked** and **unchecked** for a single expression. The following program shows how to check and uncheck a block of statements.

```
// Using checked and unchecked with statement blocks.

using System;

class CheckedBlocks {
  static void Main() {
    byte a, b;
    byte result;

    a = 127;
    b = 127;

    try {
      unchecked {
        a = 127;
        b = 127;
        result = unchecked((byte)(a * b));
        Console.WriteLine("Unchecked result: " + result);

        a = 125;
        b = 5;
        result = unchecked((byte)(a * b));
        Console.WriteLine("Unchecked result: " + result);
      }
```

```
      checked {
        a = 2;
        b = 7;
        result = checked((byte)(a * b)); // this is OK
        Console.WriteLine("Checked result: " + result);

        a = 127;
        b = 127;
        result = checked((byte)(a * b)); // this causes exception
        Console.WriteLine("Checked result: " + result); // won't execute
      }
    }
    catch (OverflowException exc) {
      Console.WriteLine(exc);
    }
  }
}
```

The output from the program is shown here:

```
Unchecked result: 1
Unchecked result: 113
Checked result: 14
System.OverflowException: Arithmetic operation resulted in an overflow.
   at CheckedBlocks.Main()
```

As you can see, the unchecked block results in the overflow being truncated. When overflow occurred in the checked block, an exception was raised.

One reason that you may need to use **checked** or **unchecked** is that the default checked/unchecked status of overflow is determined by the setting of a compiler option and the execution environment, itself. Thus, for some types of programs, it is best to specify the overflow check status explicitly.

Using I/O

T he earlier chapters of this book have used parts of the C# I/O system, such as **Console.WriteLine( )**, but have done so without much formal explanation. Because the I/O system is built upon a hierarchy of classes, it was not possible to present its theory and details without first discussing classes, inheritance, and exceptions. Now it is time to examine I/O in detail. Because C# uses the I/O system and classes defined by the .NET Framework, a discussion of I/O under C# is also a discussion of the .NET I/O system, in general.

This chapter examines both console I/O and file I/O. Be forewarned that the I/O system is quite large. This chapter describes the most important and commonly used features.

C#'s I/O Is Built Upon Streams

C# programs perform I/O through streams. A *stream* is an abstraction that either produces or consumes information. A stream is linked to a physical device by the I/O system. All streams behave in the same manner, even if the actual physical devices they are linked to differ. Thus, the I/O classes and methods can be applied to many types of devices. For example, the same methods that you use to write to the console can also be used to write to a disk file.

Byte Streams and Character Streams

At the lowest level, all C# I/O operates on bytes. This makes sense because many devices are byte oriented when it comes to I/O operations. Frequently, though, we humans prefer to communicate using characters. Recall that in C#, **char** is a 16-bit type, and **byte** is an 8-bit type. If you are using the ASCII character set, then it is easy to convert between **char** and **byte**; just ignore the high-order byte of the **char** value. But this won't work for the rest of the Unicode characters, which need both bytes (and possibly more). Thus, byte streams are not perfectly suited to handling character-based I/O. To solve this problem, the .NET Framework defines several classes that convert a byte stream into a character stream, handling the translation of **byte**-to-**char** and **char**-to-**byte** for you automatically.

The Predefined Streams

Three predefined streams, which are exposed by the properties called **Console.In**, **Console.Out**, and **Console.Error**, are available to all programs that use the **System** namespace. **Console.Out** refers to the standard output stream. By default, this is the console. When you call **Console.WriteLine( )**, for example, it automatically sends information to **Console.Out**. **Console.In** refers to standard input, which is, by default, the keyboard. **Console.Error** refers to the standard error stream, which is also the console by default. However, these streams can be redirected to any compatible I/O device. The standard streams are character streams. Thus, these streams read and write characters.

The Stream Classes

The .NET Framework defines both byte and character stream classes. However, the character stream classes are really just wrappers that convert an underlying byte stream to a character stream, handling any conversion automatically. Thus, the character streams, although logically separate, are built upon byte streams.

The core stream classes are defined within the **System.IO** namespace. To use these classes, you will usually include the following statement near the top of your program:

```
using System.IO;
```

The reason that you don't have to specify **System.IO** for console input and output is that the **Console** class is defined in the **System** namespace.

The Stream Class

The core stream class is **System.IO.Stream**. **Stream** represents a byte stream and is a base class for all other stream classes. It is also abstract, which means that you cannot instantiate a **Stream** object. **Stream** defines a set of standard stream operations. Table 14-1 shows several commonly used methods defined by **Stream**.

Several of the methods shown in Table 14-1 will throw an **IOException** if an I/O error occurs. If an invalid operation is attempted, such as attempting to write to a stream that is read-only, a **NotSupportedException** is thrown. Other exceptions are possible, depending on the specific method.

Method	Description
void Close( )	Closes the stream.
void Flush( )	Writes the contents of the stream to the physical device.
int ReadByte( )	Returns an integer representation of the next available byte of input. Returns –1 when the end of the file is encountered.
int Read(byte[ ] *buffer*, int *offset*, int *count*)	Attempts to read up to *count* bytes into *buffer* starting at *buffer[offset]*, returning the number of bytes successfully read.
long Seek(long *offset*, SeekOrigin *origin*)	Sets the current position in the stream to the specified *offset* from the specified *origin*. It returns the new position.
void WriteByte(byte *value*)	Writes a single byte to an output stream.
int Write(byte[ ] *buffer*, int *offset*, int *count*)	Writes a subrange of *count* bytes from the array *buffer*, beginning at *buffer[offset]*, returning the number of bytes written.

TABLE 14-1 Some of the Methods Defined by **Stream**

Notice that **Stream** defines methods that read and write data. However, not all streams will support both of these operations, because it is possible to open read-only or write-only streams. Also, not all streams will support position requests via **Seek( )**. To determine the capabilities of a stream, you will use one or more of **Stream**'s properties. They are shown in Table 14-2. Also shown are the **Length** and **Position** properties, which contain the length of the stream and its current position.

The Byte Stream Classes

Several concrete byte streams are derived from **Stream**. Those defined in the **System.IO** namespace are shown here:

Stream Class	Description
BufferedStream	Wraps a byte stream and adds buffering. Buffering provides a performance enhancement in many cases.
FileStream	A byte stream designed for file I/O.
MemoryStream	A byte stream that uses memory for storage.
UnmanagedMemoryStream	A byte stream that uses unmanaged memory for storage.

Several other concrete stream classes are also supported by the .NET Framework, which provide support for compressed files, sockets, and pipes, among others. It is also possible for you to derive your own stream classes. However, for the vast majority of applications, the built-in streams will be sufficient.

Property	Description
bool CanRead	This property is true if the stream can be read. This property is read-only.
bool CanSeek	This property is true if the stream supports position requests. This property is read-only.
bool CanTimeout	This property is true if the stream can time out. This property is read-only.
bool CanWrite	This property is true if the stream can be written. This property is read-only.
long Length	This property contains the length of the stream. This property is read-only.
long Position	This property represents the current position of the stream. This property is read/write.
int ReadTimeout	This property represents the length of time before a time-out will occur for read operations. This property is read/write.
int WriteTimeout	This property represents the length of time before a time-out will occur for write operations. This property is read/write.

TABLE 14-2 The Properties Defined by **Stream**

The Character Stream Wrapper Classes

To create a character stream, wrap a byte stream inside one of the character stream wrappers. At the top of the character stream hierarchy are the abstract classes **TextReader** and **TextWriter**. **TextReader** handles input, and **TextWriter** handles output. The methods defined by these two abstract classes are available to all of their subclasses. Thus, they form a minimal set of I/O functions that all character streams will have.

Table 14-3 shows the input methods in **TextReader**. In general, these methods can throw an **IOException** on error. (Some can throw other types of exceptions, too.) Of particular interest is the **ReadLine( )** method, which reads an entire line of text, returning it as a **string**. This method is useful when reading input that contains embedded spaces. **TextReader** also specifies the **Close( )** method, shown here:

void Close( )

It closes the reader and frees its resources.

TextWriter defines versions of **Write( )** and **WriteLine( )** that output all of the built-in types. For example, here are just a few of their overloaded versions:

Method	Description
void Write(int *value*)	Writes an **int**.
void Write(double *value*)	Writes a **double**.
void Write(bool *value*)	Writes a **bool**.
void WriteLine(string *value*)	Writes a **string** followed by a newline.
void WriteLine(uint *value*)	Writes a **uint** followed by a newline.
void WriteLine(char *value*)	Writes a **char** followed by a newline.

Method	Description
int Peek( )	Obtains the next character from the input stream, but does not remove that character. Returns –1 if no character is available.
int Read( )	Returns an integer representation of the next available character from the invoking input stream. Returns –1 when the end of the stream is encountered.
int Read(char[ ] *buffer*, int *index*, int *count*)	Attempts to read up to *count* characters into *buffer* starting at *buffer*[*count*], returning the number of characters successfully read.
int ReadBlock(char[ ] *buffer*, int *index*, int *count*)	Attempts to read up to *count* characters into *buffer* starting at *buffer*[*index*], returning the number of characters successfully read.
string ReadLine( )	Reads the next line of text and returns it as a string. Null is returned if an attempt is made to read at end-of-file.
string ReadToEnd( )	Reads all of the remaining characters in a stream and returns them as a string.

TABLE 14-3   The Input Methods Defined by **TextReader**

All throw an **IOException** if an error occurs while writing.

TextWriter also specifies the **Close( )** and **Flush( )** methods shown here:

```
virtual void Close( )
virtual void Flush( )
```

Flush( ) causes any data remaining in the output buffer to be written to the physical medium. **Close( )** closes the writer and frees its resources.

The **TextReader** and **TextWriter** classes are implemented by several character-based stream classes, including those shown here. Thus, these streams provide the methods and properties specified by **TextReader** and **TextWriter**.

Stream Class	Description
StreamReader	Reads characters from a byte stream. This class wraps a byte input stream.
StreamWriter	Writes characters to a byte stream. This class wraps a byte output stream.
StringReader	Reads characters from a string.
StringWriter	Writes characters to a string.

Binary Streams

In addition to the byte and character streams, there are two binary stream classes that can be used to read and write binary data directly. These streams are called **BinaryReader** and **BinaryWriter**. We will look closely at these later in this chapter when binary file I/O is discussed.

Now that you understand the general layout of the I/O system, the rest of this chapter will examine its various pieces in detail, beginning with console I/O.

Console I/O

Console I/O is accomplished through the standard streams **Console.In**, **Console.Out**, and **Console.Error**. Console I/O has been used since Chapter 2, so you are already familiar with it. As you will see, it has some additional capabilities.

Before we begin, however, it is important to emphasize a point made earlier in this book: Most real applications of C# will not be text-based, console programs. Rather, they will be graphically oriented programs or components that rely upon a windowed interface for interaction with the user, or will be server-side code. Thus, the portion of the I/O system that relates to console input and output is not widely used. Although text-based programs are excellent as teaching examples, for short utility programs, and for some types of components, they are not suitable for most real-world applications.

Reading Console Input

Console.In is an instance of **TextReader**, and you can use the methods and properties defined by **TextReader** to access it. However, you will usually use the methods provided by **Console**, which automatically read from **Console.In**. **Console** defines three input methods. The first two, **Read( )** and **ReadLine( )**, have been available since .NET Framework 1.0. The third, **ReadKey( )**, was added by .NET Framework 2.0.

To read a single character, use the **Read( )** method:

static int Read( )

Read( ) returns the next character read from the console. It waits until the user presses a key and then returns the result. The character is returned as an **int**, which must be cast to **char**. **Read( )** returns –1 on error. This method will throw an **IOException** on failure. When using **Read( )**, console input is line-buffered, so you must press ENTER before any character that you type will be sent to your program.

Here is a program that reads a character from the keyboard using **Read( )**:

```
// Read a character from the keyboard.

using System;

class KbIn {
  static void Main() {
    char ch;

    Console.Write("Press a key followed by ENTER: ");

    ch = (char) Console.Read(); // get a char

    Console.WriteLine("Your key is: " + ch);
  }
}
```

Here is a sample run:

```
Press a key followed by ENTER: t
Your key is: t
```

The fact that **Read( )** is line-buffered is a source of annoyance at times. When you press ENTER, a carriage-return, line-feed sequence is entered into the input stream. Furthermore, these characters are left pending in the input buffer until you read them. Thus, for some applications, you may need to remove them (by reading them) before the next input operation. (To read keystrokes from the console in a non-line-buffered manner, you can use **ReadKey( )**, described later in this section.)

To read a string of characters, use the **ReadLine( )** method. It is shown here:

static string ReadLine( )

ReadLine( ) reads characters until you press ENTER and returns them in a **string** object. This method will throw an **IOException** if an I/O error occurs.

Here is a program that demonstrates reading a string from **Console.In** by using **ReadLine( )**:

```
// Input from the console using ReadLine().

using System;

class ReadString {
  static void Main() {
    string str;
```

```
    Console.WriteLine("Enter some characters.");
    str = Console.ReadLine();
    Console.WriteLine("You entered: " + str);
  }
}
```

Here is a sample run:

```
Enter some characters.
This is a test.
You entered: This is a test.
```

Although the **Console** methods are the easiest way to read from **Console.In**, you can call methods on the underlying **TextReader**. For example, here is the preceding program rewritten to use the **ReadLine( )** method defined by **TextReader**:

```
// Read a string from the keyboard, using Console.In directly.

using System;

class ReadChars2 {
  static void Main() {
    string str;

    Console.WriteLine("Enter some characters.");

    str = Console.In.ReadLine(); // call TextReader's ReadLine() method

    Console.WriteLine("You entered: " + str);
  }
}
```

Notice how **ReadLine( )** is now invoked directly on **Console.In**. The key point here is that if you need access to the methods defined by the **TextReader** that underlies **Console.In**, you will invoke those methods as shown in this example.

Using ReadKey( )

The .NET Framework includes a method in **Console** that enables you to read individual keystrokes directly from the keyboard, in a non-line-buffered manner. This method is called **ReadKey( )**. When it is called, it waits until a key is pressed. When a key is pressed, **ReadKey( )** returns the keystroke immediately. The user does not need to press ENTER. Thus, **ReadKey( )** allows keystrokes to be read and processed in real time.

ReadKey( ) has these two forms:

static ConsoleKeyInfo ReadKey( )
static ConsoleKeyInfo ReadKey(bool *intercept*)

The first form waits for a key to be pressed. When that occurs, it returns the key and also displays the key on the screen. The second form also waits for and returns a keypress. However, if *intercept* is true, then the key is not displayed. If *intercept* is false, the key is displayed.

ReadKey( ) returns information about the keypress in an object of type
ConsoleKeyInfo, which is a structure. It contains the following read-only properties:

> char KeyChar
> ConsoleKey Key
> ConsoleModifiers Modifiers

KeyChar contains the **char** equivalent of the character that was pressed. **Key** contains a
value from the **ConsoleKey** enumeration, which is an enumeration of all the keys on the
keyboard. **Modifiers** describes which, if any, of the keyboard modifiers ATL, CTRL, or SHIFT
were pressed when the keystroke was generated. These modifiers are represented by the
ConsoleModifiers enumeration, which has these values: **Control**, **Shift**, and **Alt**. More than
one modifier value might be present in **Modifiers**.

The major advantage to **ReadKey( )** is that it provides a means of achieving interactive
keyboard input because it is not line buffered. To see this effect, try the following program:

```
// Read keystrokes from the console by using ReadKey().

using System;

class ReadKeys {
  static void Main() {
    ConsoleKeyInfo keypress;

    Console.WriteLine("Enter keystrokes. Enter Q to stop.");

    do {
      keypress = Console.ReadKey(); // read keystrokes

      Console.WriteLine(" Your key is: " + keypress.KeyChar);

      // Check for modifier keys.
      if((ConsoleModifiers.Alt & keypress.Modifiers) != 0)
        Console.WriteLine("Alt key pressed.");
      if((ConsoleModifiers.Control & keypress.Modifiers) != 0)
        Console.WriteLine("Control key pressed.");
      if((ConsoleModifiers.Shift & keypress.Modifiers) != 0)
        Console.WriteLine("Shift key pressed.");

    } while(keypress.KeyChar != 'Q');
  }
}
```

Here is a sample run:

```
Enter keystrokes. Enter Q to stop.
a Your key is: a
b Your key is: b
d Your key is: d
A Your key is: A
Shift key pressed.
B Your key is: B
Shift key pressed.
C Your key is: C
```

```
Shift key pressed.
● Your key is: ●
Control key pressed.
Q Your key is: Q
Shift key pressed.
```

As the output confirms, each time a key is pressed, **ReadKey( )** immediately returns the keypress. As explained, this differs from **Read( )** and **ReadLine( )**, which use line-buffered input. Therefore, if you want to achieve interactive responses from the keyboard, use **ReadKey( )**.

Writing Console Output

Console.Out and **Console.Error** are objects of type **TextWriter**. Console output is most easily accomplished with **Write( )** and **WriteLine( )**, with which you are already familiar. Versions of these methods exist that output each of the built-in types. **Console** defines its own versions of **Write( )** and **WriteLine( )** so they can be called directly on **Console**, as you have been doing throughout this book. However, you can invoke these (and other) methods on the **TextWriter** that underlies **Console.Out** and **Console.Error**, if you choose.

Here is a program that demonstrates writing to **Console.Out** and **Console.Error**. By default, both write to the console.

```
// Write to Console.Out and Console.Error.

using System;

class ErrOut {
  static void Main() {
    int a=10, b=0;
    int result;

    Console.Out.WriteLine("This will generate an exception.");
    try {
      result = a / b; // generate an exception
    } catch(DivideByZeroException exc) {
      Console.Error.WriteLine(exc.Message);
    }
  }
}
```

The output from the program is shown here:

```
This will generate an exception.
Attempted to divide by zero.
```

Sometimes newcomers to programming are confused about when to use **Console.Error**. Since both **Console.Out** and **Console.Error** default to writing their output to the console, why are there two different streams? The answer lies in the fact that the standard streams can be redirected to other devices. For example, **Console.Error** can be redirected to write to a disk file, rather than the screen. Thus, it is possible to direct error output to a log file, for example, without affecting console output. Conversely, if console output is redirected and error output is not, then error messages will appear on the console, where they can be seen. We will examine redirection later, after file I/O has been described.

FileStream and Byte-Oriented File I/O

The .NET Framework provides classes that allow you to read and write files. Of course, the most common type of files are disk files. At the operating system level, all files are byte oriented. As you would expect, there are methods to read and write bytes from and to a file. Thus, reading and writing files using byte streams is very common. You can also wrap a byte-oriented file stream within a character-based object. Character-based file operations are useful when text is being stored. Character streams are discussed later in this chapter. Byte-oriented I/O is described here.

To create a byte-oriented stream attached to a file, you will use the **FileStream** class. **FileStream** is derived from **Stream** and contains all of **Stream**'s functionality.

Remember, the stream classes, including **FileStream**, are defined in **System.IO**. Thus, you will usually include

```
using System.IO;
```

near the top of any program that uses them.

Opening and Closing a File

To create a byte stream linked to a file, create a **FileStream** object. **FileStream** defines several constructors. Perhaps its most commonly used one is shown here:

FileStream(string *path*, FileMode *mode*)

Here, *path* specifies the name of the file to open, which can include a full path specification. The *mode* parameter specifies how the file will be opened. It must be one of the values defined by the **FileMode** enumeration. These values are shown in Table 14-4. In general, this constructor opens a file for read/write access. The exception is when the file is opened using **FileMode.Append**. In this case, the file is write-only.

If a failure occurs when attempting to open the file, an exception will be thrown. If the file cannot be opened because it does not exist, **FileNotFoundException** will be thrown. If the file cannot be opened because of some type of I/O error, **IOException** will be thrown. Other exceptions include **ArgumentNullException** (the filename is null), **ArgumentException** (the filename is invalid), **ArgumentOutOfRangeException** (the mode is invalid), **SecurityException** (user does not have access rights), **PathTooLongException** (the

Value	Description
FileMode.Append	Output is appended to the end of file.
FileMode.Create	Creates a new output file. Any preexisting file by the same name will be destroyed.
FileMode.CreateNew	Creates a new output file. The file must not already exist.
FileMode.Open	Opens a preexisting file.
FileMode.OpenOrCreate	Opens a file if it exists, or creates the file if it does not already exist.
FileMode.Truncate	Opens a preexisting file, but reduces its length to zero.

TABLE 14-4   The **FileMode** Values

filename/path is too long), **NotSupportedException** (the filename specifies an unsupported device), and **DirectoryNotFoundException** (specified directory is invalid).

The exceptions **PathTooLongException**, **DirectoryNotFoundException**, and **FileNotFoundException** are subclasses of **IOException**. Thus, it is possible to catch all three by catching **IOException**.

There are many ways to handle the process of opening a file. The following shows one way. It opens a file called **test.dat** for input.

```
FileStream fin = null;

try {
  fin = new FileStream("test", FileMode.Open);
}
catch(IOException exc) { // catch all I/O exceptions
  Console.WriteLine(exc.Message);
  // Handle the error.
}
catch(Exception exc { // catch any other exception
  Console.WriteLine(exc.Message);
  // Handle the error, if possible.
  // Rethrow those exceptions that you don't handle.
}
```

Here, the first **catch** clause handles situations in which the file is not found, the path is too long, the directory does not exist, or other I/O errors occur. The second **catch**, which is a "catch all" clause for all other types of exceptions, handles the other possible errors (possibly by rethrowing the exception). You could also check for each exception individually, reporting more specifically the problem that occurred and taking remedial action specific to that error.

For the sake of simplicity, the examples in this book will catch only **IOException**, but your real-world code may (probably will) need to handle the other possible exceptions, depending upon the circumstances. Also, the exception handlers in this chapter simply report the error, but in many cases, your code should take steps to correct the problem when possible. For example, you might reprompt the user for a filename if the one previously entered is not found. You might also need to rethrow the exception.

REMEMBER *To keep the code simple, the examples in this chapter catch only **IOException**, but your own code may need to handle other possible exceptions or handle each type of I/O exception individually.*

As mentioned, the **FileStream** constructor just described opens a file that (in most cases) has read/write access. If you want to restrict access to just reading or just writing, use this constructor instead:

FileStream(string *path*, FileMode *mode*, FileAccess *access*)

As before, *path* specifies the name of the file to open, and *mode* specifies how the file will be opened. The value passed in *access* specifies how the file can be accessed. It must be one of the values defined by the **FileAccess** enumeration, which are shown here:

FileAccess.Read	FileAccess.Write	FileAccess.ReadWrite

For example, this opens a read-only file:

```
FileStream fin = new FileStream("test.dat", FileMode.Open, FileAccess.Read);
```

When you are done with a file, you must close it. This can be done by calling **Close( )**. Its general form is shown here:

void Close( )

Closing a file releases the system resources allocated to the file, allowing them to be used by another file. As a point of interest, **Close( )** works by calling **Dispose( )**, which actually frees the resources.

NOTE *The* **using** *statement, described in Chapter 20, offers a way to automatically close a file when it is no longer needed. This approach is beneficial in many file-handling situations because it provides a simple means to ensure that a file is closed when it is no longer needed. However, to clearly illustrate the fundamentals of file handling, including the point at which a file can be closed, this chapter explicitly calls* **Close( )** *in all cases.*

Reading Bytes from a FileStream

FileStream defines two methods that read bytes from a file: **ReadByte( )** and **Read( )**. To read a single byte from a file, use **ReadByte( )**, whose general form is shown here:

int ReadByte( )

Each time it is called, it reads a single byte from the file and returns it as an integer value. It returns –1 when the end of the file is encountered. Possible exceptions include **NotSupportedException** (the stream is not opened for input) and **ObjectDisposedException** (the stream is closed).

To read a block of bytes, use **Read( )**, which has this general form:

int Read(byte[ ] *array*, int *offset*, int *count*)

Read( ) attempts to read up to *count* bytes into *array* starting at *array[offset]*. It returns the number of bytes successfully read. An **IOException** is thrown if an I/O error occurs. Several other types of exceptions are possible, including **NotSupportedException**, which is thrown if reading is not supported by the stream.

The following program uses **ReadByte( )** to input and display the contents of a text file, the name of which is specified as a command-line argument. Note the program first checks that a filename has been specified before trying to open the file.

```
/* Display a text file.

   To use this program, specify the name of the file that you
   want to see. For example, to see a file called TEST.CS,
   use the following command line.

   ShowFile TEST.CS
*/

using System;
using System.IO;
```

```
class ShowFile {
  static void Main(string[] args) {
    int i;
    FileStream fin;

    if(args.Length != 1) {
      Console.WriteLine("Usage: ShowFile File");
      return;
    }

    try {
      fin = new FileStream(args[0], FileMode.Open);
    } catch(IOException exc) {
      Console.WriteLine("Cannot Open File");
      Console.WriteLine(exc.Message);
      return; // File can't be opened, so stop the program.
    }

    // Read bytes until EOF is encountered.
    try {

      do {
        i = fin.ReadByte();
        if(i != -1) Console.Write((char) i);
      } while(i != -1);

    } catch(IOException exc) {
      Console.WriteLine("Error Reading File");
      Console.WriteLine(exc.Message);
    } finally {
      fin.Close();
    }
  }
}
```

Notice that the program uses two **try** blocks. The first catches any I/O exceptions that might prevent the file from being opened. If an I/O error occurs, the program terminates. Otherwise, the second **try** block monitors the read operation for I/O exceptions. Thus, the second **try** block executes only if **fin** refers to an open file. Also, notice that the file is closed in the **finally** block associated with the second **try** block. This means that no matter how the **do** loop ends (either normally or because of an error), the file will be closed. Although not an issue in this specific example (because the entire program ends at that point anyway), the advantage to this approach, in general, is that if the code that accesses a file terminates because of some exception, the file is still closed by the **finally** block. This ensures that the file is closed in all cases.

In some situations, it may be easier to wrap the portions of a program that open the file and access the file within a single **try** block (rather than separating the two). For example, here is another, shorter way to write the **ShowFile** program:

```
// Display a text file. Compact version.

using System;
```

```
using System.IO;

class ShowFile {
  static void Main(string[] args) {
    int i;
    FileStream fin = null;

    if(args.Length != 1) {
      Console.WriteLine("Usage: ShowFile File");
      return;
    }

    // Use a single try block to open the file and then
    // read from it.
    try {
      fin = new FileStream(args[0], FileMode.Open);

      // Read bytes until EOF is encountered.
      do {
        i = fin.ReadByte();
        if(i != -1) Console.Write((char) i);
      } while(i != -1);
    } catch(IOException exc) {
      Console.WriteLine("I/O Error:\n" + exc.Message);
    } finally {
      if(fin != null) fin.Close();
    }
  }
}
```

Notice in this version that the **FileStream** reference **fin** is initialized to null. If the file can be opened by the **FileStream** constructor, **fin** will be non-null. If the constructor fails, **fin** will remain null. This is important because inside the **finally** block, **Close( )** is called only if **fin** is not null. This mechanism prevents an attempt to call **Close( )** on **fin** when it does not refer to an open file. Because of its compactness, this approach is used by many of the I/O examples in this book. Be aware, however, that it will not be appropriate in cases in which you want to deal separately with a failure to open a file, such as might occur if a user mistypes a filename. In such a situation, you might want to prompt for the correct name, for example, before entering a **try** block that accesses the file.

In general, precisely how you manage the opening, accessing, and closing of a file will be determined by your specific application. What works well in one case may not be appropriate for another. Thus, you must tailor this process to best fit the exact needs of your program.

Writing to a File

To write a byte to a file, use the **WriteByte( )** method. Its simplest form is shown here:

> void WriteByte(byte *value*)

This method writes the byte specified by *value* to the file. If the underlying stream is not opened for output, a **NotSupportedException** is thrown. If the stream is closed, **ObjectDisposedException** is thrown.

You can write an array of bytes to a file by calling **Write( )**. It is shown here:

void Write(byte[ ] *array*, int *offset*, int *count*)

Write( ) writes *count* bytes from the array *array*, beginning at *array*[*offset*], to the file. If an error occurs during writing, an **IOException** is thrown. If the underlying stream is not opened for output, a **NotSupportedException** is thrown. Several other exceptions are also possible.

As you may know, when file output is performed, often that output is not immediately written to the actual physical device. Instead, output is buffered by the operating system until a sizable chunk of data can be written all at once. This improves the efficiency of the system. For example, disk files are organized by sectors, which might be anywhere from 128 bytes long, on up. Output is usually buffered until an entire sector can be written all at once. However, if you want to cause data to be written to the physical device whether the buffer is full or not, you can call **Flush( )**, shown here:

void Flush( )

An **IOException** is thrown on failure. If the stream is closed, **ObjectDisposedException** is thrown.

Once you are done with an output file, you must remember to close it. This can be done by calling **Close( )**. Doing so ensures that any output remaining in a disk buffer is actually written to the disk. Thus, there is no reason to call **Flush( )** before closing a file.

Here is a simple example that writes to a file:

```
// Write to a file.

using System;
using System.IO;

class WriteToFile {
  static void Main(string[] args) {
    FileStream fout = null;

    try {
      // Open output file.
      fout = new FileStream("test.txt", FileMode.CreateNew);

      // Write the alphabet to the file.
      for(char c = 'A'; c <= 'Z'; c++)
        fout.WriteByte((byte) c);
    } catch(IOException exc) {
      Console.WriteLine("I/O Error:\n" + exc.Message);
    } finally {
      if(fout != null) fout.Close();
    }
  }
}
```

The program first creates a file called **test.txt** for output by using **FileMode.CreateNew**. This means that the file must not already exist. (If it does exist, an **IOException** will be thrown.) After the file is open, the uppercase alphabet is written to the file. Once this program executes, **test.txt** will contain the following output:

ABCDEFGHIJKLMNOPQRSTUVWXYZ

Using FileStream to Copy a File

One advantage to the byte-oriented I/O used by **FileStream** is that you can use it on any type of file—not just those that contain text. For example, the following program copies any type of file, including executable files. The names of the source and destination files are specified on the command line.

```
/* Copy a file one byte at a time.

   To use this program, specify the name of the source
   file and the destination file. For example, to copy a
   file called FIRST.DAT to a file called SECOND.DAT, use
   the following command line:

   CopyFile FIRST.DAT SECOND.DAT
*/

using System;
using System.IO;

class CopyFile {
  static void Main(string[] args) {
    int i;
    FileStream fin = null;
    FileStream fout = null;

    if(args.Length != 2) {
      Console.WriteLine("Usage: CopyFile From To");
      return;
    }

    try {

      // Open the files.
      fin = new FileStream(args[0], FileMode.Open);
      fout = new FileStream(args[1], FileMode.Create);

      // Copy the file.
      do {
        i = fin.ReadByte();
        if(i != -1) fout.WriteByte((byte)i);
      } while(i != -1);

    } catch(IOException exc) {
      Console.WriteLine("I/O Error:\n" + exc.Message);
    } finally {
      if(fin != null) fin.Close();
      if(fout != null) fout.Close();
    }
  }
}
```

Character-Based File I/O

Although byte-oriented file handling is quite common, it is possible to use character-based streams for this purpose. The advantage to the character streams is that they operate directly on Unicode characters. Thus, if you want to store Unicode text, the character streams are certainly your best option. In general, to perform character-based file operations, you will wrap a **FileStream** inside either a **StreamReader** or a **StreamWriter**. These classes automatically convert a byte stream into a character stream, and vice versa.

Remember, at the operating system level, a file consists of a set of bytes. Using a **StreamReader** or **StreamWriter** does not alter this fact.

StreamWriter is derived from **TextWriter**. **StreamReader** is derived from **TextReader**. Thus, **StreamWriter** and **StreamReader** have access to the methods and properties defined by their base classes.

Using StreamWriter

To create a character-based output stream, wrap a **Stream** object (such as a **FileStream**) inside a **StreamWriter**. **StreamWriter** defines several constructors. One of its most popular is shown here:

StreamWriter(Stream *stream*)

Here, *stream* is the name of an open stream. This constructor throws an **ArgumentException** if *stream* is not opened for output and an **ArgumentNullException** if *stream* is null. Once created, a **StreamWriter** automatically handles the conversion of characters to bytes. When you are done with the **StreamWriter**, you must close it. Closing the **StreamWriter** also closes the underlying stream.

Here is a simple key-to-disk utility that reads lines of text entered at the keyboard and writes them to a file called **test.txt**. Text is read until the user enters the word "stop". It uses a **FileStream** wrapped in a **StreamWriter** to output to the file.

```
// A simple key-to-disk utility that demonstrates a StreamWriter.

using System;
using System.IO;

class KtoD {
  static void Main() {
    string str;
    FileStream fout;

    // First, open the file stream.
    try {
      fout = new FileStream("test.txt", FileMode.Create);
    }
    catch(IOException exc) {
      Console.WriteLine("Error Opening File:\n" + exc.Message);
      return ;
    }
```

```
    // Wrap the file stream in a StreamWriter.
    StreamWriter fstr_out = new StreamWriter(fout);

    try {
      Console.WriteLine("Enter text ('stop' to quit).");

      do {
        Console.Write(": ");
        str = Console.ReadLine();

        if(str != "stop") {
          str = str + "\r\n"; // add newline
          fstr_out.Write(str);
        }
      } while(str != "stop");
    } catch(IOException exc) {
      Console.WriteLine("I/O Error:\n" + exc.Message);
    } finally {
      fstr_out.Close();
    }
  }
}
```

In some cases, it might be more convenient to open a file directly using **StreamWriter**. To do so, use one of these constructors:

StreamWriter(string *path*)
StreamWriter(string *path*, bool *append*)

Here, *path* specifies the name of the file to open, which can include a full path specifier. In the second form, if *append* is true, then output is appended to the end of an existing file. Otherwise, output overwrites the specified file. In both cases, if the file does not exist, it is created. Also, both throw an **IOException** if an I/O error occurs. Other exceptions are also possible.

Here is the key-to-disk program rewritten so it uses **StreamWriter** to open the output file:

```
// Open a file using StreamWriter.

using System;
using System.IO;

class KtoD {
  static void Main() {
    string str;
    StreamWriter fstr_out = null;

    try {
      // Open the file, wrapped in a StreamWriter.
      fstr_out = new StreamWriter("test.txt");

      Console.WriteLine("Enter text ('stop' to quit).");

      do {
        Console.Write(": ");
        str = Console.ReadLine();
```

```
        if(str != "stop") {
          str = str + "\r\n"; // add newline
          fstr_out.Write(str);
        }
      } while(str != "stop");
    } catch(IOException exc) {
      Console.WriteLine("I/O Error:\n" + exc.Message);
    } finally {
      if(fstr_out != null) fstr_out.Close();
    }
  }
}
```

Using a StreamReader

To create a character-based input stream, wrap a byte stream inside a **StreamReader**. **StreamReader** defines several constructors. A frequently used one is shown here:

StreamReader(Stream *stream*)

Here, *stream* is the name of an open stream. This constructor throws an **ArgumentNullException** if *stream* is null. It throws an **ArgumentException** if *stream* is not opened for input. Once created, a **StreamReader** will automatically handle the conversion of bytes to characters. When you are done with the **StreamReader**, you must close it. Closing the **StreamReader** also closes the underlying stream.

The following program creates a simple disk-to-screen utility that reads a text file called **test.txt** and displays its contents on the screen. Thus, it is the complement of the key-to-disk utility shown in the previous section:

```
// A simple disk-to-screen utility that demonstrates a StreamReader.

using System;
using System.IO;

class DtoS {
  static void Main() {
    FileStream fin;
    string s;

    try {
      fin = new FileStream("test.txt", FileMode.Open);
    }
    catch(IOException exc) {
      Console.WriteLine("Error Opening file:\n" + exc.Message);
      return ;
    }

    StreamReader fstr_in = new StreamReader(fin);

    try {
      while((s = fstr_in.ReadLine()) != null) {
        Console.WriteLine(s);
      }
    } catch(IOException exc) {
      Console.WriteLine("I/O Error:\n" + exc.Message);
```

```
    } finally {
      fstr_in.Close();
    }
  }
}
```

In the program, notice how the end of the file is determined. When the reference returned by **ReadLine( )** is null, the end of the file has been reached. Although this approach works, **StreamReader** provides an alternative means of detecting the end of the stream: the **EndOfStream** property. This read-only property is true when the end of the stream has been reached and false otherwise. Therefore, you can use **EndOfStream** to watch for the end of a file. For example, here is another way to write the **while** loop that reads the file:

```
while(!fstr_in.EndOfStream) {
  s = fstr_in.ReadLine();
  Console.WriteLine(s);
}
```

In this case, the use of **EndOfStream** makes the code a bit easier to understand but does not change the overall structure of the sequence. There are times, however, when the use of **EndOfStream** can simplify an otherwise tricky situation, adding clarity and improving structure.

As with **StreamWriter**, in some cases, you might find it easier to open a file directly using **StreamReader**. To do so, use this constructor:

StreamReader(string *path*)

Here, *path* specifies the name of the file to open, which can include a full path specifier. The file must exist. If it doesn't, a **FileNotFoundException** is thrown. If *path* is null, then an **ArgumentNullException** is thrown. If *path* is an empty string, **ArgumentException** is thrown. **IOException** and **DirectoryNotFoundException** are also possible.

Redirecting the Standard Streams

As mentioned earlier, the standard streams, such as **Console.In**, can be redirected. By far, the most common redirection is to a file. When a standard stream is redirected, input and/or output is automatically directed to the new stream, bypassing the default devices. By redirecting the standard streams, your program can read commands from a disk file, create log files, or even read input from a network connection.

Redirection of the standard streams can be accomplished in two ways. First, when you execute a program on the command line, you can use the < and > operators to redirect **Console.In** and/or **Console.Out**, respectively. For example, given this program:

```
using System;

class Test {
  static void Main() {
    Console.WriteLine("This is a test.");
  }
}
```

executing the program like this:

Test > log

will cause the line "This is a test." to be written to a file called **log**. Input can be redirected in the same way. The thing to remember when input is redirected is that you must make sure that what you specify as an input source contains sufficient input to satisfy the demands of the program. If it doesn't, the program will hang.

The < and > command-line redirection operators are not part of C#, but are provided by the operating system. Thus, if your environment supports I/O redirection (as is the case with Windows), you can redirect standard input and standard output without making any changes to your program. However, there is a second way that you can redirect the standard streams that is under program control. To do so, you will use the **SetIn( )**, **SetOut( )**, and **SetError( )** methods, shown here, which are members of **Console**:

static void SetIn(TextReader *newIn*)
static void SetOut(TextWriter *newOut*)
static void SetError(TextWriter *newError*)

Thus, to redirect input, call **SetIn( )**, specifying the desired stream. You can use any input stream as long as it is derived from **TextReader**. To redirect output, call **SetOut( )**, specifying the desired output stream, which must be derived from **TextWriter**. For example, to redirect output to a file, specify a **FileStream** that is wrapped in a **StreamWriter**. The following program shows an example:

```
// Redirect Console.Out.

using System;
using System.IO;

class Redirect {
  static void Main() {
    StreamWriter log_out = null;

    try {
      log_out = new StreamWriter("logfile.txt");

      // Redirect standard out to logfile.txt.
      Console.SetOut(log_out);

      Console.WriteLine("This is the start of the log file.");

      for(int i=0; i<10; i++) Console.WriteLine(i);

      Console.WriteLine("This is the end of the log file.");
    } catch(IOException exc) {
        Console.WriteLine("I/O Error\n" + exc.Message);
    } finally {
      if(log_out != null) log_out.Close();
    }
  }
}
```

When you run this program, you won't see any of the output on the screen, but the file **logfile.txt** will contain the following:

```
This is the start of the log file.
0
1
2
3
4
5
6
7
8
9
This is the end of the log file.
```

On your own, you might want to experiment with redirecting the other built-in streams.

Reading and Writing Binary Data

So far, we have just been reading and writing bytes or characters, but it is possible—indeed, common—to read and write other types of data. For example, you might want to create a file that contains **int**s, **double**s, or **short**s. To read and write binary values of the C# built-in types, you will use **BinaryReader** and **BinaryWriter**. When using these streams, it is important to understand that this data is read and written using its internal, binary format, not its human-readable text form.

BinaryWriter

A **BinaryWriter** is a wrapper around a byte stream that manages the writing of binary data. Its most commonly used constructor is shown here:

    BinaryWriter(Stream *output*)

Here, *output* is the stream to which data is written. To write output to a file, you can use the object created by **FileStream** for this parameter. If *output* is null, then an **ArgumentNullException** is thrown. If *output* has not been opened for writing, **ArgumentException** is thrown. When you are done using a **BinaryWriter**, you must close it. Closing a **BinaryWriter** also closes the underlying stream.

BinaryWriter defines methods that can write all of C#'s built-in types. Several are shown in Table 14-5. All can throw an **IOException**. (Other exceptions are also possible.) Notice that a **string** is written using its internal format, which includes a length specifier. **BinaryWriter** also defines the standard **Close( )** and **Flush( )** methods, which work as described earlier.

BinaryReader

A **BinaryReader** is a wrapper around a byte stream that handles the reading of binary data. Its most commonly used constructor is shown here:

    BinaryReader(Stream *input*)

Method	Description
void Write(sbyte *value*)	Writes a signed byte.
void Write(byte *value*)	Writes an unsigned byte.
void Write(byte[ ] *buffer*)	Writes an array of bytes.
void Write(short *value*)	Writes a short integer.
void Write(ushort *value*)	Writes an unsigned short integer.
void Write(int *value*)	Writes an integer.
void Write(uint *value*)	Writes an unsigned integer.
void Write(long *value*)	Writes a long integer.
void Write(ulong *value*)	Writes an unsigned long integer.
void Write(float *value*)	Writes a **float**.
void Write(double *value*)	Writes a **double**.
void Write(decimal *value*)	Writes a **decimal**.
void Write(char *ch*)	Writes a character.
void Write(char[ ] *chars*)	Writes an array of characters.
void Write(string *value*)	Writes a string using its internal representation, which includes a length specifier.

TABLE 14-5   Commonly Used Output Methods Defined by **BinaryWriter**

Here, *input* is the stream from which data is read. To read from a file, you can use the object created by **FileStream** for this parameter. If *input* has not been opened for reading or is otherwise invalid, **ArgumentException** is thrown. When you are done with a **BinaryReader** you must close it. Closing a **BinaryReader** also closes the underlying stream.

BinaryReader provides methods for reading all of C#'s simple types. Several commonly used methods are shown in Table 14-6. Notice that **ReadString( )** reads a string that is stored using its internal format, which includes a length specifier. These methods throw an **IOException** if an error occurs. (Other exceptions are also possible.)

BinaryReader also defines three versions of **Read( )**, which are shown here:

Method	Description
int Read( )	Returns an integer representation of the next available character from the invoking input stream. Returns –1 when attempting to read at the end of the file.
int Read(byte[ ] *buffer*, int *index*, int *count*)	Attempts to read up to *count* bytes into *buffer* starting at *buffer*[*index*], returning the number of bytes successfully read.
int Read(char[ ] *buffer*, int *index*, int *count*)	Attempts to read up to *count* characters into *buffer* starting at *buffer*[*index*], returning the number of characters successfully read.

These methods will throw an **IOException** on failure. Other exceptions are possible. Also defined is the standard **Close( )** method.

Method	Description
bool ReadBoolean( )	Reads a **bool**.
byte ReadByte( )	Reads a **byte**.
sbyte ReadSByte( )	Reads an **sbyte**.
byte[ ] ReadBytes(int *count*)	Reads *count* bytes and returns them as an array.
char ReadChar( )	Reads a **char**.
char[ ] ReadChars(int *count*)	Reads *count* characters and returns them as an array.
decimal ReadDecimal( )	Reads a **decimal**.
double ReadDouble( )	Reads a **double**.
float ReadSingle( )	Reads a **float**.
short ReadInt16( )	Reads a **short**.
int ReadInt32( )	Reads an **int**.
long ReadInt64( )	Reads a **long**.
ushort ReadUInt16( )	Reads a **ushort**.
uint ReadUInt32( )	Reads a **uint**.
ulong ReadUInt64( )	Reads a **ulong**.
string ReadString( )	Reads a string that is represented in its internal, binary format, which includes a length specifier. This method should only be used to read a string that has been written using a **BinaryWriter**.

TABLE 14-6   Commonly Used Input Methods Defined by **BinaryReader**

Demonstrating Binary I/O

Here is a program that demonstrates **BinaryReader** and **BinaryWriter**. It writes and then reads back various types of data to and from a file.

```
// Write and then read back binary data.

using System;
using System.IO;

class RWData {
  static void Main() {
    BinaryWriter dataOut;
    BinaryReader dataIn;

    int i = 10;
    double d = 1023.56;
    bool b = true;
    string str = "This is a test";

    // Open the file for output.
    try {
```

```
    dataOut = new
      BinaryWriter(new FileStream("testdata", FileMode.Create));
}
catch(IOException exc) {
  Console.WriteLine("Error Opening File:\n" + exc.Message);
  return;
}

// Write data to a file.
try {
  Console.WriteLine("Writing " + i);
  dataOut.Write(i);

  Console.WriteLine("Writing " + d);
  dataOut.Write(d);

  Console.WriteLine("Writing " + b);
  dataOut.Write(b);

  Console.WriteLine("Writing " + 12.2 * 7.4);
  dataOut.Write(12.2 * 7.4);

  Console.WriteLine("Writing " + str);
  dataOut.Write(str);
}
catch(IOException exc) {
  Console.WriteLine("I/O Error:\n" + exc.Message);
} finally {
  dataOut.Close();
}

Console.WriteLine();

// Now, read the data.
try {
  dataIn = new
      BinaryReader(new FileStream("testdata", FileMode.Open));
}
catch(IOException exc) {
  Console.WriteLine("Error Opening File:\n" + exc.Message);
  return;
}

try {
  i = dataIn.ReadInt32();
  Console.WriteLine("Reading " + i);

  d = dataIn.ReadDouble();
  Console.WriteLine("Reading " + d);

  b = dataIn.ReadBoolean();
  Console.WriteLine("Reading " + b);
```

```
        d = dataIn.ReadDouble();
        Console.WriteLine("Reading " + d);

        str = dataIn.ReadString();
        Console.WriteLine("Reading " + str);
      }
      catch(IOException exc) {
        Console.WriteLine("I/O Error:\n" + exc.Message);
      } finally {
        dataIn.Close();
      }
    }
  }
}
```

The output from the program is shown here:

```
Writing 10
Writing 1023.56
Writing True
Writing 90.28
Writing This is a test

Reading 10
Reading 1023.56
Reading True
Reading 90.28
Reading This is a test
```

If you examine the **testdata** file produced by this program, you will find that it contains binary data, not human-readable text.

Here is a more practical example that shows how powerful binary I/O is. The following program implements a very simple inventory program. For each item in the inventory, the program stores the item's name, the number on hand, and its cost. Next, the program prompts the user for the name of an item. It then searches the database. If the item is found, the inventory information is displayed.

```
/* Use BinaryReader and BinaryWriter to implement
   a simple inventory program. */

using System;
using System.IO;

class Inventory {
  static void Main() {
    BinaryWriter dataOut;
    BinaryReader dataIn;

    string item; // name of item
    int onhand;  // number on hand
    double cost; // cost

    try {
      dataOut = new
```

```
          BinaryWriter(new FileStream("inventory.dat", FileMode.Create));
}
catch(IOException exc) {
  Console.WriteLine("Cannot Open Inventory File For Output");
  Console.WriteLine("Reason: " + exc.Message);
  return;
}

// Write some inventory data to the file.
try {
  dataOut.Write("Hammers");
  dataOut.Write(10);
  dataOut.Write(3.95);

  dataOut.Write("Screwdrivers");
  dataOut.Write(18);
  dataOut.Write(1.50);

  dataOut.Write("Pliers");
  dataOut.Write(5);
  dataOut.Write(4.95);

  dataOut.Write("Saws");
  dataOut.Write(8);
  dataOut.Write(8.95);
}
catch(IOException exc) {
  Console.WriteLine("Error Writing Inventory File");
  Console.WriteLine("Reason: " + exc.Message);
} finally {
  dataOut.Close();
}

Console.WriteLine();

// Now, open inventory file for reading.
try {
  dataIn = new
      BinaryReader(new FileStream("inventory.dat", FileMode.Open));
}
catch(IOException exc) {
  Console.WriteLine("Cannot Open Inventory File For Input");
  Console.WriteLine("Reason: " + exc.Message);
  return;
}

// Look up item entered by user.
Console.Write("Enter item to look up: ");
string what = Console.ReadLine();
Console.WriteLine();

try {
  for(;;) {
    // Read an inventory entry.
```

```
      item = dataIn.ReadString();
      onhand = dataIn.ReadInt32();
      cost = dataIn.ReadDouble();

      // See if the item matches the one requested.
      // If so, display information.
      if(item.Equals(what, StringComparison.OrdinalIgnoreCase)) {
        Console.WriteLine(onhand + " " + item + " on hand. " +
                          "Cost: {0:C} each", cost);
        Console.WriteLine("Total value of {0}: {1:C}." ,
                          item, cost * onhand);
        break;
      }
    }
  }
  catch(EndOfStreamException) {
    Console.WriteLine("Item not found.");
  }
  catch(IOException exc) {
    Console.WriteLine("Error Reading Inventory File");
    Console.WriteLine("Reason: " + exc.Message);
  } finally {
    dataIn.Close();
  }
}
}
```

Here is a sample run:

```
Enter item to look up: Screwdrivers

18 Screwdrivers on hand. Cost: $1.50 each
Total value of Screwdrivers: $27.00.
```

In the program, notice how inventory information is stored in its binary format. Thus, the number of items on hand and the cost are stored using their binary format rather than their human-readable text-based equivalents. This makes it is possible to perform computations on the numeric data without having to convert it from its human-readable form.

There is one other point of interest in the inventory program. Notice how the end of the file is detected. Since the binary input methods throw an **EndOfStreamException** when the end of the stream is reached, the program simply reads the file until either it finds the desired item or this exception is generated. Thus, no special mechanism is needed to detect the end of the file.

Random Access Files

Up to this point, we have been using *sequential files,* which are files that are accessed in a strictly linear fashion, one byte after another. However, you can also access the contents of a file in random order. One way to do this is to use the **Seek( )** method defined by **FileStream**. This method allows you to set the *file position indicator* (also called the *file pointer* or simply the *current position*) to any point within a file.

The method **Seek( )** is shown here:

long Seek(long *offset*, SeekOrigin *origin*)

Here, *offset* specifies the new position, in bytes, of the file pointer from the location specified by *origin*. The origin will be one of these values, which are defined by the **SeekOrigin** enumeration:

Value	Meaning
SeekOrigin.Begin	Seek from the beginning of the file.
SeekOrigin.Current	Seek from the current location.
SeekOrigin.End	Seek from the end of the file.

After a call to **Seek( )**, the next read or write operation will occur at the new file position. The new position is returned. If an error occurs while seeking, an **IOException** is thrown. If the underlying stream does not support position requests, a **NotSupportedException** is thrown. Other exceptions are possible.

Here is an example that demonstrates random access I/O. It writes the uppercase alphabet to a file and then reads it back in non-sequential order.

```
// Demonstrate random access.

using System;
using System.IO;

class RandomAccessDemo {
  static void Main() {
    FileStream f = null;
    char ch;

    try {
      f = new FileStream("random.dat", FileMode.Create);

      // Write the alphabet.
      for(int i=0; i < 26; i++)
        f.WriteByte((byte)('A'+i));

      // Now, read back specific values.
      f.Seek(0, SeekOrigin.Begin); // seek to first byte
      ch = (char) f.ReadByte();
      Console.WriteLine("First value is " + ch);

      f.Seek(1, SeekOrigin.Begin); // seek to second byte
      ch = (char) f.ReadByte();
      Console.WriteLine("Second value is " + ch);

      f.Seek(4, SeekOrigin.Begin); // seek to 5th byte
      ch = (char) f.ReadByte();
      Console.WriteLine("Fifth value is " + ch);

      Console.WriteLine();
```

```
      // Now, read every other value.
      Console.WriteLine("Here is every other value: ");
      for(int i=0; i < 26; i += 2) {
        f.Seek(i, SeekOrigin.Begin); // seek to ith character
        ch = (char) f.ReadByte();
        Console.Write(ch + " ");
      }
    }
    catch(IOException exc) {
      Console.WriteLine("I/O Error\n" + exc.Message);
    } finally {
      if(f != null) f.Close();
    }

    Console.WriteLine();
  }
}
```

The output from the program is shown here:

```
First value is A
Second value is B
Fifth value is E

Here is every other value:
A C E G I K M O Q S U W Y
```

Although **Seek( )** offers the greatest flexibility, there is another way to set the current file position. You can use the **Position** property. As shown previously in Table 14-2, **Position** is a read/write property. Therefore, you can use it to obtain the current position, or to set the current position. For example, here is the code sequence from the preceding program that reads every other letter from the file, rewritten to use the **Position** property:

```
Console.WriteLine("Here is every other value: ");
for(int i=0; i < 26; i += 2) {
  f.Position = i; // seek to ith character via Position
  ch = (char) f.ReadByte();
  Console.Write(ch + " ");
}
```

Using MemoryStream

Sometimes it is useful to read input from or write output to an array. To do this, you will use **MemoryStream**. **MemoryStream** is an implementation of **Stream** that uses an array of bytes for input and/or output. **MemoryStream** defines several constructors. Here is the one we will use:

MemoryStream(byte[ ] *buffer*)

Here, *buffer* is an array of bytes that will be used for the source and/or target of I/O requests. The stream created by this constructor can be written to, read from, and supports **Seek( )**. When using this constructor, you must remember to make *buffer* large enough to hold whatever output you will be directing to it.

Here is a program that demonstrates the use of **MemoryStream**:

```
// Demonstrate MemoryStream.

using System;
using System.IO;

class MemStrDemo {
  static void Main() {
    byte[] storage = new byte[255];

    // Create a memory-based stream.
    MemoryStream memstrm = new MemoryStream(storage);

    // Wrap memstrm in a reader and a writer.
    StreamWriter memwtr = new StreamWriter(memstrm);
    StreamReader memrdr = new StreamReader(memstrm);

    try {
      // Write to storage, through memwtr.
      for(int i=0; i < 10; i++)
        memwtr.WriteLine("byte [" + i + "]: " + i);

      // Put a period at the end.
      memwtr.WriteLine(".");

      memwtr.Flush();

      Console.WriteLine("Reading from storage directly: ");

      // Display contents of storage directly.
      foreach(char ch in storage) {
        if (ch == '.') break;
        Console.Write(ch);
      }

      Console.WriteLine("\nReading through memrdr: ");

      // Read from memstrm using the stream reader.
      memstrm.Seek(0, SeekOrigin.Begin); // reset file pointer

      string str = memrdr.ReadLine();
      while(str != null) {
        str = memrdr.ReadLine();
        if(str[0] == '.') break;
        Console.WriteLine(str);
      }
    } catch(IOException exc) {
      Console.WriteLine("I/O Error\n" + exc.Message);
    } finally {
      // Release reader and writer resources.
      memwtr.Close();
      memrdr.Close();
    }
  }
}
```

The output from the program is shown here:

```
Reading from storage directly:
byte [0]: 0
byte [1]: 1
byte [2]: 2
byte [3]: 3
byte [4]: 4
byte [5]: 5
byte [6]: 6
byte [7]: 7
byte [8]: 8
byte [9]: 9

Reading through memrdr:
byte [1]: 1
byte [2]: 2
byte [3]: 3
byte [4]: 4
byte [5]: 5
byte [6]: 6
byte [7]: 7
byte [8]: 8
byte [9]: 9
```

In the program, an array of bytes called **storage** is created. This array is then used as the underlying storage for a **MemoryStream** called **memstrm**. From **memstrm** are created a **StreamReader** called **memrdr** and a **StreamWriter** called **memwtr**. Using **memwtr**, output is written to the memory-based stream. Notice that after the output has been written, **Flush( )** is called on **memwtr**. Calling **Flush( )** is necessary to ensure that the contents of **memwtr**'s buffer are actually written to the underlying array. Next, the contents of the underlying byte array are displayed manually, using a **foreach** loop. Then, using **Seek( )**, the file pointer is reset to the start of the stream, and the memory stream is read using **memrdr**.

Memory-based streams are quite useful in programming. For example, you can construct complicated output in advance, storing it in the array until it is needed. This technique is especially useful when programming for a GUI environment, such as Windows. You can also redirect a standard stream to read from an array. This might be useful for feeding test information into a program, for example.

Using StringReader and StringWriter

For some applications, it might be easier to use a **string** rather than a **byte** array for the underlying storage when performing memory-based I/O operations. When this is the case, use **StringReader** and **StringWriter**. **StringReader** inherits **TextReader**, and **StringWriter** inherits **TextWriter**. Thus, these streams have access to methods defined by those two classes. For example, you can call **ReadLine( )** on a **StringReader** and **WriteLine( )** on a **StringWriter**.

The constructor for **StringReader** is shown here:

StringReader(string *s*)

Here, *s* is the string that will be read from.

StringWriter defines several constructors. The one we will use here is this:

StringWriter( )

This constructor creates a writer that will put its output into a string. This string (in the form of a **StringBuilder**) is automatically created by **StringWriter**. You can obtain the contents of this string by calling **ToString( )**.

Here is an example that uses **StringReader** and **StringWriter**:

```
// Demonstrate StringReader and StringWriter.

using System;
using System.IO;

class StrRdrWtrDemo {
  static void Main() {
    StringWriter strwtr = null;
    StringReader strrdr = null;

    try {
      // Create a StringWriter.
      strwtr = new StringWriter();

      // Write to StringWriter.
      for(int i=0; i < 10; i++)
        strwtr.WriteLine("This is i: " + i);

      // Create a StringReader.
      strrdr = new StringReader(strwtr.ToString());

      // Now, read from StringReader.
      string str = strrdr.ReadLine();
      while(str != null) {
        str = strrdr.ReadLine();
        Console.WriteLine(str);
      }
    } catch(IOException exc) {
      Console.WriteLine("I/O Error\n" + exc.Message);
    } finally {
      // Release reader and writer resources.
      if(strrdr != null) strrdr.Close();
      if(strwtr != null) strwtr.Close();
    }
  }
}
```

The output is shown here:

```
This is i: 1
This is i: 2
This is i: 3
This is i: 4
This is i: 5
This is i: 6
```

```
This is i: 7
This is i: 8
This is i: 9
```

The program first creates a **StringWriter** called **strwtr** and outputs to it using **WriteLine( )**. Next, it creates a **StringReader** using the string contained in **strwtr**. This string is obtained by calling **ToString( )** on **strwtr**. Finally, the contents of this string are read using **ReadLine( )**.

The File Class

The .NET Framework defines a class called **File** that you will find useful when working with files because it contains several static methods that perform common file operations. For example, **File** contains methods that copy or move a file, encrypt or decrypt a file, and delete a file. It provides methods that obtain or set information about a file, such as whether it exists, its time of creation, its last access time, and its attributes (such as whether it is read-only, hidden, and so on). **File** also includes some convenience methods that let you read from a file and write to a file. In addition, you can use a **File** method to open a file and obtain a **FileStream** reference to it. Although **File** contains far too many methods to examine each one, we will look at three. The first is **Copy( )** and the other two are **Exists( )** and **GetLastAccessTime( )**. These methods will give you an idea of the convenience that the **File** methods offer. **File** is definitely a class that you will want to explore.

> **NOTE** *Another class that defines several file-related methods is **FileInfo**. It differs from **File** in one important way: it provides instance methods and properties rather than static methods to perform file operations. Therefore, if you will be performing several file operations on the same file, then **FileInfo** might offer a more efficient solution.*

Using Copy( ) to Copy a File

Earlier in this chapter you saw a program that copied a file by manually reading bytes from one file and writing them to another. Although such a task is not particularly difficult, it can be fully automated by using the **Copy( )** method defined by **File**. It has the two versions shown here:

    static void Copy(string *sourceFileName*, string *destFileName*)
    static void Copy(string *sourceFileName*, string *destFileName*, boolean *overwrite*)

Copy( ) copies the file specified by *sourceFileName* to the file specified by *destFileName*. The first version copies the file only if *destFileName* does not already exist. In the second form, if *overwrite* is passed **true**, the copy will overwrite the destination file if it exists. Both can throw several types of exceptions, including **IOException** and **FileNotFoundException**.

The following program uses **Copy( )** to copy a file. Both the source and destination filenames are specified on the command line. Notice how much shorter this version is than the copy program shown earlier. It's also more efficient.

```
/* Copy a file using File.Copy().

   To use this program, specify the name of the source
   file and the destination file. For example, to copy a
```

```
     file called FIRST.DAT to a file called SECOND.DAT, use
     the following command line:

     CopyFile FIRST.DAT SECOND.DAT
*/

using System;
using System.IO;

class CopyFile {
  static void Main(string[] args) {

    if(args.Length != 2) {
      Console.WriteLine("Usage: CopyFile From To");
      return;
    }

    // Copy the files.
    try {
      File.Copy(args[0], args[1]);
    } catch(IOException exc) {
      Console.WriteLine("Error Copying File\n" + exc.Message);
    }
  }
}
```

As you can see, this version of the program does not require that you create a
FileStream or release resources. The **Copy( )** method handles all this for you. Also notice
that this version will not overwrite an existing file. You might want to try using the second
version of **Copy( )**, which does allow the destination to be overwritten.

Using Exists( ) and GetLastAccessTime( )

Using **File** methods, it is quite easy to obtain information about a file. We will look at two
such methods: **Exists( )** and **GetLastAccessTime( )**. The **Exists( )** method determines if a file
exists. **GetLastAccessTime( )** returns the date and time at which a file was last accessed.
These two methods are shown here:

> static bool Exists(string *path*)
> static DateTime GetLastAccessTime(string *path*)

For both methods, *path* specifies the file about which to obtain information. **Exists( )** returns true
if the file exists and can be accessed by the calling process. **GetLastAccessTime( )** returns a
DateTime structure that contains the date and time the file was last accessed. (**DateTime**
is described later in this book, but its **ToString( )** method automatically creates a human-
readable form of the date and time.) A number of exceptions relating to the use of an invalid
argument or an invalid permission are possible. However, it will not throw an **IOException**.

The following program shows **Exists( )** and **GetLastAccessTime( )** in action. It determines
if a file called **test.txt** exists. If it does, the time it was last accessed is displayed.

```
// Use Exists() and GetLastAccessTime().
using System;
using System.IO;
```

```
class ExistsDemo {
  static void Main() {

    if(File.Exists("test.txt"))
      Console.WriteLine("File exists. It was last accessed at " +
                        File.GetLastAccessTime("test.txt"));
    else
      Console.WriteLine("Does Not Exist");
  }
}
```

Sample output is shown here:

```
File exists. It was last accessed at 11/1/2009 5:30:17 PM
```

You can also obtain a file's time of creation by calling **GetCreationTime( )** and the time at which it was last written to by calling **GetLastWriteTime( )**. UTC versions of these methods are also available. (UTC stands for *coordinated universal time.*) You might want to experiment with these.

Converting Numeric Strings to Their Internal Representation

Before leaving the topic of I/O, we will examine a technique useful when reading numeric strings. As you know, **WriteLine( )** provides a convenient way to output various types of data to the console, including numeric values of the built-in types, such as **int** and **double**. Thus, **WriteLine( )** automatically converts numeric values into their human-readable form. However, a parallel input method that reads and converts strings containing numeric values into their internal, binary format is not provided. For example, there is no version of **Read( )** that reads from the keyboard a string such as "100" and then automatically converts it into its corresponding binary value that can be stored in an **int** variable. Instead, there are other ways to accomplish this task. Perhaps the easiest is to use a method that is defined for all of the built-in numeric types: **Parse( )**.

Before we begin, it is necessary to state an important fact: all of C#'s built-in types, such as **int** and **double**, are actually just aliases (that is, other names) for structures defined by the .NET Framework. In fact, the C# type and .NET structure type are indistinguishable. One is just another name for the other. Because C#'s built-in types are supported by structures, they have members defined for them.

For the numeric types, the .NET structure names and their C# keyword equivalents are given here:

.NET Structure Name	C# Name
Decimal	decimal
Double	double
Single	float
Int16	short
Int32	int
Int64	long

.NET Structure Name	C# Name
UInt16	ushort
UInt32	uint
UInt64	ulong
Byte	byte
SByte	sbyte

These structures are defined inside the **System** namespace. Thus, the fully qualified name for **Int32** is **System.Int32**. These structures offer a wide array of methods that help fully integrate the built-in numeric types into C#'s object hierarchy. As a side benefit, the numeric structures also define a static method called **Parse( )** that converts a numeric string into its corresponding binary equivalent.

There are several overloaded forms of **Parse( )**. The simplest version for each numeric structure is shown here. It performs the conversion using the default locale and numeric style. (Other versions let you perform locale-specific conversions and specify the numeric style.) Notice that each method returns a binary value that corresponds to the string.

Structure	Conversion Method
Decimal	static decimal Parse(string s)
Double	static double Parse(string s)
Single	static float Parse(string s)
Int64	static long Parse(string s)
Int32	static int Parse(string s)
Int16	static short Parse(string s)
UInt64	static ulong Parse(string s)
UInt32	static uint Parse(string s)
UInt16	static ushort Parse(string s)
Byte	static byte Parse(string s)
SByte	static sbyte Parse(string s)

The **Parse( )** methods will throw a **FormatException** if *s* does not contain a valid number as defined by the invoking type. **ArgumentNullException** is thrown if *s* is null, and **OverflowException** is thrown if the value in *s* exceeds the bounds of the invoking type.

The parsing methods give you an easy way to convert a numeric value, read as a string from the keyboard or a text file, into its proper internal format. For example, the following program averages a list of numbers entered by the user. It first asks the user for the number of values to be averaged. It then reads that number using **ReadLine( )** and uses **Int32.Parse( )** to convert the string into an integer. Next, it inputs the values, using **Double.Parse( )** to convert the strings into their **double** equivalents.

```
// This program averages a list of numbers entered by the user.

using System;
using System.IO;
```

```
class AvgNums {
  static void Main() {
    string str;
    int n;
    double sum = 0.0;
    double avg, t;

    Console.Write("How many numbers will you enter: ");
    str = Console.ReadLine();
    try {
      n = Int32.Parse(str);
    } catch(FormatException exc) {
      Console.WriteLine(exc.Message);
      return;
    } catch(OverflowException exc) {
      Console.WriteLine(exc.Message);
      return;
    }

    Console.WriteLine("Enter " + n + " values.");
    for(int i=0; i < n ; i++)   {
      Console.Write(": ");
      str = Console.ReadLine();
      try {
        t = Double.Parse(str);
      } catch(FormatException exc) {
        Console.WriteLine(exc.Message);
        t = 0.0;
      } catch(OverflowException exc) {
        Console.WriteLine(exc.Message);
        t = 0;
      }
      sum += t;
    }
    avg = sum / n;
    Console.WriteLine("Average is " + avg);
  }
}
```

Here is a sample run:

```
How many numbers will you enter: 5
Enter 5 values.
: 1.1
: 2.2
: 3.3
: 4.4
: 5.5
Average is 3.3
```

One other point: You must use the right parsing method for the type of value you are trying to convert. For example, trying to use **Int32.Parse( )** on a string that contains a floating-point value will not produce the desired result.

As explained, **Parse( )** will throw an exception on failure. You can avoid generating an exception when converting numeric strings by using the **TryParse( )** method, which is defined for all of the numeric structures. Here is an example. It shows one version of **TryParse( )** as defined by **Int32**.

    static bool TryParse(string *s*, out int *result*)

The numeric string is passed in *s*. The result is returned in *result*. It performs the conversion using the default locale and numeric style. (A second version of **TryParse( )** is available that lets you specify the numeric style and locale.) If the conversion fails, such as when *s* does not contain a numeric string in the proper form, **TryParse( )** returns false. Otherwise, it returns true. Therefore, you must check the return value to confirm that the conversion was successful.

Delegates, Events, and Lambda Expressions

This chapter examines three innovative C# features: delegates, events, and lambda expressions. A *delegate* provides a way to encapsulate a method. An *event* is a notification that some action has occurred. Delegates and events are related because an event is built upon a delegate. Both expand the set of programming tasks to which C# can be applied. The *lambda expression* is a relatively new syntactic feature that offers a streamlined, yet powerful way to define what is, essentially, a unit of executable code. Lambda expressions are often used when working with delegates and events because a delegate can refer to a lambda expression. (Lambda expressions are also very important to LINQ, which is described in Chapter 19.) Also examined are anonymous methods, covariance, contravariance, and method group conversions.

Delegates

Let's begin by defining the term *delegate*. In straightforward language, a delegate is an object that can refer to a method. Therefore, when you create a delegate, you are creating an object that can hold a reference to a method. Furthermore, the method can be called through this reference. In other words, a delegate can invoke the method to which it refers. As you will see, this is a very powerful concept.

It is important to understand that the same delegate can be used to call different methods during the runtime of a program by simply changing the method to which the delegate refers. Thus, the method that will be invoked by a delegate is not determined at compile time, but rather at runtime. This is the principal advantage of a delegate.

NOTE *If you are familiar with C/C++, then it will help to know that a delegate in C# is similar to a function pointer in C/C++.*

A delegate type is declared using the keyword **delegate**. The general form of a delegate declaration is shown here:

delegate *ret-type name*(*parameter-list*);

Here, *ret-type* is the type of value returned by the methods that the delegate will be calling. The name of the delegate is specified by *name*. The parameters required by the methods called through the delegate are specified in the *parameter-list*. Once created, a delegate instance can refer to and call methods whose return type and parameter list match those specified by the delegate declaration.

A key point to understand is that a delegate can be used to call *any* method that agrees with its signature and return type. Furthermore, the method can be either an instance method associated with an object or a **static** method associated with a class. All that matters is that the return type and signature of the method agree with those of the delegate.

To see delegates in action, let's begin with the simple example shown here:

```
// A simple delegate example.

using System;

// Declare a delegate type.
delegate string StrMod(string str);

class DelegateTest {
  // Replaces spaces with hyphens.
  static string ReplaceSpaces(string s) {
    Console.WriteLine("Replacing spaces with hyphens.");
    return s.Replace(' ', '-');
  }

  // Remove spaces.
  static string RemoveSpaces(string s) {
    string temp = "";
    int i;

    Console.WriteLine("Removing spaces.");
    for(i=0; i < s.Length; i++)
      if(s[i] != ' ') temp += s[i];

    return temp;
  }

  // Reverse a string.
  static string Reverse(string s) {
    string temp = "";
    int i, j;

    Console.WriteLine("Reversing string.");
    for(j=0, i=s.Length-1; i >= 0; i--, j++)
      temp += s[i];

    return temp;
  }

  static void Main() {
    // Construct a delegate.
    StrMod strOp = new StrMod(ReplaceSpaces);
    string str;
```

```
      // Call methods through the delegate.
      str = strOp("This is a test.");
      Console.WriteLine("Resulting string: " + str);
      Console.WriteLine();

      strOp = new StrMod(RemoveSpaces);
      str = strOp("This is a test.");
      Console.WriteLine("Resulting string: " + str);
      Console.WriteLine();

      strOp = new StrMod(Reverse);
      str = strOp("This is a test.");
      Console.WriteLine("Resulting string: " + str);
  }
}
```

The output from the program is shown here:

```
Replacing spaces with hyphens.
Resulting string: This-is-a-test.

Removing spaces.
Resulting string: Thisisatest.

Reversing string.
Resulting string: .tset a si sihT
```

Let's examine this program closely. The program declares a delegate type called **StrMod**, shown here:

```
delegate string StrMod(string str);
```

Notice that **StrMod** takes one **string** parameter and returns a **string**.

Next, in **DelegateTest**, three **static** methods are declared, each with a single parameter of type **string** and a return type of **string**. Thus, they match the **StrMod** delegate. These methods perform some type of string modification. Notice that **ReplaceSpaces( )** uses one of **string**'s methods, called **Replace( )**, to replace spaces with hyphens.

In **Main( )**, a **StrMod** reference called **strOp** is created and assigned a reference to **ReplaceSpaces( )**. Pay close attention to this line:

```
StrMod strOp = new StrMod(ReplaceSpaces);
```

Notice how the method **ReplaceSpaces( )** is passed as a parameter. Only its name is used; no parameters are specified. This can be generalized. When instantiating a delegate, you specify only the name of the method to which you want the delegate to refer. Of course, the method's signature must match that of the delegate's declaration. If it doesn't, a compile-time error will result.

Next, **ReplaceSpaces( )** is called through the delegate instance **strOp**, as shown here:

```
str = strOp("This is a test.");
```

Because **strOp** refers to **ReplaceSpaces( )**, **ReplaceSpaces( )** is invoked.

Next, **strOp** is assigned a reference to **RemoveSpaces( )**, and then **strOp** is called again. This time, **RemoveSpaces( )** is invoked.

Finally, **strOp** is assigned a reference to **Reverse( )** and **strOp** is called. This results in **Reverse( )** being called.

The key point of the example is that the invocation of **strOp** results in a call to the method referred to by **strOp** at the time at which the invocation occurs. Thus, the method to call is resolved at runtime, not compile time.

Delegate Method Group Conversion

Since version 2.0, C# has included an option that significantly simplifies the syntax that assigns a method to a delegate. This feature is called *method group conversion,* and it allows you to simply assign the name of a method to a delegate, without using **new** or explicitly invoking the delegate's constructor.

For example, here is the **Main( )** method of the preceding program rewritten to use method group conversions:

```
static void Main() {
  // Construct a delegate using method group conversion.
  StrMod strOp = ReplaceSpaces; // use method group conversion
  string str;

  // Call methods through the delegate.
  str = strOp("This is a test.");
  Console.WriteLine("Resulting string: " + str);
  Console.WriteLine();

  strOp = RemoveSpaces; // use method group conversion
  str = strOp("This is a test.");
  Console.WriteLine("Resulting string: " + str);
  Console.WriteLine();

  strOp = Reverse; // use method group conversion
  str = strOp("This is a test.");
  Console.WriteLine("Resulting string: " + str);
}
```

Pay special attention to the way that **strOp** is created and assigned the method **ReplaceSpaces( )** in this line:

```
StrMod strOp = ReplaceSpaces; // use method group conversion
```

The name of the method is assigned directly to **strOp**. C# automatically provides a conversion from the method to the delegate type. This syntax can be generalized to any situation in which a method is assigned to (or converted to) a delegate type.

Because the method group conversion syntax is simpler than the old approach, it is used throughout the remainder of this book.

Using Instance Methods as Delegates

Although the preceding example used **static** methods, a delegate can also refer to instance methods. It must do so, however, through an object reference. For example, here is a rewrite of the previous example, which encapsulates the string operations inside a class called

StringOps. Notice that the method group conversion syntax can also be applied in this situation.

```
// Delegates can refer to instance methods, too.

using System;

// Declare a delegate type.
delegate string StrMod(string str);

class StringOps {
  // Replaces spaces with hyphens.
  public string ReplaceSpaces(string s) {
    Console.WriteLine("Replacing spaces with hyphens.");
    return s.Replace(' ', '-');
  }

  // Remove spaces.
  public string RemoveSpaces(string s) {
    string temp = "";
    int i;

    Console.WriteLine("Removing spaces.");
    for(i=0; i < s.Length; i++)
      if(s[i] != ' ') temp += s[i];

    return temp;
  }

  // Reverse a string.
  public string Reverse(string s) {
    string temp = "";
    int i, j;

    Console.WriteLine("Reversing string.");
    for(j=0, i=s.Length-1; i >= 0; i--, j++)
      temp += s[i];

    return temp;
  }
}

class DelegateTest {
  static void Main() {
    StringOps so = new StringOps(); // create an instance of StringOps

    // Initialize a delegate.
    StrMod strOp = so.ReplaceSpaces;
    string str;

    // Call methods through delegates.
    str = strOp("This is a test.");
    Console.WriteLine("Resulting string: " + str);
    Console.WriteLine();
```

```
    strOp = so.RemoveSpaces;
    str = strOp("This is a test.");
    Console.WriteLine("Resulting string: " + str);
    Console.WriteLine();

    strOp = so.Reverse;
    str = strOp("This is a test.");
    Console.WriteLine("Resulting string: " + str);
  }
}
```

This program produces the same output as the first, but in this case, the delegate refers to methods on an instance of **StringOps**.

Multicasting

One of the most exciting features of a delegate is its support for *multicasting*. In simple terms, multicasting is the ability to create an *invocation list,* or chain, of methods that will be automatically called when a delegate is invoked. Such a chain is very easy to create. Simply instantiate a delegate, and then use the **+** or **+=** operator to add methods to the chain. To remove a method, use **–** or **– =**. If the delegate returns a value, then the value returned by the last method in the list becomes the return value of the entire delegate invocation. Thus, a delegate that makes use of multicasting will often have a **void** return type.

Here is an example of multicasting. Notice that it reworks the preceding examples by changing the string manipulation method's return type to **void** and using a **ref** parameter to return the altered string to the caller. This makes the methods more appropriate for multicasting.

```
// Demonstrate multicasting.

using System;

// Declare a delegate type.
delegate void StrMod(ref string str);

class MultiCastDemo {
  // Replaces spaces with hyphens.
  static void ReplaceSpaces(ref string s) {
    Console.WriteLine("Replacing spaces with hyphens.");
    s = s.Replace(' ', '-');
  }

  // Remove spaces.
  static void RemoveSpaces(ref string s) {
    string temp = "";
    int i;

    Console.WriteLine("Removing spaces.");
    for(i=0; i < s.Length; i++)
      if(s[i] != ' ') temp += s[i];

    s = temp;
  }
```

```
// Reverse a string.
static void Reverse(ref string s) {
  string temp = "";
  int i, j;

  Console.WriteLine("Reversing string.");
  for(j=0, i=s.Length-1; i >= 0; i--, j++)
    temp += s[i];

  s = temp;
}

static void Main() {
  // Construct delegates.
  StrMod strOp;
  StrMod replaceSp = ReplaceSpaces;
  StrMod removeSp = RemoveSpaces;
  StrMod reverseStr = Reverse;
  string str = "This is a test";

  // Set up multicast.
  strOp = replaceSp;
  strOp += reverseStr;

  // Call multicast.
  strOp(ref str);
  Console.WriteLine("Resulting string: " + str);
  Console.WriteLine();

  // Remove replace and add remove.
  strOp -= replaceSp;
  strOp += removeSp;

  str = "This is a test."; // reset string

  // Call multicast.
  strOp(ref str);
  Console.WriteLine("Resulting string: " + str);
  Console.WriteLine();
  }
}
```

Here is the output:

```
Replacing spaces with hyphens.
Reversing string.
Resulting string: tset-a-si-sihT

Reversing string.
Removing spaces.
Resulting string: .tsetasisihT
```

In **Main( )**, four delegate instances are created. One, **strOp**, is null. The other three refer to specific string modification methods. Next, a multicast is created that calls **RemoveSpaces( )** and **Reverse( )**. This is accomplished via the following lines:

```
strOp = replaceSp;
strOp += reverseStr;
```

First, **strOp** is assigned **replaceSp**. Next, using **+=**, **reverseStr** is added. When **strOp** is invoked, both methods are invoked, replacing spaces with hyphens and reversing the string, as the output illustrates.

Next, **replaceSp** is removed from the chain, using this line:

```
strOp -= replaceSp;
```

and **removeSP** is added using this line:

```
strOp += removeSp;
```

Then, **strOp** is again invoked. This time, spaces are removed and the string is reversed.

Delegate chains are a powerful mechanism because they allow you to define a set of methods that can be executed as a unit. This can increase the structure of some types of code. Also, as you will soon see, delegate chains have a special value to events.

Covariance and Contravariance

There are two features that add flexibility to delegates: *covariance* and *contravariance*. Normally, the method that you pass to a delegate must have the same return type and signature as the delegate. However, covariance and contravariance relax this rule slightly, as it pertains to derived types. Covariance enables a method to be assigned to a delegate when the method's return type is a class derived from the class specified by the return type of the delegate. Contravariance enables a method to be assigned to a delegate when a method's parameter type is a base class of the class specified by the delegate's declaration.

Here is an example that illustrates both covariance and contravariance:

```
// Demonstrate covariance and contravariance.

using System;

class X {
  public int Val;
}

// Y is derived from X.
class Y : X { }

// This delegate returns X and takes a Y argument.
delegate X ChangeIt(Y obj);

class CoContraVariance {

  // This method returns X and has an X parameter.
```

```
static X IncrA(X obj) {
  X temp = new X();
  temp.Val = obj.Val + 1;
  return temp;
}

// This method returns Y and has a Y parameter.
static Y IncrB(Y obj) {
  Y temp = new Y();
  temp.Val = obj.Val + 1;
  return temp;
}

static void Main() {
  Y Yob = new Y();

  // In this case, the parameter to IncrA
  // is X and the parameter to ChangeIt is Y.
  // Because of contravariance, the following
  // line is OK.
  ChangeIt change = IncrA;

  X Xob = change(Yob);

  Console.WriteLine("Xob: " + Xob.Val);

  // In the next case, the return type of
  // IncrB is Y and the return type of
  // ChangeIt is X. Because of covariance,
  // the following line is OK.
  change = IncrB;

  Yob = (Y) change(Yob);

  Console.WriteLine("Yob: " + Yob.Val);
  }
}
```

The output from the program is shown here:

```
Xob: 1
Yob: 1
```

In the program, notice that class **Y** is derived from class **X**. Next, notice that the delegate **ChangeIt** is declared like this:

```
delegate X ChangeIt(Y obj);
```

ChangeIt returns **X** and has a **Y** parameter. Next, notice that the methods **IncrA( )** and **IncrB( )** are declared as shown here:

```
static X IncrA(X obj)
static Y IncrB(Y obj)
```

The **IncrA( )** method has an **X** parameter and returns **X**. The **IncrB( )** method has a **Y** parameter and returns **Y**. Given covariance and contravariance, either of these methods can be passed to **ChangeIt**, as the program illustrates.

Therefore, this line

```
ChangeIt change = IncrA;
```

uses contravariance to enable **IncrA( )** to be passed to the delegate because **IncrA( )** has an **X** parameter, but the delegate has a **Y** parameter. This works because, with contravariance, if the parameter type of the method passed to a delegate is a base class of the parameter type used by the delegate, then the method and the delegate are compatible.

The next line is also legal, but this time it is because of covariance:

```
change = IncrB;
```

In this case, the return type of **IncrB( )** is **Y**, but the return type of **ChangeIt** is **X**. However, because the return type of the method is a class derived from the return type of the delegate, the two are compatible.

System.Delegate

All delegates are classes that are implicitly derived from **System.Delegate**. You don't normally need to use its members directly, and this book makes no explicit use of **System.Delegate**. However, its members may be useful in certain specialized situations.

Why Delegates

Although the preceding examples show the "how" behind delegates, they don't really illustrate the "why." In general, delegates are useful for two main reasons. First, as shown later in this chapter, delegates support events. Second, delegates give your program a way to execute methods at runtime without having to know precisely what those methods are at compile time. This ability is quite useful when you want to create a framework that allows components to be plugged in. For example, imagine a drawing program (a bit like the standard Windows Paint accessory). Using a delegate, you could allow the user to plug in special color filters or image analyzers. Furthermore, the user could create a sequence of these filters or analyzers. Such a scheme could be easily handled using a delegate.

Anonymous Functions

You will often find that the method referred to by a delegate is used only for that purpose. In other words, the only reason for the method is so it can be invoked via a delegate. The method is never called on its own. In such a case, you can avoid the need to create a separate method by using an *anonymous function*. An anonymous function is, essentially, an unnamed block of code that is passed to a delegate constructor. One advantage to using an anonymous function is simplicity. There is no need to declare a separate method whose only purpose is to be passed to a delegate.

Beginning with version 3.0, C# defines two types of anonymous functions: *anonymous methods* and *lambda expressions.* The anonymous method was added by C# 2.0. The lambda expression was added by C# 3.0. In general, the lambda expression improves on the concept of the anonymous method and is now the preferred approach to creating an anonymous function. However, anonymous methods are still used in legacy C# code. Therefore, it is important to know how they work. Furthermore, anonymous methods are the precursor to lambda expressions and a clear understanding of anonymous methods makes it easier to understand aspects of the lambda expression. Also, there is a narrow set of cases in which an anonymous method can be used, but a lambda expression cannot. Therefore, both anonymous methods and lambda expressions are described in this chapter.

Anonymous Methods

An anonymous method is one way to create an unnamed block of code that is associated with a specific delegate instance. An anonymous method is created by following the keyword **delegate** with a block of code. To see how this is done, let's begin with a simple example. The following program uses an anonymous method that counts from 0 to 5.

```
// Demonstrate an anonymous method.

using System;

// Declare a delegate type.
delegate void CountIt();

class AnonMethDemo {

  static void Main() {

    // Here, the code for counting is passed
    // as an anonymous method.
    CountIt count = delegate {
        // This is the block of code passed to the delegate.
      for(int i=0; i <= 5; i++)
        Console.WriteLine(i);
    }; // notice the semicolon

    count();
  }
}
```

This program first declares a delegate type called **CountIt** that has no parameters and returns **void**. Inside **Main( )**, a **CountIt** instance called **count** is created, and it is passed the block of code that follows the **delegate** keyword. This block of code is the anonymous method that will be executed when **count** is called. Notice that the block of code is followed by a semicolon, which terminates the declaration statement. The output from the program is shown here:

```
0
1
2
3
4
5
```

Pass Arguments to an Anonymous Method

It is possible to pass one or more arguments to an anonymous method. To do so, follow the **delegate** keyword with a parenthesized parameter list. Then, pass the argument(s) to the delegate instance when it is called. For example, here is the preceding program rewritten so that the ending value for the count is passed:

```
// Demonstrate an anonymous method that takes an argument.

using System;

// Notice that CountIt now has a parameter.
delegate void CountIt(int end);

class AnonMethDemo2 {

  static void Main() {

    // Here, the ending value for the count
    // is passed to the anonymous method.
    CountIt count = delegate (int end) {
      for(int i=0; i <= end; i++)
        Console.WriteLine(i);
    };

    count(3);
    Console.WriteLine();
    count(5);
  }
}
```

In this version, **CountIt** now takes an integer argument. Notice how the parameter list is specified after the **delegate** keyword when the anonymous method is created. The code inside the anonymous method has access to the parameter **end** in just the same way it would if a named method were being created. The output from this program is shown next:

```
0
1
2
3

0
1
2
3
4
5
```

Return a Value from an Anonymous Method

An anonymous method can return a value. The value is returned by use of the **return** statement, which works the same in an anonymous method as it does in a named method. As you would expect, the type of the return value must be compatible with the return type specified by the delegate. For example, here the code that performs the count also computes the summation of the count and returns the result:

```
// Demonstrate an anonymous method that returns a value.

using System;

// This delegate returns a value.
delegate int CountIt(int end);

class AnonMethDemo3 {

  static void Main() {
    int result;

    // Here, the ending value for the count
    // is passed to the anonymous method.
    // A summation of the count is returned.
    CountIt count = delegate (int end) {
      int sum = 0;

      for(int i=0; i <= end; i++) {
        Console.WriteLine(i);
        sum += i;
      }
      return sum; // return a value from an anonymous method
    };

    result = count(3);
    Console.WriteLine("Summation of 3 is " + result);
    Console.WriteLine();

    result = count(5);
    Console.WriteLine("Summation of 5 is " + result);
  }
}
```

In this version, the value of **sum** is returned by the code block that is associated with the **count** delegate instance. Notice that the **return** statement is used in an anonymous method in just the same way that it is used in a named method. The output is shown here:

```
0
1
2
3
Summation of 3 is 6

0
1
2
3
4
5
Summation of 5 is 15
```

Use Outer Variables with Anonymous Methods

A local variable or parameter whose scope includes an anonymous method is called an *outer variable*. An anonymous method has access to and can use these outer variables. When an outer variable is used by an anonymous method, that variable is said to be *captured*. A captured variable will stay in existence at least until the delegate that captured it is subject to garbage collection. Thus, even though a local variable will normally cease to exist when its block is exited, if that local variable is being used by an anonymous method, then that variable will stay in existence at least until the delegate referring to that method is destroyed.

The capturing of a local variable can lead to unexpected results. For example, consider this version of the counting program. As in the previous version, the summation of the count is computed. However, in this version, a **CountIt** object is constructed and returned by a static method called **Counter( )**. This object uses the variable **sum**, which is declared in the enclosing scope provided by **Counter( )**, rather than in the anonymous method, itself. Thus, **sum** is captured by the anonymous method. Inside **Main( )**, **Counter( )** is called to obtain a **CountIt** object. Thus, **sum** will not be destroyed until the program finishes.

```
// Demonstrate a captured variable.

using System;

// This delegate returns int and takes an int argument.
delegate int CountIt(int end);

class VarCapture {

  static CountIt Counter() {
    int sum = 0;

    // Here, a summation of the count is stored
    // in the captured variable sum.
    CountIt ctObj = delegate (int end) {
      for(int i=0; i <= end; i++) {
        Console.WriteLine(i);
        sum += i;
      }
      return sum;
    };
    return ctObj;
  }

  static void Main() {
    // Get a counter.
    CountIt count = Counter();

    int result;

    result = count(3);
    Console.WriteLine("Summation of 3 is " + result);
    Console.WriteLine();
```

```
      result = count(5);
      Console.WriteLine("Summation of 5 is " + result);
    }
  }
```

The output is shown here. Pay special attention to the summation value.

```
0
1
2
3
Summation of 3 is 6

0
1
2
3
4
5
Summation of 5 is 21
```

As you can see, the count still proceeds normally. However, notice the summation value for 5. It shows 21 instead of 15! The reason for this is that **sum** is captured by **ctObj** when it is created by the **Counter( )** method. This means it remains in existence until **count** is subject to garbage collection at the end of the program. Thus, its value is not destroyed when **Counter( )** returns or with each call to the anonymous method when **count** is called in **Main( )**.

Although captured variables can result in rather counterintuitive situations, such as the one just shown, it makes sense if you think about it a bit. The key point is that when an anonymous method captures a variable, that variable cannot go out of existence until the delegate that captures it is no longer being used. If this were not the case, then the captured variable could be undefined when it is needed by the delegate.

Lambda Expressions

Although anonymous methods are still part of C#, they have been largely superceded by a better approach: the *lambda expression*. It is not an overstatement to say that the lambda expression is one of the most important features added to C# since its original 1.0 release. Based on a distinctive syntactic element, the lambda expression provides a powerful alternative to the anonymous method. Although a principal use of lambda expressions is found when working with LINQ (see Chapter 19), they are also applicable to (and commonly used with) delegates and events. This use of lambda expressions is described here.

A lambda expression is the second way that an anonymous function can be created. (The other type of anonymous function is the anonymous method, described in the preceding section.) Thus, a lambda expression can be assigned to a delegate. Because a lambda expression is more streamlined than the equivalent anonymous method, lambda expressions are now the recommended approach in almost all cases.

The Lambda Operator

All lambda expressions use the *lambda operator,* which is =>. This operator divides a lambda expression into two parts. On the left the input parameter (or parameters) is specified. On the right is the lambda body. The => operator is sometimes verbalized as "goes to" or "becomes."

C# supports two types of lambda expressions, and it is the lambda body that determines what type is being created. If the lambda body consists of a single expression, then an *expression lambda* is being created. In this case, the body is free-standing—it is not enclosed between braces. If the lambda body consists of a block of statements enclosed by braces, then a *statement lambda* is being created. A statement lambda can contain multiple statements and include such things as loops, method calls, and **if** statements. The following sections describe both kinds of lambdas.

Expression Lambdas

In an expression lambda, the expression on the right side of the **=>** acts on the parameter (or parameters) specified by the left side. The result of the expression becomes the result of the lambda operator and is returned.

Here is the general form of an expression lambda that takes only one parameter:

param => expr

When more than one parameter is required, then the following form is used:

(param-list) => expr

Therefore, when two or more parameters are needed, they must be enclosed by parentheses. If no parameters are needed, then empty parentheses must be used.

Here is a simple expression lambda:

count => count + 2

Here **count** is the parameter that is acted on by the expression **count + 2**. Thus, the result is the value of **count** increased by two. Here is another example:

n => n % 2 == 0

In this case, this expression returns true if **n** is even and false if it is odd.

To use a lambda expression involves two steps. First, declare a delegate type that is compatible with the lambda expression. Second, declare an instance of the delegate, assigning to it the lambda expression. Once this has been done, the lambda expression can be executed by calling the delegate instance. The result of the lambda expression becomes the return value.

The following program shows how to put the two expression lambdas just shown into action. It declares two delegate types. The first, called **Incr**, takes an **int** argument and returns an **int** result. The second, called **IsEven**, takes an **int** argument and returns a **bool** result. It then assigns the lambda expressions to instances of those delegates. Finally, it executes the lambda expressions through the delegate instances.

```
// Use two simple lambda expressions.

using System;

// Declare a delegate that takes an int argument
// and returns an int result.
delegate int Incr(int v);

// Declare a delegate that takes an int argument
// and returns a bool result.
```

```
delegate bool IsEven(int v);

class SimpleLambdaDemo {

  static void Main() {

    // Create an Incr delegate instance that refers to
    // a lambda expression that increases its parameter by 2.
    Incr incr = count => count + 2;

    // Now, use the incr lambda expression.
    Console.WriteLine("Use incr lambda expression: ");
    int x = -10;
    while(x <= 0) {
      Console.Write(x + " ");
      x = incr(x); // increase x by 2
    }

    Console.WriteLine("\n");

    // Create an IsEven delegate instance that refers to
    // a lambda expression that returns true if its parameter
    // is even and false otherwise.
    IsEven isEven = n => n % 2 == 0;

    // Now, use the isEven lambda expression.
    Console.WriteLine("Use isEven lambda expression: ");
    for(int i=1; i <= 10; i++)
      if(isEven(i)) Console.WriteLine(i + " is even.");

  }
}
```

The output is shown here:

```
Use incr lambda expression:
-10 -8 -6 -4 -2 0

Use isEven lambda expression:
2 is even.
4 is even.
6 is even.
8 is even.
10 is even.
```

In the program, pay special attention to these declarations:

```
Incr incr = count => count + 2;
IsEven isEven = n => n % 2 == 0;
```

The first assigns to **incr** a lambda expression that returns the result of increasing the value passed to **count** by 2. This expression can be assigned to an **Incr** delegate because it is compatible with **Incr**'s declaration. The argument used in the call to **incr** is passed to **count**. The result is returned. The second declaration assigns to **isEven** an expression that returns true if the argument is even and false otherwise. Thus, it is compatible with the **IsEven** delegate declaration.

At this point, you might be wondering how the compiler knows the type of the data used in a lambda expression. For example, in the lambda expression assigned to **incr**, how does the compiler know that **count** is an **int**? The answer is that the compiler infers the type of the parameter and the expression's result type from the delegate type. Thus, the lambda parameters and return value must be compatible with the parameter type(s) and return type of the delegate.

Although type inference is quite useful, in some cases, you might need to explicitly specify the type of a lambda parameter. To do so, simply include the type name. For example, here is another way to declare the **incr** delegate instance:

```
Incr incr = (int count) => count + 2;
```

Notice now that **count** is explicitly declared as an **int**. Also notice the use of parentheses. They are now necessary. (Parentheses can be omitted only when exactly one parameter is specified and no type specifier is used.)

Although the preceding two lambda expressions each used one parameter, lambda expressions can use any number, including zero. When using more than one parameter you *must* enclose them within parentheses. Here is an example that uses a lambda expression to determine if a value is within a specified range:

```
(low, high, val) => val >= low && val <= high;
```

Here is a delegate type that is compatible with this lambda expression:

```
delegate bool InRange(int lower, int upper, int v);
```

Thus, you could create an **InRange** delegate instance like this:

```
InRange rangeOK = (low, high, val) => val >= low && val <= high;
```

After doing so, the lambda expression can be executed as shown here:

```
if(rangeOK(1, 5, 3)) Console.WriteLine("3 is within 1 to 5.");
```

One other point: Lambda expressions can use outer variables in the same way as anonymous methods, and they are captured in the same way.

Statement Lambdas

As mentioned, there are two basic flavors of the lambda expression. The first is the expression lambda, which was discussed in the preceding section. As explained, the body of an expression lambda consists solely of a single expression. The second type of lambda expression is the *statement lambda*. A statement lambda expands the types of operations that can be handled within a lambda expression because it allows the body of lambda to contain multiple statements. For example, using a statement lambda you can use loops, **if** statements, declare variables, and so on. A statement lambda is easy to create. Simply enclose the body within braces. Aside from allowing multiple statements, it works much like the expression lambdas just discussed.

Here is an example that uses a statement lambda to compute and return the factorial of an **int** value:

```
// Demonstrate a statement lambda.
using System;

// IntOp takes one int argument and returns an int result.
delegate int IntOp(int end);

class StatementLambdaDemo {

  static void Main() {

    // A statement lambda that returns the factorial
    // of the value it is passed.
    IntOp fact = n => {
                   int r = 1;
                   for(int i=1; i <= n; i++)
                     r = i * r;
                   return r;
                 };

    Console.WriteLine("The factorial of 3 is " + fact(3));
    Console.WriteLine("The factorial of 5 is " + fact(5));
  }
}
```

The output is shown here:

```
The factorial of 3 is 6
The factorial of 5 is 120
```

In the program, notice that the statement lambda declares a variable called **r**, uses a **for** loop, and has a **return** statement. These are legal inside a statement lambda. In essence, a statement lambda closely parallels an anonymous method. Therefore, many anonymous methods will be converted to statement lambdas when updating legacy code. One other point: When a **return** statement occurs within a lambda expression, it simply causes a return from the lambda. It does not cause the enclosing method to return.

Before concluding, it is worthwhile to see another example that shows the statement lambda in action. The following program reworks the first delegate example in this chapter so it uses statement lambdas (rather than standalone methods) to accomplish various string modifications:

```
// The first delegate example rewritten to use
// statement lambdas.

using System;

// Declare a delegate type.
delegate string StrMod(string s);
```

```csharp
class UseStatementLambdas {

  static void Main() {
    // Create delegates that refer to lambda expressions
    // that perform various string modifications.

    // Replaces spaces with hyphens.
    StrMod ReplaceSpaces = s => {
            Console.WriteLine("Replacing spaces with hyphens.");
            return s.Replace(' ', '-');
          };

    // Remove spaces.
    StrMod RemoveSpaces = s => {
            string temp = "";
            int i;

            Console.WriteLine("Removing spaces.");
            for(i=0; i < s.Length; i++)
              if(s[i] != ' ') temp += s[i];

            return temp;
          };


    // Reverse a string.
    StrMod Reverse = s => {
            string temp = "";
            int i, j;

            Console.WriteLine("Reversing string.");
            for(j=0, i=s.Length-1; i >= 0; i--, j++)
            temp += s[i];

            return temp;
          };

    string str;

    // Call methods through the delegate.
    StrMod strOp = ReplaceSpaces;
    str = strOp("This is a test.");
    Console.WriteLine("Resulting string: " + str);
    Console.WriteLine();

    strOp = RemoveSpaces;
    str = strOp("This is a test.");
    Console.WriteLine("Resulting string: " + str);
    Console.WriteLine();

    strOp = Reverse;
    str = strOp("This is a test.");
```

```
    Console.WriteLine("Resulting string: " + str);
  }
}
```

The output, which is the same as the original version, is shown here:

```
Replacing spaces with hyphens.
Resulting string: This-is-a-test.

Removing spaces.
Resulting string: Thisisatest.

Reversing string.
Resulting string: .tset a si sihT
```

Events

Another important C# feature is built upon the foundation of delegates: the *event*. An event is, essentially, an automatic notification that some action has occurred. Events work like this: An object that has an interest in an event registers an event handler for that event. When the event occurs, all registered handlers are called. Event handlers are represented by delegates.

Events are members of a class and are declared using the **event** keyword. Its most commonly used form is shown here:

event *event-delegate event-name*;

Here, *event-delegate* is the name of the delegate used to support the event, and *event-name* is the name of the specific event object being declared.

Let's begin with a very simple example:

```
// A very simple event demonstration.

using System;

// Declare a delegate type for an event.
delegate void MyEventHandler();

// Declare a class that contains an event.
class MyEvent {
  public event MyEventHandler SomeEvent;

  // This is called to raise the event.
  public void OnSomeEvent() {
    if(SomeEvent != null)
      SomeEvent();
  }
}

class EventDemo {
  // An event handler.
  static void Handler() {
    Console.WriteLine("Event occurred");
  }
```

```
static void Main() {
  MyEvent evt = new MyEvent();

  // Add Handler() to the event list.
  evt.SomeEvent += Handler;

  // Raise the event.
  evt.OnSomeEvent();
  }
}
```

This program displays the following output:

```
Event occurred
```

Although simple, this program contains all the elements essential to proper event handling. Let's look at it carefully. The program begins by declaring a delegate type for the event handler, as shown here:

```
delegate void MyEventHandler();
```

All events are activated through a delegate. Thus, the event delegate type defines the return type and signature for the event. In this case, there are no parameters, but event parameters are allowed.

Next, an event class, called **MyEvent**, is created. Inside the class, an event called **SomeEvent** is declared, using this line:

```
public event MyEventHandler SomeEvent;
```

Notice the syntax. The keyword **event** tells the compiler that an event is being declared.

Also declared inside **MyEvent** is the method **OnSomeEvent( )**, which is the method a program will call to raise (or "fire") an event. (That is, this is the method called when the event occurs.) It calls an event handler through the **SomeEvent** delegate, as shown here:

```
if(SomeEvent != null)
  SomeEvent();
```

Notice that a handler is called if and only if **SomeEvent** is not **null**. Since other parts of your program must register an interest in an event in order to receive event notifications, it is possible that **OnSomeEvent( )** could be called before any event handler has been registered. To prevent calling on a **null** reference, the event delegate must be tested to ensure that it is not **null**.

Inside **EventDemo**, an event handler called **Handler( )** is created. In this simple example, the event handler simply displays a message, but other handlers could perform more meaningful actions. In **Main( )**, a **MyEvent** object is created, and **Handler( )** is registered as a handler for this event, by adding it as shown here:

```
MyEvent evt = new MyEvent();

// Add Handler() to the event list.
evt.SomeEvent += Handler;
```

Notice that the handler is added using the += operator. Events support only += and – =. In this case, **Handler( )** is a **static** method, but event handlers can also be instance methods.

Finally, the event is raised as shown here:

```
// Raise the event.
evt.OnSomeEvent();
```

Calling **OnSomeEvent( )** causes all registered event handlers to be called. In this case, there is only one registered handler, but there could be more, as the next section explains.

A Multicast Event Example

Like delegates, events can be multicast. This enables multiple objects to respond to an event notification. Here is an event multicast example:

```
// An event multicast demonstration.

using System;

// Declare a delegate type for an event.
delegate void MyEventHandler();

// Declare a class that contains an event.
class MyEvent {
  public event MyEventHandler SomeEvent;

  // This is called to raise the event.
  public void OnSomeEvent() {
    if(SomeEvent != null)
      SomeEvent();
  }
}

class X {
  public void Xhandler() {
    Console.WriteLine("Event received by X object");
  }
}

class Y {
  public void Yhandler() {
    Console.WriteLine("Event received by Y object");
  }
}

class EventDemo2 {
  static void Handler() {
    Console.WriteLine("Event received by EventDemo");
  }

  static void Main() {
    MyEvent evt = new MyEvent();
    X xOb = new X();
    Y yOb = new Y();
```

```
    // Add handlers to the event list.
    evt.SomeEvent += Handler;
    evt.SomeEvent += xOb.Xhandler;
    evt.SomeEvent += yOb.Yhandler;

    // Raise the event.
    evt.OnSomeEvent();
    Console.WriteLine();

    // Remove a handler.
    evt.SomeEvent -= xOb.Xhandler;
    evt.OnSomeEvent();
  }
}
```

The output from the program is shown here:

```
Event received by EventDemo
Event received by X object
Event received by Y object

Event received by EventDemo
Event received by Y object
```

This example creates two additional classes, called **X** and **Y**, which also define event handlers compatible with **MyEventHandler**. Thus, these handlers can also become part of the event chain. Notice that the handlers in **X** and **Y** are not **static**. This means that objects of each must be created, and the handler linked to each instance must be added to the event chain. The differences between instance and **static** handlers are examined in the next section.

Instance Methods vs. Static Methods as Event Handlers

Although both instance methods and **static** methods can be used as event handlers, they do differ in one important way. When a **static** method is used as a handler, an event notification applies to the class. When an instance method is used as an event handler, events are sent to specific object instances. Thus, each object of a class that wants to receive an event notification must register individually. In practice, most event handlers are instance methods, but, of course, this is subject to the specific application. Let's look at an example of each.

The following program creates a class called **X** that defines an instance method as an event handler. This means that each **X** object must register individually to receive events. To demonstrate this fact, the program multicasts an event to three objects of type **X**.

```
/* Individual objects receive notifications when instance
   event handlers are used. */

using System;

// Declare a delegate type for an event.
delegate void MyEventHandler();

// Declare a class that contains an event.
class MyEvent {
```

```
  public event MyEventHandler SomeEvent;

  // This is called to raise the event.
  public void OnSomeEvent() {
    if(SomeEvent != null)
      SomeEvent();
  }
}

class X {
  int id;

  public X(int x) { id = x; }

  // This is an instance method that will be used as an event handler.
  public void Xhandler() {
    Console.WriteLine("Event received by object " + id);
  }
}

class EventDemo3 {
  static void Main() {
    MyEvent evt = new MyEvent();
    X o1 = new X(1);
    X o2 = new X(2);
    X o3 = new X(3);

    evt.SomeEvent += o1.Xhandler;
    evt.SomeEvent += o2.Xhandler;
    evt.SomeEvent += o3.Xhandler;

    // Raise the event.
    evt.OnSomeEvent();
  }
}
```

The output from this program is shown here:

```
Event received by object 1
Event received by object 2
Event received by object 3
```

As the output shows, each object registers its interest in an event separately, and each receives a separate notification.

Alternatively, when a **static** method is used as an event handler, events are handled independently of any object, as the following program shows:

```
/* A class receives the notification when
   a static method is used as an event handler. */

using System;

// Declare a delegate type for an event.
```

```
delegate void MyEventHandler();

// Declare a class that contains an event.
class MyEvent {
  public event MyEventHandler SomeEvent;

  // This is called to raise the event.
  public void OnSomeEvent() {
    if(SomeEvent != null)
      SomeEvent();
  }
}

class X {

  /* This is a static method that will be used as
     an event handler. */
  public static void Xhandler() {
    Console.WriteLine("Event received by class.");
  }
}

class EventDemo4 {
  static void Main() {
    MyEvent evt = new MyEvent();

    evt.SomeEvent += X.Xhandler;

    // Raise the event.
    evt.OnSomeEvent();
  }
}
```

The output from this program is shown here:

```
Event received by class.
```

In the program, notice that no object of type **X** is ever created. However, since **Xhandler( )** is a **static** method of **X**, it can be attached to **SomeEvent** and executed when **OnSomeEvent( )** is called.

Using Event Accessors

The form of **event** used in the preceding examples created events that automatically manage the event handler invocation list, including the adding and subtracting of event handlers to and from the list. Thus, you did not need to implement any of the list management functionality yourself. Because they manage the details for you, these types of events are by far the most commonly used. It is possible, however, to provide the event handler list operations yourself, perhaps to implement some type of specialized event storage mechanism.

To take control of the event handler list, you will use an expanded form of the **event** statement, which allows the use of *event accessors*. The accessors give you control over how the event handler list is implemented. This form is shown here:

```
event event-delegate event-name {
  add {
    // code to add an event to the chain
  }

  remove {
    // code to remove an event from the chain
  }
}
```

This form includes the two event accessors **add** and **remove**. The **add** accessor is called when an event handler is added to the event chain, by using **+=**. The **remove** accessor is called when an event handler is removed from the chain, by using **– =**.

When **add** or **remove** is called, it receives the handler to add or remove as a parameter. As with other types of accessors, this parameter is called **value**. By implementing **add** and **remove**, you can define a custom event-handler storage scheme. For example, you could use an array, a stack, or a queue to store the handlers.

Here is an example that uses the accessor form of **event**. It uses an array to hold the event handlers. Because the array is only three elements long, only three event handlers can be held in the chain at any one time.

```
// Create a custom means of managing the event invocation list.

using System;

// Declare a delegate type for an event.
delegate void MyEventHandler();

// Declare a class that holds up to 3 events.
class MyEvent {
  MyEventHandler[] evnt = new MyEventHandler[3];

  public event MyEventHandler SomeEvent {
    // Add an event to the list.
    add {
      int i;

      for(i=0; i < 3; i++)
        if(evnt[i] == null) {
          evnt[i] = value;
          break;
        }
      if (i == 3) Console.WriteLine("Event list full.");
    }

    // Remove an event from the list.
    remove {
      int i;

      for(i=0; i < 3; i++)
        if(evnt[i] == value) {
```

```
            evnt[i] = null;
            break;
        }
      if (i == 3) Console.WriteLine("Event handler not found.");
    }
  }

  // This is called to raise the events.
  public void OnSomeEvent() {
    for(int i=0; i < 3; i++)
      if(evnt[i] != null) evnt[i]();
  }

}

// Create some classes that use MyEventHandler.
class W {
  public void Whandler() {
    Console.WriteLine("Event received by W object");
  }
}

class X {
  public void Xhandler() {
    Console.WriteLine("Event received by X object");
  }
}

class Y {
  public void Yhandler() {
    Console.WriteLine("Event received by Y object");
  }
}

class Z {
  public void Zhandler() {
    Console.WriteLine("Event received by Z object");
  }
}

class EventDemo5 {
  static void Main() {
    MyEvent evt = new MyEvent();
    W wOb = new W();
    X xOb = new X();
    Y yOb = new Y();
    Z zOb = new Z();

    // Add handlers to the event list.
    Console.WriteLine("Adding events.");
    evt.SomeEvent += wOb.Whandler;
    evt.SomeEvent += xOb.Xhandler;
    evt.SomeEvent += yOb.Yhandler;
```

```
      // Can't store this one -- full.
      evt.SomeEvent += zOb.Zhandler;
      Console.WriteLine();

      // Raise the events.
      evt.OnSomeEvent();
      Console.WriteLine();

      // Remove a handler.
      Console.WriteLine("Remove xOb.Xhandler.");
      evt.SomeEvent -= xOb.Xhandler;
      evt.OnSomeEvent();

      Console.WriteLine();

      // Try to remove it again.
      Console.WriteLine("Try to remove xOb.Xhandler again.");
      evt.SomeEvent -= xOb.Xhandler;
      evt.OnSomeEvent();

      Console.WriteLine();

      // Now, add Zhandler.
      Console.WriteLine("Add zOb.Zhandler.");
      evt.SomeEvent += zOb.Zhandler;
      evt.OnSomeEvent();

   }
}
```

The output from the program is shown here:

```
Adding events.
Event list full.

Event received by W object
Event received by X object
Event received by Y object

Remove xOb.Xhandler.
Event received by W object
Event received by Y object

Try to remove xOb.Xhandler again.
Event handler not found.
Event received by W object
Event received by Y object

Add zOb.Zhandler.
Event received by W object
Event received by Z object
Event received by Y object
```

Let's examine this program closely. First, an event handler delegate called **MyEventHandler** is defined. Next, the class **MyEvent** is declared. It begins by defining a three-element array of event handlers called **evnt**, as shown here:

```
MyEventHandler[] evnt = new MyEventHandler[3];
```

This array will be used to store the event handlers that are added to the event chain. The elements in **evnt** are initialized to **null** by default.

Next, the event **SomeEvent** is declared. It uses the accessor form of the **event** statement, as shown here:

```
public event MyEventHandler SomeEvent {
  // Add an event to the list.
  add {
    int i;

    for(i=0; i < 3; i++)
      if(evnt[i] == null) {
        evnt[i] = value;
        break;
      }
    if (i == 3) Console.WriteLine("Event queue full.");
  }

  // Remove an event from the list.
  remove {
    int i;

    for(i=0; i < 3; i++)
      if(evnt[i] == value) {
        evnt[i] = null;
        break;
      }
    if (i == 3) Console.WriteLine("Event handler not found.");
  }
}
```

When an event handler is added, **add** is called and a reference to the handler (contained in **value**) is put into the first unused (that is, null) element of **evnt**. If no element is free, then an error is reported. (Of course, throwing an exception when the list is full would be a better approach for real-world code.) Since **evnt** is only three elements long, only three event handlers can be stored. When an event handler is removed, **remove** is called and the **evnt** array is searched for the reference to the handler passed in **value**. If it is found, its element in the array is assigned **null**, thus removing the handler from the list.

When an event is raised, **OnSomeEvent( )** is called. It cycles through the **evnt** array, calling each event handler in turn.

As the preceding example shows, it is relatively easy to implement a custom event-handler storage mechanism if one is needed. For most applications, though, the default storage provided by the non-accessor form of **event** is better. The accessor-based form of **event** can be useful in certain specialized situations, however. For example, if you have a program in which event handlers need to be executed in order of their priority and not in the order in which they are added to the chain, then you could use a priority queue to store the handlers.

> **NOTE** *In multithreaded applications, you will usually need to synchronize access to the event accessors. For information on multithreaded programming, see Chapter 23.*

Miscellaneous Event Features

Events can be specified in interfaces. Implementing classes must supply the event. Events can also be specified as **abstract**. A derived class must implement the event. Accessor-based events cannot, however, be **abstract**. An event can be specified as **sealed**. Finally, an event can be virtual, which means that it can be overridden in a derived class.

Use Anonymous Methods and Lambda Expressions with Events

Anonymous methods and lambda expressions are especially useful when working with events because often the event handler is not called by any code other than the event handling mechanism. As a result, there is usually no reason to create a standalone method. Thus, the use of lambda expressions or anonymous methods can significantly streamline event handling code.

Since lambda expressions are now the preferred approach, we will start there. Here is an example that uses a lambda expression as an event handler:

```
// Use a lambda expression as an event handler.
using System;

// Declare a delegate type for an event.
delegate void MyEventHandler(int n);

// Declare a class that contains an event.
class MyEvent {
  public event MyEventHandler SomeEvent;

  // This is called to raise the event.
  public void OnSomeEvent(int n) {
    if(SomeEvent != null)
      SomeEvent(n);
  }
}

class LambdaEventDemo {
  static void Main() {
    MyEvent evt = new MyEvent();

    // Use a lambda expression as an event handler.
    evt.SomeEvent += (n) =>
      Console.WriteLine("Event received. Value is " + n);

    // Raise the event twice.
    evt.OnSomeEvent(1);
    evt.OnSomeEvent(2);
  }
}
```

The output is shown here:

```
Event received. Value is 1
Event received. Value is 2
```

In the program, pay special attention to the way the lambda expression is used as an event handler, as shown here:

```
evt.SomeEvent += (n) =>
  Console.WriteLine("Event received. Value is " + n);
```

The syntax for using a lambda expression event handler is the same as that for using a lambda expression with any other type of delegate.

Although lambda expressions are now the preferred way to construct an anonymous function, you can still use an anonymous method as an event handler if you so choose. For example, here is the event handler from the previous example rewritten to use an anonymous method:

```
// Use an anonymous method as an event handler.
evt.SomeEvent += delegate(int n)  {
  Console.WriteLine("Event received. Value is" + n);
};
```

As you can see, the syntax for using an anonymous event handler is the same as that for any anonymous method.

.NET Event Guidelines

C# allows you to write any type of event you desire. However, for component compatibility with the .NET Framework, you will need to follow the guidelines Microsoft has established for this purpose. At the core of these guidelines is the requirement that event handlers have two parameters. The first is a reference to the object that generated the event. The second is a parameter of type **EventArgs** that contains any other information required by the handler. Thus, .NET-compatible event handlers will have this general form:

> void *handler*(object *sender*, EventArgs *e*) {
>   // ...
> }

Typically, the *sender* parameter is passed **this** by the calling code. The **EventArgs** parameter contains additional information and can be ignored if it is not needed.

The **EventArgs** class itself does not contain fields that you use to pass additional data to a handler. Instead, **EventArgs** is used as a base class from which you will derive a class that contains the necessary fields. **EventArgs** does include one **static** field called **Empty**, which is an **EventArgs** object that contains no data.

Here is an example that creates a .NET-compatible event:

```
// A .NET-compatible event.

using System;

// Derive a class from EventArgs.
class MyEventArgs : EventArgs {
  public int EventNum;
```

```
}

// Declare a delegate type for an event.
delegate void MyEventHandler(object sender, MyEventArgs e);

// Declare a class that contains an event.
class MyEvent {
  static int count = 0;

  public event MyEventHandler SomeEvent;

  // This raises SomeEvent.
  public void OnSomeEvent() {
    MyEventArgs arg = new MyEventArgs();

    if(SomeEvent != null) {
      arg.EventNum = count++;
      SomeEvent(this, arg);
    }
  }
}

class X {
  public void Handler(object sender, MyEventArgs e) {
    Console.WriteLine("Event " + e.EventNum +
                      " received by an X object.");
    Console.WriteLine("Source is " + sender);
    Console.WriteLine();
  }
}

class Y {
  public void Handler(object sender, MyEventArgs e) {
    Console.WriteLine("Event " + e.EventNum +
                      " received by a Y object.");
    Console.WriteLine("Source is " + sender);
    Console.WriteLine();
  }
}

class EventDemo6 {
  static void Main() {
    X ob1 = new X();
    Y ob2 = new Y();
    MyEvent evt = new MyEvent();

    // Add Handler() to the event list.
    evt.SomeEvent += ob1.Handler;
    evt.SomeEvent += ob2.Handler;

    // Raise the event.
    evt.OnSomeEvent();
    evt.OnSomeEvent();
  }
}
```

Here is the output:

```
Event 0 received by an X object.
Source is MyEvent

Event 0 received by a Y object.
Source is MyEvent

Event 1 received by an X object.
Source is MyEvent

Event 1 received by a Y object.
Source is MyEvent
```

In this example, **MyEventArgs** is derived from **EventArgs**. **MyEventArgs** adds just one field of its own: **EventNum**. The event handler delegate **MyEventHandler** now takes the two parameters required by the .NET Framework. As explained, the first is an object reference to the generator of the event. The second is a reference to **EventArgs** or a class derived from **EventArgs**. The event handler in the **X** and **Y** classes, **Handler( )**, also has the same types of parameters.

Inside **MyEvent**, a **MyEventHandler** called **SomeEvent** is declared. In the **OnSomeEvent( )** method, **SomeEvent** is called with the first argument being **this**, and the second argument being a **MyEventArgs** instance. Thus, the proper arguments are passed to **MyEventHandler** to fulfill the requirements for .NET compatibility.

Use EventHandler<TEventArgs> and EventHandler

The previous program declared its own event delegate. However, there is no need to do this because the .NET Framework provides a built-in generic delegate called **EventHandler<TEventArgs>**. (See Chapter 18 for a discussion of generic types.) Here, the type of **TEventArgs** specifies the type of the argument passed to the **EventArgs** parameter of the event. For example, in the preceding program, **SomeEvent** in **MyEvent** could have been declared like this:

```
public event EventHandler<MyEventArgs> SomeEvent;
```

In general, it is better to use this approach rather than defining your own delegate.

For many events, the **EventArgs** parameter is unused. To help facilitate the creation of code in these situations, the .NET Framework includes a non-generic delegate called **EventHandler**, which can be used to declare event handlers in which no extra information is needed. Here is an example that uses **EventHandler**:

```
// Use the built-in EventHandler delegate.

using System;

// Declare a class that contains an event.
class MyEvent {
  public event EventHandler SomeEvent; // uses EventHandler delegate

  // This is called to raise SomeEvent.
  public void OnSomeEvent() {
```

```
      if(SomeEvent != null)
        SomeEvent(this, EventArgs.Empty);
  }
}

class EventDemo7 {
  static void Handler(object sender, EventArgs e) {
    Console.WriteLine("Event occurred");
    Console.WriteLine("Source is " + sender);
  }

  static void Main() {
    MyEvent evt = new MyEvent();

    // Add Handler() to the event list.
    evt.SomeEvent += Handler;

    // Raise the event.
    evt.OnSomeEvent();
  }
}
```

In this case, the **EventArgs** parameter is unused and is passed the placeholder object
EventArgs.Empty. The output is shown here:

```
Event occurred
Source is MyEvent
```

Applying Events: A Case Study

Events are frequently used in message-based environments such as Windows. In such an
environment, a program simply waits until it receives a message, and then it takes the
appropriate action. Such an architecture is well suited for C#-style event handling because it
is possible to create event handlers for various messages and then simply invoke a handler
when a message is received. For example, the left-button mouse click message could be tied
to an event called **LButtonClick**. When a left-button click is received, a method called
OnLButtonClick( ) can be called, and all registered handlers will be notified.

Although developing a Windows program that demonstrates this approach is beyond
the scope of this chapter, it is possible to give an idea of how such an approach would work.
The following program creates an event handler that processes keystrokes. The event is
called **KeyPress**, and each time a key is pressed, the event is raised by calling **OnKeyPress( )**.
Notice that .NET-compatible events are created and that lambda expressions provide the
event handlers.

```
// A keypress event example.

using System;

// Derive a custom EventArgs class that holds the key.
class KeyEventArgs : EventArgs {
  public char ch;
}
```

```
// Declare a keypress event class.
class KeyEvent {
  public event EventHandler <KeyEventArgs> KeyPress;

  // This is called when a key is pressed.
  public void OnKeyPress(char key) {
    KeyEventArgs k = new KeyEventArgs();

    if(KeyPress != null) {
      k.ch = key;
      KeyPress(this, k);
    }
  }
}

// Demonstrate KeyEvent.
class KeyEventDemo {
  static void Main() {
    KeyEvent kevt = new KeyEvent();
    ConsoleKeyInfo key;
    int count = 0;

    // Use a lambda expression to display the keypress.
    kevt.KeyPress += (sender, e) =>
      Console.WriteLine(" Received keystroke: " + e.ch);

    // Use a lambda expression to count keypresses.
    kevt.KeyPress += (sender, e) =>
      count++; // count is an outer variable

    Console.WriteLine("Enter some characters. " +
                      "Enter a period to stop.");
    do {
      key = Console.ReadKey();
      kevt.OnKeyPress(key.KeyChar);
    } while(key.KeyChar != '.');

    Console.WriteLine(count + " keys pressed.");
  }
}
```

Here is a sample run:

```
Enter some characters. Enter a period to stop.
t Received keystroke: t
e Received keystroke: e
s Received keystroke: s
t Received keystroke: t
. Received keystroke: .
5 keys pressed.
```

The program begins by deriving a class from **EventArgs** called **KeyEventArgs**, which is used to pass a keystroke to an event handler. Next, a delegate called **KeyHandler** defines the event handler for keystroke events. The class **KeyEvent** encapsulates the keypress event. It defines the event **KeyPress**.

In **Main( )**, a **KeyEvent** object called **kevt** is created. Next, an event handler based on a lambda expression is added to **kvet.KeyPress** that displays each key as it is entered, as shown here:

```
kevt.KeyPress += (sender, e) =>
  Console.WriteLine(" Received keystroke: " + e.ch);
```

Next, another lambda expression–based handler is added to **kvet.KeyPress** by the following code. It counts the number of keypresses.

```
kevt.KeyPress += (sender, e) =>
  count++; // count is an outer variable
```

Notice that **count** is a local variable declared in **Main( )** that is initialized to zero.

Next, a loop is started that calls **kevt.OnKeyPress( )** when a key is pressed. This causes the registered event handlers to be notified. When the loop ends, the number of keypresses is displayed. Although quite simple, this example illustrates the essence of event handling. The same basic approach will be used for other event handling situations. Of course, in some cases, anonymous event handlers will not be appropriate and named methods will need to be employed.

Namespaces, the Preprocessor, and Assemblies

This chapter discusses three C# features that give you greater control over the organization and accessibility of a program. These are namespaces, the preprocessor, and assemblies.

Namespaces

The namespace was mentioned briefly in Chapter 2 because it is a concept fundamental to C#. In fact, every C# program makes use of a namespace in one way or another. We didn't need to examine namespaces in detail before now because C# automatically provides a default, global namespace for your program. Thus, the programs in earlier chapters simply used the global namespace. In the real world, however, many programs will need to create their own namespaces or interact with other namespaces. Here, they are examined in detail.

A *namespace* defines a declarative region that provides a way to keep one set of names separate from another. In essence, names declared in one namespace will not conflict with the same names declared in another. The namespace used by the .NET Framework library (which is the C# library) is **System**. This is why you have included

```
using System;
```

near the top of every program. As explained in Chapter 14, the I/O classes are defined within a namespace subordinate to **System** called **System.IO**. There are many other namespaces subordinate to **System** that hold other parts of the C# library.

Namespaces are important because there has been an explosion of variable, method, property, and class names over the past few years. These include library routines, third-party code, and your own code. Without namespaces, all of these names would compete for slots in the global namespace and conflicts would arise. For example, if your program defined a class called **Finder**, it could conflict with another class called **Finder** supplied by a third-party library that your program uses. Fortunately, namespaces prevent this type of problem because a namespace restricts the visibility of names declared within it.

Declaring a Namespace

A namespace is declared using the **namespace** keyword. The general form of **namespace** is shown here:

```
namespace name {
  // members
}
```

Here, *name* is the name of the namespace. A namespace declaration defines a scope. Anything declared immediately inside the namespace is in scope throughout the namespace. Within a namespace, you can declare classes, structures, delegates, enumerations, interfaces, or another namespace.

Here is an example of a **namespace** that creates a namespace called **Counter**. It localizes the name used to implement a simple countdown counter class called **CountDown**.

```
// Declare a namespace for counters.

namespace Counter {
  // A simple countdown counter.
  class CountDown {
    int val;

    public CountDown(int n) {
      val = n;
    }

    public void Reset(int n) {
      val = n;
    }

    public int Count() {
      if(val > 0) return val--;
      else return 0;
    }
  }
} // This is the end of the Counter namespace.
```

Notice how the class **CountDown** is declared within the scope defined by the **Counter** namespace. To follow along with the example, put this code into a file called **Counter.cs**.

Here is a program that demonstrates the use of the **Counter** namespace:

```
// Demonstrate the Counter namespace.

using System;

class NSDemo {
  static void Main() {
    // Notice how CountDown is qualified by Counter.
    Counter.CountDown cd1 = new Counter.CountDown(10);
    int i;

    do {
      i = cd1.Count();
      Console.Write(i + " ");
```

```
    } while(i > 0);
    Console.WriteLine();

    // Again, notice how CountDown is qualified by Counter.
    Counter.CountDown cd2 = new Counter.CountDown(20);

    do {
      i = cd2.Count();
      Console.Write(i + " ");
    } while(i > 0);
    Console.WriteLine();

    cd2.Reset(4);
    do {
      i = cd2.Count();
      Console.Write(i + " ");
    } while(i > 0);
    Console.WriteLine();
  }
}
```

The output from the program is shown here:

```
10 9 8 7 6 5 4 3 2 1 0
20 19 18 17 16 15 14 13 12 11 10 9 8 7 6 5 4 3 2 1 0
4 3 2 1 0
```

To compile this program, you must include both the preceding code and the code contained in the **Counter** namespace. Assuming you called the preceding code **NSDemo.cs** and put the source code for the **Counter** namespace into a file called **Counter.cs** as mentioned earlier, then you can use this command line to compile the program:

```
csc NSDemo.cs counter.cs
```

Some important aspects of this program warrant close examination. First, since **CountDown** is declared within the **Counter** namespace, when an object is created, **CountDown** must be qualified with **Counter**, as shown here:

```
Counter.CountDown cd1 = new Counter.CountDown(10);
```

This rule can be generalized. Whenever you use a member of a namespace, you must qualify it with the namespace name. If you don't, the member of the namespace won't be found by the compiler.

Second, once an object of type **Counter** has been created, it is not necessary to further qualify it or any of its members with the namespace. Thus, **cd1.Count( )** can be called directly without namespace qualification, as this line shows:

```
i = cd1.Count();
```

Third, for the sake of illustration, this example uses two separate files. One holds the **Counter** namespace and the other holds the **NSDemo** program. However, both could have been contained in the same file. Furthermore, a single file can contain two or more named namespaces, with each namespace defining its own declarative region. When a named namespace ends, the outer namespace resumes, which in the case of the **Counter** is the global namespace. For clarity, subsequent examples will show all namespaces required by a program within the same file, but remember that separate files would be equally valid (and more commonly used in production code).

REMEMBER *For clarity, the remaining namespace examples in this chapter show all namespaces required by a program within the same file. In real-world code, however, a namespace will often be defined in its own file, as the preceding example illustrates.*

Namespaces Prevent Name Conflicts

The key point about a namespace is that names declared within it won't conflict with similar names declared outside of it. For example, the following program defines two namespaces. The first is **Counter**, shown earlier. The second is called **Counter2**. Both contain classes called **CountDown**, but because they are in separate namespaces, the two classes do not conflict. Also notice how both namespaces are specified within the same file. As just explained, a single file can contain multiple namespace declarations. Of course, separate files for each namespace could also have been used.

```csharp
// Namespaces prevent name conflicts.

using System;

// Declare the Counter namespace.
namespace Counter {
  // A simple countdown counter.
  class CountDown {
    int val;

    public CountDown(int n) {
      val = n;
    }

    public void Reset(int n) {
      val = n;
    }

    public int Count() {
      if(val > 0) return val--;
      else return 0;
    }
  }
}

// Declare the Counter2 namespace.
namespace Counter2 {
  /* This CountDown is in the Counter2 namespace and
     does not conflict with the one in Counter. */
  class CountDown {
    public void Count() {
      Console.WriteLine("This is Count() in the " +
                        "Counter2 namespace.");
    }
```

```
    }
}

class NSDemo2 {
  static void Main() {
    // This is CountDown in the Counter namespace.
    Counter.CountDown cd1 = new Counter.CountDown(10);

    // This is CountDown in the Counter2 namespace.
    Counter2.CountDown cd2 = new Counter2.CountDown();

    int i;

    do {
      i = cd1.Count();
      Console.Write(i + " ");
    } while(i > 0);
    Console.WriteLine();

    cd2.Count();
  }
}
```

The output is shown here:

```
10 9 8 7 6 5 4 3 2 1 0
This is Count() in the Counter2 namespace.
```

As the output confirms, the **CountDown** class inside **Counter** is separate from the **CountDown** class in the **Counter2** namespace, and no name conflicts arise. Although this example is quite simple, it is easy to see how putting classes into a namespace helps prevent name conflicts between your code and code written by others.

using

If your program includes frequent references to the members of a namespace, having to specify the namespace each time you need to refer to a member quickly becomes tedious. The **using** directive alleviates this problem. Throughout this book, you have been using it to bring the C# **System** namespace into view, so you are already familiar with it. As you would expect, **using** can also be employed to bring namespaces that you create into view.

There are two forms of the **using** directive. The first is shown here:

using *name*;

Here, *name* specifies the name of the namespace you want to access. This is the form of **using** that you have already seen. All of the members defined within the specified namespace are brought into view and can be used without qualification. A **using** directive must be specified at the top of each file, prior to any other declarations, or at the start of a namespace body.

The following program reworks the counter example to show how you can employ **using** to bring a namespace that you create into view:

```
// Demonstrate the using directive.

using System;
```

```
// Bring Counter into view.
using Counter;

// Declare a namespace for counters.
namespace Counter {
  // A simple countdown counter.
  class CountDown {
    int val;

    public CountDown(int n) {
      val = n;
    }

    public void Reset(int n) {
      val = n;
    }

    public int Count() {
      if(val > 0) return val--;
      else return 0;
    }
  }
}

class NSDemo3 {
  static void Main() {
    // now, CountDown can be used directly.
    CountDown cd1 = new CountDown(10);
    int i;

    do {
      i = cd1.Count();
      Console.Write(i + " ");
    } while(i > 0);
    Console.WriteLine();

    CountDown cd2 = new CountDown(20);

    do {
      i = cd2.Count();
      Console.Write(i + " ");
    } while(i > 0);
    Console.WriteLine();

    cd2.Reset(4);
    do {
      i = cd2.Count();
      Console.Write(i + " ");
    } while(i > 0);
    Console.WriteLine();
  }
}
```

This version of the program contains two important changes. The first is this **using** statement, near the top of the program:

```
using Counter;
```

This brings the **Counter** namespace into view. The second change is that it is no longer necessary to qualify **CountDown** with **Counter**, as this statement in **Main( )** shows:

```
CountDown cd1 = new CountDown(10);
```

Because **Counter** is now in view, **CountDown** can be used directly.

The program illustrates one other important point: Using one namespace does not override another. When you bring a namespace into view, it simply lets you use its contents without qualification. Thus, in the example, both **System** and **Counter** have been brought into view.

A Second Form of using

The **using** directive has a second form that creates another name, called an alias, for a type or a namespace. This form is shown here:

using *alias* = *name*;

Here, *alias* becomes another name for the type (such as a class type) or namespace specified by *name*. Once the alias has been created, it can be used in place of the original name.

Here the example from the preceding section has been reworked so that an alias for **Counter.CountDown** called **MyCounter** is created:

```
// Demonstrate a using alias.

using System;

// Create an alias for Counter.CountDown.
using MyCounter = Counter.CountDown;

// Declare a namespace for counters.
namespace Counter {
  // A simple countdown counter.
  class CountDown {
    int val;

    public CountDown(int n) {
      val = n;
    }

    public void Reset(int n) {
      val = n;
    }

    public int Count() {
      if(val > 0) return val--;
      else return 0;
    }
  }
}

class NSDemo4 {
```

```
static void Main() {
  // Here, MyCounter is used as a name for Counter.CountDown.
  MyCounter cd1 = new MyCounter(10);
  int i;

  do {
    i = cd1.Count();
    Console.Write(i + " ");
  } while(i > 0);
  Console.WriteLine();

  MyCounter cd2 = new MyCounter(20);

  do {
    i = cd2.Count();
    Console.Write(i + " ");
  } while(i > 0);
  Console.WriteLine();

  cd2.Reset(4);
  do {
    i = cd2.Count();
    Console.Write(i + " ");
  } while(i > 0);
  Console.WriteLine();
  }
}
```

The **MyCounter** alias is created using this statement:

```
using MyCounter = Counter.CountDown;
```

Once **MyCounter** has been specified as another name for **Counter.CountDown**, it can be used to declare objects without any further namespace qualification. For example, in the program, this line

```
MyCounter cd1 = new MyCounter(10);
```

creates a **CountDown** object.

Namespaces Are Additive

There can be more than one namespace declaration of the same name. This allows a namespace to be split over several files or even separated within the same file. For example, the following program defines two **Counter** namespaces. One contains the **CountDown** class. The other contains the **CountUp** class. When compiled, the contents of both **Counter** namespaces are added together.

```
// Namespaces are additive.

using System;

// Bring Counter into view.
using Counter;
```

```
// Here is one Counter namespace.
namespace Counter {
  // A simple countdown counter.
  class CountDown {
    int val;

    public CountDown(int n) {
      val = n;
    }

    public void Reset(int n) {
      val = n;
    }

    public int Count() {
      if(val > 0) return val--;
      else return 0;
    }
  }
}

// Here is another Counter namespace.
namespace Counter {
  // A simple count-up counter.
  class CountUp {
    int val;
    int target;

    public int Target {
      get{
        return target;
      }
    }

    public CountUp(int n) {
      target = n;
      val = 0;
    }

    public void Reset(int n) {
      target = n;
      val = 0;
    }

    public int Count() {
      if(val < target) return val++;
      else return target;
    }
  }
}

class NSDemo5 {
  static void Main() {
    CountDown cd = new CountDown(10);
```

```
      CountUp cu = new CountUp(8);
      int i;

      do {
        i = cd.Count();
        Console.Write(i + " ");
      } while(i > 0);
      Console.WriteLine();

      do {
        i = cu.Count();
        Console.Write(i + " ");
      } while(i < cu.Target);

  }
}
```

This program produces the following output:

```
10 9 8 7 6 5 4 3 2 1 0
0 1 2 3 4 5 6 7 8
```

Notice one other thing: The directive

```
using Counter;
```

brings into view the entire contents of the **Counter** namespace. Thus, both **CountDown** and **CountUp** can be referred to directly, without namespace qualification. It doesn't matter that the **Counter** namespace was split into two parts.

Namespaces Can Be Nested

One namespace can be nested within another. Consider this program:

```
// Namespaces can be nested.

using System;

namespace NS1 {
  class ClassA {
    public ClassA() {
      Console.WriteLine("constructing ClassA");
    }
  }
  namespace NS2 { // a nested namespace
    class ClassB {
      public ClassB() {
        Console.WriteLine("constructing ClassB");
      }
    }
  }
}

class NestedNSDemo {
  static void Main() {
```

```
    NS1.ClassA a = new NS1.ClassA();

// NS2.ClassB b = new NS2.ClassB(); // Error!!! NS2 is not in view

    NS1.NS2.ClassB b = new NS1.NS2.ClassB(); // this is right
  }
}
```

This program produces the following output:

```
constructing ClassA
constructing ClassB
```

In the program, the namespace **NS2** is nested within **NS1**. Thus, to refer to **ClassB**, you must qualify it with both the **NS1** and **NS2** namespaces. **NS2**, by itself, is insufficient. As shown, the namespace names are separated by a period. Therefore, to refer to **ClassB** within **Main( )**, you must use **NS1.NS2.ClassB**.

Namespaces can be nested by more than two levels. When this is the case, a member in a nested namespace must be qualified with all of the enclosing namespace names.

You can specify a nested namespace using a single **namespace** statement by separating each namespace with a period. For example,

```
namespace OuterNS {
  namespace InnerNS {
    // ...
  }
}
```

can also be specified like this:

```
namespace OuterNS.InnerNS {
  // ...
}
```

The Global Namespace

If you don't declare a namespace for your program, then the default global namespace is used. This is why you have not needed to use **namespace** for the programs in the preceding chapters. Although the global namespace is convenient for the short, sample programs found in this book, most real-world code will be contained within a declared namespace. The main reason for encapsulating your code within a declared namespace is that it prevents name conflicts. Namespaces are another tool that you have to help you organize programs and make them viable in today's complex, networked environment.

Using the :: Namespace Alias Qualifier

Although namespaces help prevent name conflicts, they do not completely eliminate them. One way that a conflict can still occur is when the same name is declared within two different namespaces, and you then try to bring both namespaces into view. For example, assume that two different namespaces contain a class called **MyClass**. If you attempt to bring these two namespaces into view via **using** statements, **MyClass** in the first namespace will conflict with **MyClass** in the second namespace, causing an ambiguity error. In this situation, you can use the **::** *namespace alias qualifier* to explicitly specify which namespace is intended.

The :: operator has this general form:

namespace-alias::identifier

Here, *namespace-alias* is the name of a namespace alias and *identifier* is the name of a member of that namespace.

To understand why the namespace alias qualifier is needed, consider the following program. It creates two namespaces, **Counter** and **AnotherCounter**, and both declare a class called **CountDown**. Furthermore, both namespaces are brought into view by **using** statements. Finally, in **Main( )**, an attempt is made to instantiate an object of type **CountDown**.

```csharp
// Demonstrate why the :: qualifier is needed.
//
// This program will not compile.

using System;

// Use both the Counter and AnotherCounter namespace.
using Counter;
using AnotherCounter;

// Declare a namespace for counters.
namespace Counter {
  // A simple countdown counter.
  class CountDown {
    int val;

    public CountDown(int n) {
      val = n;
    }

    // ...
  }
}

// Declare another namespace for counters.
namespace AnotherCounter {
  // Declare another class called CountDown, which
  // is in the AnotherCounter namespace.
  class CountDown {
    int val;

    public CountDown(int n) {
      val = n;
    }

    // ...
  }
}

class WhyAliasQualifier {
  static void Main() {
    int i;
```

```
  // The following line is inherently ambiguous!
  // Does it refer to CountDown in Counter or
  // to CountDown in AnotherCounter?
  CountDown cd1 = new CountDown(10); // Error! ! !

  // ...
  }
}
```

If you try to compile this program, you will receive an error message stating that this line in **Main( )** is ambiguous:

```
CountDown cd1 = new CountDown(10); // Error! ! !
```

The trouble is that both namespaces, **Counter** and **AnotherCounter**, declare a class called **CountDown**, and both namespaces have been brought into view. Thus, to which version of **CountDown** does the preceding declaration refer? The :: qualifier was designed to handle these types of problems.

To use the ::, you must first define an alias for the namespace you want to qualify. Then, simply qualify the ambiguous element with the alias. For example, here is one way to fix the preceding program:

```
// Demonstrate the :: qualifier.

using System;

using Counter;
using AnotherCounter;

// Give Counter an alias called Ctr.
using Ctr = Counter;

// Declare a namespace for counters.
namespace Counter {
  // A simple countdown counter.
  class CountDown {
    int val;

    public CountDown(int n) {
      val = n;
    }

    // ...
  }
}

// Another counter namespace.
namespace AnotherCounter {
  // Declare another class called CountDown, which
  // is in the AnotherCounter namespace.
  class CountDown {
    int val;
```

```
    public CountDown(int n) {
      val = n;
    }

    // ...
  }
}

class AliasQualifierDemo {
  static void Main() {

    // Here, the :: operator
    // tells the compiler to use the CountDown
    // that is in the Counter namespace.
    Ctr::CountDown cd1 = new Ctr::CountDown(10);

    // ...
  }
}
```

In this version, the alias **Ctr** is specified for **Counter** by the following line:

```
using Ctr = Counter;
```

Then, inside **Main( )**, this alias is used to qualify **CountDown**, as shown here:

```
Ctr::CountDown cd1 = new Ctr::CountDown(10);
```

The use of the :: qualifier removes the ambiguity because it specifies that the **CountDown** in **Ctr** (which stands for **Counter**) is desired, and the program now compiles.

You can use the :: qualifier to refer to the global namespace by using the predefined identifier **global**. For example, in the following program, a class called **CountDown** is declared in both the **Counter** namespace and in the global namespace. To access the version of **CountDown** in the global namespace, the predefined alias **global** is used.

```
// Use the global alias.

using System;

// Give Counter an alias called Ctr.
using Ctr = Counter;

// Declare a namespace for counters.
namespace Counter {
  // A simple countdown counter.
  class CountDown {
    int val;

    public CountDown(int n) {
      val = n;
    }

    // ...
  }
```

```
}

// Declare another class called CountDown, which
// is in the global namespace.
class CountDown {
  int val;

  public CountDown(int n) {
    val = n;
  }

  // ...
}

class GlobalAliasQualifierDemo {
  static void Main() {

    // Here, the :: qualifier tells the compiler
    // to use the CountDown in the Counter namespace.
    Ctr::CountDown cd1 = new Ctr::CountDown(10);

    // Next, create CountDown object from global namespace.
    global::CountDown cd2 = new global::CountDown(10);

    // ...
  }
}
```

Notice how the **global** identifier is used to access the version of **CountDown** in the default namespace:

```
global::CountDown cd2 = new global::CountDown(10);
```

This same approach can be generalized to any situation in which you need to specify the default namespace.

One final point: You can also use the namespace alias qualifier with **extern** aliases, which are described in Chapter 20.

The Preprocessor

C# defines several *preprocessor directives,* which affect the way that your program's source file is interpreted by the compiler. These directives affect the text of the source file in which they occur, prior to the translation of the program into object code. The term *preprocessor directive* comes from the fact that these instructions were traditionally handled by a separate compilation phase called the *preprocessor.* Today's modern compiler technology no longer requires a separate preprocessing stage to handle the directives, but the name has stuck.

C# defines the following preprocessor directives:

#define	#elif	#else	#endif
#endregion	#error	#if	#line
#pragma	#region	#undef	#warning

All preprocessor directives begin with a # sign. In addition, each preprocessor directive must be on its own line.

Given C#'s modern, object-oriented architecture, there is not as much need for the preprocessor directives as there is in older languages. Nevertheless, they can be of value from time to time, especially for conditional compilation. Each directive is examined in turn.

#define

The **#define** directive defines a character sequence called a *symbol*. The existence or nonexistence of a symbol can be determined by **#if** or **#elif** and is used to control compilation. Here is the general form for **#define**:

#define *symbol*

Notice that there is no semicolon in this statement. There may be any number of spaces between the **#define** and the symbol, but once the symbol begins, it is terminated only by a newline. For example, to define the symbol **EXPERIMENTAL**, use this directive:

```
#define EXPERIMENTAL
```

NOTE   *In C/C++ you can use **#define** to perform textual substitutions, such as defining a name for a value, and to create function-like macros. C# does not support these uses of **#define**. In C#, **#define** is used only to define a symbol.*

#if and #endif

The **#if** and **#endif** directives enable conditional compilation of a sequence of code based upon whether an expression involving one or more symbols evaluates to true. A symbol is true if it has been defined. It is false otherwise. Thus, if a symbol has been defined by a **#define** directive, it will evaluate as true.

The general form of **#if** is

#if *symbol-expression*
   statement sequence
#endif

If the expression following **#if** is true, the code that is between it and **#endif** is compiled. Otherwise, the intervening code is skipped. The **#endif** directive marks the end of an **#if** block.

A symbol expression can be as simple as just the name of a symbol. You can also use these operators in a symbol expression: **!**, **= =**, **!=**, **&&**, and **| |**. Parentheses are also allowed. Here's an example:

```
// Demonstrate #if, #endif, and #define.

#define EXPERIMENTAL

using System;

class Test {
  static void Main() {

    #if EXPERIMENTAL
      Console.WriteLine("Compiled for experimental version.");
```

```
    #endif

    Console.WriteLine("This is in all versions.");
  }
}
```

This program displays the following:

```
Compiled for experimental version.
This is in all versions.
```

The program defines the symbol **EXPERIMENTAL**. Thus, when the **#if** is encountered, the symbol expression evaluates to true, and the first **WriteLine( )** statement is compiled. If you remove the definition of **EXPERIMENTAL** and recompile the program, the first **WriteLine( )** statement will not be compiled, because the **#if** will evaluate to false. In all cases, the second **WriteLine( )** statement is compiled because it is not part of the **#if** block.

As explained, you can use operators in a symbol expression in an **#if**. For example,

```
// Use an operator in a symbol expression.

#define EXPERIMENTAL
#define TRIAL

using System;

class Test {
  static void Main() {

    #if EXPERIMENTAL
      Console.WriteLine("Compiled for experimental version.");
    #endif

    #if EXPERIMENTAL && TRIAL
       Console.Error.WriteLine("Testing experimental trial version.");
    #endif

    Console.WriteLine("This is in all versions.");
  }
}
```

The output from this program is shown here:

```
Compiled for experimental version.
Testing experimental trial version.
This is in all versions.
```

In this example, two symbols are defined, **EXPERIMENTAL** and **TRIAL**. The second **WriteLine( )** statement is compiled only if both are defined.

You can use the ! to compile code when a symbol is not defined. For example,

```
#if !EXPERIMENTAL
  Console.WriteLine("Code is not experimental!");
#endif
```

The call to **WriteLine( )** will be compiled only if **EXPERIMENTAL** *has not* been defined.

#else and #elif

The **#else** directive works much like the **else** that is part of the C# language: It establishes an alternative if **#if** fails. The previous example can be expanded as shown here:

```
// Demonstrate #else.

#define EXPERIMENTAL

using System;

class Test {
  static void Main() {

    #if EXPERIMENTAL
      Console.WriteLine("Compiled for experimental version.");
    #else
      Console.WriteLine("Compiled for release.");
    #endif

    #if EXPERIMENTAL && TRIAL
       Console.Error.WriteLine("Testing experimental trial version.");
    #else
       Console.Error.WriteLine("Not experimental trial version.");
    #endif

    Console.WriteLine("This is in all versions.");
  }
}
```

The output is shown here:

```
Compiled for experimental version.
Not experimental trial version.
This is in all versions.
```

Since **TRIAL** is not defined, the **#else** portion of the second conditional code sequence is used.

Notice that **#else** marks both the end of the **#if** block and the beginning of the **#else** block. This is necessary because there can only be one **#endif** associated with any **#if**. Furthermore, there can be only one **#else** associated with any **#if**.

The **#elif** directive means "else if" and establishes an if-else-if chain for multiple compilation options. **#elif** is followed by a symbol expression. If the expression is true, that block of code is compiled and no other **#elif** expressions are tested. Otherwise, the next block in the series is checked. If no **#elif** succeeds, then if there is a **#else**, the code sequence associated with the **#else** is compiled. Otherwise, no code in the entire **#if** is compiled.

The general form for **#elif** is

    #if *symbol-expression*
      statement sequence
    #elif *symbol-expression*
      statement sequence
    #elif *symbol-expression*

     statement sequence
   `// . . .`
   `#endif`

Here's an example:

```
// Demonstrate #elif.

#define RELEASE

using System;

class Test {
  static void Main() {

    #if EXPERIMENTAL
      Console.WriteLine("Compiled for experimental version.");
    #elif RELEASE
      Console.WriteLine("Compiled for release.");
    #else
      Console.WriteLine("Compiled for internal testing.");
    #endif

    #if TRIAL && !RELEASE
       Console.WriteLine("Trial version.");
    #endif

    Console.WriteLine("This is in all versions.");
  }
}
```

    The output is shown here:

```
Compiled for release.
This is in all versions.
```

#undef

The **#undef** directive removes a previously defined symbol. That is, it "undefines" a symbol. The general form for **#undef** is

    `#undef` *symbol*

    Here's an example:

```
#define SMALL

#if SMALL
  // ...
#undef SMALL
// at this point SMALL is undefined.
```

After the **#undef** directive, **SMALL** is no longer defined.
    #undef is used principally to allow symbols to be localized to only those sections of code that need them.

#error

The **#error** directive forces the compiler to stop compilation. It is used for debugging. The general form of the **#error** directive is

#error *error-message*

When the **#error** directive is encountered, the error message is displayed. For example, when the compiler encounters this line:

```
#error This is a test error!
```

compilation stops and the error message "This is a test error!" is displayed.

#warning

The **#warning** directive is similar to **#error**, except that a warning rather than an error is produced. Thus, compilation is not stopped. The general form of the **#warning** directive is

#warning *warning-message*

#line

The **#line** directive sets the line number and filename for the file that contains the **#line** directive. The number and the name are used when errors or warnings are output during compilation. The general form for **#line** is

#line *number "filename"*

where *number* is any positive integer, which becomes the new line number, and the optional *filename* is any valid file identifier, which becomes the new filename. **#line** is primarily used for debugging and special applications.

#line allows two options. The first is **default**, which returns the line numbering to its original condition. It is used like this:

```
#line default
```

The second is **hidden**. When stepping through a program, the **hidden** option allows a debugger to bypass lines between a

```
#line hidden
```

directive and the next **#line** directive that does not include the **hidden** option.

#region and #endregion

The **#region** and **#endregion** directives let you define a region that will be expanded or collapsed when using outlining in the Visual Studio IDE. The general form is shown here:

#region *text*
  // code sequence
#endregion *text*

Here, *text* is an optional string.

#pragma

The **#pragma** directive gives instructions, such as specifying an option, to the compiler. It has this general form:

#pragma *option*

Here, *option* is the instruction passed to the compiler.

There are currently two options supported by **#pragma**. The first is **warning**, which is used to enable or disable specific compiler warnings. It has these two forms:

#pragma warning disable *warnings*

#pragma warning restore *warnings*

Here, *warnings* is a comma-separated list of warning numbers. To disable a warning, use the **disable** option. To enable a warning, use the **restore** option. If no *warnings* are specified, then all warnings are affected.

For example, this **#pragma** statement disables warning 168, which indicates when a variable is declared but not used:

```
#pragma warning disable 168
```

The second **#pragma** option is **checksum**. It is used to generate checksums for ASP.NET projects. It has this general form.

#pragma checksum *"filename" "{GUID}" "check-sum"*

Here, *filename* is the name of the file, *GUID* is the globally unique identifier associated with *filename,* and *check-sum* is a hexadecimal number that contains the checksum. This string must contain an even number of digits.

Assemblies and the internal Access Modifier

An integral part of C# programming is the assembly. An *assembly* is a file (or files) that contains all deployment and version information for a program. Assemblies are fundamental to the .NET environment. They provide mechanisms that support safe component interaction, cross-language interoperability, and versioning. An assembly also defines a scope.

An assembly is composed of four sections. The first is the assembly *manifest*. The manifest contains information about the assembly, itself. This data includes such things as the name of the assembly, its version number, type mapping information, and cultural settings. The second section is *type metadata,* which is information about the data types used by the program. Among other benefits, type metadata aids in cross-language interoperability. The third part of an assembly is the *program code,* which is stored in Microsoft Intermediate Language (MSIL) format. The fourth constituent of an assembly is the resources used by the program.

Fortunately, when using C#, assemblies are produced automatically, with little or no extra effort on your part. The reason for this is that the **exe** file created when you compile a C# program is actually an assembly that contains your program's executable code as well as other types of information. Thus, when you compile a C# program, an assembly is automatically produced.

There are many other features and topics that relate to assemblies, but a discussion of these is outside the scope of this book. (Assemblies are an integral part of .NET development, but are not technically a feature of the C# language.) However, there is one part of C# that relates directly to the assembly: the **internal** access modifier, which is examined next.

The internal Access Modifier

In addition to the access modifiers **public**, **private**, and **protected**, which you have been using throughout this book, C# also defines **internal**. The **internal** modifier declares that a member is known throughout all files in an assembly, but unknown outside that assembly. Thus, in simplified terms, a member marked as **internal** is known throughout a program, but not elsewhere. The **internal** access modifier is particularly useful when creating software components.

The **internal** modifier can be applied to classes and members of classes and to structures and members of structures. The **internal** modifier can also be applied to interface and enumeration declarations.

You can use **protected** in conjunction with **internal** to produce the **protected internal** access modifier pair. The **protected internal** access level can be given only to class members. A member declared with **protected internal** access is accessible within its own assembly or to derived types.

Here is an example that uses **internal**:

```
// Use internal.

using System;

class InternalTest {
  internal int x;
}

class InternalDemo {
  static void Main() {
    InternalTest ob = new InternalTest();

    ob.x = 10; // can access -- in same file

    Console.WriteLine("Here is ob.x: " + ob.x);

  }
}
```

Inside **InternalTest**, the field **x** is declared **internal**. This means that it is accessible within the program, as its use in **InternalDemo** shows, but unavailable outside the program.

17

Runtime Type ID, Reflection, and Attributes

This chapter discusses three interrelated and powerful features: runtime type identification, reflection, and attributes. *Runtime type ID* is the mechanism that lets you identify a type during the execution of a program. *Reflection* is the feature that enables you to obtain information about a type. Using this information, you can construct and use objects at runtime. This feature is very powerful because it lets a program add functionality dynamically, during execution. An *attribute* describes a characteristic of some element of a C# program. For example, you can specify attributes for classes, methods, and fields, among others. Attributes can be interrogated at runtime, and the attribute information obtained. Attributes use both runtime type identification and reflection.

Runtime Type Identification

Runtime type identification (RTTI) allows the type of an object to be determined during program execution. RTTI is useful for many reasons. For example, you can discover precisely what type of object is being referred to by a base-class reference. Another use of RTTI is to test in advance whether a cast will succeed, preventing an invalid cast exception. Runtime type identification is also a key component of reflection.

C# includes three keywords that support runtime type identification: **is**, **as**, and **typeof**. Each is examined in turn.

Testing a Type with is

You can determine if an object is of a certain type by using the **is** operator. Its general form is shown here:

    expr is *type*

Here, *expr* is an expression that describes an object whose type is being tested against *type*. If the type of *expr* is the same as, or compatible with, *type*, then the outcome of this operation is true. Otherwise, it is false. Thus, if the outcome is true, *expr* is some form of *type*. As it applies to **is**, one type is compatible with another if both are the same type, or if a reference, boxing, or unboxing conversion exists.

Here is an example that uses **is**:

```
// Demonstrate is.

using System;

class A {}
class B : A {}

class UseIs {
  static void Main() {
    A a = new A();
    B b = new B();

    if(a is A) Console.WriteLine("a is an A");
    if(b is A)
      Console.WriteLine("b is an A because it is derived from A");
    if(a is B)
      Console.WriteLine("This won't display -- a not derived from B");

    if(b is B) Console.WriteLine("b is a B");
    if(a is object) Console.WriteLine("a is an object");
  }
}
```

The output is shown here:

```
a is an A
b is an A because it is derived from A
b is a B
a is an object
```

Most of the **is** expressions are self-explanatory, but two may need a little discussion.
First, notice this statement:

```
if(b is A)
  Console.WriteLine("b is an A because it is derived from A");
```

The **if** succeeds because **b** is an object of type **B**, which is derived from type **A**. Thus, **b** *is* an
A. However, the reverse is not true. When this line is executed,

```
if(a is B)
  Console.WriteLine("This won't display -- a not derived from B");
```

the **if** does not succeed, because **a** is of type **A**, which is not derived from **B**. Thus, **a** *is not* a **B**.

Using as

Sometimes you will want to try a conversion at runtime, but not throw an exception if the
conversion fails (which is the case when a cast is used). To do this, use the **as** operator,
which has this general form:

expr as *type*

Here, *expr* is the expression being converted to *type*. If the conversion succeeds, then a reference to *type* is returned. Otherwise, a null reference is returned. The **as** operator can be used to perform only reference, boxing, unboxing, or identity conversions.

The **as** operator offers a streamlined alternative to **is** in some cases. For example, consider the following program that uses **is** to prevent an invalid cast from occurring:

```
// Use is to avoid an invalid cast.

using System;

class A {}
class B : A {}

class CheckCast {
  static void Main() {
    A a = new A();
    B b = new B();

    // Check to see if a can be cast to B.
    if(a is B)  // if so, do the cast
      b = (B) a;
    else // if not, skip the cast
      b = null;

    if(b==null)
      Console.WriteLine("The cast in b = (B) a is NOT allowed.");
    else
      Console.WriteLine("The cast in b = (B) a is allowed");
  }
}
```

This program displays the following output:

```
The cast in b = (B) a is NOT allowed.
```

As the output shows, since **a** is not a **B**, the cast of **a** to **B** is invalid and is prevented by the **if** statement. However, this approach requires two steps. First, the validity of the cast must be confirmed. Second, the cast must be made. These two steps can be combined into one through the use of **as**, as the following program shows:

```
// Demonstrate as.

using System;

class A {}
class B : A {}

class CheckCast {
  static void Main() {
    A a = new A();
    B b = new B();

    b = a as B; // cast, if possible
```

```
      if(b==null)
        Console.WriteLine("The cast in b = (B) a is NOT allowed.");
      else
        Console.WriteLine("The cast in b = (B) a is allowed");
  }
}
```

Here is the output, which is the same as before:

```
The cast in b = (B) a is NOT allowed.
```

In this version, the **as** statement checks the validity of the cast and then, if valid, performs the cast, all in one statement.

Using typeof

Although useful in their own ways, the **as** and **is** operators simply test the compatibility of two types. Often, you will need to obtain information about a type. To do this, C# supplies the **typeof** operator. It retrieves a **System.Type** object for a given type. Using this object, you can determine the type's characteristics.

The **typeof** operator has this general form:

typeof(*type*)

Here, *type* is the type being obtained. The **Type** object returned encapsulates the information associated with *type*.

Once you have obtained a **Type** object for a given type, you can obtain information about it through the use of various properties, fields, and methods defined by **Type**. **Type** is a large class with many members, and a discussion is deferred until the next section, where reflection is examined. However, to briefly demonstrate **Type**, the following program uses three of its properties: **FullName**, **IsClass**, and **IsAbstract**. To obtain the full name of the type, use **FullName**. **IsClass** returns true if the type is a class. **IsAbstract** returns true if a class is abstract.

```
// Demonstrate typeof.

using System;
using System.IO;

class UseTypeof {
  static void Main() {
    Type t = typeof(StreamReader);

    Console.WriteLine(t.FullName);

    if(t.IsClass) Console.WriteLine("Is a class.");
    if(t.IsAbstract) Console.WriteLine("Is abstract.");
    else Console.WriteLine("Is concrete.");
  }
}
```

This program outputs the following:

```
System.IO.StreamReader
Is a class.
Is concrete.
```

This program obtains a **Type** object that describes **StreamReader**. It then displays the full name, and determines if it is a class and whether it is abstract.

Reflection

Reflection is the feature that enables you to obtain information about a type. The term *reflection* comes from the way the process works: A **Type** object mirrors the underlying type that it represents. To obtain information, you ask the **Type** object questions, and it returns (reflects) the information associated with the type back to you. Reflection is a powerful mechanism because it allows you to learn and use the capabilities of types that are known only at runtime.

Many of the classes that support reflection are part of the .NET Reflection API, which is in the **System.Reflection** namespace. Thus, you will normally include the following in programs that use reflection:

```
using System.Reflection;
```

The Reflection Core: System.Type

System.Type is at the core of the reflection subsystem because it encapsulates a type. It contains many properties and methods that you will use to obtain information about a type at runtime. **Type** is derived from an abstract class called **System.Reflection.MemberInfo**.

MemberInfo defines the following read-only properties:

Property	Description
Type DeclaringType	Obtains the type of the class or interface in which the member is declared.
MemberTypes MemberType	Obtains the kind of the member. This value indicates if the member is a field, method, property, event, or constructor, among others.
int MetadataToken	Obtains a value associated with a specific metadata.
Module Module	Obtains a **Module** object that represents the module (an executable file) in which the reflected type resides.
string Name	The name of the member.
Type ReflectedType	The type of the object being reflected.

Notice that the return type of **MemberType** is **MemberTypes**. **MemberTypes** is an enumeration that defines values that indicate the various member types. Among others, these include

MemberTypes.Constructor
MemberTypes.Method
MemberTypes.Field
MemberTypes.Event
MemberTypes.Property

Thus, the type of a member can be determined by checking **MemberType**. For example, if **MemberType** equals **MemberTypes.Method**, then that member is a method.

MemberInfo includes two abstract methods: **GetCustomAttributes( )** and **IsDefined( )**. These both relate to attributes. The first obtains a list of the custom attributes associated with the invoking object. The second determines if an attribute is defined for the invoking object. The .NET Framework Version 4.0 adds a method called **GetCustomAttributesData( )**, which returns information about custom attributes. (Attributes are described later in this chapter.)

To the methods and properties defined by **MemberInfo**, **Type** adds a great many of its own. For example, here are several commonly used methods defined by **Type**:

Method	Purpose
ConstructorInfo[ ] GetConstructors( )	Obtains a list of the constructors for the specified type.
EventInfo[ ] GetEvents( )	Obtains a list of events for the specified type.
FieldInfo[ ] GetFields( )	Obtains a list of the fields for the specified type.
Type[ ] GetGenericArguments( )	Obtains a list of the type arguments bound to a closed constructed generic type or the type parameters if the specified type is a generic type definition. For an open constructed type, the list may contain both type arguments and type parameters. (See Chapter 18 for a discussion of generics.)
MemberInfo[ ] GetMembers( )	Obtains a list of the members for the specified type.
MethodInfo[ ] GetMethods( )	Obtains a list of methods for the specified type.
PropertyInfo[ ] GetProperties( )	Obtains a list of properties for the specified type.

Here are several commonly used, read-only properties defined by **Type**:

Property	Purpose
Assembly Assembly	Obtains the assembly for the specified type.
TypeAttributes Attributes	Obtains the attributes for the specified type.
Type BaseType	Obtains the immediate base type for the specified type.
string FullName	Obtains the complete name of the specified type.
bool IsAbstract	Is true if the specified type is abstract.
bool isArray	Is true if the specified type is an array.
bool IsClass	Is true if the specified type is a class.
bool IsEnum	Is true if the specified type is an enumeration.
bool IsGenericParameter	Is true if the specified type is a generic type parameter. (See Chapter 18 for a discussion of generics.)
bool IsGenericType	Is true if the specified type is a generic type. (See Chapter 18 for a discussion of generics.)
string Namespace	Obtains the namespace of the specified type.

Using Reflection

Using **Type**'s methods and properties, it is possible to obtain detailed information about a type at runtime. This is an extremely powerful feature, because once you have obtained information about a type, you can invoke its constructors, call its methods, and use its properties. Thus, reflection enables you to use code that was not available at compile time.

The Reflection API is quite large, and it is not possible to cover the entire topic here. (Complete coverage of reflection could easily fill an entire book!) However, because the Reflection API is logically designed, once you understand how to use a part of it, the rest just falls into place. With this thought in mind, the following sections demonstrate four key reflection techniques: obtaining information about methods, invoking methods, constructing objects, and loading types from assemblies.

Obtaining Information About Methods

Once you have a **Type** object, you can obtain a list of the public methods supported by the type by using **GetMethods( )**. One form is shown here:

    MethodInfo[ ] GetMethods( )

It returns an array of **MethodInfo** objects that describe the methods supported by the invoking type. **MethodInfo** is in the **System.Reflection** namespace.

MethodInfo is derived from the abstract class **MethodBase**, which inherits **MemberInfo**. Thus, the properties and methods defined by all three of these classes are available for your use. For example, to obtain the name of a method, use the **Name** property. Two members that are of particular interest at this time are **ReturnType** and **GetParameters( )**.

The return type of a method is found in the read-only **ReturnType** property, which is an object of **Type**.

The method **GetParameters( )** returns a list of the parameters associated with a method. It has this general form:

    ParameterInfo[ ] GetParameters( );

The parameter information is held in a **ParameterInfo** object. **ParameterInfo** defines properties and methods that describe the parameter. Two properties that are of particular value are **Name**, which is a string that contains the name of the parameter, and **ParameterType**, which describes the parameter's type. The parameter's type is encapsulated within a **Type** object.

Here is a program that uses reflection to obtain the methods supported by a class called **MyClass**. For each method, it displays the return type and name of the method, and the name and type of any parameters that each method may have.

```
// Analyze methods using reflection.

using System;
using System.Reflection;

class MyClass {
  int x;
  int y;
```

```
    public MyClass(int i, int j) {
      x = i;
      y = j;
    }

    public int Sum() {
      return x+y;
    }

    public bool IsBetween(int i) {
      if(x < i && i < y) return true;
      else return false;
    }

    public void Set(int a, int b) {
      x = a;
      y = b;
    }

    public void Set(double a, double b) {
      x = (int) a;
      y = (int) b;
    }

    public void Show() {
      Console.WriteLine(" x: {0}, y: {1}", x, y);
    }
}

class ReflectDemo {
  static void Main() {
    Type t = typeof(MyClass); // get a Type object representing MyClass

    Console.WriteLine("Analyzing methods in " + t.Name);
    Console.WriteLine();

    Console.WriteLine("Methods supported: ");

    MethodInfo[] mi = t.GetMethods();

    // Display methods supported by MyClass.
    foreach(MethodInfo m in mi) {
      // Display return type and name.
      Console.Write("   " + m.ReturnType.Name +
                    " " + m.Name + "(");

      // Display parameters.
      ParameterInfo[] pi = m.GetParameters();

      for(int i=0; i < pi.Length; i++) {
        Console.Write(pi[i].ParameterType.Name +
                      " " + pi[i].Name);
        if(i+1 < pi.Length) Console.Write(", ");
      }
```

```
        Console.WriteLine(")");

        Console.WriteLine();
      }
    }
}
```

The output is shown here:

```
Analyzing methods in MyClass

Methods supported:
    Int32 Sum()

    Boolean IsBetween(Int32 i)

    Void Set(Int32 a, Int32 b)

    Void Set(Double a, Double b)

    Void Show()

    Type GetType()

    String ToString()

    Boolean Equals(Object obj)

    Int32 GetHashCode()
```

Notice that in addition to the methods defined by **MyClass**, the public, non-static methods defined by **object** are also displayed. This is because all types in C# inherit **object**. Also notice that the .NET structure names are used for the type names. Observe that **Set( )** is displayed twice. This is because **Set( )** is overloaded. One version takes **int** arguments. The other takes **double** arguments.

Let's look at this program closely. First, notice that **MyClass** defines a public constructor and a number of public methods, including the overloaded **Set( )** method.

Inside **Main( )**, a **Type** object representing **MyClass** is obtained using this line of code:

```
Type t = typeof(MyClass); // get a Type object representing MyClass
```

Recall that **typeof** returns a **Type** object that represents the specified type, which in this case is **MyClass**.

Using **t** and the Reflection API, the program then displays information about the methods supported by **MyClass**. First, a list of the methods is obtained by the following statement:

```
MethodInfo[] mi = t.GetMethods();
```

Next, a **foreach** loop is established that cycles through **mi**. With each pass, the return type, name, and parameters for each method are displayed by the following code:

```
// Display return type and name.
Console.Write("   " + m.ReturnType.Name +
              " " + m.Name + "(");
```

```
// Display parameters.
ParameterInfo[] pi = m.GetParameters();

for(int i=0; i < pi.Length; i++) {
  Console.Write(pi[i].ParameterType.Name +
                " " + pi[i].Name);
  if(i+1 < pi.Length) Console.Write(", ");
}
```

In this sequence, the parameters associated with each method are obtained by calling **GetParameters( )** and stored in the **pi** array. Then a **for** loop cycles through the **pi** array, displaying the type and name of each parameter. The key point is that this information is obtained dynamically at runtime without relying on prior knowledge of **MyClass**.

A Second Form of GetMethods( )

A second form of **GetMethods( )** lets you specify various flags that filter the methods that are retrieved. It has this general form:

MethodInfo[ ] GetMethods(BindingFlags *bindingAttr*)

This version obtains only those methods that match the criteria you specify. **BindingFlags** is an enumeration. Here are several commonly used values:

Value	Meaning
DeclaredOnly	Retrieves only those methods defined by the specified class. Inherited methods are not included.
Instance	Retrieves instance methods.
NonPublic	Retrieves nonpublic methods.
Public	Retrieves public methods.
Static	Retrieves **static** methods.

You can OR together two or more flags. In fact, minimally you must include either **Instance** or **Static** with **Public** or **NonPublic**. Failure to do so will result in no methods being retrieved.

One of the main uses of the **BindingFlags** form of **GetMethods( )** is to enable you to obtain a list of the methods defined by a class without also retrieving the inherited methods. This is especially useful for preventing the methods defined by **object** from being obtained. For example, try substituting this call to **GetMethods( )** into the preceding program:

```
// Now, only methods declared by MyClass are obtained.
MethodInfo[] mi = t.GetMethods(BindingFlags.DeclaredOnly |
                               BindingFlags.Instance |
                               BindingFlags.Public) ;
```

After making this change, the program produces the following output:

```
Analyzing methods in MyClass

Methods supported:
   Int32 Sum()
```

```
Boolean IsBetween(Int32 i)

Void Set(Int32 a, Int32 b)

Void Set(Double a, Double b)

Void Show()
```

As you can see, only those methods explicitly defined by **MyClass** are displayed.

Calling Methods Using Reflection

Once you know what methods a type supports, you can call one or more of them. To do this, you will use the **Invoke( )** method that is contained in **MethodInfo**. One of its forms is shown here:

object Invoke(object *obj*, object[ ] *parameters*)

Here, *obj* is a reference to the object on which the method is invoked. (For **static** methods, you can pass **null** to *obj*.) Any arguments that need to be passed to the method are specified in the array *parameters*. If no arguments are needed, *parameters* must be **null**. Also, *parameters* must contain exactly the same number of elements as there are arguments. Therefore, if two arguments are needed, then *parameters* must be two elements long. It can't, for example, be three or four elements long. The value returned by the invoked method is returned by **Invoke( )**.

To call a method, simply call **Invoke( )** on an instance of **MethodInfo** that was obtained by calling **GetMethods( )**. The following program demonstrates the procedure:

```
// Invoke methods using reflection.

using System;
using System.Reflection;

class MyClass {
  int x;
  int y;

  public MyClass(int i, int j) {
    x = i;
    y = j;
  }

  public int Sum() {
    return x+y;
  }

  public bool IsBetween(int i) {
    if((x < i) && (i < y)) return true;
    else return false;
  }

  public void Set(int a, int b) {
    Console.Write("Inside Set(int, int). ");
    x = a;
```

```
      y = b;
      Show();
    }

    // Overload set.
    public void Set(double a, double b) {
      Console.Write("Inside Set(double, double). ");
      x = (int) a;
      y = (int) b;
      Show();
    }

    public void Show() {
      Console.WriteLine("Values are x: {0}, y: {1}", x, y);
    }
}

class InvokeMethDemo {
    static void Main() {
      Type t = typeof(MyClass);
      MyClass reflectOb = new MyClass(10, 20);
      int val;

      Console.WriteLine("Invoking methods in " + t.Name);
      Console.WriteLine();
      MethodInfo[] mi = t.GetMethods();

      // Invoke each method.
      foreach(MethodInfo m in mi) {
        // Get the parameters.
        ParameterInfo[] pi = m.GetParameters();

        if(m.Name.Equals("Set", StringComparison.Ordinal) &&
           pi[0].ParameterType == typeof(int)) {
          object[] args = new object[2];
          args[0] = 9;
          args[1] = 18;
          m.Invoke(reflectOb, args);
        }
        else if(m.Name.Equals("Set", StringComparison.Ordinal) &&
                pi[0].ParameterType == typeof(double)) {
          object[] args = new object[2];
          args[0] = 1.12;
          args[1] = 23.4;
          m.Invoke(reflectOb, args);
        }
        else if(m.Name.Equals("Sum", StringComparison.Ordinal)) {
          val = (int) m.Invoke(reflectOb, null);
          Console.WriteLine("sum is " + val);
        }
        else if(m.Name.Equals("IsBetween", StringComparison.Ordinal)) {
          object[] args = new object[1];
          args[0] = 14;
          if((bool) m.Invoke(reflectOb, args))
```

```
          Console.WriteLine("14 is between x and y");
      }
      else if(m.Name.Equals("Show", StringComparison.Ordinal)) {
        m.Invoke(reflectOb, null);
      }
    }
  }
}
```

The output is shown here:

```
Invoking methods in MyClass

sum is 30
14 is between x and y
Inside Set(int, int). Values are x: 9, y: 18
Inside Set(double, double). Values are x: 1, y: 23
Values are x: 1, y: 23
```

Look closely at how the methods are invoked. First, a list of methods is obtained. Then, inside the **foreach** loop, parameter information is retrieved. Next, using a series of if/else statements, each method is executed with the proper type and number of arguments. Pay special attention to the way that the overloaded **Set( )** method is executed by the following code:

```
if(m.Name.Equals("Set", StringComparison.Ordinal) &&
   pi[0].ParameterType == typeof(int)) {
  object[] args = new object[2];
  args[0] = 9;
  args[1] = 18;
  m.Invoke(reflectOb, args);
}
else if(m.Name.Equals("Set", StringComparison.Ordinal) &&
        pi[0].ParameterType == typeof(double)) {
  object[] args = new object[2];
  args[0] = 1.12;
  args[1] = 23.4;
  m.Invoke(reflectOb, args);
}
```

If the name of the method is **Set**, then the type of the first parameter is tested to determine which version of the method was found. If it was **Set(int, int)**, then **int** arguments are loaded into **args**. Otherwise, **double** arguments are used.

Obtaining a Type's Constructors

In the previous example, there is no advantage to using reflection to invoke methods on **MyClass** since an object of type **MyClass** was explicitly created. It would be easier to just call its methods normally. However, the power of reflection starts to become apparent when an object is created dynamically at runtime. To do this, you will need to first obtain a list of the constructors. Then, you will create an instance of the type by invoking one of the constructors. This mechanism allows you to instantiate an object at runtime without naming it in a declaration statement.

To obtain the public, non-static constructors for a type, call **GetConstructors( )** on a **Type** object. One commonly used form is shown here:

ConstructorInfo[ ] GetConstructors( )

It returns an array of **ConstructorInfo** objects that describe the constructors.

ConstructorInfo is derived from the abstract class **MethodBase**, which inherits **MemberInfo**. It also defines several members of its own. The method we are interested in is **GetParameters( )**, which returns a list of the parameters associated with a constructor. It works just like **GetParameters( )** defined by **MethodInfo**, described earlier.

Once an appropriate constructor has been found, an object is created by calling the **Invoke( )** method defined by **ConstructorInfo**. One form is shown here:

object Invoke(object[ ] *parameters*)

Any arguments that need to be passed to the method are specified in the array *parameters*. If no arguments are needed, pass **null** to *parameters*. In all cases, *parameters* must contain exactly the same number of elements as there are arguments and the types of arguments must be compatible with the types of the parameters. **Invoke( )** returns a reference to the object that was constructed.

The following program uses reflection to create an instance of **MyClass**:

```
// Create an object using reflection.

using System;
using System.Reflection;

class MyClass {
  int x;
  int y;

  public MyClass(int i) {
    Console.WriteLine("Constructing MyClass(int, int). ");
    x = y = i;
  }

  public MyClass(int i, int j) {
    Console.WriteLine("Constructing MyClass(int, int). ");
    x = i;
    y = j;
    Show();
  }

  public int Sum() {
    return x+y;
  }

  public bool IsBetween(int i) {
    if((x < i) && (i < y)) return true;
    else return false;
  }

  public void Set(int a, int b) {
    Console.Write("Inside Set(int, int). ");
```

```
      x = a;
      y = b;
      Show();
  }

  // Overload Set.
  public void Set(double a, double b) {
    Console.Write("Inside Set(double, double). ");
    x = (int) a;
    y = (int) b;
    Show();
  }

  public void Show() {
    Console.WriteLine("Values are x: {0}, y: {1}", x, y);
  }

}

class InvokeConsDemo {
  static void Main() {
    Type t = typeof(MyClass);
    int val;

    // Get constructor info.
    ConstructorInfo[] ci = t.GetConstructors();

    Console.WriteLine("Available constructors: ");
    foreach(ConstructorInfo c in ci) {
      // Display return type and name.
      Console.Write("    " + t.Name + "(");

      // Display parameters.
      ParameterInfo[] pi = c.GetParameters();

      for(int i=0; i < pi.Length; i++) {
        Console.Write(pi[i].ParameterType.Name +
                      " " + pi[i].Name);
        if(i+1 < pi.Length) Console.Write(", ");
      }

      Console.WriteLine(")");
    }
    Console.WriteLine();

    // Find matching constructor.
    int x;

    for(x=0; x < ci.Length; x++) {
      ParameterInfo[] pi = ci[x].GetParameters();
      if(pi.Length == 2) break;
    }

    if(x == ci.Length) {
```

```
        Console.WriteLine("No matching constructor found.");
        return;
      }
      else
        Console.WriteLine("Two-parameter constructor found.\n");

      // Construct the object.
      object[] consargs = new object[2];
      consargs[0] = 10;
      consargs[1] = 20;
      object reflectOb = ci[x].Invoke(consargs);

      Console.WriteLine("\nInvoking methods on reflectOb.");
      Console.WriteLine();
      MethodInfo[] mi = t.GetMethods();

      // Invoke each method.
      foreach(MethodInfo m in mi) {
        // Get the parameters.
        ParameterInfo[] pi = m.GetParameters();

        if(m.Name.Equals("Set", StringComparison.Ordinal) &&
            pi[0].ParameterType == typeof(int)) {
          // This is Set(int, int).
          object[] args = new object[2];
          args[0] = 9;
          args[1] = 18;
          m.Invoke(reflectOb, args);
        }
        else if(m.Name.Equals("Set", StringComparison.Ordinal) &&
                pi[0].ParameterType == typeof(double)) {
          // This is Set(double, double).
          object[] args = new object[2];
          args[0] = 1.12;
          args[1] = 23.4;
          m.Invoke(reflectOb, args);
        }
        else if(m.Name.Equals("Sum", StringComparison.Ordinal)) {
          val = (int) m.Invoke(reflectOb, null);
          Console.WriteLine("sum is " + val);
        }
        else if(m.Name.Equals("IsBetween", StringComparison.Ordinal)) {
          object[] args = new object[1];
          args[0] = 14;
          if((bool) m.Invoke(reflectOb, args))
            Console.WriteLine("14 is between x and y");
        }
        else if(m.Name.Equals("Show")) {
          m.Invoke(reflectOb, null);
        }
      }
    }
  }
}
```

The output is shown here:

```
Available constructors:
  MyClass(Int32 i)
  MyClass(Int32 i, Int32 j)

Two-parameter constructor found.

Constructing MyClass(int, int).
Values are x: 10, y: 20

Invoking methods on reflectOb.

sum is 30
14 is between x and y
Inside Set(int, int). Values are x: 9, y: 18
Inside Set(double, double). Values are x: 1, y: 23
Values are x: 1, y: 23
```

Let's look at how reflection is used to construct a **MyClass** object. First, a list of the public constructors is obtained using the following statement:

```
ConstructorInfo[] ci = t.GetConstructors();
```

Next, for the sake of illustration, the constructors are displayed. Then the list is searched for a constructor that takes two arguments, using this code:

```
for(x=0; x < ci.Length; x++) {
  ParameterInfo[] pi =  ci[x].GetParameters();
  if(pi.Length == 2) break;
}
```

If the constructor is found (as it will be in this case), an object is instantiated by the following sequence:

```
// Construct the object.
object[] consargs = new object[2];
consargs[0] = 10;
consargs[1] = 20;
object reflectOb = ci[x].Invoke(consargs);
```

After the call to **Invoke( )**, **reflectOb** will refer to an object of type **MyClass**. The program then executes methods on that instance.

One important point needs to be made. In this example, for the sake of simplicity, it was assumed that the only two-argument constructor was one that took two **int** arguments. Obviously, in real-world code this would need to be verified by checking the parameter type of each argument.

Obtaining Types from Assemblies

In the preceding example, everything about **MyClass** has been discovered using reflection except for one item: the type **MyClass**, itself. That is, although the preceding examples dynamically determined information about **MyClass**, they still relied upon the fact that the type name **MyClass** was known in advance and used in a **typeof** statement to obtain a **Type** object upon which all of the reflection methods either directly or indirectly operated. Although this might be useful in a number of circumstances, the full power of reflection is found when the types available to a program are determined dynamically by analyzing the contents of other assemblies.

As you know from Chapter 16, an assembly carries with it type information about the classes, structures, and so on, that it contains. The Reflection API allows you to load an assembly, discover information about it, and create instances of any of its publicly available types. Using this mechanism, a program can search its environment, utilizing functionality that might be available without having to explicitly define that functionality at compile time. This is an extremely potent, and exciting, concept. For example, you can imagine a program that acts as a "type browser," displaying the types available on a system. Another application could be a design tool that lets you visually "wire together" a program that is composed of the various types supported by the system. Since all information about a type is discoverable, there is no inherent limitation to the ways reflection can be applied.

To obtain information about an assembly, you will first create an **Assembly** object. The **Assembly** class does not define a public constructor. Instead, an **Assembly** object is obtained by calling one of its methods. The one we will use is **LoadFrom( )**, which loads an assembly given its filename. The form we will use is shown here:

static Assembly LoadFrom(string *assemblyFile*)

Here, *assemblyFile* specifies the filename of the assembly.

Once you have obtained an **Assembly** object, you can discover the types that it defines by calling **GetTypes( )** on it. Here is its general form:

Type[ ] GetTypes( )

It returns an array of the types contained in the assembly.

To demonstrate the discovery of types in an assembly, you will need two files. The first will contain a set of classes that will be discovered by the second. To begin, create a file called **MyClasses.cs** that contains the following:

```csharp
// A file that contains three classes. Call this file MyClasses.cs.

using System;

class MyClass {
  int x;
  int y;

  public MyClass(int i) {
    Console.WriteLine("Constructing MyClass(int). ");
    x = y = i;
    Show();
  }

  public MyClass(int i, int j) {
    Console.WriteLine("Constructing MyClass(int, int). ");
    x = i;
    y = j;
```

```
      Show();
  }

  public int Sum() {
    return x+y;
  }

  public bool IsBetween(int i) {
    if((x < i) && (i < y)) return true;
    else return false;
  }

  public void Set(int a, int b) {
    Console.Write("Inside Set(int, int). ");
    x = a;
    y = b;
    Show();
  }

  // Overload Set.
  public void Set(double a, double b) {
    Console.Write("Inside Set(double, double). ");
    x = (int) a;
    y = (int) b;
    Show();
  }

  public void Show() {
    Console.WriteLine("Values are x: {0}, y: {1}", x, y);
  }
}

class AnotherClass {
  string msg;

  public AnotherClass(string str) {
    msg = str;
  }

  public void Show() {
    Console.WriteLine(msg);
  }
}

class Demo {
  static void Main() {
    Console.WriteLine("This is a placeholder.");
  }
}
```

This file contains **MyClass**, which we have been using in the previous examples. It also adds a second class called **AnotherClass** and a third class called **Demo**. Thus, the assembly produced by this program will contain three classes. Next, compile this file so the file **MyClasses.exe** is produced. This is the assembly that will be interrogated.

The program that will discover information about **MyClasses.exe** is shown here. Enter it at this time.

```
/* Locate an assembly, determine types, and create
   an object using reflection. */

using System;
using System.Reflection;

class ReflectAssemblyDemo {
  static void Main() {
    int val;

    // Load the MyClasses.exe assembly.
    Assembly asm = Assembly.LoadFrom("MyClasses.exe");

    // Discover what types MyClasses.exe contains.
    Type[] alltypes = asm.GetTypes();
    foreach(Type temp in alltypes)
      Console.WriteLine("Found: " + temp.Name);

    Console.WriteLine();

    // Use the first type, which is MyClass in this case.
    Type t = alltypes[0]; // use first class found
    Console.WriteLine("Using: " + t.Name);

    // Obtain constructor info.
    ConstructorInfo[] ci = t.GetConstructors();

    Console.WriteLine("Available constructors: ");
    foreach(ConstructorInfo c in ci) {
      // Display return type and name.
      Console.Write("   " + t.Name + "(");

      // Display parameters.
      ParameterInfo[] pi = c.GetParameters();

      for(int i=0; i < pi.Length; i++) {
        Console.Write(pi[i].ParameterType.Name +
                      " " + pi[i].Name);
        if(i+1 < pi.Length) Console.Write(", ");
      }

      Console.WriteLine(")");
    }
    Console.WriteLine();

    // Find matching constructor.
    int x;
```

```
for(x=0; x < ci.Length; x++) {
  ParameterInfo[] pi =  ci[x].GetParameters();
  if(pi.Length == 2) break;
}

if(x == ci.Length) {
  Console.WriteLine("No matching constructor found.");
  return;
}
else
  Console.WriteLine("Two-parameter constructor found.\n");

// Construct the object.
object[] consargs = new object[2];
consargs[0] = 10;
consargs[1] = 20;
object reflectOb = ci[x].Invoke(consargs);

Console.WriteLine("\nInvoking methods on reflectOb.");
Console.WriteLine();
MethodInfo[] mi = t.GetMethods();

// Invoke each method.
foreach(MethodInfo m in mi) {
  // Get the parameters.
  ParameterInfo[] pi = m.GetParameters();

  if(m.Name.Equals("Set", StringComparison.Ordinal) &&
     pi[0].ParameterType == typeof(int)) {
    // This is Set(int, int).
    object[] args = new object[2];
    args[0] = 9;
    args[1] = 18;
    m.Invoke(reflectOb, args);
  }
  else if(m.Name.Equals("Set", StringComparison.Ordinal) &&
     pi[0].ParameterType == typeof(double)) {
    // This is Set(double, double).
    object[] args = new object[2];
    args[0] = 1.12;
    args[1] = 23.4;
    m.Invoke(reflectOb, args);
  }
  else if(m.Name.Equals("Sum", StringComparison.Ordinal)) {
    val = (int) m.Invoke(reflectOb, null);
    Console.WriteLine("sum is " + val);
  }
  else if(m.Name.Equals("IsBetween", StringComparison.Ordinal)) {
    object[] args = new object[1];
    args[0] = 14;
    if((bool) m.Invoke(reflectOb, args))
      Console.WriteLine("14 is between x and y");
  }
  else if(m.Name.Equals("Show", StringComparison.Ordinal)) {
```

```
        m.Invoke(reflectOb, null);
    }
  }

  }
}
```

The output from the program is shown here:

```
Found: MyClass
Found: AnotherClass
Found: Demo

Using: MyClass
Available constructors:
   MyClass(Int32 i)
   MyClass(Int32 i, Int32 j)

Two-parameter constructor found.

Constructing MyClass(int, int).
Values are x: 10, y: 20

Invoking methods on reflectOb.

sum is 30
14 is between x and y
Inside Set(int, int). Values are x: 9, y: 18
Inside Set(double, double). Values are x: 1, y: 23
Values are x: 1, y: 23
```

As the output shows, all three classes contained within **MyClasses.exe** were found. The first one, which in this case was **MyClass**, was then used to instantiate an object and execute methods.

The types in **MyClasses.exe** are discovered using this sequence of code, which is near the start of **Main( )**:

```
// Load the MyClasses.exe assembly.
Assembly asm = Assembly.LoadFrom("MyClasses.exe");

// Discover what types MyClasses.exe contains.
Type[] alltypes = asm.GetTypes();
foreach(Type temp in alltypes)
  Console.WriteLine("Found: " + temp.Name);
```

You can use such a sequence whenever you need to dynamically load and interrogate an assembly.

On a related point, an assembly need not be an **exe** file. Assemblies can also be contained in dynamic link library (DLL) files that use the **dll** extension. For example, if you were to compile **MyClasses.cs** using this command line,

```
csc /t:library MyClasses.cs
```

then the output file would be **MyClasses.dll**. One advantage to putting code into a DLL is that no **Main( )** method is required. All **exe** files require an entry point, such as **Main( )**, that defines where execution begins. This is why the **Demo** class contained a placeholder **Main( )** method. Such a method is not required by a DLL. If you try making **MyClass** into a DLL, you will need to change the call to **LoadFrom( )** as shown here:

```
Assembly asm = Assembly.LoadFrom("MyClasses.dll");
```

Fully Automating Type Discovery

Before we leave the topic of reflection, one last example will be instructive. Even though the preceding program was able to fully use **MyClass** without explicitly specifying **MyClass** in the program, it still relied upon prior knowledge of the contents of **MyClass**. For example, the program knew the names of its methods, such as **Set** and **Sum**. However, using reflection it is possible to utilize a type about which you have no prior knowledge. To do this, you must discover all information necessary to construct an object and to generate method calls. Such an approach would be useful to a visual design tool, for example, because it could utilize the types available on the system.

To see how the full dynamic discovery of a type can be accomplished, consider the following example, which loads the **MyClasses.exe** assembly, constructs a **MyClass** object, and then calls all of the methods declared by **MyClass**, all without assuming any prior knowledge:

```
// Utilize MyClass without assuming any prior knowledge.

using System;
using System.Reflection;

class ReflectAssemblyDemo {
  static void Main() {
    int val;
    Assembly asm = Assembly.LoadFrom("MyClasses.exe");

    Type[] alltypes = asm.GetTypes();

    Type t = alltypes[0]; // use first class found

    Console.WriteLine("Using: " + t.Name);

    ConstructorInfo[] ci = t.GetConstructors();

    // Use first constructor found.
    ParameterInfo[] cpi = ci[0].GetParameters();
    object reflectOb;

    if(cpi.Length > 0) {
      object[] consargs = new object[cpi.Length];

      // Initialize args.
      for(int n=0; n < cpi.Length; n++)
        consargs[n] = 10 + n * 20;

      // Construct the object.
      reflectOb = ci[0].Invoke(consargs);
    } else
```

```
  reflectOb = ci[0].Invoke(null);


Console.WriteLine("\nInvoking methods on reflectOb.");
Console.WriteLine();

// Ignore inherited methods.
MethodInfo[] mi = t.GetMethods(BindingFlags.DeclaredOnly |
                               BindingFlags.Instance |
                               BindingFlags.Public) ;

// Invoke each method.
foreach(MethodInfo m in mi) {
  Console.WriteLine("Calling {0} ", m.Name);

  // Get the parameters.
  ParameterInfo[] pi = m.GetParameters();

  // Execute methods.
  switch(pi.Length) {
    case 0: // no args
      if(m.ReturnType == typeof(int)) {
        val = (int) m.Invoke(reflectOb, null);
        Console.WriteLine("Result is " + val);
      }
      else if(m.ReturnType == typeof(void)) {
        m.Invoke(reflectOb, null);
      }
      break;
    case 1: // one arg
      if(pi[0].ParameterType == typeof(int)) {
        object[] args = new object[1];
        args[0] = 14;
        if((bool) m.Invoke(reflectOb, args))
          Console.WriteLine("14 is between x and y");
        else
          Console.WriteLine("14 is not between x and y");
      }
      break;
    case 2: // two args
      if((pi[0].ParameterType == typeof(int)) &&
         (pi[1].ParameterType == typeof(int))) {
        object[] args = new object[2];
        args[0] = 9;
        args[1] = 18;
        m.Invoke(reflectOb, args);
      }
      else if((pi[0].ParameterType == typeof(double)) &&
              (pi[1].ParameterType == typeof(double))) {
        object[] args = new object[2];
        args[0] = 1.12;
        args[1] = 23.4;
        m.Invoke(reflectOb, args);
      }
      break;
```

```
    }
    Console.WriteLine();
  }

 }
}
```

Here is the output produced by the program:

```
Using: MyClass
Constructing MyClass(int).
Values are x: 10, y: 10

Invoking methods on reflectOb.

Calling Sum
Result is 20

Calling IsBetween
14 is not between x and y

Calling Set
Inside Set(int, int). Values are x: 9, y: 18

Calling Set
Inside Set(double, double). Values are x: 1, y: 23

Calling Show
Values are x: 1, y: 23
```

The operation of the program is straightforward, but a couple of points are worth mentioning. First, notice that only the methods explicitly declared by **MyClass** are obtained and used. This is accomplished by using the **BindingFlags** form of **GetMethods( )**. The reason for this is to prevent calling the methods inherited from **object**. Second, notice how the number of parameters and return type of each method are obtained dynamically. A **switch** statement determines the number of parameters. Within each **case**, the parameter type(s) and return type are checked. A method call is then constructed based on this information.

Attributes

C# allows you to add declarative information to a program in the form of an *attribute*. An attribute defines additional information (metadata) that is associated with a class, structure, method, and so on. For example, you might define an attribute that determines the type of button that a class will display. Attributes are specified between square brackets, preceding the item to which they apply. Thus, an attribute is not a member of a class. Rather, an attribute specifies supplemental information that is attached to an item.

Attribute Basics

An attribute is supported by a class that inherits **System.Attribute**. Thus, all attribute classes must be subclasses of **Attribute**. Although **Attribute** defines substantial functionality, this functionality is not always needed when working with attributes. By convention, attribute classes often use the suffix **Attribute**. For example, **ErrorAttribute** would be a name for an attribute class that described an error.

When an attribute class is declared, it is preceded by an attribute called **AttributeUsage**. This built-in attribute specifies the types of items to which the attribute can be applied. Thus, the usage of an attribute can be restricted to methods, for example.

Creating an Attribute

In an attribute class, you will define the members that support the attribute. Often attribute classes are quite simple, containing just a small number of fields or properties. For example, an attribute might define a remark that describes the item to which the attribute is being attached. Such an attribute might look like this:

```
[AttributeUsage(AttributeTargets.All)]
public class RemarkAttribute : Attribute {
  string pri_remark; // underlies Remark property

  public RemarkAttribute(string comment) {
    pri_remark = comment;
  }

  public string Remark {
    get {
      return pri_remark;
    }
  }
}
```

Let's look at this class, line by line.

The name of this attribute is **RemarkAttribute**. Its declaration is preceded by the **AttributeUsage** attribute, which specifies that **RemarkAttribute** can be applied to all types of items. Using **AttributeUsage**, it is possible to narrow the list of items to which an attribute can be attached, and we will examine its capabilities later in this chapter.

Next, **RemarkAttribute** is declared and it inherits **Attribute**. Inside **RemarkAttribute** there is one private field, **pri_remark**, which supports one public, read-only property: **Remark**. This property holds the description that will be associated with the attribute. (**Remark** could also have been declared as an auto-implemented property with a private set accessor, but a read-only property is used for the purposes of illustration.) There is one public constructor that takes a string argument and assigns it to **Remark**.

At this point, no other steps are needed, and **RemarkAttribute** is ready for use.

Attaching an Attribute

Once you have defined an attribute class, you can attach the attribute to an item. An attribute precedes the item to which it is attached and is specified by enclosing its constructor inside square brackets. For example, here is how **RemarkAttribute** can be associated with a class:

```
[RemarkAttribute("This class uses an attribute.")]
class UseAttrib {
  // ...
}
```

This constructs a **RemarkAttribute** that contains the comment, "This class uses an attribute." This attribute is then associated with **UseAttrib**.

When attaching an attribute, it is not actually necessary to specify the **Attribute** suffix. For example, the preceding class could be declared this way:

```
[Remark("This class uses an attribute.")]
class UseAttrib {
  // ...
}
```

Here, only the name **Remark** is used. Although the short form is correct, it is usually safer to use the full name when attaching attributes, because it avoids possible confusion and ambiguity.

Obtaining an Object's Attributes

Once an attribute has been attached to an item, other parts of the program can retrieve the attribute. To retrieve an attribute, you will often use one of two methods. The first is **GetCustomAttributes( )**, which is defined by **MemberInfo** and inherited by **Type**. It retrieves a list of all attributes attached to an item. Here is one of its forms:

object[ ] GetCustomAttributes(bool *inherit*)

If *inherit* is true, then the attributes of all base classes through the inheritance chain will be included. Otherwise, only those attributes defined for the specified type will be found.

The second method is **GetCustomAttribute( )**, which is defined by **Attribute**. One of its forms is shown here:

static Attribute GetCustomAttribute(MemberInfo *element*, Type *attributeType*)

Here, *element* is a **MemberInfo** object that describes the item for which the attributes are being obtained. The attribute desired is specified by *attributeType*. You will use this method when you know the name of the attribute you want to obtain, which is often the case. For example, assuming that the **UseAttrib** class has the **RemarkAttribute**, to obtain a reference to the **RemarkAttribute**, you can use a sequence like this:

```
// Get a MemberInfo instance associated with a
// class that has the RemarkAttribute.
Type t = typeof(UseAttrib);

// Retrieve the RemarkAttribute.
Type tRemAtt = typeof(RemarkAttribute);
RemarkAttribute ra = (RemarkAttribute)
     Attribute.GetCustomAttribute(t, tRemAtt);
```

This sequence works because **MemberInfo** is a base class of **Type**. Thus, **t** is a **MemberInfo** instance.

Once you have a reference to an attribute, you can access its members. This makes information associated with an attribute available to a program that uses an element to which an attribute is attached. For example, the following statement displays the **Remark** property:

```
Console.WriteLine(ra.Remark);
```

The following program puts together all of the pieces and demonstrates the use of **RemarkAttribute**:

```csharp
// A simple attribute example.

using System;
using System.Reflection;

[AttributeUsage(AttributeTargets.All)]
public class RemarkAttribute : Attribute {
  string pri_remark; // underlies Remark property

  public RemarkAttribute(string comment) {
    pri_remark = comment;
  }

  public string Remark {
    get {
      return pri_remark;
    }
  }
}

[RemarkAttribute("This class uses an attribute.")]
class UseAttrib {
  // ...
}

class AttribDemo {
  static void Main() {
    Type t = typeof(UseAttrib);

    Console.Write("Attributes in " + t.Name + ": ");

    object[] attribs = t.GetCustomAttributes(false);
    foreach(object o in attribs) {
      Console.WriteLine(o);
    }

    Console.Write("Remark: ");

    // Retrieve the RemarkAttribute.
    Type tRemAtt = typeof(RemarkAttribute);
    RemarkAttribute ra = (RemarkAttribute)
        Attribute.GetCustomAttribute(t, tRemAtt);

    Console.WriteLine(ra.Remark);
  }
}
```

The output from the program is shown here:

```
Attributes in UseAttrib: RemarkAttribute
Remark: This class uses an attribute.
```

Positional vs. Named Parameters

In the preceding example, **RemarkAttribute** was initialized by passing the description string to the constructor, using the normal constructor syntax. In this case, the **comment** parameter to **RemarkAttribute( )** is called a *positional parameter*. This term relates to the fact that the argument is linked to a parameter by its position in the argument list. Thus, the first argument is passed to the first parameter, the second argument is passed to the second parameter, and so on.

However, for an attribute, you can also create *named parameters*, which can be assigned initial values by using their name. In this case, it is the name of the parameter, not its position, that is important.

NOTE *Although named attribute parameters are conceptually similar to named arguments in methods, the specifics differ.*

A named parameter is supported by either a public field or property, which must be read-write and non-static. Any such field or property is automatically able to be used as a named parameter. A named parameter is given a value by an assignment statement that is located within the argument list when the attribute's constructor is invoked. Here is the general form of an attribute specification that includes named parameters:

[*attrib(positional-param-list, named-param1 = value, named-param2 = value, ...)*]

The positional parameters (if they exist) come first. Next, each named parameter is assigned a value. The order of the named parameters is not important. Named parameters do not need to be given a value. In this case, their default value will be used.

To understand how to use a named parameter, it is best to work through an example. Here is a version of **RemarkAttribute** that adds a field called **Supplement**, which can be used to hold a supplemental remark:

```
[AttributeUsage(AttributeTargets.All)]
public class RemarkAttribute : Attribute {
  string pri_remark; // underlies Remark property

  // This can be used as a named parameter:
  public string Supplement;

  public RemarkAttribute(string comment) {
    pri_remark = comment;
    Supplement = "None";
  }

  public string Remark {
    get {
      return pri_remark;
    }
  }
}
```

As you can see, **Supplement** is initialized to the string "None" by the constructor. There is no way of using the constructor to assign it a different initial value. However, because **Supplement** is a public field of **RemarkAttribute**, it can be used as a named parameter, as shown here:

```
[RemarkAttribute("This class uses an attribute.",
        Supplement = "This is additional info.")]
class UseAttrib {
  // ...
}
```

Pay close attention to the way **RemarkAttribute**'s constructor is called. First, the positional argument is specified as it was before. Next is a comma, followed by the named parameter, **Supplement**, which is assigned a value. Finally, the closing **)** ends the call to the constructor. Thus, the named parameter is initialized within the call to the constructor. This syntax can be generalized. Position parameters must be specified in the order in which they appear. Named parameters are specified by assigning values to their name.

Here is a program that demonstrates the **Supplement** field:

```
// Use a named attribute parameter.

using System;
using System.Reflection;

[AttributeUsage(AttributeTargets.All)]
public class RemarkAttribute : Attribute {
  string pri_remark; // underlies Remark property

  public string Supplement; // this is a named parameter

  public RemarkAttribute(string comment) {
    pri_remark = comment;
    Supplement = "None";
  }

  public string Remark {
    get {
      return pri_remark;
    }
  }
}

[RemarkAttribute("This class uses an attribute.",
                Supplement = "This is additional info.")]
class UseAttrib {
  // ...
}

class NamedParamDemo {
  static void Main() {
    Type t = typeof(UseAttrib);

    Console.Write("Attributes in " + t.Name + ": ");
```

```
    object[] attribs = t.GetCustomAttributes(false);
    foreach(object o in attribs) {
      Console.WriteLine(o);
    }

    // Retrieve the RemarkAttribute.
    Type tRemAtt = typeof(RemarkAttribute);
    RemarkAttribute ra = (RemarkAttribute)
          Attribute.GetCustomAttribute(t, tRemAtt);

    Console.Write("Remark: ");
    Console.WriteLine(ra.Remark);

    Console.Write("Supplement: ");
    Console.WriteLine(ra.Supplement);
  }
}
```

The output from the program is shown here:

```
Attributes in UseAttrib: RemarkAttribute
Remark: This class uses an attribute.
Supplement: This is additional info.
```

Before moving on, it is important to emphasize that **pri_remark** *cannot* be used as a named parameter because it is private to **RemarkAttribute**. The **Remark** property *cannot* be used as a named parameter because it is read-only. Remember that only public, read-write fields and properties can be used as named parameters.

A public, read-write property can be used as a named parameter in the same way as a field. For example, here an auto-implemented **int** property called **Priority** is added to **RemarkAttribute**:

```
// Use a property as a named attribute parameter.

using System;
using System.Reflection;

[AttributeUsage(AttributeTargets.All)]
public class RemarkAttribute : Attribute {
  string pri_remark; // underlies Remark property

  public string Supplement; // this is a named parameter

  public RemarkAttribute(string comment) {
    pri_remark = comment;
    Supplement = "None";
    Priority = 1;
  }

  public string Remark {
    get {
      return pri_remark;
    }
  }
```

```
    // Use a property as a named parameter.
    public int Priority { get; set; }
}

[RemarkAttribute("This class uses an attribute.",
                 Supplement = "This is additional info.",
                 Priority = 10)]
class UseAttrib {
  // ...
}

class NamedParamDemo {
  static void Main() {
    Type t = typeof(UseAttrib);

    Console.Write("Attributes in " + t.Name + ": ");

    object[] attribs = t.GetCustomAttributes(false);
    foreach(object o in attribs) {
      Console.WriteLine(o);
    }

    // Retrieve the RemarkAttribute.
    Type tRemAtt = typeof(RemarkAttribute);
    RemarkAttribute ra = (RemarkAttribute)
         Attribute.GetCustomAttribute(t, tRemAtt);

    Console.Write("Remark: ");
    Console.WriteLine(ra.Remark);

    Console.Write("Supplement: ");
    Console.WriteLine(ra.Supplement);

    Console.WriteLine("Priority: " + ra.Priority);
  }
}
```

The output is shown here:

```
Attributes in UseAttrib: RemarkAttribute
Remark: This class uses an attribute.
Supplement: This is additional info.
Priority: 10
```

There is one point of interest in the program. Notice the attribute specified before **UseAttrib** that is shown here:

```
[RemarkAttribute("This class uses an attribute.",
                 Supplement = "This is additional info.",
                 Priority = 10)]
```

The named attributes **Supplement** and **Priority** are *not* in any special order. These two assignments can be reversed without any change to the attribute.

One last point: For both positional and named parameters, the type of an attribute parameter must be either one of the built-in primitive types, **object**, **Type**, an enumeration, or a one-dimensional array of one of these types.

Three Built-in Attributes

C# defines many built-in attributes, but three are especially important because they apply to a wide variety of situations: **AttributeUsage**, **Conditional**, and **Obsolete**. They are examined here.

AttributeUsage

As mentioned earlier, the **AttributeUsage** attribute specifies the types of items to which an attribute can be applied. **AttributeUsage** is another name for the **System.AttributeUsageAttribute** class. **AttributeUsage** has the following constructor:

AttributeUsage(AttributeTargets *validOn*)

Here, *validOn* specifies the item or items upon which the attribute can be used. **AttributeTargets** is an enumeration that defines the following values:

All	Assembly	Class	Constructor
Delegate	Enum	Event	Field
GenericParameter	Interface	Method	Module
Parameter	Property	ReturnValue	Struct

Two or more of these values can be ORed together. For example, to specify an attribute that can be applied only to fields and properties, use

```
AttributeTargets.Field | AttributeTargets.Property
```

AttributeUsage supports two named parameters. The first is **AllowMultiple**, which is a **bool** value. If this value is true, then the attribute can be applied more than one time to a single item. The second is **Inherited**, which is also a **bool** value. If this value is true, then the attribute is inherited by derived classes. Otherwise, it is not inherited. The default setting is false for **AllowMultiple** and true for **Inherited**.

AttributeUsage also specifies a read-only property called **ValidOn**, which returns a value of type **AttributeTargets**, which specifies what types of items the attribute can be used on. The default is **AttributeTargets.All**.

The Conditional Attribute

The attribute **Conditional** is perhaps C#'s most interesting built-in attribute. It allows you to create *conditional methods*. A conditional method is invoked only when a specific symbol has been defined via **#define**. Otherwise, the method is bypassed. Thus, a conditional method offers an alternative to conditional compilation using **#if**.

Conditional is another name for **System.Diagnostics.ConditionalAttribute**. To use the **Conditional** attribute, you must include the **System.Diagnostics** namespace.

Let's begin with an example:

```
// Demonstrate the Conditional attribute.

#define TRIAL

using System;
using System.Diagnostics;

class Test {

  [Conditional("TRIAL")]
  void Trial() {
    Console.WriteLine("Trial version, not for distribution.");
  }

  [Conditional("RELEASE")]
  void Release() {
    Console.WriteLine("Final release version.");
  }

  static void Main() {
    Test t = new Test();

    t.Trial(); // called only if TRIAL is defined
    t.Release(); // called only if RELEASE is defined
  }
}
```

The output from this program is shown here:

```
Trial version, not for distribution.
```

Let's look closely at this program to understand why this output is produced. First, notice the program defines the symbol **TRIAL**. Next, notice how the methods **Trial( )** and **Release( )** are coded. They are both preceded with the **Conditional** attribute, which has this general form:

[Conditional *symbol*]

where *symbol* is the symbol that determines whether the method will be executed. If the symbol is defined, then when the method is called, it will be executed. If the symbol is not defined, then the method is not executed.

Inside **Main( )**, both **Trial( )** and **Release( )** are called. However, only **TRIAL** is defined. Thus, **Trial( )** is executed. The call to **Release( )** is ignored. If you define **RELEASE**, then **Release( )** will also be called. If you remove the definition for **TRIAL**, then **Trial( )** will not be called.

The **Conditional** attribute can also be applied to an attribute class (that is, a class that inherits **Attribute**). In this case, if the symbol is defined when the attribute is encountered during compilation, the attribute is applied. Otherwise, it is not.

Conditional methods have a few restrictions. First, they must return **void**. Second, they must be members of a class or structure, not an interface. Third, they cannot be preceded with the **override** keyword.

The Obsolete Attribute

The **Obsolete** attribute, which is short for **System.ObsoleteAttribute**, lets you mark a program element as obsolete. Here is one of its forms:

[Obsolete("*message*")]

Here, *message* is displayed when that program element is compiled. Here is a short example:

```
// Demonstrate the Obsolete attribute.

using System;

class Test {

  [Obsolete("Use MyMeth2, instead.")]
  public static int MyMeth(int a, int b) {
    return a / b;
  }

  // Improved version of MyMeth.
  public static int MyMeth2(int a, int b) {
    return b == 0 ? 0 : a /b;
  }

  static void Main() {
   // Warning displayed for this.
    Console.WriteLine("4 / 3 is " + Test.MyMeth(4, 3));

   // No warning here.
    Console.WriteLine("4 / 3 is " + Test.MyMeth2(4, 3));
  }
}
```

When the call to **MyMeth( )** is encountered in **Main( )** when this program is compiled, a warning will be generated that tells the user to use **MyMeth2( )** instead.

A second form of **Obsolete** is shown here:

[Obsolete("*message*", *error*)]

Here, *error* is a Boolean value. If it is true, then use of the obsolete item generates a compilation error rather than a warning. The difference is, of course, that a program containing an error cannot be compiled into an executable program.

Generics

This chapter examines one of C#'s most sophisticated and powerful features: *generics*. Interestingly, although generics are now an indispensable part of C# programming, they were not included in the original 1.0 release. Instead, they were added by C# 2.0. It is not an overstatement to say that the addition of generics fundamentally changed the character of C#. Not only did it add a new syntactic element, it also added new capabilities and resulted in many changes and upgrades to the library. Although it has been a few years since the inclusion of generics in C#, the effects still reverberate throughout the language.

The generics feature is so important because it enables the creation of classes, structures, interfaces, methods, and delegates that work in a type-safe manner with various kinds of data. As you may know, many algorithms are logically the same no matter what type of data they are being applied to. For example, the mechanism that supports a queue is the same whether the queue is storing items of type **int**, **string**, **object**, or a user-defined class. Prior to generics, you might have created several different versions of the same algorithm to handle different types of data. Through the use of generics, you can define a solution once, independently of any specific type of data, and then apply that solution to a wide variety of data types without any additional effort.

This chapter describes the syntax, theory, and use of generics. It also shows how generics provide type safety for some previously difficult cases. Once you have completed this chapter, you will want to examine Chapter 25, which covers Collections. There you will find many examples of generics at work in the generic collection classes.

What Are Generics?

At its core, the term *generics* means *parameterized types*. Parameterized types are important because they enable you to create classes, structures, interfaces, methods, and delegates in which the type of data upon which they operate is specified as a parameter. Using generics, it is possible to create a single class, for example, that automatically works with different types of data. A class, structure, interface, method, or delegate that operates on a parameterized type is called *generic*, as in *generic class* or *generic method*.

It is important to understand that C# has always given you the ability to create generalized code by operating through references of type **object**. Because **object** is the base class of all other classes, an **object** reference can refer to any type of object. Thus, in pre-generics code, generalized code used **object** references to operate on a variety of different kinds of objects.

The problem was that it could not do so with type safety because casts were needed to convert between the **object** type and the actual type of the data. This was a potential source of errors because it was possible to accidentally use an incorrect cast. Generics avoid this problem by providing the type safety that was lacking. Generics also streamline the process because it is no longer necessary to employ casts to translate between **object** and the type of data that is actually being operated upon. Thus, generics expand your ability to re-use code, and let you do so safely and easily.

NOTE *A Warning to C++ and Java Programmers: Although C# generics are similar to templates in C++ and generics in Java, they are not the same as either. In fact, there are some fundamental differences among these three approaches to generics. If you have a background in C++ or Java, it is important to not jump to conclusions about how generics work in C#.*

A Simple Generics Example

Let's begin with a simple example of a generic class. The following program defines two classes. The first is the generic class **Gen**, and the second is **GenericsDemo**, which uses **Gen**.

```
// A simple generic class.

using System;

// In the following Gen class, T is a type parameter
// that will be replaced by a real type when an object
// of type Gen is created.
class Gen<T> {
  T ob; // declare a variable of type T

  // Notice that this constructor has a parameter of type T.
  public Gen(T o) {
    ob = o;
  }

  // Return ob, which is of type T.
  public T GetOb() {
    return ob;
  }

  // Show type of T.
  public void ShowType() {
    Console.WriteLine("Type of T is " + typeof(T));
  }
}

// Demonstrate the generic class.
class GenericsDemo {
  static void Main() {
    // Create a Gen reference for int.
    Gen<int> iOb;

    // Create a Gen<int> object and assign its reference to iOb.
    iOb = new Gen<int>(102);
```

```
    // Show the type of data used by iOb.
    iOb.ShowType();

    // Get the value in iOb.
    int v = iOb.GetOb();
    Console.WriteLine("value: " + v);

    Console.WriteLine();

    // Create a Gen object for strings.
    Gen<string> strOb = new Gen<string>("Generics add power.");

    // Show the type of data stored in strOb.
    strOb.ShowType();

    // Get the value in strOb.
    string str = strOb.GetOb();
    Console.WriteLine("value: " + str);
  }
}
```

The output produced by the program is shown here:

```
Type of T is System.Int32
value: 102

Type of T is System.String
value: Generics add power.
```

Let's examine this program carefully.

First, notice how **Gen** is declared by the following line.

```
class Gen<T> {
```

Here, **T** is the name of a *type parameter*. This name is used as a placeholder for the actual type that will be specified when a **Gen** object is created. Thus, **T** is used within **Gen** whenever the type parameter is needed. Notice that **T** is contained within < >. This syntax can be generalized. Whenever a type parameter is being declared, it is specified within angle brackets. Because **Gen** uses a type parameter, **Gen** is a *generic class*.

In the declaration of **Gen**, there is no special significance to the name **T**. Any valid identifier could have been used, but **T** is traditional. Other commonly used type parameter names include **V** and **E**. Of course, you can also use descriptive names for type parameters, such as **TValue** or **TKey**. When using a descriptive name, it is common practice to use **T** as the first letter.

Next, **T** is used to declare a variable called **ob**, as shown here:

```
T ob; // declare a variable of type T
```

As explained, **T** is a placeholder for the actual type that will be specified when a **Gen** object is created. Thus, **ob** will be a variable of the type *bound to* **T** when a **Gen** object is instantiated. For example, if type **string** is specified for **T**, then in that instance, **ob** will be of type **string**.

Now consider **Gen**'s constructor:

```
public Gen(T o) {
  ob = o;
}
```

Notice that its parameter, **o**, is of type **T**. This means that the actual type of **o** is determined by the type bound to **T** when a **Gen** object is created. Also, because both the parameter **o** and the instance variable **ob** are of type **T**, they will both be of the same actual type when a **Gen** object is created.

The type parameter **T** can also be used to specify the return type of a method, as is the case with the **GetOb( )** method, shown here:

```
public T GetOb() {
  return ob;
}
```

Because **ob** is also of type **T**, its type is compatible with the return type specified by **GetOb( )**.

The **ShowType( )** method displays the type of **T** by passing **T** to the **typeof** operator. Because a real type will be substituted for **T** when an object of type **Gen** is created, **typeof** will obtain type information about the actual type.

The **GenericsDemo** class demonstrates the generic **Gen** class. It first creates a version of **Gen** for type **int**, as shown here:

```
Gen<int> iOb;
```

Look closely at this declaration. First, notice that the type **int** is specified within the angle brackets after **Gen**. In this case, **int** is a *type argument* that is bound to **Gen**'s type parameter, **T**. This creates a version of **Gen** in which all uses of **T** are replaced by **int**. Thus, for this declaration, **ob** is of type **int**, and the return type of **GetOb( )** is of type **int**.

The next line assigns to **iOb** a reference to an instance of an **int** version of the **Gen** class:

```
iOb = new Gen<int>(102);
```

Notice that when the **Gen** constructor is called, the type argument **int** is also specified. This is necessary because the type of the variable (in this case **iOb**) to which the reference is being assigned is of type **Gen<int>**. Thus, the reference returned by **new** must also be of type **Gen<int>**. If it isn't, a compile-time error will result. For example, the following assignment will cause a compile-time error:

```
iOb = new Gen<double>(118.12); // Error!
```

Because **iOb** is of type **Gen<int>**, it can't be used to refer to an object of **Gen<double>**. This type checking is one of the main benefits of generics because it ensures type safety.

The program then displays the type of **ob** within **iOb**, which is **System.Int32**. This is the .NET structure that corresponds to **int**. Next, the program obtains the value of **ob** by use of the following line:

```
int v = iOb.GetOb();
```

Because the return type of **GetOb( )** is **T**, which was replaced by **int** when **iOb** was declared, the return type of **GetOb( )** is also **int**. Thus, this value can be assigned to an **int** variable.

Next, **GenericsDemo** declares an object of type **Gen<string>**:

```
Gen<string> strOb = new Gen<string>("Generics add power.");
```

Because the type argument is **string**, **string** is substituted for **T** inside **Gen**. This creates a **string** version of **Gen**, as the remaining lines in the program demonstrate.

Before moving on, a few terms need to be defined. When you specify a type argument such as **int** or **string** for **Gen**, you are creating what is referred to in C# as a *closed constructed type*. Thus, **Gen<int>** is a closed constructed type. In essence, a generic type, such as **Gen<T>**, is an abstraction. It is only after a specific version, such as **Gen<int>**, has been constructed that a concrete type has been created. In C# terminology, a construct such as **Gen<T>** is called an *open constructed type*, because the type parameter **T** (rather than an actual type, such as **int**) is specified.

More generally, C# defines the concepts of an *open type* and a *closed type*. An open type is a type parameter or any generic type whose type argument is (or involves) a type parameter. Any type that is not an open type is a closed type. A *constructed type* is a generic type for which all type arguments have been supplied. If those type arguments are all closed types, then it is a closed constructed type. If one or more of those type arguments are open types, it is an open constructed type.

Generic Types Differ Based on Their Type Arguments

A key point to understand about generic types is that a reference of one specific version of a generic type is not type-compatible with another version of the same generic type. For example, assuming the program just shown, the following line of code is in error and will not compile:

```
iOb = strOb; // Wrong!
```

Even though both **iOb** and **strOb** are of type **Gen<T>**, they are references to different types because their type arguments differ.

How Generics Improve Type Safety

At this point, you might be asking yourself the following question. Given that the same functionality found in the generic **Gen** class can be achieved without generics, by simply specifying **object** as the data type and employing the proper casts, what is the benefit of making **Gen** generic? The answer is that generics automatically ensure the type safety of all operations involving **Gen**. In the process, generics eliminate the need for you to use casts and type-check code by hand.

To understand the benefits of generics, first consider the following program that creates a non-generic equivalent of **Gen**:

```
// NonGen is functionally equivalent to Gen but does not use generics.

using System;

class NonGen {
  object ob; // ob is now of type object

  // Pass the constructor a reference of type object.
  public NonGen(object o) {
```

```
      ob = o;
    }

    // Return type object.
    public object GetOb() {
      return ob;
    }

    // Show type of ob.
    public void ShowType() {
      Console.WriteLine("Type of ob is " + ob.GetType());
    }
  }

// Demonstrate the non-generic class.
class NonGenDemo {
  static void Main() {
    NonGen iOb;

    // Create NonGen object.
    iOb = new NonGen(102);

    // Show the type of data stored in iOb.
    iOb.ShowType();

    // Get the value in iOb.
    // This time, a cast is necessary.
    int v = (int) iOb.GetOb();
    Console.WriteLine("value: " + v);

    Console.WriteLine();

    // Create another NonGen object and store a string in it.
    NonGen strOb = new NonGen("Non-Generics Test");

    // Show the type of data stored in strOb.
    strOb.ShowType();

    // Get the value of strOb.
    // Again, notice that a cast is necessary.
    String str = (string) strOb.GetOb();
    Console.WriteLine("value: " + str);

    // This compiles, but is conceptually wrong!
    iOb = strOb;

    // The following line results in a runtime exception.
    // v = (int) iOb.GetOb(); // runtime error!
  }
}
```

This program produces the following output:

```
Type of ob is System.Int32
value: 102
```

```
Type of ob is System.String
value: Non-Generics Test
```

As you can see, the output is similar to the previous version of the program.

There are several things of interest in this version. First, notice that **NonGen** replaces all uses of **T** with **object**. This makes **NonGen** able to store any type of object, as can the generic version. However, this approach is bad for two reasons. First, explicit casts must be employed to retrieve the stored data. Second, many kinds of type mismatch errors cannot be found until runtime. Let's look closely at each problem.

We will begin with this line:

```
int v = (int) iOb.GetOb();
```

Because the return type of **GetOb( )** is now **object**, the cast to **int** is necessary to enable the value returned by **GetOb( )** to be unboxed and stored in **v**. If you remove the cast, the program will not compile. In the generic version of the program, this cast was not needed because **int** was specified as a type argument when **iOb** was constructed. In the non-generic version, the cast must be employed. This is not only an inconvenience, but a potential source of error.

Now, consider the following sequence from near the end of the program:

```
// This compiles, but is conceptually wrong!
iOb = strOb;

// The following line results in a runtime exception.
// v = (int) iOb.GetOb(); // runtime error!
```

Here, **strOb** is assigned to **iOb**. However, **strOb** refers to an object that contains a string, not an integer. This assignment is syntactically valid because all **NonGen** references are the same, and any **NonGen** reference can refer to any other **NonGen** object. However, the statement is semantically wrong, as the commented-out line shows. In that line, the return type of **GetOb( )** is cast to **int** and then an attempt is made to assign this value to **v**. The trouble is that **iOb** now refers to an object that stores a **string**, not an **int**. Unfortunately, without generics, the compiler won't catch this error. Instead, a runtime exception will occur when the cast to **int** is attempted. To see this for yourself, try removing the comment symbol from the start of the line and then compiling and running the program. A runtime error will occur.

The preceding sequence can't occur when generics are used. If this sequence were attempted in the generic version of the program, the compiler would catch it and report an error, thus preventing a serious bug that results in a runtime exception. The ability to create type-safe code in which type-mismatch errors are caught at compile time is a key advantage of generics. Although using **object** references to create "generic" code has always been possible in C#, that code was not type-safe and its misuse could result in runtime exceptions. Generics prevent this from occurring. In essence, through generics, what were once runtime errors have become compile-time errors. This is a major benefit.

There is one other point of interest in the **NonGen** program. Notice how the type of the **NonGen** instance variable **ob** is obtained by **ShowType( )**:

```
Console.WriteLine("Type of ob is " + ob.GetType());
```

Recall from Chapter 11 that **object** defines several methods that are available to all data types. One of these methods is **GetType( )**, which returns a **Type** object that describes the type of the invoking object at runtime. Thus, even though the type of **ob** is specified as **object** in the program's source code, at runtime, the actual type of object being referred to is known. This is why the CLR will generate an exception if you try an invalid cast during program execution.

A Generic Class with Two Type Parameters

You can declare more than one type parameter in a generic type. To specify two or more type parameters, simply use a comma-separated list. For example, the following **TwoGen** class is a variation of the **Gen** class that has two type parameters:

```
// A simple generic class with two type parameters: T and V.

using System;

class TwoGen<T, V> {
  T ob1;
  V ob2;

  // Notice that this constructor has parameters of type T and V.
  public TwoGen(T o1, V o2) {
    ob1 = o1;
    ob2 = o2;
  }

  // Show types of T and V.
  public void showTypes() {
    Console.WriteLine("Type of T is " + typeof(T));
    Console.WriteLine("Type of V is " + typeof(V));
  }

  public T getob1() {
    return ob1;
  }

  public V GetObj2() {
    return ob2;
  }
}

// Demonstrate two generic type parameters.
class SimpGen {
  static void Main() {

    TwoGen<int, string> tgObj =
      new TwoGen<int, string>(119, "Alpha Beta Gamma");

    // Show the types.
    tgObj.showTypes();

    // Obtain and show values.
    int v = tgObj.getob1();
    Console.WriteLine("value: " + v);
```

```
    string str = tgObj.GetObj2();
    Console.WriteLine("value: " + str);
  }
}
```

The output from this program is shown here:

```
Type of T is System.Int32
Type of V is System.String
value: 119
value: Alpha Beta Gamma
```

Notice how **TwoGen** is declared:

```
class TwoGen<T, V> {
```

It specifies two type parameters: **T** and **V**, separated by a comma. Because it has two type parameters, two type arguments must be specified when a **TwoGen** object is created, as shown here:

```
TwoGen<int, string> tgObj =
  new TwoGen<int, string>(119, "Alpha Beta Gamma");
```

In this case, **int** is substituted for **T** and **string** is substituted for **V**.

Although the two type arguments differ in this example, it is possible for both types to be the same. For example, the following line of code is valid:

```
TwoGen<string, string> x = new TwoGen<string, string>("Hello", "Goodbye");
```

In this case, both **T** and **V** would be of type **string**. Of course, if the type arguments were always the same, then two type parameters would be unnecessary.

The General Form of a Generic Class

The generics syntax shown in the preceding examples can be generalized. Here is the syntax for declaring a generic class:

class *class-name<type-param-list>* { // ...

Here is the syntax for declaring a reference to a generics class:

class-name<type-arg-list> var-name =
    new *class-name<type-arg-list>(cons-arg-list)*;

Constrained Types

In the preceding examples, the type parameters could be replaced by any type. For example, given this declaration

```
class Gen<T> {
```

any type can be specified for **T**. Thus, it is legal to create **Gen** objects in which **T** is replaced by **int**, **double**, **string**, **FileStream**, or any other type. Although having no restrictions on the type argument is fine for many purposes, sometimes it is useful to limit the types that can be used as a type argument. For example, you might want to create a method that operates on the contents of a stream, including a **FileStream** or **MemoryStream**. This situation seems perfect for generics, but you need some way to ensure that only stream types are used as type arguments. You don't want to allow a type argument of **int**, for example. You also need some way to tell the compiler that the methods defined by a stream will be available for use. For example, your generic code needs some way to know that it can call the **Read( )** method.

To handle such situations, C# provides *constrained types*. When specifying a type parameter, you can specify a constraint that the type parameter must satisfy. This is accomplished through the use of a **where** clause when specifying the type parameter, as shown here:

class *class-name*<*type-param*> where *type-param* : *constraints* { // ...

Here, *constraints* is a comma-separated list of constraints.

C# defines the following types of constraints.

- You can require that a certain base class be present in a type argument by using a *base class constraint*. This constraint is specified by naming the desired base class. There is a variation of this constraint, called a *naked type constraint,* in which a type parameter (rather than an actual type) specifies the base class. This enables you to establish a relationship between two type parameters.

- You can require that one or more interfaces be implemented by a type argument by using an *interface constraint.* This constraint is specified by naming the desired interface.

- You can require that the type argument supply a parameterless constructor. This is called a *constructor constraint*. It is specified by **new( )**.

- You can specify that a type argument be a reference type by specifying the *reference type constraint:* **class**.

- You can specify that the type argument be a value type by specifying the *value type constraint:* **struct**.

Of these constraints, the base class constraint and the interface constraint are probably the most often used, but all are important. Each constraint is examined in the following sections.

Using a Base Class Constraint

The base class constraint enables you to specify a base class that a type argument must inherit. A base class constraint serves two important purposes. First, it lets you use the members of the base class specified by the constraint within the generic class. For example, you can call a method or use a property of the base class. Without a base class constraint, the compiler has no way to know what type of members a type argument might have. By supplying a base class constraint, you are letting the compiler know that all type arguments will have the members defined by that base class.

The second purpose of a base class constraint is to ensure that only type arguments that support the specified base class are used. This means that for any given base class constraint, the type argument must be either the base class, itself, or a class derived from that base class. If you attempt to use a type argument that does not match or inherit the specified base class, a compile-time error will result.

The base class constraint uses this form of the **where** clause:

where *T* : *base-class-name*

Here, *T* is the name of the type parameter, and *base-class-name* is the name of the base class. Only one base class can be specified.

Here is a simple example that demonstrates the base class constraint mechanism:

```
// A simple demonstration of a base class constraint.

using System;

class A {
  public void Hello() {
    Console.WriteLine("Hello");
  }
}

// Class B inherits A.
class B : A { }

// Class C does not inherit A.
class C { }

// Because of the base class constraint, all type arguments
// passed to Test must have A as a base class.
class Test<T> where T : A {
  T obj;

  public Test(T o) {
    obj = o;
  }

  public void SayHello() {
    // OK to call Hello() because it's declared
    // by the base class A.
    obj.Hello();
  }
}

class BaseClassConstraintDemo {
  static void Main() {
    A a = new A();
    B b = new B();
    C c = new C();

    // The following is valid because A is the specified base class.
    Test<A> t1 = new Test<A>(a);

    t1.SayHello();

    // The following is valid because B inherits A.
    Test<B> t2 = new Test<B>(b);
```

```
      t2.SayHello();


    // The following is invalid because C does not inherit A.
//    Test<C> t3 = new Test<C>(c); // Error!
//    t3.SayHello(); // Error!
  }
}
```

In this program, class **A** is inherited by **B**, but not by **C**. Notice also that **A** declares a method called **Hello( )**. Next, notice that **Test** is a generic class that is declared like this:

```
class Test<T> where T : A {
```

The **where** clause stipulates that any type argument specified for **T** must have **A** as a base class.

Now notice that **Test** declares the method **SayHello( )**, shown next:

```
public void SayHello() {
  // OK to call Hello() because it's declared
  // by the base class A.
  obj.Hello();
}
```

This method calls **Hello( )** on **obj**, which is a **T** object. The key point is that the only reason that **Hello( )** can be called is because the base class constraint requires that any type argument bound to **T** must be **A** or inherit **A**, and **A** declares **Hello( )**. Thus, any valid **T** will define **Hello( )**. If the base class constraint had not been used, the compiler would have no way of knowing that a method called **Hello( )** could be called on an object of type **T**. You can prove this for yourself by removing the **where** clause. The program will no longer compile because the **Hello( )** method will be unknown.

In addition to enabling access to members of the base class, the base class constraint enforces that only types that inherit the base class can be passed as type arguments. This is why the following two lines are commented-out:

```
//    Test<C> t3 = new Test<C>(c); // Error!
//    t3.SayHello(); // Error!
```

Because **C** does not inherit **A**, it can't be used as a type argument when constructing a **Test** object. You can prove this by removing the comment symbols and trying to recompile.

Before continuing, let's review the two effects of a base class constraint: A base class constraint enables a generic class to access the members of the base class. It also ensures that only those type arguments that fulfill this constraint are valid, thus preserving type safety.

Although the preceding example shows the "how" of base class constraints, it does not show the "why." To better understand the value of base type constraints, let's work through another, more practical example. Assume you want to create a mechanism that manages lists of telephone numbers. Furthermore, assume you want to use different lists for different groupings of numbers. Specifically, you want one list for friends, another for suppliers, and so on. To accomplish this, you might start by creating a base class called **PhoneNumber** that stores a name and a phone number linked to that name. Such a class might look like this:

```
// A base class that stores a name and phone number.
class PhoneNumber {
  public PhoneNumber(string n, string num) {
    Name = n;
    Number = num;
  }

  // Auto-implemented properties that hold a name and phone number.
  public string Number { get; set; }
  public string Name { get; set; }
}
```

Next, you create two classes that inherit **PhoneNumber**: **Friend** and **Supplier**. They are shown here:

```
// A class of phone numbers for friends.
class Friend : PhoneNumber {

  public Friend(string n, string num, bool wk) :
    base(n, num)
  {
    IsWorkNumber = wk;
  }

  public bool IsWorkNumber { get; private set; }
  // ...
}

// A class of phone numbers for suppliers.
class Supplier : PhoneNumber {
  public Supplier(string n, string num) :
    base(n, num) { }

  // ...
}
```

Notice that **Friend** adds a property called **IsWorkNumber**, which returns true if the telephone number is a work number.

To manage telephone lists, you create a class called **PhoneList**. Because you want this class to manage any type of phone list, you make it generic. Furthermore, because part of the list management is looking up numbers given names, and vice versa, you add the constraint that requires that the type of objects stored in the list must be instances of a class derived from **PhoneNumber**.

```
// PhoneList can manage any type of phone list
// as long as it is derived from PhoneNumber.
class PhoneList<T> where T : PhoneNumber {
  T[] phList;
  int end;

  public PhoneList() {
    phList = new T[10];
```

```
      end = 0;
    }

    // Add an entry to the list.
    public bool Add(T newEntry) {
      if(end == 10) return false;

      phList[end] = newEntry;
      end++;

      return true;
    }

    // Given a name, find and return the phone info.
    public T FindByName(string name) {

      for(int i=0; i<end; i++) {
        // Name can be used because it is a member of
        // PhoneNumber, which is the base class constraint.
        if(phList[i].Name == name)
          return phList[i];
      }

      // Name not in list.
      throw new NotFoundException();
    }

    // Given a number, find and return the phone info.
    public T FindByNumber(string number) {

      for(int i=0; i<end; i++) {
        // Number can be used because it is also a member of
        // PhoneNumber, which is the base class constraint.
        if(phList[i].Number == number)
          return phList[i];
      }

      // Number not in list.
      throw new NotFoundException();
    }

    // ...
}
```

The base class constraint enables code inside **PhoneList** to access the properties **Name** and **Number** for any type of telephone list. It also guarantees that only valid types are used to construct a **PhoneList** object. Notice that **PhoneList** throws a **NotFoundException** if a name or number is not found. This is a custom exception that is declared as shown here:

```
class NotFoundException : Exception {
  /* Implement all of the Exception constructors. Notice that
     the constructors simply execute the base class constructor.
     Because NotFoundException adds nothing to Exception,
     there is no need for any further actions. */
```

```
  public NotFoundException() : base() { }
  public NotFoundException(string message) : base(message) { }
  public NotFoundException(string message, Exception innerException) :
    base(message, innerException) { }
  protected NotFoundException(
    System.Runtime.Serialization.SerializationInfo info,
    System.Runtime.Serialization.StreamingContext context) :
      base(info, context) { }
}
```

Although only the default constructor is used by this example, **NotFoundException** implements all of the constructors defined by **Exception** for the sake of illustration. Notice that these constructors simply invoke the equivalent base class constructor defined by **Exception**. Because **NotFoundException** adds nothing to **Exception**, there is no reason for any further action.

The following program puts together all the pieces and demonstrates **PhoneList**. Notice that a class called **EmailFriend** is also created. This class does not inherit **PhoneNumber**. Thus, it *cannot* be used to create a **PhoneList**.

```
// A more practical demonstration of a base class constraint.

using System;

// A custom exception that is thrown if a name or number is not found.
class NotFoundException : Exception {
  /* Implement all of the Exception constructors. Notice that
     the constructors simply execute the base class constructor.
     Because NotFoundException adds nothing to Exception,
     there is no need for any further actions. */
  public NotFoundException() : base() { }
  public NotFoundException(string message) : base(message) { }
  public NotFoundException(string message, Exception innerException) :
    base(message, innerException) { }
  protected NotFoundException(
    System.Runtime.Serialization.SerializationInfo info,
    System.Runtime.Serialization.StreamingContext context) :
      base(info, context) { }
}
// A base class that stores a name and phone number.
class PhoneNumber {

  public PhoneNumber(string n, string num) {
    Name = n;
    Number = num;
  }

  public string Number { get; set; }
  public string Name { get; set; }

}

// A class of phone numbers for friends.
class Friend : PhoneNumber {
```

```
  public Friend(string n, string num, bool wk) :
    base(n, num)
  {
    IsWorkNumber = wk;
  }

  public bool IsWorkNumber { get; private set; }

  // ...
}

// A class of phone numbers for suppliers.
class Supplier : PhoneNumber {
  public Supplier(string n, string num) :
    base(n, num) { }

  // ...
}

// Notice that this class does not inherit PhoneNumber.
class EmailFriend {
  // ...
}

// PhoneList can manage any type of phone list
// as long as it is derived from PhoneNumber.
class PhoneList<T> where T : PhoneNumber {
  T[] phList;
  int end;

  public PhoneList() {
    phList = new T[10];
    end = 0;
  }

  // Add an entry to the list.
  public bool Add(T newEntry) {
    if(end == 10) return false;

    phList[end] = newEntry;
    end++;

    return true;
  }

  // Given a name, find and return the phone info.
  public T FindByName(string name) {

    for(int i=0; i<end; i++) {
      // Name can be used because it is a member of
      // PhoneNumber, which is the base class constraint.
      if(phList[i].Name == name)
        return phList[i];
    }
```

```
      // Name not in list.
      throw new NotFoundException();
    }

    // Given a number, find and return the phone info.
    public T FindByNumber(string number) {

      for(int i=0; i<end; i++) {
        // Number can be used because it is also a member of
        // PhoneNumber, which is the base class constraint.
        if(phList[i].Number == number)
          return phList[i];
      }

      // Number not in list.
      throw new NotFoundException();
    }

    // ...
}

// Demonstrate base class constraints.
class UseBaseClassConstraint {
  static void Main() {

    // The following code is OK because Friend
    // inherits PhoneNumber.
    PhoneList<Friend> plist = new PhoneList<Friend>();
    plist.Add(new Friend("Tom", "555-1234", true));
    plist.Add(new Friend("Gary", "555-6756", true));
    plist.Add(new Friend("Matt", "555-9254", false));

    try {
      // Find the number of a friend given a name.
      Friend frnd = plist.FindByName("Gary");

      Console.Write(frnd.Name + ": " + frnd.Number);

      if(frnd.IsWorkNumber)
        Console.WriteLine(" (work)");
      else
        Console.WriteLine();
    } catch(NotFoundException) {
      Console.WriteLine("Not Found");
    }

    Console.WriteLine();

    // The following code is also OK because Supplier
    // inherits PhoneNumber.
    PhoneList<Supplier> plist2 = new PhoneList<Supplier>();
    plist2.Add(new Supplier("Global Hardware", "555-8834"));
    plist2.Add(new Supplier("Computer Warehouse", "555-9256"));
    plist2.Add(new Supplier("NetworkCity", "555-2564"));
```

```
      try {
        // Find the name of a supplier given a number.
        Supplier sp = plist2.FindByNumber("555-2564");
        Console.WriteLine(sp.Name + ": " + sp.Number);
      } catch(NotFoundException) {
          Console.WriteLine("Not Found");
      }

      // The following declaration is invalid because EmailFriend
      // does NOT inherit PhoneNumber.
//    PhoneList<EmailFriend> plist3 =
//        new PhoneList<EmailFriend>(); // Error!
    }
}
```

The output from the program is shown here:

```
Gary: 555-6756 (work)

NetworkCity: 555-2564
```

You might want to try experimenting with this program a bit. For example, try creating different types of telephone lists. Also, try using **IsWorkNumber** from within **PhoneList**. As you will see, the compiler won't let you do it. The reason is that **IsWorkNumber** is a property defined by **Friend**, not by **PhoneNumber**. Thus, **PhoneList** has no knowledge of it.

Using an Interface Constraint

The interface constraint enables you to specify an interface that a type argument must implement. The interface constraint serves the same two important purposes as the base class constraint. First, it lets you use the members of the interface within the generic class. Second, it ensures that only type arguments that implement the specified interface are used. This means that for any given interface constraint, the type argument must be either the interface or a type that implements that interface.

The interface constraint uses this form of the **where** clause:

where *T* : *interface-name*

Here, *T* is the name of the type parameter, and *interface-name* is the name of the interface. More than one interface can be specified by using a comma-separated list. If a constraint includes both a base class and interface, then the base class must be listed first.

The following program illustrates the interface constraint by reworking the telephone list example shown in the previous section. In this version, the **PhoneNumber** class has been converted into an interface called **IPhoneNumber**. This interface is then implemented by **Friend** and **Supplier**.

```
// Use an interface constraint.

using System;

// A custom exception that is thrown if a name or number is not found.
class NotFoundException : Exception {
  /* Implement all of the Exception constructors. Notice that
```

```
    the constructors simply execute the base class constructor.
    Because NotFoundException adds nothing to Exception,
    there is no need for any further actions. */
  public NotFoundException() : base() { }
  public NotFoundException(string message) : base(message) { }
  public NotFoundException(string message, Exception innerException) :
    base(message, innerException) { }
  protected NotFoundException(
    System.Runtime.Serialization.SerializationInfo info,
    System.Runtime.Serialization.StreamingContext context) :
      base(info, context) { }
}

// An interface that supports a name and phone number.
public interface IPhoneNumber {

  string Number {
    get;
    set;
  }

  string Name {
    get;
    set;
  }
}

// A class of phone numbers for friends.
// It implements IPhoneNumber.
class Friend : IPhoneNumber {

  public Friend(string n, string num, bool wk) {
    Name = n;
    Number = num;

    IsWorkNumber = wk;
  }

  public bool IsWorkNumber { get; private set; }

  // Implement IPhoneNumber.
  public string Number { get; set; }
  public string Name { get; set; }

  // ...
}

// A class of phone numbers for suppliers.
class Supplier : IPhoneNumber {

  public Supplier(string n, string num) {
    Name = n;
    Number = num;
  }
```

```csharp
    // Implement IPhoneNumber.
    public string Number { get; set; }
    public string Name { get; set; }

    // ...
}

// Notice that this class does not implement IPhoneNumber.
class EmailFriend {
    // ...
}

// PhoneList can manage any type of phone list
// as long as it implements IPhoneNumber.
class PhoneList<T> where T : IPhoneNumber {
  T[] phList;
  int end;

  public PhoneList() {
    phList = new T[10];
    end = 0;
  }

  public bool Add(T newEntry) {
    if(end == 10) return false;

    phList[end] = newEntry;
    end++;

    return true;
  }

  // Given a name, find and return the phone info.
  public T FindByName(string name) {

    for(int i=0; i<end; i++) {
      // Name can be used because it is a member of
      // IPhoneNumber, which is the interface constraint.
      if(phList[i].Name == name)
        return phList[i];
    }

    // Name not in list.
    throw new NotFoundException();
  }

  // Given a number, find and return the phone info.
  public T FindByNumber(string number) {

    for(int i=0; i<end; i++) {
      // Number can be used because it is also a member of
      // IPhoneNumber, which is the interface constraint.
      if(phList[i].Number == number)
        return phList[i];
    }
```

```
      // Number not in list.
      throw new NotFoundException();
    }

  // ...
}

// Demonstrate interface constraints.
class UseInterfaceConstraint {
  static void Main() {

    // The following code is OK because Friend
    // implements IPhoneNumber.
    PhoneList<Friend> plist = new PhoneList<Friend>();
    plist.Add(new Friend("Tom", "555-1234", true));
    plist.Add(new Friend("Gary", "555-6756", true));
    plist.Add(new Friend("Matt", "555-9254", false));

    try {
      // Find the number of a friend given a name.
      Friend frnd = plist.FindByName("Gary");

      Console.Write(frnd.Name + ": " + frnd.Number);

      if(frnd.IsWorkNumber)
        Console.WriteLine(" (work)");
      else
        Console.WriteLine();
    } catch(NotFoundException) {
      Console.WriteLine("Not Found");
    }

    Console.WriteLine();

    // The following code is also OK because Supplier
    // implements IPhoneNumber.
    PhoneList<Supplier> plist2 = new PhoneList<Supplier>();
    plist2.Add(new Supplier("Global Hardware", "555-8834"));
    plist2.Add(new Supplier("Computer Warehouse", "555-9256"));
    plist2.Add(new Supplier("NetworkCity", "555-2564"));

    try {
      // Find the name of a supplier given a number.
      Supplier sp = plist2.FindByNumber("555-2564");
      Console.WriteLine(sp.Name + ": " + sp.Number);
    } catch(NotFoundException) {
        Console.WriteLine("Not Found");
    }

    // The following declaration is invalid because EmailFriend
    // does NOT implement IPhoneNumber.
//    PhoneList<EmailFriend> plist3 =
//        new PhoneList<EmailFriend>(); // Error!
  }
}
```

In this version of the program, the interface constraint specified by **PhoneList** requires that a type argument implement the **IPhoneList** interface. Because both **Friend** and **Supplier** implement **IPhoneList**, they are valid types to be bound to **T**. However, **EmailFriend** does not implement **IPhoneList** and cannot be bound to **T**. To prove this, remove the comment symbols from the last two lines in **Main( )**. As you will see, the program will not compile.

Using the new( ) Constructor Constraint

The **new( )** constructor constraint enables you to instantiate an object of a generic type. Normally, you cannot create an instance of a generic type parameter. However, the **new( )** constraint changes this because it requires that a type argument supply a public parameterless constructor. This can be the default constructor provided automatically when no explicit constructor is declared or a parameterless constructor explicitly defined by you. With the **new( )** constraint in place, you can invoke the parameterless constructor to create an object.

Here is a simple example that illustrates the use of **new( )**:

```
// Demonstrate a new() constructor constraint.

using System;

class MyClass {

  public MyClass() {
    // ...
  }

  //...
}

class Test<T> where T : new() {
  T obj;

  public Test() {
    // This works because of the new() constraint.
    obj = new T(); // create a T object
  }

  // ...
}

class ConsConstraintDemo {
  static void Main() {

    Test<MyClass> x = new Test<MyClass>();

  }
}
```

First, notice the declaration of the **Test** class, shown here:

```
class Test<T> where T : new() {
```

Because of the **new( )** constraint, any type argument must supply a parameterless constructor.

Next, examine the **Test** constructor, shown here:

```
public Test() {
  // This works because of the new() constraint.
  obj = new T(); // create a T object
}
```

A new object of type **T** is created and a reference to it is assigned to **obj**. This statement is valid only because the **new( )** constraint ensures that a constructor will be available. To prove this, try removing the **new( )** constraint and then attempt to recompile the program. As you will see, an error will be reported.

In **Main( )**, an object of type **Test** is instantiated, as shown here:

```
Test<MyClass> x = new Test<MyClass>();
```

Notice that the type argument is **MyClass**, and that **MyClass** defines a parameterless constructor. Thus, it is valid for use as a type argument for **Test**. It must be emphasized that it was not necessary for **MyClass** to explicitly declare a parameterless constructor. Its default constructor would also satisfy the constraint. However, if a class needs other constructors in addition to a parameterless one, then it would be necessary to also explicitly declare a parameterless version, too.

There are three important points about using **new( )**. First, it can be used with other constraints, but it must be the last constraint in the list. Second, **new( )** allows you to construct an object using only the parameterless constructor, even when other constructors are available. In other words, it is not permissible to pass arguments to the constructor of a type parameter. Third, you cannot use **new( )** in conjunction with a value type constraint, described next.

The Reference Type and Value Type Constraints

The next two constraints enable you to indicate that a type argument must be either a reference type or a value type. These are useful in the few cases in which the difference between reference and value types is important to generic code. Here is the general form of the reference type constraint:

where T : class

In this form of the **where** clause, the keyword **class** specifies that T must be a reference type. Thus, an attempt to use a value type, such as **int** or **bool**, for T will result in a compilation error.

Here is the general form of the value type constraint:

where T : struct

In this case, the keyword **struct** specifies that T must be a value type. (Recall that structures are value types.) Thus, an attempt to use a reference type, such as **string**, for T will result in a compilation error. In both cases, when additional constraints are present, **class** or **struct** must be the first constraint in the list.

Here is an example that demonstrates the reference type constraint:

```
// Demonstrate a reference constraint.

using System;

class MyClass {
  //...
}

// Use a reference constraint.
class Test<T> where T : class {
  T obj;

  public Test() {
    // The following statement is legal only
    // because T is guaranteed to be a reference
    // type, which can be assigned the value null.
    obj = null;
  }

  // ...
}

class ClassConstraintDemo {
  static void Main() {

    // The following is OK because MyClass is a class.
    Test<MyClass> x = new Test<MyClass>();

    // The next line is in error because int is a value type.
//    Test<int> y = new Test<int>();
  }
}
```

First, notice how **Test** is declared:

```
class Test<T> where T : class {
```

The **class** constraint requires that any type argument for **T** be a reference type. In this program, this is necessary because of what occurs inside the **Test** constructor:

```
public Test() {
  // The following statement is legal only
  // because T is guaranteed to be a reference
  // type, which can be assigned the value null.
  obj = null;
}
```

Here, **obj** (which is of type **T**) is assigned the value **null**. This assignment is valid only for reference types. As a general rule, you cannot assign **null** to a value type. (The exception to this rule is the *nullable type*, which is a special structure type that encapsulates a value type and allows the value **null**. See Chapter 20 for details.) Therefore, without the constraint, the assignment would not have been valid and the compile would have failed. This is one case in which the difference between value types and reference types might be important to a generic routine.

The value type constraint is the complement of the reference type constraint. It simply ensures that any type argument is a value type, including a **struct** or an **enum**. (In this context, a nullable type is not considered a value type.) Here is an example:

```
// Demonstrate a value type constraint.

using System;

struct MyStruct {
  //...
}

class MyClass {
  // ...
}

class Test<T> where T : struct {
  T obj;

  public Test(T x) {
    obj = x;
  }

  // ...
}

class ValueConstraintDemo {
  static void Main() {

    // Both of these declarations are legal.

    Test<MyStruct> x = new Test<MyStruct>(new MyStruct());

    Test<int> y = new Test<int>(10);

    // But, the following declaration is illegal!
//    Test<MyClass> z = new Test<MyClass>(new MyClass());
  }
}
```

In this program, **Test** is declared as shown here:

```
class Test<T> where T : struct {
```

Because **T** of **Test** now has the **struct** constraint, **T** can be bound only to value type arguments. This means that **Test<MyStruct>** and **Test<int>** are valid, but **Test<MyClass>** is not. To prove this, try removing the comment symbols from the start of the last line in the program and recompiling. An error will be reported.

Using a Constraint to Establish a Relationship Between Two Type Parameters

There is a variation of the base class constraint that allows you to establish a relationship between two type parameters. For example, consider the following generic class declaration:

```
class Gen<T, V> where V : T {
```

In this declaration, the **where** clause tells the compiler that the type argument bound to **V** must be identical to or inherit from the type argument bound to **T**. If this relationship is not present when an object of type **Gen** is declared, then a compile-time error will result. A constraint that uses a type parameter, such as that just shown, is called a *naked type constraint*. The following example illustrates this constraint:

```
// Create relationship between two type parameters.

using System;

class A {
  //...
}

class B : A {
  // ...
}

// Here, V must be or inherit from T.
class Gen<T, V> where V : T {
  // ...
}

class NakedConstraintDemo {
  static void Main() {

    // This declaration is OK because B inherits A.
    Gen<A, B> x = new Gen<A, B>();

    // This declaration is in error because
    // A does not inherit B.
//    Gen<B, A> y = new Gen<B, A>();

  }
}
```

First, notice that class **B** inherits class **A**. Next, examine the two **Gen** declarations in **Main( )**. As the comments explain, the first declaration

```
Gen<A, B> x = new Gen<A, B>();
```

is legal because **B** inherits **A**. However, the second declaration

```
//    Gen<B, A> y = new Gen<B, A>();
```

is illegal because **A** does not inherit **B**.

Using Multiple Constraints

There can be more than one constraint associated with a type parameter. When this is the case, use a comma-separated list of constraints. In this list, the first constraint must be **class** or **struct** (if present) or the base class (if one is specified). It is illegal to specify both a **class** or **struct** constraint and a base class constraint. Next in the list must be any interface constraints. The **new( )** constraint must be last. For example, this is a valid declaration.

```
class Gen<T> where T : MyClass, IMyInterface, new() { // ...
```

In this case, **T** must be replaced by a type argument that inherits **MyClass**, implements **IMyInterface**, and has a parameterless constructor.

When using two or more type parameters, you can specify a constraint for each parameter by using a separate **where** clause. Here is an example:

```
// Use multiple where clauses.

using System;

// Gen has two type arguments and both have a where clause.
class Gen<T, V> where T : class
                where V : struct {
  T ob1;
  V ob2;

  public Gen(T t, V v) {
    ob1 = t;
    ob2 = v;
  }
}

class MultipleConstraintDemo {
  static void Main() {
    // This is OK because string is a class and
    // int is a value type.
    Gen<string, int> obj = new Gen<string, int>("test", 11);

    // The next line is wrong because bool is not
    // a reference type.
//    Gen<bool, int> obj = new Gen<bool, int>(true, 11);
  }
}
```

In this example, **Gen** takes two type arguments and both have a **where** clause. Pay special attention to its declaration:

```
class Gen<T, V> where T : class
                where V : struct {
```

Notice the only thing that separates the first **where** clause from the second is whitespace. No other punctuation is required or valid.

Creating a Default Value of a Type Parameter

When writing generic code, there will be times when the difference between value types and reference types is an issue. One such situation occurs when you want to give a variable of a type parameter a default value. For reference types, the default value is **null**. For non-**struct** value types, the default value is 0, or **false** for **bool**. The default value for a **struct** is an object of that **struct** with all fields set to their defaults. Thus, trouble occurs if you want to give a variable of a type parameter a default value. What value would you use: **null**, 0, **false**, or something else?

For example, given a generic class called **Test** declared like this:

```
class Test<T> {
  T obj;
  // ...
```

if you want to give **obj** a default value, neither

```
obj = null; // works only for reference types
```

nor

```
obj = 0; // works only for numeric types and enums
```

works in all classes.

The solution to this problem is to use another form of **default**, shown here:

default(*type*)

This is the operator form of **default**, and it produces a default value of the specified *type*, no matter what type is used. Thus, continuing with the example, to assign **obj** a default value of type **T**, you would use this statement:

```
obj = default(T);
```

This will work for all type arguments, whether they are value or reference types.

Here is a short program that demonstrates **default**:

```
// Demonstrate the default operator.

using System;

class MyClass {
  //...
}

// Construct a default value of T.
class Test<T> {
  public T obj;

  public Test() {
    // The following statement would work only for reference types.
//    obj = null; // can't use

    // The following statement will work only for numeric value types.
//    obj = 0; // can't use
```

```
    // This statement works for both reference and value types.
    obj = default(T); // Works!
  }

  // ...
}

class DefaultDemo {
  static void Main() {

    // Construct Test using a reference type.
    Test<MyClass> x = new Test<MyClass>();

    if(x.obj == null)
      Console.WriteLine("x.obj is null.");

    // Construct Test using a value type.
    Test<int> y = new Test<int>();

    if(y.obj == 0)
      Console.WriteLine("y.obj is 0.");
  }
}
```

The output is shown here:

```
x.obj is null.
y.obj is 0.
```

Generic Structures

C# allows you to create generic structures. The syntax is the same as for generic classes. For example, in the following program, the **XY** structure, which stores X, Y coordinates, is generic:

```
// Demonstrate a generic struct.
using System;

// This structure is generic.
struct XY<T> {
  T x;
  T y;

  public XY(T a, T b) {
    x = a;
    y = b;
  }

  public T X {
    get { return x; }
    set { x = value; }
  }

  public T Y {
    get { return y; }
```

```
    set { y = value; }
  }
}

class StructTest {
  static void Main() {
    XY<int> xy = new XY<int>(10, 20);
    XY<double> xy2 = new XY<double>(88.0, 99.0);

    Console.WriteLine(xy.X + ", " + xy.Y);

    Console.WriteLine(xy2.X + ", " + xy2.Y);
  }
}
```

The output is shown here:

```
10, 20
88, 99
```

Like generic classes, generic structures can have constraints. For example, this version of **XY** restricts type arguments to value types:

```
struct XY<T> where T : struct {
// ...
```

Creating a Generic Method

As the preceding examples have shown, methods inside a generic class can make use of a class' type parameter and are, therefore, automatically generic relative to the type parameter. However, it is possible to declare a generic method that uses one or more type parameters of its own. Furthermore, it is possible to create a generic method that is enclosed within a non-generic class.

Let's begin with an example. The following program declares a non-generic class called **ArrayUtils** and a static generic method within that class called **CopyInsert( )**. The **CopyInsert( )** method copies the contents of one array to another, inserting a new element at a specified location in the process. It can be used with any type of array.

```
// Demonstrate a generic method.

using System;

// A class of array utilities. Notice that this is not
// a generic class.
class ArrayUtils {

  // Copy an array, inserting a new element
  // in the process. This is a generic method.
  public static bool CopyInsert<T>(T e, uint idx,
                                    T[] src, T[] target) {

    // See if target array is big enough.
    if(target.Length < src.Length+1)
      return false;
```

```
      // Copy src to target, inserting e at idx in the process.
      for(int i=0, j=0; i < src.Length; i++, j++) {
        if(i == idx) {
          target[j] = e;
          j++;
        }
        target[j] = src[i];
      }

      return true;
    }
  }

  class GenMethDemo {
    static void Main() {
      int[] nums = { 1, 2, 3 };
      int[] nums2 = new int[4];

      // Display contents of nums.
      Console.Write("Contents of nums: ");
      foreach(int x in nums)
        Console.Write(x + " ");

      Console.WriteLine();

      // Operate on an int array.
      ArrayUtils.CopyInsert(99, 2, nums, nums2);

      // Display contents of nums2.
      Console.Write("Contents of nums2: ");
      foreach(int x in nums2)
        Console.Write(x + " ");

      Console.WriteLine();


      // Now, use copyInsert on an array of strings.
      string[] strs = { "Generics", "are", "powerful."};
      string[] strs2 = new string[4];

      // Display contents of strs.
      Console.Write("Contents of strs: ");
      foreach(string s in strs)
        Console.Write(s + " ");

      Console.WriteLine();

      // Insert into a string array.
      ArrayUtils.CopyInsert("in C#", 1, strs, strs2);

      // Display contents of strs2.
      Console.Write("Contents of strs2: ");
      foreach(string s in strs2)
        Console.Write(s + " ");
```

```
     Console.WriteLine();

     // This call is invalid because the first argument
     // is of type double, and the third and fourth arguments
     // have element types of int.
//     ArrayUtils.CopyInsert(0.01, 2, nums, nums2);
  }
}
```

The output from the program is shown here:

```
Contents of nums: 1 2 3
Contents of nums2: 1 2 99 3
Contents of strs: Generics are powerful.
Contents of strs2: Generics in C# are powerful.
```

Let's examine **CopyInsert( )** closely. First, notice how it is declared by this line:

```
public static bool CopyInsert<T>(T e, uint idx,
                                 T[] src, T[] target) {
```

The type parameter is declared *after* the method name, but *before* the parameter list. Also notice that **CopyInsert( )** is static, enabling it to be called independently of any object. Understand, though, that generic methods can be either static or non-static. There is no restriction in this regard.

Now, notice how **CopyInsert( )** is called within **Main( )** by use of the normal call syntax, without the need to specify type arguments. This is because the types of the arguments are automatically discerned, and the type of **T** is adjusted accordingly. This process is called *type inference*. For example, in the first call:

```
ArrayUtils.CopyInsert(99, 2, nums, nums2);
```

the type of **T** becomes **int** because 99 and the element types of **nums** and **nums2** are **int**. In the second call, **string** types are used, and **T** is replaced by **string**.

Now, notice the commented-out code, shown here:

```
//     ArrayUtils.CopyInsert(0.01, 2, nums, nums2);
```

If you remove the comments and then try to compile the program, you will receive an error. The reason is that the type of the first argument is **double**, but the element types of **nums** and **nums2** are **int**. However, all three types must be substituted for the same type parameter, **T**. This causes a type-mismatch, which results in a compile-time error. This ability to enforce type safety is one of the most important advantages of generic methods.

The syntax used to create **CopyInsert( )** can be generalized. Here is the general form of a generic method:

ret-type meth-name<type-param-list>(param-list) { // ...

In all cases, *type-param-list* is a comma-separated list of type parameters. Notice that for a generic method, the type parameter list follows the method name.

Using Explicit Type Arguments to Call a Generic Method

Although implicit type inference is adequate for most invocations of a generic method, it is possible to explicitly specify the type argument. To do so, specify the type argument after the method name when calling the method. For example, here **CopyInsert( )** is explicitly passed type **string**:

```
ArrayUtils.CopyInsert<string>("in C#", 1, strs, strs2);
```

You will need to explicitly specify the type when the compiler cannot infer the type for the **T** parameter or if you want to override the type inference.

Using a Constraint with a Generic Method

You can add constraints to the type arguments of a generic method by specifying them after the parameter list. For example, the following version of **CopyInsert( )** will work only with reference types:

```
public static bool CopyInsert<T>(T e, uint idx,
                                 T[] src, T[] target) where T : class {
```

If you were to try this version in the program shown earlier, then the following call to **CopyInsert( )** would not compile because **int** is a value type, not a reference type:

```
// Now wrong because T must be reference type!
ArrayUtils.CopyInsert(99, 2, nums, nums2); // Now illegal!
```

Generic Delegates

Like methods, delegates can also be generic. To declare a generic delegate, use this general form:

delegate *ret-type delegate-name<type-parameter-list>(arg-list)*;

Notice the placement of the type parameter list. It immediately follows the delegate's name. The advantage of generic delegates is that they let you define, in a type-safe manner, a generalized form that can then be matched to any compatible method.

The following program demonstrates a generic delegate called **SomeOp** that has one type parameter called **T**. It returns type **T** and takes an argument of type **T**.

```
// A simple generic delegate.

using System;

// Declare a generic delegate.
delegate T SomeOp<T>(T v);

class GenDelegateDemo {
  // Return the summation of the argument.
  static int Sum(int v) {
    int result = 0;
    for(int i=v; i>0; i--)
```

```
        result += i;

      return result;
    }

  // Return a string containing the reverse of the argument.
  static string Reflect(string str) {
    string result = "";

    foreach(char ch in str)
      result = ch + result;

    return result;
  }

  static void Main() {
    // Construct an int delegate.
    SomeOp<int> intDel = Sum;
    Console.WriteLine(intDel(3));

    // Construct a string delegate.
    SomeOp<string> strDel = Reflect;
    Console.WriteLine(strDel("Hello"));
  }
}
```

The output is shown here:

```
6
olleH
```

Let's look closely at this program. First, notice how the **SomeOp** delegate is declared:

```
delegate T SomeOp<T>(T v);
```

Notice that **T** can be used as the return type even though the type parameter **T** is specified after the name **SomeOp**.

Inside **GenDelegateDemo**, the methods **Sum( )** and **Reflect( )** are declared, as shown here:

```
static int Sum(int v) {
```

```
static string Reflect(string str) {
```

The **Sum( )** method returns the summation of the integer value passed as an argument. The **Reflect( )** method returns a string that is the reverse of the string passed as an argument.

Inside **Main( )**, a delegate called **intDel** is instantiated and assigned a reference to **Sum( )**:

```
SomeOp<int> intDel = Sum;
```

Because **Sum( )** takes an **int** argument and returns an **int** value, **Sum( )** is compatible with an **int** instance of **SomeOp**.

In similar fashion, the delegate **strDel** is created and assigned a reference to **Reflect( )**:

```
SomeOp<string> strDel = Reflect;
```

Because **Reflect( )** takes a **string** argument and returns a **string** result, it is compatible with the string version of **SomeOp**.

Because of the type safety inherent in generics, you cannot assign incompatible methods to delegates. For example, assuming the preceding program, the following statement would be in error:

```
SomeOp<int> intDel = Reflect; // Error!
```

Because **Reflect( )** takes a **string** argument and returns a **string** result, it cannot be assigned to an **int** version of **SomeOp**.

Generic Interfaces

In addition to generic classes and methods, you can also have generic interfaces. Generic interfaces are specified just like generic classes. Here is an example that reworks the **ISeries** interface developed in Chapter 12. (Recall that **ISeries** defines the interface to a class that generates a series of numbers.) The data type upon which it operates is now specified by a type parameter.

```
// Demonstrate a generic interface.

using System;

public interface ISeries<T> {
  T GetNext(); // return next element in series
  void Reset(); // restart the series
  void SetStart(T v); // set the starting element
}

// Implement ISeries.
class ByTwos<T> : ISeries<T> {
  T start;
  T val;

  // This delegate defines the form of a method
  // that will be called when the next element in
  // the series is needed.
  public delegate T IncByTwo(T v);

  // This delegate reference will be assigned the
  // method passed to the ByTwos constructor.
  IncByTwo incr;

  public ByTwos(IncByTwo incrMeth) {
    start = default(T);
    val = default(T);
    incr = incrMeth;
  }
```

```
    public T GetNext() {
      val = incr(val);
      return val;
    }

    public void Reset() {
      val = start;
    }

    public void SetStart(T v) {
      start = v;
      val = start;
    }
}

class ThreeD {
  public int x, y, z;

  public ThreeD(int a, int b, int c) {
    x = a;
    y = b;
    z = c;
  }
}

class GenIntfDemo {
  // Define plus two for int.
  static int IntPlusTwo(int v) {
    return v + 2;
  }

  // Define plus two for double.
  static double DoublePlusTwo(double v) {
    return v + 2.0;
  }

  // Define plus two for ThreeD.
  static ThreeD ThreeDPlusTwo(ThreeD v) {
    if(v==null) return new ThreeD(0, 0, 0);
    else return new ThreeD(v.x + 2, v.y + 2, v.z + 2);
  }

  static void Main() {

    // Demonstrate int series.
    ByTwos<int> intBT = new ByTwos<int>(IntPlusTwo);

    for(int i=0; i < 5; i++)
      Console.Write(intBT.GetNext() + "  ");

    Console.WriteLine();
```

```
    // Demonstrate double series.
    ByTwos<double> dblBT = new ByTwos<double>(DoublePlusTwo);

    dblBT.SetStart(11.4);

    for(int i=0; i < 5; i++)
      Console.Write(dblBT.GetNext() + "   ");

    Console.WriteLine();


    // Demonstrate ThreeD series.
    ByTwos<ThreeD> ThrDBT = new ByTwos<ThreeD>(ThreeDPlusTwo);

    ThreeD coord;
    for(int i=0; i < 5; i++) {
      coord = ThrDBT.GetNext();
      Console.Write(coord.x + "," +
                    coord.y + "," +
                    coord.z + "   ");
    }

    Console.WriteLine();
  }
}
```

The output is shown here:

```
2   4   6   8   10
13.4   15.4   17.4   19.4   21.4
0,0,0   2,2,2   4,4,4   6,6,6   8,8,8
```

There are several things of interest in the preceding example. First, notice how **ISeries** is declared:

```
public interface ISeries<T> {
```

As mentioned, a generic interface uses a syntax similar to that of a generic class.

Now, notice how **ByTwos**, which implements **ISeries**, is declared:

```
class ByTwos<T> : ISeries<T> {
```

The type parameter **T** is specified by **ByTwos** and is also specified in **ISeries**. This is important. A class that implements a generic version of a generic interface must, itself, be generic. For example, the following declaration would be illegal because **T** is not defined:

```
class ByTwos : ISeries<T> { // Wrong!
```

The type argument required by the **ISeries** interface must be passed to **ByTwos**. Otherwise, there is no way for the interface to receive the type argument.

Next, the current value of the series, **val**, and the starting value, **start**, are declared to be objects of the generic type **T**. Then, a delegate called **IncByTwo** is declared. This delegate defines the form of a method that will be used to increase an object of type **T** by two. In order for **ByTwos** to work with any type of data, there must be some way to define what an increase by two means for each type of data. This is achieved by passing to the **ByTwos** constructor a reference to a method that performs an increase by two. This reference is stored in **incr**. When the next element in the series is needed, that method is called through the **incr** delegate to obtain the next value in the series.

Notice the class **ThreeD**. It encapsulates three-dimensional (X,Z,Y) coordinates. It is used to demonstrate **ByTwos** on a class type.

In **GenIntfDemo**, three increment methods are declared; one for **int**, one for **double**, and one for objects of type **ThreeD**. These are passed to the **ByTwos** constructor when objects of their respective types are created. Pay special attention to **ThreeDPlusTwo( )**, shown here:

```
// Define plus two for ThreeD.
static ThreeD ThreeDPlusTwo(ThreeD v) {
  if(v==null) return new ThreeD(0, 0, 0);
  else return new ThreeD(v.x + 2, v.y + 2, v.z + 2);
}
```

Notice that it first checks if **v** is **null**. If it is, then it returns a new **ThreeD** object in which all fields are set to zero. The reason for this is that **v** is set to **default(T)** by the **ByTwos** constructor. This value is zero for value types and **null** for object types. Thus, (unless **SetStart( )** has been called) for the first increment, **v** will contain **null** instead of a reference to an object. This means that for the first increment, a new object is required.

A type parameter for a generic interface can have constraints in the same way as it can for a generic class. For example, this version of **ISeries** restricts its use to reference types:

```
public interface ISeries<T> where T : class {
```

When this version of **ISeries** is implemented, the implementing class must also specify the same constraint for **T**, as shown here:

```
class ByTwos<T> : ISeries<T> where T : class {
```

Because of the reference constraint, this version of **ISeries** cannot be used on value types. Thus, in the preceding program, only **ByTwos<ThreeD>** would be valid. **ByTwos<int>** and **ByTwos<double>** would be invalid.

Comparing Instances of a Type Parameter

Sometimes you will want to compare two instances of a type parameter. For example, you might want to write a generic method called **IsIn( )** that returns true if some value is contained within an array. To accomplish this, you might first try something like this:

```
// This won't work!
public static bool IsIn<T>(T what, T[] obs) {
  foreach(T v in obs)
    if(v == what) // Error!
```

```
      return true;

  return false;
}
```

Unfortunately, this attempt won't work. Because **T** is a generic type, the compiler has no way to know precisely how two objects should be compared for equality. Should a bitwise comparison be done? Should only certain fields be compared? Should reference equality be used? The compiler has no way to answer these questions. Fortunately, there is a solution.

To enable two objects of a generic type parameter to be compared, they must implement the **IComparable** or **IComparable<T>**, and/or **IEquatable<T>** interfaces. Both versions of **IComparable** define the **CompareTo( )** method and **IEquatable<T>** defines the **Equals( )** method. The **IComparable** interfaces are intended for use when you need to determine the relative order of two objects. **IEquatable** is used for determining the equality of two objects. These interfaces are defined by the **System** namespace, and they are implemented by all of C#'s built-in types, including **int**, **string**, and **double**. They are also easy to implement for classes that you create. Let's begin with **IEquatable<T>**.

The **IEquatable<T>** interface is declared like this:

```
public interface IEquatable<T>
```

The type of data being compared is passed as a type argument to **T**. It defines the **Equals( )** method, which is shown here:

```
bool Equals(T other)
```

It compares the invoking object to *other*. It returns true if the two objects are equal and false otherwise.

When implementing **IEquatable<T>**, you will usually also need to override **GetHashCode( )** and **Equals(Object)** defined by **Object**, so they act in a manner compatible with your implementation of **Equals( )**. The program that follows shows an example.

Using **IEquatable<T>**, here is a corrected version of **IsIn( )**:

```
// Require IEquatable<T> interface.
public static bool IsIn<T>(T what, T[] obs) where T : IEquatable<T> {
  foreach(T v in obs)
    if(v.Equals(what)) // Uses Equals().
      return true;

  return false;
}
```

Notice the use of the constraint

```
where T : IEquatable<T>
```

This constraint ensures that only types that implement **IEquatable** are valid type arguments for **IsIn( )**. Inside **IsIn( )**, **Equals( )** is used to determine if one object is equal to another.

To determine the relative order of two elements, use the **IComparable** interface. It has two forms: generic and non-generic. The generic form has the advantage of being type-safe, so it is the form used here. **IComparable<T>** is declared like this:

```
public interface IComparable<T>
```

The type of data being compared is passed as a type argument to **T**. It defines **CompareTo( )**, which is shown here:

　　int CompareTo(T *other*)

It compares the invoking object to *other*. It returns zero if the two objects are equal, a positive value if the invoking object is greater than *other*, and a negative value if the invoking object is less than *other*.

　　To use **CompareTo( )**, you must specify a constraint that requires the type argument to implement the **IComparable<T>** interface. Then, when you need to compare two instances of the type parameter, simply call **CompareTo( )**.

　　Here is an example that uses **IComparable<T>**. It is a method called **InRange( )** that returns true if an object is within the range of elements contained in a sorted array.

```
// Require IComparable<T> interface. This method assumes
// a sorted array. It returns true if what is inside the range
// of elements passed to obs.
public static bool InRange<T>(T what, T[] obs) where T : IComparable<T> {
  if(what.CompareTo(obs[0]) < 0 ||
     what.CompareTo(obs[obs.Length-1]) > 0) return false;
  return true;
}
```

　　The following program shows **IsIn( )** and **InRange( )** in action:

```
// Demonstrate IComparable<T> and IEquatable<T>.

using System;

// Now MyClass implements IComparable<T> and IEquatable<T>.
class MyClass : IComparable<MyClass>, IEquatable<MyClass> {
  public int Val;

  public MyClass(int x) { Val = x; }

  // Implement IComparable<T>.
  public int CompareTo(MyClass other) {
    return Val - other.Val; // Now, no cast is needed.
  }

  // Implement IEquatable<T>.
  public bool Equals(MyClass other) {
    return Val == other.Val;
  }

  // An override of Equals(Object).
  public override bool Equals(Object obj) {
    if(obj is MyClass)
      return Equals((MyClass) obj);
    return false;
  }
```

```csharp
    // An override of GetHashCode().
    public override int GetHashCode() {
      return Val.GetHashCode();
    }
}

class CompareDemo {

  // Require IEquatable<T> interface.
  public static bool IsIn<T>(T what, T[] obs) where T : IEquatable<T> {
    foreach(T v in obs)
      if(v.Equals(what)) // Uses Equals()
        return true;

    return false;
  }

  // Require IComparable<T> interface. This method assumes
  // a sorted array. It returns true if what is inside the range
  // of elements passed to obs.
  public static bool InRange<T>(T what, T[] obs) where T : IComparable<T> {
    if(what.CompareTo(obs[0]) < 0 ||
       what.CompareTo(obs[obs.Length-1]) > 0) return false;
    return true;
  }

  // Demonstrate comparisons.
  static void Main() {

    // Use IsIn() with int.
    int[] nums = { 1, 2, 3, 4, 5 };

    if(IsIn(2, nums))
      Console.WriteLine("2 is found.");

    if(IsIn(99, nums))
      Console.WriteLine("This won't display.");


    // Use IsIn() with MyClass.
    MyClass[] mcs = { new MyClass(1), new MyClass(2),
                      new MyClass(3), new MyClass(4) };

    if(IsIn(new MyClass(3), mcs))
      Console.WriteLine("MyClass(3) is found.");

    if(IsIn(new MyClass(99), mcs))
      Console.WriteLine("This won't display.");


    // Use InRange() with int.
    if(InRange(2, nums))
```

```
      Console.WriteLine("2 is within the range of nums.");
    if(InRange(1, nums))
      Console.WriteLine("1 is within the range of nums.");
    if(InRange(5, nums))
      Console.WriteLine("5 is within the range of nums.");
    if(!InRange(0, nums))
      Console.WriteLine("0 is NOT within the range of nums.");
    if(!InRange(6, nums))
      Console.WriteLine("6 is NOT within the range of nums.");

    // Use InRange() with MyClass.
    if(InRange(new MyClass(2), mcs))
      Console.WriteLine("MyClass(2) is within the range of mcs.");
    if(InRange(new MyClass(1), mcs))
      Console.WriteLine("MyClass(1) is within the range of mcs.");
    if(InRange(new MyClass(4), mcs))
      Console.WriteLine("MyClass(4) is within the range of mcs.");
    if(!InRange(new MyClass(0), mcs))
      Console.WriteLine("MyClass(0) is NOT within the range of mcs.");
    if(!InRange(new MyClass(5), mcs))
      Console.WriteLine("MyClass(5) is NOT within the range of mcs.");
  }
}
```

The output is shown here:

```
2 is found.
MyClass(3) is found.
2 is within the range of nums.
1 is within the range of nums.
5 is within the range of nums.
0 is NOT within the range of nums.
6 is NOT within the range of nums.
MyClass(2) is within the range of mcs.
MyClass(1) is within the range of mcs.
MyClass(4) is within the range of mcs.
MyClass(0) is NOT within the range of mcs.
MyClass(5) is NOT within the range of mcs.
```

NOTE *If a type parameter specifies a reference or a base class constraint, then = = and ! = can be applied to instances of that type parameter, but they only test for reference equality. To compare values, you must require **IComparable**, **IComparable<T>**, or **IEquatable<T>**.*

Generic Class Hierarchies

Generic classes can be part of a class hierarchy in just the same way as non-generic classes. Thus, a generic class can act as a base class or be a derived class. The key difference between generic and non-generic hierarchies is that in a generic hierarchy, any type arguments needed by a generic base class must be passed up the hierarchy by all derived classes. This is similar to the way that constructor arguments must be passed up a hierarchy.

Using a Generic Base Class

Here is a simple example of a hierarchy that uses a generic base class:

```
// A simple generic class hierarchy.
using System;

// A generic base class.
class Gen<T> {
  T ob;

  public Gen(T o) {
    ob = o;
  }

  // Return ob.
  public T GetOb() {
    return ob;
  }
}

// A class derived from Gen.
class Gen2<T> : Gen<T> {
  public Gen2(T o) : base(o) {
    // ...
  }
}

class GenHierDemo {
  static void Main() {
    Gen2<string> g2 = new Gen2<string>("Hello");

    Console.WriteLine(g2.GetOb());
  }
}
```

In this hierarchy, **Gen2** inherits the generic class **Gen**. Notice how **Gen2** is declared by the following line:

```
class Gen2<T> : Gen<T> {
```

The type parameter **T** is specified by **Gen2** and is also passed to **Gen**. This means that whatever type is passed to **Gen2** will also be passed to **Gen**. For example, this declaration

```
Gen2<string> g2 = new Gen2<string>("Hello");
```

passes **string** as the type parameter to **Gen**. Thus, the **ob** inside the **Gen** portion of **Gen2** will be of type **string**.

Notice also that **Gen2** does not use the type parameter **T** except to pass it along to the **Gen** base class. Thus, even if a derived class would otherwise not need to be generic, it still must specify the type parameter(s) required by its generic base class.

Of course, a derived class is free to add its own type parameters, if needed. For example, here is a variation on the preceding hierarchy in which **Gen2** adds a type parameter of its own:

```
// A derived class can add its own type parameters.
using System;

// A generic base class.
class Gen<T> {
  T ob; // declare a variable of type T

  // Pass the constructor a reference of type T.
  public Gen(T o) {
    ob = o;
  }

  // Return ob.
  public T GetOb() {
    return ob;
  }
}

// A derived class of Gen that defines a second
// type parameter, called V.
class Gen2<T, V> : Gen<T> {
  V ob2;

  public Gen2(T o, V o2) : base(o) {
    ob2 = o2;
  }

  public V GetObj2() {
    return ob2;
  }
}

// Create an object of type Gen2.
class GenHierDemo2 {
  static void Main() {

    // Create a Gen2 object for string and int.
    Gen2<string, int> x =
      new Gen2<string, int>("Value is: ", 99);

    Console.Write(x.GetOb());
    Console.WriteLine(x.GetObj2());
  }
}
```

Notice the declaration of this version of **Gen2**, which is shown here:

```
class Gen2<T, V> : Gen<T> {
```

Here, **T** is the type passed to **Gen**, and **V** is the type that is specific to **Gen2**. **V** is used to declare an object called **ob2** and as a return type for the method **GetObj2( )**. In **Main( )**, a

Gen2 object is created in which type parameter **T** is **string**, and type parameter **V** is **int**. The program displays the following, expected, result:

```
Value is: 99
```

A Generic Derived Class

It is perfectly acceptable for a non-generic class to be the base class of a generic derived class. For example, consider this program:

```
// A non-generic class can be the base class of a generic derived class.
using System;

// A non-generic class.
class NonGen {
  int num;

  public NonGen(int i) {
    num = i;
  }

  public int GetNum() {
    return num;
  }
}

// A generic derived class.
class Gen<T> : NonGen {
  T ob;

  public Gen(T o, int i) : base (i) {
    ob = o;
  }

  // Return ob.
  public T GetOb() {
    return ob;
  }
}

// Create a Gen object.
class HierDemo3 {
  static void Main() {

    // Create a Gen object for string.
    Gen<String> w = new Gen<String>("Hello", 47);

    Console.Write(w.GetOb() + " ");
    Console.WriteLine(w.GetNum());
  }
}
```

The output from the program is shown here:

```
Hello 47
```

In the program, notice how **Gen** inherits **NonGen** in the following declaration:

```
class Gen<T> : NonGen {
```

Because **NonGen** is not generic, no type argument is specified. Thus, even though **Gen** declares the type parameter **T**, it is not needed by (nor can it be used by) **NonGen**. Thus, **NonGen** is inherited by **Gen** in the normal way. No special conditions apply.

Overriding Virtual Methods in a Generic Class

A virtual method in a generic class can be overridden just like any other method. For example, consider this program in which the virtual method **GetOb( )** is overridden:

```
// Overriding a virtual method in a generic class.
using System;

// A generic base class.
class Gen<T> {
  protected T ob;

  public Gen(T o) {
    ob = o;
  }

  // Return ob. This method is virtual.
  public virtual T GetOb() {
    Console.Write("Gen's GetOb(): " );
    return ob;
  }
}

// A derived class of Gen that overrides GetOb().
class Gen2<T> : Gen<T> {

  public Gen2(T o) : base(o) {  }

  // Override GetOb().
  public override T GetOb() {
    Console.Write("Gen2's GetOb(): ");
    return ob;
  }
}

// Demonstrate generic method override.
class OverrideDemo {
  static void Main() {

    // Create a Gen object for int.
    Gen<int> iOb = new Gen<int>(88);

    // This calls Gen's version of GetOb().
    Console.WriteLine(iOb.GetOb());
```

```
      // Now, create a Gen2 object and assign its
      // reference to iOb (which is a Gen<int> variable).
      iOb = new Gen2<int>(99);

      // This calls Gen2's version of GetOb().
      Console.WriteLine(iOb.GetOb());
   }
}
```

The output is shown here:

```
Gen's GetOb(): 88
Gen2's GetOb(): 99
```

As the output confirms, the overridden version of **GetOb( )** is called for an object of type **Gen2**, but the base class version is called for an object of type **Gen**.

Notice one other thing: This line

```
iOb = new Gen2<int>(99);
```

is valid because **iOb** is a variable of type **Gen<int>**. Thus, it can refer to any object of type **Gen<int>** or any object of a class derived from **Gen<int>**, including **Gen2<int>**. Of course, **iOb** couldn't be used to refer to an object of type **Gen2<double>**, for example, because of the type mismatch.

Overloading Methods That Use Type Parameters

Methods that use type parameters to declare method parameters can be overloaded. However, the rules are a bit more stringent than they are for methods that don't use type parameters. In general, a method that uses a type parameter as the data type of a parameter can be overloaded as long as the signatures of the two versions differ. This means the type and/or number of their parameters must differ. However, the determination of type difference is not based on the generic type parameter, but on the type argument substituted for the type parameter when a constructed type is created. Therefore, it is possible to overload a method that uses type parameters in such a way that it "looks right," but won't work in all specific cases.

For example, consider this generic class:

```
// Ambiguity can result when overloading methods that
// use type parameters.
//
// This program will not compile.

using System;

// A generic class that contains a potentially ambiguous
// overload of the Set() method.
class Gen<T, V> {
  T ob1;
  V ob2;
```

```
// ...

// In some cases, these two methods
// will not differ in their parameter types.
public void Set(T o) {
  ob1 = o;
}

public void Set(V o) {
  ob2 = o;
}
}

class AmbiguityDemo {
  static void Main() {
    Gen<int, double> ok = new Gen<int, double>();

    Gen<int, int> notOK = new Gen<int, int>();

    ok.Set(10); // is valid, type args differ

    notOK.Set(10); // ambiguous, type args are the same!
  }
}
```

Let's examine this program closely. First, notice that **Gen** declares two type parameters: **T** and **V**. Inside **Gen**, **Set( )** is overloaded based on parameters of type **T** and **V**, as shown here:

```
public void Set(T o) {
  ob1 = o;
}

public void Set(V o) {
  ob2 = o;
}
```

This looks reasonable because **T** and **V** appear to be different types. However, this overloading creates a potential ambiguity problem.

As **Gen** is written, there is no requirement that **T** and **V** actually be different types. For example, it is perfectly correct (in principle) to construct a **Gen** object as shown here:

```
Gen<int, int> notOK = new Gen<int, int>();
```

In this case, both **T** and **V** will be replaced by **int**. This makes both versions of **Set( )** identical, which is, of course, an error. Thus, when the attempt to call **Set( )** on **notOK** occurs later in **Main( )**, a compile-time ambiguity error is reported.

In general, you can overload methods that use type parameters as long as there is no constructed type that results in a conflict. Like methods, constructors, operators, and indexers that use type parameters can also be overloaded, and the same rules apply.

Covariance and Contravariance in Generic Type Parameters

In Chapter 15, covariance and contravariance were described as they relate to non-generic delegates. That form of contravariance and covariance is still fully supported by C# 4.0 and is quite useful. However, C# 4.0 expands the covariance and contravariance features to include generic type parameters that are used by generic interfaces and generic delegates. One of their principal uses is to streamline certain types of situations encountered when using generic interfaces and delegates defined by the .NET Framework, and some interfaces and delegates defined by the library have been upgraded to use type parameter covariance and contravariance. Of course, they can also be beneficial in interfaces and delegates that you create.

This section explains the generic type parameter covariance and contravariance mechanisms and shows examples of both.

Using Covariance in a Generic Interface

As it applies to a generic interface, covariance is the feature that enables a method to return a type that is derived from the class specified by a type parameter. In the past, because of the strict type-checking applied to generics, the return type had to match the type parameter precisely. Covariance relaxes this rule in a type-safe way. A covariant type parameter is declared by preceding its name with the keyword **out**.

To understand the implications of covariance, it is helpful to work through an example. First, here is a very simple interface called **IMyCoVarGenIF** that uses covariance:

```
// This generic interface supports covariance.
public interface IMyCoVarGenIF<out T> {
  T GetObject();
}
```

Pay special attention to the way that the type parameter **T** is declared. It is preceded by the keyword **out**. When used in this context, **out** specifies that **T** is covariant. Because **T** is covariant, **GetObject( )** can return a reference of type **T** or a reference of any class derived from **T**.

Although covariant on **T**, **IMyCoVarGenIF** is implemented just like any other generic interface. For example, here it is implemented by **MyClass**:

```
// Implement the IMyCoVarGenIF interface.
class MyClass<T> : IMyCoVarGenIF<T> {
  T obj;

  public MyClass(T v) { obj = v; }

  public T GetObject() { return obj; }
}
```

Notice that **out** is not specified again in the interface clause of **MyClass**. Not only is it not needed, but also it would be an error to attempt to specify it again.

Now, assume the following simple class hierarchy:

```
// Create a simple class hierarchy.
class Alpha {
  string name;
```

```
  public Alpha(string n) { name = n; }

  public string GetName() { return name; }
  // ...
}

class Beta : Alpha {
  public Beta(string n) : base(n) { }
  // ...
}
```

Notice that **Beta** is derived from **Alpha**.

Given the foregoing, the following sequence is legal:

```
// Create a IMyCoVarGenIF reference to a MyClass<Alpha> object.
// This is legal with or without covariance.
IMyCoVarGenIF<Alpha> AlphaRef =
    new MyClass<Alpha>(new Alpha("Alpha #1"));

Console.WriteLine("Name of object referred to by AlphaRef is " +
                  AlphaRef.GetObject().GetName());

// Now create a MyClass<Beta> object and assign it to AlphaRef.
// *** This line is legal because of covariance. ***
AlphaRef = new MyClass<Beta>(new Beta("Beta #1"));

Console.WriteLine("Name of object referred to by AlphaRef is now " +
                  AlphaRef.GetObject().GetName());
```

First, an **IMyCoVarGenIF<Alpha>** interface variable called **AlphaRef** is created and is assigned a reference to a **MyClass<Alpha>** object. This is legal because **MyClass** implements **IMyCoVarGenIF**, and both specify **Alpha** for a type argument. Next, the name of the object is displayed by calling **GetName( )** on the object returned by **GetObject( )**. Again, this works because the return type of **GetName( )** is **Alpha** (in this case) and **T** is of type **Alpha**. Next, **AlphaRef** is assigned a reference to an instance of **MyClass<Beta>**. This is legal because **Beta** is derived from **Alpha**, and **T** is covariant in **IMyCoVarGenIF**. If either of these were not the case, the statement would be illegal.

For your convenience, the entire sequence is assembled into the program shown here:

```
// Demonstrate generic interface covariance.
using System;

// This generic interface supports covariance.
public interface IMyCoVarGenIF<out T> {
  T GetObject();
}

// Implement the IMyCoVarGenIF interface.
class MyClass<T> : IMyCoVarGenIF<T> {
  T obj;

  public MyClass(T v) { obj = v; }
```

```
    public T GetObject() { return obj; }
}

// Create a simple class hierarchy.
class Alpha {
  string name;

  public Alpha(string n) { name = n; }

  public string GetName() { return name; }
  // ...
}

class Beta : Alpha {
  public Beta(string n) : base(n) { }
  // ...
}

class VarianceDemo {
  static void Main() {
    // Create a IMyCoVarGenIF reference to a MyClass<Alpha> object.
    // This is legal with or without covariance.
    IMyCoVarGenIF<Alpha> AlphaRef =
        new MyClass<Alpha>(new Alpha("Alpha #1"));

    Console.WriteLine("Name of object referred to by AlphaRef is " +
                    AlphaRef.GetObject().GetName());

    // Now create a MyClass<Beta> object and assign it to AlphaRef.
    // *** This line is legal because of covariance. ***
    AlphaRef = new MyClass<Beta>(new Beta("Beta #1"));

    Console.WriteLine("Name of object referred to by AlphaRef is now " +
                    AlphaRef.GetObject().GetName());
  }
}
```

The output is

```
Name of object referred to by AlphaRef is Alpha #1
Name of object referred to by AlphaRef is now Beta #1
```

It is important to stress that **AlphaRef** can be assigned a reference to a **MyClass<Beta>** object only because **T** is covariant in **IMyCoVarGenIF**. To prove this, remove **out** from in **IMyCoVarGenIF**'s declaration of **T**, and then attempt to recompile the program. The compilation will fail because the default strict type-checking will not allow the assignment.

It is possible for one generic interface to be inherited by another. In other words, a generic interface with a covariant type parameter can be extended. For example,

```
public interface IMyCoVarGenIF2<out T> : IMyCoVarGenIF<T> {
  // ...
}
```

Notice that **out** is specified only in the extending interface's declaration. Specifying **out** in the base interface clause is not necessary or legal. One last point: it is legal for **IMyCoVarGenIF2** to not specify **T** as covariant. However, doing so eliminates the covariance that extending **IMyCoVarGetIF** could provide. Of course, making **IMyCoVarGenIF2** invariant may be required for some uses.

Here are some restrictions that apply to covariance. A covariant type parameter can be applied only to a method return type. Thus, **out** cannot be applied to a type parameter that is used to declare a method parameter. Covariance works only with reference types. A covariant type cannot be used as a constraint in an interface method. For example, this interface is illegal:

```
public interface IMyCoVarGenIF2<out T> {
  void M<V>() where V:T; // Error, covariant T cannot be used as constraint
}
```

Using Contravariance in a Generic Interface

As it applies to a generic interface, contravariance is the feature that lets a method use an argument whose type is a base class of the type specified by the type parameter for that parameter. In the past, because of the strict type-checking applied to generics, a method's argument type had to match the type parameter precisely. Contravariance relaxes this rule in a type-safe way. A contravariant type parameter is declared by preceding the type parameter with the keyword **in**.

To understand the effects of contravariance, we will again work through an example. To begin, here is a contravariant generic interface called **IMyContraVarGenIF**. Notice that its type parameter **T** is contravariant and it uses T in the declaration of a method called **Show( )**.

```
// This generic interface supports contravariance.
public interface IMyContraVarGenIF<in T> {
  void Show(T obj);
}
```

Notice that **T** is specified as contravariant by preceding it with **in**. Also, notice that the parameter type of **obj** is **T**.

Next, **MyClass** implements **IMyContraVarGenIF**, as shown here:

```
// Implement the IMyContraVarGenIF interface.
class MyClass<T> : IMyContraVarGenIF<T> {
  public void Show(T x) { Console.WriteLine(x); }
}
```

Here, **Show( )** simply displays the string representation of **x** (as obtained by **WriteLine( )**'s implicit call to **ToString( )**).

Next, a class hierarchy is declared:

```
// Create a simple class hierarchy.
class Alpha {
  public override string ToString() {
    return "This is an Alpha object.";
  }
```

```
  // ...
}

class Beta : Alpha {
  public override string ToString() {
    return "This is a Beta object.";
  }
  // ...
}
```

Notice that these versions of **Alpha** and **Beta** differ from the previous example for the sake of illustration. Also notice that **ToString( )** is overridden to return the type of object.

Given the foregoing, the following sequence is legal:

```
// Create an IMyContraVarGenIF<Alpha> reference to a
// MyClass<Alpha> object.
// This is legal with or without contravariance.
IMyContraVarGenIF<Alpha> AlphaRef = new MyClass<Alpha>();

// Create an IMyContraVarGenIF<beta> reference to a
// MyClass<Beta> object.
// This is legal with or without contravariance.
IMyContraVarGenIF<Beta> BetaRef = new MyClass<Beta>();

// Create an IMyContraVarGenIF<beta> reference to
// a MyClass<Alpha> object.
// *** This is legal because of contravariance. ***
IMyContraVarGenIF<Beta> BetaRef2 = new MyClass<Alpha>();

// This call is legal with or without contravariance.
BetaRef.Show(new Beta());

// Assign AlphaRef to BetaRef.
//  *** This is legal because of contravariance. ***
BetaRef = AlphaRef;

BetaRef.Show(new Beta());
```

First, notice that two **IMyContraVarGenIF** reference variables are created and are assigned references to **MyClass** objects whose type parameters match that of the interface references. The first uses **Alpha**. The second uses **Beta**. These declarations do not require contravariance and are legal in all cases.

Next, an **IMyContraVarGenIF<Beta>** reference is created, but it is assigned a reference to a **MyClass<Alpha>** object. This is legal only because **T** is contravariant.

As you would expect, the next line, which calls **BetaRef.Show( )** with a **Beta** argument, is legal because **T** in **MyClass<Beta>** is **Beta**, and the argument to **Show( )** is **Beta**.

The next line assigns **AlphaRef** to **BetaRef**. This is legal only because of contravariance. In this case, **BetaRef** is of type **MyClass<Beta>**, but **AlphaRef** is of type **MyClass<Alpha>**. Because **Alpha** is a base class of **Beta**, contravariance makes this conversion legal. To prove to yourself that contravariance is required in the program, try removing **in** from the declaration of **T** in **IMyContraVarGenIF**. Then attempt to recompile the program. As you will see, errors will result.

For your convenience, all the pieces are assembled into the following program:

```
// Demonstrate generic interface contravariance.
using System;

// This generic interface supports contravariance.
public interface IMyContraVarGenIF<in T> {
  void Show(T obj);
}

// Implement the IMyContraVarGenIF interface.
class MyClass<T> : IMyContraVarGenIF<T> {
  public void Show(T x) { Console.WriteLine(x); }
}

// Create a simple class hierarchy.
class Alpha {
  public override string ToString() {
    return "This is an Alpha object.";
  }
  // ...
}

class Beta : Alpha {
  public override string ToString() {
    return "This is a Beta object.";
  }
  // ...
}

class VarianceDemo {
  static void Main() {
    // Create an IMyContraVarGenIF<Alpha> reference to a
    // MyClass<Alpha> object.
    // This is legal with or without contravariance.
    IMyContraVarGenIF<Alpha> AlphaRef = new MyClass<Alpha>();

    // Create an IMyContraVarGenIF<beta> reference to a
    // MyClass<Beta> object.
    // This is legal with or without contravariance.
    IMyContraVarGenIF<Beta> BetaRef = new MyClass<Beta>();

    // Create an IMyContraVarGenIF<beta> reference to
    // a MyClass<Alpha> object.
    // *** This is legal because of contravariance. ***
    IMyContraVarGenIF<Beta> BetaRef2 = new MyClass<Alpha>();

    // This call is legal with or without contravariance.
    BetaRef.Show(new Beta());

    // Assign AlphaRef to BetaRef.
    //  *** This is legal because of contravariance. ***
    BetaRef = AlphaRef;
```

```
      BetaRef.Show(new Beta());
  }
}
```

The output is shown here:

```
This is a Beta object.
This is a Beta object.
```

A contravariant interface can be extended. The process is similar to that described for extending a covariant interface. To access the contravariant nature of the extended interface, the extending interface must specify **in** for the type parameter that corresponds to the contravariant type parameter in the base interface. For example,

```
public interface IMyContraVarGenIF2<in T> : IMyContraVarGenIF<T> {
  // ...
}
```

Notice that **in** is not required (nor would it be legal) to be specified in the base interface clause. Furthermore, it is not required that **IMyContraVarGenIF2** be contravariant. In other words, it is not required that **IMyContraVarGenIF2** modify **T** with **in**. Of course, any benefits that could result from the contravariant **IMyContraVarGen** interface would be lost relative to the **IMyContraVarGenIF2** interface.

Contravariance works only with reference types, and a contravariant type parameter can be applied only to method arguments. Thus, **in** cannot be applied to a type parameter that is used for a return type.

Variant Delegates

As explained in Chapter 15, non-generic delegates already support covariance and contravariance as they relate to method return types and parameter types. Beginning with C# 4.0, these features are expanded for generic delegates to include type parameter covariance and contravariance. These features work in a fashion similar to that just described for interfaces.

Here is an example of a contravariant delegate:

```
// Declare a generic delegate that is contravariant on T.
delegate bool SomeOp<in T>(T obj);
```

This delegate can be assigned a method whose parameter is **T** or a class from which **T** is derived.

Here is an example of a covariant delegate:

```
// Declare a generic delegate that is covariant on T.
delegate T AnotherOp<out T, V>(V obj);
```

This delegate can be assigned a method whose return type is **T** or a class derived from **T**. In this case, **V** is simply an invariant type parameter.

The following program puts these delegates into action:

```
// Demonstrate covariance and contravariance with a generic delegate.

using System;
```

```csharp
// Declare a generic delegate that is contravariant on T.
delegate bool SomeOp<in T>(T obj);

// Declare a generic delegate that is covariant on T.
delegate T AnotherOp<out T, V>(V obj);

class Alpha {
  public int Val { get; set; }

  public Alpha(int v) { Val = v; }
}

class Beta : Alpha {
  public Beta(int v) : base(v) { }
}

class GenDelegateVarianceDemo {
  // Return true if obj.Val is even.
  static bool IsEven(Alpha obj) {
    if((obj.Val % 2) == 0) return true;
    return false;
   }

  static Beta ChangeIt(Alpha obj) {
    return new Beta(obj.Val +2);
  }

  static void Main() {
    Alpha objA = new Alpha(4);
    Beta objB = new Beta(9);

    // First demonstrate contravariance.

    // Declare a SomeOp<Alpha> delegate and set it to IsEven.
    SomeOp<Alpha> checkIt = IsEven;

    // Declare a SomeOp<Beta> delegate.
    SomeOp<Beta> checkIt2;

    // Now, assign the SomeOp<Alpha> delegate the SomeOp<Beta> delegate.
    // *** This is legal only because of contravariance. ***
    checkIt2 = checkIt;

    // Call through the delegate.
    Console.WriteLine(checkIt2(objB));


    // Now, demonstrate covariance.

    // First, declare two AnotherOp delegates.
    // Here, the return type is Beta and the parameter type is Alpha.
    // Notice that modifyIt is set to ChangeIt.
```

```
    AnotherOp<Beta, Alpha> modifyIt = ChangeIt;

    // Here, the return type is Alpha and the parameter type is Alpha.
    AnotherOp<Alpha, Alpha> modifyIt2;

    // Now, assign modifyIt to modifyIt2.
    // *** This statement is legal only because of covariance. ***
    modifyIt2 = modifyIt;

    // Actually call the method and display the results.
    objA = modifyIt2(objA);
    Console.WriteLine(objA.Val);
  }
}
```

The output is shown here:

```
False
6
```

The comments in the program explain each operation. It is important to stress, however, that for both **SomeOp** and **AnotherOp**, the use of **in** and **out**, respectively, is necessary for the program to compile. Without these modifiers, compilation errors would result at the indicated lines because no implicit conversions would be available.

How Generic Types Are Instantiated

One question that is often raised when working with generics is whether the use of a generic class leads to code-bloat at runtime. The simple answer is no. The reason is that C# implements generics in a highly efficient manner that creates new constructed types only when they are needed. Here is how the process works.

When a generic class is compiled into MSIL, it retains all of its type parameters in their generic form. At runtime, when a specific instance of the class is required, the JIT compiler constructs a specific, executable code version of the class in which the type parameters are replaced by the type arguments. Each instance of the class that uses the same type arguments will use the same executable code version.

For example, given some generic class called **Gen<T>**, then all **Gen<int>** objects will use the same executable code. Thus, code-bloat is reduced and only those versions of the class that are actually used in the program will be created. When a different constructed type is needed, a new version of the class is compiled.

In general, a new executable version of a generic class is created for each constructed type in which the type argument is a value type, such as **int** or **double**. Thus, each object of **Gen<int>** will use one version of **Gen** and each object of type **Gen<double>** will use another version of **Gen**, with each version of **Gen** tailored to the specific value type. However, there will be *only one version* of a generic class that handles all cases in which the type argument is a reference type. This is because the size (in bytes) of all references is the same. Thus, only one version is needed to handle all types of references. This optimization also reduces code-bloat.

Some Generic Restrictions

Here are a few restrictions that you need to keep in mind when using generics:

- Properties, operators, and indexers cannot be generic. However, these items can be used in a generic class and can make use of the generic type parameters of that class.

- The **extern** modifier cannot be applied to a generic method.

- Pointer types cannot be used as type arguments.

- If a generic class contains a **static** field, then *each constructed type has its own copy* of that field. This means that each instance of the *same constructed type* shares the same **static** field. However, a different constructed type shares a different copy of that field. Thus, a **static** field is not shared by all constructed types.

Final Thoughts on Generics

Generics are a powerful element of C# because they streamline the creation of type-safe, reusable code. Although the generic syntax can seem a bit overwhelming at first, it will quickly become second nature. Likewise, learning how and when to use constraints takes a bit of practice, but becomes easier over time. Generics are now an integral part of C# programming. It's worth the effort it takes to master this important feature.

LINQ

L INQ is without question one of the most exciting features in C#. It was added by C# 3.0, and it represented a major addition to the language. Not only did it add an entirely new syntactic element, several new keywords, and a powerful new capability, but also it significantly increased the scope of the language, expanding the range of tasks to which C# can be applied. Simply put, the addition of LINQ was a pivotal event in the evolution of C#.

LINQ stands for *Language-Integrated Query*. It encompasses a set of features that lets you retrieve information from a data source. As you may know, the retrieval of data constitutes an important part of many programs. For example, a program might obtain information from a customer list, look up product information in a catalog, or access an employee's record. In many cases, such data is stored in a database that is separate from the application. For example, a product catalog might be stored in a relational database. In the past, interacting with such a database would involve generating queries using SQL (Structured Query Language). Other sources of data, such as XML, required their own approaches. Therefore, prior to C# 3.0, support for such queries was not built into C#. The addition of LINQ changed this.

LINQ gives to C# the ability to generate queries for any LINQ-compatible data source. Furthermore, the syntax used for the query is the same—no matter what data source is used. This means the syntax used to query data in a relational database is the same as that used to query data stored in an array, for example. It is not necessary to use SQL or any other non-C# mechanism. The query capability is fully integrated into the C# language.

In addition to using LINQ with SQL, LINQ can be used with XML files and ADO.NET Datasets. Perhaps equally important, it can also be used with C# arrays and collections (described in Chapter 25). Therefore, LINQ gives you a uniform way to access data in general. This is a powerful, innovative concept in its own right, but the benefits of LINQ do not stop there. LINQ also offers a different way to think about and approach many types of programming tasks—not just traditional database access. As a result, many solutions can be crafted in terms of LINQ.

LINQ is supported by a set of interrelated features, including the query syntax added to the C# language, lambda expressions, anonymous types, and extension methods. Lambda expressions are described in Chapter 15. The others are examined here.

> **NOTE** *LINQ in C# is essentially a language within a language. As a result, the subject of LINQ is quite large, involving many features, options, and alternatives. Although this chapter describes LINQ in significant detail, it is not possible to explore all facets, nuances, and applications of this powerful feature. To do so would require an entire book of its own. Instead, this chapter focuses on the core elements of LINQ and presents numerous examples. Going forward, LINQ is definitely a subsystem that you will want to study in greater detail.*

LINQ Fundamentals

At LINQ's core is the *query*. A query specifies what data will be obtained from a data source. For example, a query on a customer mailing list might request the addresses of all customers that reside in a specific city, such as Chicago or Tokyo. A query on an inventory database might request a list of out-of-stock items. A query on a log of Internet usage could ask for a list of the websites with the highest hit counts. Although these queries differ in their specifics, all can be expressed using the same LINQ syntactic elements.

After a query has been created, it can be executed. One way this is done is by using the query in a **foreach** loop. Executing a query causes its results to be obtained. Thus, using a query involves two key steps. First, the form of the query is created. Second, the query is executed. Therefore, the query defines *what* to retrieve from a data source. Executing the query actually *obtains the results*.

In order for a source of data to be used by LINQ, it must implement the **IEnumerable** interface. There are two forms of this interface: one generic, one not. In general, it is easier if the data source implements the generic version, **IEnumerable<T>**, where **T** specifies the type of data being enumerated. The rest of the chapter assumes that a data source implements **IEnumerable<T>**. This interface is declared in **System.Collections.Generic**. A class that implements **IEnumerable<T>** supports enumeration, which means that its contents can be obtained one at a time, in sequence. All C# arrays implicitly support **IEnumerable<T>**. Thus, arrays can be used to demonstrate the central concepts of LINQ. Understand, however, that LINQ is not limited to arrays.

A Simple Query

At this point, it will be helpful to work through a simple LINQ example. The following program uses a query to obtain the positive values contained in an array of integers:

```
// Create a simple LINQ query.
using System;
using System.Linq;

class SimpQuery {
  static void Main() {

    int[] nums = { 1, -2, 3, 0, -4, 5 };
```

```
    // Create a query that obtains only positive numbers.
    var posNums = from n in nums
                  where n > 0
                  select n;

    Console.Write("The positive values in nums: ");

    // Execute the query and display the results.
    foreach(int i in posNums) Console.Write(i + " ");

    Console.WriteLine();
  }
}
```

This program produces the following output:

```
The positive values in nums: 1 3 5
```

As you can see, only the positive values in the **nums** array are displayed. Although quite simple, this program demonstrates the key features of LINQ. Let's examine it closely.

The first thing to notice in the program is the **using** directive:

```
using System.Linq;
```

To use the LINQ features, you must include the **System.Linq** namespace.

Next, an array of **int** called **nums** is declared. All arrays in C# are implicitly convertible to **IEnumerable<T>**. This makes any C# array usable as a LINQ data source.

Next, a query is declared that retrieves those elements in **nums** that are positive. It is shown here:

```
var posNums = from n in nums
              where n > 0
              select n;
```

The variable **posNums** is called the *query variable*. It refers to the set of rules defined by the query. Notice it uses **var** to implicitly declare **posNums**. As you know, this makes **posNums** an implicitly typed variable. In queries, it is often convenient to use implicitly typed variables, although you can also explicitly declare the type (which must be some form of **IEnumerable<T>**). The variable **posNums** is then assigned the query expression.

All queries begin with **from**. This clause specifies two items. The first is the *range variable*, which will receive elements obtained from the data source. In this case, the range variable is **n**. The second item is the data source, which in this case is the **nums** array. The type of the range variable is inferred from the data source. In this case, the type of **n** is **int**. Generalizing, here is the syntax of the **from** clause:

from *range-variable* in *data-source*

The next clause in the query is **where**. It specifies a condition that an element in the data source must meet in order to be obtained by the query. Its general form is shown here:

where *boolean-expression*

The *boolean-expression* must produce a **bool** result. (This expression is also called a *predicate*.) There can be more than one **where** clause in a query. In the program, this **where** clause is used:

```
where n > 0
```

It will be true only for an element whose value is greater than zero. This expression will be evaluated for every **n** in **nums** when the query executes. Only those values that satisfy this condition will be obtained. In other words, a **where** clause acts as a filter on the data source, allowing only certain items through.

All queries end with either a **select** clause or a **group** clause. This example employs the **select** clause. It specifies precisely what is obtained by the query. For simple queries, such as the one in this example, the range value is selected. Therefore, it returns those integers from **nums** that satisfy the **where** clause. In more sophisticated situations, it is possible to finely tune what is selected. For example, when querying a mailing list, you might return just the last name of each recipient, rather than the entire address. Notice that the **select** clause ends with a semicolon. Because **select** ends a query, it ends the statement and requires a semicolon. Notice, however, that the other clauses in the query do not end with a semicolon.

At this point, a query variable called **posNums** has been created, but no results have been obtained. It is important to understand that a query simply defines a set of rules. It is not until the query is executed that results are obtained. Furthermore, the same query can be executed two or more times, with the possibility of differing results if the underlying data source changes between executions. Therefore, simply declaring the query **posNums** does not mean that it contains the results of the query.

To execute the query, the program uses the **foreach** loop shown here:

```
foreach(int i in posNums) Console.WriteLine(i + " ");
```

Notice that **posNums** is specified as the collection being iterated over. When the **foreach** executes, the rules defined by the query specified by **posNums** are executed. With each pass through the loop, the next element returned by the query is obtained. The process ends when there are no more elements to retrieve. In this case, the type of the iteration variable **i** is explicitly specified as **int** because this is the type of the elements retrieved by the query. Explicitly specifying the type of the iteration variable is fine in this situation, since it is easy to know the type of the value selected by the query. However, in more complicated situations, it will be easier (or in some cases, necessary) to implicitly specify the type of the iteration variable by using **var**.

A Query Can Be Executed More Than Once

Because a query defines a set of rules that are used to retrieve data, but does not, itself, produce results, the same query can be run multiple times. If the data source changes between runs, then the results of the query may differ. Therefore, once you define a query, executing it will always produce the most current results. Here is an example. In the following version of the preceding program, the contents of the **nums** array are changed between two executions of **posNums**:

```
// Create a simple query.
using System;
using System.Linq;
using System.Collections.Generic;
```

```
class SimpQuery {
  static void Main() {

    int[] nums =  { 1, -2, 3, 0, -4, 5 };

    // Create a query that obtains only positive numbers.
    var posNums = from n in nums
                  where n > 0
                  select n;

    Console.Write("The positive values in nums: ");

    // Execute the query and display the results.
    foreach(int i in posNums) Console.Write(i + " ");
    Console.WriteLine();

    // Change nums.
    Console.WriteLine("\nSetting nums[1] to 99.");
    nums[1] = 99;

    Console.Write("The positive values in nums after change: ");

    // Execute the query a second time.
    foreach(int i in posNums) Console.Write(i + " ");
    Console.WriteLine();
  }
}
```

The following output is produced:

```
The positive values in nums: 1 3 5

Setting nums[1] to 99.
The positive values in nums after change: 1 99 3 5
```

As the output confirms, after the value in **nums[1]** was changed from –2 to 99, the result of rerunning the query reflects the change. This is a key point that must be emphasized. Each execution of a query produces its own results, which are obtained by enumerating the current contents of the data source. Therefore, if the data source changes, so, too, might the results of executing a query. The benefits of this approach are quite significant. For example, if you are obtaining a list of pending orders for an online store, then you want each execution of your query to produce all orders, including those just entered.

How the Data Types in a Query Relate

As the preceding examples have shown, a query involves variables whose types relate to one another. These are the query variable, the range variable, and the data source. Because the correspondence among these types is both important and a bit confusing at first, they merit a closer look.

The type of the range variable must agree with the type of the elements stored in the data source. Thus, the type of the range variable is dependent upon the type of the data source. In many cases, C# can infer the type of the range variable. As long as the data source implements **IEnumerable<T>**, the type inference can be made because **T** describes the type of the elements in the data source. However, if the data source implements the non-generic version of **IEnumerable**, then you will need to explicitly specify the type of the range variable. This is done by specifying its type in the **from** clause. For example, assuming the preceding examples, this shows how to explicitly declare **n** to be an **int**:

```
var posNums = from int n in nums
  // ...
```

Of course, the explicit type specification is not needed here because all arrays are implicitly convertible to **IEnumerable<T>**, which enables the type of the range variable to be inferred.

The type of object returned by a query is an instance of **IEnumerable<T>**, where **T** is the type of the elements. Thus, the type of the query variable must be an instance of **IEnumerable<T>**. The value of **T** is determined by the type of the value specified by the **select** clause. In the case of the preceding examples, **T** is **int** because **n** is an **int**. (As explained, **n** is an **int** because **int** is the type of elements stored in **nums**.) Therefore, the query could have been written like this, with the type explicitly specified as **IEnumerable <int>**:

```
IEnumerable<int> posNums = from n in nums
                          where n > 0
                          select n;
```

The key point is that the type of the item selected by **select** must agree with the type argument passed to **IEnumerable<T>** used to declare the query variable. Often query variables use **var** rather than explicitly specifying the type because this lets the compiler infer the proper type from the **select** clause. As you will see, this approach is particularly useful when **select** returns something other than an individual element from the data source.

When a query is executed by the **foreach** loop, the type of the iteration variable must be the same as the type specified by the **select** clause. In the preceding examples, this type was explicitly specified as **int**, but you can let the compiler infer the type by declaring this variable as **var**. As you will see, there are also some cases in which **var** must be used because the data type has no name.

The General Form of a Query

All queries share a general form, which is based on a set of contextual keywords, shown here:

ascending	by	descending	equals
from	group	in	into
join	let	on	orderby
select	where		

Of these, the following begin query clauses:

from	group	join	let
orderby	select	where	

A query must begin with the keyword **from** and end with either a **select** or **group** clause. The **select** clause determines what type of value is enumerated by the query. The **group** clause returns the data by groups, with each group being able to be enumerated individually. As the preceding examples have shown, the **where** clause specifies criteria that an item must meet in order for it to be returned. The remaining clauses help you fine-tune a query. The follows sections examine each query clause.

Filter Values with where

As explained, **where** is used to filter the data returned by a query. The preceding examples have shown only its simplest form, in which a single condition is used. A key point to understand is that you can use **where** to filter data based on more than one condition. One way to do this is through the use of multiple **where** clauses. For example, consider the following program that displays only those values in the array that are both positive and less than 10:

```
// Use multiple where clauses.
using System;
using System.Linq;

class TwoWheres {
  static void Main() {

    int[] nums =  { 1, -2, 3, -3, 0, -8, 12, 19, 6, 9, 10 };

    // Create a query that obtains positive values less than 10.
    var posNums = from n in nums
                  where n > 0
                  where n < 10
                  select n;

    Console.Write("The positive values less than 10: ");

    // Execute the query and display the results.
    foreach(int i in posNums) Console.Write (i + " ");
    Console.WriteLine();
  }
}
```

The output is shown here:

```
The positive values less than 10: 1 3 6 9
```

As you can see, only positive values less than 10 are retrieved. This outcome is achieved by the use of the following two **where** clauses:

```
where n > 0
where n < 10
```

The first **where** requires that an element be greater than zero. The second requires the element to be less than 10. Thus, an element must be between 1 and 9 (inclusive) to satisfy both clauses.

Although it is not wrong to use two **where** clauses as just shown, the same effect can be achieved in a more compact manner by using a single **where** in which both tests are combined into a single expression. Here is the query rewritten to use this approach:

```
var posNums = from n in nums
              where n > 0 && n < 10
              select n;
```

In general, a **where** condition can use any valid C# expression that evaluates to a Boolean result. For example, the following program defines an array of **string**s. Several of the strings define Internet addresses. The query **netAddrs** retrieves only those strings that have more than four characters and that end with ".net". Thus, it finds those strings that contain Internet addresses that use the **.net** top-level domain name.

```
// Demonstrate another where clause.
using System;
using System.Linq;

class WhereDemo2 {

  static void Main() {

    string[] strs = { ".com", ".net", "hsNameA.com", "hsNameB.net",
                      "test", ".network", "hsNameC.net", "hsNameD.com" };

    // Create a query that obtains Internet addresses that
    // end with .net.
    var netAddrs = from addr in strs
                   where addr.Length > 4 && addr.EndsWith(".net",
                       StringComparison.Ordinal)
                   select addr;

    // Execute the query and display the results.
    foreach(var str in netAddrs) Console.WriteLine(str);
  }
}
```

The output is shown here:

```
hsNameB.net
hsNameC.net
```

Notice that the program makes use of one of **string**'s methods called **EndsWith( )** within the **where** clause. It returns true if the invoking string ends with the character sequence specified as an argument.

Sort Results with orderby

Often you will want the results of a query to be sorted. For example, you might want to obtain a list of past-due accounts, in order of the remaining balance, from greatest to least. Or, you might want to obtain a customer list, alphabetized by name. Whatever the purpose, LINQ gives you an easy way to produce sorted results: the **orderby** clause.

You can use **orderby** to sort on one or more criteria. We will begin with the simplest case: sorting on a single item. The general form of **orderby** that sorts based on a single criterion is shown here:

orderby *sort-on how*

The item on which to sort is specified by *sort-on*. This can be as inclusive as the entire element stored in the data source or as restricted as a portion of a single field within the element. The value of *how* determines if the sort is ascending or descending, and it must be either **ascending** or **descending**. The default direction is ascending, so you won't normally specify **ascending**.

Here is an example that uses **orderby** to retrieve the values in an **int** array in ascending order:

```
// Demonstrate orderby.
using System;
using System.Linq;

class OrderbyDemo {

  static void Main() {

    int[] nums =  { 10, -19, 4, 7, 2, -5, 0 };

    // Create a query that obtains the values in sorted order.
    var posNums = from n in nums
                  orderby n
                  select n;

    Console.Write("Values in ascending order: ");

    // Execute the query and display the results.
    foreach(int i in posNums) Console.Write(i + " ");

    Console.WriteLine();
  }
}
```

The output is shown here:

```
Values in ascending order: -19 -5 0 2 4 7 10
```

To change the order to descending, simply specify the **descending** option, as shown here:

```
var posNums = from n in nums
              orderby n descending
              select n;
```

If you try this, you will see that the order of the values is reversed.

Although sorting on a single criterion is often what is needed, you can use **orderby** to sort on multiple items by using this form:

orderby *sort-onA direction, sort-onB direction, sort-onC direction,* ...

In this form, *sort-onA* is the item on which the primary sorting is done. Then, each group of equivalent items is sorted on *sort-onB*, and each of those groups is sorted on *sort-onC*, and so on. Thus, each subsequent *sort-on* specifies a "then by" item on which to sort. In all cases, *direction* is optional, defaulting to **ascending**. Here is an example that uses three sort criteria to sort bank account information by last name, then by first name, and finally by account balance:

```csharp
// Sort on multiple criteria with orderby.
using System;
using System.Linq;

class Account {
  public string FirstName { get; private set; }
  public string LastName { get; private set; }
  public double Balance { get; private set; }
  public string AccountNumber { get; private set; }

  public Account(string fn, string ln, string accnum, double b) {
    FirstName = fn;
    LastName = ln;
    AccountNumber = accnum;
    Balance = b;
  }
}

class OrderbyDemo {

  static void Main() {

    // Create some data.
    Account[] accounts = { new Account("Tom", "Smith", "132CK", 100.23),
                           new Account("Tom", "Smith", "132CD", 10000.00),
                           new Account("Ralph", "Jones", "436CD", 1923.85),
                           new Account("Ralph", "Jones", "454MM", 987.132),
                           new Account("Ted", "Krammer", "897CD", 3223.19),
                           new Account("Ralph", "Jones", "434CK", -123.32),
                           new Account("Sara", "Smith", "543MM", 5017.40),
                           new Account("Sara", "Smith", "547CD", 34955.79),
                           new Account("Sara", "Smith", "843CK", 345.00),
                           new Account("Albert", "Smith", "445CK", 213.67),
                           new Account("Betty", "Krammer","968MM",5146.67),
                           new Account("Carl", "Smith", "078CD", 15345.99),
                           new Account("Jenny", "Jones", "108CK", 10.98)
                         };

    // Create a query that obtains the accounts in sorted order.
    // Sorting first by last name, then within same last names sorting by
    // by first name, and finally by account balance.
    var accInfo = from acc in accounts
                  orderby acc.LastName, acc.FirstName, acc.Balance
                  select acc;
```

```
        Console.WriteLine("Accounts in sorted order: ");

        string str = "";

        // Execute the query and display the results.
        foreach(Account acc in accInfo) {
          if(str != acc.FirstName) {
            Console.WriteLine();
            str = acc.FirstName;
          }

          Console.WriteLine("{0}, {1}\tAcc#: {2}, {3,10:C}",
                            acc.LastName, acc.FirstName,
                            acc.AccountNumber, acc.Balance);
        }
        Console.WriteLine();
    }
}
```

The output is shown here:

```
Accounts in sorted order:

Jones, Jenny        Acc#: 108CK,     $10.98

Jones, Ralph        Acc#: 434CK,    ($123.32)
Jones, Ralph        Acc#: 454MM,    $987.13
Jones, Ralph        Acc#: 436CD,  $1,923.85

Krammer, Betty      Acc#: 968MM,  $5,146.67

Krammer, Ted        Acc#: 897CD,  $3,223.19

Smith, Albert       Acc#: 445CK,    ($213.67)

Smith, Carl         Acc#: 078CD, $15,345.99

Smith, Sara         Acc#: 843CK,    $345.00
Smith, Sara         Acc#: 543MM,  $5,017.40
Smith, Sara         Acc#: 547CD, $34,955.79

Smith, Tom          Acc#: 132CK,    $100.23
Smith, Tom          Acc#: 132CD, $10,000.00
```

In the query, look closely at how the **orderby** clause is written:

```
var accInfo = from acc in accounts
              orderby acc.LastName, acc.FirstName, acc.Balance
              select acc;
```

Here is how it works. First, the results are sorted by last name, and then entries with the same last name are sorted by the first name. Finally, groups of entries with the same first and last name are sorted by the account balance. This is why the list of accounts under the name Jones is shown in this order:

```
Jones, Jenny        Acc#: 108CK,      $10.98

Jones, Ralph        Acc#: 434CK,    ($123.32)
Jones, Ralph        Acc#: 454MM,     $987.13
Jones, Ralph        Acc#: 436CD,   $1,923.85
```

As the output confirms, the list is sorted by last name, then by first name, and finally by account balance.

When using multiple criteria, you can reverse the condition of any sort by applying the **descending** option. For example, this query causes the results to be shown in order of decreasing balance:

```
var accInfo = from acc in accounts
              orderby x.LastName, x.FirstName, x.Balance descending
              select acc;
```

When using this version, the list of Jones entries will be displayed like this:

```
Jones, Jenny        Acc#: 108CK,      $10.98

Jones, Ralph        Acc#: 436CD,   $1,923.85
Jones, Ralph        Acc#: 454MM,     $987.13
Jones, Ralph        Acc#: 434CK,    ($123.32)
```

As you can see, now the accounts for Ralph Jones are displayed from greatest to least.

A Closer Look at select

The **select** clause determines what type of elements are obtained by a query. Its general form is shown here:

select *expression*

So far we have been using **select** to return the range variable. Thus, *expression* has simply named the range variable. However, **select** is not limited to this simple action. It can return a specific portion of the range variable, the result of applying some operation or transformation to the range variable, or even a new type of object that is constructed from pieces of the information retrieved from the range variable. This is called *projecting*.

To begin examining the other capabilities of **select**, consider the following program. It displays the square roots of the positive values contained in an array of **double** values.

```
// Use select to return the square root of all positive values
// in an array of doubles.
using System;
using System.Linq;

class SelectDemo {

  static void Main() {
```

```
      double[] nums =  { -10.0, 16.4, 12.125, 100.85, -2.2, 25.25, -3.5 } ;

      // Create a query that returns the square roots of the
      // positive values in nums.
      var sqrRoots = from n in nums
                     where n > 0
                     select Math.Sqrt(n);

      Console.WriteLine("The square roots of the positive values" +
                        " rounded to two decimal places:");

      // Execute the query and display the results.
      foreach(double r in sqrRoots) Console.WriteLine("{0:#.##}", r);
   }
}
```

The output is shown here:

```
The square roots of the positive values rounded to two decimal places:
4.05
3.48
10.04
5.02
```

In the query, pay special attention to the **select** clause:

```
select Math.Sqrt(n);
```

It returns the square root of the range variable. It does this by obtaining the result of passing the range variable to **Math.Sqrt( )**, which returns the square root of its argument. This means that the sequence obtained when the query is executed will contain the square roots of the positive values in **nums**. If you generalize this concept, the power of **select** becomes apparent. You can use **select** to generate any type of sequence you need, based on the values obtained from the data source.

Here is a program that shows another way to use **select**. It creates a class called **EmailAddress** that contains two properties. The first holds a person's name. The second contains an e-mail address. The program then creates an array that contains several **EmailAddress** entries. The program uses a query to obtain a list of just the e-mail addresses by themselves.

```
// Return a portion of the range variable.
using System;
using System.Linq;

class EmailAddress {
  public string Name { get; set; }
  public string Address { get; set; }

  public EmailAddress(string n, string a) {
    Name = n;
    Address = a;
  }
}
```

```
class SelectDemo2 {
  static void Main() {

    EmailAddress[] addrs = {
        new EmailAddress("Herb", "Herb@HerbSchildt.com"),
        new EmailAddress("Tom", "Tom@HerbSchildt.com"),
        new EmailAddress("Sara", "Sara@HerbSchildt.com")
    };

    // Create a query that selects e-mail addresses.
    var eAddrs = from entry in addrs
                 select entry.Address;

    Console.WriteLine("The e-mail addresses are");

    // Execute the query and display the results.
    foreach(string s in eAddrs) Console.WriteLine("  " + s);
  }
}
```

The output is shown here:

```
The e-mail addresses are
  Herb@HerbSchildt.com
  Tom@HerbSchildt.com
  Sara@HerbSchildt.com
```

Pay special attention to the **select** clause:

```
select entry.Address;
```

Instead of returning the entire range variable, it returns only the **Address** portion. This fact is evidenced by the output. This means the query returns a sequence of strings, not a sequence of **EmailAddress** objects. This is why the **foreach** loop specifies **s** as a **string**. As explained, the type of sequence returned by a query is determined by the type of value returned by the **select** clause.

One of the more powerful features of **select** is its ability to return a sequence that contains elements created during the execution of the query. For example, consider the following program. It defines a class called **ContactInfo**, which stores a name, e-mail address, and telephone number. It also defines the **EmailAddress** class used by the preceding example. Inside **Main( )**, an array of **ContactInfo** is created. Then, a query is declared in which the data source is an array of **ContactInfo**, but the sequence returned contains **EmailAddress** objects. Thus, the type of the sequence returned by **select** is not **ContactInfo**, but rather **EmailAddress**, and these objects are created during the execution of the query.

```
// Use a query to obtain a sequence of EmailAddresses
// from a list of ContactInfo.
using System;
using System.Linq;

class ContactInfo {
  public string Name { get; set; }
  public string Email { get; set; }
```

```
    public string Phone { get; set; }

    public ContactInfo(string n, string a, string p) {
      Name = n;
      Email = a;
      Phone = p;
    }
}

class EmailAddress {
  public string Name { get; set; }
  public string Address { get; set; }

  public EmailAddress(string n, string a) {
    Name = n;
    Address = a;
  }
}

class SelectDemo3 {
  static void Main() {

    ContactInfo[] contacts = {
        new ContactInfo("Herb", "Herb@HerbSchildt.com", "555-1010"),
        new ContactInfo("Tom", "Tom@HerbSchildt.com", "555-1101"),
        new ContactInfo("Sara", "Sara@HerbSchildt.com", "555-0110")
    };

    // Create a query that creates a list of EmailAddress objects.
    var emailList = from entry in contacts
                    select new EmailAddress(entry.Name, entry.Email);

    Console.WriteLine("The e-mail list is");

    // Execute the query and display the results.
    foreach(EmailAddress e in emailList)
      Console.WriteLine("  {0}: {1}", e.Name, e.Address );
  }
}
```

The output is shown here:

```
The e-mail list is
  Herb: Herb@HerbSchildt.com
  Tom: Tom@HerbSchildt.com
  Sara: Sara@HerbSchildt.com
```

In the query, pay special attention to the **select** clause:

```
select new EmailAddress(entry.Name, entry.Email);
```

It creates a new **EmailAddress** object that contains the name and e-mail address obtained from a **ContactInfo** object in the **contacts** array. The key point is that new **EmailAddress** objects are created by the query in its **select** clause, during the query's execution.

Use Nested from Clauses

A query can contain more than one **from** clause. Thus, a query can contain nested **from** clauses. One common use of a nested **from** clause is found when a query needs to obtain data from two different sources. Here is a simple example. It uses two **from** clauses to iterate over two different character arrays. It produces a sequence that contains all possible combinations of the two sets of characters.

```
// Use two from clauses to create a list of all
// possible combinations of the letters A, B, and C
// with the letters X, Y, and Z.
using System;
using System.Linq;


// This class holds the result of the query.
class ChrPair {
  public char First;
  public char Second;

  public ChrPair(char c, char c2) {
    First = c;
    Second = c2;
  }
}

class MultipleFroms {
  static void Main() {

    char[] chrs = { 'A', 'B', 'C' };
    char[] chrs2 = { 'X', 'Y', 'Z' };

    // Notice that the first from iterates over chrs and
    // the second from iterates over chrs2.
    var pairs = from ch1 in chrs
                from ch2 in chrs2
                select new ChrPair(ch1, ch2);

    Console.WriteLine("All combinations of ABC with XYZ: ");

    foreach(var p in pairs)
      Console.WriteLine("{0} {1}", p.First, p.Second);
  }
}
```

The output is shown here:

```
All combinations of ABC with XYZ:
A X
A Y
A Z
B X
B Y
```

```
B Z
C X
C Y
C Z
```

The program begins by creating a class called **ChrPair** that will hold the results of the query. It then creates two character arrays, called **chrs** and **chrs2**. It uses the following query to produce all possible combinations of the two sequences:

```
var pairs = from ch1 in chrs
            from ch2 in chrs2
            select new ChrPair(ch1, ch2);
```

The nested **from** clauses cause both **chrs** and **chrs2** to be iterated over. Here is how it works. First, a character is obtained from **chrs** and stored in **ch1**. Then, the **chrs2** array is enumerated. With each iteration of the inner **from**, a character from **chrs2** is stored in **ch2** and the **select** clause is executed. The result of the **select** clause is a new object of type **ChrPair** that contains the character pair **ch1, ch2** produced by each iteration of the inner **from**. Thus, a **ChrPair** is produced in which each possible combination of characters is obtained.

Another common use of a nested **from** is to iterate over a data source that is contained within another data source. An example of this is found in the section, "Use **let** to Create a Variable in a Query," later in this chapter.

Group Results with group

One of the most powerful query features is provided by the **group** clause because it enables you to create results that are grouped by keys. Using the sequence obtained from a group, you can easily access all of the data associated with a key. This makes **group** an easy and effective way to retrieve data that is organized into sequences of related items. The **group** clause is one of only two clauses that can end a query. (The other is **select**.)

The **group** clause has the following general form:

group *range-variable* by *key*

It returns data grouped into sequences, with each sequence sharing the key specified by *key*.

The result of **group** is a sequence that contains elements of type **IGrouping<TKey, TElement>**, which is declared in the **System.Linq** namespace. It defines a collection of objects that share a common key. The type of query variable in a query that returns a group is **IEnumerable<IGrouping<TKey, TElement>>**. **IGrouping** defines a read-only property called **Key**, which returns the key associated with each sequence.

Here is an example that illustrates the use of **group**. It declares an array that contains a list of websites. It then creates a query that groups the list by top-level domain name, such as **.org** or **.com**.

```
// Demonstrate the group clause.
using System;
using System.Linq;

class GroupDemo {

  static void Main() {
```

```
        string[] websites = { "hsNameA.com", "hsNameB.net", "hsNameC.net",
                              "hsNameD.com", "hsNameE.org", "hsNameF.org",
                              "hsNameG.tv",  "hsNameH.net", "hsNameI.tv" };

        // Create a query that groups websites by top-level domain name.
        var webAddrs = from addr in websites
                       where addr.LastIndexOf('.') != -1
                       group addr by addr.Substring(addr.LastIndexOf('.'));

        // Execute the query and display the results.
        foreach(var sites in webAddrs) {
          Console.WriteLine("Web sites grouped by " + sites.Key);
          foreach(var site in sites)
            Console.WriteLine("  " + site);
          Console.WriteLine();
        }
      }
    }
```

The output is shown here:

```
Web sites grouped by .com
  hsNameA.com
  hsNameD.com

Web sites grouped by .net
  hsNameB.net
  hsNameC.net
  hsNameH.net

Web sites grouped by .org
  hsNameE.org
  hsNameF.org

Web sites grouped by .tv
  hsNameG.tv
  hsNameI.tv
```

As the output shows, the data is grouped based on the top-level domain name of a website. Notice how this is achieved by the **group** clause:

```
var webAddrs = from addr in websites
               where addr.LastIndexOf('.') != -1
               group addr by addr.Substring(addr.LastIndexOf('.'));
```

The key is obtained by use of the **LastIndexOf( )** and **Substring( )** methods defined by **string**. (These are described in Chapter 7. The version of **Substring( )** used here returns the substring that starts at the specified index and runs to the end of the invoking string.) The index of the last period in a website name is found using **LastIndexOf( )**. Using this index, the **Substring( )** method obtains the remainder of the string, which is the part of the website name that contains the top-level domain name. One other point: Notice the use of the **where** clause to filter out any strings that don't contain a period. The **LastIndexOf( )** method returns –1 if the specified string is not contained in the invoking string.

Because the sequence obtained when **webAddrs** is executed is a list of groups, you will need to use two **foreach** loops to access the members of each group. The outer loop obtains each group. The inner loop enumerates the members within the group. The iteration variable of the outer **foreach** loop must be an **IGrouping** instance compatible with the key and element type. In the example both the keys and elements are **string**. Therefore, the type of the **sites** iteration variable of the outer loop is **IGrouping<string, string>**. The type of the iteration variable of the inner loop is **string**. For brevity, the example implicitly declares these variables, but they could have been explicitly declared as shown here:

```
foreach(IGrouping<string, string> sites in webAddrs) {
  Console.WriteLine("Web sites grouped by " + sites.Key);
  foreach(string site in sites)
    Console.WriteLine("  " + site);
  Console.WriteLine();
}
```

Use into to Create a Continuation

When using **select** or **group**, you will sometimes want to generate a temporary result that will be used by a subsequent part of the query to produce the final result. This is called a *query continuation* (or just a *continuation* for short), and it is accomplished through the use of **into** with a **select** or **group** clause. It has the following general form:

into *name query-body*

where *name* is the name of the range variable that iterates over the temporary result and is used by the continuing query, specified by *query-body*. This is why **into** is called a query continuation when used with **select** or **group**—it continues the query. In essence, a query continuation embodies the concept of building a new query that queries the results of the preceding query.

NOTE *There is also a form of **into** that can be used with **join**, which creates a group join. This is described later in this chapter.*

Here is an example that uses **into** with **group**. The following program reworks the **GroupDemo** example shown earlier, which creates a list of websites grouped by top-level domain name. In this case, the initial results are queried by a range variable called **ws**. This result is then filtered to remove all groups that have fewer than three elements.

```
// Use into with group.
using System;
using System.Linq;

class IntoDemo {

  static void Main() {

    string[] websites = { "hsNameA.com", "hsNameB.net", "hsNameC.net",
                          "hsNameD.com", "hsNameE.org", "hsNameF.org",
                          "hsNameG.tv",  "hsNameH.net", "hsNameI.tv" };
```

```
    // Create a query that groups websites by top-level domain name,
    // but select only those groups that have more than two members.
    // Here, ws is the range variable over the set of groups
    // returned when the first half of the query is executed.
    var webAddrs = from addr in websites
                   where addr.LastIndexOf('.') != -1
                   group addr by addr.Substring(addr.LastIndexOf('.'))
                        into ws
                   where ws.Count() > 2
                   select ws;

    // Execute the query and display the results.
    Console.WriteLine("Top-level domains with more than 2 members.\n");

    foreach(var sites in webAddrs) {
      Console.WriteLine("Contents of " + sites.Key + " domain:");
      foreach(var site in sites)
        Console.WriteLine("  " + site);
      Console.WriteLine();
    }
  }
}
```

The following output is produced:

```
Top-level domains with more than 2 members.

Contents of .net domain:
  hsNameB.net
  hsNameC.net
  hsNameH.net
```

As the output shows, only the **.net** group is returned because it is the only group that has more than two elements.

In the program, pay special attention to this sequence of clauses in the query:

```
group addr by addr.Substring(addr.LastIndexOf('.'))
         into ws
where ws.Count() > 2
select ws;
```

First, the results of the **group** clause are stored (creating a temporary result) and the **where** clause operates on the stored results. At this point, **ws** will range over each group obtained by **group**. Next, the **where** clause filters the query so the final result contains only those groups that contain more than two members. This determination is made by calling **Count( )**, which is an *extension method* that is implemented for all **IEnumerable** objects. It returns the number of elements in a sequence. (You'll learn more about extension methods later in this chapter.) The resulting sequence of groups is returned by the **select** clause.

Use let to Create a Variable in a Query

In a query, you will sometimes want to retain a value temporarily. For example, you might want to create an enumerable variable that can, itself, be queried. Or, you might want to store a value that will be used later on in a **where** clause. Whatever the purpose, these types of actions can be accomplished through the use of **let**.

The **let** clause has this general form:

let *name* = *expression*

Here, *name* is an identifier that is assigned the value of *expression.* The type of *name* is inferred from the type of the expression.

Here is an example that shows how **let** can be used to create another enumerable data source. The query takes as input an array of strings. It then converts those strings into **char** arrays. This is accomplished by use of another **string** method called **ToCharArray( )**, which returns an array containing the characters in the string. The result is assigned to a variable called **chrArray**, which is then used by a nested **from** clause to obtain the individual characters in the array. The query then sorts the characters and returns the resulting sequence.

```
// Use a let clause and a nested from clause.
using System;
using System.Linq;

class LetDemo {

  static void Main() {

    string[] strs = { "alpha", "beta", "gamma" };

    // Create a query that obtains the characters in the
    // strings, returned in sorted order. Notice the use
    // of a nested from clause.
    var chrs = from str in strs
               let chrArray = str.ToCharArray()
                 from ch in chrArray
                 orderby ch
                 select ch;

    Console.WriteLine("The individual characters in sorted order:");

    // Execute the query and display the results.
    foreach(char c in chrs) Console.Write(c + " ");

    Console.WriteLine();
  }
}
```

The output is shown here:

```
The individual characters in sorted order:
a a a a a b e g h l m m p t
```

In the program, notice how the **let** clause assigns to **chrArray** a reference to the array returned by **str.ToCharArray( )**:

```
let chrArray = str.ToCharArray()
```

After the **let** clause, other clauses can make use of **chrArray**. Furthermore, because all arrays in C# are convertible to **IEnumerable<T>**, **chrArray** can be used as a data source for a second, nested **from** clause. This is what happens in the example. It uses the nested **from** to enumerate the individual characters in the array, sorting them into ascending sequence and returning the result.

You can also use a **let** clause to hold a non-enumerable value. For example, the following is a more efficient way to write the query used in the **IntoDemo** program shown in the preceding section.

```
var webAddrs = from addr in websites
               let idx = addr.LastIndexOf('.')
               where idx != -1
               group addr by addr.Substring(idx)
                         into ws
               where ws.Count() > 2
               select ws;
```

In this version, the index of the last occurrence of a period is assigned to **idx**. This value is then used by **Substring( )**. This prevents the search for the period from having to be conducted twice.

Join Two Sequences with join

When working with databases, it is common to want to create a sequence that correlates data from two different data sources. For example, an online store might have one database that associates the name of an item with its item number, and a second database that associates the item number with its in-stock status. Given this situation, you might want to generate a list that shows the in-stock status of items by name, rather than by item number. You can do this by correlating the data in the two databases. Such an action is easy to accomplish in LINQ through the use of the **join** clause.

The general form of **join** is shown here (in context with the **from**):

> from *range-varA* in *data-sourceA*
>   join *range-varB* in *data-sourceB*
>   on *range-varA.property* equals *range-varB.property*

The key to using **join** is to understand that each data source must contain data in common, and that the data can be compared for equality. Thus, in the general form, *data-sourceA* and *data-sourceB* must have something in common that can be compared. The items being compared are specified by the **on** section. Thus, when *range-varA.property* is equal to *range-varB.property*, the correlation succeeds. In essence, **join** acts like a filter, allowing only those elements that share a common value to pass through.

When using **join**, often the sequence returned is a composite of portions of the two data sources. Therefore, **join** lets you generate a new list that contains elements from two different data sources. This enables you to organize data in a new way.

The following program creates a class called **Item**, which encapsulates an item's name with its number. It creates another class called **InStockStatus**, which links an item number with a Boolean property that indicates whether or not the item is in stock. It also creates a class called **Temp**, which has two fields: one **string** and one **bool**. Objects of this class will hold the result of the query. The query uses **join** to produce a list in which an item's name is associated with its in-stock status.

```
// Demonstrate join.
using System;
using System.Linq;

// A class that links an item name with its number.
class Item {
  public string Name { get; set; }
  public int ItemNumber { get; set; }

  public Item(string n, int inum) {
    Name = n;
    ItemNumber = inum;
  }
}

// A class that links an item number with its in-stock status.
class InStockStatus {
  public int ItemNumber { get; set; }
  public bool InStock { get; set; }

  public InStockStatus(int n, bool b) {
    ItemNumber = n;
    InStock = b;
  }
}

// A class that encapsulates a name with its status.
class Temp {
  public string Name { get; set; }
  public bool InStock { get; set; }

  public Temp(string n, bool b) {
    Name = n;
    InStock  = b;
  }
}

class JoinDemo {
  static void Main() {

    Item[] items = {
        new Item("Pliers", 1424),
        new Item("Hammer", 7892),
        new Item("Wrench", 8534),
        new Item("Saw", 6411)
    };
```

```
    InStockStatus[] statusList = {
        new InStockStatus(1424, true),
        new InStockStatus(7892, false),
        new InStockStatus(8534, true),
        new InStockStatus(6411, true)
    };


    // Create a query that joins Item with InStockStatus to
    // produce a list of item names and availability. Notice
    // that a sequence of Temp objects is produced.
    var inStockList = from item in items
                      join entry in statusList
                        on item.ItemNumber equals entry.ItemNumber
                      select new Temp(item.Name, entry.InStock);

    Console.WriteLine("Item\tAvailable\n");

    // Execute the query and display the results.
    foreach(Temp t in inStockList)
      Console.WriteLine("{0}\t{1}", t.Name, t.InStock);
  }
}
```

The output is shown here:

```
Item    Available

Pliers  True
Hammer  False
Wrench  True
Saw     True
```

To understand how **join** works, let's walk through each line in the query. The query begins in the normal fashion with this **from** clause:

```
var inStockList = from item in items
```

This clause specifies that **item** is the range variable for the data source specified by **items**. The **items** array contains objects of type **Item**, which encapsulate a name and a number for an inventory item.

Next comes the **join** clause shown here:

```
join entry in statusList
  on item.ItemNumber equals entry.ItemNumber
```

This clause specifies that **entry** is the range variable for the **statusList** data source. The **statusList** array contains objects of type **InStockStatus**, which link an item number with its status. Thus, **items** and **statusList** have a property in common: the item number. This is used by the **on/equals** portion of the **join** clause to describe the correlation. Thus, **join** matches items from the two data sources when their item numbers are equal.

Finally, the **select** clause returns a **Temp** object that contains an item's name along with its in-stock status:

```
select new Temp(item.Name, entry.InStock);
```

Therefore, the sequence obtained by the query consists of **Temp** objects.

Although the preceding example is fairly straightforward, **join** supports substantially more sophisticated operations. For example, you can use **into** with **join** to create a *group join*, which creates a result that consists of an element from the first sequence and a group of all matching elements from the second sequence. (You'll see an example of this a bit later in this chapter.) In general, the time and effort needed to fully master **join** is well worth the investment because it gives you the ability to reorganize data at runtime. This is a powerful capability. This capability is made even more powerful by the use of anonymous types, described in the next section.

Anonymous Types

C# provides a feature called the *anonymous type* that directly relates to LINQ. As the name implies, an anonymous type is a class that has no name. Its primary use is to create an object returned by the **select** clause. Often, the outcome of a query is a sequence of objects that are either a composite of two (or more) data sources (such as in the case of **join**) or include a subset of the members of one data source. In either case, often the type of the object being returned is needed only because of the query and is not used elsewhere in the program. In this case, using an anonymous type eliminates the need to declare a class that will be used simply to hold the outcome of the query.

An anonymous type is created through the use of this general form:

new { *nameA = valueA, nameB = valueB, ...* }

Here, the names specify identifiers that translate into read-only properties that are initialized by the values. For example,

```
new { Count = 10, Max = 100, Min = 0 }
```

This creates a class type that has three public read-only properties: **Count**, **Max**, and **Min**. These are given the values 10, 100, and 0, respectively. These properties can be referred to by name by other code. Notice that an anonymous type uses object initializers to initialize the properties. As explained in Chapter 8, object initializers provide a way to initialize an object without explicitly invoking a constructor. This is necessary in the case of anonymous types because there is no way to explicitly call a constructor. (Recall that constructors have the same name as their class. In the case of an anonymous class, there is no name. So, how would you invoke the constructor?)

Because an anonymous type has no name, you must use an implicitly typed variable to refer to it. This lets the compiler infer the proper type. For example,

```
var myOb = new { Count = 10, Max = 100, Min = 0 }
```

creates a variable called **myOb** that is assigned a reference to the object created by the anonymous type expression. This means that the following statements are legal:

```
Console.WriteLine("Count is " + myOb.Count);

if(i <= myOb.Max && i >= myOb.Min) // ...
```

Remember, when an anonymous type is created, the identifiers that you specify become read-only public properties. Thus, they can be used by other parts of your code.

Although the term *anonymous type* is used, it's not quite completely true! The type is anonymous relative to you, the programmer. However, the compiler does give it an internal name. Thus, anonymous types do not violate C#'s strong type checking rules.

To fully understand the value of anonymous types, consider this rewrite of the previous program that demonstrated **join**. Recall that in the previous version, a class called **Temp** was needed to encapsulate the result of the **join**. Through the use of an anonymous type, this "placeholder" class is no longer needed and no longer clutters the source code to the program. The output from the program is unchanged from before.

```
// Use an anonymous type to improve the join demo program.
using System;
using System.Linq;

// A class that links an item name with its number.
class Item {
  public string Name { get; set; }
  public int ItemNumber { get; set; }

  public Item(string n, int inum) {
    Name = n;
    ItemNumber = inum;
  }
}

// A class that links an item number with its in-stock status.
class InStockStatus {
  public int ItemNumber { get; set; }
  public bool InStock { get; set; }

  public InStockStatus(int n, bool b) {
    ItemNumber = n;
    InStock = b;
  }
}

class AnonTypeDemo {
  static void Main() {

    Item[] items = {
        new Item("Pliers", 1424),
        new Item("Hammer", 7892),
        new Item("Wrench", 8534),
        new Item("Saw", 6411)
    };

    InStockStatus[] statusList = {
        new InStockStatus(1424, true),
        new InStockStatus(7892, false),
        new InStockStatus(8534, true),
        new InStockStatus(6411, true)
    };
```

```
    // Create a query that joins Item with InStockStatus to
    // produce a list of item names and availability.
    // Now, an anonymous type is used.
    var inStockList = from item in items
                      join entry in statusList
                         on item.ItemNumber equals entry.ItemNumber
                      select new { Name = item.Name,
                                   InStock =  entry.InStock };

    Console.WriteLine("Item\tAvailable\n");

    // Execute the query and display the results.
    foreach(var t in inStockList)
      Console.WriteLine("{0}\t{1}", t.Name, t.InStock);
  }
}
```

Pay special attention to the **select** clause:

```
select new { Name = item.Name,
             InStock =  entry.InStock };
```

It returns an object of an anonymous type that has two read-only properties, **Name** and **InStock**. These are given the values specified by the item's name and availability. Because of the anonymous type, there is no longer any need for the **Temp** class.

One other point. Notice the **foreach** loop that executes the query. It now uses **var** to declare the iteration variable. This is necessary because the type of the object contained in **inStockList** has no name. This situation is one of the reasons that C# includes implicitly typed variables. They are needed to support anonymous types.

Before moving on, there is one more aspect of anonymous types that warrants a mention. In some cases, including the one just shown, you can simplify the syntax of the anonymous type through the use of a *projection initializer*. In this case, you simply specify the name of the initializer by itself. This name automatically becomes the name of the property. For example, here is another way to code the **select** clause used by the preceding program:

```
select new { item.Name, entry.InStock };
```

Here, the property names are still **Name** and **InStock**, just as before. The compiler automatically "projects" the identifiers **Name** and **InStock**, making them the property names of the anonymous type. Also as before, the properties are given the values specified by **item.Name** and **entry.InStock**.

Create a Group Join

As mentioned earlier, you can use **into** with **join** to create a *group join*, which creates a sequence in which each entry in the result consists of an entry from the first sequence and a group of all matching elements from the second sequence. No example was presented then because often a group join makes use of an anonymous type. Now that anonymous types have been covered, an example of a simple group join can be given.

The following example uses a group join to create a list in which various transports, such as cars, boats, and planes, are organized by their general transportation category, which is land, sea, or air. The program first creates a class called **Transport** that links a transport type with its classification. Inside **Main( )**, it creates two input sequences. The first is an array of strings that contains the names of the general means by which one travels, which are land, sea, and air. The second is an array of **Transport**, which encapsulates various means of transportation. It then uses a group join to produce a list of transports that are organized by their category.

```csharp
// Demonstrate a simple group join.
using System;
using System.Linq;

// This class links the name of a transport, such as Train,
// with its general classification, such as land, sea, or air.
class Transport {
  public string Name { get; set; }
  public string How { get; set; }

  public Transport(string n, string h) {
    Name = n;
    How = h;
  }
}

class GroupJoinDemo {
  static void Main() {

    // An array of transport classifications.
    string[] travelTypes = {
        "Air",
        "Sea",
        "Land"
    };

    // An array of transports.
    Transport[] transports = {
        new Transport("Bicycle", "Land"),
        new Transport("Balloon", "Air"),
        new Transport("Boat", "Sea"),
        new Transport("Jet", "Air"),
        new Transport("Canoe", "Sea"),
        new Transport("Biplane", "Air"),
        new Transport("Car", "Land"),
        new Transport("Cargo Ship", "Sea"),
        new Transport("Train", "Land")
    };

    // Create a query that uses a group join to produce
    // a list of item names and IDs organized by category.
    var byHow = from how in travelTypes
                join trans in transports
                on how equals trans.How
                into lst
                select new { How = how, Tlist = lst };
```

```
    // Execute the query and display the results.
    foreach(var t in byHow) {
      Console.WriteLine("{0} transportation includes:", t.How);

      foreach(var m in t.Tlist)
        Console.WriteLine("  " + m.Name);

      Console.WriteLine();
    }
  }
}
```

The output is shown here:

```
Air transportation includes:
  Balloon
  Jet
  Biplane

Sea transportation includes:
  Boat
  Canoe
  Cargo Ship

Land transportation includes:
  Bicycle
  Car
  Train
```

The key part of the program is, of course, the query, which is shown here:

```
var byHow = from how in travelTypes
                join trans in transports
                on how equals trans.How
                into lst
                select new { How = how, Tlist = lst };
```

Here is how it works. The **from** statement uses **how** to range over the **travelTypes** array. Recall that **travelTypes** contains an array of the general travel classifications: air, land, and sea. The **join** clause joins each travel type with those transports that use that type. For example, the type Land is joined with Bicycle, Car, and Train. However, because of the **into** clause, for each travel type, the **join** produces a list of the transports that use that travel type. This list is represented by **lst**. Finally, **select** returns an anonymous type that encapsulates each value of **how** (the travel type) with a list of transports. This is why the two **foreach** loops shown here are needed to display the results of the query:

```
foreach(var t in byHow) {
  Console.WriteLine("{0} transportation includes:", t.How);

  foreach(var m in t.Tlist)
    Console.WriteLine("  " + m.Name);

  Console.WriteLine();
}
```

The outer loop obtains an object that contains the name of the travel type and the list of the transports for that type. The inner loop displays the individual transports.

The Query Methods

The query syntax described by the preceding sections is the way you will probably write most queries in C#. It is convenient, powerful, and compact. It is, however, not the only way to write a query. The other way is to use the *query methods*. These methods can be called on any enumerable object, such as an array.

The Basic Query Methods

The query methods are defined by **System.Linq.Enumerable** and are implemented as *extension methods* that extend the functionality of **IEnumerable<T>**. (Query methods are also defined by **System.Linq.Queryable**, which extends the functionality of **IQueryable<T>**, but this interface is not used in this chapter.) An extension method adds functionality to another class, but without the use of inheritance. Support for extension methods is relatively new, being added by C# 3.0, and we will look more closely at them later in this chapter. For now, it is sufficient to understand that query methods can be called only on an object that implements **IEnumerable<T>**.

The **Enumerable** class provides many query methods, but at the core are those that correspond to the query keywords described earlier. These methods are shown here, along with the keywords to which they relate. Understand that these methods have overloaded forms and only their simplest form is shown. However, this is also the form that you will often use.

Query Keyword	Equivalent Query Method
select	Select(*selector*)
where	Where(*predicate*)
orderby	OrderBy(*keySelector*) or OrderByDescending(*keySelector*)
join	Join(*inner*, *outerKeySelector*, *innerKeySelector*, *resultSelector*)
group	GroupBy(*keySelector*)

Except for **Join( )**, these query methods take one argument, which is an object of some form of the generic type **Func<T, TResult>**. This is a built-in delegate type that is declared like this:

delegate TResult Func<in T, out TResult>(T *arg*)

Here, **TResult** specifies the result type of the delegate and **T** specifies the element type. In these query methods, the *selector*, *predicate*, or *keySelector* argument determines what action the query method takes. For example, in the case of **Where( )**, it determines how the query filters the data. Each of these query methods returns an enumerable object. Thus, the result of one can be used to execute a call on another, allowing the methods to be chained together.

The **Join( )** method takes four arguments. The first is a reference to the second sequence to be joined. The first sequence is the one on which **Join( )** is called. The key selector for the first sequence is passed via *outerKeySelector*, and the key selector for the second sequence is passed via *innerKeySelector*. The result of the join is described by *resultSelector*. The type of *outerKeySelector* is **Func<TOuter, TKey>**, and the type of *innerKeySelector* is **Func<TInner, TKey>**. The *resultSelector* argument is of type **Func<TOuter, TInner, TResult>**. Here, **TOuter** is the element type of the invoking sequence; **TInner** is the element type of the passed sequence; and **TResult** is the type of the resulting elements. An enumerable object is returned that contains the result of the join.

Although an argument to a query method such as **Where( )** is a method compatible with the specified form of the **Func** delegate, it does not need to be an explicitly declared method. In fact, most often it won't be. Instead, you will usually use a lambda expression. As explained in Chapter 15, a lambda expression offers a streamlined, yet powerful way to define what is, essentially, an anonymous method. The C# compiler automatically converts a lambda expression into a form that can be passed to a **Func** parameter. Because of the convenience offered by lambda expressions, they are used by all of the examples in this section.

Create Queries by Using the Query Methods

By using the query methods in conjunction with lambda expressions, it is possible to create queries that do not use the C# query syntax. Instead, the query methods are called. Let's begin with a simple example. It reworks the first program in this chapter so that it uses calls to **Where( )** and **Select( )** rather than the query keywords.

```
// Use the query methods to create a simple query.
// This is a reworked version of the first program in this chapter.
using System;
using System.Linq;

class SimpQuery {
  static void Main() {

    int[] nums =  { 1, -2, 3, 0, -4, 5 };

    // Use Where() and Select() to create a simple query.
    var posNums = nums.Where(n => n > 0).Select(r => r);

    Console.Write("The positive values in nums: ");

    // Execute the query and display the results.
    foreach(int i in posNums) Console.Write(i + " ");
    Console.WriteLine();
  }
}
```

The output, shown here, is the same as the original version:

```
The positive values in nums: 1 3 5
```

In the program, pay special attention to this line:

```
var posNums = nums.Where(n => n > 0).Select(r => r);
```

This creates a query called **posNums** that creates a sequence of the positive values in **nums**. It does this by use of the **Where( )** method (to filter the values) and **Select( )** (to select the values). The **Where( )** method can be invoked on **nums** because all arrays implement **IEnumerable<T>**, which supports the query extension methods.

Technically, the **Select( )** method in the preceding example is not necessary because in this simple case, the sequence returned by **Where( )** already contains the result. However, you can use more sophisticated selection criteria, just as you did with the query syntax. For example, this query returns the positive values in **nums** increased by an order of magnitude:

```
var posNums = nums.Where(n => n > 0).Select(r => r * 10);
```

As you might expect, you can chain together other operations. For example, this query selects the positive values, sorts them into descending order, and returns the resulting sequence:

```
var posNums = nums.Where(n => n > 0).OrderByDescending(j => j);
```

Here, the expression **j => j** specifies that the ordering is dependent on the input parameter, which is an element from the sequence obtained from **Where( )**.

Here is an example that demonstrates the **GroupBy( )** method. It reworks the **group** example shown earlier.

```
// Demonstrate the GroupBy() query method.
// This program reworks the earlier version that used
// the query syntax.
using System;
using System.Linq;

class GroupByDemo {

  static void Main() {

    string[] websites = { "hsNameA.com", "hsNameB.net", "hsNameC.net",
                          "hsNameD.com", "hsNameE.org", "hsNameF.org",
                          "hsNameG.tv",  "hsNameH.net", "hsNameI.tv" };

    // Use query methods to group websites by top-level domain name.
    var webAddrs = websites.Where(w => w.LastIndexOf('.') != -1).
         GroupBy(x => x.Substring(x.LastIndexOf(".")));

    // Execute the query and display the results.
    foreach(var sites in webAddrs) {
      Console.WriteLine("Web sites grouped by " + sites.Key);
      foreach(var site in sites)
        Console.WriteLine("  " + site);
      Console.WriteLine();
    }
  }
}
```

This version produces the same output as the earlier version. The only difference is how the query is created. In this version, the query methods are used.

Here is another example. Recall the **join** query used in the **JoinDemo** example shown earlier:

```
var inStockList = from item in items
                  join entry in statusList
                    on item.ItemNumber equals entry.ItemNumber
                  select new Temp(item.Name, entry.InStock);
```

This query produces a sequence that contains objects that encapsulate the name and the in-stock status of an inventory item. This information is synthesized from joining the two lists **items** and **statusList**. The following version reworks this query so that it uses the **Join( )** method rather than the C# query syntax:

```
// Use Join() to produce a list of item names and status.
var inStockList = items.Join(statusList,
                    k1 => k1.ItemNumber,
                    k2 => k2.ItemNumber,
                    (k1, k2) => new Temp(k1.Name, k2.InStock) );
```

Although this version uses the named class called **Temp** to hold the resulting object, an anonymous type could have been used instead. This approach is shown next:

```
var inStockList = items.Join(statusList,
                    k1 => k1.ItemNumber,
                    k2 => k2.ItemNumber,
                    (k1, k2) => new { k1.Name, k2.InStock} );
```

Query Syntax vs. Query Methods

As the preceding section has explained, C# has two ways of creating queries: the query syntax and the query methods. What is interesting, and not readily apparent by simply looking at a program's source code, is that the two approaches are more closely related than you might at first assume. The reason is that the query syntax is compiled into calls to the query methods. Thus, when you write something like

```
where x < 10
```

the compiler translates it into

```
Where(x => x < 10)
```

Therefore, the two approaches to creating a query ultimately lead to the same place.

Given that the two approaches are ultimately equivalent, the following question naturally arises: Which approach is best for a C# program? The answer: In general, you will want to use the query syntax. It is fully integrated into the C# language, supported by keywords and syntax, and is cleaner.

More Query-Related Extension Methods

In addition to the methods that correspond to the query keywords supported by C#, the .NET Framework provides several other query-related extension methods that are often helpful in a query. These query-related methods are defined for **IEnumerable<T>** by **Enumerable**. Here is a sampling of several commonly used methods. Because many of the methods are overloaded, only their general form is shown.

Method	Description
All(*predicate*)	Returns true if all elements in a sequence satisfy a specified condition.
Any(*predicate*)	Returns true if any element in a sequence satisfies a specified condition.
Average( )	Returns the average of the values in a numeric sequence.
Contains(*value*)	Returns true if the sequence contains the specified object.
Count( )	Returns the length of a sequence. This is the number of elements that it contains.
First( )	Returns the first element in a sequence.
Last( )	Returns the last element in a sequence.
Max( )	Returns the maximum value in a sequence.
Min( )	Returns the minimum value in a sequence.
Sum( )	Returns the summation of the values in a numeric sequence.

You have already seen **Count( )** in action earlier in this chapter. Here is a program that demonstrates the others:

```
// Use several of the extension methods defined by Enumerable.
using System;
using System.Linq;

class ExtMethods {
  static void Main() {

    int[] nums = { 3, 1, 2, 5, 4 };

    Console.WriteLine("The minimum value is " + nums.Min());
    Console.WriteLine("The maximum value is " + nums.Max());

    Console.WriteLine("The first value is " + nums.First());
    Console.WriteLine("The last value is " + nums.Last());

    Console.WriteLine("The sum is " + nums.Sum());
    Console.WriteLine("The average is " + nums.Average());

    if(nums.All(n => n > 0))
      Console.WriteLine("All values are greater than zero.");

    if(nums.Any(n => (n % 2) == 0))
      Console.WriteLine("At least one value is even.");

    if(nums.Contains(3))
      Console.WriteLine("The array contains 3.");
  }
}
```

The output is shown here:

```
The minimum value is 1
The maximum value is 5
The first value is 3
The last value is 4
The sum is 15
The average is 3
All values are greater than zero.
At least one value is even.
The array contains 3.
```

You can also use the query-related extension methods within a query based on the C# query syntax. In fact, it is quite common to do so. For example, this program uses **Average( )** to obtain a sequence that contains only those values that are less than the average of the values in an array.

```
// Use Average() with the query syntax.
using System;
using System.Linq;

class ExtMethods2 {
  static void Main() {

    int[] nums =  { 1, 2, 4, 8, 6, 9, 10, 3, 6, 7 };

    var ltAvg = from n in nums
                let x = nums.Average()
                where n < x
                select n;

    Console.WriteLine("The average is " + nums.Average());

    Console.Write("These values are less than the average: ");

    // Execute the query and display the results.
    foreach(int i in ltAvg) Console.Write(i + " ");

    Console.WriteLine();
  }
}
```

The output is shown here:

```
The average is 5.6
These values are less than the average: 1 2 4 3
```

Pay special attention to the query:

```
    var ltAvg = from n in nums
                let x = nums.Average()
                where n < x
                select n;
```

Notice in the **let** statement, **x** is set equal to the average of the values in **nums**. This value is obtained by calling **Average( )** on **nums**.

Deferred vs. Immediate Query Execution

In LINQ, queries have two different modes of execution: immediate and deferred. As explained early in this chapter, a query defines a set of rules that are not actually executed until a **foreach** statement executes. This is called *deferred execution*.

However, if you use one of the extension methods that produces a non-sequence result, then the query must be executed to obtain that result. For example, consider the **Count( )** method. In order for **Count( )** to return the number of elements in the sequence, the query must be executed, and this is done automatically when **Count( )** is called. In this case, *immediate execution* takes place, with the query being executed automatically in order to obtain the result. Therefore, even though you don't explicitly use the query in a **foreach** loop, the query is still executed.

Here is a simple example. It obtains the number of positive elements in the sequence.

```
// Use immediate execution.
using System;
using System.Linq;

class ImmediateExec {
  static void Main() {

    int[] nums =  { 1, -2, 3, 0, -4, 5 };

    // Create a query that obtains the number of positive
    // values in nums.
    int len = (from n in nums
               where n > 0
               select n).Count();

    Console.WriteLine("The number of positive values in nums: " + len);
  }
}
```

The output is

```
The number of positive values in nums: 3
```

In the program, notice that no explicit **foreach** loop is specified. Instead, the query automatically executes because of the call to **Count( )**.

As a point of interest, the query in the preceding program could also have been written like this:

```
var posNums = from n in nums
              where n > 0
              select n;

int len = posNums.Count(); // query executes here
```

In this case, **Count( )** is called on the query variable. At that point, the query is executed to obtain the count.

Other methods that cause immediate execution of a query include **ToArray( )** and **ToList( )**. Both are extension methods defined by **Enumerable**. **ToArray( )** returns the results of a query in an array. **ToList( )** returns the results of a query in the form of a **List** collection. (See Chapter 25 for a discussion of collections.) In both cases, the query is executed to obtain the results. For example, the following sequence obtains an array of the results generated by the **posNums** query just shown. It then displays the results.

```
int[] pnums = posNum.ToArray(); // query executes here

foreach(int i in pnums)
  Console.Write(i + " ");
}
```

Expression Trees

Another LINQ-related feature is the *expression tree*. An expression tree is a representation of a lambda expression as data. Thus, an expression tree, itself, cannot be executed. It can, however, be converted into an executable form. Expression trees are encapsulated by the **System.Linq.Expressions.Expression<TDelegate>** class. Expression trees are useful in situations in which a query will be executed by something outside the program, such as a database that uses SQL. By representing the query as data, the query can be converted into a format understood by the database. This process is used by the LINQ to SQL feature provided by Visual C#, for example. Thus, expression trees help C# support a variety of data sources.

You can obtain an executable form of an expression tree by calling the **Compile( )** method defined by **Expression**. It returns a reference that can be assigned to a delegate and then executed. You can declare your own delegate type or use one of the predefined **Func** delegate types defined within the **System** namespace. Two forms of the **Func** delegate were mentioned earlier, when the query methods were described, but there are several others.

Expression trees have one key restriction: Only expression lambdas can be represented by expression trees. They cannot be used to represent statement lambdas.

Here is a simple example of an expression tree in action. It creates an expression tree whose data represents a method that determines if one integer is a factor of another. It then compiles the expression tree into executable code. Finally, it demonstrates the compiled code.

```
// A simple expression tree.
using System;
using System.Linq;
using System.Linq.Expressions;

class SimpleExpTree {
  static void Main() {

    // Represent a lambda expression as data.
    Expression<Func<int, int, bool>>
      IsFactorExp = (n, d) => (d != 0) ? (n % d) == 0 : false;

    // Compile the expression data into executable code.
    Func<int, int, bool> IsFactor = IsFactorExp.Compile();

    // Execute the expression.
    if(IsFactor(10, 5))
      Console.WriteLine("5 is a factor of 10.");

    if(!IsFactor(10, 7))
```

```
        Console.WriteLine("7 is not a factor of 10.");

      Console.WriteLine();
  }
}
```

The output is shown here:

```
5 is a factor of 10.
7 is not a factor of 10.
```

The program illustrates the two key steps in using an expression tree. First, it creates an expression tree by using this statement:

```
Expression<Func<int, int, bool>>
  IsFactorExp = (n, d) => (d != 0) ? (n % d) == 0 : false;
```

This constructs a representation of a lambda expression in memory. As explained, this representation is data, not code. This representation is referred to by **IsFactorExp**. The following statement converts the expression data into executable code:

```
Func<int, int, bool> IsFactor = IsFactorExp.Compile();
```

After this statement executes, the **IsFactor** delegate can be called to determine if one value is a factor of another.

One other point: Notice that **Func<int, int, bool>** indicates the delegate type. This form of **Func** specifies two parameters of type **int** and a return type of **bool**. This is the form of **Func** that is compatible with the lambda expression used in the program because that expression requires two parameters. Other lambda expressions may require different forms of **Func**, based on the number of parameters they require. In general, the specific form of **Func** must match the requirements of the lambda expression.

Extension Methods

As mentioned earlier, extension methods provide a means by which functionality can be added to a class without using the normal inheritance mechanism. Although you won't often create your own extension methods (because the inheritance mechanism offers a better solution in many cases), it is still important that you understand how they work because of their integral importance to LINQ.

An extension method is a static method that must be contained within a static, non-generic class. The type of its first parameter determines the type of objects on which the extension method can be called. Furthermore, the first parameter must be modified by **this**. The object on which the method is invoked is passed automatically to the first parameter. It is not explicitly passed in the argument list. A key point is that even though an extension method is declared **static**, it can still be called on an object, just as if it were an instance method.

Here is the general form of an extension method:

static *ret-type name*(this *invoked-on-type ob, param-list*)

Of course, if there are no arguments other than the one passed implicitly to *ob*, then *param-list* will be empty. Remember, the first parameter is automatically passed the object on which the method is invoked. In general, an extension method will be a public member of its class.

Here is an example that creates three simple extension methods:

```
// Create and use some extension methods.
using System;
using System.Globalization;
static class MyExtMeths {

  // Return the reciprocal of a double.
  public static double Reciprocal(this double v) {
    return 1.0 / v;
  }

  // Reverse the case of letters within a string and
  // return the result.
  public static string RevCase(this string str) {
    string temp = "";

    foreach(char ch in str) {
      if(Char.IsLower(ch)) temp += Char.ToUpper(ch, CultureInfo.CurrentCulture);
      else temp += Char.ToLower(ch, CultureInfo.CurrentCulture);
    }
    return temp;
  }

  // Return the absolute value of n / d.
  public static double AbsDivideBy(this double n, double d) {
    return Math.Abs(n / d);
  }
}

class ExtDemo {
  static void Main() {
    double val = 8.0;
    string str = "Alpha Beta Gamma";

    // Call the Reciprocal() extension method.
    Console.WriteLine("Reciprocal of {0} is {1}",
                      val, val.Reciprocal());

    // Call the RevCase() extension method.
    Console.WriteLine(str + " after reversing case is " +
                      str.RevCase());

    // Use AbsDivideBy();
    Console.WriteLine("Result of val.AbsDivideBy(-2): " +
                      val.AbsDivideBy(-2));
  }
}
```

The output is shown here:

```
Reciprocal of 8 is 0.125
Alpha Beta Gamma after reversing case is aLPHA bETA gAMMA
Result of val.AbsDivideBy(-2): 4
```

In the program, notice that each extension method is contained in a static class called **MyExtMeths**. As explained, an extension method must be declared within a static class. Furthermore, this class must be in scope in order for the extension methods that it contains to be used. (This is why you needed to include the **System.Linq** namespace to use the LINQ-related extension methods.) Next, notice the calls to the extension methods. They are invoked on an object, in just the same way that an instance method is called. The main difference is that the invoking object is passed to the first parameter of the extension method. Therefore, when the expression

```
val.AbsDivideBy(-2)
```

executes, **val** is passed to the **n** parameter of **AbsDivideBy( )** and –2 is passed to the **d** parameter.

As a point of interest, because the methods **Reciprocal( )** and **AbsDivideBy( )** are defined for **double**, it is legal to invoke them on a **double** literal, as shown here:

```
8.0.Reciprocal()
8.0.AbsDivideBy(-1)
```

Furthermore, **RevCase( )** can be invoked like this:

```
"AbCDe".RevCase()
```

Here, the reversed-case version of a string literal is returned.

PLINQ

The .NET Framework 4.0 adds a new capability to LINQ called PLINQ. PLINQ provides support for parallel programming. This feature enables a query to automatically take advantage of multiple processors. PLINQ and other features related to parallel programming are described in Chapter 24.

Unsafe Code, Pointers, Nullable Types, Dynamic Types, and Miscellaneous Topics

This chapter covers a feature of C# whose name usually takes programmers by surprise: unsafe code. Unsafe code often involves the use of pointers. Together, unsafe code and pointers enable C# to be used to create applications that one might normally associate with C++: high-performance, systems code. Moreover, the inclusion of unsafe code and pointers gives C# capabilities that are lacking in Java.

Also covered in this chapter are nullable types, partial class and partial method definitions, fixed-size buffers, and the new **dynamic** type. The chapter concludes by discussing the few keywords that have not been covered by the preceding chapters.

Unsafe Code

C# allows you to write what is called "unsafe" code. Although this statement might seem shocking, it really isn't. Unsafe code is not code that is poorly written; it is code that does not execute under the full management of the common language runtime (CLR). As explained in Chapter 1, C# is normally used to create managed code. It is possible, however, to write code that does not execute under the full control of the CLR. This unmanaged code is not subject to the same controls and constraints as managed code, so it is called "unsafe" because it is not possible to verify that it won't perform some type of harmful action. Thus, the term *unsafe* does not mean that the code is inherently flawed. It simply means that it is possible for the code to perform actions that are not subject to the supervision of the managed context.

Given that unsafe code might cause problems, you might ask why anyone would want to create such code. The answer is that managed code prevents the use of *pointers*. If you are familiar with C or C++, then you know that pointers are variables that hold the addresses of other objects. Thus, pointers are a bit like references in C#. The main difference is that a pointer can point anywhere in memory; a reference always refers to an object of its type. Because a pointer can point anywhere in memory, it is possible to misuse a pointer. It is also easy to introduce a coding error when using pointers. This is why C# does not support pointers when creating managed code. Pointers are, however, both useful and necessary for some types of programming (such as system-level utilities), and C# does allow you to create and use pointers. However, all pointer operations must be marked as unsafe since they execute outside the managed context.

The declaration and use of pointers in C# parallels that of C/C++—if you know how to use pointers in C/C++, then you can use them in C#. But remember, the essence of C# is the creation of managed code. Its ability to support unmanaged code allows it to be applied to a special class of problems. It is not for normal C# programming. In fact, to compile unmanaged code, you must use the **/unsafe** compiler option.

Since pointers are at the core of unsafe code, we will begin there.

Pointer Basics

A pointer is a variable that holds the address of some other object, such as another variable. For example, if **x** contains the address of **y**, then **x** is said to "point to" **y**. When a pointer points to a variable, the value of that variable can be obtained or changed through the pointer. Operations through pointers are often referred to as *indirection.*

Declaring a Pointer

Pointer variables must be declared as such. The general form of a pointer variable declaration is

> *type* * *var-name*;

Here, *type* is the pointer's *referent type,* which must be a nonreference type. Thus, you cannot declare a pointer to a class object. A pointer's referent type is also sometimes called its *base type.* Notice the placement of the *. It follows the type name. *var-name* is the name of the pointer variable.

Here is an example. To declare **ip** to be a pointer to an **int**, use this declaration:

```
int* ip;
```

For a **float** pointer, use

```
float* fp;
```

In general, in a declaration statement, following a type name with an * creates a pointer type.

The type of data that a pointer will point to is determined by its referent type. Thus, in the preceding examples, **ip** can be used to point to an **int**, and **fp** can be used to point to a **float**. Understand, however, that there is nothing that actually prevents a pointer from pointing elsewhere. This is why pointers are potentially unsafe.

If you come from a C/C++ background, then you need to be aware of an important difference between the way C# and C/C++ declare pointers. When you declare a pointer type in C/C++, the * is not distributive over a list of variables in a declaration. Thus, in C/C++, this statement

```
int* p, q;
```

declares an **int** pointer called **p** and an **int** called **q**. It is equivalent to the following two declarations:

```
int* p;
int q;
```

However, in C#, the * *is* distributive and the declaration

```
int* p, q;
```

creates two pointer variables. Thus, in C# it is the same as these two declarations:

```
int* p;
int* q;
```

This is an important difference to keep in mind when porting C/C++ code to C#.

The * and & Pointer Operators

Two operators are used with pointers: * and &. The & is a unary operator that returns the memory address of its operand. (Recall that a unary operator requires only one operand.) For example,

```
int* ip;
int num = 10;

ip = &num;
```

puts into **ip** the memory address of the variable **num**. This address is the location of the variable in the computer's internal memory. It has *nothing* to do with the *value* of **num**. Thus, **ip** *does not* contain the value 10 (**num**'s initial value). It contains the address at which **num** is stored. The operation of & can be remembered as returning "the address of" the variable it precedes. Therefore, the preceding assignment statement could be verbalized as "**ip** receives the address of **num**."

The second operator is *, and it is the complement of &. It is a unary operator that evaluates to the value of the variable located at the address specified by its operand. That is, it refers to the value of the variable pointed to by a pointer. Continuing with the same example, if **ip** contains the memory address of the variable **num**, then

```
int val = *ip;
```

will place into **val** the value 10, which is the value of **num**, which is pointed to by **ip**. The operation of * can be remembered as "at address." In this case, then, the statement could be read as "**val** receives the value at address **ip**."

The * can also be used on the left side of an assignment statement. In this usage, it sets the value pointed to by the pointer. For example,

```
*ip = 100;
```

This statement assigns 100 to the variable pointed to by **ip**, which is **num** in this case. Thus, this statement can be read as "at address **ip**, put the value 100."

Using unsafe

Any code that uses pointers must be marked as unsafe by using the **unsafe** keyword. You can mark types (such as classes and structures), members (such as methods and operators), or individual blocks of code as unsafe. For example, here is a program that uses pointers inside **Main( )**, which is marked unsafe:

```
// Demonstrate pointers and unsafe.

using System;

class UnsafeCode {
  // Mark Main as unsafe.
  unsafe static void Main() {
    int count = 99;
    int* p; // create an int pointer

    p = &count; // put address of count into p

    Console.WriteLine("Initial value of count is " + *p);

    *p = 10; // assign 10 to count via p

    Console.WriteLine("New value of count is " + *p);
  }
}
```

The output of this program is shown here:

```
Initial value of count is 99
New value of count is 10
```

Using fixed

The **fixed** modifier is often used when working with pointers. It prevents a managed variable from being moved by the garbage collector. This is needed when a pointer refers to a field in a class object, for example. Because the pointer has no knowledge of the actions of the garbage collector, if the object is moved, the pointer will point to the wrong object. Here is the general form of **fixed**:

> fixed (*type* * *p* = &*fixedObj*) {
>   // use fixed object
> }

Here, *p* is a pointer that is being assigned the address of an object. The object will remain at its current memory location until the block of code has executed. You can also use a single statement for the target of a **fixed** statement. The **fixed** keyword can be used only in an unsafe context. You can declare more than one fixed pointer at a time using a comma-separated list.

Here is an example of **fixed**:

```
// Demonstrate fixed.

using System;

class Test {
  public int num;
  public Test(int i) { num = i; }
}
```

```
class FixedCode {
  // Mark Main as unsafe.
  unsafe static void Main() {
    Test o = new Test(19);

    fixed (int* p = &o.num) { // use fixed to put address of o.num into p

      Console.WriteLine("Initial value of o.num is " + *p);

      *p = 10; // assign 10 to o.num via p

      Console.WriteLine("New value of o.num is " + *p);
    }
  }
}
```

The output from this program is shown here:

```
Initial value of o.num is 19
New value of o.num is 10
```

Here, **fixed** prevents **o** from being moved. Because **p** points to **o.num**, if **o** were moved, then **p** would point to an invalid location.

Accessing Structure Members Through a Pointer

A pointer can point to an object of a structure type as long as the structure does not contain reference types. When you access a member of a structure through a pointer, you must use the arrow operator, which is –>, rather than the dot (.) operator. For example, given this structure,

```
struct MyStruct {
  public int a;
  public int b;
  public int Sum() { return a + b; }
}
```

you would access its members through a pointer, like this:

```
MyStruct o = new MyStruct();
MyStruct* p; // declare a pointer

p = &o;
p->a = 10; // use the -> operator
p->b = 20; // use the -> operator

Console.WriteLine("Sum is " + p->Sum());
```

Pointer Arithmetic

There are only four arithmetic operators that can be used on pointers: ++, – –, +, and –. To understand what occurs in pointer arithmetic, we will begin with an example. Let **p1** be an **int** pointer with a current value of 2,000 (that is, it contains the address 2,000). After this expression,

```
p1++;
```

the contents of **p1** will be 2,004, not 2,001! The reason is that each time **p1** is incremented, it will point to the *next* **int**. Since **int** in C# is 4 bytes long, incrementing **p1** increases its value by 4. The reverse is true of decrements. Each decrement decreases **p1**'s value by 4. For example,

```
p1--;
```

will cause **p1** to have the value 1,996, assuming it previously was 2,000.

Generalizing from the preceding example, each time that a pointer is incremented, it will point to the memory location of the next element of its referent type. Each time it is decremented, it will point to the location of the previous element of its referent type.

Pointer arithmetic is not limited to only increment and decrement operations. You can also add or subtract integers to or from pointers. The expression

```
p1 = p1 + 9;
```

makes **p1** point to the ninth element of **p1**'s referent type, beyond the one it is currently pointing to.

Although you cannot add pointers, you can subtract one pointer from another (provided they are both of the same referent type). The remainder will be the number of elements of the referent type that separate the two pointers.

Other than addition and subtraction of a pointer and an integer, or the subtraction of two pointers, no other arithmetic operations can be performed on pointers. For example, you cannot add or subtract **float** or **double** values to or from pointers. Also, you cannot use pointer arithmetic with **void*** pointers.

To see the effects of pointer arithmetic, execute the next short program. It prints the actual physical addresses to which an integer pointer (**ip**) and a floating-point pointer (**fp**) are pointing. Observe how each changes, relative to its referent type, each time the loop is repeated.

```
// Demonstrate the effects of pointer arithmetic.

using System;

class PtrArithDemo {
  unsafe static void Main() {
    int x;
    int i;
    double d;

    int* ip = &i;
    double* fp = &d;

    Console.WriteLine("int      double\n");

    for(x=0; x < 10; x++) {
      Console.WriteLine((uint) (ip) + " " + (uint) (fp));
      ip++;
      fp++;
    }
  }
}
```

Sample output is shown here. Your output may differ, but the intervals will be the same.

```
int      double

1243464  1243468
1243468  1243476
1243472  1243484
1243476  1243492
1243480  1243500
1243484  1243508
1243488  1243516
1243492  1243524
1243496  1243532
1243500  1243540
```

As the output shows, pointer arithmetic is performed relative to the referent type of the pointer. Since an **int** is 4 bytes and a **double** is 8 bytes, the addresses change in increments of these values.

Pointer Comparisons

Pointers can be compared using the relational operators, such as = =, <, and >. However, for the outcome of a pointer comparison to be meaningful, usually the two pointers must have some relationship to each other. For example, if **p1** and **p2** are pointers that point to two separate and unrelated variables, then any comparison between **p1** and **p2** is generally meaningless. However, if **p1** and **p2** point to variables that are related to each other, such as elements of the same array, then **p1** and **p2** can be meaningfully compared.

Pointers and Arrays

In C#, pointers and arrays are related. For example, within a **fixed** statement, the name of an array without any index generates a pointer to the start of the array when used as an initializer. Consider the following program:

```
/* An array name without an index yields a pointer to the
   start of the array. */

using System;

class PtrArray {
  unsafe static void Main() {
    int[] nums = new int[10];

    fixed(int* p = &nums[0], p2 = nums) {
      if(p == p2)
        Console.WriteLine("p and p2 point to same address.");
    }
  }
}
```

The output is shown here:

```
p and p2 point to same address.
```

As the output shows, the expression

```
&nums[0]
```

is the same as

```
nums
```

Since the second form is shorter, most programmers use it when a pointer to the start of an array is needed.

Indexing a Pointer

When a pointer refers to an array, the pointer can be indexed as if it were an array. This syntax provides an alternative to pointer arithmetic that can be more convenient in some situations. Here is an example:

```
// Index a pointer as if it were an array.

using System;

class PtrIndexDemo {
  unsafe static void Main() {
    int[] nums = new int[10];

    // Index a pointer.
    Console.WriteLine("Index pointer like array.");
    fixed (int* p = nums) {
      for(int i=0; i < 10; i++)
        p[i] = i; // index pointer like array

      for(int i=0; i < 10; i++)
        Console.WriteLine("p[{0}]: {1} ", i, p[i]);
    }

    // Use pointer arithmetic.
    Console.WriteLine("\nUse pointer arithmetic.");
    fixed (int* p = nums) {
      for(int i=0; i < 10; i++)
        *(p+i) = i; // use pointer arithmetic

      for(int i=0; i < 10; i++)
        Console.WriteLine("*(p+{0}): {1} ", i, *(p+i));
    }
  }
}
```

The output is shown here:

```
Index pointer like array.
p[0]: 0
p[1]: 1
p[2]: 2
p[3]: 3
```

```
p[4]: 4
p[5]: 5
p[6]: 6
p[7]: 7
p[8]: 8
p[9]: 9

Use pointer arithmetic.
*(p+0): 0
*(p+1): 1
*(p+2): 2
*(p+3): 3
*(p+4): 4
*(p+5): 5
*(p+6): 6
*(p+7): 7
*(p+8): 8
*(p+9): 9
```

As the program illustrates, a pointer expression with this general form

*(ptr + i)

can be rewritten using array-indexing syntax like this:

ptr[i]

There are two important things to understand about indexing a pointer: First, no boundary checking is applied. Thus, it is possible to access an element beyond the end of the array to which the pointer refers. Second, a pointer does not have a **Length** property. So, using the pointer, there is no way of knowing how long the array is.

Pointers and Strings

Although strings are implemented as objects in C#, it is possible to access the characters in a string through a pointer. To do so, you will assign a pointer to the start of the string to a **char*** pointer using a **fixed** statement like this:

fixed(char* *p* = *str*) { // ...

After the **fixed** statement executes, **p** will point to the start of the array of characters that make up the string. This array is *null-terminated*, which means that it ends with a zero. You can use this fact to test for the end of the array. Null-terminated character arrays are the way that strings are implemented in C/C++. Thus, obtaining a **char*** pointer to a **string** allows you to operate on strings in much the same way as does C/C++.

Here is a program that demonstrates accessing a string through a **char*** pointer:

```
// Use fixed to get a pointer to the start of a string.

using System;

class FixedString {
  unsafe static void Main() {
    string str = "this is a test";
```

```
    // Point p to start of str.
    fixed(char* p = str) {

      // Display the contents of str via p.
      for(int i=0; p[i] != 0; i++)
        Console.Write(p[i]);
    }

    Console.WriteLine();

  }
}
```

The output is shown here:

```
this is a test
```

Multiple Indirection

You can have a pointer point to another pointer that points to the target value. This situation is called *multiple indirection,* or *pointers to pointers.* Pointers to pointers can be confusing. Figure 20-1 helps clarify the concept of multiple indirection. As you can see, the value of a normal pointer is the address of the variable that contains the value desired. In the case of a pointer to a pointer, the first pointer contains the address of the second pointer, which points to the variable that contains the value desired.

Multiple indirection can be carried on to whatever extent desired, but more than a pointer to a pointer is rarely needed. In fact, excessive indirection is difficult to follow and prone to conceptual errors.

A variable that is a pointer to a pointer must be declared as such. You do this by placing an additional asterisk after the type name. For example, the following declaration tells the compiler that **q** is a pointer to a pointer of type **int**:

```
int** q;
```

You should understand that **q** is not a pointer to an integer, but rather a pointer to an **int** pointer.

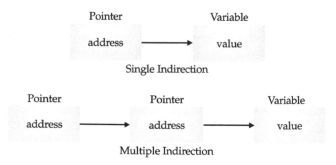

FIGURE 20-1 Single and multiple indirection

To access the target value indirectly pointed to by a pointer to a pointer, you must apply the asterisk operator twice, as in this example:

```
using System;

class MultipleIndirect {
  unsafe static void Main() {
    int x;   // holds an int value
    int* p;  // holds an int pointer
    int** q; // holds a pointer to an int pointer

    x = 10;
    p = &x; // put address of x into p
    q = &p; // put address of p into q

    Console.WriteLine(**q); // display the value of x
  }
}
```

The output is the value of **x**, which is 10. In the program, **p** is declared as a pointer to an **int** and **q** as a pointer to an **int** pointer.

One last point: Do not confuse multiple indirection with high-level data structures, such as linked lists. These are two fundamentally different concepts.

Arrays of Pointers

Pointers can be arrayed like any other data type. The declaration for an **int** pointer array of size 3 is

```
int * [] ptrs = new int * [3];
```

To assign the address of an **int** variable called **myvar** to the third element of the pointer array, write

```
ptrs[2] = &myvar;
```

To find the value of **myvar**, write

```
*ptrs[2]
```

sizeof

When working in an unsafe context, you might occasionally find it useful to know the size, in bytes, of one of C#'s value types. To obtain this information, use the **sizeof** operator. It has this general form:

sizeof(*type*)

Here, type is the *type* whose size is being obtained. In general, **sizeof** is intended primarily for special-case situations, especially when working with a blend of managed and unmanaged code.

stackalloc

You can allocate memory from the stack by using **stackalloc**. It can be used only when initializing local variables and has this general form:

type* p = stackalloc *type*[*size*]

Here, *p* is a pointer that receives the address of the memory that is large enough to hold *size* number of objects of *type*. Also, *type* must be a nonreference type. If there is not room on the stack to allocate the memory, a **System.StackOverflowException** is thrown. Finally, **stackalloc** can be used only in an unsafe context.

Normally, memory for objects is allocated from the *heap,* which is a region of free memory. Allocating memory from the stack is the exception. Variables allocated on the stack are not garbage-collected. Rather, they exist only while the method in which they are declared is executing. When the method is left, the memory is freed. One advantage to using **stackalloc** is that you don't need to worry about the memory being moved about by the garbage collector.

Here is an example that uses **stackalloc**:

```
// Demonstrate stackalloc.

using System;

class UseStackAlloc {
  unsafe static void Main() {
    int* ptrs = stackalloc int[3];

    ptrs[0] = 1;
    ptrs[1] = 2;
    ptrs[2] = 3;

    for(int i=0; i < 3; i++)
      Console.WriteLine(ptrs[i]);
  }
}
```

The output is shown here:

```
1
2
3
```

Creating Fixed-Size Buffers

There is a second use of the **fixed** keyword that enables you to create fixed-sized, single-dimensional arrays. In the C# documentation, these are referred to as *fixed-size buffers.* A fixed-size buffer is always a member of a **struct**. The purpose of a fixed-size buffer is to allow the creation of a **struct** in which the array elements that make up the buffer are contained within the **struct**. Normally, when you include an array member in a **struct**, only a reference to the array is actually held within the **struct**. By using a fixed-size buffer, you cause the entire array to be contained within the **struct**. This results in a structure that can be used in situations in which the size of a **struct** is important, such as in mixed-language programming, interfacing to data not created by a C# program, or whenever a nonmanaged **struct** containing an array is required. Fixed-size buffers can be used only within an unsafe context.

To create a fixed-size buffer, use this form of **fixed**:

fixed *type buf-name*[*size*];

Here, *type* is the data type of the array; *buf-name* is the name of the fixed-size buffer; and *size* is the number of elements in the buffer. Fixed-size buffers can be specified only within a **struct**.

To understand why a fixed-size buffer might be useful, consider a situation in which you want to pass bank account information to an account management program that is written in C++. Furthermore, assume that each account record uses the following organization:

Name	An 8-bit, ASCII character string, 80 bytes long
Balance	A **double**, 8 bytes long
ID	A **long**, 8 bytes long

In C++, each structure, itself, contains the **Name** array. This differs from C#, which would normally just store a reference to the array. Thus, representing this data in a C# **struct** requires the use of a fixed-size buffer, as shown here:

```
// Use a fixed-size buffer.
unsafe struct FixedBankRecord {
  public fixed byte Name[80]; // create a fixed-size buffer
  public double Balance;
  public long ID;
}
```

By using a fixed-size buffer for **Name**, each instance of **FixedBankRecord** will contain all 80 bytes of the **Name** array, which is the way that a C++ **struct** would be organized. Thus, the overall size of **FixedBankRecord** is 96, which is the sum of its members. Here is a program that demonstrates this fact:

```
// Demonstrate a fixed-size buffer.

using System;

// Create a fixed-size buffer.
unsafe struct FixedBankRecord {
  public fixed byte Name[80]; // create a fixed-size buffer
  public double Balance;
  public long ID;
}

class FixedSizeBuffer {
  // Mark Main as unsafe.
  unsafe static void Main() {
    Console.WriteLine("Size of FixedBankRecord is " +
                      sizeof(FixedBankRecord));
  }
}
```

The output is shown here:

```
Size of FixedBankRecord is 96
```

Although the size of **FixedBankRecord** is the exact sum of its members, this may not be the case for all **struct**s that have fixed-size buffers. C# is free to pad the overall length of structure so that it aligns on an even boundary (such as a word boundary) for efficiency reasons. Therefore, the overall length of a **struct** might be a few bytes greater than the sum of its fields, even when fixed-size buffers are used. In most cases, an equivalent C++ **struct** would also use the same padding. However, be aware that a difference in this regard may be possible.

One last point: In the program, notice how the fixed-size buffer for **Name** is created:

```
public fixed byte Name[80]; // create a fixed-size buffer
```

Pay special attention to how the dimension of the array is specified. The brackets containing the array size follow the array name. This is C++-style syntax, and it differs from normal C# array declarations. This statement allocates 80 bytes of storage within each **FixedBankRecord** object.

Nullable Types

Beginning with version 2.0, C# has included a feature that provides an elegant solution to what is both a common and irritating problem. The feature is the *nullable type*. The problem is how to recognize and handle fields that do not contain values (in other words, unassigned fields). To understand the problem, consider a simple customer database that keeps a record of the customer's name, address, customer ID, invoice number, and current balance. In such a situation, it is possible to create a customer entry in which one or more of those fields would be unassigned. For example, a customer may simply request a catalog. In this case, no invoice number would be needed and the field would be unused.

In the past, handling the possibility of unused fields required the use of either placeholder values or an extra field that simply indicated whether a field was in use. Of course, placeholder values could work only if there was a value that would otherwise be invalid, which won't be the case in all situations. Adding an extra field to indicate if a field is in use works in all cases, but having to manually create and manage such a field is an annoyance. The nullable type solves both problems.

Nullable Basics

A nullable type is a special version of a value type that is represented by a structure. In addition to the values defined by the underlying type, a nullable type can also store the value **null**. Thus, a nullable type has the same range and characteristics as its underlying type. It simply adds the ability to represent a value that indicates that a variable of that type is unassigned. Nullable types are objects of **System.Nullable<T>**, where **T** must be a non-nullable value type.

REMEMBER   *Only value types have nullable equivalents.*

A nullable type can be specified two different ways. First, you can explicitly declare objects of type **Nullable<T>**, which is defined in the **System** namespace. For example, this creates **int** and **bool** nullable types:

```
System.Nullable<int> count;
System.Nullable<bool> done;
```

The second way to declare a nullable type is much shorter and is more commonly used. Simply follow the type name with a **?**. For example, the following shows the more common way to declare a nullable **int** and **bool** type:

```
int? count;
bool? done;
```

When using nullable types, you will often see a nullable object created like this:

```
int? count = null;
```

This explicitly initializes **count** to **null**. This satisfies the constraint that a variable must be given a value before it is used. In this case, the value simply means undefined.

You can assign a value to a nullable variable in the normal way because a conversion from the underlying type to the nullable type is predefined. For example, this assigns the value 100 to **count**.

```
count = 100;
```

There are two ways to determine if a variable of a nullable type is **null** or contains a value. First, you can test its value against **null**. For example, using **count** declared by the preceding statement, the following determines if it has a value:

```
if(count != null) // has a value
```

If **count** is not **null**, then it contains a value.

The second way to determine if a nullable type contains a value is to use the **HasValue** read-only property defined by **Nullable<T>**. It is shown here:

```
bool HasValue
```

HasValue will return true if the instance on which it is called contains a value. It will return false otherwise. Using the **HasValue** property, here is the second way to determine if the nullable object **count** has a value:

```
if(count.HasValue) // has a value
```

Assuming that a nullable object contains a value, you can obtain its value by using the **Value** read-only property defined by **Nullable<T>**, which is shown here:

```
T Value
```

It returns the value of the nullable instance on which it is called. If you try to obtain a value from a variable that is **null**, a **System.InvalidOperationException** will be thrown. It is also possible to obtain the value of a nullable instance by casting it into its underlying type.

The following program puts together the pieces and demonstrates the basic mechanism that handles a nullable type:

```
// Demonstrate a nullable type.

using System;

class NullableDemo {
  static void Main() {
```

```
      int? count = null;

      if(count.HasValue)
        Console.WriteLine("count has this value: " + count.Value);
      else
        Console.WriteLine("count has no value");

      count = 100;

      if(count.HasValue)
        Console.WriteLine("count has this value: " + count.Value);
      else
        Console.WriteLine("count has no value");
    }
}
```

The output is shown here:

```
count has no value
count has this value: 100
```

Nullable Objects in Expressions

A nullable object can be used in expressions that are valid for its underlying type. Furthermore, it is possible to mix nullable objects and non-nullable objects within the same expression. This works because of the predefined conversion that exists from the underlying type to the nullable type. When non-nullable and nullable types are mixed in an operation, the outcome is a nullable value.

The following program illustrates the use of nullable types in expressions:

```
// Use nullable objects in expressions.

using System;

class NullableDemo {
  static void Main() {
    int? count = null;
    int? result = null;

    int incr = 10; // notice that incr is a non-nullable type

    // result contains null, because count is null.
    result = count + incr;

    if(result.HasValue)
      Console.WriteLine("result has this value: " + result.Value);
    else
      Console.WriteLine("result has no value");

    // Now, count is given a value and result will contain a value.
    count = 100;
    result = count + incr;
```

```
    if(result.HasValue)
      Console.WriteLine("result has this value: " + result.Value);
    else
      Console.WriteLine("result has no value");

  }
}
```

The output is shown here:

```
result has no value
result has this value: 110
```

The ?? Operator

If you attempt to use a cast to convert a nullable object to its underlying type, a **System.InvalidOperationException** will be thrown if the nullable object contains a **null** value. This can occur, for example, when you use a cast to assign the value of a nullable object to a variable of its underlying type. You can avoid the possibility of this exception being thrown by using the **??** operator, which is called the *null coalescing operator*. It lets you specify a default value that will be used when the nullable object contains **null**. It also eliminates the need for the cast.

The **??** operator has this general form:

nullable-object **??** *default-value*

If *nullable-object* contains a value, then the value of the **??** is that value. Otherwise, the value of the **??** operation is *default-value*.

For example, in the following code **balance** is **null**. This causes **currentBalance** to be assigned the value 0.0 and no exception will be thrown.

```
double? balance = null;
double currentBalance;

currentBalance = balance ?? 0.0;
```

In the next sequence, **balance** is given the value 123.75:

```
double? balance = 123.75;
double currentBalance;

currentBalance = balance ?? 0.0;
```

Now, **currentBalance** will contain the value of **balance**, which is 123.75.

One other point: The right-hand expression of the **??** is evaluated only if the left-hand expression does not contain a value. The following program demonstrates this fact:

```
// Using ??

using System;

class NullableDemo2 {
```

```
// Return a zero balance.
static double GetZeroBal() {
  Console.WriteLine("In GetZeroBal().");
    return 0.0;
}

static void Main() {
  double? balance = 123.75;
  double currentBalance;

  // Here, GetZeroBal( ) is not called because balance
  // contains a value.
  currentBalance = balance ?? GetZeroBal();

  Console.WriteLine(currentBalance);
}
}
```

In this program, the method **GetZeroBal( )** is not called because **balance** contains a value. As explained, when the left-hand expression of **??** contains a value, the right-hand expression is not evaluated.

Nullable Objects and the Relational and Logical Operators

Nullable objects can be used in relational expressions in just the same way as their corresponding non-nullable types. However, there is one additional rule that applies. When two nullable objects are compared using the **<**, **>**, **<=**, or **>=** operators, the result is false if either of the objects is **null**. For example, consider this sequence:

```
byte? lower = 16;
byte? upper = null;

// Here, lower is defined, but upper isn't.
if(lower < upper) // false
```

Here, the result of the test for less than is false. However, somewhat counterintuitively, so is the inverse comparison:

```
if(lower > upper) // .. also false!
```

Thus, when one (or both) of the nullable objects used in a comparison is **null**, the result of that comparison is always false; **null** does not participate in an ordering relationship.

You can test whether a nullable object contains **null**, however, by using the **==** or **!=** operator. For example, this is a valid test that will result in a true outcome:

```
if(upper == null) // ...
```

When a logical expression involves two **bool?** objects, the outcome of that expression will be one of three values: **true**, **false**, or **null** (undefined). Here are the entries that are added to the truth table for the **&** and **|** operators that apply to **bool?**.

P	Q	P | Q	P & Q
true	null	true	null
false	null	null	false
null	true	true	null
null	false	null	false
null	null	null	null

One other point: When the ! operator is applied to a **bool?** value that is **null**, the outcome is **null**.

Partial Types

Beginning with C# 2.0, a class, structure, or interface definition can be broken into two or more pieces, with each piece residing in a separate file. This is accomplished through the use of the **partial** contextual keyword. When your program is compiled, the pieces are united.

When used to create a partial type, the **partial** modifier has this general form:

partial *type typename* { // ...

Here, *typename* is the name of the class, structure, or interface that is being split into pieces. Each part of a partial type must be modified by **partial**.

Here is an example that divides a simple XY coordinate class into three separate files. The first file is shown here:

```
partial class XY {
  public XY(int a, int b) {
    X = a;
    Y = b;
  }
}
```

The second file is shown next:

```
partial class XY {
  public int X { get; set; }
}
```

The third file is

```
partial class XY {
  public int Y { get; set; }
}
```

The following file demonstrates the use of **XY**:

```
// Demonstrate partial class definitions.
using System;
```

```
class Test {
  static void Main() {
    XY xy = new XY(1, 2);

    Console.WriteLine(xy.X + "," + xy.Y);
  }
}
```

To use **XY**, all files must be included in the compile. For example, assuming the **XY** files are called **xy1.cs**, **xy2.cs**, and **xy3.cs**, and that the **Test** class is contained in a file called **test.cs**, then to compile **Test**, use the following command line:

```
csc test.cs xy1.cs xy2.cs xy3.cs
```

One last point: It is legal to have partial generic classes. However, the type parameters of each partial declaration must match the other parts.

Partial Methods

As the preceding section described, you can use **partial** to create a partial type. Beginning with C# 3.0, there is a second use of **partial** that lets you create a *partial method* within a partial type. A partial method has its declaration in one part and its implementation in another part. Thus, in a partial class or structure, **partial** can be used to allow the declaration of a method to be separate from its implementation.

The key aspect of a partial method is that the implementation is not required! When the partial method is not implemented by another part of the class or structure, then all calls to the partial method are silently ignored. This makes it possible for a class to specify, but not require, optional functionality. If that functionality is not implemented, then it is simply ignored.

Here is an expanded version of the preceding program that creates a partial method called **Show( )**. It is called by another method called **ShowXY( )**. (For convenience, all pieces of the partial class **XY** are shown in one file, but they could have been organized into separate files, as illustrated in the preceding section.)

```
// Demonstrate a partial method.
using System;

partial class XY {
  public XY(int a, int b) {
    X = a;
    Y = b;
  }

  // Declare a partial method.
  partial void Show();
}

partial class XY {
  public int X { get; set; }
```

```
      // Implement a partial method.
      partial void Show() {
        Console.WriteLine("{0}, {1}", X, Y);
      }
    }

    partial class XY {
      public int Y { get; set; }

      // Call a partial method.
      public void ShowXY() {
        Show();
      }
    }

    class Test {
      static void Main() {
        XY xy = new XY(1, 2);

        xy.ShowXY();
      }
    }
```

Notice that **Show( )** is declared in one part of **XY** and implemented by another part.
The implementation displays the values of **X** and **Y**. This means that when **Show( )** is called
by **ShowXY( )**, the call has effect, and it will, indeed, display **X** and **Y**. However, if you
comment-out the implementation of **Show( )**, then the call to **Show( )** within **ShowXY( )**
does nothing.

Partial methods have several restrictions, including these: They must return **void**. They
cannot have access modifiers. They cannot be virtual. They cannot use **out** parameters.

Create a Dynamic Type with dynamic

As first mentioned in Chapter 3, C# is a strongly typed language. In general, this means that
all operations are checked at compile time, and actions not supported by a type will not be
compiled. Although strong typing is a great benefit to the programmer, helping ensure
resilient, reliable programs, it can be problematic in situations in which the type of an object
is not known until runtime. This situation might be encountered when using reflection,
accessing a COM object, or when needing interoperability with a dynamic language, such
as IronPython, for example. Prior to C# 4.0, these situations could be difficult to handle. To
address this problem, C# 4.0 added a new data type called **dynamic**.

With an important exception, the **dynamic** type is similar to **object** because it can be
used to refer to any type of object. The difference between **object** and **dynamic** is that all
type checking related to a **dynamic** type is deferred until runtime. (With **object**, type
checking still occurs at compile time.) The benefit of waiting until runtime is that, at compile
time, a **dynamic** object is assumed to support any operation, including the use of operators,
calls to methods, access to fields, and so on. This enables code to be compiled without error.
Of course, if at runtime the object's actual type does not support the operation, then a
runtime exception will occur.

The following program shows **dynamic** in action:

```
// Demonstrate the use of dynamic.

using System;
using System.Globalization;

class DynDemo {
  static void Main() {
    // Declare two dynamic variables.
    dynamic str;
    dynamic val;

    // Implicit conversion to dynamic types is supported.
    // Therefore the following assignments are legal.
    str = "This is a string";
    val = 10;

    Console.WriteLine("str contains " + str);
    Console.WriteLine("val contains " + val + '\n');

    str = str.ToUpper(CultureInfo.CurrentCulture);
    Console.WriteLine("str now contains " + str);

    val = val + 2;
    Console.WriteLine("val now contains " + val + '\n');


    string str2 = str.ToLower(CultureInfo.CurrentCulture);
    Console.WriteLine("str2 contains " + str2);

    // Implicit conversions from dynamic types are supported.
    int x = val * 2;
    Console.WriteLine("x contains " + x);
  }
}
```

The output from the program is shown here:

```
str contains This is a string
val contains 10

str now contains THIS IS A STRING
val now contains 12

str2 contains this is a string
x contains 24
```

In the program, notice how the two variables, **str** and **val**, are declared using the **dynamic** type. This means that type checking on actions involving these two variables will not occur at compile time. As a result, any operation can be applied to them. In this case, **str** calls the **String** methods, **ToUpper( )** and **ToLower( )**, and **val** uses the addition and multiplication operators. Although these actions are compatible with the types of objects assigned to the variables in this example, the compiler has no way of knowing this. It simply accepts them without question. This, of course, simplifies the coding of dynamic routines, but allows the possibility that such actions will produce a runtime error.

In this example, the program behaves correctly at runtime because the objects assigned to these references support the actions used in the program. Specifically, because **val** is assigned an integer value, integer operations such as addition are supported. Because **str** is assigned a **string**, string operations are supported. Understand, however, that it is your responsibility to ensure that all operations applied to a **dynamic** type are actually supported by the type of object being referred to. If they aren't, a program crash will occur.

One other thing to notice in the preceding example: any type of object reference can be assigned to a **dynamic** variable. This is because an implicit conversion is provided from any type to **dynamic**. Also, a **dynamic** type is automatically converted to any other type. Of course, if at runtime such a conversion is invalid, then a runtime error will result. For example, if you add this line to the end of the preceding example,

```
bool b = val;
```

a runtime error will result because there is no implicit conversion defined from **int** (which is the runtime type of **val** in this case) to **bool**. Therefore, even though this line will compile without error, it will result in a runtime error.

Before leaving this example, try a short experiment. Change the type of **str** and **val** to **object**, and then try recompiling. As you will see, compile-time errors result. This is because **object** does not support the actions that are performed on the variables, and this is caught during compilation. This is the primary difference between **object** and **dynamic**. Even though both can be used to refer to any other type of object, only those actions supported by **object** can be used on a variable of type **object**. By using **dynamic**, you can specify whatever action you like as long as that action is supported by the actual object being referred to at runtime.

To see how **dynamic** can simplify certain tasks, we will work through a simple example that uses it with reflection. As explained in Chapter 17, one way to invoke a method on an object of a class that was obtained at runtime via reflection is to call the **Invoke( )** method. Although this works, it would be more convenient to invoke that method by name in cases in which the method name is known. For example, you might have a situation in which you know that a certain assembly contains a specific class, which supports methods whose names and actions are known. However, because this assembly is subject to change, you always want to make sure that you are using the latest version. One way to accomplish this is to use reflection to examine the assembly, construct an object of the class, and then invoke the methods defined by the class. By using **dynamic**, you can now invoke those methods by name (since the names are known) rather than through the **Invoke( )** method.

To begin, put the following code in a file called **MyClass.cs**. This is the code that will be dynamically loaded via reflection.

```
public class DivBy {
  public bool IsDivBy(int a, int b) {
    if((a % b) == 0) return true;
    return false;
  }
}
```

```
  public bool IsEven(int a) {
    if((a % 2) == 0) return true;
    return false;
  }
}
```

Next, compile this file into a DLL called **MyClass.dll**. If you are using the command-line compiler, then you can use this line:

```
csc /t:library MyClass.cs
```

Now, create the following program that uses **MyClass.dll**, as shown here:

```
// Use dynamic with reflection.

using System;
using System.Reflection;

class DynRefDemo {
  static void Main() {

    Assembly asm = Assembly.LoadFrom("MyClass.dll");

    Type[] all = asm.GetTypes();

    // Find the DivBy class.
    int i;
    for(i = 0; i < all.Length; i++)
      if(all[i].Name == "DivBy") break;

    if(i == all.Length) {
      Console.WriteLine("DivBy not found in assembly.");
      return;
    }

    Type t = all[i];

    // Now, find the default constructor.
    ConstructorInfo[] ci = t.GetConstructors();

    int j;
    for(j = 0; j < ci.Length; j++)
      if(ci[j].GetParameters().Length == 0) break;

    if(j == ci.Length) {
      Console.WriteLine("Default constructor not found.");
      return;
    }

    // Create a DivBy object dynamically.
    dynamic obj = ci[j].Invoke(null);

    // Now, invoke methods on obj by name. This is legal because
    // obj is of type dynamic, and the calls to the methods are
```

```
    // type-checked at runtime, not compile time.
    if(obj.IsDivBy(15, 3))
      Console.WriteLine("15 is evenly divisible by 3.");
    else
      Console.WriteLine("15 is NOT evenly divisible by 3.");

    if(obj.IsEven(9))
      Console.WriteLine("9 is even.");
    else
      Console.WriteLine("9 is NOT even.");
  }
}
```

As you can see, the program dynamically loads **MyClass.dll** and then uses reflection to construct a **DivBy** object. The object constructed is assigned to **obj**, which is of type **dynamic**. Because it is **dynamic**, the methods **IsDivBy( )** and **IsEven( )** can be called on **obj** by name, rather than through the **Invoke( )** method. This works, of course, because in this example, **obj** does, in fact, refer to a **DivBy** object. If it did not, the program would fail.

Although the preceding example is, obviously, contrived and simplified, it does illustrate in principle the benefit the **dynamic** type brings to situations in which types are obtained at runtime. In cases in which a type has known characteristics, including methods, operators, fields, and properties, you can use the characteristics by name, through a **dynamic** type, as in the preceding example. Doing so can make your code cleaner, shorter, and easier to understand.

There is another thing to keep in mind when using **dynamic**. When a program is compiled, **dynamic** is actually replaced with **object** and runtime information is included to describe the usage. Because **dynamic** is compiled into type **object**, for the purposes of overloading, **dynamic** and **object** are seen as the same. Therefore, the following two overloaded methods will generate a compile-time error:

```
static void f(object v) { // ... }
static void f(dynamic v) { // ... } // Error!
```

One last point: **dynamic** is supported by the Dynamic Language Runtime (DLR), which was added by .NET 4.0.

COM Interoperability

C# 4.0 adds features that streamline the ability to interact with unmanaged code that is defined by the Component Object Model (COM), especially that used by Office Automation. Some of these features, such as the **dynamic** type, and named and optional properties, are applicable beyond COM interoperability. COM in general, and Office Automation in particular, is a very large and, at times, complex topic. It is far beyond the scope of this book to discuss it. Therefore, the topic of COM interoperability is also outside the scope of this book.

The preceding notwithstanding, two features related to COM interoperability warrant a brief mention. The first is the use of indexed properties. The second is the ability to pass value arguments to COM methods that require a reference.

As you know, a C# property is normally associated with only one value, with a single **get** and **set** accessor. However, this is not the case with all COM properties. To address this situation, beginning with C# 4.0, when working with a COM object, you can use an *indexed property* to access a COM property that has more than one parameter. This is done by indexing the property name, much as though it were an indexer. For example, assuming an object called **myXLApp** that is an object of type **Microsoft.Office.Interop.Execl.Application**, in the past, to set cells C1 through C3 with the string "OK" in an Excel spreadsheet, you could use a statement like this:

```
myXLapp.get_Range("C1", "C3").set_Value(Type.Missing, "OK");
```

Here, the range is obtained by calling **get_Range( )**, specifying the beginning and ending of the range. The values are set by calling **set_Value( )**, specifying the type (which is optional) and the value. These methods use the **Range** and **Value** properties. The reason methods are used is that both of these properties have two parameters. Thus, in the past, you could not refer to them as properties, but needed to use the methods shown. Also, the **Type.Missing** argument is simply a placeholder that was passed to indicate that the default type be used. However, beginning with C# 4.0, the preceding statement can be written more conveniently as

```
myXLapp.Range["C1", "C3"].Value = "OK";
```

In this case, the range values are passed using the indexer syntax, and the **Type.Missing** placeholder is not needed because this parameter now defaults.

Normally, when a method defines a **ref** parameter, you must pass a reference to that parameter. However, when working with COM, you can pass a value to a **ref** parameter without having to first wrap it in an object. This is because the compiler will automatically create a temporary argument for you that is already wrapped in an object, and **ref** is not needed in the argument list.

Friend Assemblies

It is possible to make one assembly the *friend* of another. A friend has access to the **internal** members of the assembly of which it is a friend. This feature makes it possible to share members between selected assemblies without making those members public. To declare a friend assembly, you must use the **InternalsVisibleTo** attribute.

Miscellaneous Keywords

To conclude Part I, the few remaining keywords defined by C# that have not been described elsewhere are briefly discussed.

lock

The **lock** keyword is used when creating multithreaded programs. It is examined in detail in Chapter 23, where multithreaded programming is discussed. A brief description is given here for the sake of completeness.

In C#, a program can contain more than one *thread of execution*. When this is the case, the program is said to be *multithreaded*, and pieces of the program are executed concurrently. Thus, pieces of the program execute independently and simultaneously. This raises the prospect of a special type of problem: What if two threads try to use a resource that can be used by only one thread at a time? To solve this problem, you can create a *critical code section* that will be executed by one and only one thread at a time. This is accomplished by **lock**. Its general form is shown here:

```
lock(obj) {
  // critical section
}
```

Here, *obj* is the object on which the lock is synchronized. If one thread has already entered the critical section, then a second thread will wait until the first thread exits the critical section. When the first thread leaves the critical section, the lock is released and the second thread can be granted the lock, at which point the second thread can execute the critical section.

NOTE *lock is discussed in detail in Chapter 23.*

---

readonly

You can create a read-only field in a class by declaring it as **readonly**. A **readonly** field can be given a value only by using an initializer when it is declared or by assigning it a value within a constructor. Once the value has been set, it can't be changed outside the constructor. Thus, a **readonly** field is a good way to create a fixed value that has its value set by a constructor. For example, you might use a **readonly** field to represent an array dimension that is used frequently throughout a program. Both static and non-static **readonly** fields are allowed.

NOTE *Although similar, **readonly** fields are not the same as **const** fields, which are described in the following section.*

Here is an example that creates a **readonly** field:

```
// Demonstrate readonly.

using System;

class MyClass {
  public static readonly int SIZE = 10;
}

class DemoReadOnly {
  static void Main() {
    int[] source = new int[MyClass.SIZE];
    int[] target = new int[MyClass.SIZE];

    // Give source some values.
    for(int i=0; i < MyClass.SIZE; i++)
      source[i] = i;

    foreach(int i in source)
      Console.Write(i + " ");

    Console.WriteLine();
```

```
    // Reverse copy source into target.
    for(int i = MyClass.SIZE-1, j = 0; i > 0; i--, j++)
      target[j] = source[i];

    foreach(int i in target)
      Console.Write(i + " ");

    Console.WriteLine();

//  MyClass.SIZE = 100; // Error!!! can't change
  }
}
```

Here, **MyClass.SIZE** is initialized to 10. After that, it can be used, but not changed. To prove this, try removing the comment symbol from before the last line and then compiling the program. As you will see, an error will result.

const and volatile

The **const** modifier is used to declare fields or local variables that cannot be changed. These variables must be given initial values when they are declared. Thus, a **const** variable is essentially a constant. For example,

```
const int i = 10;
```

creates a **const** variable called **i** that has the value 10. Although a **const** field is similar to a **readonly** field, the two are not the same. A **const** field cannot be set within a constructor, but a **readonly** field can.

The **volatile** modifier tells the compiler that a field's value may be changed by two or more concurrently executing threads. In this situation, one thread may not know when the field has been changed by another thread. This is important because the C# compiler will automatically perform certain optimizations that work only when a field is accessed by a single thread of execution. To prevent these optimizations from being applied to a shared field, declare it **volatile**. This tells the compiler that it must obtain the value of this field each time it is accessed.

The using Statement

In addition to the **using** *directive* discussed earlier in this book, **using** has a second form that is called the **using** *statement.* It has these general forms:

```
using (obj) {
  // use obj
}

using (type obj = initializer) {
  // use obj
}
```

Here, *obj* is an expression that must evaluate to an object that implements the **System.IDisposable** interface. It specifies a variable that will be used inside the **using** block. In the first form, the object is declared outside the **using** statement. In the second form, the object is declared within the **using** statement. When the block concludes, the **Dispose( )** method (defined by the **System.IDisposable** interface) will be called on *obj*. **Dispose( )** is called even if the **using** block ends because of an exception. Thus, a **using** statement provides a means by which objects are automatically disposed when they are no longer needed. Remember, the **using** statement applies only to objects that implement the **System.IDisposable** interface.

Here is an example of each form of the **using** statement:

```
// Demonstrate using statement.

using System;
using System.IO;

class UsingDemo {
  static void Main() {
    try {
      StreamReader sr = new StreamReader("test.txt");

      // Use object inside using statement.
      using(sr) {
        // ...
      }
    } catch(IOException exc) {
      // ...
    }

    try {
      // Create a StreamReader inside the using statement.
      using(StreamReader sr2 = new StreamReader("test.txt")) {
        // ...
      }
    } catch(IOException exc) {
      // ...
    }
  }
}
```

The class **StreamReader** implements the **IDisposable** interface (through its base class **TextReader**). Thus, it can be used in a **using** statement. When the **using** statement ends, **Dispose( )** is automatically called on the stream variable, thus closing the stream.

As the preceding example illustrates, **using** is particularly useful when working with files because the file is automatically closed at the end of the **using** block, even if the block ends because of an exception. As a result, closing a file via **using** often simplifies file-handling code. Of course, **using** is not limited to just files. There are many other resources in the .NET Framework that implement **IDisposable**. All can be managed via **using**.

extern

The **extern** keyword has two uses. Each is examined here.

Declaring extern Methods

The first use of **extern** indicates that a method is provided by unmanaged code that is not part of the program. In other words, that method is supplied by external code.

To declare a method as external, simply precede its declaration with the **extern** modifier. The declaration must not include any body. Thus, the general form of an **extern** declaration is as shown here:

extern *ret-type meth-name(arg-list)*;

Notice that no braces are used.

In this use, **extern** is often used with the **DllImport** attribute, which specifies the DLL that contains the method. **DllImport** is in the **System.Runtime.InteropServices** namespace. It supports several options, but for most uses, it is sufficient to simply specify the name of the DLL that contains the **extern** method. In general, **extern** methods should be coded in C. (If you use C++, then the name of the method within the DLL might be altered with the addition of type decorations.)

To best understand how to use **extern** methods, it is helpful to work through an example. The example consists of two files. The first is the C file shown here, which defines a method called **AbsMax( )**. Call this file **ExtMeth.c**.

```
#include <stdlib.h>

int __declspec(dllexport) AbsMax(int a, int b) {
  return abs(a) < abs(b) ? abs(b) : abs(a);
}
```

The **AbsMax( )** method compares the absolute values of its two parameters and returns the maximum. Notice the use of **__declspec(dllexport)**. This is a Microsoft-specific extension to the C language that tells the compiler to export the **AbsMax( )** method within the DLL that contains it. You must use this command line to compile **ExtMeth.c**.

```
CL /LD /MD ExtMeth.c
```

This creates a DLL file called **ExtMeth.dll**.

Next is a program that uses **AbsMax( )**:

```
using System;
using System.Runtime.InteropServices;

class ExternMeth {

  // Here an extern method is declared.
  [DllImport("ExtMeth.dll")]
  public extern static int AbsMax(int a, int b);

  static void Main() {

    // Use the extern method.
    int max = AbsMax(-10, -20);
    Console.WriteLine(max);

  }
}
```

Notice the use of the **DllImport** attribute. It tells the compiler what DLL contains the **extern** method **AbsMax( )**. In this case, the file is **ExtMeth.dll**, which is the file DLL created when the C file was compiled. When the program is run, the value 20 is displayed, as expected.

Declaring an extern Assembly Alias

A second form of **extern** provides an alias for an external assembly. It is used in cases in which a program includes two separate assemblies that both contain the same type name. For example, if an assembly called **test1** contains a class called **MyClass** and **test2** also contains a class called **MyClass**, then a conflict will arise if both classes need to be used within the same program.

To solve this problem, you must create an alias for each assembly. This is a two-step process. First, you must specify the aliases using the **/r** compiler option. For example:

```
/r:Asm1=test1.dll
/r:Asm2=test2.dll
```

Second, you must specify **extern** statements that refer to these aliases. Here is the form of **extern** that creates an assembly alias:

> extern alias *assembly-name*;

Continuing the example, these lines must appear in your program:

```
extern alias Asm1;
extern alias Asm2;
```

Now, either version of **MyClass** can be accessed by qualifying it with its alias.

Here is a complete example that demonstrates an **extern** alias. It contains three files. The first is shown here. It should be put in a file called **test1.cs**.

```
using System;

namespace MyNS {
  public class MyClass {
    public MyClass() {
      Console.WriteLine("Constructing from MyClass1.dll.");
    }
  }
}
```

The second file is called **test2.cs**. It is shown here:

```
using System;

namespace MyNS {
  public class MyClass {
    public MyClass() {
      Console.WriteLine("Constructing from MyClass2.dll.");
    }
  }
}
```

Notice that both **test1.cs** and **test2.cs** define a namespace called **MyNS**, and that within that namespace, both files define a class called **MyClass**. Thus, without an **extern** alias, no program could have access to both versions of **MyClass**.

The third file, **test3.cs**, which is shown next, uses **MyClass** from both **test1.cs** and **test2.cs**. It is able to do this because of the **extern** alias statements.

```
// extern alias statements must be at the top of the file.
extern alias Asm1;
extern alias Asm2;

using System;

class Demo {
  static void Main() {
    Asm1::MyNS.MyClass t = new Asm1::MyNS.MyClass();
    Asm2::MyNS.MyClass t2 = new Asm2::MyNS.MyClass();
  }
}
```

Start by compiling **test1.cs** and **test2.cs** into DLLs. This can be done easily from the command line by using these commands:

```
csc /t:library test1.cs
csc /t:library test2.cs
```

Next, compile **test3.cs** by using this command line:

```
csc /r:Asm1=test1.dll /r:Asm2=test2.dll test3.cs
```

Notice the use of the **/r** option, which tells the compiler to reference the metadata found in the associated file. In this case, the alias **Asm1** is linked with **test1.dll** and the alias **Asm2** is linked with **test2.dll**.

Within **test3.cs**, the aliases are specified by these two **extern** statements at the top of the file:

```
extern alias Asm1;
extern alias Asm2;
```

Within **Main( )**, the aliases are used to disambiguate the references to **MyClass**. Notice how the alias is used to refer to **MyClass**:

```
Asm1::MyNS.MyClass
```

The alias is specified first, followed by the namespace resolution operator, followed by the name of the namespace that contains the ambiguous class, followed by the dot operator and the class name. This same general form works with other **extern** aliases.

The output from the program is shown here:

```
Constructing from MyClass1.dll.
Constructing from MyClass2.dll.
```

Exploring the C# Library

P art II explores the C# library. As explained in Part I, the class library used by C# is the .NET Framework class library. As a result, the material in this section applies not only to C#, but to the .NET Framework as a whole.

The .NET Framework class library is organized into namespaces. To use a portion of the library, you will normally import its namespace by including a **using** directive. Of course, you can also fully qualify the name of the item with its namespace name, but most often, it is simply easier to import the entire namespace.

The .NET library is very large, and it is beyond the scope of this book to examine each part of it. (A complete description would easily fill a very large book!) Instead, Part II examines several core elements of the library, many of which are contained in the **System** namespace. Also discussed are the collection classes, multithreading, and networking.

NOTE *The I/O classes are discussed in Chapter 14.*

Exploring the System Namespace

This chapter explores the **System** namespace. **System** is a top-level namespace of the .NET Framework class library. It directly contains those classes, structures, interfaces, delegates, and enumerations that are most commonly used by a C# program or that are deemed otherwise integral to the .NET Framework. Thus, **System** defines the core of the library.

System also contains many nested namespaces that support specific subsystems, such as **System.Net**. Several of these subsystems are described later in this book. This chapter is concerned only with the members of **System**, itself.

The Members of System

In addition to a large number of exception classes, **System** contains the following classes:

ActivationContext	Activator	AppDomain
AppDomainManager	AppDomainSetup	ApplicationId
ApplicationIdentity	Array	AssemblyLoadEventArgs
Attribute	AttributeUsageAttribute	BitConverter
Buffer	CharEnumerator	CLSCompliantAttribute
Console	ConsoleCancelEventArgs	ContextBoundObject
ContextStaticAttribute	Convert	DBNull
Delegate	Enum	Environment
EventArgs	Exception	FileStyleUriParser
FlagsAttribute	FtpStyleUriParser	GC
GenericUriParser	GopherStyleUriParser	HttpStyleUriParser
Lazy<T>	Lazy<T, TMetadata>	LdapStyleUriParser
LoaderOptimizationAttribute	LocalDataStoreSlot	MarshalByRefObject

Math	MTAThreadAttribute	MulticastDelegate
NetPipeStyleUriParser	NetTcpStyleUriParser	NewsStyleUriParser
NonSerializedAttribute	Nullable	Object
ObsoleteAttribute	OperatingSystem	ParamArrayAttribute
Random	ResolveEventArgs	SerializableAttribute
STAThreadAttribute	String	StringComparer
ThreadStaticAttribute	TimeZone	TimeZoneInfo
TimeZoneInfo.AdjustmentRule	Tuple	Tuple<...> (various forms)
Type	UnhandledExceptionEventArgs	Uri
UriBuilder	UriParser	UriTemplate
UriTemplateEquivalenceComparer	UriTemplateMatch	UriTemplateTable
UriTypeConverter	ValueType	Version
WeakReference		

System defines the following structures:

ArgIterator	ArraySegment<T>	Boolean
Byte	Char	ConsoleKeyInfo
DateTime	DateTimeOffset	Decimal
Double	Guid	Int16
Int32	Int64	IntPtr
ModuleHandle	Nullable<T>	RuntimeArgumentHandle
RuntimeFieldHandle	RuntimeMethodHandle	RuntimeTypeHandle
Sbyte	Single	TimeSpan
TimeZoneInfo.TransitionTime	TypedReference	UInt16
UInt32	UInt64	UIntPtr
Void		

System defines the following interfaces:

_AppDomain	IappDomainSetup	IAsyncResult
ICloneable	IComparable	IComparable<T>
IConvertible	ICustomFormatter	IDisposable
IEquatable<T>	IFormatProvider	IFormattable
IObservable<T>	IObserver<T>	IServiceProvider

System defines the following delegates:

Action	Action<...> (various forms)	AppDomainInitializer
AssemblyLoadEventHandler	AsyncCallback	Comparison<T>
ConsoleCancelEventHandler	Converter<TInput, VOutput>	CrossAppDomainDelegate
EventHandler	EventHandler<TEventArgs>	Func<...> (various forms)
Predicate<T>	ResolveEventHandler	UnhandledExceptionEventHandler

System defines these enumerations:

ActivationContext.contextForm	AppDomainManagerInitializationOptions	AttributeTargets
Base64FormattingOptions	ConsoleColor	ConsoleKey
ConsoleModifiers	ConsoleSpecialKey	DateTimeKind
DayOfWeek	Environment.SpecialFolder	Environment.SpecialFolderOption
EnvironmentVariableTarget	GCCollectionMode	GCNotificationStatus
GenericUriParserOptions	LoaderOptimization	MidpointRounding
PlatformID	StringComparison	StringSplitOptions
TypeCode	UriComponents	UriFormat
UriHostNameType	UriIdnScope	UriKind
UriPartial		

As the preceding tables show, **System** is quite large. It is not possible to examine all of its constituents in detail in a single chapter. Furthermore, several of **System**'s members, such as **Nullable<T>**, **Type**, **Exception**, and **Attribute**, are discussed in Part I. Finally, because **System.String**, which defines the C# **string** type, is such a large and important topic, it is covered in Chapter 22 along with formatting. For these reasons, this chapter explores only those members that are commonly used by a wide range of applications and that are not fully covered elsewhere.

The Math Class

Math defines several standard mathematical operations, such as square root, sine, cosine, and logarithms. The **Math** class is **static**, which means all of the methods defined by **Math** are **static** and no object of type **Math** can be constructed. It also means **Math** is implicitly sealed and cannot be inherited. The methods defined by **Math** are shown in Table 21-1. All angles are in radians.

Math also defines these two fields:

public const double E
public const double PI

E is the value of the natural logarithm base, commonly referred to as *e*. **PI** is the value of pi.

Method	Meaning
public static double Abs(double *value*)	Returns the absolute value of *value*.
public static float Abs(float *value*)	Returns the absolute value of *value*.
public static decimal Abs(decimal *value*)	Returns the absolute value of *value*.
public static int Abs(int *value*)	Returns the absolute value of *value*.
public static short Abs(short *value*)	Returns the absolute value of *value*.
public static long Abs(long *value*)	Returns the absolute value of *value*.
public static sbyte Abs(sbyte *value*)	Returns the absolute value of *value*.
public static double Acos(double *d*)	Returns the arc cosine of *d*. The value of *d* must be between –1 and 1.
public static double Asin(double *d*)	Returns the arc sine of *d*. The value of *d* must be between –1 and 1.
public static double Atan(double *d*)	Returns the arc tangent of *d*.
public static double Atan2(double *y*, double *x*)	Returns the arc tangent of *y/x*.
public static long BigMul(int *a*, int *b*)	Returns the result of *a* * *b* as a **long** value, thus avoiding overflow.
public static double Ceiling(double *a*)	Returns the smallest integer (represented as a floating-point value) not less than *a*. For example, given 1.02, **Ceiling( )** returns 2.0. Given –1.02, **Ceiling( )** returns –1.
public static decimal Ceiling(decimal *d*)	Returns the smallest integer (represented as a **decimal** value) not less than *d*. For example, given 1.02, **Ceiling( )** returns 2.0. Given –1.02, **Ceiling( )** returns –1.
public static double Cos(double *d*)	Returns the cosine of *d*.
public static double Cosh(double *value*)	Returns the hyperbolic cosine of *value*.
public static int DivRem(int *a*, int *b*, out int *result*)	Returns the result of *a / b*. The remainder is returned in *result*.
public static long DivRem(long *a*, long *b*, out long *result*)	Returns the result of *a / b*. The remainder is returned in *result*.
public static double Exp(double *d*)	Returns the natural logarithm base *e* raised to the *d* power.
public static decimal Floor(decimal *d*)	Returns the largest integer (represented as a **decimal** value) not greater than *d*. For example, given 1.02, **Floor( )** returns 1.0. Given –1.02, **Floor( )** returns –2.
public static double Floor(double *d*)	Returns the largest integer (represented as a floating-point value) not greater than *d*. For example, given 1.02, **Floor( )** returns 1.0. Given –1.02, **Floor( )** returns –2.
public static double IEEERemainder(double *x*, double *y*)	Returns the remainder of *x / y*.
public static double Log(double *d*)	Returns the natural logarithm for *d*.
public static double Log(double *a*, double *newBase*)	Returns the logarithm for *a* using base *newBase*.

TABLE 21-1 Methods Defined by **Math**

Method	Meaning
public static double Log10(double *d*)	Returns the base 10 logarithm for *d*.
public static double Max(double *val1*, double *val2*)	Returns the greater of *val1* and *val2*.
public static float Max(float *val1*, float *val2*)	Returns the greater of *val1* and *val2*.
public static decimal Max(decimal *val1*, decimal *val2*)	Returns the greater of *val1* and *val2*.
public static int Max(int *val1*, int *val2*)	Returns the greater of *val1* and *val2*.
public static short Max(short *val1*, short *val2*)	Returns the greater of *val1* and *val2*.
public static long Max(long *val1*, long *val2*)	Returns the greater of *val1* and *val2*.
public static uint Max(uint *val1*, uint *val2*)	Returns the greater of *val1* and *val2*.
public static ushort Max(ushort *val1*, ushort *val2*)	Returns the greater of *val1* and *val2*.
public static ulong Max(ulong *val1*, ulong *val2*)	Returns the greater of *val1* and *val2*.
public static byte Max(byte *val1*, byte *val2*)	Returns the greater of *val1* and *val2*.
public static sbyte Max(sbyte *val1*, sbyte *val2*)	Returns the greater of *val1* and *val2*.
public static double Min(double *val1*, double *val2*)	Returns the lesser of *val1* and *val2*.
public static float Min(float *val1*, float *val2*)	Returns the lesser of *val1* and *val2*.
public static decimal Min(decimal *val1*, decimal *val2*)	Returns the lesser of *val1* and *val2*.
public static int Min(int *val1*, int *val2*)	Returns the lesser of *val1* and *val2*.
public static short Min(short *val1*, short *val2*)	Returns the lesser of *val1* and *val2*.
public static long Min(long *val1*, long *val2*)	Returns the lesser of *val1* and *val2*.
public static uint Min(uint *val1*, uint *val2*)	Returns the lesser of *val1* and *val2*.
public static ushort Min(ushort *val1*, ushort *val2*)	Returns the lesser of *val1* and *val2*.
public static ulong Min(ulong *val1*, ulong *val2*)	Returns the lesser of *val1* and *val2*.
public static byte Min(byte *val1*, byte *val2*)	Returns the lesser of *val1* and *val2*.
public static sbyte Min(sbyte *val1*, sbyte *val2*)	Returns the lesser of *val1* and *val2*.
public static double Pow(double *x*, double *y*)	Returns *x* raised to the *y* power(x^y).

TABLE 21-1 Methods Defined by **Math** (*continued*)

Method	Meaning
public static double Round(double *a*)	Returns *a* rounded to the nearest whole number.
public static decimal Round(decimal *d*)	Returns *d* rounded to the nearest whole number.
public static double Round(double *value*, int *digits*)	Returns *value* rounded to the number of fractional digits specified by *digits*.
public static decimal Round(decimal *d*, int *decimals*)	Returns *d* rounded to the number of fractional digits specified by *decimals*.
public static double Round(double *value*, MidpointRounding *mode*)	Returns *value* rounded to the nearest whole number using the rounding mode specified by *mode*.
public static decimal Round(decimal *d*, MidpointRounding *mode*)	Returns *d* rounded to the nearest whole number using the rounding mode specified by *mode*.
public static double Round(double *value*, int *digits*, MidpointRounding *mode*)	Returns *value* rounded to the number of fractional digits specified by *digits*. It uses the rounding mode specified by *mode*.
public static decimal Round(decimal *d*, int *decimals*, MidpointRounding *mode*)	Returns *d* rounded to the number of fractional digits specified by *decimals*. It uses the rounding mode specified by *mode*.
public static int Sign(double *value*)	Returns –1 if *value* is less than zero, 0 if *value* is zero, and 1 if *value* is greater than zero.
public static int Sign(float *value*)	Returns –1 if *value* is less than zero, 0 if *value* is zero, and 1 if *value* is greater than zero.
public static int Sign(decimal *value*)	Returns –1 if *value* is less than zero, 0 if *value* is zero, and 1 if *value* is greater than zero.
public static int Sign(int *value*)	Returns –1 if *value* is less than zero, 0 if *value* is zero, and 1 if *value* is greater than zero.
public static int Sign(short *value*)	Returns –1 if *value* is less than zero, 0 if *value* is zero, and 1 if *value* is greater than zero.
public static int Sign(long *value*)	Returns –1 if *value* is less than zero, 0 if *value* is zero, and 1 if *value* is greater than zero.
public static int Sign(sbyte *value*)	Returns –1 if *value* is less than zero, 0 if *value* is zero, and 1 if *value* is greater than zero.
public static double Sin(double *a*)	Returns the sine of *a*.
public static double Sinh(double *value*)	Returns the hyperbolic sine of *value*.
public static double Sqrt(double *d*)	Returns the square root of *d*.
public static double Tan(double *a*)	Returns the tangent of *a*.
public static double Tanh(double *value*)	Returns the hyperbolic tangent of *value*.
public static double Truncate(double *d*)	Returns the whole number portion of *d*.
public static decimal Truncate(decimal *d*)	Returns the whole number portion of *d*.

TABLE 21-1 Methods Defined by **Math** *(continued)*

Here is an example that uses **Sqrt( )** to help implement the Pythagorean theorem. It computes the length of the hypotenuse given the lengths of the two opposing sides of a right triangle.

```
// Implement the Pythagorean Theorem.

using System;

class Pythagorean {
  static void Main() {
    double s1;
    double s2;
    double hypot;
    string str;

    Console.WriteLine("Enter length of first side: ");
    str = Console.ReadLine();
    s1 = Double.Parse(str);

    Console.WriteLine("Enter length of second side: ");
    str = Console.ReadLine();
    s2 = Double.Parse(str);

    hypot = Math.Sqrt(s1*s1 + s2*s2);

    Console.WriteLine("Hypotenuse is " + hypot);
  }
}
```

Here is a sample run:

```
Enter length of first side: 3
Enter length of second side: 4
Hypotenuse is 5
```

Next is an example that uses the **Pow( )** method to compute the initial investment required to achieve a desired future value given the annual rate of return and the number of years. The formula to compute the initial investment is shown here:

$$InitialInvestment = FutureValue / (1 + InterestRate)^{Years}$$

Because **Pow( )** requires **double** arguments, the interest rate and the number of years are held in **double** values. The future value and initial investment use the **decimal** type.

```
/* Compute the initial investment needed to attain
   a known future value given annual rate of return
   and the time period in years. */

using System;

class InitialInvestment {
  static void Main() {
    decimal initInvest; // initial investment
    decimal futVal;     // future value
```

```
        double numYears;     // number of years
        double intRate;      // annual rate of return as a decimal

        string str;

        Console.Write("Enter future value: ");
        str = Console.ReadLine();
        try {
          futVal = Decimal.Parse(str);
        } catch(FormatException exc) {
          Console.WriteLine(exc.Message);
          return;
        }

        Console.Write("Enter interest rate (such as 0.085): ");
        str = Console.ReadLine();
        try {
          intRate = Double.Parse(str);
        } catch(FormatException exc) {
          Console.WriteLine(exc.Message);
          return;
        }

        Console.Write("Enter number of years: ");
        str = Console.ReadLine();
        try {
          numYears = Double.Parse(str);
        } catch(FormatException exc) {
          Console.WriteLine(exc.Message);
          return;
        }

        initInvest = futVal / (decimal) Math.Pow(intRate+1.0, numYears);

        Console.WriteLine("Initial investment required: {0:C}",
                          initInvest);
    }
}
```

Here is a sample run:

```
Enter future value: 10000
Enter interest rate (such as 0.085): 0.07
Enter number of years: 10
Initial investment required: $5,083.49
```

The .NET Structures Corresponding to the Built-in Value Types

The structures that correspond to C#'s built-in value types were introduced in Chapter 14 when they were used to convert strings holding human-readable numeric values into their equivalent binary values. Here these structures are examined in detail.

The .NET structure names and their C# keyword equivalents are shown in the following table:

.NET Structure Name	C# Name
System.Boolean	bool
System.Char	char
System.Decimal	decimal
System.Double	double
System.Single	float
System.Int16	short
System.Int32	int
System.Int64	long
System.UInt16	ushort
System.UInt32	uint
System.UInt64	ulong
System.Byte	byte
System.Sbyte	sbyte

By using the members defined by these structures, you can perform operations relating to the value types. The following sections examine each of these structures.

NOTE *Some methods defined by the structures that correspond to the built-in value types take a parameter of type* **IFormatProvider** *or* **NumberStyles**. **IFormatProvider** *is briefly described later in this chapter.* **NumberStyles** *is an enumeration found in the* **System.Globalization** *namespace. The topic of formatting is discussed in Chapter 22.*

The Integer Structures

The integer structures are

Byte	SByte	Int16	UInt16
Int32	UInt32	Int64	UInt64

Each of these structures contains the same methods. The ones for **Int32** are shown in Table 21-2 as an example, but the others are similar except for the integer type that they represent.

The integer structures also define the following **const** fields:

MaxValue
MinValue

For each structure, these fields contain the largest and smallest value that type of integer can hold.

All of the integer structures implement the following interfaces: **IComparable**, **IComparable<T>**, **IConvertible**, **IFormattable**, and **IEquatable<T>**, where T is replaced by the corresponding data type. For example, **T** will be replaced with **int** for **Int32**.

Method	Meaning
public int CompareTo(object *value*)	Compares the numerical value of the invoking object with that of *value*. Returns zero if the values are equal. Returns a negative value if the invoking object has a lower value. Returns a positive value if the invoking object has a greater value.
public int CompareTo(int *value*)	Compares the numerical value of the invoking object with that of *value*. Returns zero if the values are equal. Returns a negative value if the invoking object has a lower value. Returns a positive value if the invoking object has a greater value.
public override bool Equals(object *obj*)	Returns true if the value of the invoking object equals the value of *obj*.
public bool Equals(int *obj*)	Returns true if the value of the invoking object equals the value of *obj*.
public override int GetHashCode( )	Returns the hash code for the invoking object.
public TypeCode GetTypeCode( )	Returns the **TypeCode** enumeration value for **Int32**, which is **TypeCode.Int32**.
public static int Parse(string s)	Returns the binary equivalent of the numeric string in s. If the string does not represent a numeric value as defined by the structure type, an exception is thrown.
public static int Parse(string s, IFormatProvider *provider*)	Returns the binary equivalent of the numeric string in s using the culture-specific information provided by *provider*. If the string does not represent a numeric value as defined by the structure type, an exception is thrown.
public static int Parse(string s, NumberStyles *style*)	Returns the binary equivalent of the numeric string in s using the style information provided by *style*. If the string does not represent a numeric value as defined by the structure type, an exception is thrown.
public static int Parse(string s, NumberStyles *style*, IFormatProvider *provider*)	Returns the binary equivalent of the numeric string in s using the style information provided by *style* and the culture-specific format information provided by *provider*. If the string does not represent a numeric value as defined by the structure type, an exception is thrown.
public override string ToString( )	Returns the string representation of the value of the invoking object.
public string ToString(string *format*)	Returns the string representation of the value of the invoking object as specified by the format string passed in *format*.
public string ToString(IFormatProvider *provider*)	Returns the string representation of the value of the invoking object using the culture-specific information specified in *provider*.
public string ToString(string *format*, IFormatProvider *provider*)	Returns the string representation of the value of the invoking object using the culture-specific information specified in *provider* and the format specified by *format*.

TABLE 21-2   Methods Supported by the **Int32** Structure

Method	Meaning
public static bool TryParse(string s, out int *result*)	Attempts to convert the numeric string in s into a binary value. If successful, the value is stored in *result* and true is returned. If no conversion takes place, false is returned. This differs from **Parse( )**, which throws an exception on failure.

public static bool
   TryParse(string s,
      NumberStyles *style*,
      IFormatProvider *provider*,
      out int *result*)
	Attempts to convert the numeric string in s into a binary value using the style information provided by *style* and the culture-specific format information provided by *provider*. If successful, the value is stored in *result* and true is returned. If no conversion takes place, false is returned. This differs from **Parse( )**, which throws an exception on failure.

TABLE 21-2   Methods Supported by the **Int32** Structure *(continued)*

The Floating-Point Structures

There are two floating-point structures: **Double** and **Single**. **Single** represents **float**. Its methods are shown in Table 21-3, and its fields are shown in Table 21-4. **Double** represents **double**. Its methods are shown in Table 21-5, and its fields are shown in Table 21-6. As is the case with the integer structures, you can specify culture-specific information and format information in a call to **Parse( )** or **ToString( )**.

The floating-point structures implement the following interfaces: **IComparable**, **IComparable<T>**, **IConvertible**, **IFormattable**, and **IEquatable<T>**, where **T** is replaced by either **double** for **Double** or **float** for **Single**.

Method	Meaning
public int CompareTo(object *value*)	Compares the numerical value of the invoking object with that of *value*. Returns zero if the values are equal. Returns a negative value if the invoking object has a lower value. Returns a positive value if the invoking object has a greater value.
public int CompareTo(float *value*)	Compares the numerical value of the invoking object with that of *value*. Returns zero if the values are equal. Returns a negative value if the invoking object has a lower value. Returns a positive value if the invoking object has a greater value.
public override bool Equals(object *obj*)	Returns true if the value of the invoking object equals the value of *obj*.
public bool Equals(float *obj*)	Returns true if the value of the invoking object equals the value of *obj*.
public override int GetHashCode( )	Returns the hash code for the invoking object.
public TypeCode GetTypeCode( )	Returns the **TypeCode** enumeration value for **Single**, which is **TypeCode.Single**.
public static bool IsInfinity(float *f*)	Returns true if *f* represents infinity (either positive or negative). Otherwise, returns false.
public static bool IsNaN(float *f*)	Returns true if *f* is not a number. Otherwise, returns false.

TABLE 21-3   Methods Supported by **Single**

Method	Meaning
public static bool IsPositiveInfinity(float *f*)	Returns true if *f* represents positive infinity. Otherwise, returns false.
public static bool IsNegativeInfinity(float *f*)	Returns true if *f* represents negative infinity. Otherwise, returns false.
public static float Parse(string *s*)	Returns the binary equivalent of the numeric string in *s*. If the string does not represent a **float** value, an exception is thrown.

public static float
    Parse(string *s*,
        IFormatProvider *provider*)
	Returns the binary equivalent of the numeric string in *s* using the culture-specific information provided by *provider*. If the string does not represent a **float** value, an exception is thrown.

public static float Parse(string *s*, NumberStyles *style*)	Returns the binary equivalent of the numeric string in *s* using the style information provided by *style*. If the string does not represent a **float** value, an exception is thrown.

public static float
    Parse(string *s*,
        NumberStyles *style*,
        IFormatProvider *provider*)
	Returns the binary equivalent of the numeric string in *s* using the style information provided by *style* and the culture-specific format information provided by *provider*. If the string does not represent a **float** value, an exception is thrown.

public override string ToString( )	Returns the string representation of the value of the invoking object in the default format.
public string ToString(string *format*)	Returns the string representation of the value of the invoking object as specified by the format string passed in *format*.
public string ToString(IFormatProvider *provider*)	Returns the string representation of the value of the invoking object using the culture-specific information specified in *provider*.

public string
    ToString(string *format*,
        IFormatProvider *provider*)
	Returns the string representation of the value of the invoking object using the culture-specific information specified in *provider* and the format specified by *format*.

public static bool TryParse(string *s*, out float *result*)	Attempts to convert the numeric string in *s* into a **float** value. If successful, the value is stored in *result* and true is returned. If no conversion takes place, false is returned. This differs from **Parse( )**, which throws an exception on failure.

public static bool
    TryParse(string *s*,
        NumberStyles *style*,
        IFormatProvider *provider*,
        out float *result*)
	Attempts to convert the numeric string in *s* into a **float** value using the style information provided by *style* and the culture-specific format information provided by *provider*. If successful, the value is stored in *result* and true is returned. If no conversion takes place, false is returned. This differs from **Parse( )**, which throws an exception on failure.

TABLE 21-3 Methods Supported by **Single** *(continued)*

TABLE 21-4
Fields Supported
by **Single**

Field	Meaning
public const float Epsilon	The smallest non-zero positive value.
public const float MaxValue	The largest value that a **float** can hold.
public const float MinValue	The smallest value that a **float** can hold.
public const float NaN	A value that is not a number.
public const float NegativeInfinity	A value representing negative infinity.
public const float PositiveInfinity	A value representing positive infinity

Method	Meaning
public int CompareTo(object *value*)	Compares the numerical value of the invoking object with that of *value*. Returns zero if the values are equal. Returns a negative value if the invoking object has a lower value. Returns a positive value if the invoking object has a greater value.
public int CompareTo(double *value*)	Compares the numerical value of the invoking object with that of *value*. Returns zero if the values are equal. Returns a negative value if the invoking object has a lower value. Returns a positive value if the invoking object has a greater value.
public override bool Equals(object *obj*)	Returns true if the value of the invoking object equals the value of *obj*.
public bool Equals(double *obj*)	Returns true if the value of the invoking object equals the value of *obj*.
public override int GetHashCode( )	Returns the hash code for the invoking object.
public TypeCode GetTypeCode( )	Returns the **TypeCode** enumeration value for **Double**, which is **TypeCode.Double**.
public static bool IsInfinity(double *d*)	Returns true if *d* represents infinity (either positive or negative). Otherwise, returns false.
public static bool IsNaN(double *d*)	Returns true if *d* is not a number. Otherwise, returns false.
public static bool IsPositiveInfinity(double *d*)	Returns true if *d* represents positive infinity. Otherwise, returns false.
public static bool IsNegativeInfinity(double *d*)	Returns true if *d* represents negative infinity. Otherwise, returns false.
public static double Parse(string *s*)	Returns the binary equivalent of the numeric string in *s*. If the string does not represent a **double** value, an exception is thrown.
public static double Parse(string *s*, IFormatProvider *provider*)	Returns the binary equivalent of the numeric string in *s* using the culture-specific information provided by *provider*. If the string does not represent a **double** value, an exception is thrown.
public static double Parse(string *s*, NumberStyles *style*)	Returns the binary equivalent of the numeric string in *s* using the style information provided by *style*. If the string does not represent a **double** value, an exception is thrown.
public static double Parse(string *s*, NumberStyles *style*, IFormatProvider *provider*)	Returns the binary equivalent of the numeric string in *s* using the style information provided by *style* and the culture-specific format information provided by *provider*. If the string does not represent a **double** value, an exception is thrown.

TABLE 21-5   Methods Supported by **Double**

Method	Meaning
public override string ToString( )	Returns the string representation of the value of the invoking object in the default format.
public string ToString(string *format*)	Returns the string representation of the value of the invoking object as specified by the format string passed in *format*.
public string ToString(IFormatProvider *provider*)	Returns the string representation of the value of the invoking object using the culture-specific information specified in *provider*.
public string ToString(string *format*, IFormatProvider *provider*)	Returns the string representation of the value of the invoking object using the culture-specific information specified in *provider* and the format specified by *format*.
public static bool TryParse(string *s*, out double *result*)	Attempts to convert the numeric string in *s* into a **double** value. If successful, the value is stored in *result* and true is returned. If no conversion takes place, false is returned. This differs from **Parse( )**, which throws an exception on failure.
public static bool TryParse(string *s*, NumberStyles *style*, IFormatProvider *provider*, out double *result*)	Attempts to convert the numeric string in *s* into a **double** value using the style information provided by *style* and the culture-specific format information provided by *provider*. If successful, the value is stored in *result* and true is returned. If no conversion takes place, false is returned. This differs from **Parse( )**, which throws an exception on failure.

TABLE 21-5 Methods Supported by **Double** *(continued)*

Decimal

The **Decimal** structure is a bit more complicated than its integer and floating-point relatives. It contains many constructors, fields, methods, and operators that help integrate **decimal** with the other numeric types supported by C#. For example, several of the methods provide conversions between **decimal** and the other numeric types.

Decimal offers eight public constructors. The following six are the most commonly used:

```
public Decimal(int value)
public Decimal(uint value)
public Decimal(long value)
public Decimal(ulong value)
```

TABLE 21-6
Fields Supported by
Double

Field	Meaning
public const double Epsilon	The smallest non-zero positive value.
public const double MaxValue	The largest value that a **double** can hold.
public const double MinValue	The smallest value that a **double** can hold.
public const double NaN	A value that is not a number.
public const double NegativeInfinity	A value representing negative infinity.
public const double PositiveInfinity	A value representing positive infinity.

public Decimal(float *value*)
public Decimal(double *value*)

Each constructs a **Decimal** from the specified value.

You can also construct a **Decimal** by specifying its constituent parts using this constructor:

public Decimal(int *lo*, int *mid*, int *hi*, bool *isNegative*, byte *scale*)

A decimal value consists of three parts. The first is a 96-bit integer, the second is a sign flag, and the third is a scaling factor. The 96-bit integer is passed in 32-bit chunks through *lo, mid,* and *hi*. The sign is passed through *isNegative*, which is **false** for a positive number and **true** for a negative number. The scaling factor is passed in *scale*, which must be a value between 0 and 28. This factor specifies the power of 10 (that is, 10^{scale}) by which the number is divided, thus yielding its fractional component.

Instead of passing each component separately, you can specify the constituents of a **Decimal** in an array of integers, using this constructor:

public Decimal(int[ ] *bits*)

The first three **ints** in *bits* contain the 96-bit integer value. In *bits*[3], bit 31 specifies the sign flag (0 for positive, 1 for negative), and bits 16 through 23 contain the scale factor.

Decimal implements the following interfaces: **IComparable, IComparable<decimal>, IConvertible, IFormattable, IEquatable<decimal>**, and **IDeserializationCallback**.

Here is an example that constructs a **decimal** value by hand:

```
// Manually create a decimal number.

using System;

class CreateDec {
  static void Main() {
    decimal d = new decimal(12345, 0, 0, false, 2);

    Console.WriteLine(d);
  }
}
```

The output is shown here:

```
123.45
```

In this example, the value of the 96-bit integer is 12345. Its sign is positive, and it has two decimal fractions.

The methods defined by **Decimal** are shown in Table 21-7. The fields defined by **Decimal** are shown in Table 21-8. **Decimal** also defines a large number of operators and conversions that allow **decimal** values to be used in expressions with other numeric types. The rules governing the use of **decimal** in expressions and assignments are described in Chapter 3.

Method	Meaning
public static decimal Add(decimal *d1*, decimal *d2*)	Returns *d1* + *d2*.
public static decimal Ceiling(decimal *d*)	Returns the smallest integer (represented as a **decimal** value) not less than *d*. For example, given 1.02, **Ceiling( )** returns 2.0. Given –1.02, **Ceiling( )** returns –1.
public static int Compare(decimal *d1*, decimal *d2*)	Compares the numerical value of *d1* with that of *d2*. Returns zero if the values are equal. Returns a negative value if *d1* is less than *d2*. Returns a positive value if *d1* is greater than *d2*.
public int CompareTo(object *value*)	Compares the numerical value of the invoking object with that of *value*. Returns zero if the values are equal. Returns a negative value if the invoking object has a lower value. Returns a positive value if the invoking object has a greater value.
public int CompareTo(decimal *value*)	Compares the numerical value of the invoking object with that of *value*. Returns zero if the values are equal. Returns a negative value if the invoking object has a lower value. Returns a positive value if the invoking object has a greater value.
public static decimal Divide(decimal *d1*, decimal *d2*)	Returns *d1* / *d2*.
public bool Equals(decimal *value*)	Returns true if the value of the invoking object equals the value of *value*.
public override bool Equals(object *value*)	Returns true if the value of the invoking object equals the value of *value*.
public static bool Equals(decimal *d1*, decimal *d2*)	Returns true if *d1* equals *d2*.
public static decimal Floor(decimal *d*)	Returns the largest integer (represented as a **decimal** value) not greater than *d*. For example, given 1.02, **Floor( )** returns 1.0. Given –1.02, **Floor( )** returns –2.
public static decimal FromOACurrency(long *cy*)	Converts the OLE Automation currency value in *cy* into its **decimal** equivalent and returns the result.
public static int[ ] GetBits(decimal *d*)	Returns the binary representation of *d* as an array of **int**. The organization of this array is as described in the text.
public override int GetHashCode( )	Returns the hash code for the invoking object.
public TypeCode GetTypeCode( )	Returns the **TypeCode** enumeration value for **Decimal**, which is **TypeCode.Decimal**.
public static decimal Multiply(decimal *d1*, decimal *d2*)	Returns *d1* * *d2*.
public static decimal Negate(decimal *d*)	Returns –*d*.
public static decimal Parse(string *s*)	Returns the binary equivalent of the numeric string in *s*. If the string does not represent a **decimal** value, an exception is thrown.

TABLE 21-7 Methods Defined by **Decimal**

Method	Meaning

public static decimal
    Parse(string s,
        IFormatProvider *provider*)
	Returns the binary equivalent of the numeric string in *s* using the culture-specific information provided by *provider*. If the string does not represent a **decimal** value, an exception is thrown.

public static decimal Parse(string s, NumberStyles *style*)	Returns the binary equivalent of the numeric string in *s*, using the style information provided by *style*. If the string does not represent a **decimal** value, an exception is thrown.

public static decimal
    Parse(string s,
        NumberStyles *style*,
        IFormatProvider *provider*)
	Returns the binary equivalent of the numeric string in *s* using the style information provided by *style* and the culture-specific format information provided by *provider*. If the string does not represent a **decimal** value, an exception is thrown.

public static decimal Remainder(decimal *d1*, decimal *d2*)	Returns the remainder of the integer division *d1* / *d2*.
public static decimal Round(decimal *d*)	Returns the value of *d* rounded to the nearest whole number.
public static decimal Round(decimal *d*, int *decimals*)	Returns the value of *d* rounded to the number of decimal places specified by *decimals,* which must be between 0 and 28.

public static decimal
    Round(decimal *d*,
        MidPointRounding *mode*)
	Returns the value of *d* rounded to the nearest whole number using the rounding mode specified by *mode*. The rounding mode applies only to those conditions in which *d* is at the midpoint between two whole numbers.

public static decimal
    Round(decimal *d*, int *decimals*,
        MidPointRounding *mode*)
	Returns the value of *d* rounded to the number of decimal places specified by *decimals* (which must be between 0 and 28), using the rounding mode specified by *mode*. The rounding mode applies only to those conditions in which *d* is at the midpoint between two rounded values.

public static decimal Subtract(decimal *d1*, decimal *d2*)	Returns *d1* – *d2*.
public static byte ToByte(decimal *value*)	Returns the **byte** equivalent of *value*. Any fractional component is truncated. An **OverflowException** occurs if *value* is not within the range of a **byte**.
public static double ToDouble(decimal *d*)	Returns the **double** equivalent of *d*. A loss of precision may occur because **double** has fewer significant digits than does **decimal**.
public static short ToInt16(decimal *value*)	Returns the **short** equivalent of *value*. Any fractional component is truncated. An **OverflowException** occurs if *value* is not within the range of a **short**.
public static int ToInt32(decimal *d*)	Returns the **int** equivalent of *d*. Any fractional component is truncated. An **OverflowException** occurs if *d* is not within the range of an **int**.
public static long ToInt64(decimal *d*)	Returns the **long** equivalent of *d*. Any fractional component is truncated. An **OverflowException** occurs if *d* is not within the range of a **long**.

TABLE 21-7   Methods Defined by **Decimal** *(continued)*

Method	Meaning
public static long ToOACurrency(decimal *value*)	Converts *value* into the equivalent OLE Automation currency value and returns the result.
public static sbyte ToSByte(decimal *value*)	Returns the **sbyte** equivalent of *value*. Any fractional component is truncated. An **OverflowException** occurs if *value* is not within the range of an **sbyte**.
public static float ToSingle(decimal *d*)	Returns the **float** equivalent of *d*. A loss of precision may occur because **float** has fewer significant digits than does **decimal**.
public override string ToString( )	Returns the string representation of the value of the invoking object in the default format.
public string ToString(string *format*)	Returns the string representation of the value of the invoking object as specified by the format string passed in *format*.
public string ToString(IFormatProvider *provider*)	Returns the string representation of the value of the invoking object using the culture-specific information specified in *provider*.
public string ToString(string *format*, IFormatProvider *provider*)	Returns the string representation of the value of the invoking object using the culture-specific information specified in *provider* and the format specified by *format*.
public static ushort ToUInt16(decimal *value*)	Returns the **ushort** equivalent of *value*. Any fractional component is truncated. An **OverflowException** occurs if *value* is not within the range of a **ushort**.
public static uint ToUInt32(decimal *d*)	Returns the **uint** equivalent of *d*. Any fractional component is truncated. An **OverflowException** occurs if *d* is not within the range of a **uint**.
public static ulong ToUInt64(decimal *d*)	Returns the **ulong** equivalent of *d*. Any fractional component is truncated. An **OverflowException** occurs if *d* is not within the range of a **ulong**.
public static decimal Truncate(decimal *d*)	Returns the whole-number portion of *d*. Thus, it truncates any fractional digits.
public static bool TryParse(string *s*, out decimal *result*)	Attempts to convert the numeric string in *s* into a **decimal** value. If successful, the value is stored in *result* and **true** is returned. If no conversion takes place, **false** is returned. This differs from **Parse( )**, which throws an exception on failure.
public static bool TryParse(string *s*, NumberStyles *style*, IFormatProvider *provider*, out decimal *result*)	Attempts to convert the numeric string in *s* into a **decimal** value using the style information provided by *style* and the culture-specific format information provided by *provider*. If successful, the value is stored in *result* and **true** is returned. If no conversion takes place, **false** is returned. This differs from **Parse( )**, which throws an exception on failure.

TABLE 21-7   Methods Defined by **Decimal** *(continued)*

	Field	Meaning
TABLE 21-8 Fields Supported by **Decimal**	public static readonly decimal MaxValue	The largest value that a **decimal** can hold.
	public static readonly decimal MinusOne	The **decimal** representation of –1.
	public static readonly decimal MinValue	The smallest value that a **decimal** can hold.
	public static readonly decimal One	The **decimal** representation of 1.
	public static readonly decimal Zero	The **decimal** representation of 0.

Char

The structure corresponding to the **char** type is **Char**. It is quite useful because it supplies a large number of methods that allow you to process and categorize characters. For example, you can convert a lowercase character to uppercase by calling **ToUpper( )**. You can determine if a character is a digit by calling **IsDigit( )**.

The methods defined by **Char** are shown in Table 21-9. Notice that several, such as **ConvertFromUtf32( )** and **ConvertToUtf32( )**, give you the ability to work with both UTF-16 and UTF-32 Unicode characters. In the past, all Unicode characters could be represented by 16 bits, which is the size of a **char**. However, a few years ago the Unicode character set was expanded and more than 16 bits are required. Each Unicode character is represented by a *code point*. The way that a code point is encoded depends on the Unicode Transformation Format (UTF) being used. In UTF-16, the most common code points require one 16-bit value, but some need two 16-bit values. When two 16-bit values are needed, two **char** values are used to represent it. The first character is called the *high surrogate* and the second is called the *low surrogate*. In UTF-32, each code point uses one 32-bit value. **Char** provides the necessary conversions between UTF-16 and UTF-32.

One other point about the **Char** methods. The default forms of **ToUpper( )** and **ToLower( )** use the current cultural settings to determine how to upper- or lowercase a character. At the time of this writing, the recommended style is to explicitly specify the cultural setting by using a second form of these methods that has a **CultureInfo** parameter. **CultureInfo** is in **System.Globalization**. You can pass the property **CultureInfo.CurrentCulture** to specify the current culture.

Char defines the following fields:

```
public const char MaxValue
public const char MinValue
```

These represent the largest and smallest values that a **char** variable can hold.

Char implements the following interfaces: **IComparable**, **IComparable<char>**, **IConvertible**, and **IEquatable<char>**.

Method	Meaning
public int CompareTo(char *value*)	Compares the character in the invoking object with that of *value*. Returns zero if the characters are equal. Returns a negative value if the invoking object has a lower value. Returns a positive value if the invoking object has a greater value.
public int CompareTo(object *value*)	Compares the character in the invoking object with that of *value*. Returns zero if the characters are equal. Returns a negative value if the invoking object has a lower value. Returns a positive value if the invoking object has a greater value.
public static string ConvertFromUtf32(int *utf32*)	Converts the Unicode UTF-32 code point in *utf32* into a UTF-16 string and returns the result.
pubic static int ConvertToUtf32(char *highSurrogate*, char *lowSurrogate*)	Converts the high and low UTF-16 surrogates specified by *highSurrogate* and *lowSurrogate* into a UTF-32 codepoint. The result is returned.
pubic static int ConvertToUtf32(string *s*, int *index*)	Converts the UTF-16 character or surrogate pair at s[*index*] into its UTF-32 code point. The result is returned.
public bool Equals(char *obj*)	Returns true if the value of the invoking object equals the value of *obj*.
public override bool Equals(object *obj*)	Returns true if the value of the invoking object equals the value of *obj*.
public override int GetHashCode( )	Returns the hash code for the invoking object.
public static double GetNumericValue(char *c*)	Returns the numeric value of *c* if *c* is a digit. Otherwise, returns –1.
public static double GetNumericValue(string *s*, int *index*)	Returns the numeric value of s[*index*] if that character is a digit. Otherwise, returns –1.
public TypeCode GetTypeCode( )	Returns the **TypeCode** enumeration value for **Char**, which is **TypeCode.Char**.
public static UnicodeCategory GetUnicodeCategory(char *c*)	Returns the **UnicodeCategory** enumeration value for *c*. **UnicodeCategory** is an enumeration defined by **System.Globalization** that categorizes Unicode characters.
public static UnicodeCategory GetUnicodeCategory(string *s*, int *index*)	Returns the **UnicodeCategory** enumeration value for s[*index*]. **UnicodeCategory** is an enumeration defined by **System.Globalization** that categorizes Unicode characters.
public static bool IsControl(char *c*)	Returns true if *c* is a control character. Otherwise, returns false.
public static bool IsControl(string *s*, int *index*)	Returns true if s[*index*] is a control character. Otherwise, returns false.
public static bool IsDigit(char *c*)	Returns true if *c* is a digit. Otherwise, returns false.
public static bool IsDigit(string *s*, int *index*)	Returns true if s[*index*] is a digit. Otherwise, returns false.
public static bool IsHighSurrogate(char *c*)	Returns true if *c* is a valid high surrogate. Otherwise, returns false.
public static bool IsHighSurrogate(string *s*, int *index*)	Returns true if s[*index*] is a valid high surrogate. Otherwise, returns false.

TABLE 21-9   Methods Defined by **Char**

Method	Meaning
public static bool IsLetter(char c)	Returns true if c is a letter of the alphabet. Otherwise, returns false.
public static bool IsLetter(string s, int index)	Returns true if s[index] is a letter of the alphabet. Otherwise, returns false.
public static bool IsLetterOrDigit(char c)	Returns true if c is either a letter of the alphabet or a digit. Otherwise, returns false.
public static bool IsLetterOrDigit(string s, int index)	Returns true if s[index] is either a letter of the alphabet or a digit. Otherwise, returns false.
public static bool IsLower(char c)	Returns true if c is a lowercase letter of the alphabet. Otherwise, returns false.
public static bool IsLower(string s, int index)	Returns true if s[index] is a lowercase letter of the alphabet. Otherwise, returns false.
public static bool IsLowSurrogate(char c)	Returns true if c is a valid low surrogate. Otherwise, returns false.
public static bool IsLowSurrogate(string s, int index)	Returns true if s[index] is a valid low surrogate. Otherwise, returns false.
public static bool IsNumber(char c)	Returns true if c is a number. Otherwise, returns false.
public static bool IsNumber(string s, int index)	Returns true if s[index] is a number. Otherwise, returns false.
public static bool IsPunctuation(char c)	Returns true if c is a punctuation character. Otherwise, returns false.
public static bool IsPunctuation(string s, int index)	Returns true if s[index] is a punctuation character. Otherwise, returns false.
public static bool IsSeparator(char c)	Returns true if c is a separator character, such as a space. Otherwise, returns false.
public static bool IsSeparator(string s, int index)	Returns true if s[index] is a separator character, such as a space. Otherwise, returns false.
public static bool IsSurrogate(char c)	Returns true if c is a Unicode surrogate character. Otherwise, returns false.
public static bool IsSurrogate(string s, int index)	Returns true if s[index] is a Unicode surrogate character. Otherwise, returns false.
public static bool IsSurrogatePair(char highSurrogate, char lowSurrogate)	Returns true if highSurrogate and lowSurrogate form a valid surrogate pair. Otherwise, returns false.
public static bool IsSurrogatePair(string s, int index)	Returns true if the two consecutive characters starting at index within s form a valid surrogate pair. Otherwise, returns false.
public static bool IsSymbol(char c)	Returns true if c is a symbolic character, such as the currency symbol. Otherwise, returns false.
public static bool IsSymbol(string s, int index)	Returns true if s[index] is a symbolic character, such as the currency symbol. Otherwise, returns false.
public static bool IsUpper(char c)	Returns true if c is an uppercase letter. Otherwise, returns false.
public static bool IsUpper(string s, int index)	Returns true if s[index] is an uppercase letter. Otherwise, returns false.

TABLE 21-9 Methods Defined by **Char** (continued)

Method	Meaning
public static bool IsWhiteSpace(char c)	Returns true if c is a whitespace character, such as a space or tab. Otherwise, returns false.
public static bool IsWhiteSpace(string s, int index)	Returns true if s[index] is a whitespace character, such as a space or tab. Otherwise, returns false.
public static char Parse(string s)	Returns the **char** equivalent of the character in s. If s contains more than one character, a **FormatException** is thrown.
public static char ToLower(char c)	Returns the lowercase equivalent of c if c is an uppercase letter. Otherwise, c is returned unchanged.
public static char ToLower(char c, CultureInfo culture)	Returns the lowercase equivalent of c if c is an uppercase letter. Otherwise, c is returned unchanged. The conversion is handled in accordance with the specified cultural information. **CultureInfo** is a class defined in **System.Globalization**.
public static char ToLowerInvariant(char c)	Returns the lowercase version of c independently of the cultural settings.
public override string ToString( )	Returns the string representation of the value of the invoking **Char**.
public static string ToString(char c)	Returns the string representation of c.
public string ToString(IFormatProvider provider)	Returns the string representation of the invoking **Char** using the specified culture information.
public static char ToUpper(char c)	Returns the uppercase equivalent of c if c is a lowercase letter. Otherwise, c is returned unchanged.
public static char ToUpper(char c, CultureInfo culture)	Returns the uppercase equivalent of c if c is a lowercase letter. Otherwise, c is returned unchanged. The conversion is handled in accordance with the specified cultural information. **CultureInfo** is a class defined in **System.Globalization**.
public static char ToUpperInvariant(char c)	Returns the uppercase version of c independently of the cultural settings.
public static bool TryParse(string s, out char result)	Attempts to convert the character in s into its **char** equivalent. If successful, the value is stored in result and true is returned. If s contains more than one character, false is returned. This differs from **Parse( )**, which throws an exception on failure.

TABLE 21-9   Methods Defined by **Char** (continued)

Here is a program that demonstrates several of the methods defined by **Char**:

```
// Demonstrate several Char methods.

using System;
using System.Globalization;

class CharDemo {
  static void Main() {
    string str = "This is a test. $23";
    int i;
```

```
    for(i=0; i < str.Length; i++) {
      Console.Write(str[i] + " is");
      if(Char.IsDigit(str[i]))
        Console.Write(" digit");
      if(Char.IsLetter(str[i]))
        Console.Write(" letter");
      if(Char.IsLower(str[i]))
        Console.Write(" lowercase");
      if(Char.IsUpper(str[i]))
        Console.Write(" uppercase");
      if(Char.IsSymbol(str[i]))
        Console.Write(" symbol");
      if(Char.IsSeparator(str[i]))
        Console.Write(" separator");
      if(Char.IsWhiteSpace(str[i]))
        Console.Write(" whitespace");
      if(Char.IsPunctuation(str[i]))
        Console.Write(" punctuation");

      Console.WriteLine();
    }

    Console.WriteLine("Original: " + str);

    // Convert to uppercase.
    string newstr = "";
    for(i=0; i < str.Length; i++)
      newstr += Char.ToUpper(str[i], CultureInfo.CurrentCulture);

    Console.WriteLine("Uppercased: " + newstr);

  }
}
```

The output is shown here:

```
T is letter uppercase
h is letter lowercase
i is letter lowercase
s is letter lowercase
  is separator whitespace
i is letter lowercase
s is letter lowercase
  is separator whitespace
a is letter lowercase
  is separator whitespace
t is letter lowercase
e is letter lowercase
s is letter lowercase
t is letter lowercase
. is punctuation
  is separator whitespace
$ is symbol
```

```
2 is digit
3 is digit
Original: This is a test. $23
Uppercased: THIS IS A TEST. $23
```

The Boolean Structure

The **Boolean** structure supports the **bool** data type. The methods defined by **Boolean** are shown in Table 21-10. It defines these fields:

public static readonly string FalseString
public static readonly string TrueString

These contain the human-readable forms of **true** and **false**. For example, if you output **FalseString** using a call to **WriteLine( )**, the string "False" is displayed.

Boolean implements the following interfaces: **IComparable**, **IComparable<bool>**, **IConvertible**, and **IEquatable<bool>**.

Method	Meaning
public int CompareTo(bool *value*)	Compares the value of the invoking object with that of *value*. Returns zero if the values are equal. Returns a negative value if the invoking object is false and *value* is true. Returns a positive value if the invoking object is true and *value* is false.
public int CompareTo(object *obj*)	Compares the value of the invoking object with that of *obj*. Returns zero if the values are equal. Returns a negative value if the invoking object is false and *obj* is true. Returns a positive value if the invoking object is true and *obj* is false.
public bool Equals(bool *obj*)	Returns true if the value of the invoking object equals the value of *obj*.
public override bool Equals(object *obj*)	Returns true if the value of the invoking object equals the value of *obj*.
public override int GetHashCode( )	Returns the hash code for the invoking object.
public TypeCode GetTypeCode( )	Returns the **TypeCode** enumeration value for **Boolean**, which is **TypeCode.Boolean**.
public static bool Parse(string *value*)	Returns the **bool** equivalent of the string in *value*. If the string is neither **Boolean.TrueString** nor **Boolean.FalseString**, a **FormatException** is thrown. However, case differences are ignored.
public override string ToString( )	Returns the string representation of the value of the invoking object, which will be either **TrueString** or **FalseString**.
public string ToString(IFormatProvider *provider*)	Returns the string representation of the value of the invoking object, which will be either **TrueString** or **FalseString**. The *provider* parameter is ignored.
public static bool TryParse(string *value*, out bool *result*)	Attempts to convert the string in *value* into its **bool** equivalent. If successful, the value is stored in *result* and true is returned. If the string is neither **Boolean.TrueString** nor **Boolean.FalseString**, false is returned. (Case differences are ignored.) This differs from **Parse( )**, which throws an exception on failure.

TABLE 21-10   Methods Defined by **Boolean**

The Array Class

One very useful class in **System** is **Array**. **Array** is a base class for all arrays in C#. Thus, its methods can be applied to arrays of any of the built-in types or to arrays of types that you create. **Array** defines the properties shown in Table 21-11. It defines the methods shown in Table 21-12.

    Array implements the following interfaces: **ICloneable**, **ICollection**, **IEnumerable**, **IStructuralComparable**, **IStructuralEquatable**, and **IList**. All but **ICloneable** are defined in the **System.Collections** namespace and are described in Chapter 24.

    Several methods use a parameter of type **IComparer** or **IComparer\<T>**. The **IComparer** interface is in **System.Collections**. It defines a method called **Compare( )**, which compares the values of two objects. It is shown here:

    int Compare(object *x*, object *y*)

It returns greater than zero if *x* is greater than *y*, less than zero if *x* is less than *y*, and zero if the two values are equal.

    IComparer\<T> is in **System.Collections.Generic**. It defines a generic form of **Compare( )**, which is shown here:

    int Compare(T *x*, T *y*)

It works the same as its non-generic relative: returning greater than zero if *x* is greater than *y*, less than zero if *x* is less than *y*, and zero if the two values are equal. The advantage to **IComparer\<T>** is type safety, because the type of data being operated upon is explicitly specified. Thus, no casts from **object** are required.

    The next few sections demonstrate several commonly used array operations.

Property	Meaning
public bool IsFixedSize { get; }	A read-only property that is true if the array is of fixed size and false if the array is dynamic. This value is true for arrays.
public bool IsReadOnly { get; }	A read-only property that is true if the **Array** object is read-only and false if it is not. This value is false for arrays.
public bool IsSynchronized { get; }	A read-only property that is true if the array is safe for use in a multithreaded environment and false if it is not. This value is false for arrays.
public int Length { get; }	An **int** read-only property that contains the number of elements in the array.
public long LongLength { get; }	A **long** read-only property that contains the number of elements in the array.
public int Rank { get; }	A read-only property that contains the number of dimensions in the array.
public object SyncRoot { get; }	A read-only property that contains the object that synchronizes access to the array.

TABLE 21-11   Properties Defined by **Array**

Method	Meaning
public static ReadOnlyCollection<T> AsReadOnly<T>(T[ ] *array*)	Returns a read-only collection that wraps the array specified by *array*.
public static int BinarySearch(Array *array*, object *value*)	Searches the array specified by *array* for the value specified by *value*. Returns the index of the first match. If *value* is not found, returns a negative value. The array must be sorted and one-dimensional.
public static int BinarySearch<T>(T[ ] *array*, T *value*)	Searches the array specified by *array* for the value specified by *value*. Returns the index of the first match. If *value* is not found, returns a negative value. The array must be sorted and one-dimensional.
public static int BinarySearch(Array *array*, object *value*, IComparer *comparer*)	Searches the array specified by *array* for the value specified by *value*, using the comparison method specified by *comparer*. Returns the index of the first match. If *value* is not found, returns a negative value. The array must be sorted and one-dimensional.
public static int BinarySearch<T>(T[ ] *array*, T *value*, IComparer<T> *comparer*)	Searches the array specified by *array* for the value specified by *value*, using the comparison method specified by *comparer*. Returns the index of the first match. If *value* is not found, returns a negative value. The array must be sorted and one-dimensional.
public static int BinarySearch(Array *array*, int *index*, int *length*, object *value*)	Searches a portion of the array specified by *array* for the value specified by *value*. The search begins at the index specified by *index* and is restricted to *length* elements. Returns the index of the first match. If *value* is not found, returns a negative value. The array must be sorted and one-dimensional.
public static int BinarySearch<T>(T[ ] *array*, int *index*, int *length*, T *value*)	Searches a portion of the array specified by *array* for the value specified by *value*. The search begins at the index specified by *index* and is restricted to *length* elements. Returns the index of the first match. If *value* is not found, returns a negative value. The array must be sorted and one-dimensional.
public static int BinarySearch(Array *array*, int *index*, int *length*, object *value*, IComparer *comparer*)	Searches a portion of the array specified by *array* for the value specified by *value*, using the comparison method specified by *comparer*. The search begins at the index specified by *index* and is restricted to *length* elements. Returns the index of the first match. If *value* is not found, returns a negative value. The array must be sorted and one-dimensional.
public static int BinarySearch<T>(T [ ] *array*, int *index*, int *length*, T *value*, IComparer<T> *comparer*)	Searches a portion of the array specified by *array* for the value specified by *value*, using the comparison method specified by *comparer*. The search begins at the index specified by *index* and is restricted to *length* elements. Returns the index of the first match. If *value* is not found, returns a negative value. The array must be sorted and one-dimensional.

TABLE 21-12 Methods Defined by **Array**

Method	Meaning
public static void Clear(Array *array*, int *index*, int *length*)	Sets the specified elements of *array* to zero, **null**, or **false**, depending on whether the element type is a value type, a reference type, or Boolean. The elements to be zeroed begin at the index specified by *index* and run for *length* elements.
public object Clone( )	Returns a copy of the invoking array. The copy refers to the same elements as does the original. This is called a "shallow copy." Thus, changes to the elements affect both arrays since they both use the same elements.
public static void ConstrainedCopy(Array *sourceArray*, int *sourceIndex*, Array *destinationArray*, int *destinationIndex*, int *length*)	Copies *length* elements from *sourceArray* (beginning at *sourceIndex*) to *destinationArray* (beginning at *destinationIndex*). If both arrays are reference types, then **ConstrainedCopy( )** makes a "shallow copy," which means that both arrays will refer to the same elements. If an error occurs during the copy, *destinationArray* is unchanged.
public static TOutput[ ] ConvertAll<TInput, TOutput>(TInput[ ] *array*, Converter<TInput, TOutput> *converter*)	Converts *array* from type **TInput** to **TOutput** and returns the resulting array. The original array is unaffected. The conversion is performed by the specified converter.
public static void Copy(Array *sourceArray*, Array *destinationArray*, int *length*)	Beginning at the start of each array, copies *length* elements from *sourceArray* to *destinationArray*. When both arrays are reference types, then **Copy( )** makes a "shallow copy," which means that both arrays will refer to the same elements. If an error occurs during the copy, *destinationArray* is undefined.
public static void Copy(Array *sourceArray*, Array *destinationArray*, long *length*)	Beginning at the start of each array, copies *length* elements from *sourceArray* to *destinationArray*. When both arrays are reference types, then **Copy( )** makes a "shallow copy," which means that both arrays will refer to the same elements. If an error occurs during the copy, *destinationArray* is undefined.
public static void Copy(Array *sourceArray*, int *sourceIndex*, Array *destinationArray*, int *destinationIndex*, int *length*)	Copies *length* elements from *sourceArray*[*sourceIndex*] to *destinationArray*[*destinationIndex*]. When both arrays are reference types, then **Copy( )** makes a "shallow copy," which means that both arrays will refer to the same elements. If an error occurs during the copy, *destinationArray* is undefined.
public static void Copy(Array *sourceArray*, long *sourceIndex*, Array *destinationArray*, long *destinationIndex*, long *length*)	Copies *length* elements from *sourceArray*[*sourceIndex*] to *destinationArray*[*destinationIndex*]. When both arrays are reference types, then **Copy( )** makes a "shallow copy," which means that both arrays will refer to the same elements. If an error occurs during the copy, *destinationArray* is undefined.
public void CopyTo(Array *array*, int *index*)	Copies the elements of the invoking array to *array*, beginning at *array*[*index*]. If an error occurs during the copy, *array* is undefined.

TABLE 21-12   Methods Defined by **Array** *(continued)*

Method	Meaning
public void CopyTo(Array *array*, long *index*)	Copies the elements of the invoking array to *array*, beginning at *array*[*index*]. If an error occurs during the copy, *array* is undefined.
public static Array CreateInstance(Type *elementType*, int *length*)	Returns a reference to a one-dimensional array that contains *length* elements of type *elementType*.

public static Array
    CreateInstance(Type *elementType*,
            int *length1*,
            int *length2*)
	Returns a reference to a *length1*-by-*length2* two-dimensional array. Each element is of type *elementType*.

public static Array
    CreateInstance(Type elementType,
            int *length1*,
            int *length2*,
            int *length3*)
	Returns a reference to a *length1*-by-*length2*-by-*length3* three-dimensional array. Each element is of type *elementType*.

public static Array
    CreateInstance(Type *elementType*,
            params int[ ] *lengths*)
	Returns a reference to a multi-dimensional array that has the dimensions specified in *lengths*. Each element is of type *elementType*.

public static Array
    CreateInstance(Type *elementType*,
            params long[ ] *lengths*)
	Returns a reference to a multi-dimensional array that has the dimensions specified in *lengths*. Each element is of type *elementType*.

public static Array
    CreateInstance(Type *elementType*,
            int[ ] *lengths*,
            int[ ] *lowerBounds*)
	Returns a reference to a multi-dimensional array that has the dimensions specified in *lengths*. Each element is of type *elementType*. The starting index of each dimension is specified in *lowerBounds*. Thus, it is possible to create arrays that begin at some index other than zero.

public static bool Exists<T>(T[ ] *array*, Predicate<T> *match*)	Returns true if *array* contains at least one element that satisfies the predicate specified by *match*. Returns false if no elements satisfy *match*.
public static T Find<T>(T[ ] *array*, Predicate<T> *match*)	Returns the first element in *array* that satisfies the predicate specified by *match*. If no element satisfies *match*, then **default(T)** is returned.

public static T[ ]
    FindAll<T>(T[ ] *array*,
            Predicate<T> *match*)
	Returns an array that contains all elements in *array* that satisfy the predicate specified by *match*. If no element satisfies *match*, then a zero-length array is returned.

public static int
    FindIndex<T>(T[ ] *array*,
            Predicate<T> *match*)
	Returns the index of the first element in *array* that satisfies the predicate specified by *match*. If no element satisfies *match*, −1 is returned.

public static int
    FindIndex<T>(T[ ] *array*,
            int *startIndex*,
            Predicate<T> *match*)
	Returns the index of the first element in *array* that satisfies the predicate specified by *match*. The search begins at *array*[*startIndex*]. If no element satisfies *match*, −1 is returned.

TABLE 21-12   Methods Defined by **Array** (continued)

Method	Meaning

public static int
    FindIndex<T>(T[ ] *array*,
             int *startIndex*,
             int *count*,
             Predicate<T> *match*)
	Returns the index of the first element in *array* that satisfies the predicate specified by *match*. The search begins at *array*[*startIndex*] and runs for *count* elements. If no element satisfies *match*, –1 is returned.

public static T
    FindLast<T>(T[ ] *array*,
            Predicate<T> *match*)
	Returns the last element in *array* that satisfies the predicate specified by *match*. If no element satisfies *match*, then **default(T)** is returned.

public static int
    FindLastIndex<T>(T[ ] *array*,
               Predicate<T> *match*)
	Returns the index of the last element in *array* that satisfies the predicate specified by *match*. If no element satisfies *match*, –1 is returned.

public static int
    FindLastIndex<T>(T[ ] *array*,
               int *startIndex*,
               Predicate<T> *match*)
	Returns the index of the last element in *array* that satisfies the predicate specified by *match*. The search proceeds in reverse order, beginning at *array*[*startIndex*] and stopping at *array*[0]. If no element satisfies *match*, –1 is returned.

public static int
    FindLastIndex<T>(T[ ] *array*,
               Int *startIndex*,
               Int *count*,
               Predicate<T> *match*)
	Returns the index of the last element in *array* that satisfies the predicate specified by *match*. The search proceeds in reverse order, beginning at *array*[*startIndex*] and running for *count* elements. If no element satisfies *match*, –1 is returned.

public static void
    ForEach<T>(T[ ] *array*,
             Action<T> *action*)
	Applies the method specified by *action* to each element of *array*.

public IEnumerator GetEnumerator( )	Returns an enumerator object for the array. An enumerator enables you to cycle through an array. Enumerators are described in Chapter 25.
public int GetLength(int *dimension*)	Returns the length of the specified dimension. The dimension is zero-based. Thus, to get the length of the first dimension, pass 0; to obtain the length of the second dimension, pass 1; and so on.
public long GetLongLength(int *dimension*)	Returns the length of the specified dimension as a **long**. The dimension is zero-based. Thus, to get the length of the first dimension, pass 0; to obtain the length of the second dimension, pass 1; and so on.
public int GetLowerBound(int *dimension*)	Returns the first index of the specified dimension, which is usually zero. The parameter *dimension* is zero-based. Thus, to get the start index of the first dimension, pass 0; to obtain the start index of the second dimension, pass 1; and so on.
public int GetUpperBound(int *dimension*)	Returns the last index of the specified dimension. The parameter *dimension* is zero-based. Thus, to get the last index of the first dimension, pass 0; to obtain the last index of the second dimension, pass 1, and so on.

TABLE 21-12 Methods Defined by **Array** (*continued*)

Method	Meaning
public object GetValue(int *index*)	Returns the value of the element at index *index* within the invoking array. The array must be one-dimensional.
public object GetValue(long *index*)	Returns the value of the element at index *index* within the invoking array. The array must be one-dimensional.
public object GetValue(int *index1*, int *index2*)	Returns the value of the element at [*index1*, *index2*] within the invoking array. The array must be two-dimensional.
public object GetValue(long *index1*, long *index2*)	Returns the value of the element at [*index1*, *index2*] within the invoking array. The array must be two-dimensional.
public object GetValue(int *index1*, int *index2*, int *index3*)	Returns the value of the element at [*index1*, *index2*, *index3*] within the invoking array. The array must be three-dimensional.
public object GetValue(long *index1*, long *index2*, long *index3*)	Returns the value of the element at [*index1*, *index2*, *index3*] within the invoking array. The array must be three-dimensional.
public object GetValue(params int[ ] *indices*)	Returns the value of the element at the specified indices within the invoking array. The array must have as many dimensions as *indices* has elements.
public object GetValue(params long[ ] *indices*)	Returns the value of the element at the specified indices within the invoking array. The array must have as many dimensions as *indices* has elements.
public static int IndexOf(Array *array*, object *value*)	Returns the index of the first element within the one-dimensional array *array* that has the value specified by *value*. Returns –1 if the value is not found. (If the array has a lower bound other than 0, then the failure value is the lower bound –1.)
public static int IndexOf<T>(T[ ] *array*, T *value*)	Returns the index of the first element within the one-dimensional array *array* that has the value specified by *value*. Returns –1 if the value is not found.
public static int IndexOf(Array *array*, object *value*, int *startIndex*)	Returns the index of the first element within the one-dimensional array *array* that has the value specified by *value*. The search begins at *array*[*startIndex*]. Returns –1 if the value is not found. (If the array has a lower bound other than 0, then the failure value is the lower bound –1.)
public static int IndexOf<T>(T[ ] *array*, T *value*, int *startIndex*)	Returns the index of the first element within the one-dimensional array *array* that has the value specified by *value*. The search begins at *array*[*startIndex*]. Returns –1 if the value is not found.
public static int IndexOf(Array *array*, object *value*, int *startIndex*, int *count*)	Returns the index of the first element within the one-dimensional array *array* that has the value specified by *value*. The search begins at *array*[*startIndex*] and runs for *count* elements. Returns –1 if the value is not found within the specified range. (If the array has a lower bound other than 0, then the failure value is the lower bound –1.)

TABLE 21-12   Methods Defined by **Array** (continued)

Method	Meaning
public static int IndexOf<T>(T[ ] array, T value, int startIndex, int count)	Returns the index of the first element within the one-dimensional array array that has the value specified by value. The search begins at array[startIndex] and runs for count elements. Returns –1 if the value is not found within the specified range.
public void Initialize( )	Initializes each element in the invoking array by calling the element's default constructor. This method can be used only on arrays of value types that have constructors.
public static int LastIndexOf(Array array, object value)	Returns the index of the last element within the one-dimensional array array that has the value specified by value. Returns –1 if the value is not found. (If the array has a lower bound other than 0, then the failure value is the lower bound –1.)
public static int LastIndexOf<T>(T[ ] array, T value)	Returns the index of the last element within the one-dimensional array array that has the value specified by value. Returns –1 if the value is not found.
public static int LastIndexOf(Array array, object value, int startIndex)	Returns the index of the last element within a range of the one-dimensional array array that has the value specified by value. The search proceeds in reverse order, beginning at array[startIndex] and stopping at array[0]. Returns –1 if the value is not found. (If the array has a lower bound other than 0, then the failure value is the lower bound –1.)
public static int LastIndexOf<T>(T[ ] array, T value, int startIndex)	Returns the index of the last element within a range of the one-dimensional array array that has the value specified by value. The search proceeds in reverse order, beginning at array[startIndex] and stopping at array[0]. Returns –1 if the value is not found.
public static int LastIndexOf(Array array, object value, int startIndex, int count)	Returns the index of the last element within a range of the one-dimensional array array that has the value specified by value. The search proceeds in reverse order, beginning at array[startIndex] and running for count elements. Returns –1 if the value is not found within the specified range. (If the array has a lower bound other than 0, then the failure value is the lower bound –1.)
public static int LastIndexOf<T>(T[ ] array, T value, int startIndex, int count)	Returns the index of the last element within a range of the one-dimensional array array that has the value specified by value. The search proceeds in reverse order, beginning at array[startIndex] and running for count elements. Returns –1 if the value is not found within the specified range.
public static void Resize<T>(ref T[ ] array, int newSize)	Sets the size of array to newSize.
public static void Reverse(Array array)	Reverses the elements in array.

TABLE 21-12   Methods Defined by **Array** (continued)

Method	Meaning
public static void Reverse(Array *array*, int *index*, int *length*)	Reverses a range of elements in *array*. The range reversed begins at *array*[*index*] and runs for *length* elements.
public void SetValue(object *value*, int *index*)	Sets the value of the element at index *index* within the invoking array to *value*. The array must be one-dimensional.
public void SetValue(object *value*, long *index*)	Sets the value of the element at index *index* within the invoking array to *value*. The array must be one-dimensional.
public void SetValue(object *value*, int *index1*, int *index2*)	Sets the value of the element at indices [*index1*, *index2*] within the invoking array to *value*. The array must be two-dimensional.
public void SetValue(object *value*, long *index1*, long *index2*)	Sets the value of the element at indices [*index1*, *index2*] within the invoking array to *value*. The array must be two-dimensional.
public void SetValue(object *value*, int *index1*, int *index2*, int *index3*)	Sets the value of the element at indices [*index1*, *index2*, *index3*] within the invoking array to *value*. The array must be three-dimensional.
public void SetValue(object *value*, long *index1*, long *index2*, long *index3*)	Sets the value of the element at indices [*index1*, *index2*, *index3*] within the invoking array to *value*. The array must be three-dimensional.
public void SetValue(object *value*, params int[ ] *indices*)	Sets the value of the element at the specified indices within the invoking array to *value*. The array must have as many dimensions as *indices* has elements.
public void SetValue(object *value*, params long[ ] *indices*)	Sets the value of the element at the specified indices within the invoking array to *value*. The array must have as many dimensions as *indices* has elements.
public static void Sort(Array *array*)	Sorts *array* into ascending order. The array must be one-dimensional.
public static void Sort<T>(T[ ] *array*)	Sorts *array* into ascending order. The array must be one-dimensional.
public static void Sort(Array *array*, IComparer *comparer*)	Sorts *array* into ascending order using the comparison method specified by *comparer*. The array must be one-dimensional.
public static void Sort<T>(T[ ] *array*, Comparison<T> *comparison*)	Sorts *array* into ascending order using the comparison method specified by *comparison*. The array must be one-dimensional.
public static void Sort<T>(T[ ] *array*, IComparer<T> *comparer*)	Sorts *array* into ascending order using the comparison method specified by *comparer*. The array must be one-dimensional.
public static void Sort(Array *keys*, Array *items*)	Sorts a pair of one-dimensional arrays into ascending order. The *keys* array contains the sort keys. The *items* array contains the values linked to those keys. Thus, the two arrays contain key/value pairs. After the sort, both arrays are in ascending-key order.

TABLE 21-12 Methods Defined by **Array** (continued)

Method	Meaning

public static void
    Sort<TKey, TValue>(TKey[ ] *keys,*
                  TValue[ ] *items*)
	Sorts a pair of one-dimensional arrays into ascending order. The *keys* array contains the sort keys. The *items* array contains the values linked to those keys. Thus, the two arrays contain key/value pairs. After the sort, both arrays are in ascending-key order.

public static void Sort(Array *keys,*
                  Array *items,*
                  IComparer *comparer*)
	Sorts a pair of one-dimensional arrays into ascending order using the comparison method specified by *comparer.* The *keys* array contains the sort keys. The *items* array contains the values linked to those keys. Thus, the two arrays contain key/value pairs. After the sort, both arrays are in ascending-key order.

public static void
    Sort<TKey, TValue>(TKey[ ] *keys,*
                  TValue[ ] *items,*
                  IComparer<TKey> *comparer*)
	Sorts a pair of one-dimensional arrays into ascending order using the comparison method specified by *comparer.* The *keys* array contains the sort keys. The *items* array contains the values linked to those keys. Thus, the two arrays contain key/value pairs. After the sort, both arrays are in ascending-key order.

public static void Sort(Array *array,*
                  int *index,*
                  int *length*)
	Sorts a range of *array* into ascending order. The range begins at *array*[*index*] and runs for *length* elements. The array must be one-dimensional.

public static void Sort<T>(T[ ] *array,*
                  int *index,*
                  int *length*)
	Sorts a range of *array* into ascending order. The range begins at *array*[*index*] and runs for *length* elements. The array must be one-dimensional.

public static void Sort(Array *array,*
                  int *index,*
                  int *length,*
                  IComparer *comparer*)
	Sorts a range of *array* into ascending order using the comparison method specified by *comparer.* The range begins at *array*[*index*] and runs for *length* elements. The array must be one-dimensional.

public static void
    Sort<T>(T[ ] *array,*
                  int *index,*
                  int *length,*
                  IComparer<T> *comparer*)
	Sorts a range of *array* into ascending order using the comparison method specified by *comparer.* The range begins at *array*[*index*] and runs for *length* elements. The array must be one-dimensional.

public static void Sort(Array *keys,*
                  Array *items,*
                  int *index,*
                  int *length*)
	Sorts a range within a pair of one-dimensional arrays into ascending order. Within both arrays, the range to sort begins at the index passed in *index* and runs for *length* elements. The *keys* array contains the sort keys. The *items* array contains the values linked to those keys. Thus, the two arrays contain key/value pairs. After the sort, both ranges are in ascending-key order.

public static void
    Sort<TKey, TValue>(TKey[ ] *keys,*
                  TValue[ ] *items,*
                  int *index,*
                  int *length*)
	Sorts a range within a pair of one-dimensional arrays into ascending order. Within both arrays, the range to sort begins at the index passed in *index* and runs for *length* elements. The *keys* array contains the sort keys. The *items* array contains the values linked to those keys. Thus, the two arrays contain key/value pairs. After the sort, both ranges are in ascending-key order.

TABLE 21-12   Methods Defined by **Array** *(continued)*

Method	Meaning
public static void Sort(Array *keys*, Array *items*, int *index*, int *length*, IComparer *comparer*)	Sorts a range within a pair of one-dimensional arrays into ascending order using the comparison method specified by *comparer*. Within both arrays, the range to sort begins at the index passed in *index* and runs for *length* elements. The *keys* array contains the sort keys. The *items* array contains the values linked to those keys. Thus, the two arrays contain key/value pairs. After the sort, both ranges are in ascending-key order.
public static void Sort<TKey, TValue>(TKey[ ] *keys*, TValue *items*, int *index*, int *length*, IComparer<TKey> *comparer*)	Sorts a range within a pair of one-dimensional arrays into ascending order using the comparison method specified by *comparer*. Within both arrays, the range to sort begins at the index passed in *index* and runs for *length* elements. The *keys* array contains the sort keys. The *items* array contains the values linked to those keys. Thus, the two arrays contain key/value pairs. After the sort, both ranges are in ascending-key order.
public static bool TrueForAll<T>(T[ ] *array*, Predicate<T> *match*)	Returns true if the predicate specified by *match* is satisfied by all elements in *array*. If one or more elements fail to satisfy *match*, then false is returned.

TABLE 21-12   Methods Defined by **Array** *(continued)*

Sorting and Searching Arrays

Often you will want to sort the contents of an array. To handle this, **Array** supports a rich complement of sorting methods. Using **Sort( )**, you can sort an entire array, a range within an array, or a pair of arrays that contain corresponding key/value pairs. Once an array has been sorted, you can efficiently search it using **BinarySearch( )**. Here is a program that demonstrates the **Sort( )** and **BinarySearch( )** methods by sorting an array of **int**s:

```
// Sort an array and search for a value.

using System;

class SortDemo {
  static void Main() {
    int[] nums = { 5, 4, 6, 3, 14, 9, 8, 17, 1, 24, -1, 0 };

    // Display original order.
    Console.Write("Original order: ");
    foreach(int i in nums)
      Console.Write(i + " ");
    Console.WriteLine();

    // Sort the array.
    Array.Sort(nums);

    // Display sorted order.
    Console.Write("Sorted order:   ");
    foreach(int i in nums)
```

```
      Console.Write(i + " ");
    Console.WriteLine();


    // Search for 14.
    int idx = Array.BinarySearch(nums, 14);

    Console.WriteLine("Index of 14 is " + idx);
  }
}
```

The output is shown here:

```
Original order: 5 4 6 3 14 9 8 17 1 24 -1 0
Sorted order:   -1 0 1 3 4 5 6 8 9 14 17 24
Index of 14 is 9
```

In the preceding example, the array has an element type of **int**, which is a value type. All methods defined by **Array** are automatically available to all of the built-in value types. However, this may not be the case for arrays of object references. To sort or search an array of object references, the class type of those objects must implement either the **IComparable** or **IComparable<T>** interface. If the class does not implement one of these interfaces, a runtime exception will occur when attempting to sort or search the array. Fortunately, both **IComparable** and **IComparable<T>** are easy to implement.

IComparable defines just one method:

int CompareTo(object *obj*)

This method compares the invoking object against the value in *obj*. It returns greater than zero if the invoking object is greater than *obj*, zero if the two objects are equal, and less than zero if the invoking object is less than *obj*.

IComparable<T> is the generic version of **IComparable**. It defines the generic version of **CompareTo( )**:

int CompareTo(T *other*)

The generic version of **CompareTo( )** works like the non-generic version. It compares the invoking object against the value in *other*. It returns greater than zero if the invoking object is greater than *other*, zero if the two objects are equal, and less than zero if the invoking object is less than *other*. The advantage of using **IComparable<T>** is type-safety because the type of data being operated upon is explicitly specified. There is no need to cast the object being compared from **object** into the desired type. Here is an example that illustrates sorting and searching an array of user-defined class objects:

```
// Sort and search an array of objects.

using System;

class MyClass : IComparable<MyClass> {
  public int i;

  public MyClass(int x) { i = x; }
```

```
    // Implement IComparable<MyClass>.
    public int CompareTo(MyClass v) {
      return i - v.i;
    }

}

class SortDemo {
  static void Main() {
    MyClass[] nums = new MyClass[5];

    nums[0] = new MyClass(5);
    nums[1] = new MyClass(2);
    nums[2] = new MyClass(3);
    nums[3] = new MyClass(4);
    nums[4] = new MyClass(1);

    // Display original order.
    Console.Write("Original order: ");
    foreach(MyClass o in nums)
      Console.Write(o.i + " ");
    Console.WriteLine();

    // Sort the array.
    Array.Sort(nums);

    // Display sorted order.
    Console.Write("Sorted order:    ");
    foreach(MyClass o in nums)
      Console.Write(o.i + " ");
    Console.WriteLine();

    // Search for MyClass(2).
    MyClass x = new MyClass(2);
    int idx = Array.BinarySearch(nums, x);

    Console.WriteLine("Index of MyClass(2) is " + idx);
  }
}
```

The output is shown here:

```
Original order: 5 2 3 4 1
Sorted order:    1 2 3 4 5
Index of MyClass(2) is 1
```

When sorting or searching an array of strings, you may need to explicitly specify how those strings are compared. For example, if the array will be sorted using one cultural setting and searched under another, then explicitly specifying the comparison method may be necessary to avoid errors. Or, you might want to sort an array of strings using a cultural setting that is different than the current setting. To handle these (and other) types of situations, you can pass an instance of **StringComparer** to the **IComparer** parameter supported by several overloads of **Sort( )** and **BinarySearch( )**.

NOTE *See Chapter 22 for a discussion of issues related to string comparisons.*

StringComparer is declared in **System**, and among other interfaces, it implements the **IComparer** and **IComparer<T>** interfaces. Thus, an instance of **StringComparer** can be passed to an **IComparer** parameter as an argument. **StringComparer** defines several read-only properties that return an instance of **StringComparer** and that support various types of string comparisons. They are shown here:

Property	Comparison
public static StringComparer CurrentCulture {get; }	Case-sensitive, culture-sensitive
public static StringComparer CurrentCultureIgnoreCase {get; }	Case-insensitive, culture-sensitive
public static StringComparer InvariantCulture {get; }	Case-sensitive, uses the invariant culture
public static StringComparer InvariantCultureIgnoreCase {get; }	Case-insensitive, uses the invariant culture
public static StringComparer Ordinal {get; }	Case-sensitive, ordinal comparison
public static StringComparer OrdinalIgnoreCase {get; }	Case-insensitive, ordinal comparison

By explicitly passing a **StringComparer**, you unambiguously determine how sorting or searching will be accomplished. For example, the following sorts and searches an array of strings by using **StringComparer.Ordinal**:

```
string[] strs = { "xyz", "one" , "beta", "Alpha" };
// ...
Array.Sort(strs, StringComparer.Ordinal);
int idx = Array.BinarySearch(strs, "beta", StringComparer.Ordinal);
```

Reversing an Array

Sometimes it is useful to reverse the contents of an array. For example, you might want to change an array that has been sorted into ascending order into one sorted in descending order. Reversing an array is easy: Simply call **Reverse( )**. Using **Reverse( )**, you can reverse all or part of an array. The following program demonstrates the process:

```
// Reverse an array.

using System;

class ReverseDemo {
  static void Main() {
    int[] nums = { 1, 2, 3, 4, 5 };

    // Display original order.
    Console.Write("Original order: ");
```

```
    foreach(int i in nums)
      Console.Write(i + " ");
    Console.WriteLine();

    // Reverse the entire array.
    Array.Reverse(nums);

    // Display reversed order.
    Console.Write("Reversed order: ");
    foreach(int i in nums)
      Console.Write(i + " ");
    Console.WriteLine();

    // Reverse a range.
    Array.Reverse(nums, 1, 3);

    // Display reversed order.
    Console.Write("Range reversed: ");
    foreach(int i in nums)
      Console.Write(i + " ");
    Console.WriteLine();
  }
}
```

The output is shown here:

```
Original order: 1 2 3 4 5
Reversed order: 5 4 3 2 1
Range reversed: 5 2 3 4 1
```

Copying an Array

Copying all or part of one array to another is another common array operation. To copy an array, use **Copy( )**. **Copy( )** can put elements at the start of the destination array or in the middle, depending upon which version of **Copy( )** you use. **Copy( )** is demonstrated by the following program:

```
// Copy an array.

using System;

class CopyDemo {
  static void Main() {
    int[] source = { 1, 2, 3, 4, 5 };
    int[] target = { 11, 12, 13, 14, 15 };
    int[] source2 = { -1, -2, -3, -4, -5 };

    // Display source.
    Console.Write("source: ");
    foreach(int i in source)
      Console.Write(i + " ");
    Console.WriteLine();

    // Display original target.
    Console.Write("Original contents of target: ");
```

```
      foreach(int i in target)
        Console.Write(i + " ");
      Console.WriteLine();

      // Copy the entire array.
      Array.Copy(source, target, source.Length);

      // Display copy.
      Console.Write("target after copy:  ");
      foreach(int i in target)
        Console.Write(i + " ");
      Console.WriteLine();

      // Copy into middle of target.
      Array.Copy(source2, 2, target, 3, 2);

      // Display copy.
      Console.Write("target after copy:  ");
      foreach(int i in target)
        Console.Write(i + " ");
      Console.WriteLine();
  }
}
```

The output is shown here:

```
source: 1 2 3 4 5
Original contents of target: 11 12 13 14 15
target after copy:  1 2 3 4 5
target after copy:  1 2 3 -3 -4
```

Using a Predicate

A *predicate* is a delegate of type **System.Predicate** that returns either true or false, based upon some condition. It is declared as shown here:

public delegate bool Predicate<in T> (T *obj*)

The object to be tested against the condition is passed in *obj*. If *obj* satisfies that condition, the predicate must return true. Otherwise, it must return false. Predicates are used by several methods in **Array**, including **Exists( )**, **Find( )**, **FindIndex( )**, and **FindAll( )**.

The following program demonstrates using a predicate to determine if an array of integers contains a negative value. If a negative value is found, the program then obtains the first negative value in the array. To accomplish this, the program uses **Exists( )** and **Find( )**.

```
// Demonstrate Predicate delegate.

using System;

class PredDemo {

  // A predicate method.
  // It returns true if v is negative.
```

```
static bool IsNeg(int v) {
  if(v < 0) return true;
  return false;
}

static void Main() {
  int[] nums = { 1, 4, -1, 5, -9 };

  Console.Write("Contents of nums: ");
  foreach(int i in nums)
    Console.Write(i + " ");
  Console.WriteLine();

  // First see if nums contains a negative value.
  if(Array.Exists(nums, PredDemo.IsNeg)) {
    Console.WriteLine("nums contains a negative value.");

    // Now, find first negative value.
    int x = Array.Find(nums, PredDemo.IsNeg);
    Console.WriteLine("First negative value is : " + x);
  }
  else
    Console.WriteLine("nums contains no negative values.");
}
}
```

The output is shown here:

```
Contents of nums: 1 4 -1 5 -9
nums contains a negative value.
First negative value is : -1
```

In the program, the method passed to **Exists( )** and **Find( )** for the predicate is **IsNeg( )**. Notice that **IsNeg( )** is declared like this:

```
static bool IsNeg(int v) {
```

The methods **Exists( )** and **Find( )** will automatically pass the elements of the array (in sequence) to **v**. Thus, each time **IsNeg( )** is called, **v** will contain the next element in the array.

Using an Action

The **Action** delegate is used by **Array.ForEach( )** to perform an action on each element of an array. There are various forms of **Action**, each taking a different number of type parameters. The one used here is

public delegate void Action<in T> (T *obj*)

The object to be acted upon is passed in *obj*. When used with **ForEach( )**, each element of the array is passed to *obj* in turn. Thus, through the use of **ForEach( )** and **Action**, you can, in a single statement, perform an operation over an entire array.

The following program demonstrates both **ForEach( )** and **Action**. It first creates an array of **MyClass** objects, and then uses the method **Show( )** to display the values. Next, it uses **Neg( )** to negate the values. Finally, it uses **Show( )** again to display the negated values. These operations all occur through calls to **ForEach( )**.

```
// Demonstrate an Action.

using System;

class MyClass {
  public int i;

  public MyClass(int x) { i = x; }
}

class ActionDemo {

  // An Action method.
  // It displays the value it is passed.
  static void Show(MyClass o) {
    Console.Write(o.i + " ");
  }

  // Another Action method.
  // It negates the value it is passed.
  static void Neg(MyClass o) {
    o.i = -o.i;
  }

  static void Main() {
    MyClass[] nums = new MyClass[5];

    nums[0] = new MyClass(5);
    nums[1] = new MyClass(2);
    nums[2] = new MyClass(3);
    nums[3] = new MyClass(4);
    nums[4] = new MyClass(1);

    Console.Write("Contents of nums: ");

    // Use action to show the values.
    Array.ForEach(nums, ActionDemo.Show);

    Console.WriteLine();

    // Use action to negate the values.
    Array.ForEach(nums, ActionDemo.Neg);

    Console.Write("Contents of nums negated: ");

    // Use action to negate the values again.
    Array.ForEach(nums, ActionDemo.Show);

    Console.WriteLine();
  }
}
Contents of nums: 5 2 3 4 1
Contents of nums negated: -5 -2 -3 -4 -1
```

BitConverter

In programming, one often needs to convert a built-in data type into an array of bytes. For example, some hardware device might require an integer value, but that value must be sent one byte at a time. The reverse situation also frequently occurs. Sometimes data will be received as an ordered sequence of bytes that needs to be converted into one of the built-in types. For example, a device might output integers, sent as a stream of bytes. Whatever your conversion needs, .NET provides the **BitConverter** class to meet them.

BitConverter is a **static** class. It contains the methods shown in Table 21-13. It defines the following field:

    public static readonly bool IsLittleEndian

This field is **true** if the current environment stores a word with the least significant byte first and the most significant byte last. This is called "little-endian" format. **IsLittleEndian** is **false** if the current environment stores a word with the most significant byte first and the least significant byte last. This is called "big-endian" format. Intel Pentium–based machines use little-endian format.

Method	Meaning
public static long DoubleToInt64Bits(double *value*)	Converts *value* into a **long** integer and returns the result.
public static byte[ ] GetBytes(bool *value*)	Converts *value* into a 1-byte array and returns the result.
public static byte[ ] GetBytes(char *value*)	Converts *value* into a 2-byte array and returns the result.
public static byte[ ] GetBytes(double *value*)	Converts *value* into an 8-byte array and returns the result.
public static byte[ ] GetBytes(float *value*)	Converts *value* into a 4-byte array and returns the result.
public static byte[ ] GetBytes(int *value*)	Converts *value* into a 4-byte array and returns the result.
public static byte[ ] GetBytes(long *value*)	Converts *value* into an 8-byte array and returns the result.
public static byte[ ] GetBytes(short *value*)	Converts *value* into a 2-byte array and returns the result.
public static byte[ ] GetBytes(uint *value*)	Converts *value* into a 4-byte array and returns the result.
public static byte[ ] GetBytes(ulong *value*)	Converts *value* into an 8-byte array and returns the result.
public static byte[ ] GetBytes(ushort *value*)	Converts *value* into a 2-byte array and returns the result.
public static double Int64BitsToDouble(long *value*)	Converts *value* into a **double** value and returns the result.
public static bool ToBoolean(byte[ ] *value*, int *startIndex*)	Converts the byte at *value*[*startIndex*] into its **bool** equivalent and returns the result. A non-zero value is converted to true; zero is converted to false.
public static char ToChar(byte[ ] *value*, int *startIndex*)	Converts two bytes starting at *value*[*startIndex*] into its **char** equivalent and returns the result.
public static double ToDouble(byte[ ] *value*, int *startIndex*)	Converts eight bytes starting at *value*[*startIndex*] into its **double** equivalent and returns the result.

TABLE 21-13 Methods Defined by **BitConverter**

Method	Meaning
public static short ToInt16(byte[ ] *value*, int *startIndex*)	Converts two bytes starting at *value*[*startIndex*] into its **short** equivalent and returns the result.
public static int ToInt32(byte[ ] *value*, int *startIndex*)	Converts four bytes starting at *value*[*startIndex*] into its **int** equivalent and returns the result.
public static long ToInt64(byte[ ] *value*, int *startIndex*)	Converts eight bytes starting at *value*[*startIndex*] into its **long** equivalent and returns the result.
public static float ToSingle(byte[ ] *value*, int *startIndex*)	Converts four bytes starting at *value*[*startIndex*] into its **float** equivalent and returns the result.
public static string ToString(byte[ ] *value*)	Converts the bytes in *value* into a string. The string contains the hexadecimal values associated with the bytes, separated by hyphens.
public static string ToString(byte[ ] *value*, int *startIndex*)	Converts the bytes in *value*, beginning at *value*[*startIndex*], into a string. The string contains the hexadecimal values associated with the bytes, separated by hyphens.

public static string
    ToString(byte[ ] *value*, int *startIndex*,
        int *length*)
	Converts the bytes in *value*, beginning at *value*[*startIndex*] and running for *length* bytes, into a string. The string contains the hexadecimal values associated with the bytes, separated by hyphens.

public static ushort ToUInt16(byte[ ] *value*, int *startIndex*)	Converts two bytes starting at *value*[*startIndex*] into its **ushort** equivalent and returns the result.
public static uint ToUInt32(byte[ ] *value*, int *startIndex*)	Converts four bytes starting at *value*[*startIndex*] into its **uint** equivalent and returns the result.
public static ulong ToUInt64(byte[ ] *value*, int *startIndex*)	Converts eight bytes starting at *value*[*startIndex*] into its **ulong** equivalent and returns the result.

TABLE 21-13   Methods Defined by **BitConverter** *(continued)*

Generating Random Numbers with Random

To generate a sequence of pseudorandom numbers, you will use the **Random** class. Sequences of random numbers are useful in a variety of situations, including simulations and modeling. The starting point of the sequence is determined by a *seed* value, which can be automatically provided by **Random** or explicitly specified.

Random defines these two constructors:

    public Random( )
    public Random(int *Seed*)

The first version creates a **Random** object that uses the system time to compute the seed value. The second uses the value of *Seed* as the seed value.

Random defines the methods shown in Table 21-14.

Method	Meaning
public virtual int Next( )	Returns the next random integer, which will be between 0 and **Int32.MaxValue**-1, inclusive.
public virtual int Next(int *maxValue*)	Returns the next random integer that is between 0 and *maxValue*-1, inclusive.
public virtual int Next(int *minValue*, int *maxValue*)	Returns the next random integer that is between *minValue* and *maxValue*-1, inclusive.
public virtual void NextBytes(byte[ ] *buffer*)	Fills *buffer* with a sequence of random integers. Each byte in the array will be between 0 and **Byte.MaxValue**-1, inclusive.
public virtual double NextDouble( )	Returns the next random value from the sequence represented as a floating-point number that is greater than or equal to 0.0 and less than 1.0.
protected virtual double Sample( )	Returns the next random value from the sequence represented as a floating-point number that is greater than or equal to 0.0 and less than 1.0. To create a skewed or specialized distribution, override this method in a derived class.

TABLE 21-14   Methods Defined by **Random**

Here is a program that demonstrates **Random** by creating a pair of computerized dice:

```
// An automated pair of dice.

using System;

class RandDice {
  static void Main() {
    Random ran = new Random();

    Console.Write(ran.Next(1, 7) + " ");
    Console.WriteLine(ran.Next(1, 7));
  }
}
```

Here are three sample runs:

```
5 2
4 4
1 6
```

The program works by first creating a **Random** object. Then it requests the two random values, each between 1 and 6.

Memory Management and the GC Class

The **GC** class encapsulates the garbage-collection facility. The methods defined by **GC** are shown in Table 21-15. It defines the read-only property shown here:

public static int MaxGeneration { get; }

MaxGeneration contains the maximum generation number available to the system. A generation number indicates the age of an allocation. Newer allocations have a lower number than older ones. Generation numbers help improve the efficiency of the garbage collector.

Method	Meaning
public static void AddMemoryPressure(long *bytesAllocated*)	Indicates that *bytesAllocated* number of bytes of unmanaged memory have been allocated.
public static void CancelFullGCNotification( )	Cancels garbage collection notification.
public static void Collect( )	Initiates garbage collection.
public static void Collect(int *generation*)	Initiates garbage collection for memory with generation numbers of 0 through *generation*.
public static void Collect(int *generation*, GCCollectionMode *mode*)	Initiates garbage collection for memory with generation numbers of 0 through *generation* as specified by *mode*.
public static int CollectionCount(int *generation*)	Returns the number of garbage collections that have taken place for memory having the generation number specified by *generation*.
public static int GetGeneration(object *obj*)	Returns the generation number for the memory referred to by *obj*.
public static int GetGeneration(WeakReference *wo*)	Returns the generation number for the memory referred to by the weak reference specified by *wo*. A weak reference does not prevent the object from being garbage-collected.
public static long GetTotalMemory(bool *forceFullCollection*)	Returns the total number of bytes currently allocated. If *forceFullCollection* is true, garbage collection occurs first.
public static void KeepAlive(object *obj*)	Creates a reference to *obj*, thus preventing it from being garbage-collected. This reference ends when **KeepAlive( )** executes.
public static void RegisterForFullGCNotification(int *maxGenerationThreshold*, int *largeObjectHeapThreshold*)	Enables garbage-collection notifications. The value of *maxGenerationThreshold* specifies the number of generation 2 objects in the normal heap that will trigger notification. The value of *largeObjectHeapThreshold* specifies the number of objects in the large object heap that will trigger notification. Both values must be between 1 and 99.
public static void RemoveMemoryPressure(long *bytesAllocated*)	Indicates that *bytesAllocated* number of bytes of unmanaged memory have been released.
public static void ReRegisterForFinalize(object *obj*)	Causes the finalizer (i.e., the destructor) for *obj* to be called. This method undoes the effects of **SuppressFinalize( )**.
public static void SuppressFinalize(object *obj*)	Prevents the finalizer (i.e., the destructor) for *obj* from being called.

TABLE 21-15   Methods Defined by **GC**

Method	Meaning
public static GCNotificationStatus WaitForFullGCApproach( )	Waits for the notification that a full garbage-collection cycle is about to occur. **GCNotificationStatus** is an enumeration defined in **System**.
public static GCNotificationStatus WaitForFullGCApproach(int *millisecondsTimeout*)	Waits up to *millisecondsTimeout* milliseconds for the notification that a full garbage-collection cycle is about to occur. **GCNotificationStatus** is an enumeration defined in **System**.
public static GCNotificationStatus WaitForFullGCComplete( )	Waits for the notification that a full garbage-collection cycle has completed. **GCNotificationStatus** is an enumeration defined in **System**.
public static GCNotificationStatus WaitForFullGCComplete(int *millisecondsTimeout*)	Waits up to *millisecondsTimeout* milliseconds for the notification that a full garbage-collection cycle has completed. **GCNotificationStatus** is an enumeration defined in **System**.
public static void WaitForPendingFinalizers( )	Halts execution of the invoking thread until all pending finalizers (i.e., destructors) have been called.

TABLE 21-15   Methods Defined by **GC** *(continued)*

For most applications, you will not use any of the capabilities of **GC**. However, in specialized cases, they can be very useful. For example, you might want to use **Collect( )** to force garbage collection to occur at a time of your choosing. Normally, garbage collection occurs at times unspecified by your program. Since garbage collection takes time, you might not want it to occur during some time-critical task, or you might want to take advantage of idle time to perform garbage collection and other types of "housekeeping" chores. You can also register for notifications about the approach and completion of garbage collection.

There are two methods that are especially important if you have unmanaged code in your project. **AddMemoryPressure( )** and **RemoveMemoryPressure( )**. These are used to indicate that a large amount of unmanaged memory has been allocated or released by the program. They are important because the memory management system has no oversight on unmanaged memory. If a program allocates a large amount of unmanaged memory, then performance might be affected because the system has no way of knowing that free memory has been reduced. By calling **AddMemoryPressure( )** when allocating large amounts of unmanaged memory, you let the CLR know that memory has been reduced. By calling **RemoveMemoryPressure( )**, you let the CLR know the memory has been freed. Remember: **RemoveMemoryPressure( )** must be called only to indicate that memory reported by a call to **AddMemoryPressure( )** has been released.

Object

Object is the class that underlies the C# **object** type. The members of **Object** were discussed in Chapter 11, but because of its central role in C#, its methods are repeated in Table 21-16 for your convenience. **Object** defines one constructor, which is shown here:

    public Object( )

It constructs an empty object.

Method	Purpose
public virtual bool Equals(object *obj*)	Returns true if the invoking object is the same as the one referred to by *obj*. Returns false otherwise.
public static bool Equals(object *objA*, object *objB*)	Returns true if *objA* is the same as *objB*. Returns false otherwise.
protected Finalize( )	Performs shutdown actions prior to garbage collection. In C#, **Finalize( )** is accessed through a destructor.
public virtual int GetHashCode( )	Returns the hash code associated with the invoking object.
public Type GetType( )	Obtains the type of an object at runtime.
protected object MemberwiseClone( )	Makes a "shallow copy" of the object. This is one in which the members are copied, but objects referred to by members are not.
public static bool ReferenceEquals(object *objA*, object *objB*)	Returns true if *objA* and *objB* refer to the same object. Returns false otherwise.
public virtual string ToString( )	Returns a string that describes the object.

TABLE 21-16   Methods Defined by **Object**

Tuple

.NET Framework 4.0 adds a convenient way to create groups (tuples) of objects. At the core is the static class **Tuple**, which defines several **Create( )** methods that create tuples, and various **Tuple<...>** classes that encapsulate tuples. For example, here is a version of **Create( )** that returns a tuple with three members:

```
public static Tuple<T1, T2, T3>
    Create<T1, T2, T3>(T1 item1, T2 item2, T3 item3)
```

Notice that the method returns a **Tuple<T1, T2, T3>** object. This object encapsulates *item1*, *item2*, and *item3*. In general, tuples are useful whenever you want to treat a group of values as a unit. For example, you might pass a tuple to a method, return a tuple from a method, or store tuples in a collection or array.

The IComparable and IComparable<T> Interfaces

Many classes will need to implement either the **IComparable** or **IComparable<T>** interface because they enable one object to be compared to another (for the purpose of ordering) by various methods defined by the .NET Framework. Chapter 18 introduced the **IComparable** and **IComparable<T>** interfaces, where they were used to enable two objects of a generic type parameter to be compared. They were also mentioned in the discussion of **Array**, earlier in this chapter. However, because of their importance and applicability to many situations, they are formally examined here.

IComparable is especially easy to implement because it consists of just this one method:

```
int CompareTo(object obj)
```

This method compares the invoking object against the value in *obj*. It returns greater than zero if the invoking object is greater than *obj*, zero if the two objects are equal, and less than zero if the invoking object is less than *obj*.

The generic version of **IComparable** is declared like this:

public interface IComparable<in T>

In this version, the type of data being compared is passed as a type argument to **T**. This causes the declaration of **CompareTo( )** to be changed, as shown next:

int CompareTo(T *other*)

Here, the type of data that **CompareTo( )** operates on can be explicitly specified. This makes **IComparable<T>** type-safe. For this reason, **IComparable<T>** is now preferable to **IComparable**.

The IEquatable<T> Interface

IEquatable<T>is implemented by those classes that need to define how two objects should be compared for equality. It defines only one method, **Equals( )**, which is shown here:

bool Equals(T *other*)

The method returns true if *other* is equal to the invoking object and false otherwise.

IEquatable<T> is implemented by several classes and structures in the .NET Framework, including the numeric structures and the **String** class. When implementing **IEquatable<T>,** you will usually also need to override **Equals(Object)** and **GetHashCode( )** defined by **Object**.

The IConvertible Interface

The **IConvertible** interface is implemented by all of the value-type structures, **string**, and **DateTime**. It specifies various type conversions. Normally, classes that you create will not need to implement this interface.

The ICloneable Interface

By implementing the **ICloneable** interface, you enable a copy of an object to be made. **ICloneable** defines only one method, **Clone( )**, which is shown here:

object Clone( )

This method makes a copy of the invoking object. How you implement **Clone( )** determines how the copy is made. In general, there are two types of copies: deep and shallow. When a deep copy is made, the copy and original are completely independent. Thus, if the original object contained a reference to another object *O*, then a copy of *O* will also be made. In a shallow copy, members are copied, but objects referred to by members are not. If an object refers to some other object *O*, then after a shallow copy, both the copy and the original will refer to the same *O*, and any changes to *O* affect both the copy and the original. Usually, you will implement **Clone( )** so that it performs a deep copy. Shallow copies can be made by using **MemberwiseClone( )**, which is defined by **Object**.

Here is an example that illustrates **ICloneable**. It creates a class called **Test** that contains a reference to an object of a class called **X**. **Test** uses **Clone( )** to create a deep copy.

```
// Demonstrate ICloneable.

using System;

class X {
  public int a;

  public X(int x) { a = x; }
}

class Test : ICloneable {
  public X o;
  public int b;

  public Test(int x, int y) {
    o = new X(x);
    b = y;
  }

  public void Show(string name) {
    Console.Write(name + " values are ");
    Console.WriteLine("o.a: {0}, b: {1}", o.a, b);
  }

  // Make a deep copy of the invoking object.
  public object Clone() {
    Test temp = new Test(o.a, b);
    return temp;
  }

}

class CloneDemo {
  static void Main() {
    Test ob1 = new Test(10, 20);

    ob1.Show("ob1");

    Console.WriteLine("Make ob2 a clone of ob1.");
    Test ob2 = (Test) ob1.Clone();

    ob2.Show("ob2");

    Console.WriteLine("Changing ob1.o.a to 99 and ob1.b to 88.");
    ob1.o.a = 99;
    ob1.b = 88;

    ob1.Show("ob1");
    ob2.Show("ob2");
  }
}
```

The output is shown here:

```
ob1 values are o.a: 10, b: 20
Make ob2 a clone of ob1.
```

```
ob2 values are o.a: 10, b: 20
Changing ob1.o.a to 99 and ob1.b to 88.
ob1 values are o.a: 99, b: 88
ob2 values are o.a: 10, b: 20
```

As the output shows, **ob2** is a clone of **ob1**, but **ob1** and **ob2** are completely separate objects. Changing one does not affect the other. This is accomplished by constructing a new **Test** object, which allocates a new **X** object for the copy. The new **X** instance is given the same value as the **X** object in the original.

To implement a shallow copy, simply have **Clone( )** call **MemberwiseClone( )** defined by **Object**. For example, try changing **Clone( )** in the preceding program as shown here:

```
// Make a shallow copy of the invoking object.
public object Clone() {
  Test temp = (Test) MemberwiseClone();
  return temp;
}
```

After making this change, the output of the program will look like this:

```
ob1 values are o.a: 10, b: 20
Make ob2 a clone of ob1.
ob2 values are o.a: 10, b: 20
Changing ob1.o.a to 99 and ob1.b to 88.
ob1 values are o.a: 99, b: 88
ob2 values are o.a: 99, b: 20
```

Notice that **o** in **ob1** and **o** in **ob2** both refer to the same **X** object. Changing one affects both. Of course, the **int** field **b** in each is still separate because the value types are not accessed via references.

IFormatProvider and IFormattable

The **IFormatProvider** interface defines one method called **GetFormat( )**, which returns an object that controls the formatting of data into a human-readable string. The general form of **GetFormat( )** is shown here:

object GetFormat(Type *formatType*)

Here, *formatType* specifies the format object to obtain.

The **IFormattable** interface supports the formatting of human-readable output. **IFormattable** defines this method:

string ToString(string *format*, IFormatProvider *formatProvider*)

Here, *format* specifies formatting instructions and *formatProvider* specifies the format provider.

NOTE *Formatting is described in detail in Chapter 22.*

IObservable<T> and IObserver<T>

.NET Framework 4.0 adds two interfaces that support the observer pattern. These are
IObservable<T> and **IObserver<T>**. In the observer pattern, one class (the observable)
provides notifications to another (the observer). This is accomplished by registering an
object of the observing class with an object of the observable class. An observer is registered
by calling **Subscribe( )**, which is specified by **IObservable<T>**, passing in the **IObserver<T>**
object that will receive notification. More than one observer can be registered to receive
notifications. To send notifications to all registered observers, three methods defined by
IObserver<T> are used. **OnNext( )** sends data to the observer, **OnError( )** indicates an error,
and **OnCompleted( )** indicates the observable object has stopped sending notifications.

Strings and Formatting

Thin chapter examines the **String** class, which underlies C#'s **string** type. As all
programmers know, string handling is a part of almost any program. For this reason,
the **String** class defines an extensive set of methods, properties, and fields that give
you detailed control of the construction and manipulation of strings. Closely related to
string handling is the formatting of data into its human-readable form. Using the formatting
subsystem, you can format the C# numeric types, date and time, and enumerations.

Strings in C#

An overview of C#'s string handling was presented in Chapter 7, and that discussion is
not repeated here. However, it is worthwhile to review how strings are implemented in
C# before examining the **String** class.

In all computer languages, a *string* is a sequence of characters, but precisely how such
a sequence is implemented varies from language to language. In some computer languages,
such as C++, strings are arrays of characters, but this is not the case with C#. Instead, C#
strings are objects of the built-in **string** data type. Thus, **string** is a reference type. Moreover,
string is C#'s name for **System.String**, the standard .NET string type. Thus, a C# string has
access to all of the methods, properties, fields, and operators defined by **String**.

Once a string has been created, the character sequence that comprises a string cannot
be altered. This restriction allows C# to implement strings more efficiently. Though this
restriction probably sounds like a serious drawback, it isn't. When you need a string that is
a variation on one that already exists, simply create a new string that contains the desired
changes, and discard the original string if it is no longer needed. Since unused string objects
are automatically garbage-collected, you don't need to worry about what happens to the
discarded strings. It must be made clear, however, that **string** reference variables may, of
course, change the object to which they refer. It is just that the character sequence of a
specific **string** object cannot be changed after it is created.

To create a string that can be changed, C# offers a class called **StringBuilder**, which is in
the **System.Text** namespace. For most purposes, however, you will want to use **string**, not
StringBuilder.

The String Class

String is defined in the **System** namespace. It implements the **IComparable**, **IComparable<string>**, **ICloneable**, **IConvertible**, **IEnumerable**, **IEnumerable<char>**, and **IEquatable<string>** interfaces. **String** is a sealed class, which means that it cannot be inherited. **String** provides string-handling functionality for C#. It underlies C#'s built-in **string** type and is part of the .NET Framework. The next few sections examine **String** in detail.

The String Constructors

The **String** class defines several constructors that allow you to construct a string in a variety of ways. To create a string from a character array, use one of these constructors:

public String(char[ ] *value*)
public String(char[ ] *value*, int *startIndex*, int *length*)

The first form constructs a string that contains the characters in *value*. The second form uses *length* characters from *value*, beginning at the index specified by *startIndex*.

You can create a string that contains a specific character repeated a number of times using this constructor:

public String(char *c*, int *count*)

Here, *c* specifies the character that will be repeated *count* times.

You can construct a string given a pointer to a character array using one of these constructors:

public String(char* *value*)
public String(char* *value*, int *startIndex*, int *length*)

The first form constructs a string that contains the characters pointed to by *value*. It is assumed that *value* points to a null-terminated array, which is used in its entirety. The second form uses *length* characters from the array pointed to by *value*, beginning at the index specified by *startIndex*. Because they use pointers, these constructors can be used only in unsafe code.

You can construct a string given a pointer to an array of bytes using one of these constructors:

public String(sbyte* *value*)
public String(sbyte* *value*, int *startIndex*, int *length*)
public String(sbyte* *value*, int *startIndex*, int *length*, Encoding *enc*)

The first form constructs a string that contains the bytes pointed to by *value*. It is assumed that *value* points to a null-terminated array, which is used in its entirety. The second form uses *length* characters from the array pointed to by *value*, beginning at the index specified by *startIndex*. The third form lets you specify how the bytes are encoded. The **Encoding** class is in the **System.Text** namespace. Because they use pointers, these constructors can be used only in unsafe code.

A string literal automatically creates a string object. For this reason, a **string** object is often initialized by assigning it a string literal, as shown here:

```
string str = "a new string";
```

The String Field, Indexer, and Property

The **String** class defines one field, shown here:

public static readonly string Empty

Empty specifies an empty string, which is a string that contains no characters. This differs from a null **String** reference, which simply refers to no object.

There is one read-only indexer defined for **String**, which is shown here:

public char this[int *index*] { get; }

This indexer allows you to obtain the character at a specified index. Like arrays, the indexing for strings begins at zero. Since **String** objects are immutable, it makes sense that **String** supports a read-only indexer.

There is one read-only property:

public int Length { get; }

Length returns the number of characters in the string.

The String Operators

The **String** class overloads two operators: = = and !=. To test two strings for equality, use the = = operator. Normally, when the = = operator is applied to object references, it determines if both references refer to the same object. This differs for objects of type **String**. When the = = is applied to two **String** references, the contents of the strings, themselves, are compared for equality. The same is true for the != operator: the contents of the strings are compared. However, the other relational operators, such as < or >=, compare the references, just like they do for other types of objects. To determine if one string is greater than or less than another, use the **Compare( )** or **CompareTo( )** method defined by **String**.

As you will see, many string comparisons make use of cultural information. This is not the case with the = = and != operators. They simply compare the ordinal values of the characters within the strings. (In other words, they compare the binary values of the characters, unmodified by cultural norms.) Thus, these operators are case-sensitive and culture-insensitive.

The String Methods

The **String** class defines a large number of methods, and many of the methods have two or more overloaded forms. For this reason it is neither practical nor useful to list them all. Instead, several of the more commonly used methods will be presented, along with examples that illustrate them.

Comparing Strings

Perhaps the most frequently used string-handling operation is the comparison of one string to another. Before we examine any of the comparison methods, a key point needs to be made. String comparisons can be performed in two general ways by the .NET Framework. First, a comparison can reflect the customs and norms of a given culture, which is often the cultural setting in force when the program executes. This is the default behavior of some, but not all, of the comparison methods. Second, comparisons can be performed independently of cultural settings, using only the ordinal values of the characters that comprise the string. In general, string comparisons that are culture-sensitive use dictionary order (and linguistic features) to determine whether one string is greater than, equal to, or less than another. Ordinal string comparisons simply order strings based on the unmodified value of each character.

Choosing a comparison approach is an important decision. As a general rule (and with exceptions), if the strings are being compared for the purposes of displaying output to a user (such as showing a set of sorted strings in dictionary order), then a culture-sensitive comparison is often the right choice. However, if the strings contain fixed information that is not intended to be modified based on cultural differences, such as a filename, a keyword, a website URL, or a security-related value, then an ordinal comparison should usually be used. Of course, it is ultimately the specifics of your application that will dictate what approach is required.

NOTE *Because of the differences between culture-sensitive comparisons and ordinal comparisons, and the implications of each, it is strongly suggested that you consult Microsoft's currently recommended best practices in this regard. Choosing the wrong approach can, in some cases, make your program malfunction when it is used in an environment that differs from the development environment.*

String provides a wide array of comparison methods. These are shown in Table 22-1. Of the comparison methods, the **Compare( )** method is the most versatile. It can compare two strings in their entirety or in parts. It can use case-sensitive comparisons or ignore case. You can also specify how the comparison is performed by using a version that has a **StringComparison** parameter, or what cultural information governs the comparison using a version that has a **CultureInfo** parameter. The overloads of **Compare( )** that do not include a **StringComparison** are case-sensitive and culture-sensitive. Overloads that don't specify a **CultureInfo** parameter use the cultural information defined by the current execution environment. Although we won't make use of the **CultureInfo** parameter in this chapter, the **StringComparison** parameter is of immediate importance.

Method	Description
public static int 　　Compare(string *strA*, string *strB*)	Compares the string referred to by *strA* with *strB*. Returns greater than zero if *strA* is greater than *strB*, less than zero if *strA* is less than *strB*, and zero if *strA* and *strB* are equal. The comparison is case- and culture-sensitive.
public static int 　　Compare(string *strA*, string *strB*, 　　　　bool *ignoreCase*)	Compares the string referred to by *strA* with *strB*. Returns greater than zero if *strA* is greater than *strB*, less than zero if *strA* is less than *strB*, and zero if *strA* and *strB* are equal. If *ignoreCase* is **true**, the comparison ignores case differences. Otherwise, case differences matter. The comparison is culture-sensitive.
public static int 　　Compare(string *strA*, string *strB*, 　　　　StringComparison 　　　　*comparisonType*)	Compares the string referred to by *strA* with *strB*. Returns greater than zero if *strA* is greater than *strB*, less than zero if *strA* is less than *strB*, and zero if *strA* and *strB* are equal. How the comparison is performed is specified by *comparisonType*.

TABLE 22-1 The **String** Comparison Methods

Method	Description

public static int
    Compare(string *strA*, string *strB*,
        bool *ignoreCase*,
        CultureInfo *culture*)
	Compares the string referred to by *strA* with *strB* using the cultural information passed in *culture*. Returns greater than zero if *strA* is greater than *strB*, less than zero if *strA* is less than *strB*, and zero if *strA* and *strB* are equal. If *ignoreCase* is **true**, the comparison ignores case differences. Otherwise, case differences matter. The **CultureInfo** class is defined in the **System.Globalization** namespace.

public static int
    Compare(string *strA*, int *indexA*,
        string *strB*, int *indexB*,
        int *length*)
	Compares portions of the strings referred to by *strA* and *strB*. The comparison begins at *strA*[*indexA*] and *strB*[*indexB*] and runs for *length* characters. Returns greater than zero if *strA* is greater than *strB*, less than zero if *strA* is less than *strB*, and zero if *strA* and *strB* are equal. The comparison is case- and culture-sensitive.

public static int
    Compare(string *strA*, int *indexA*,
        string *strB*, int *indexB*,
        int *length*,
        bool *ignoreCase*)
	Compares portions of the strings referred to by *strA* and *strB*. The comparison begins at *strA*[*indexA*] and *strB*[*indexB*] and runs for *length* characters. Returns greater than zero if *strA* is greater than *strB*, less than zero if *strA* is less than *strB*, and zero if *strA* and *strB* are equal. If *ignoreCase* is **true**, the comparison ignores case differences. Otherwise, case differences matter. The comparison is culture-sensitive.

public static int
    Compare(string *strA*, int *indexA*,
        string *strB*, int *indexB*,
        int *length*,
        StringComparison
            comparisonType)
	Compares portions of the strings referred to by *strA* and *strB*. The comparison begins at *strA*[*indexA*] and *strB*[*indexB*] and runs for *length* characters. Returns greater than zero if *strA* is greater than *strB*, less than zero if *strA* is less than *strB*, and zero if *strA* and *strB* are equal. How the comparison is performed is specified by *comparisonType*.

public static int
    Compare(string *strA*, int *indexA*,
        string *strB*, int *indexB*,
        int *length*,
        bool *ignoreCase*,
        CultureInfo *culture*)
	Compares portions of the strings referred to by *strA* and *strB* using the cultural information passed in *culture*. The comparison begins at *strA*[*indexA*] and *strB*[*indexB*] and runs for *length* characters. Returns greater than zero if *strA* is greater than *strB*, less than zero if *strA* is less than *strB*, and zero if *strA* and *strB* are equal. If *ignoreCase* is **true**, the comparison ignores case differences. Otherwise, case differences matter. The **CultureInfo** class is defined in the **System.Globalization** namespace.

public static int
    Compare(string *strA*, string *strB*,
        CultureInfo *culture*,
        CompareOptions *options*)
	Compares the string referred to by *strA* with the string referred to by *strB* using the cultural information passed in *culture* and the comparison options passed in *options*. Returns greater than zero if *strA* is greater than *strB*, less than zero if *strA* is less than *strB*, and zero if *strA* and *strB* are equal. **CultureInfo** and **CompareOptions** are defined in **System.Globalization**.

TABLE 22-1   The **String** Comparison Methods *(continued)*

Method	Description
public static int Compare(string *strA*, int *indexA*, string *strB*, int *indexB*, int *length*, CultureInfo *culture*, CompareOptions *options*)	Compares portions of the strings referred to by *strA* and *strB* using the cultural information passed in *culture* and the comparison options passed in *options*. The comparison begins at *strA*[*indexA*] and *strB*[*indexB*] and runs for *length* characters. Returns greater than zero if *strA* is greater than *strB*, less than zero if *strA* is less than *strB*, and zero if *strA* and *strB* are equal. **CultureInfo** and **CompareOptions** are defined in the **System.Globalization** namespace.
public static int CompareOrdinal(string *strA*, string *strB*)	Compares the strings referred to by *strA* and *strB* independently of culture, region, or language. Returns greater than zero if *strA* is greater than *strB*, less than zero if *strA* is less than *strB*, and zero if *strA* and *strB* are equal.
public static int CompareOrdinal(string *strA*, int *indexA*, string *strB*, int *indexB*, int *length*)	Compares portions of the strings referred to by *strA* and *strB* independently of culture, region, or language. The comparison begins at *strA*[*indexA*] and *strB*[*indexB*] and runs for *length* characters. Returns greater than zero if *strA* is greater than *strB*, less than zero if *strA* is less than *strB*, and zero if *strA* and *strB* are equal.
public int CompareTo(object *value*)	Compares the invoking string with the string representation of *value*. Returns greater than zero if the invoking string is greater than *value*, less than zero if the invoking string is less than *value*, and zero if the two are equal. The comparison is case- and culture-sensitive.
public int CompareTo(string *strB*)	Compares the invoking string with *strB*. Returns greater than zero if the invoking string is greater than *strB*, less than zero if the invoking string is less than *strB*, and zero if the two are equal. The comparison is case- and culture-sensitive.
public override bool Equals(object *obj*)	Returns true if the invoking string contains the same character sequence as the string representation of *obj*. The comparison is ordinal, meaning that it is case-sensitive and culture-insensitive.
public bool Equals(string *value*)	Returns true if the invoking string contains the same character sequence as *value*. The comparison is ordinal, meaning that it is case-sensitive and culture-insensitive.
public bool Equals(string *value*, StringComparison *comparisonType*)	Returns true if the invoking string contains the same character sequence as *value*. How the comparison is performed is specified by *comparisonType*.
public static bool Equals(string *a*, string *b*)	Returns true if *a* contains the same character sequence as *b*. The comparison is ordinal, meaning that it is case-sensitive and culture-insensitive.
public static bool Equals(string *a*, string *b*, StringComparison *comparisonType*)	Returns true if *a* contains the same character sequence as *b*. How the comparison is performed is specified by *comparisonType*.

TABLE 22-1   The **String** Comparison Methods *(continued)*

StringComparison is an enumeration that defines the values shown in Table 22-2. Using these values, it is possible to craft a comparison that meets the specific needs of your application. Thus, the addition of the **StringComparison** parameter expands the capabilities of **Compare( )** and other methods, such as **Equals( )**. It also lets you specify in an unambiguous way precisely what type of comparison you intend. Because of the differences between culture-sensitive and ordinal comparisons, it important to be as clear as possible in this regard. For this reason, the examples in this book will explicitly specify the **StringComparison** parameter in calls to methods that support such a parameter.

In all cases, **Compare( )** returns less than zero when the first string is less than the second, greater than zero when the first string is greater than the second, and zero when the two strings compare as equal. Even though **Compare( )** returns zero when it determines two strings are equal, it is usually better to use **Equals( )** (or the = = operator) to determine equality. The reason is that **Compare( )** determines equality based on sort order. When a culture-sensitive comparison is performed, two strings might compare as equal in terms of sort order, but not be equal otherwise. By default, **Equals( )** determines equality based on the ordinal values of the characters and is culture-insensitive. Thus, by default, it compares two strings for absolute, character-by-character equality. Thus, it works like the = = operator.

Although **Compare( )** is more versatile, when performing simple ordinal comparisons, the **CompareOrdinal( )** method is a bit easier to use. Finally, notice that **CompareTo( )** performs only a culture-sensitive comparison. At the time of this writing, there is no overload that lets you specify a different approach.

The following program demonstrates **Compare( )**, **Equals( )**, **CompareOrdinal( )**, and the = = and != operators. Notice that the first two comparisons clearly show the difference

Value	Description
CurrentCulture	Comparisons are performed using the currently active cultural settings.
CurrentCultureIgnoreCase	Case-insensitive comparisons are performed using the currently active cultural settings.
InvariantCulture	Comparisons are performed using an invariant (that is, universal and unchanging) culture.
InvariantCultureIngoreCase	Case-insensitive comparisons are performed using an invariant (that is, universal and unchanging) culture.
Ordinal	Comparisons are performed using the ordinal values of the characters in the string. Thus, dictionary-order may not result and cultural conventions are ignored.
OrdinalIgnoreCase	Case-insensitive comparisons are performed using the ordinal values of the characters in the string. Thus, dictionary-order may not result and cultural conventions are ignored.

TABLE 22-2   The **StringComparison** Enumeration Values

between culture-sensitive comparisons and ordinal comparisons in an English-language environment.

```csharp
// Demonstrate string comparisons.
using System;

class CompareDemo {
  static void Main() {
    string str1 = "alpha";
    string str2 = "Alpha";
    string str3 = "Beta";
    string str4 = "alpha";
    string str5 = "alpha, beta";

    int result;

    // First, demonstrate the differences between culture-sensitive
    // and ordinal comparison.
    result = String.Compare(str1, str2, StringComparison.CurrentCulture);
    Console.Write("Using a culture-sensitive comparison: ");
    if(result < 0)
      Console.WriteLine(str1 + " is less than " + str2);
    else if(result > 0)
      Console.WriteLine(str1 + " is greater than " + str2);
    else
      Console.WriteLine(str1 + " equals " + str2);

    result = String.Compare(str1, str2, StringComparison.Ordinal);
    Console.Write("Using an ordinal comparison: ");
    if(result < 0)
      Console.WriteLine(str1 + " is less than " + str2);
    else if(result > 0)
      Console.WriteLine(str1 + " is greater than " + str2);
    else
      Console.WriteLine(str1 + " equals " + str4);

    // Use the CompareOrdinal() method.
    result = String.CompareOrdinal(str1, str2);
    Console.Write("Using CompareOrdinal(): ");
    if(result < 0)
      Console.WriteLine(str1 + " is less than " + str2);
    else if(result > 0)
      Console.WriteLine(str1 + " is greater than " + str2);
    else
      Console.WriteLine(str1 + " equals " + str4);

    Console.WriteLine();

    // Use == to determine if two strings are equal.
    // This comparison is ordinal.
    if(str1 == str4) Console.WriteLine(str1 + " == " + str4);

    // Use != on strings.
    if(str1 != str3) Console.WriteLine(str1 + " != " + str3);
    if(str1 != str2) Console.WriteLine(str1 + " != " + str2);
```

```
      Console.WriteLine();

      // Use Equals() to perform an ordinal, case-insensitive comparison.
      if(String.Equals(str1, str2, StringComparison.OrdinalIgnoreCase))
        Console.WriteLine("Using Equals() with OrdinalIgnoreCase, " +
                          str1 + " equals " + str2);

      Console.WriteLine();

      // Compare a portion of a string.
      if(String.Compare(str2, 0, str5, 0, 3,
                        StringComparison.CurrentCulture) > 0)  {
        Console.WriteLine("Using the current culture, the first " +
                          "3 characters of " + str2 +
                          "\nare greater than the first " +
                          "3 characters of " + str5);
      }
    }
  }
}
```

The output is shown here:

```
Using a culture-sensitive comparison: alpha is less than Alpha
Using an ordinal comparison: alpha is greater than Alpha
Using CompareOrdinal(): alpha is greater than Alpha

alpha == alpha
alpha != Beta
alpha != Alpha

Using Equals() with OrdinalIgnoreCase, alpha equals Alpha

Using the current culture, the first 3 characters of Alpha
are greater than the first 3 characters of alpha, beta
```

Concatenating Strings

There are two ways to concatenate (join together) two or more strings. First, you can use the +
operator, as demonstrated in Chapter 7. Second, you can use one of the various concatenation
methods defined by **String**. Although using + is the easiest approach in many cases, the
concatenation methods give you an alternative.

The method that performs concatenation is called **Concat( )**. One of its simplest forms is
shown here:

   public static string Concat(string *str0*, string *str1*)

This method returns a string that contains *str1* concatenated to the end of *str0*. Another form
of **Concat( )**, shown here, concatenates three strings:

   public static string Concat(string *str0*, string *str1*, string *str2*)

In this version, a string that contains the concatenation of *str0, str1,* and *str2* is returned.
There is also a form that concatenates four strings:

   public static string Concat(string *str0*, string *str1*, string *str2*, string *str3*)

This version returns the concatenation of all four strings.

The version of **Concat( )** shown next concatenates an arbitrary number of strings:

public static string Concat(params string[ ] *values*)

Here, *values* refers to a variable number of arguments that are concatenated, and the result is returned. Because this version of **Concat( )** can be used to concatenate any number of strings, including two, three, or four strings, you might wonder why the other forms just shown exist. The reason is efficiency; passing up to four arguments is more efficient than using a variable-length argument list.

The following program demonstrates the variable-length argument version of **Concat( )**:

```
// Demonstrate Concat().

using System;

class ConcatDemo {
  static void Main() {

    string result = String.Concat("This ", "is ", "a ",
                                  "test ", "of ", "the ",
                                  "String ", "class.");

    Console.WriteLine("result: " + result);

  }
}
```

The output is shown here:

```
result: This is a test of the String class.
```

There are also versions of the **Concat( )** method that take **object** references, rather than **string** references. These obtain the string representation of the objects with which they are called and return a string containing the concatenation of those strings. (The string representations are obtained by calling **ToString( )** on the objects.) These versions of **Concat( )** are shown here:

public static string Concat(object *arg0*)
public static string Concat(object *arg0*, object *arg1*)
public static string Concat(object *agr0*, object *arg1*, object *arg2*)
public static string Concat(object *arg0*, object *arg1*, object *arg2*, object *arg3*)
public static string Concat(params object[ ] *args*)

The first method simply returns the string equivalent of *arg0*. The other methods return a string that contains the concatenation of their arguments. The **object** forms of **Concat( )** are very convenient because they let you avoid having to manually obtain string representations prior to concatenation. To see how useful these methods can be, consider the following program:

```
// Demonstrate the object form of Concat().

using System;
```

```
class MyClass {
  public static int Count = 0;

  public MyClass() { Count++; }
}

class ConcatDemo {
  static void Main() {

    string result = String.Concat("The value is " + 19);
    Console.WriteLine("result: " + result);

    result = String.Concat("hello ", 88, " ", 20.0, " ",
                           false, " ",  23.45M);
    Console.WriteLine("result: " + result);

    MyClass mc = new MyClass();

    result = String.Concat(mc, " current count is ",
                           MyClass.Count);
    Console.WriteLine("result: " + result);
  }
}
```

The output is shown here:

```
result: The value is 19
result: hello 88 20 False 23.45
result: MyClass current count is 1
```

In this example, **Concat( )** concatenates the string representations of various types of data. For each argument, the **ToString( )** method associated with that argument is called to obtain a string representation. Thus, in this call to **concat( )**:

```
string result = String.Concat("The value is " + 19);
```

Int32.ToString( ) is invoked to obtain the string representation of the integer value 19. **Concat( )** then concatenates the strings and returns the result.

Also notice how an object of the user-defined class **MyClass** can be used in this call to **Concat( )**:

```
result = String.Concat(mc, " current count is ",
                       MyClass.Count);
```

In this case, the string representation of **mc**, which is of type **MyClass**, is returned. By default, this is simply its class name. However, if you override the **ToString( )** method, then **MyClass** can return a different string. For example, try adding this version of **ToString( )** to **Myclass** in the preceding program:

```
public override string ToString() {
  return "An object of type MyClass";
}
```

When this version is used, the last line in the output will be

```
result: An object of type MyClass current count is 1
```

Version 4.0 of the .NET Framework adds two more forms of **Concat( )**, which are shown here:

public static string Concat<T>(IEnumerable<T> *values*)
public static string Concat(IEnumerable<string> *values*)

The first form returns a string that contains the concatenation of the string representation of the values in *values*, which can be any type of object that implements **IEnumerable<T>**. The second form concatenates the strings specified by *values*. (Understand, however, that if you are doing a large amount of string concatenations, then using a **StringBuilder** may be a better choice.)

Searching a String

String offers many methods that allow you to search a string. For example, you can search for either a substring or a character. You can also search for the first or last occurrence of either. It is important to keep in mind that a search can be either culture-sensitive or ordinal.

To find the first occurrence of a string or a character, use the **IndexOf( )** method. It defines several overloaded forms. Here is one that searches for the first occurrence of a character within a string:

public int IndexOf(char *value*)

This method returns the index of the first occurrence of the character *value* within the invoking string. It returns –1 if *value* is not found. The search to find the character ignores cultural settings. Thus, to find the first occurrence of a character, an ordinal search is used.

Here are two of forms of **IndexOf( )** that let you search for the first occurrence of a string:

public int IndexOf(String *value*)
public int IndexOf(String *value*, StringComparison *comparisonType*)

The first form uses a culture-sensitive search to find the first occurrence of the string referred to by *value*. The second form lets you specify a **StringComparison** value that specifies how the search is conducted. Both return –1 if the item is not found.

To search for the last occurrence of a character or a string, use the **LastIndexOf( )** method. It also defines several overloaded forms. This one searches for the last occurrence of a character within the invoking string:

public int LastIndexOf(char *value*)

This method uses an ordinal search and returns the index of the last occurrence of the character *value* within the invoking string or –1 if *value* is not found.

Here are two forms of **LastIndexOf( )** that let you search for the last occurrence of a string:

public int LastIndexOf(string *value*)
public int LastIndexOf(string *value*, StringComparison *comparisonType*)

The first form uses a culture-sensitive search to find the first occurrence of the string referred to by *value*. The second form lets you specify a **StringComparison** value that specifies how the search is conducted. Both return –1 if the item is not found.

String offers two interesting supplemental search methods: **IndexOfAny( )** and **LastIndexOfAny( )**. These search for the first or last character that matches any of a set of characters. Here are their simplest forms:

```
public int IndexOfAny(char[ ] anyOf)
public int LastIndexOfAny(char[ ] anyOf)
```

IndexOfAny( ) returns the index of the first occurrence of any character in *anyOf* that is found within the invoking string. **LastIndexOfAny( )** returns the index of the last occurrence of any character in *anyOf* that is found within the invoking string. Both return –1 if no match is found. In both cases, an ordinal search is used.

When working with strings, it is often useful to know if a string begins with or ends with a given substring. To accomplish this task, use the **StartsWith( )** and **EndsWith( )** methods. Here are their two simplest forms:

```
public bool StartsWith(string value)
public bool EndsWith(string value)
```

StartsWith( ) returns true if the invoking string begins with the string passed in *value*. **EndsWith( )** returns true if the invoking string ends with the string passed in *value*. Both return false on failure. These use culture-sensitive searches. To specify how the searches are conducted, you can use a version of these methods that has a **StringComparison** parameter. Here are examples:

```
public bool StartsWith(string value, StringComparison comparisonType)
public bool EndsWith(string value, StringComparison comparisonType)
```

They work like the previous versions, but let you explicitly specify how the search is conducted.

Here is a program that demonstrates several of the string search methods. For purposes of illustration, all use ordinal searching:

```
// Search strings.

using System;

class StringSearchDemo {
  static void Main() {
    string str = "C# has powerful string handling.";
    int idx;

    Console.WriteLine("str: " + str);

    idx = str.IndexOf('h');
    Console.WriteLine("Index of first 'h': " + idx);

    idx = str.LastIndexOf('h');
    Console.WriteLine("Index of last 'h': " + idx);

    idx = str.IndexOf("ing", StringComparison.Ordinal);
    Console.WriteLine("Index of first \"ing\": " + idx);

    idx = str.LastIndexOf("ing", StringComparison.Ordinal);
    Console.WriteLine("Index of last \"ing\": " + idx);
```

```
      char[] chrs = { 'a', 'b', 'c' };
      idx = str.IndexOfAny(chrs);
      Console.WriteLine("Index of first 'a', 'b', or 'c': " + idx);

      if(str.StartsWith("C# has", StringComparison.Ordinal))
        Console.WriteLine("str begins with \"C# has\"");

      if(str.EndsWith("ling.", StringComparison.Ordinal))
        Console.WriteLine("str ends with \"ling.\"");
  }
}
```

The output from the program is shown here:

```
str: C# has powerful string handling.
Index of first 'h': 3
Index of last 'h': 23
Index of first "ing": 19
Index of last "ing": 28
Index of first 'a', 'b', or 'c': 4
str begins with "C# has"
str ends with "ling."
```

A string search method that you will find useful in many circumstances is **Contains()**. Its general form is shown here:

   public bool Contains(string *value*)

It returns true if the invoking string contains the string specified by *value,* and false otherwise. It uses ordinal searching. This method is especially useful when all you need to know is if a specific substring exists within another string. Here is an example that demonstrates its use.

```
// Demonstrate Contains().

using System;

class ContainsDemo {
  static void Main() {
    string str = "C# combines power with performance.";

    if(str.Contains("power"))
      Console.WriteLine("The sequence power was found.");

    if(str.Contains("pow"))
      Console.WriteLine("The sequence pow was found.");

    if(!str.Contains("powerful"))
      Console.WriteLine("The sequence powerful was not found.");
  }
}
```

The output is shown here:

```
The sequence power was found.
The sequence pow was found.
The sequence powerful was not found.
```

As the output shows, **Contains( )** searches for a matching sequence, not for whole words. Thus, both "pow" and "power" are found. However, because there are no sequences that match "powerful", it is (correctly) not found.

Several of the search methods have additional forms that allow you to begin a search at a specified index or to specify a range to search within. All versions of the **String** search methods are shown in Table 22-3.

Method	Description
public bool Contains(string *value*)	Returns true if the invoking string contains the string specified by *value*. False is returned if *value* is not found. Ordinal searching is used.
public bool EndsWith(string *value*)	Returns true if the invoking string ends with the string passed in *value*. Otherwise, false is returned. Culture-sensitive searching is used.

public bool
    EndsWith(string *value*,
             StringComparison
                 comparisonType)
	Returns true if the invoking string ends with the string passed in *value*. Otherwise, false is returned. How the search is performed is specified by *comparisonType*.

public bool
    EndsWith(string *value*,
             bool *ignoreCase*,
             CultureInfo *culture*)
	Returns true if the invoking string ends with the string passed in *value*. Otherwise, false is returned. If *ignoreCase* is **true**, the search ignores case differences. Otherwise, case differences matter. The search is conducted using the cultural information passed in *culture*.

public int IndexOf(char *value*)	Returns the index of the first occurrence of *value* within the invoking string. Returns –1 if *value* is not found. Ordinal searching is used.
public int IndexOf(string *value*)	Returns the index of the first occurrence of *value* within the invoking string. Returns –1 if *value* is not found. Culture-sensitive searching is used.
public int IndexOf(char *value*, int *startIndex*)	Returns the index of the first occurrence of *value* within the invoking string. Searching begins at the index specified by *startIndex*. Returns –1 if *value* is not found. Ordinal searching is used.
public int IndexOf(string *value*, int *startIndex*)	Returns the index of the first occurrence of *value* within the invoking string. Searching begins at the index specified by *startIndex*. Returns –1 if *value* is not found. Culture-sensitive searching is used.

public int
    IndexOf(char *value*,
             int *startIndex*,
             int *count*)
	Returns the index of the first occurrence of *value* within the invoking string. Searching begins at the index specified by *startIndex* and runs for *count* elements. Returns –1 if *value* is not found. Ordinal searching is used.

public int
    IndexOf(string *value*,
             int *startIndex*,
             int *count*)
	Returns the index of the first occurrence of *value* within the invoking string. Searching begins at the index specified by *startIndex* and runs for *count* elements. Returns –1 if *value* is not found. Culture-sensitive searching is used.

public int
    IndexOf(string *value*,
             StringComparison
                 comparisonType)
	Returns the index of the first occurrence of *value* within the invoking string. How the search is performed is specified by *comparisonType*. Returns –1 if *value* is not found.

TABLE 22-3   The Search Methods Offered by **String**

Method	Description

public int
  IndexOf(string *value*,
        int *startIndex*,
        StringComparison
           comparisonType)
	Returns the index of the first occurrence of *value* within the invoking string. Searching begins at the index specified by *startIndex*. How the search is performed is specified by *comparisonType*. Returns –1 if *value* is not found.

public int
  IndexOf(string *value*,
        int *startIndex*,
        int *count*,
        StringComparison
           comparisonType)
	Returns the index of the first occurrence of *value* within the invoking string. Searching begins at the index specified by *startIndex* and runs for *count* elements. How the search is performed is specified by *comparisonType*. Returns –1 if *value* is not found.

public int IndexOfAny(char[ ] *anyOf*)	Returns the index of the first occurrence of any character in *anyOf* that is found within the invoking string. Returns –1 if no match is found. Ordinal searching is used.
public int IndexOfAny(char[ ] *anyOf*, int *startIndex*)	Returns the index of the first occurrence of any character in *anyOf* that is found within the invoking string. Searching begins at the index specified by *startIndex*. Returns –1 if no match is found. Ordinal searching is used.

public int IndexOfAny(char[ ] *anyOf*,
          int *startIndex*,
          int *count*)
	Returns the index of the first occurrence of any character in *anyOf* that is found within the invoking string. Searching begins at the index specified by *startIndex* and runs for *count* elements. Returns –1 if no match is found. Ordinal searching is used.

public int LastIndexOf(char *value*)	Returns the index of the last occurrence of *value* within the invoking string. Returns –1 if *value* is not found. Ordinal searching is used.
public int LastIndexOf(string *value*)	Returns the index of the last occurrence of *value* within the invoking string. Returns –1 if *value* is not found. Culture-sensitive searching is used.
public int LastIndexOf(char *value*, int *startIndex*)	Returns the index of the last occurrence of *value* within a range of the invoking string. The search proceeds in reverse order, beginning at the index specified by *startIndex* and stopping at zero. Returns –1 if the *value* is not found. Ordinal searching is used.
public int LastIndexOf(string *value*, int *startIndex*)	Returns the index of the last occurrence of *value* within a range of the invoking string. The search proceeds in reverse order, beginning at the index specified by *startIndex* and stopping at zero. Returns –1 if *value* is not found. Culture-sensitive searching is used.

public int
  LastIndexOf(char *value*,
        int *startIndex*,
        int *count*)
	Returns the index of the last occurrence of *value* within the invoking string. The search proceeds in reverse order, beginning at the index specified by *startIndex* and running for *count* elements. Returns –1 if *value* is not found. Ordinal searching is used.

TABLE 22-3 The Search Methods Offered by **String** *(continued)*

Method	Description

public int
LastIndexOf(string *value*,
      int *startIndex*,
      int *count*)
	Returns the index of the last occurrence of *value* within the invoking string. The search proceeds in reverse order, beginning at the index specified by *startIndex* and running for *count* elements. Returns –1 if *value* is not found. Culture-sensitive searching is used.

public int
LastIndexOf(string *value*,
      StringComparison
        comparisonType)
	Returns the index of the last occurrence of *value* within the invoking string. How the search is performed is specified by *comparisonType*. Returns –1 if *value* is not found.

public int
LastIndexOf(strlng *value*,
      int *startIndex*,
      StringComparison
        comparisonType)
	Returns the index of the last occurrence of *value* within a range of the Invoking string. The search proceeds in reverse order, beginning at the index specified by *startIndex* and stopping at zero. How the search is performed is specified by *comparisonType*. Returns –1 if *value* is not found.

public int
LastIndexOf(string *value*,
      int *startIndex*,
      int *count*,
      StringComparison
        comparisonType)
	Returns the index of the last occurrence of *value* within the invoking string. The search proceeds in reverse order, beginning at the index specified by *startIndex* and running for *count* elements. How the search is performed is specified by *comparisonType*. Returns –1 if *value* is not found.

public int LastIndexOfAny(char[ ] *anyOf*)	Returns the index of the last occurrence of any character in *anyOf* that is found within the invoking string. Returns –1 if no match is found. Ordinal searching is used.
public int LastIndexOfAny(char[ ] *anyOf*, int *startIndex*)	Returns the index of the last occurrence of any character in *anyOf* that is found within the invoking string. The search proceeds in reverse order, beginning at the index specified by *startIndex* and stopping at zero. Returns –1 if no match is found. Ordinal searching is used.

public int
LastIndexOfAny(char[ ] *anyOf*,
      int *startIndex*,
      int *count*)
	Returns the index of the last occurrence of any character in *anyOf* that is found within the invoking string. The search proceeds in reverse order, beginning at the index specified by *startIndex* and running for *count* elements. Returns –1 if no match is found. Ordinal searching is used.

public bool StartsWith(string *value*)	Returns true if the invoking string begins with the string passed in *value*. Otherwise, false is returned. Culture-sensitive searching is used.

public bool
StartsWith(string *value*,
      StringComparison
        comparisonType)
	Returns true if the invoking string begins with the string passed in *value*. Otherwise, false is returned. How the search is performed is specified by *comparisonType*.

public bool
StartsWith(string *value*,
      bool *ignoreCase*,
      CultureInfo *culture*)
	Returns true if the invoking string begins with the string passed in *value*. Otherwise, false is returned. If *ignoreCase* is **true**, the search ignores case differences. Otherwise, case differences matter. The search is conducted using the cultural information passed in *culture*.

TABLE 22-3   The Search Methods Offered by **String** (*continued*)

Splitting and Joining Strings

Two fundamental string-handling operations are split and join. A *split* decomposes a string into its constituent parts. A *join* constructs a string from a set of parts. To split a string, **String** defines **Split( )**. To join a set of strings, **String** provides **Join( )**.

There are several versions of **Split( )**. Two commonly used forms, which have been available since C# 1.0, are shown here:

public string[ ] Split(params char[ ] *separator*)
public string[ ] Split(char[ ] *separator*, int *count*)

The first form splits the invoking string into pieces and returns an array containing the substrings. The characters that delimit each substring are passed in *separator*. If *separator* is null or refers to an empty string, then whitespace is used as the separator. In the second form, no more than *count* substrings will be returned.

There are several forms of the **Join( )** method. Here are two that have been available since version 2.0 of the .NET Framework:

public static string Join(string *separator*, params string[ ] *value*)
public static string Join(string *separator*, string[ ] *value*, int *startIndex*, int *count*)

The first form returns a string that contains the concatenation of the strings in *value*. The second form returns a string that contains the concatenation of *count* strings in *value*, beginning at *value*[*startIndex*]. For both versions, each string is separated from the next by the string specified by *separator*.

The following program shows **Split( )** and **Join( )** in action:

```
// Split and join strings.

using System;

class SplitAndJoinDemo {
  static void Main() {
    string str = "One if by land, two if by sea.";
    char[] seps = {' ', '.', ',' };

    // Split the string into parts.
    string[] parts = str.Split(seps);
    Console.WriteLine("Pieces from split: ");
    for(int i=0; i < parts.Length; i++)
      Console.WriteLine(parts[i]);

    // Now, join the parts.
    string whole = String.Join(" | ", parts);
    Console.WriteLine("Result of join: ");
    Console.WriteLine(whole);
  }
}
```

Here is the output:

```
Pieces from split:
One
if
by
land
```

```
two
if
by
sea

Result of join:
One | if | by | land |   | two | if | by | sea |
```

There is one important thing to notice in this output: the empty string that occurs between "land" and "two". This is caused by the fact that in the original string, the word "land" is followed by a comma and a space, as in "land, two". However, both the comma and the space are specified as separators. Thus, when this string is split, the empty string that exists between the two separators (the comma and the space) is returned.

There are several additional forms of **Split( )** that take a parameter of type **StringSplitOptions**. This parameter controls whether empty strings are part of the resulting split. Here are these forms of **Split( )**:

> public string[ ] Split(char[ ] *separator,* StringSplitOptions *options*)
> public string[ ] Split(string[ ] *separator,* StringSplitOptions *options*)
> public string[ ] Split(char[ ] *separator,* int *count ,* StringSplitOptions *options*)
> public string[ ] Split(string[ ] *separator,* int *count ,* StringSplitOptions *options*)

The first two forms split the invoking string into pieces and return an array containing the substrings. The characters that delimit each substring are passed in *separator*. If *separator* is null, then whitespace is used as the separator. In the third and fourth forms, no more than *count* substrings will be returned. For all versions, the value of *options* determines how to handle empty strings that result when two separators are adjacent to each other. The **StringSplitOptions** enumeration defines only two values: **None** and **RemoveEmptyEntries**. If *options* is **None**, then empty strings are included in the result (as the previous program showed). If *options* is **RemoveEmptyEntries**, empty strings are excluded from the result.

To understand the effects of removing empty entries, try replacing this line in the preceding program:

```
string[] parts = str.Split(seps);
```

with the following.

```
string[] parts = str.Split(seps, StringSplitOptions.RemoveEmptyEntries);
```

When you run the program, the output will be as shown next:

```
Pieces from split:
One
if
by
land
two
if
by
sea
Result of join:
One | if | by | land | two | if | by | sea
```

As you can see, the empty string that previously resulted because of the combination of the comma and space after "land" has been removed.

Splitting a string is an important string-manipulation procedure, because it is often used to obtain the individual *tokens* that comprise the string. For example, a database program might use **Split( )** to decompose a query such as "show me all balances greater than 100" into its individual parts, such as "show" and "100". In the process, the separators are removed. Thus, "show" (without any leading or trailing spaces) is obtained, not "show ". The following program illustrates this concept. It tokenizes strings containing binary mathematical operations, such as 10 + 5. It then performs the operation and displays the result.

```csharp
// Tokenize strings.

using System;

class TokenizeDemo {
  static void Main() {
    string[] input = {
                       "100 + 19",
                       "100 / 3.3",
                       "-3 * 9",
                       "100 - 87"
                     };
    char[] seps = {' '};

    for(int i=0; i < input.Length; i++) {
      // split string into parts
      string[] parts = input[i].Split(seps);
      Console.Write("Command: ");
      for(int j=0; j < parts.Length; j++)
        Console.Write(parts[j] + " ");

      Console.Write(", Result: ");
      double n = Double.Parse(parts[0]);
      double n2 = Double.Parse(parts[2]);

      switch(parts[1]) {
        case "+":
          Console.WriteLine(n + n2);
          break;
        case "-":
          Console.WriteLine(n - n2);
          break;
        case "*":
          Console.WriteLine(n * n2);
          break;
        case "/":
          Console.WriteLine(n / n2);
          break;
      }
    }
  }
}
```

Here is the output:

```
Command: 100 + 19 , Result: 119
Command: 100 / 3.3 , Result: 30.3030303030303
Command: -3 * 9 , Result: -27
Command: 100 - 87 , Result: 13
```

Beginning with .NET Framework 4.0, the following additional forms of **Join( )** are also defined:

public static string Join(string *separator*, params object[ ] *values*)
public static string Join(string *separator*, IEnumerable<string>[ ] *values*)
public static string Join<T>(string *separator*, IEnumerable<T>[ ] *values*)

The first form returns a string that contains the concatenation of the string representation of the objects in *values*. The second form returns a string that contains the concatenation of the collection of strings referred to by *values*. The third form returns a string that contains the concatenation of the string representation of the collection of objects in *values*. In all cases, each string is separated from the next by *separator*.

Padding and Trimming Strings

Sometimes you will want to remove leading and trailing spaces from a string. This type of operation, called *trimming*, is often needed by command processors. For example, a database might recognize the word "print". However, a user might enter this command with one or more leading or trailing spaces. Any such spaces must be removed before the string can be recognized by the database. Conversely, sometimes you will want to pad a string with spaces so that it meets some minimal length. For example, if you are preparing formatted output, you might need to ensure that each line is a certain length in order to maintain an alignment. Fortunately, C# includes methods that make these types of operations easy.

To trim a string, use one of these **Trim( )** methods:

public string Trim( )
public string Trim(params char[ ] *trimChars*)

The first form removes leading and trailing whitespace from the invoking string. The second form removes leading and trailing occurrences of the characters specified by *trimChars*. In both cases, the resulting string is returned.

You can pad a string by adding characters to either the left or the right side of the string. To pad a string on the left, use one of the methods shown here:

public string PadLeft(int *totalWidth*)
public string PadLeft(int *totalWidth*, char *paddingChar*)

The first form adds spaces on the left as needed to the invoking string so that its total length equals *totalWidth*. The second form adds the character specified by *paddingChar* as needed to the invoking string so that its total length equals *totalWidth*. In both cases, the resulting string is returned. If *totalWidth* is less than the length of the invoking string, a copy of the invoking string is returned unaltered.

To pad a string to the right, use one of these methods:

public string PadRight(int *totalWidth*)
public string PadRight(int *totalWidth*, char *paddingChar*)

The first form adds spaces on the right as needed to the invoking string so that its total length equals *totalWidth*. The second form adds the characters specified by *paddingChar* as needed to the invoking string so that its total length equals *totalWidth*. In both cases, the resulting string is returned. If *totalWidth* is less than the length of the invoking string, a copy of the invoking string is returned unaltered.

The following program demonstrates trimming and padding:

```
// Trimming and padding.

using System;

class TrimPadDemo {
  static void Main() {
    string str = "test";

    Console.WriteLine("Original string: " + str);

    // Pad on left with spaces.
    str = str.PadLeft(10);
    Console.WriteLine("|" + str + "|");

    // Pad on right with spaces.
    str = str.PadRight(20);
    Console.WriteLine("|" + str + "|");

    // Trim spaces.
    str = str.Trim();
    Console.WriteLine("|" + str + "|");

    // Pad on left with #s.
    str = str.PadLeft(10, '#');
    Console.WriteLine("|" + str + "|");

    // Pad on right with #s.
    str = str.PadRight(20, '#');
    Console.WriteLine("|" + str + "|");

    // Trim #s.
    str = str.Trim('#');
    Console.WriteLine("|" + str + "|");
  }
}
```

The output is shown here:

```
Original string: test
|      test|
|      test            |
|test|
|######test|
|######test##########|
|test|
```

Inserting, Removing, and Replacing

You can insert a string into another using the **Insert( )** method, shown here:

> public string Insert(int *startIndex*, string *value*)

Here, the string referred to by *value* is inserted into the invoking string at the index specified by *startIndex*. The resulting string is returned.

You can remove a portion of a string using **Remove( )**, shown next:

> public string Remove(int *startIndex*)
> public string Remove(int *startIndex*, int *count*)

The first form begins at the index specified by *startIndex* and removes all remaining characters in the string. The second form begins at *startIndex* and removes *count* number of characters. In both cases, the resulting string is returned.

You can replace a portion of a string by using **Replace( )**. It has these forms:

> public string Replace(char *oldChar*, char *newChar*)
> public string Replace(string *oldValue*, string *newValue*)

The first form replaces all occurrences of *oldChar* in the invoking string with *newChar*. The second form replaces all occurrences of the string referred to by *oldValue* in the invoking string with the string referred to by *newValue*. In both cases, the resulting string is returned.

Here is an example that demonstrates **Insert( )**, **Remove( )**, and **Replace( )**:

```
// Inserting, replacing, and removing.

using System;

class InsRepRevDemo {
  static void Main() {
    string str = "This test";

    Console.WriteLine("Original string: " + str);

    // Insert
    str = str.Insert(5, "is a ");
    Console.WriteLine(str);

    // Replace string
    str = str.Replace("is", "was");
    Console.WriteLine(str);

    // Replace characters
    str = str.Replace('a', 'X');
    Console.WriteLine(str);

    // Remove
    str = str.Remove(4, 5);
    Console.WriteLine(str);
  }
}
```

The output is shown here:

```
Original string: This test
This is a test
Thwas was a test
ThwXs wXs X test
ThwX X test
```

Changing Case

String offers two convenient methods that enable you to change the case of letters within a string. These are called **ToUpper( )** and **ToLower( )**. Here are their simplest forms:

```
public string ToLower( )
public string ToUpper( )
```

ToLower( ) lowercases all letters within the invoking string. **ToUpper( )** uppercases all letters within the invoking string. The resulting string is returned. For both, the transformation is culture-sensitive. There are also versions of these methods that allow you to specify cultural settings that determine how the methods perform their conversions. These are shown here:

```
public string ToLower(CultureInfo culture)
public string ToUpper(CultureInfo culture)
```

Using these forms lets you avoid ambiguity in your source code about what rules you want to follow when changing case, and these are the forms recommended for use.

Also available are the methods **ToUpperInvariant( )** and **ToLowerInvariant( )**, shown here:

```
public string ToUpperInvariant( )
public string ToLowerInvariant( )
```

These work like **ToUpper( )** and **ToLower( )** except that they use the invariant culture to perform the transformations to upper- or lowercase.

Using the Substring( ) Method

You can obtain a portion of a string by using the **Substring( )** method. It has these two forms:

```
public string Substring(int startIndex)
public string Substring(int startIndex, int length)
```

In the first form, the substring begins at the index specified by *startIndex* and runs to the end of the invoking string. In the second form, the substring begins at *startIndex* and runs for *length* characters. In each case, the substring is returned.

The following program demonstrates the **Substring( )** method:

```
// Use Substring().

using System;
```

```
class SubstringDemo {
  static void Main() {
    string str = "ABCDEFGHIJKLMNOPQRSTUVWXYZ";

    Console.WriteLine("str: " + str);

    Console.Write("str.Substring(15): ");
    string substr = str.Substring(15);
    Console.WriteLine(substr);

    Console.Write("str.Substring(0, 15): ");
    substr = str.Substring(0, 15);
    Console.WriteLine(substr);
  }
}
```

The following output is produced:

```
str: ABCDEFGHIJKLMNOPQRSTUVWXYZ
str.Substring(15): PQRSTUVWXYZ
str.Substring(0, 15): ABCDEFGHIJKLMNO
```

The String Extension Methods

As mentioned earlier, **String** implements **IEnumerable<T>**. This means that beginning with C# 3.0, a **String** object can call the extension methods defined by **Enumerable** and **Queryable**, which are both in the **System.Linq** namespace. These extension methods primarily provide support for LINQ, but some can also be used for other purposes, such as certain types of string handling. See Chapter 19 for a discussion of extension methods.

Formatting

When a human-readable form of a built-in type, such as **int** or **double**, is needed, a string representation must be created. Although C# automatically supplies a default format for this representation, it is also possible to specify a format of your own choosing. For example, as you saw in Part I, it is possible to output numeric data using a dollars and cents format. A number of methods format data, including **Console.WriteLine( )**, **String.Format( )**, and the **ToString( )** method defined for the numeric structure types. The same approach to formatting is used by all three; once you have learned to format data for one, you can apply it to the others.

Formatting Overview

Formatting is governed by two components: *format specifiers* and *format providers*. The form that the string representation of a value will take is controlled through the use of a format specifier. Thus, it is the format specifier that dictates how the human-readable form of the data will look. For example, to output a numeric value using scientific notation, you will use the E format specifier.

In many cases, the precise format of a value will be affected by the culture and language in which the program is running. For example, in the United States, money is represented in dollars. In Europe, money is represented in euros. To handle the cultural and language differences, C# uses format providers. A format provider defines the way that a format specifier will be interpreted. A format provider is created by implementing the **IFormatProvider** interface, which defines the **GetFormat( )** method. Format providers are predefined for the built-in numeric types and many other types in the .NET Framework. In general, you can format data without having to worry about specifying a format provider, and format providers are not examined further in this book.

To format data, include a format specifier in a call to a method that supports formatting. The use of format specifiers was introduced in Chapter 3, but is worthwhile reviewing here. The discussion that follows uses **Console.WriteLine( )**, but the same basic approach applies to other methods that support formatting.

To format data using **WriteLine( )**, use the version of **WriteLine( )** shown here:

WriteLine(*"format string"*, *arg0*, *arg1*, … , *argN*);

In this version, the arguments to **WriteLine( )** are separated by commas and not **+** signs. The *format string* contains two items: regular, printing characters that are displayed as-is, and format items (also called format commands).

Format items take this general form:

{*argnum*, *width*: *fmt*}

Here, *argnum* specifies the number of the argument (starting from zero) to display. The minimum width of the field is specified by *width,* and the format specifier is represented by a string in *fmt*. Both *width* and *fmt* are optional. Thus, in its simplest form, a format item simply indicates which argument to display. For example, {0} indicates *arg0,* {1} specifies *arg1,* and so on.

During execution, when a format item is encountered in the format string, the corresponding argument, as specified by *argnum,* is substituted and displayed. Thus, it is the position of a format item within the format string that determines where its matching data will be displayed. It is the argument number that determines which argument will be formatted.

If *fmt* is present, then the data is displayed using the specified format. Otherwise, the default format is used. If *width* is present, then output is padded with spaces to ensure that the minimum field width is attained. If *width* is positive, output is right-justified. If *width* is negative, output is left-justified.

The remainder of this chapter examines formatting and format specifiers in detail.

The Numeric Format Specifiers

There are several format specifiers defined for numeric data. They are shown in Table 22-4. Each format specifier can include an optional precision specifier. For example, to specify that a value be represented as a fixed-point value with two decimal places, use F2.

As explained, the precise effect of certain format specifiers depends upon the cultural settings. For example, the currency specifier, C, automatically displays a value in the monetary format of the selected culture. For most users, the default cultural information matches their locale and language. Thus, the same format specifier can be used without concern about the cultural context in which the program is executed.

Specifier	Format	Meaning of Precision Specifier
C	Currency (that is, a monetary value).	Specifies the number of decimal places.
c	Same as C.	
D	Whole number numeric data. (Use with integers only.)	Minimum number of digits. Leading zeros will be used to pad the result, if necessary.
d	Same as D.	
E	Scientific notation (uses uppercase E).	Specifies the number of decimal places. The default is six.
e	Scientific notation (uses lowercase e).	Specifies the number of decimal places. The default is six.
F	Fixed-point notation.	Specifies the number of decimal places.
f	Same as F.	
G	Use either E or F format, whichever is shorter.	See E and F.
g	Use either e or f format, whichever is shorter.	See e and f.
N	Fixed-point notation, with comma separators.	Specifies the number of decimal places.
n	Same as N.	
P	Percentage	Specifies the number of decimal places.
p	Same as P.	
R or r	Numeric value that can be parsed, using **Parse( )**, back into its equivalent internal form. (This is called the "round-trip" format.)	Not used.
X	Hexadecimal (uses uppercase letters A through F).	Minimum number of digits. Leading zeros will be used to pad the result, if necessary.
x	Hexadecimal (uses lowercase letters a through f).	Minimum number of digits. Leading zeros will be used to pad the result if necessary

TABLE 22-4   The Numeric Format Specifiers

Here is a program that demonstrates several of the numeric format specifiers:

```
// Demonstrate various format specifiers.

using System;

class FormatDemo {
  static void Main() {
    double v = 17688.65849;
    double v2 = 0.15;
    int x = 21;

    Console.WriteLine("{0:F2}", v);

    Console.WriteLine("{0:N5}", v);
```

```
      Console.WriteLine("{0:e}", v);

      Console.WriteLine("{0:r}", v);

      Console.WriteLine("{0:p}", v2);

      Console.WriteLine("{0:X}", x);

      Console.WriteLine("{0:D12}", x);

      Console.WriteLine("{0:C}", 189.99);
   }
}
```

The output is shown here:

```
17688.66
17,688.65849
1.768866e+004
17688.65849
15.00 %
15
000000000021
$189.99
```

Notice the effect of the precision specifier in several of the formats.

Understanding Argument Numbers

It is important to understand that the argument associated with a format item is determined by the argument number, not the argument's position in the argument list. This means the same argument can be output more than once within the same call to **WriteLine( )**. It also means that arguments can be displayed in a sequence different than they are specified in the argument list. For example, consider the following program:

```
using System;

class FormatDemo2 {
  static void Main() {

    // Format the same argument three different ways:
    Console.WriteLine("{0:F2}  {0:F3}  {0:e}", 10.12345);

    // Display arguments in non-sequential order.
    Console.WriteLine("{2:d} {0:d} {1:d}", 1, 2, 3);
  }
}
```

The output is shown here:

```
10.12  10.123  1.012345e+001
3 1 2
```

In the first **WriteLine( )** statement, the same argument, 10.12345, is formatted three different ways. This is possible because each format specifier refers to the first (and only) argument. In the second **WriteLine( )** statement, the three arguments are displayed in non-sequential order. Remember, there is no rule that format specifiers must use the arguments in sequence. Any format specifier can refer to any argument.

Using String.Format( ) and ToString( ) to Format Data

Although embedding format commands into **WriteLine( )** is a convenient way to format output, sometimes you will want to create a string that contains the formatted data, but not immediately display that string. Doing so lets you format data in advance, allowing you to output it later, to the device of your choosing. This is especially useful in a GUI environment, such as Windows, in which console-based I/O is rarely used, or for preparing output for a web page.

In general, there are two ways to obtain the formatted string representation of a value. One way is to use **String.Format( )**. The other is to pass a format specifier to the **ToString( )** method of the built-in numeric types. Each approach is examined here.

Using String.Format( ) to Format Values

You can obtain a formatted value by calling one of the **Format( )** methods defined by **String**. They are shown in Table 22-5. **Format( )** works much like **WriteLine( )**, except that it returns a formatted string rather than outputting it to the console.

Method	Description
public static string Format(string *format*, object *arg0*)	Formats *arg0* according to the format command in *format*. Returns a copy of *format* in which formatted data has been substituted for the format command.
public static string Format(string *format*, object *arg0*, object *arg1*)	Formats *arg0* and *arg1* according to the corresponding format commands in *format*. Returns a copy of *format* in which formatted data has been substituted for the format commands.
public static string Format(string *format*, object *arg0*, object *arg1*, object *arg2*)	Formats *arg0*, *arg1*, and *arg2* according to the corresponding format commands in *format*. Returns a copy of *format* in which formatted data has been substituted for the format commands.
public static string Format(string *format*, params object[ ] *args*)	Formats the values passed in *args* according to the format commands in *format*. Returns a copy of *format* in which formatted data has been substituted for each format command.
public static string Format(IFormatProvider *provider*, string *format*, params object[ ] *args*)	Formats the values passed in *args* according to the format commands in *format* using the format provider specified by *provider*. Returns a copy of *format* in which formatted data has been substituted for each format command.

TABLE 22-5   The **Format( )** Methods

Here is the previous format demonstration program rewritten to use **String.Format( )**. It produces the same output as the earlier version.

```
// Use String.Format() to format a value.

using System;

class FormatDemo {
  static void Main() {
    double v = 17688.65849;
    double v2 = 0.15;
    int x = 21;

    string str = String.Format("{0:F2}", v);
    Console.WriteLine(str);

    str = String.Format("{0:N5}", v);
    Console.WriteLine(str);

    str = String.Format("{0:e}", v);
    Console.WriteLine(str);

    str = String.Format("{0:r}", v);
    Console.WriteLine(str);

    str = String.Format("{0:p}", v2);
    Console.WriteLine(str);

    str = String.Format("{0:X}", x);
    Console.WriteLine(str);

    str = String.Format("{0:D12}", x);
    Console.WriteLine(str);

    str = String.Format("{0:C}", 189.99);
    Console.WriteLine(str);
  }
}
```

Like **WriteLine( )**, **String.Format( )** lets you embed regular text along with format specifiers, and you can use more than one format item and value. For example, consider this program, which displays the running sum and product of the numbers 1 through 10:

```
// A closer look at Format().

using System;

class FormatDemo2 {
  static void Main() {
    int i;
    int sum = 0;
    int prod = 1;
    string str;
```

```
    // Display the running sum and product for the
    // numbers 1 through 10.
    for(i=1; i <= 10; i++) {
      sum += i;
      prod *= i;
      str = String.Format("Sum:{0,3:D}  Product:{1,8:D}",
                             sum, prod);
      Console.WriteLine(str);
    }
  }
}
```

The output is shown here:

```
Sum:  1  Product:        1
Sum:  3  Product:        2
Sum:  6  Product:        6
Sum: 10  Product:       24
Sum: 15  Product:      120
Sum: 21  Product:      720
Sum: 28  Product:     5040
Sum: 36  Product:    40320
Sum: 45  Product:   362880
Sum: 55  Product:  3628800
```

In the program, pay close attention to this statement:

```
str = String.Format("Sum:{0,3:D}  Product:{1,8:D}",
                       sum, prod);
```

This call to **Format( )** contains two format items, one for **sum** and one for **prod**. Notice that the argument numbers are specified just as they are when using **WriteLine( )**. Also, notice that regular text, such as "Sum:" is included. This text is passed through and becomes part of the output string.

Using ToString( ) to Format Data

For all of the built-in numeric structure types, such as **Int32** or **Double**, you can use **ToString( )** to obtain a formatted string representation of the value. To do so, you will use this general form of **ToString( )**:

ToString("*format string*")

It returns the string representation of the invoking object as specified by the format specifier passed in *format string*. For example, the following program creates a monetary representation of the value 188.99 through the use of the C format specifier:

```
string str = 189.99.ToString("C");
```

Notice how the format specifier is passed directly to **ToString( )**. Unlike embedded format commands used by **WriteLine( )** or **Format( )**, which supply an argument-number and field-width component, **ToString( )** requires only the format specifier, itself.

Here is a rewrite of the previous format program that uses **ToString( )** to obtain formatted strings. It produces the same output as the earlier versions.

```
// Use ToString() to format values.

using System;

class ToStringDemo {
  static void Main() {
    double v = 17688.65849;
    double v2 = 0.15;
    int x = 21;

    string str = v.ToString("F2");
    Console.WriteLine(str);

    str = v.ToString("N5");
    Console.WriteLine(str);

    str = v.ToString("e");
    Console.WriteLine(str);

    str = v.ToString("r");
    Console.WriteLine(str);

    str = v2.ToString("p");
    Console.WriteLine(str);

    str = x.ToString("X");
    Console.WriteLine(str);

    str = x.ToString("D12");
    Console.WriteLine(str);

    str = 189.99.ToString("C");
    Console.WriteLine(str);
  }
}
```

Creating a Custom Numeric Format

Although the predefined numeric format specifiers are quite useful, C# gives you the ability to define your own, custom format using a feature sometimes called *picture format*. The term *picture format* comes from the fact that you create a custom format by specifying an example (that is, a picture) of how you want the output to look. This approach was mentioned briefly in Part I. Here it is examined in detail.

The Custom Format Placeholder Characters

When you create a custom format, you specify that format by creating an example (or picture) of what you want the data to look like. To do this, you use the characters shown in Table 22-6 as placeholders. Each is examined in turn.

Placeholder	Meaning
#	Digit
.	Decimal point
,	Thousands separator
%	Percentage, which is the value being formatted multiplied by 100
0	Pads with leading and trailing zeros
;	Separates sections that describe the format for positive, negative, and zero values
E0 E+0 E-0 e0 e+0 e-0	Scientific notation

TABLE 22-6   Custom Format Placeholder Characters

The period specifies where the decimal point will be located.

The # placeholder specifies a digit position. The # can occur on the left or right side of the decimal point, or by itself. When one or more #s occur on the right side of the decimal point, they specify the number of decimal digits to display. The value is rounded if necessary. When the # occurs to the left of the decimal point, it specifies the digit positions for the whole-number part of the value. Leading zeros will be added if necessary. If the whole-number portion of the value has more digits than there are #s, the entire whole-number portion will be displayed. In no cases will the whole-number portion of a value be truncated. If there is no decimal point, then the # causes the value to be rounded to its integer value. A zero value that is not significant, such as a trailing zero, will not be displayed. This causes a somewhat odd quirk, however, because a format such as #.## displays nothing at all if the value being formatted is zero. To output a zero value, use the 0 placeholder described next.

The 0 placeholder causes a leading or trailing 0 to be added to ensure that a minimum number of digits will be present. It can be used on both the right and left side of the decimal point. For example,

```
Console.WriteLine("{0:00##.#00}", 21.3);
```

displays this output:

```
0021.300
```

Values containing more digits will be displayed in full on the left side of the decimal point and rounded on the right side.

You can insert commas into large numbers by specifying a pattern that embeds a comma within a sequence of #s. For example, this:

```
Console.WriteLine("{0:#,###.#}", 3421.3);
```

displays

```
3,421.3.
```

It is not necessary to specify each comma for each position. Specifying one comma causes it to be inserted into the value every third digit from the left. For example,

```
Console.WriteLine("{0:#,###.#}", 8763421.3);
```

produces this output:

```
8,763,421.3.
```

Commas have a second meaning. When they occur on the immediate left of the decimal point, they act as a scaling factor. Each comma causes the value to be divided by 1,000. For example,

```
Console.WriteLine("Value in thousands: {0:#,###,.#}", 8763421.3);
```

produces this output:

```
Value in thousands: 8,763.4
```

As the output shows, the value is scaled in terms of thousands.

In addition to the placeholders, a custom format specifier can contain other characters. Any other characters are simply passed through, appearing in the formatted string exactly as they appear in the format specifier. For example, this **WriteLine( )** statement:

```
Console.WriteLine("Fuel efficiency is {0:##.# mpg}", 21.3);
```

produces this output:

```
Fuel efficiency is 21.3 mpg
```

You can also use the escape sequences, such as \t or \n, if necessary.

The *E* and *e* placeholders cause a value to be displayed in scientific notation. At least one 0, but possibly more, must follow the *E* or *e*. The 0s indicate the number of decimal digits that will be displayed. The decimal component will be rounded to fit the format. Using an uppercase *E* causes an uppercase *E* to be displayed; using a lowercase *e* causes a lowercase *e* to be displayed. To ensure that a sign character precedes the exponent, use the *E+* or *e+* forms. To display a sign character for negative values only, use *E, e, E–,* or *e–*.

The ";" is a separator that enables you to specify different formats for positive, negative, and zero values. Here is the general form of a custom format specifier that uses the ";":

positive-fmt;negative-fmt;zero-fmt

Here is an example:

```
Console.WriteLine("{0:#.##;(#.##);0.00}", num);
```

If **num** is positive, the value is displayed with two decimal places. If **num** is negative, the value is displayed with two decimal places and is between a set of parentheses. If **num** is zero, the string 0.00 is displayed. When using the separators, you don't need to supply all parts. If you just want to specify how positive and negative values will look, omit the zero format. (In this case, zero is formatted as a positive value.) Alternatively, you can omit the negative format. In this case, the positive format and the zero format will be separated by two semicolons. This causes the positive format to also be used for negative values.

The following program demonstrates just a few of the many possible custom formats that you can create:

```
// Using custom formats.

using System;

class PictureFormatDemo {
  static void Main() {
    double num = 64354.2345;

    Console.WriteLine("Default format: " + num);

    // Display with 2 decimal places.
    Console.WriteLine("Value with two decimal places: " +
                      "{0:#.##}", num);

    // Display with commas and 2 decimal places.
    Console.WriteLine("Add commas: {0:#,###.##}", num);

    // Display using scientific notation.
    Console.WriteLine("Use scientific notation: " +
                      "{0:#.###e+00}", num);

    // Scale the value by 1000.
    Console.WriteLine("Value in 1,000s: " +
                      "{0:#0,}", num);

    /* Display positive, negative, and zero
       values differently. */
    Console.WriteLine("Display positive, negative, " +
                      "and zero values differently.");
    Console.WriteLine("{0:#.#;(#.##);0.00}", num);
    num = -num;
    Console.WriteLine("{0:#.##;(#.##);0.00}", num);
    num = 0.0;
    Console.WriteLine("{0:#.##;(#.##);0.00}", num);

    // Display a percentage.
    num = 0.17;
    Console.WriteLine("Display a percentage: {0:#%}", num);
  }
}
```

The output is shown here:

```
Default format: 64354.2345
Value with two decimal places: 64354.23
Add commas: 64,354.23
Use scientific notation: 6.435e+04
Value in 1,000s: 64
Display positive, negative, and zero values differently.
64354.2
(64354.23)
0.00
Display a percentage: 17%
```

Formatting Date and Time

In addition to formatting numeric values, another data type to which formatting is often applied is **DateTime**. **DateTime** is a structure that represents date and time. Date and time values can be displayed in a variety of ways. Here are just a few examples:

06/05/2005
Friday, January 1, 2010
12:59:00
12:59:00 PM

Also, the date and time representations can vary from country to country. For these reasons, the .NET Framework provides an extensive formatting subsystem for time and date values.

Date and time formatting is handled through format specifiers. The format specifiers for date and time are shown in Table 22-7. Because the specific date and time representation may vary from country to country and by language, the precise representation generated will be influenced by the cultural settings.

Specifier	Format
D	Date in long form.
d	Date in short form.
F	Date and time in long form.
f	Date and time in short form.
G	Date in short form, time in long form.
g	Date in short form, time in short form.
M	Month and day.
m	Same as M.
O	A form of date and time that includes the time zone. The string produced by the O format can be parsed back into the equivalent date and time. This is called the "round trip" format.
o	Same as O.
R	Date and time in standard, GMT form.
r	Same as R.
s	A sortable form of date and time.
T	Time in long form.
t	Time in short form.
U	Long form, universal form of date and time. Time is displayed as UTC.
u	Short form, universal form of date and time that is sortable.
Y	Month and year.
y	Same as Y.

TABLE 22-7 The Date and Time Format Specifiers

Here is a program that demonstrates the date and time format specifiers:

```
// Format time and date information.

using System;

class TimeAndDateFormatDemo {
  static void Main() {
    DateTime dt = DateTime.Now; // obtain current time

    Console.WriteLine("d format: {0:d}", dt);
    Console.WriteLine("D format: {0:D}", dt);

    Console.WriteLine("t format: {0:t}", dt);
    Console.WriteLine("T format: {0:T}", dt);

    Console.WriteLine("f format: {0:f}", dt);
    Console.WriteLine("F format: {0:F}", dt);

    Console.WriteLine("g format: {0:g}", dt);
    Console.WriteLine("G format: {0:G}", dt);

    Console.WriteLine("m format: {0:m}", dt);
    Console.WriteLine("M format: {0:M}", dt);

    Console.WriteLine("o format: {0:o}", dt);
    Console.WriteLine("O format: {0:O}", dt);

    Console.WriteLine("r format: {0:r}", dt);
    Console.WriteLine("R format: {0:R}", dt);

    Console.WriteLine("s format: {0:s}", dt);

    Console.WriteLine("u format: {0:u}", dt);
    Console.WriteLine("U format: {0:U}", dt);

    Console.WriteLine("y format: {0:y}", dt);
    Console.WriteLine("Y format: {0:Y}", dt);
  }
}
```

Sample output is shown here:

```
d format: 2/11/2010
D format: Thursday, February 11, 2010
t format: 11:21 AM
T format: 11:21:23 AM
f format: Thursday, February 11, 2010 11:21 AM
F format: Thursday, February 11, 2010 11:21:23 AM
g format: 2/11/2010 11:21 AM
G format: 2/11/2010 11:21:23 AM
m format: February 11
M format: February 11
o format: 2010-02-11T11:21:23.3768153-06:00
O format: 2010-02-11T11:21:23.3768153-06:00
r format: Thu, 11 Feb 2010 11:21:23 GMT
```

```
R format: Thu, 11 Feb 2010 11:21:23 GMT
s format: 2010-02-11T11:21:23
u format: 2010-02-11 11:21:23Z
U format: Thursday, February 11, 2010 5:21:23 PM
y format: February, 2010
Y format: February, 2010
```

The next program creates a very simple clock. The time is updated once every second. At the top of each hour, the computer's bell is sounded. It uses the **ToString( )** method of **DateTime** to obtain the formatted time prior to outputting it. If the top of the hour has been reached, then the alert character (\a) is appended to the formatted time, thus ringing the bell.

```
// A simple clock.

using System;

class SimpleClock {
  static void Main() {
    string t;
    int seconds;

    DateTime dt = DateTime.Now;
    seconds = dt.Second;

    for(;;) {
      dt = DateTime.Now;

      // update time if seconds change
      if(seconds != dt.Second) {
        seconds = dt.Second;

        t = dt.ToString("T");

        if(dt.Minute==0 && dt.Second==0)
          t = t + "\a"; // ring bell at top of hour

        Console.WriteLine(t);
      }
    }
  }
}
```

Creating a Custom Date and Time Format

Although the standard date and time format specifiers will apply to the vast majority of situations, you can create your own, custom formats. The process is similar to creating custom formats for the numeric types, as described earlier. In essence, you simply create an example (picture) of what you want the date and time information to look like. To create a custom date and time format, you will use one or more of the placeholders shown in Table 22-8.

If you examine Table 22-8, you will see that the placeholders *d, f, g, m, M, s,* and *t* are the same as the date and time format specifiers shown in Table 22-7. In general, if one of these characters is used by itself, it is interpreted as a format specifier. Otherwise, it is assumed to be a placeholder. If you want to use one of these characters by itself, but have it interpreted as a placeholder, then precede the character with a %.

Placeholder	Replaced By
d	Day of month as a number between 1 and 31.
dd	Day of month as a number between 1 and 31. A leading zero prefixes the values 1 through 9.
ddd	Abbreviated weekday name.
dddd	Full weekday name.
f, ff, fff, ffff, fffff, ffffff, fffffff	Fractional seconds, with the number of decimal places specified by the number of *fs*. (If uppercase Fs are used, trailing zeros are not displayed.)
g	Era.
h	Hour as a number between 1 and 12.
hh	Hour as a number between 1 and 12. A leading zero prefixes the values 1 through 9.
H	Hour as a number between 0 and 23.
HH	Hour as a number between 0 and 23. A leading zero prefixes the values 0 through 9.
K	Time zone offset in hours. It uses the value of the **DateTime.Kind** property to automatically adjust for local time and UTC time. (This specifier is now recommended over the z-based specifiers.)
m	Minutes.
mm	Minutes. A leading zero prefixes the values 0 through 9.
M	Month as a number between 1 and 12.
MM	Month as a number between 1 and 12. A leading zero prefixes the values 1 through 9.
MMM	Abbreviated month name.
MMMM	Full month name.
s	Seconds.
ss	Seconds. A leading zero prefixes the values 0 through 9.
t	A or P, indicating A.M. or P.M.
tt	A.M. or P.M.
y	Year as two digits, unless only one digit is needed.
yy	Year as two digits. A leading zero prefixes the values 0 through 9.
yyy	Year as at least three digits.
yyyy	Year using four digits.
yyyyy	Year using five digits.
z	Time zone offset in hours.
zz	Time zone offset in hours. A leading zero prefixes the values 0 through 9.
zzz	Time zone offset in hours and minutes.
:	Separator for time components.
/	Separator for date components.
%*fmt*	The standard format associated with *fmt*.

TABLE 22-8 The Custom Date and Time Placeholder Characters

The following program demonstrates several custom time and date formats:

```
// Format time and date information.

using System;

class CustomTimeAndDateFormatsDemo {
  static void Main() {
    DateTime dt = DateTime.Now;

    Console.WriteLine("Time is {0:hh:mm tt}", dt);
    Console.WriteLine("24 hour time is {0:HH:mm}", dt);
    Console.WriteLine("Date is {0:ddd MMM dd, yyyy}", dt);

    Console.WriteLine("Era: {0:gg}", dt);

    Console.WriteLine("Time with seconds: " +
                      "{0:HH:mm:ss tt}", dt);

    Console.WriteLine("Use m for day of month: {0:m}", dt);
    Console.WriteLine("Use m for minutes: {0:%m}", dt);
  }
}
```

The output is shown here:

```
Time is 11:19 AM
24 hour time is 11:19
Date is Thu Feb 11, 2010
Era: A.D.
Time with seconds: 11:19:40 AM
Use m for day of month: February 11
Use m for minutes: 19
```

Formatting Time Spans

Beginning with .NET Framework 4.0, you can also format objects of type **TimeSpan**.
TimeSpan is a structure that represents a span of time. A **TimeSpan** object can be obtained
in various ways, one of which is by subtracting one **DateTime** object from another. Although
it is not common to format a **TimeSpan** value, it warrants a brief mention.

By default, **TimeSpan** supports three standard format specifiers: **c**, **g**, and **G**. These
correspond to an invariant form, a culture-sensitive short form, and a culture-sensitive long
form, which always includes days. **TimeSpan** also supports custom format specifiers. These
are shown in Table 22-9. In general, if one of these characters is used by itself, precede the
character with a %.

Placeholder	Replaced By
d, dd, ddd, dddd, ddddd, dddddd, ddddddd	Whole days. If more than one *d* is specified, then at least that number of digits will be displayed, with leading zeros as needed.
h, hh	Hours (not counting those that are part of whole days). If *hh* is specified, then two digits are displayed, with a leading zero as needed.
m, mm	Minutes (not counting those that are part of whole hours). If *mm* is specified, then two digits are displayed, with a leading zero as needed.
s, ss	Seconds (not counting those that are part of whole minutes). If *ss* is specified, then two digits are displayed, with a leading zero as needed.
f, ff, fff, ffff, fffff, ffffff, fffffff	Fractional seconds. The number of *f*s specify the precision. Remaining digits will be truncated.
F, FF, FFF, FFFF, FFFFF, FFFFFF, FFFFFFF	Fractional seconds. The number of *F*s specify the number of significant digits to display. Trailing zeros are not displayed. Remaining digits will be truncated.

TABLE 22-9   The Custom **TimeSpan** Placeholder Characters

The following program demonstrates the formatting of **TimeSpan** objects by displaying the approximate amount of time it takes a **for** loop to display 1,000 integers:

```
// Format a TimeSpan.

using System;

class TimeSpanDemo {

  static void Main() {
    DateTime start = DateTime.Now;

    // Output the numbers 1 through 1000.
    for(int i = 1; i <= 1000; i++) {
      Console.Write(i + " ");
      if((i % 10) == 0) Console.WriteLine();
    }

    Console.WriteLine();

    DateTime end = DateTime.Now;

    TimeSpan span = end - start;

    Console.WriteLine("Run time: {0:c}", span);
    Console.WriteLine("Run time: {0:g}", span);
    Console.WriteLine("Run time: {0:G}", span);

    Console.WriteLine("Run time: 0.{0:fff} seconds", span);
  }
}
```

Sample output is shown here:

```
. . .
981 982 983 984 985 986 987 988 989 990
991 992 993 994 995 996 997 998 999 1000

Run time: 00:00:00.0140000
Run time: 0:00:00.014
Run time: 0:00:00:00.0140000
Run time: 0.014 seconds
```

Formatting Enumerations

C# allows you to format the values defined by an enumeration. In general, enumeration values can be displayed using their name or their value. The enumeration format specifiers are shown in Table 22-10. Pay special attention to the G and F formats. Enumerations that will be used to represent bit-fields can be preceded by the **Flags** attribute. Typically, bit-fields hold values that represent individual bits and are arranged in powers of two. If the **Flags** attribute is present, then the G specifier will display the names of all of the values that comprise the value, assuming the value is valid. The F specifier will display the names of all of the values that comprise the value if the value can be constructed by ORing together two or more fields defined by the enumeration.

Specifier	Meaning
D	Displays the value as a decimal integer.
d	Same as D.
F	Displays the name of the value. However, if the value can be created by ORing together two or more values defined by the enumeration, then the names of each part of the value will be displayed. (This applies whether or not the **Flags** attribute has been specified.) Otherwise, the value is displayed as an integer.
f	Same as F.
G	Displays the name of the value. If the enumeration is preceded by the **Flags** attribute, then all names that are part of the value will be displayed (assuming a valid value). An invalid value is displayed as an integer.
g	Same as G.
X	Displays the value as a hexadecimal integer. Leading zeros will be added to ensure that at least eight digits are shown.
x	Same as X.

TABLE 22-10   The Enumeration Format Specifiers

The following program demonstrates the enumeration specifiers:

```
// Format an enumeration.

using System;

class EnumFmtDemo {
  enum Direction { North, South, East, West }
  [Flags] enum Status { Ready=0x1, OffLine=0x2,
                        Waiting=0x4, TransmitOK=0x8,
                        RecieveOK=0x10, OnLine=0x20 }

  static void Main() {
    Direction d = Direction.West;

    Console.WriteLine("{0:G}", d);
    Console.WriteLine("{0:F}", d);
    Console.WriteLine("{0:D}", d);
    Console.WriteLine("{0:X}", d);

    Status s = Status.Ready | Status.TransmitOK;

    Console.WriteLine("{0:G}", s);
    Console.WriteLine("{0:F}", s);
    Console.WriteLine("{0:D}", s);
    Console.WriteLine("{0:X}", s);
  }
}
```

The output is shown here:

```
West
West
3
00000003
Ready, TransmitOK
Ready, TransmitOK
9
00000009
```

Multithreaded Programming, Part One

Although C# contains many exciting features, one of its most powerful is its built-in support for *multithreaded programming*. A multithreaded program contains two or more parts that can run concurrently. Each part of such a program is called a *thread*, and each thread defines a separate path of execution. Thus, multithreading is a specialized form of multitasking.

Multithreaded programming relies on a combination of features defined by the C# language and by classes in the .NET Framework. Because support for multithreading is built into C#, many of the problems associated with multithreading in other languages are minimized or eliminated. As you will see, C#'s support of multithreading is both clean and easy to understand.

With the release of version 4.0 of the .NET Framework, two important additions were made that relate to multithreaded applications. The first is the Task Parallel Library (TPL), and the other is Parallel LINQ (PLINQ). Both provide support for parallel programming, and both can take advantage of multiple-processor (multicore) computers. In addition, the TPL streamlines the creation and management of multithreaded applications. Because of this, TPL-based multithreading is now the recommended approach for multithreading in most cases. However, a working knowledge of the original multithreading subsystem is still important for several reasons. First, there is much preexisting (legacy) code that uses the original approach. If you will be working on or maintaining this code, you need to know how the original threading system operated. Second, TPL-based code may still use elements of the original threading system, especially its synchronization features. Third, although the TPL is based on an abstraction called the *task*, it still implicitly relies on threads and the thread-based features described here. Therefore, to fully understand and utilize the TPL, a solid understanding of the material in this chapter is needed.

Finally, it is important to state that multithreading is a very large topic. It is far beyond the scope of this book to cover it in detail. This and the following chapter present an overview of the topic and show several fundamental techniques. Thus, it serves as an introduction to this important topic and provides a foundation upon which you can build.

Multithreading Fundamentals

There are two distinct types of multitasking: process-based and thread-based. It is important to understand the difference between the two. A *process* is, in essence, a program that is executing. Thus, *process-based multitasking* is the feature that allows your computer to run two or more programs concurrently. For example, process-based multitasking allows you to run a word processor at the same time you are using a spreadsheet or browsing the Internet. In process-based multitasking, a program is the smallest unit of code that can be dispatched by the scheduler.

A *thread* is a dispatchable unit of executable code. The name comes from the concept of a "thread of execution." In a *thread-based* multitasking environment, all processes have at least one thread, but they can have more. This means that a single program can perform two or more tasks at once. For instance, a text editor can be formatting text at the same time that it is printing, as long as these two actions are being performed by two separate threads.

The differences between process-based and thread-based multitasking can be summarized like this: Process-based multitasking handles the concurrent execution of programs. Thread-based multitasking deals with the concurrent execution of pieces of the same program.

The principal advantage of multithreading is that it enables you to write very efficient programs because it lets you utilize the idle time that is present in most programs. As you probably know, most I/O devices, whether they be network ports, disk drives, or the keyboard, are much slower than the CPU. Thus, a program will often spend a majority of its execution time waiting to send or receive information to or from a device. By using multithreading, your program can execute another task during this idle time. For example, while one part of your program is sending a file over the Internet, another part can be reading keyboard input, and still another can be buffering the next block of data to send.

A thread can be in one of several states. In general terms, it can be *running*. It can be *ready to run* as soon as it gets CPU time. A running thread can be *suspended,* which is a temporary halt to its execution. It can later be *resumed.* A thread can be *blocked* when waiting for a resource. A thread can be *terminated,* in which case its execution ends and cannot be resumed.

The .NET Framework defines two types of threads: *foreground* and *background.* By default, when you create a thread, it is a foreground thread, but you can change it to a background thread. The only difference between foreground and background threads is that a background thread will be automatically terminated when all foreground threads in its process have stopped.

Along with thread-based multitasking comes the need for a special type of feature called *synchronization,* which allows the execution of threads to be coordinated in certain well-defined ways. C# has a complete subsystem devoted to synchronization, and its key features are also described here.

All processes have at least one thread of execution, which is usually called the *main thread* because it is the one that is executed when your program begins. Thus, the main thread is the thread that all of the preceding example programs in the book have been using. From the main thread, you can create other threads.

C# and the .NET Framework support both process-based and thread-based multitasking. Thus, using C#, you can create and manage both processes and threads. However, little programming effort is required to start a new process because each process is largely separate from the next. Rather, it is C#'s support for multithreading that is important. Because support for multithreading is built in, C# makes it easier to construct high-performance, multithreaded programs than do some other languages.

The classes that support multithreaded programming are defined in the **System.Threading** namespace. Thus, you will usually include this statement at the start of any multithreaded program:

```
using System.Threading;
```

The Thread Class

The multithreading system is built upon the **Thread** class, which encapsulates a thread of execution. The **Thread** class is *sealed*, which means that it cannot be inherited. **Thread** defines several methods and properties that help manage threads. Throughout this chapter, several of its most commonly used members will be examined.

Creating and Starting a Thread

There are a number of ways to create and start a thread. This section describes the basic mechanism. Various options are described later in this chapter.

To create a thread, instantiate an object of type **Thread**, which is a class defined in **System.Threading**. The simplest **Thread** constructor is shown here:

public Thread(ThreadStart *start*)

Here, *start* specifies the method that will be called to begin execution of the thread. In other words, it specifies the thread's entry point. **ThreadStart** is a delegate defined by the .NET Framework as shown here:

public delegate void ThreadStart( )

Thus, your entry point method must have a **void** return type and take no arguments.

Once created, the new thread will not start running until you call its **Start( )** method, which is defined by **Thread**. The **Start( )** method has two forms. The one used here is

public void Start( )

Once started, the thread will run until the entry point method returns. Thus, when the thread's entry point method returns, the thread automatically stops. If you try to call **Start( )** on a thread that has already been started, a **ThreadStateException** will be thrown.

Here is an example that creates a new thread and starts it running:

```
// Create a thread of execution.

using System;
using System.Threading;

class MyThread {
  public int Count;
  string thrdName;

  public MyThread(string name) {
    Count = 0;
    thrdName = name;
  }
```

```
    // Entry point of thread.
    public void Run() {
      Console.WriteLine(thrdName + " starting.");

      do {
        Thread.Sleep(500);
        Console.WriteLine("In " + thrdName +
                         ", Count is " + Count);
        Count++;
      } while(Count < 10);

      Console.WriteLine(thrdName + " terminating.");
    }
}

class MultiThread {
  static void Main() {
    Console.WriteLine("Main thread starting.");

    // First, construct a MyThread object.
    MyThread mt = new MyThread("Child #1");

    // Next, construct a thread from that object.
    Thread newThrd = new Thread(mt.Run);

    // Finally, start execution of the thread.
    newThrd.Start();

    do {
      Console.Write(".");
      Thread.Sleep(100);
    } while (mt.Count != 10);

    Console.WriteLine("Main thread ending.");
  }
}
```

Let's look closely at this program. **MyThread** defines a class that will be used to create a second thread of execution. Inside its **Run( )** method, a loop is established that counts from 0 to 9. Notice the call to **Sleep( )**, which is a **static** method defined by **Thread**. The **Sleep( )** method causes the thread from which it is called to suspend execution for the specified period of milliseconds. The form used by the program is shown here:

public static void Sleep(int *millisecondsTimeout*)

The number of milliseconds to suspend is specified in *millisecondsTimeout*. If *millisecondsTimeout* is zero, the calling thread is suspended only to allow a waiting thread to execute.

Inside **Main( )**, a new **Thread** object is created by the following sequence of statements:

```
// First, construct a MyThread object.
MyThread mt = new MyThread("Child #1");

// Next, construct a thread from that object.
Thread newThrd = new Thread(mt.Run);
```

```
// Finally, start execution of the thread.
newThrd.Start();
```

As the comments suggest, first an object of **MyThread** is created. This object is then used to construct a **Thread** object by passing the **mt.Run( )** method as the entry point. Finally, execution of the new thread is started by calling **Start( )**. This causes **mt.Run( )** to begin executing in its own thread. After calling **Start( )**, execution of the main thread returns to **Main( )**, and it enters **Main( )**'s **do** loop. Both threads continue running, sharing the CPU, until their loops finish. The output produced by this program is as follows. (The precise output that you see may vary slightly because of differences in your execution environment, operating system, and task load.)

```
Main thread starting.
Child #1 starting.
.....In Child #1, Count is 0
.....In Child #1, Count is 1
.....In Child #1, Count is 2
.....In Child #1, Count is 3
.....In Child #1, Count is 4
.....In Child #1, Count is 5
.....In Child #1, Count is 6
.....In Child #1, Count is 7
.....In Child #1, Count is 8
.....In Child #1, Count is 9
Child #1 terminating.
Main thread ending.
```

Often in a multithreaded program, you will want the main thread to be the last thread to finish running. Technically, a program continues to run until all of its foreground threads have finished. Thus, having the main thread finish last is not a requirement. It is, however, good practice to follow because it clearly defines your program's endpoint. The preceding program tries to ensure that the main thread will finish last by checking the value of **Count** within **Main( )**'s **do** loop, stopping when **Count** equals 10, and through the use of calls to **Sleep( )**. However, this is an imperfect approach. Later in this chapter, you will see better ways for one thread to wait until another finishes.

Some Simple Improvements

While the preceding program is perfectly valid, some easy improvements will make it more efficient. First, it is possible to have a thread begin execution as soon as it is created. In the case of **MyThread**, this is done by instantiating a **Thread** object inside **MyThread**'s constructor. Second, there is no need for **MyThread** to store the name of the thread since **Thread** defines a property called **Name** that can be used for this purpose. **Name** is defined like this:

> public string Name { get; set; }

Since **Name** is a read-write property, you can use it to set the name of a thread or to retrieve the thread's name.

Here is a version of the preceding program that makes these three improvements:

```
// An alternate way to start a thread.

using System;
```

```
using System.Threading;

class MyThread {
  public int Count;
  public Thread Thrd;

  public MyThread(string name) {
    Count = 0;
    Thrd = new Thread(this.Run);
    Thrd.Name = name; // set the name of the thread
    Thrd.Start(); // start the thread
  }

  // Entry point of thread.
  void Run() {
    Console.WriteLine(Thrd.Name + " starting.");

    do {
      Thread.Sleep(500);
      Console.WriteLine("In " + Thrd.Name +
                          ", Count is " + Count);
      Count++;
    } while(Count < 10);

    Console.WriteLine(Thrd.Name + " terminating.");
  }
}

class MultiThreadImproved {
  static void Main() {
    Console.WriteLine("Main thread starting.");

    // First, construct a MyThread object.
    MyThread mt = new MyThread("Child #1");

    do {
      Console.Write(".");
      Thread.Sleep(100);
    } while (mt.Count != 10);

    Console.WriteLine("Main thread ending.");
  }
}
```

This version produces the same output as before. Notice that the thread object is stored in **Thrd** inside **MyThread**.

Creating Multiple Threads

The preceding examples have created only one child thread. However, your program can spawn as many threads as it needs. For example, the following program creates three child threads:

```csharp
// Create multiple threads of execution.

using System;
using System.Threading;

class MyThread {
  public int Count;
  public Thread Thrd;

  public MyThread(string name) {
    Count = 0;
    Thrd = new Thread(this.Run);
    Thrd.Name = name;
    Thrd.Start();
  }

  // Entry point of thread.
  void Run() {
    Console.WriteLine(Thrd.Name + " starting.");

    do {
      Thread.Sleep(500);
      Console.WriteLine("In " + Thrd.Name +
                        ", Count is " + Count);
      Count++;
    } while(Count < 10);

    Console.WriteLine(Thrd.Name + " terminating.");
  }
}

class MoreThreads {
  static void Main() {
    Console.WriteLine("Main thread starting.");

    // Construct three threads.
    MyThread mt1 = new MyThread("Child #1");
    MyThread mt2 = new MyThread("Child #2");
    MyThread mt3 = new MyThread("Child #3");

    do {
      Console.Write(".");
      Thread.Sleep(100);
    } while (mt1.Count < 10 ||
             mt2.Count < 10 ||
             mt3.Count < 10);

    Console.WriteLine("Main thread ending.");
  }
}
```

Sample output from this program is shown next:

```
Main thread starting.
.Child #1 starting.
Child #2 starting.
Child #3 starting.
....In Child #1, Count is 0
In Child #2, Count is 0
In Child #3, Count is 0
.....In Child #1, Count is 1
In Child #2, Count is 1
In Child #3, Count is 1
.....In Child #1, Count is 2
In Child #2, Count is 2
In Child #3, Count is 2
.....In Child #1, Count is 3
In Child #2, Count is 3
In Child #3, Count is 3
.....In Child #1, Count is 4
In Child #2, Count is 4
In Child #3, Count is 4
.....In Child #1, Count is 5
In Child #2, Count is 5
In Child #3, Count is 5
.....In Child #1, Count is 6
In Child #2, Count is 6
In Child #3, Count is 6
.....In Child #1, Count is 7
In Child #2, Count is 7
In Child #3, Count is 7
.....In Child #1, Count is 8
In Child #2, Count is 8
In Child #3, Count is 8
.....In Child #1, Count is 9
Child #1 terminating.
In Child #2, Count is 9
Child #2 terminating.
In Child #3, Count is 9
Child #3 terminating.
Main thread ending.
```

As you can see, once started, all three child threads share the CPU. Again, because of differences among system configurations, operating systems, and other environmental factors, when you run the program, the output you see may differ slightly from that shown here.

Determining When a Thread Ends

Often it is useful to know when a thread has ended. In the preceding examples, this was accomplished by watching the **Count** variable—hardly a satisfactory or generalizable solution. Fortunately, **Thread** provides two means by which you can determine whether a thread has ended. First, you can interrogate the read-only **IsAlive** property for the thread. It is defined like this:

```
public bool IsAlive { get; }
```

IsAlive returns true if the thread upon which it is called is still running. It returns false otherwise. To try **IsAlive**, substitute this version of **MoreThreads** for the one shown in the preceding program:

```
// Use IsAlive to wait for threads to end.
class MoreThreads {
  static void Main() {
    Console.WriteLine("Main thread starting.");

    // Construct three threads.
    MyThread mt1 = new MyThread("Child #1");
    MyThread mt2 = new MyThread("Child #2");
    MyThread mt3 = new MyThread("Child #3");

    do {
      Console.Write(".");
      Thread.Sleep(100);
    } while (mt1.Thrd.IsAlive &&
             mt2.Thrd.IsAlive &&
             mt3.Thrd.IsAlive);

    Console.WriteLine("Main thread ending.");
  }
}
```

This version produces the same output as before. The only difference is that it uses **IsAlive** to wait for the child threads to terminate.

Another way to wait for a thread to finish is to call **Join( )**. Its simplest form is shown here:

```
public void Join( )
```

Join( ) waits until the thread on which it is called terminates. Its name comes from the concept of the calling thread waiting until the specified thread *joins* it. A **ThreadStateException** will be thrown if the thread has not been started. Additional forms of **Join( )** allow you to specify a maximum amount of time that you want to wait for the specified thread to terminate.

Here is a program that uses **Join( )** to ensure that the main thread is the last to stop:

```
// Use Join().

using System;
using System.Threading;

class MyThread {
  public int Count;
  public Thread Thrd;

  public MyThread(string name) {
    Count = 0;
    Thrd = new Thread(this.Run);
    Thrd.Name = name;
    Thrd.Start();
  }
```

```
  // Entry point of thread.
  void Run() {
    Console.WriteLine(Thrd.Name + " starting.");

    do {
      Thread.Sleep(500);
      Console.WriteLine("In " + Thrd.Name +
                        ", Count is " + Count);
      Count++;
    } while(Count < 10);

    Console.WriteLine(Thrd.Name + " terminating.");
  }
}

// Use Join() to wait for threads to end.
class JoinThreads {
  static void Main() {
    Console.WriteLine("Main thread starting.");

    // Construct three threads.
    MyThread mt1 = new MyThread("Child #1");
    MyThread mt2 = new MyThread("Child #2");
    MyThread mt3 = new MyThread("Child #3");

    mt1.Thrd.Join();
    Console.WriteLine("Child #1 joined.");

    mt2.Thrd.Join();
    Console.WriteLine("Child #2 joined.");

    mt3.Thrd.Join();
    Console.WriteLine("Child #3 joined.");

    Console.WriteLine("Main thread ending.");
  }
}
```

Sample output from this program is shown here. Remember when you try the program, your output may vary slightly.

```
Main thread starting.
Child #1 starting.
Child #2 starting.
Child #3 starting.
In Child #1, Count is 0
In Child #2, Count is 0
In Child #3, Count is 0
In Child #1, Count is 1
In Child #2, Count is 1
In Child #3, Count is 1
In Child #1, Count is 2
In Child #2, Count is 2
In Child #3, Count is 2
```

```
In Child #1, Count is 3
In Child #2, Count is 3
In Child #3, Count is 3
In Child #1, Count is 4
In Child #2, Count is 4
In Child #3, Count is 4
In Child #1, Count is 5
In Child #2, Count is 5
In Child #3, Count is 5
In Child #1, Count is 6
In Child #2, Count is 6
In Child #3, Count is 6
In Child #1, Count is 7
In Child #2, Count is 7
In Child #3, Count is 7
In Child #1, Count is 8
In Child #2, Count is 8
In Child #3, Count is 8
In Child #1, Count is 9
Child #1 terminating.
In Child #2, Count is 9
Child #2 terminating.
In Child #3, Count is 9
Child #3 terminating.
Child #1 joined.
Child #2 joined.
Child #3 joined.
Main thread ending.
```

As you can see, after the calls to **Join( )** return, the threads have stopped executing.

Passing an Argument to a Thread

In the early days of the .NET Framework, it was not possible to pass an argument to a thread when the thread was started because the method that serves as the entry point to a thread could not have a parameter. If information needed to be passed to a thread, various workarounds (such as using a shared variable) were required. However, this deficiency was subsequently remedied, and today it is possible to pass an argument to a thread. To do so, you must use different forms of **Start( )**, the **Thread** constructor, and the entry point method.

An argument is passed to a thread through this version of **Start( )**:

public void Start(object *parameter*)

The object passed to *parameter* is automatically passed to the thread's entry point method. Thus, to pass an argument to a thread, you pass it to **Start( )**.

To make use of the parameterized version of **Start( )**, you must use the following form of the **Thread** constructor:

public Thread(ParameterizedThreadStart *start*)

Here, *start* specifies the method that will be called to begin execution of the thread. Notice in this version, the type of *start* is **ParameterizedThreadStart** rather than **ThreadStart**, as used by the preceding examples. **ParameterizedThreadStart** is a delegate that is declared as shown here:

public delegate void ParameterizedThreadStart(object *obj*)

As you can see, this delegate takes an argument of type **object**. Therefore, to use this form of the **Thread** constructor, the thread entry point method must have an **object** parameter. Here is an example that demonstrates the passing of an argument to a thread:

```csharp
// Passing an argument to the thread method.

using System;
using System.Threading;

class MyThread {
  public int Count;
  public Thread Thrd;

  // Notice that MyThread is also passed an int value.
  public MyThread(string name, int num) {
    Count = 0;

    // Explicitly invoke ParameterizedThreadStart constructor
    // for the sake of illustration.
    Thrd = new Thread(this.Run);

    Thrd.Name = name;

     // Here, Start() is passed num as an argument.
    Thrd.Start(num);
  }

  // Notice that this version of Run() has
  // a parameter of type object.
  void Run(object num) {
    Console.WriteLine(Thrd.Name +
                      " starting with count of " + num);

    do {
      Thread.Sleep(500);
      Console.WriteLine("In " + Thrd.Name +
                        ", Count is " + Count);
      Count++;
    } while(Count < (int) num);

    Console.WriteLine(Thrd.Name + " terminating.");
  }
}

class PassArgDemo {
  static void Main() {

    // Notice that the iteration count is passed
    // to these two MyThread objects.
```

```
    MyThread mt = new MyThread("Child #1", 5);
    MyThread mt2 = new MyThread("Child #2", 3);

    do {
      Thread.Sleep(100);
    } while (mt.Thrd.IsAlive | mt2.Thrd.IsAlive);

    Console.WriteLine("Main thread ending.");
  }
}
```

The output is shown here. (The actual output you see may vary.)

```
Child #1 starting with count of 5
Child #2 starting with count of 3
In Child #2, Count is 0
In Child #1, Count is 0
In Child #1, Count is 1
In Child #2, Count is 1
In Child #2, Count is 2
Child #2 terminating.
In Child #1, Count is 2
In Child #1, Count is 3
In Child #1, Count is 4
Child #1 terminating.
Main thread ending.
```

As the output shows, the first thread iterates five times and the second thread iterates three times. The iteration count is specified in the **MyThread** constructor and then passed to the thread entry method **Run( )** through the use of the **ParameterizedThreadStart** version of **Start( )**.

The IsBackground Property

As mentioned earlier, the .NET Framework defines two types of threads: foreground and background. The only difference between the two is that a process won't end until all of its foreground threads have ended, but background threads are terminated automatically after all foreground threads have stopped. By default, a thread is created as a foreground thread. It can be changed to a background thread by using the **IsBackground** property defined by **Thread**, as shown here:

    public bool IsBackground { get; set; }

To set a thread to background, simply assign **IsBackground** a **true** value. A value of **false** indicates a foreground thread.

Thread Priorities

Each thread has a priority setting associated with it. A thread's priority determines, in part, how frequently a thread gains access to the CPU. In general, low-priority threads gain access to the CPU less often than high-priority threads. As a result, within a given period of time, a low-priority thread will often receive less CPU time than a high-priority thread. As you might expect, how much CPU time a thread receives profoundly affects its execution characteristics and its interaction with other threads currently executing in the system.

It is important to understand that factors other than a thread's priority can also affect how frequently a thread gains access to the CPU. For example, if a high-priority thread is waiting on some resource, perhaps for keyboard input, it will be blocked, and a lower-priority thread will run. Thus, in this situation, a low-priority thread may gain greater access to the CPU than the high-priority thread over a specific period. Finally, precisely how task scheduling is implemented by the operating system affects how CPU time is allocated.

When a child thread is started, it receives a default priority setting. You can change a thread's priority through the **Priority** property, which is a member of **Thread**. This is its general form:

   public ThreadPriority Priority{ get; set; }

ThreadPriority is an enumeration that defines the following five priority settings:

   ThreadPriority.Highest
   ThreadPriority.AboveNormal
   ThreadPriority.Normal
   ThreadPriority.BelowNormal
   ThreadPriority.Lowest

The default priority setting for a thread is **ThreadPriority.Normal**.

To understand how priorities affect thread execution, we will use an example that executes two threads, one having a higher priority than the other. The threads are created as instances of the **MyThread** class. The **Run( )** method contains a loop that counts the number of iterations. The loop stops when either the count reaches 1,000,000,000 or the static variable **stop** is **true**. Initially, **stop** is set to **false**. The first thread to count to 1,000,000,000 sets **stop** to **true**. This causes the second thread to terminate with its next time slice. Each time through the loop, the string in **currentName** is checked against the name of the executing thread. If they don't match, it means that a task-switch occurred. Each time a task-switch happens, the name of the new thread is displayed and **currentName** is given the name of the new thread. This allows you to watch how often each thread has access to the CPU. After both threads stop, the number of iterations for each loop is displayed.

```
// Demonstrate thread priorities.

using System;
using System.Threading;

class MyThread {
  public int Count;
  public Thread Thrd;

  static bool stop = false;
  static string currentName;

  /* Construct a new thread. Notice that this
     constructor does not actually start the
     threads running. */
  public MyThread(string name) {
    Count = 0;
```

```
    Thrd = new Thread(this.Run);
    Thrd.Name = name;
    currentName = name;
  }

  // Begin execution of new thread.
  void Run() {
    Console.WriteLine(Thrd.Name + " starting.");
    do {
      Count++;

      if(currentName != Thrd.Name) {
        currentName = Thrd.Name;
        Console.WriteLine("In " + currentName);
      }

    } while(stop == false && Count < 1000000000);
    stop = true;

    Console.WriteLine(Thrd.Name + " terminating.");
  }
}

class PriorityDemo {
  static void Main() {
    MyThread mt1 = new MyThread("High Priority");
    MyThread mt2 = new MyThread("Low Priority");

    // Set the priorities.
    mt1.Thrd.Priority = ThreadPriority.AboveNormal;
    mt2.Thrd.Priority = ThreadPriority.BelowNormal;

    // Start the threads.
    mt1.Thrd.Start();
    mt2.Thrd.Start();

    mt1.Thrd.Join();
    mt2.Thrd.Join();

    Console.WriteLine();
    Console.WriteLine(mt1.Thrd.Name + " thread counted to " +
                      mt1.Count);
    Console.WriteLine(mt2.Thrd.Name + " thread counted to " +
                      mt2.Count);
  }
}
```

Here is sample output:

```
High Priority starting.
In High Priority
Low Priority starting.
In Low Priority
In High Priority
```

```
In Low Priority
In High Priority
In Low Priority
In High Priority
In Low Priority
In High Priority
In Low Priority
In High Priority
High Priority terminating.
Low Priority terminating.

High Priority thread counted to 1000000000
Low Priority thread counted to 23996334
```

In this run, of the CPU time allotted to the program, the high-priority thread got approximately 98 percent. Of course, the precise output you see may vary, depending on the speed of your CPU and the number of other tasks running on the system. Which version of Windows you are running will also have an effect.

Because multithreaded code can behave differently in different environments, you should never base your code on the execution characteristics of a single environment. For example, in the preceding example, it would be a mistake to assume that the low-priority thread will always execute at least a small amount of time before the high-priority thread finishes. In a different environment, the high-priority thread might complete before the low-priority thread has executed even once, for example.

Synchronization

When using multiple threads, you will sometimes need to coordinate the activities of two or more of the threads. The process by which this is achieved is called *synchronization*. The most common reason for using synchronization is when two or more threads need access to a shared resource that can be used by only one thread at a time. For example, when one thread is writing to a file, a second thread must be prevented from doing so at the same time. Another situation in which synchronization is needed is when one thread is waiting for an event that is caused by another thread. In this case, there must be some means by which the first thread is held in a suspended state until the event has occurred. Then the waiting thread must resume execution.

The key to synchronization is the concept of a *lock,* which controls access to a block of code within an object. When an object is locked by one thread, no other thread can gain access to the locked block of code. When the thread releases the lock, the object is available for use by another thread.

The lock feature is built into the C# language. Thus, all objects can be synchronized. Synchronization is supported by the keyword **lock**. Since synchronization was designed into C# from the start, it is much easier to use than you might first expect. In fact, for many programs, the synchronization of objects is almost transparent.

The general form of **lock** is shown here:

```
lock(lockObj) {
   // statements to be synchronized
}
```

Here, *lockObj* is a reference to the object being synchronized. If you want to synchronize only a single statement, the curly braces are not needed. A **lock** statement ensures that the section of code protected by the lock for the given object can be used only by the thread that obtains the lock. All other threads are blocked until the lock is removed. The lock is released when the block is exited.

The object you lock on is an object that represents the resource being synchronized. In some cases, this will be an instance of the resource itself or simply an arbitrary instance of **object** that is being used to provide synchronization. A key point to understand about **lock** is that the lock-on object should not be publically accessible. Why? Because it is possible that another piece of code that is outside your control could lock on the object and never release it. In the past, it was common to use a construct such as **lock(this)**. However, this only works if **this** refers to a private object. Because of the potential for error and conceptual mistakes in this regard, **lock(this)** is no longer recommended for general use. Instead, it is better to simply create a private object on which to lock. This is the approach used by the examples in this chapter. Be aware that you will still find many examples of **lock(this)** in legacy C# code. In some cases, it will be safe. In others, it will need to be changed to avoid problems.

The following program demonstrates synchronization by controlling access to a method called **SumIt( )**, which sums the elements of an integer array:

```
// Use lock to synchronize access to an object.

using System;
using System.Threading;

class SumArray {
  int sum;
  object lockOn = new object(); // a private object to lock on

  public int SumIt(int[] nums) {
    lock(lockOn) { // lock the entire method
      sum = 0; // reset sum

      for(int i=0; i < nums.Length; i++) {
        sum += nums[i];
        Console.WriteLine("Running total for " +
               Thread.CurrentThread.Name +
               " is " + sum);
        Thread.Sleep(10); // allow task-switch
      }
      return sum;
    }
  }
}

class MyThread {
  public Thread Thrd;
  int[] a;
  int answer;

  // Create one SumArray object for all instances of MyThread.
```

```
      static SumArray sa = new SumArray();

      // Construct a new thread.
      public MyThread(string name, int[] nums) {
        a = nums;
        Thrd = new Thread(this.Run);
        Thrd.Name = name;
        Thrd.Start(); // start the thread
      }

      // Begin execution of new thread.
      void Run() {
        Console.WriteLine(Thrd.Name + " starting.");

        answer = sa.SumIt(a);

        Console.WriteLine("Sum for " + Thrd.Name +
                          " is " + answer);

        Console.WriteLine(Thrd.Name + " terminating.");
      }
    }

    class Sync {
      static void Main() {
        int[] a = {1, 2, 3, 4, 5};

        MyThread mt1 = new MyThread("Child #1", a);
        MyThread mt2 = new MyThread("Child #2", a);

        mt1.Thrd.Join();
        mt2.Thrd.Join();
      }
    }
```

Here is sample output from the program. (The actual output you see may vary slightly.)

```
Child #1 starting.
Running total for Child #1 is 1
Child #2 starting.
Running total for Child #1 is 3
Running total for Child #1 is 6
Running total for Child #1 is 10
Running total for Child #1 is 15
Running total for Child #2 is 1
Sum for Child #1 is 15
Child #1 terminating.
Running total for Child #2 is 3
Running total for Child #2 is 6
Running total for Child #2 is 10
Running total for Child #2 is 15
Sum for Child #2 is 15
Child #2 terminating.
```

As the output shows, both threads compute the proper sum of 15.

Let's examine this program in detail. The program creates three classes. The first is **SumArray**. It defines the method **SumIt( )**, which sums an integer array. The second class is **MyThread**, which uses a **static** object called **sa** that is of type **SumArray**. Thus, only one object of **SumArray** is shared by all objects of type **MyThread**. This object is used to obtain the sum of an integer array. Notice that **SumArray** stores the running total in a field called **sum**. Thus, if two threads use **SumIt( )** concurrently, both will be attempting to use **sum** to hold the running total. Because this will cause errors, access to **SumIt( )** must be synchronized. Finally, the class **Sync** creates two threads and has them compute the sum of an integer array.

Inside **SumIt( )**, the **lock** statement prevents simultaneous use of the method by different threads. Notice that **lock** uses **lockOn** as the object being synchronized. This is a private object that is used solely for synchronization. **Sleep( )** is called to purposely allow a task-switch to occur, if one can—but it can't in this case. Because the code within **SumIt( )** is locked, it can be used by only one thread at a time. Thus, when the second child thread begins execution, it does not enter **SumIt( )** until after the first child thread is done with it. This ensures the correct result is produced.

To understand the effects of **lock** fully, try removing it from the body of **SumIt( )**. After doing this, **SumIt( )** is no longer synchronized, and any number of threads can use it concurrently on the same object. The problem with this is that the running total is stored in **sum**, which will be changed by each thread that calls **SumIt( )**. Thus, when two threads call **SumIt( )** at the same time on the same object, incorrect results are produced because **sum** reflects the summation of both threads, mixed together. For example, here is sample output from the program after **lock** has been removed from **SumIt( )**:

```
Child #1 starting.
Running total for Child #1 is 1
Child #2 starting.
Running total for Child #2 is 1
Running total for Child #1 is 3
Running total for Child #2 is 5
Running total for Child #1 is 8
Running total for Child #2 is 11
Running total for Child #1 is 15
Running total for Child #2 is 19
Running total for Child #1 is 24
Running total for Child #2 is 29
Sum for Child #1 is 29
Child #1 terminating.
Sum for Child #2 is 29
Child #2 terminating.
```

As the output shows, both child threads are using **SumIt( )** at the same time on the same object, and the value of **sum** is corrupted.

The effects of **lock** are summarized here:

- For any given object, once a lock has been acquired, the object is locked and no other thread can acquire the lock.

- Other threads trying to acquire the lock on the same object will enter a wait state until the code is unlocked.

- When a thread leaves the locked block, the object is unlocked.

An Alternative Approach

Although locking a method's code, as shown in the previous example, is an easy and effective means of achieving synchronization, it will not work in all cases. For example, you might want to synchronize access to a method of a class you did not create, which is itself not synchronized. This can occur if you want to use a class that was written by a third party and for which you do not have access to the source code. Thus, it is not possible for you to add a **lock** statement to the appropriate method within the class. How can access to an object of this class be synchronized? Fortunately, the solution to this problem is simple: Lock access to the object from code outside the object by specifying the object in a **lock** statement. For example, here is an alternative implementation of the preceding program. Notice that the code within **SumIt( )** is no longer locked and no longer declares the **lockOn** object. Instead, calls to **SumIt( )** are locked within **MyThread**.

```
// Another way to use lock to synchronize access to an object.

using System;
using System.Threading;

class SumArray {
  int sum;

  public int SumIt(int[] nums) {
    sum = 0; // reset sum

    for(int i=0; i < nums.Length; i++) {
      sum += nums[i];
      Console.WriteLine("Running total for " +
              Thread.CurrentThread.Name +
              " is " + sum);
      Thread.Sleep(10); // allow task-switch
    }
    return sum;
  }
}

class MyThread {
  public Thread Thrd;
  int[] a;
  int answer;

  /* Create one SumArray object for all
     instances of MyThread. */
  static SumArray sa = new SumArray();

  // Construct a new thread.
  public MyThread(string name, int[] nums) {
    a = nums;
    Thrd = new Thread(this.Run);
    Thrd.Name = name;
    Thrd.Start(); // start the thread
  }
```

```
    // Begin execution of new thread.
    void Run() {
      Console.WriteLine(Thrd.Name + " starting.");

      // Lock calls to SumIt().
      lock(sa) answer = sa.SumIt(a);

      Console.WriteLine("Sum for " + Thrd.Name +
                          " is " + answer);

      Console.WriteLine(Thrd.Name + " terminating.");
    }
}

class Sync {
  static void Main() {
    int[] a = {1, 2, 3, 4, 5};

    MyThread mt1 = new MyThread("Child #1", a);
    MyThread mt2 = new MyThread("Child #2", a);

    mt1.Thrd.Join();
    mt2.Thrd.Join();
  }
}
```

Here, the call to **sa.SumIt( )** is locked, rather than the code inside **SumIt( )** itself. The code that accomplishes this is shown here:

```
// Lock calls to SumIt().
lock(sa) answer = sa.SumIt(a);
```

Because **sa** is a private object, it is safe to lock on. Using this approach, the program produces the same correct results as the original approach.

The Monitor Class and lock

The C# keyword **lock** is really just shorthand for using the synchronization features defined by the **Monitor** class, which is defined in the **System.Threading** namespace. **Monitor** defines several methods that control or manage synchronization. For example, to obtain a lock on an object, call **Enter( )**. To release a lock, call **Exit( )**. The simplest form of **Enter( )** is shown here, along with the **Exit( )** method:

> public static void Enter(object *obj*)
> public static void Exit(object *obj*)

Here, *obj* is the object being synchronized. If the object is not available when **Enter( )** is called, the calling thread will wait until it becomes available. You will seldom use **Enter( )** or **Exit( )**, however, because a **lock** block automatically provides the equivalent. For this reason, **lock** is the preferred method of obtaining a lock on an object when programming in C#.

One method in **Monitor** that you may find useful on occasion is **TryEnter( )**. One of its forms is shown here:

> public static bool TryEnter(object *obj*)

It returns true if the calling thread obtains a lock on *obj* and false if it doesn't. In no case does the calling thread wait. You could use this method to implement an alternative if the desired object is unavailable.

Monitor also defines these three methods: **Wait( )**, **Pulse( )**, and **PulseAll( )**. They are described in the next section.

Thread Communication Using Wait( ), Pulse( ), and PulseAll( )

Consider the following situation. A thread called *T* is executing inside a **lock** block and needs access to a resource, called *R*, that is temporarily unavailable. What should *T* do? If *T* enters some form of polling loop that waits for *R*, then *T* ties up the lock, blocking other threads' access to it. This is a less than optimal solution because it partially defeats the advantages of programming for a multithreaded environment. A better solution is to have *T* temporarily relinquish the lock, allowing another thread to run. When *R* becomes available, *T* can be notified and resume execution. Such an approach relies upon some form of interthread communication in which one thread can notify another that it is blocked and be notified when it can resume execution. C# supports interthread communication with the **Wait( )**, **Pulse( )**, and **PulseAll( )** methods.

The **Wait( )**, **Pulse( )**, and **PulseAll( )** methods are defined by the **Monitor** class. These methods can be called only from within a locked block of code. Here is how they are used. When a thread is temporarily blocked from running, it calls **Wait( )**. This causes the thread to go to sleep and the lock for that object to be released, allowing another thread to acquire the lock. At a later point, the sleeping thread is awakened when some other thread enters the same lock and calls **Pulse( )** or **PulseAll( )**. A call to **Pulse( )** resumes the first thread in the queue of threads waiting for the lock. A call to **PulseAll( )** signals the release of the lock to all waiting threads.

Here are two commonly used forms of **Wait( )**:

```
public static bool Wait(object obj)
public static bool Wait(object obj, int millisecondsTimeout)
```

The first form waits until notified. The second form waits until notified or until the specified period of milliseconds has expired. For both, *obj* specifies the object upon which to wait.

Here are the general forms for **Pulse( )** and **PulseAll( )**:

```
public static void Pulse(object obj)
public static void PulseAll(object obj)
```

Here, *obj* is the object being released.

A **SynchronizationLockException** will be thrown if **Wait( )**, **Pulse( )**, or **PulseAll( )** is called from code that is not within synchronized code, such as a **lock** block.

An Example That Uses Wait( ) and Pulse( )

To understand the need for and the application of **Wait( )** and **Pulse( )**, we will create a program that simulates the ticking of a clock by displaying the words "Tick" and "Tock" on the screen. To accomplish this, we will create a class called **TickTock** that contains two methods: **Tick( )** and **Tock( )**. The **Tick( )** method displays the word "Tick" and **Tock( )** displays "Tock". To run the clock, two threads are created, one that calls **Tick( )** and one that calls **Tock( )**. The goal is to make the two threads execute in a way that the output from the program displays a consistent "Tick Tock"—that is, a repeated pattern of one "Tick" followed by one "Tock."

```
// Use Wait() and Pulse() to create a ticking clock.

using System;
using System.Threading;

class TickTock {
  object lockOn = new object();

  public void Tick(bool running) {
    lock(lockOn) {
      if(!running) { // stop the clock
        Monitor.Pulse(lockOn); // notify any waiting threads
        return;
      }

      Console.Write("Tick ");
      Monitor.Pulse(lockOn); // let Tock() run

      Monitor.Wait(lockOn); // wait for Tock() to complete
    }
  }

  public void Tock(bool running) {
    lock(lockOn) {
      if(!running) { // stop the clock
        Monitor.Pulse(lockOn); // notify any waiting threads
        return;
      }

      Console.WriteLine("Tock");
      Monitor.Pulse(lockOn); // let Tick() run

      Monitor.Wait(lockOn); // wait for Tick() to complete
    }
  }
}

class MyThread {
  public Thread Thrd;
  TickTock ttOb;

  // Construct a new thread.
  public MyThread(string name, TickTock tt) {
    Thrd = new Thread(this.Run);
    ttOb = tt;
    Thrd.Name = name;
    Thrd.Start();
  }

  // Begin execution of new thread.
  void Run() {
```

```
        if(Thrd.Name == "Tick") {
          for(int i=0; i<5; i++) ttOb.Tick(true);
          ttOb.Tick(false);
        }
        else {
          for(int i=0; i<5; i++) ttOb.Tock(true);
          ttOb.Tock(false);
        }
      }
    }

class TickingClock {
  static void Main() {
    TickTock tt = new TickTock();
    MyThread mt1 = new MyThread("Tick", tt);
    MyThread mt2 = new MyThread("Tock", tt);

    mt1.Thrd.Join();
    mt2.Thrd.Join();
    Console.WriteLine("Clock Stopped");
  }
}
```

Here is the output produced by the program:

```
Tick Tock
Tick Tock
Tick Tock
Tick Tock
Tick Tock
Clock Stopped
```

Let's take a close look at this program. In **Main( )**, a **TickTock** object called **tt** is created, and this object is used to start two threads of execution. Inside the **Run( )** method of **MyThread**, if the name of the thread is "Tick," calls to **Tick( )** are made. If the name of the thread is "Tock," the **Tock( )** method is called. Five calls that pass **true** as an argument are made to each method. The clock runs as long as **true** is passed. A final call that passes **false** to each method stops the clock.

The most important part of the program is found in the **Tick( )** and **Tock( )** methods. We will begin with the **Tick( )** method, which, for convenience, is shown here:

```
public void Tick(bool running) {
  lock(lockOn) {
    if(!running) { // stop the clock
      Monitor.Pulse(lockOn); // notify any waiting threads
      return;
    }

    Console.Write("Tick ");
    Monitor.Pulse(lockOn); // let Tock() run

    Monitor.Wait(lockOn); // wait for Tock() to complete
  }
}
```

First, notice that the code in **Tick( )** is contained within a **lock** block. Recall, **Wait( )** and **Pulse( )** can be used only inside synchronized blocks. The method begins by checking the value of the **running** parameter. This parameter is used to provide a clean shutdown of the clock. If it is **false**, then the clock has been stopped. If this is the case, a call to **Pulse( )** is made to enable any waiting thread to run. We will return to this point in a moment. Assuming the clock is running when **Tick( )** executes, the word "Tick" is displayed, and then a call to **Pulse( )** takes place followed by a call to **Wait( )**. The call to **Pulse( )** allows a thread waiting on the same lock to run. The call to **Wait( )** causes **Tick( )** to suspend until another thread calls **Pulse( )**. Thus, when **Tick( )** is called, it displays one "Tick," lets another thread run, and then suspends.

The **Tock( )** method is an exact copy of **Tick( )**, except that it displays "Tock." Thus, when entered, it displays "Tock," calls **Pulse( )**, and then waits. When viewed as a pair, a call to **Tick( )** can be followed only by a call to **Tock( )**, which can be followed only by a call to **Tick( )**, and so on. Therefore, the two methods are mutually synchronized.

The reason for the call to **Pulse( )** when the clock is stopped is to allow a final call to **Wait( )** to succeed. Remember, both **Tick( )** and **Tock( )** execute a call to **Wait( )** after displaying their message. The problem is that when the clock is stopped, one of the methods will still be waiting. Thus, a final call to **Pulse( )** is required in order for the waiting method to run. As an experiment, try removing this call to **Pulse( )** inside **Tick( )** and watch what happens. As you will see, the program will "hang," and you will need to press CTRL-C to exit. The reason for this is that when the final call to **Tock( )** calls **Wait( )**, there is no corresponding call to **Pulse( )** that lets **Tock( )** conclude. Thus, **Tock( )** just sits there, waiting forever.

Before moving on, if you have any doubt that the calls to **Wait( )** and **Pulse( )** are actually needed to make the "clock" run right, substitute this version of **TickTock** into the preceding program. It has all calls to **Wait( )** and **Pulse( )** removed.

```
// A nonfunctional version of TickTock.
class TickTock {

  object lockOn = new object();

  public void Tick(bool running) {
    lock(lockOn) {
      if(!running) { // stop the clock
        return;
      }

      Console.Write("Tick ");
    }
  }

  public void Tock(bool running) {
    lock(lockOn) {
      if(!running) { // stop the clock
        return;
      }

      Console.WriteLine("Tock");
    }
  }
}
```

After the substitution, the output produced by the program will look like this:

```
Tick Tick Tick Tick Tick Tock
Tock
Tock
Tock
Tock
Clock Stopped
```

Clearly, the **Tick( )** and **Tock( )** methods are no longer synchronized!

Deadlock and Race Conditions

When developing multithreaded programs, you must be careful to avoid deadlock and race conditions. *Deadlock* is, as the name implies, a situation in which one thread is waiting for another thread to do something, but that other thread is waiting on the first. Thus, both threads are suspended, waiting for each other, and neither executes. This situation is analogous to two overly polite people both insisting that the other step through a door first!

Avoiding deadlock seems easy, but it's not. For example, deadlock can occur in roundabout ways. Consider the **TickTock** class. As explained, if a final **Pulse( )** is not executed by **Tick( )** or **Tock( )**, then one or the other will be waiting indefinitely and the program is deadlocked. Often the cause of the deadlock is not readily understood simply by looking at the source code to the program, because concurrently executing threads can interact in complex ways at runtime. To avoid deadlock, careful programming and thorough testing is required. In general, if a multithreaded program occasionally "hangs," deadlock is the likely cause.

A *race condition* occurs when two (or more) threads attempt to access a shared resource at the same time, without proper synchronization. For example, one thread may be writing a new value to a variable while another thread is incrementing the variable's current value. Without synchronization, the new value of the variable will depend on the order in which the threads execute. (Does the second thread increment the original value or the new value written by the first thread?) In situations like this, the two threads are said to be "racing each other," with the final outcome determined by which thread finishes first. Like deadlock, a race condition can occur in difficult-to-discover ways. The solution is prevention: careful programming that properly synchronizes access to shared resources.

Using MethodImplAttribute

It is possible to synchronize an entire method by using the **MethodImplAttribute** attribute. This approach can be used as an alternative to the **lock** statement in cases in which the entire contents of a method are to be locked. **MethodImplAttribute** is defined within the **System.Runtime.CompilerServices** namespace. The constructor that applies to synchronization is shown here:

public MethodImplAttribute(MethodImplOptions *methodImplOptions*)

Here, *methodImplOptions* specifies the implementation attribute. To synchronize a method, specify **MethodImplOptions.Synchronized**. This attribute causes the entire method to be locked on the instance (that is, via **this**). (In the case of **static** methods, the type is locked on.) Thus, it must not be used on a public object or with a public class.

Here is a rewrite of the **TickTock** class that uses **MethodImplAttribute** to provide synchronization:

```
// Use MethodImplAttribute to synchronize a method.

using System;
using System.Threading;
using System.Runtime.CompilerServices;

// Rewrite of TickTock to use MethodImplOptions.Synchronized.
class TickTock {

  /* The following attribute synchronizes the entire
     Tick() method. */
  [MethodImplAttribute(MethodImplOptions.Synchronized)]
  public void Tick(bool running) {
    if(!running) { // stop the clock
      Monitor.Pulse(this); // notify any waiting threads
      return;
    }

    Console.Write("Tick ");
    Monitor.Pulse(this); // let Tock() run

    Monitor.Wait(this); // wait for Tock() to complete
  }


  /* The following attribute synchronizes the entire
     Tock() method. */
  [MethodImplAttribute(MethodImplOptions.Synchronized)]
  public void Tock(bool running) {
    if(!running) { // stop the clock
      Monitor.Pulse(this); // notify any waiting threads
      return;
    }

    Console.WriteLine("Tock");
    Monitor.Pulse(this); // let Tick() run

    Monitor.Wait(this); // wait for Tick() to complete
  }
}

class MyThread {
  public Thread Thrd;
  TickTock ttOb;

  // Construct a new thread.
  public MyThread(string name, TickTock tt) {
    Thrd = new Thread(this.Run);
    ttOb = tt;
    Thrd.Name = name;
    Thrd.Start();
  }

  // Begin execution of new thread.
```

```
    void Run() {
      if(Thrd.Name == "Tick") {
        for(int i=0; i<5; i++) ttOb.Tick(true);
        ttOb.Tick(false);
      }
      else {
        for(int i=0; i<5; i++) ttOb.Tock(true);
        ttOb.Tock(false);
      }
    }
}

class TickingClock {
  static void Main() {
    TickTock tt = new TickTock();
    MyThread mt1 = new MyThread("Tick", tt);
    MyThread mt2 = new MyThread("Tock", tt);

    mt1.Thrd.Join();
    mt2.Thrd.Join();
    Console.WriteLine("Clock Stopped");
  }
}
```

The proper Tick Tock output is the same as before.

As long as the method being synchronized is not defined by a public class or called on a public object, then whether you use **lock** or **MethodImplAttribute** is your decision. Both produce the same results. Because **lock** is a keyword built into C#, that is the approach the examples in this book will use.

REMEMBER *Do not use MethodImplAttribute with public classes or public instances. Instead, use lock, locking on a private object (as explained earlier).*

Using a Mutex and a Semaphore

Although C#'s **lock** statement is sufficient for many synchronization needs, some situations, such as restricting access to a shared resource, are sometimes more conveniently handled by other synchronization mechanisms built into the .NET Framework. The two described here are related to each other: mutexes and semaphores.

The Mutex

A *mutex* is a mutually exclusive synchronization object. This means it can be acquired by one and only one thread at a time. The mutex is designed for those situations in which a shared resource can be used by only one thread at a time. For example, imagine a log file that is shared by several processes, but only one process can write to that file at any one time. A mutex is the perfect synchronization device to handle this situation.

The mutex is supported by the **System.Threading.Mutex** class. It has several constructors. Two commonly used ones are shown here:

    public Mutex( )
    public Mutex(bool *initiallyOwned*)

The first version creates a mutex that is initially unowned. In the second version, if *initiallyOwned* is true, the initial state of the mutex is owned by the calling thread. Otherwise, it is unowned.

To acquire the mutex, your code will call **WaitOne( )** on the mutex. This method is inherited by **Mutex** from the **Thread.WaitHandle** class. Here is its simplest form:

```
public bool WaitOne( );
```

It waits until the mutex on which it is called can be acquired. Thus, it blocks execution of the calling thread until the specified mutex is available. It always returns true.

When your code no longer needs ownership of the mutex, it releases it by calling **ReleaseMutex( )**, shown here:

```
public void ReleaseMutex( )
```

This releases the mutex on which it is called, enabling the mutex to be acquired by another thread.

To use a mutex to synchronize access to a shared resource, you will use **WaitOne( )** and **ReleaseMutex( )**, as shown in the following sequence:

```
Mutex myMtx = new Mutex();

// ...

myMtx.WaitOne(); // wait to acquire the mutex

// Access the shared resource.

myMtx.ReleaseMutex(); // release the mutex
```

When the call to **WaitOne( )** takes place, execution of the thread will suspend until the mutex can be acquired. When the call to **ReleaseMutex( )** takes place, the mutex is released and another thread can acquire it. Using this approach, access to a shared resource can be limited to one thread at a time.

The following program puts this framework into action. It creates two threads, **IncThread** and **DecThread**, which both access a shared resource called **SharedRes.Count**. **IncThread** increments **SharedRes.Count** and **DecThread** decrements it. To prevent both threads from accessing **SharedRes.Count** at the same time, access is synchronized by the **Mtx** mutex, which is also part of the **SharedRes** class.

```
// Use a Mutex.

using System;
using System.Threading;

// This class contains a shared resource (Count),
// and a mutex (Mtx) to control access to it.
class SharedRes {
  public static int Count = 0;
  public static Mutex Mtx = new Mutex();
}

// This thread increments SharedRes.Count.
```

```csharp
class IncThread {
  int num;
  public Thread Thrd;

  public IncThread(string name, int n) {
    Thrd = new Thread(this.Run);
    num = n;
    Thrd.Name = name;
    Thrd.Start();
  }

  // Entry point of thread.
  void Run() {

    Console.WriteLine(Thrd.Name + " is waiting for the mutex.");

    // Acquire the Mutex.
    SharedRes.Mtx.WaitOne();

    Console.WriteLine(Thrd.Name + " acquires the mutex.");

    do {
      Thread.Sleep(500);
      SharedRes.Count++;
      Console.WriteLine("In " + Thrd.Name +
                        ", SharedRes.Count is " + SharedRes.Count);
      num--;
    } while(num > 0);

    Console.WriteLine(Thrd.Name + " releases the mutex.");

    // Release the Mutex.
    SharedRes.Mtx.ReleaseMutex();
  }
}

// This thread decrements SharedRes.Count.
class DecThread {
  int num;
  public Thread Thrd;

  public DecThread(string name, int n) {
    Thrd = new Thread(new ThreadStart(this.Run));
    num = n;
    Thrd.Name = name;
    Thrd.Start();
  }

  // Entry point of thread.
  void Run() {

    Console.WriteLine(Thrd.Name + " is waiting for the mutex.");
```

```
    // Acquire the Mutex.
    SharedRes.Mtx.WaitOne();

    Console.WriteLine(Thrd.Name + " acquires the mutex.");

    do {
      Thread.Sleep(500);
      SharedRes.Count--;
      Console.WriteLine("In " + Thrd.Name +
                        ", SharedRes.Count is " + SharedRes.Count);
      num--;
    } while(num > 0);

    Console.WriteLine(Thrd.Name + " releases the mutex.");

    // Release the Mutex.
    SharedRes.Mtx.ReleaseMutex();
  }
}

class MutexDemo {
  static void Main() {

    // Construct three threads.
    IncThread mt1 = new IncThread("Increment Thread", 5);

    Thread.Sleep(1); // let the Increment thread start

    DecThread mt2 = new DecThread("Decrement Thread", 5);

    mt1.Thrd.Join();
    mt2.Thrd.Join();
  }
}
```

The output is shown here:

```
Increment Thread is waiting for the mutex.
Increment Thread acquires the mutex.
Decrement Thread is waiting for the mutex.
In Increment Thread, SharedRes.Count is 1
In Increment Thread, SharedRes.Count is 2
In Increment Thread, SharedRes.Count is 3
In Increment Thread, SharedRes.Count is 4
In Increment Thread, SharedRes.Count is 5
Increment Thread releases the mutex.
Decrement Thread acquires the mutex.
In Decrement Thread, SharedRes.Count is 4
In Decrement Thread, SharedRes.Count is 3
In Decrement Thread, SharedRes.Count is 2
In Decrement Thread, SharedRes.Count is 1
In Decrement Thread, SharedRes.Count is 0
Decrement Thread releases the mutex.
```

As the output shows, access to **SharedRes.Count** is synchronized, with only one thread at a time being able to change its value.

To prove that the **Mtx** mutex was needed to produce the preceding output, try commenting out the calls to **WaitOne( )** and **ReleaseMutex( )** in the preceding program. When you run the program, you will see the following sequence (the actual output you see may vary):

```
In Increment Thread, SharedRes.Count is 1
In Decrement Thread, SharedRes.Count is 0
In Increment Thread, SharedRes.Count is 1
In Decrement Thread, SharedRes.Count is 0
In Increment Thread, SharedRes.Count is 1
In Decrement Thread, SharedRes.Count is 0
In Increment Thread, SharedRes.Count is 1
In Decrement Thread, SharedRes.Count is 0
In Increment Thread, SharedRes.Count is 1
```

As this output shows, without the mutex, increments and decrements to **SharedRes.Count** are interspersed rather than sequenced.

The mutex created by the previous example is known only to the process that creates it. However, it is possible to create a mutex that is known systemwide. To do so, you must create a named mutex, using one of these constructors:

  public Mutex(bool *initiallyOwned*, string *name*)
  public Mutex(bool *initiallyOwned*, string *name*, out bool *createdNew*)

In both forms, the name of the mutex is passed in *name*. In the first form, if *initiallyOwned* is **true**, then ownership of the mutex is requested. However, because a systemwide mutex might already be owned by another process, it is better to specify **false** for this parameter. In the second form, on return *createdNew* will be **true** if ownership was requested and acquired. It will be **false** if ownership was denied. (There is also a third form of the **Mutex** constructor that allows you to specify a **MutexSecurity** object, which controls access.) Using a named mutex enables you to manage interprocess synchronization.

One other point: It is legal for a thread that has acquired a mutex to make one or more additional calls to **WaitOne( )** prior to calling **ReleaseMutex( )**, and these additional calls will succeed. That is, redundant calls to **WaitOne( )** will not block a thread that already owns the mutex. However, the number of calls to **WaitOne( )** must be balanced by the same number of calls to **ReleaseMutex( )** before the mutex is released.

The Semaphore

A semaphore is similar to a mutex except that it can grant more than one thread access to a shared resource at the same time. Thus, the semaphore is useful when a collection of resources is being synchronized. A semaphore controls access to a shared resource through the use of a counter. If the counter is greater than zero, then access is allowed. If it is zero, access is denied. What the counter is counting are *permits*. Thus, to access the resource, a thread must be granted a permit from the semaphore.

In general, to use a semaphore, the thread that wants access to the shared resource tries to acquire a permit. If the semaphore's counter is greater than zero, the thread acquires a permit, which causes the semaphore's count to be decremented. Otherwise, the thread will block until a permit can be acquired. When the thread no longer needs access to the shared resource, it releases the permit, which causes the semaphore's count to be incremented. If there is another thread waiting for a permit, then that thread will acquire a permit at that time. The number of simultaneous accesses permitted is specified when the semaphore is created. If you create a semaphore that allows only one access, then a semaphore acts just like a mutex.

Semaphores are especially useful in situations in which a shared resource consists of a group or *pool*. For example, a collection of network connections, any of which can be used for communication, is a resource pool. A thread needing a network connection doesn't care which one it gets. In this case, a semaphore offers a convenient mechanism to manage access to the connections.

The semaphore is implemented by **System.Threading.Semaphore**. It has several constructors. The simplest form is shown here:

> public Semaphore(int *initialCount*, int *maximumCount*)

Here, *initialCount* specifies the initial value of the semaphore permit counter, which is the number of permits available. The maximum value of the counter is passed in *maximumCount*. Thus, *maximumCount* represents the maximum number of permits that can granted by the semaphore. The value in *initialCount* specifies how many of these permits are initially available.

Using a semaphore is similar to using a mutex, described earlier. To acquire access, your code will call **WaitOne( )** on the semaphore. This method is inherited by **Semaphore** from the **WaitHandle** class. **WaitOne( )** waits until the semaphore on which it is called can be acquired. Thus, it blocks execution of the calling thread until the specified semaphore can grant permission.

When your code no longer needs ownership of the semaphore, it releases it by calling **Release( )**, which is shown here:

> public int Release( )
> public int Release(int *releaseCount*)

The first form releases one permit. The second form releases the number of permits specified by *releaseCount*. Both return the permit count that existed prior to the release.

It is possible for a thread to call **WaitOne( )** more than once before calling **Release( )**. However, the number of calls to **WaitOne( )** must be balanced by the same number of calls to **Release( )** before the permit is released. Alternatively, you can call the **Release(int)** form, passing a number equal to the number of times that **WaitOne( )** was called.

Here is an example that illustrates the semaphore. In the program, the class **MyThread** uses a semaphore to allow only two **MyThread** threads to be executed at any one time. Thus, the resource being shared is the CPU.

```
// Use a Semaphore.

using System;
using System.Threading;

// This thread allows only two instances of itself
// to run at any one time.
class MyThread {
  public Thread Thrd;
```

```
    // This creates a semaphore that allows up to two
    // permits to be granted and that initially has
    // two permits available.
    static Semaphore sem = new Semaphore(2, 2);

    public MyThread(string name) {
      Thrd = new Thread(this.Run);
      Thrd.Name = name;
      Thrd.Start();
    }

    // Entry point of thread.
    void Run() {

      Console.WriteLine(Thrd.Name + " is waiting for a permit.");

      sem.WaitOne();

      Console.WriteLine(Thrd.Name + " acquires a permit.");

      for(char ch='A'; ch < 'D'; ch++) {
        Console.WriteLine(Thrd.Name + " : " + ch + " ");
        Thread.Sleep(500);
      }

      Console.WriteLine(Thrd.Name + " releases a permit.");

      // Release the semaphore.
      sem.Release();
    }
}


class SemaphoreDemo {
  static void Main() {

    // Construct three threads.
    MyThread mt1 = new MyThread("Thread #1");
    MyThread mt2 = new MyThread("Thread #2");
    MyThread mt3 = new MyThread("Thread #3");

    mt1.Thrd.Join();
    mt2.Thrd.Join();
    mt3.Thrd.Join();
  }
}
```

MyThread declares the semaphore **sem**, as shown here:

```
static Semaphore sem = new Semaphore(2, 2);
```

This creates a semaphore that can grant up to two permits and that initially has both permits available.

In **MyThread.Run( )**, notice that execution cannot continue until a permit is granted by the semaphore, **sem**. If no permits are available, then execution of that thread suspends. When a permit does become available, execution resumes and the thread can run. In **Main( )**, three **MyThread** threads are created. However, only the first two get to execute. The third must wait until one of the other threads terminates. The output, shown here, verifies this. (The actual output you see may vary slightly.)

```
Thread #1 is waiting for a permit.
Thread #1 acquires a permit.
Thread #1 : A
Thread #2 is waiting for a permit.
Thread #2 acquires a permit.
Thread #2 : A
Thread #3 is waiting for a permit.
Thread #1 : B
Thread #2 : B
Thread #1 : C
Thread #2 : C
Thread #1 releases a permit.
Thread #3 acquires a permit.
Thread #3 : A
Thread #2 releases a permit.
Thread #3 : B
Thread #3 : C
Thread #3 releases a permit.
```

The semaphore created by the previous example is known only to the process that creates it. However, it is possible to create a semaphore that is known systemwide. To do so, you must create a named semaphore. To do this, use one of these constructors:

> public Semaphore(int *initialCount*, int *maximumCount*, string *name*)
> public Semaphore(int *initialCount*, int *maximumCount*, string *name*,
>   out bool *createdNew*)

In both forms, the name of the semaphore is passed in *name*. In the first form, if a semaphore by the specified name does not already exist, it is created using the values of *initialCount* and *maximumCount*. If it does already exist, then the values of *initialCount* and *maximumCount* are ignored. In the second form, on return, *createdNew* will be **true** if the semaphore was created. In this case, the values of *initialCount* and *maximumCount* will be used to create the semaphore. If *createdNew* is **false**, then the semaphore already exists and the values of *initialCount* and *maximumCount* are ignored. (There is also a third form of the **Semaphore** constructor that allows you to specify a **SemaphoreSecurity** object, which controls access.) Using a named semaphore enables you to manage interprocess synchronization.

Using Events

C# supports another type of synchronization object: the event. There are two types of events: manual reset and auto reset. These are supported by the classes **ManualResetEvent** and **AutoResetEvent**. These classes are derived from the top-level class **EventWaitHandle**. These classes are used in situations in which one thread is waiting for some event to occur in another thread. When the event takes place, the second thread signals the first, allowing it to resume execution.

The constructors for **ManualResetEvent** and **AutoResetEvent** are shown here:

public ManualResetEvent(bool *initialState*)
public AutoResetEvent(bool *initialState*)

Here, if *initialState* is true, the event is initially signaled. If *initialState* is false, the event is initially non-signaled.

Events are easy to use. For a **ManualResetEvent**, the procedure works like this. A thread that is waiting for some event simply calls **WaitOne( )** on the event object representing that event. **WaitOne( )** returns immediately if the event object is in a signaled state. Otherwise, it suspends execution of the calling thread until the event is signaled. After another thread performs the event, that thread sets the event object to a signaled state by calling **Set( )**. Thus, a call **Set( )** can be understood as signaling that an event has occurred. After the event object is set to a signaled state, the call to **WaitOne( )** will return and the first thread will resume execution. The event is returned to a non-signaled state by calling **Reset( )**.

The difference between **AutoResetEvent** and **ManualResetEvent** is how the event gets reset. For **ManualResetEvent**, the event remains signaled until a call to **Reset( )** is made. For **AutoResetEvent**, the event automatically changes to a non-signaled state as soon as a thread waiting on that event receives the event notification and resumes execution. Thus, a call to **Reset( )** is not necessary when using **AutoResetEvent**.

Here is an example that illustrates **ManualResetEvent**:

```
// Use a manual event object.

using System;
using System.Threading;

// This thread signals the event passed to its constructor.
class MyThread {
  public Thread Thrd;
  ManualResetEvent mre;

  public MyThread(string name, ManualResetEvent evt) {
    Thrd = new Thread(this.Run);
    Thrd.Name = name;
    mre = evt;
    Thrd.Start();
  }

  // Entry point of thread.
  void Run() {
    Console.WriteLine("Inside thread " + Thrd.Name);

    for(int i=0; i<5; i++) {
      Console.WriteLine(Thrd.Name);
      Thread.Sleep(500);
    }

    Console.WriteLine(Thrd.Name + " Done!");
```

```
      // Signal the event.
      mre.Set();
    }
}

class ManualEventDemo {
  static void Main() {
    ManualResetEvent evtObj = new ManualResetEvent(false);

    MyThread mt1 = new MyThread("Event Thread 1", evtObj);

    Console.WriteLine("Main thread waiting for event.");

    // Wait for signaled event.
    evtObj.WaitOne();

    Console.WriteLine("Main thread received first event.");


    // Reset the event.
    evtObj.Reset();


    mt1 = new MyThread("Event Thread 2", evtObj);

    // Wait for signaled event.
    evtObj.WaitOne();

    Console.WriteLine("Main thread received second event.");
  }
}
```

The output is shown here. (The actual output you see may vary slightly.)

```
Inside thread Event Thread 1
Event Thread 1
Main thread waiting for event.
Event Thread 1
Event Thread 1
Event Thread 1
Event Thread 1
Event Thread 1 Done!
Main thread received first event.
Inside thread Event Thread 2
Event Thread 2
Event Thread 2
Event Thread 2
Event Thread 2
Event Thread 2
Event Thread 2 Done!
Main thread received second event.
```

First, notice that **MyThread** is passed a **ManualResetEvent** in its constructor. When **MyThread**'s **Run( )** method finishes, it calls **Set( )** on that event object, which puts the event object into a signaled state. Inside **Main( )**, a **ManualResetEvent** called **evtObj** is created with an initially unsignaled state. Then, a **MyThread** instance is created and passed **evtObj**. Next, the main thread waits on the event object. Because the initial state of **evtObj** is not signaled, this causes the main thread to wait until the instance of **MyThread** calls **Set( )**, which puts **evtObj** into a signaled state. This allows the main thread to run again. Then the event is reset and the process is repeated for the second thread. Without the use of the event object, all threads would have run simultaneously and their output would have been jumbled. To verify this, try commenting out the call to **WaitOne( )** inside **Main( )**.

In the preceding program, if an **AutoResetEvent** object rather than a **ManualResetEvent** object were used, then the call to **Reset( )** in **Main( )** would not be necessary. The reason is that the event is automatically set to a non-signaled state when a thread waiting on the event is resumed. To try this, simply change all references to **ManualResetEvent** to **AutoResetEvent** and remove the calls to **Reset( )**. This version will execute the same as before.

The Interlocked Class

One other class that is related to synchronization is **Interlocked**. This class offers an alternative to the other synchronization features when all you need to do is change the value of a shared variable. The methods provided by **Interlocked** guarantee that their operation is performed as a single, uninterruptable operation. Thus, no other synchronization is needed. **Interlocked** provides static methods that add two integers, increment an integer, decrement an integer, compare and set an object, exchange objects, and obtain a 64-bit value. All of these operations take place without interruption.

The following program demonstrates two **Interlocked** methods: **Increment( )** and **Decrement( )**. Here are the forms of these methods that will be used:

public static int Increment(ref int *location*)

public static int Decrement(ref int *location*)

Here, *location* is the variable to be incremented or decremented.

```
// Use Interlocked operations.

using System;
using System.Threading;

// A shared resource.
class SharedRes {
  public static int Count = 0;
}

// This thread increments SharedRes.Count.
class IncThread {
  public Thread Thrd;

  public IncThread(string name) {
    Thrd = new Thread(this.Run);
    Thrd.Name = name;
```

```
      Thrd.Start();
    }

    // Entry point of thread.
    void Run() {

      for(int i=0; i<5; i++) {
        Interlocked.Increment(ref SharedRes.Count);
        Console.WriteLine(Thrd.Name + " Count is " + SharedRes.Count);
      }
    }
  }
}

// This thread decrements SharedRes.Count.
class DecThread {
  public Thread Thrd;

  public DecThread(string name) {
    Thrd = new Thread(this.Run);
    Thrd.Name = name;
    Thrd.Start();
  }

  // Entry point of thread.
  void Run() {

    for(int i=0; i<5; i++) {
      Interlocked.Decrement(ref SharedRes.Count);
      Console.WriteLine(Thrd.Name + " Count is " + SharedRes.Count);
    }
  }
}

class InterlockedDemo {
  static void Main() {

    // Construct two threads.
    IncThread mt1 = new IncThread("Increment Thread");
    DecThread mt2 = new DecThread("Decrement Thread");

    mt1.Thrd.Join();
    mt2.Thrd.Join();
  }
}
```

Synchronization Classes Added by .NET 4.0

The synchronization classes discussed by the foregoing sections, such as **Semaphore** and **AutoResetEvent**, have been available in earlier versions of the .NET Framework, with some going as far back as .NET 1.1. As a result, these classes form the core of .NET's support for synchronization. However, with the release of .NET 4.0, several new synchronization alternatives have been added. They are shown here:

Class	Purpose
Barrier	Causes threads to wait at a specified point (called the barrier) until all threads arrive.
CountdownEvent	Raises a signal when a countdown completes.
ManualResetEventSlim	A lightweight version of **ManualResetEvent**.
SemaphoreSlim	A lightweight version of **Semaphore**.

If you understand how to use the core synchronization classes described earlier, then you will have no trouble using these additions.

Terminating a Thread Via Abort( )

It is sometimes useful to stop a thread prior to its normal conclusion, even when the new cancellation subsystem is used. For example, a debugger may need to stop a thread that has run wild. Once a thread has been terminated, it is removed from the system and cannot be restarted.

To terminate a thread prior to its normal conclusion, use **Thread.Abort( )**. Its simplest form is shown here:

public void Abort( )

Abort( ) causes a **ThreadAbortException** to be thrown to the thread on which **Abort( )** is called. This exception causes the thread to terminate. This exception can also be caught by your code (but is automatically rethrown in order to stop the thread). **Abort( )** may not always be able to stop a thread immediately, so if it is important that a thread be stopped before your program continues, you will need to follow a call to **Abort( )** with a call to **Join( )**. Also, in rare cases, it is possible that **Abort( )** won't be able to stop a thread. One way this could happen is if a **finally** block goes into an infinite loop.

The following example shows how to stop a thread by use of **Abort( )**:

```
// Stopping a thread by use of Abort().

using System;
using System.Threading;

class MyThread {
  public Thread Thrd;

  public MyThread(string name) {
    Thrd = new Thread(this.Run);
    Thrd.Name = name;
    Thrd.Start();
  }

  // This is the entry point for thread.
  void Run() {
    Console.WriteLine(Thrd.Name + " starting.");
```

```
    for(int i = 1; i <= 1000; i++) {
      Console.Write(i + " ");
      if((i%10)==0) {
        Console.WriteLine();
        Thread.Sleep(250);
      }
    }
    Console.WriteLine(Thrd.Name + " exiting.");
  }
}

class StopDemo {
  static void Main() {
    MyThread mt1 = new MyThread("My Thread");

    Thread.Sleep(1000); // let child thread start executing

    Console.WriteLine("Stopping thread.");
    mt1.Thrd.Abort();

    mt1.Thrd.Join(); // wait for thread to terminate

    Console.WriteLine("Main thread terminating.");
  }
}
```

The output from this program is shown here:

```
My Thread starting.
1 2 3 4 5 6 7 8 9 10
11 12 13 14 15 16 17 18 19 20
21 22 23 24 25 26 27 28 29 30
31 32 33 34 35 36 37 38 39 40
Stopping thread.
Main thread terminating.
```

NOTE *Abort( ) should not be used as the normal means of stopping a thread. It is meant for specialized situations. Usually, a thread should end because its entry point method returns.*

An Abort( ) Alternative

You might find a second form of **Abort( )** useful in some cases. Its general form is shown here:

   public void Abort(object *stateInfo*)

Here, *stateInfo* contains any information that you want to pass to the thread when it is being stopped. This information is accessible through the **ExceptionState** property of **ThreadAbortException**. You might use this to pass a termination code to a thread. The following program demonstrates this form of **Abort( )**:

```
// Using Abort(object).

using System;
using System.Threading;
```

```
class MyThread {
  public Thread Thrd;

  public MyThread(string name) {
    Thrd = new Thread(this.Run);
    Thrd.Name = name;
    Thrd.Start();
  }

  // This is the entry point for thread.
  void Run() {
    try {
      Console.WriteLine(Thrd.Name + " starting.");

      for(int i = 1; i <= 1000; i++) {
        Console.Write(i + " ");
        if((i%10)==0) {
          Console.WriteLine();
          Thread.Sleep(250);
        }
      }
      Console.WriteLine(Thrd.Name + " exiting normally.");
    } catch(ThreadAbortException exc) {
      Console.WriteLine("Thread aborting, code is " +
                        exc.ExceptionState);
    }
  }
}

class UseAltAbort {
  static void Main() {
    MyThread mt1 = new MyThread("My Thread");

    Thread.Sleep(1000); // let child thread start executing

    Console.WriteLine("Stopping thread.");
    mt1.Thrd.Abort(100);

    mt1.Thrd.Join(); // wait for thread to terminate

    Console.WriteLine("Main thread terminating.");
  }
}
```

The output is shown here:

```
My Thread starting.
1 2 3 4 5 6 7 8 9 10
11 12 13 14 15 16 17 18 19 20
21 22 23 24 25 26 27 28 29 30
31 32 33 34 35 36 37 38 39 40
Stopping thread.
Thread aborting, code is 100
Main thread terminating.
```

As the output shows, the value 100 is passed to **Abort( )**. This value is then accessed through the **ExceptionState** property of the **ThreadAbortException** caught by the thread when it is terminated.

Canceling Abort( )

A thread can override a request to abort. To do so, the thread must catch the **ThreadAbortException** and then call **ResetAbort( )**. This prevents the exception from being automatically rethrown when the thread's exception handler ends. **ResetAbort( )** is declared like this:

    public static void ResetAbort( )

A call to **ResetAbort( )** can fail if the thread does not have the proper security setting to cancel the abort.

    The following program demonstrates **ResetAbort( )**:

```
// Using ResetAbort().

using System;
using System.Threading;

class MyThread {
  public Thread Thrd;

  public MyThread(string name) {
    Thrd = new Thread(this.Run);
    Thrd.Name = name;
    Thrd.Start();
  }

  // This is the entry point for thread.
  void Run() {
    Console.WriteLine(Thrd.Name + " starting.");

    for(int i = 1; i <= 1000; i++) {
      try {
        Console.Write(i + " ");
        if((i%10)==0) {
          Console.WriteLine();
          Thread.Sleep(250);
        }
      } catch(ThreadAbortException exc) {
        if((int)exc.ExceptionState == 0) {
          Console.WriteLine("Abort Cancelled! Code is " +
                            exc.ExceptionState);
          Thread.ResetAbort();
        }
        else
          Console.WriteLine("Thread aborting, code is " +
                            exc.ExceptionState);
      }
    }
    Console.WriteLine(Thrd.Name + " exiting normally.");
```

```
    }
  }

class ResetAbort {
  static void Main() {
    MyThread mt1 = new MyThread("My Thread");

    Thread.Sleep(1000); // let child thread start executing

    Console.WriteLine("Stopping thread.");
    mt1.Thrd.Abort(0); // this won't stop the thread

    Thread.Sleep(1000); // let child execute a bit longer

    Console.WriteLine("Stopping thread.");
    mt1.Thrd.Abort(100); // this will stop the thread

    mt1.Thrd.Join(); // wait for thread to terminate

    Console.WriteLine("Main thread terminating.");
  }
}
```

The output is shown here:

```
My Thread starting.
1 2 3 4 5 6 7 8 9 10
11 12 13 14 15 16 17 18 19 20
21 22 23 24 25 26 27 28 29 30
31 32 33 34 35 36 37 38 39 40
Stopping thread.
Abort Cancelled! Code is 0
41 42 43 44 45 46 47 48 49 50
51 52 53 54 55 56 57 58 59 60
61 62 63 64 65 66 67 68 69 70
71 72 73 74 75 76 77 78 79 80
Stopping thread.
Thread aborting, code is 100
Main thread terminating.
```

In this example, if **Abort( )** is called with an argument that equals zero, then the abort request is cancelled by the thread by calling **ResetAbort( )**, and the thread's execution continues. Any other value causes the thread to stop.

Suspending and Resuming a Thread

In early versions of the .NET Framework, a thread could be suspended by calling **Thread.Suspend( )** and resumed by calling **Thread.Resume( )**. Today, however, both of these methods are marked as obsolete and should not be used for new code. One reason is that **Suspend( )** is inherently dangerous because it can be used to suspend a thread that is currently holding a lock, thus preventing the lock from being released, resulting in deadlock. This can cause a systemwide problem. You must use C#'s other synchronization features, such as a mutex, to suspend and resume a thread.

Determining a Thread's State

The state of a thread can be obtained from the **ThreadState** property provided by **Thread**.
It is shown here:

    public ThreadState ThreadState{ get; }

The state of the thread is returned as a value defined by the **ThreadState** enumeration. It
defines the following values:

ThreadState.Aborted	ThreadState.AbortRequested
ThreadState.Background	ThreadState.Running
ThreadState.Stopped	ThreadState.StopRequested
ThreadState.Suspended	ThreadState.SuspendRequested
ThreadState.Unstarted	ThreadState.WaitSleepJoin

All but one of these values is self-explanatory. The one that needs some explanation is
ThreadState.WaitSleepJoin. A thread enters this state when it is waiting because of a call
to **Wait( )**, **Sleep( )**, or **Join( )**.

Using the Main Thread

As mentioned at the start of this chapter, all C# programs have at least one thread of
execution, called the *main thread,* which is given to the program automatically when it
begins running. The main thread can be handled just like all other threads.

To access the main thread, you must obtain a **Thread** object that refers to it. You do this
through the **CurrentThread** property, which is a member of **Thread**. Its general form is
shown here:

    public static Thread CurrentThread{ get; }

This property returns a reference to the thread in which it is used. Therefore, if you use
CurrentThread while execution is inside the main thread, you will obtain a reference to the
main thread. Once you have this reference, you can control the main thread just like any
other thread.

The following program obtains a reference to the main thread and then gets and sets the
main thread's name and priority:

```
// Control the main thread.

using System;
using System.Threading;

class UseMain {
  static void Main() {
    Thread Thrd;

    // Get the main thread.
    Thrd = Thread.CurrentThread;
```

```
  // Display main thread's name.
  if(Thrd.Name == null)
    Console.WriteLine("Main thread has no name.");
  else
    Console.WriteLine("Main thread is called: " + Thrd.Name);

  // Display main thread's priority.
  Console.WriteLine("Priority: " + Thrd.Priority);

  Console.WriteLine();

  // Set the name and priority.
  Console.WriteLine("Setting name and priority.\n");
  Thrd.Name = "Main Thread";
  Thrd.Priority = ThreadPriority.AboveNormal;

  Console.WriteLine("Main thread is now called: " +
                  Thrd.Name);

  Console.WriteLine("Priority is now: " +
                  Thrd.Priority);
  }
}
```

The output from the program is shown here:

```
Main thread has no name.
Priority: Normal

Setting name and priority.

Main thread is now called: Main Thread
Priority is now: AboveNormal
```

One word of caution: You need to be careful about what operations you perform on the main thread. For example, if you add this call to **Join( )** to the end of **Main( )**,

```
Thrd.Join();
```

the program will never terminate because it will be waiting for the main thread to end!

Additional Multithreading Features Added by .NET 4.0

Version 4.0 of the .NET Framework adds new multithreading features that you might find useful. The most important is the new cancellation system. The cancellation system supports a mechanism by which a thread can be cancelled easily in a well-defined, structured way. It is based on the concept of a *cancellation token,* which is used to specify the cancellation state of a thread. Cancellation tokens are supported by the **CancellationTokenSource** class and the **CancellationToken** structure. Because the cancellation system is fully integrated into the new Task Parallel Library, it is described in Chapter 24, where the TPL is discussed.

System.Threading adds a structure called **SpinWait**. It provides the methods **SpinOnce( )** and **SpinUntil( )** that give you greater control over spin waiting. In general, on single-processor systems, **SpinWait** will yield. On multiprocessor systems, it will use a loop. Another spin-related element is the **SpinLock**, which uses a loop to wait until a lock is available.

The **Thread** class adds a method called **Yield( )** that simply yields the remainder of a thread's timeslice. It is shown here:

    public static bool Yield( )

It returns true if a context switch occurred, and false otherwise. A context switch will not occur if there is not another thread that is ready to run.

Multithreading Tips

The key to effectively utilizing multithreading is to think concurrently rather than serially. For example, when you have two subsystems within a program that can execute concurrently, consider making them into individual threads. A word of caution is in order, however. If you create too many threads, you can actually degrade your program's performance rather than enhance it. Remember, there is some overhead associated with context switching. If you create too many threads, more CPU time will be spent changing contexts than in executing your program! Finally, for new code consider using the Task Parallel Library to accomplish multithreading.

Starting a Separate Task

Although thread-based multitasking is what you will use most often when programming in C#, it is possible to utilize process-based multitasking where appropriate. When using process-based multitasking, instead of starting another thread within the same program, one program starts the execution of another program. In C#, you do this by using the **Process** class. **Process** is defined within the **System.Diagnostics** namespace. To conclude this chapter, a brief look at starting and managing another process is offered.

The easiest way to start another process is to use the **Start( )** method defined by **Process**. Here is one of its simplest forms:

    public static Process Start(string *fileName*)

Here, *fileName* specifies the name of an executable file that will be executed or a file that is associated with an executable.

When a process that you create ends, call **Close( )** to free the memory associated with that process. It is shown here:

    public void Close( )

You can terminate a process in two ways. If the process is a Windows GUI application, then to terminate the process, call **CloseMainWindow( )**, shown here:

    public bool CloseMainWindow( )

This method sends a message to the process, instructing it to stop. It returns true if the message was received. It returns false if the application was not a GUI app, or does not have a main window. Furthermore, **CloseMainWindow( )** is only a request to shut down. If the application ignores the request, the application will not be terminated.

To positively terminate a process, call **Kill( )**, as shown here:

public void Kill( )

Use **Kill( )** carefully. It causes an uncontrolled termination of the process. Any unsaved data associated with the process will most likely be lost.

You can wait for a process to end by calling **WaitForExit( )**. Its two forms are shown here:

public void WaitForExit( )
public bool WaitForExit(int *milliseconds*)

The first form waits until the process terminates. The second waits for only the specified number of milliseconds. The second form returns true if the process has terminated and false if it is still running.

The following program demonstrates how to create, wait for, and close a process. It starts the standard Windows utility program **WordPad.exe**. It then waits for WordPad to end.

```
// Starting a new process.

using System;
using System.Diagnostics;

class StartProcess {
  static void Main() {
    Process newProc = Process.Start("wordpad.exe");

    Console.WriteLine("New process started.");

    newProc.WaitForExit();

    newProc.Close(); // free resources

    Console.WriteLine("New process ended.");
  }
}
```

When you run this program, WordPad will start, and you will see the message, "New process started." The program will then wait until you close WordPad. Once WordPad has been terminated, the final message, "New process ended.", is displayed.

Multithreading, Part Two: Exploring the Task Parallel Library and PLINQ

Perhaps the most important new feature added to the .NET Framework by version 4.0 is the *Task Parallel Library (TPL)*. This library enhances multithreaded programming in two important ways. First, it simplifies the creation and use of multiple threads. Second, it automatically makes use of multiple processors. In other words, by using the TPL you enable your applications to automatically scale to make use of the number of available processors. These two features make the TPL the recommended approach to multithreading in most cases.

Another parallel programming feature added by .NET 4.0 is PLINQ, which stands for *Parallel Language Integrated Query*. PLINQ enables you to write queries that automatically make use of multiple processors and parallelism when appropriate. As you will see, it is trivially easy to request parallel execution of a query. Thus, through the use of PLINQ, it is possible to add parallelism to a query with little effort.

The primary reason that TPL and PLINQ are such important advances is because of the growing importance of parallelism in modern programming. Today, multicore processors are becoming commonplace. Furthermore, the demand for better program performance is increasing. As a result, there has been a growing need for a mechanism that enables software to take advantage of multiple processors to increase performance. The trouble is that in the past, it was not always easy to do so in a clean, scalable manner. The TPL and PLINQ change this, making it easier (and safer) to best utilize system resources.

The TPL is defined in the **System.Threading.Tasks** namespace. However, when working with the TPL, you will also often need to include **System.Threading** because it provides support for synchronization and other multithreading features such as the **Interlocked** class.

This chapter explores both the TPL and PLINQ. Understand, however, that these are large topics, and it is not possible to cover them in detail. Instead, the fundamentals of each is described and several basic techniques are demonstrated. Thus, the information in this chapter will help you get started. If you will be focusing on parallel programming, then these are areas of the .NET framework that you will want to study in greater detail.

> **NOTE** *Although the use of the TPL and PLINQ is now recommended for most multithreading applications, threading based on the* **Thread** *class as described in Chapter 23 is still in widespread use. Furthermore, much of what is described in Chapter 23 applies to the TPL. Therefore, an understanding of the material in Chapter 23 is still required to fully master multithreading in C#.*

Two Approaches to Parallel Programming

When using the TPL, there are two basic ways in which you can add parallelism to a program. The first is called *data parallelism*. With this approach, one operation on a collection of data is broken into two or more concurrent threads of execution, each operating on a portion of the data. For example, if a transformation is applied to each element in an array, then through the use of data parallelism, it is possible for two or more threads to be operating on different ranges of the array concurrently. As you can imagine, such parallel actions could result in substantial increases in speed over a strictly sequential approach. Although data parallelism has always been possible by using the **Thread** class, it was difficult and time-consuming to construct scalable solutions. The TPL changes this. With the TPL, scalable data parallelism is easy to add to your program.

The second way to add parallelism is through the use of *task parallelism*. This approach executes two or more operations concurrently. Thus, task parallelism is the type of parallelism that has been accomplished in the past via the **Thread** class. The advantages that the TPL adds are ease-of-use and the ability to automatically scale execution to multiple processors.

The Task Class

At the core of the TPL is the **Task** class. With the TPL, the basic unit of execution is encapsulated by **Task**, not **Thread**. **Task** differs from **Thread** in that **Task** is an abstraction that represents an asynchronous operation. **Thread** encapsulates a thread of execution. Of course, at the system level, a thread is still the basic unit of execution that can be scheduled by the operating system. However, the correspondence between a **Task** instance and a thread of execution is not necessarily one-to-one. Furthermore, task execution is managed by a task scheduler, which works with a thread pool. This means that several tasks might share the same thread, for example. The **Task** class (and all of the TPL) is defined in **System.Threading.Tasks**.

Creating a Task

There are various ways to create a new **Task** and start its execution. We will begin by first creating a **Task** using a constructor and then starting it by calling the **Start( )** method. **Task** defines several constructors. Here is the one we will be using:

   public Task(Action *action*)

Here, *action* is the entry point of the code that represents the task. **Action** is a delegate defined in **System**. It has several forms. Here is the form we will use now:

   public delegate void Action( )

Thus, the entry point must be a method that takes no parameters and returns **void**. (As you will see later, it is possible to specify an argument to **Action**.)

Once a task has been created, you can start it by calling **Start( )**. One version is shown here:

public void Start( )

After a call to **Start( )**, the task scheduler schedules it for execution.

The following program puts the preceding discussion into action. It creates a separate task based on the **MyTask( )** method. After **Main( )** starts, the task is created and then started. Both **MyTask( )** and **Main( )** execute concurrently.

```
// Create and run a task.

using System;
using System.Threading;
using System.Threading.Tasks;

class DemoTask {

  // A method to be run as a task.
  static void MyTask() {
    Console.WriteLine("MyTask() starting");

    for(int count = 0; count < 10; count++) {
      Thread.Sleep(500);
      Console.WriteLine("In MyTask(), count is " + count);
    }

    Console.WriteLine("MyTask terminating");
  }

  static void Main() {

    Console.WriteLine("Main thread starting.");

    // Construct a task.
    Task tsk = new Task(MyTask);

    // Run the task.
    tsk.Start();

    // Keep Main() alive until MyTask() finishes.
    for(int i = 0; i < 60; i++) {
      Console.Write(".");
      Thread.Sleep(100);
    }

    Console.WriteLine("Main thread ending.");
  }
}
```

The output is shown here. (The precise output that you see may differ slightly based on task load, operating system, etc.)

```
Main thread starting.
.MyTask() starting
```

```
.....In MyTask(), count is 0
.....In MyTask(), count is 1
.....In MyTask(), count is 2
.....In MyTask(), count is 3
.....In MyTask(), count is 4
.....In MyTask(), count is 5
.....In MyTask(), count is 6
.....In MyTask(), count is 7
.....In MyTask(), count is 8
.....In MyTask(), count is 9
MyTask terminating
.........Main thread ending.
```

It is important to understand that, by default, a task executes in a background thread. Thus, when the creating thread ends, the task will end. This is why **Thread.Sleep( )** was used to keep the main thread alive until **MyTask( )** completed. As you would expect and will soon see, there are far better ways of waiting for a task to finish.

In the foregoing example, the task to be concurrently executed is specified by a **static** method. However, there is no requirement to this effect. For example, the following program reworks the previous one so that **MyTask( )** is encapsulated within a class:

```
// Use an instance method as a task.

using System;
using System.Threading;
using System.Threading.Tasks;

class MyClass {

  // A method to be run as a task.
  public void MyTask() {
    Console.WriteLine("MyTask() starting");

    for(int count = 0; count < 10; count++) {
      Thread.Sleep(500);
      Console.WriteLine("In MyTask(), count is " + count);
    }

    Console.WriteLine("MyTask terminating");
  }
}

class DemoTask {

  static void Main() {

    Console.WriteLine("Main thread starting.");

    // Construct a MyClass object.
    MyClass mc = new MyClass();

    // Construct a task on mc.MyTask().
    Task tsk = new Task(mc.MyTask);
```

```
    // Run the task.
    tsk.Start();

    // Keep Main() alive until MyTask() finishes.
    for(int i = 0; i < 60; i++) {
      Console.Write(".");
      Thread.Sleep(100);
    }

    Console.WriteLine("Main thread ending.");
  }
}
```

The output is the same as before. The only difference is that **MyTask( )** is now called on an instance of **MyClass**.

One other important point about tasks needs to be made now: once a task completes, it cannot be restarted. Thus, there is no way to rerun a task without re-creating it.

Use a Task ID

Unlike **Thread**, **Task** does not include a name property. It does, however, have an ID property called **Id**, which can be used to identify the task. **Id** is a read-only property of type **int**. It is shown here:

public int Id { get; }

A task is given an ID when it is created. The ID values are unique, but unordered. Therefore, the ID of a task begun before another might not be lower in value.

You can find the ID of the currently executing task by using the **CurrentId** property. This is a read-only **static** property, which is declared like this:

public static Nullable<int> CurrentID { get; }

It returns the ID of the currently executing task or null if the invoking code is not a task.

The following program creates two tasks and shows which task is executing:

```
// Demonstrate the Id and CurrentId properties.

using System;
using System.Threading;
using System.Threading.Tasks;

class DemoTask {

  // A method to be run as a task.
  static void MyTask() {
    Console.WriteLine("MyTask() #" + Task.CurrentId + " starting");

    for(int count = 0; count < 10; count++) {
      Thread.Sleep(500);
      Console.WriteLine("In MyTask() #" + Task.CurrentId +
                       ", count is " + count );
    }
```

```
      Console.WriteLine("MyTask #" + Task.CurrentId + " terminating");
    }

  static void Main() {

    Console.WriteLine("Main thread starting.");

    // Construct two tasks.
    Task tsk = new Task(MyTask);
    Task tsk2 = new Task(MyTask);

    // Run the tasks.
    tsk.Start();
    tsk2.Start();

    Console.WriteLine("Task ID for tsk is " + tsk.Id);
    Console.WriteLine("Task ID for tsk2 is " + tsk2.Id);

    // Keep Main() alive until the other tasks finish.
    for(int i = 0; i < 60; i++) {
      Console.Write(".");
      Thread.Sleep(100);
    }

    Console.WriteLine("Main thread ending.");
  }
}
```

The output is shown here:

```
Main thread starting.
Task ID for tsk is 1
Task ID for tsk2 is 2
.MyTask() #1 starting
MyTask() #2 starting
.....In MyTask() #1, count is 0
In MyTask() #2, count is 0
.....In MyTask() #2, count is 1
In MyTask() #1, count is 1
.....In MyTask() #1, count is 2
In MyTask() #2, count is 2
.....In MyTask() #2, count is 3
In MyTask() #1, count is 3
.....In MyTask() #1, count is 4
In MyTask() #2, count is 4
....In MyTask() #1, count is 5
In MyTask() #2, count is 5
.....In MyTask() #2, count is 6
.In MyTask() #1, count is 6
....In MyTask() #2, count is 7
.In MyTask() #1, count is 7
....In MyTask() #1, count is 8
In MyTask() #2, count is 8
```

```
.....In MyTask() #1, count is 9
MyTask #1 terminating
In MyTask() #2, count is 9
MyTask #2 terminating
.........Main thread ending.
```

Using Wait Methods

In the preceding examples, the **Main( )** thread ended last because the calls to **Thread.Sleep( )** ensured this outcome, but this is not a satisfactory approach. The best way to wait for a task to end is to use one of the wait methods that **Task** provides. The simplest one is called **Wait( )**, and it pauses execution of the calling thread until the invoking task completes. Here is its most straightforward form:

    public void Wait( )

This method can throw two exceptions. The first is **ObjectDisposedException**. It is thrown if the task has been released via a call to **Dispose( )**. The second is **AggregateException**. It is thrown when a task throws an exception or is cancelled. In general, you will want to watch for and handle this exception. Because a task might produce more than one exception (if it has child tasks, for example), they are aggregated into a single exception of type **AggregateException**. You can then examine the inner exception(s) associated with this exception to determine what happened. For now, the following examples will simply let any task-based exceptions be handled by the runtime.

The following reworked version of the preceding program shows **Wait( )** in action. It is used inside **Main( )** to suspend execution until both **tsk** and **tsk2** finish.

```
// Use Wait().

using System;
using System.Threading;
using System.Threading.Tasks;

class DemoTask {

  // A method to be run as a task.
  static void MyTask() {
    Console.WriteLine("MyTask() #" + Task.CurrentId + " starting");

    for(int count = 0; count < 10; count++) {
      Thread.Sleep(500);
      Console.WriteLine("In MyTask() #" + Task.CurrentId +
                        ", count is " + count );
    }

    Console.WriteLine("MyTask #" + Task.CurrentId + " terminating");
  }

  static void Main() {

    Console.WriteLine("Main thread starting.");
```

```
    // Construct two tasks.
    Task tsk = new Task(MyTask);
    Task tsk2 = new Task(MyTask);

    // Run the tasks.
    tsk.Start();
    tsk2.Start();

    Console.WriteLine("Task ID for tsk is " + tsk.Id);
    Console.WriteLine("Task ID for tsk2 is " + tsk2.Id);

    // Suspend Main() until both tsk and tsk2 finish.
    tsk.Wait();
    tsk2.Wait();

    Console.WriteLine("Main thread ending.");
  }
}
```

Here is the output:

```
Main thread starting.
Task ID for tsk is 1
Task ID for tsk2 is 2
MyTask() #1 starting
MyTask() #2 starting
In MyTask() #1, count is 0
In MyTask() #2, count is 0
In MyTask() #1, count is 1
In MyTask() #2, count is 1
In MyTask() #1, count is 2
In MyTask() #2, count is 2
In MyTask() #1, count is 3
In MyTask() #2, count is 3
In MyTask() #1, count is 4
In MyTask() #2, count is 4
In MyTask() #1, count is 5
In MyTask() #2, count is 5
In MyTask() #1, count is 6
In MyTask() #2, count is 6
In MyTask() #1, count is 7
In MyTask() #2, count is 7
In MyTask() #1, count is 8
In MyTask() #2, count is 8
In MyTask() #1, count is 9
MyTask #1 terminating
In MyTask() #2, count is 9
MyTask #2 terminating
Main thread ending.
```

As the output shows, **Main( )** suspends execution until both **tsk** and **tsk2** terminate. It is important to understand that in this program, the sequence in which **tsk** and **tsk2** finish is not important relative to the calls to **Wait( )**. For example, if **tsk2** completed first, the call to

tsk.Wait( ) would still wait until **tsk** finished. Then, the call to **tsk2.Wait( )** would execute and return immediately, since **tsk2** was already done.

Although using two separate calls to **Wait( )** works in this case, there is a simpler way: use **WaitAll( )**. This method waits on a group of tasks. It will not return until all have finished. Here is its simplest form:

public static void WaitAll(params Task[ ] *tasks*)

The tasks that you want to wait for are passed via *tasks*. Because this is a **params** parameter, you can pass an array of **Task** objects or list of tasks separately. Various exceptions are possible, including **AggregateException**.

To see **WaitAll( )** in action, in the preceding program try replacing this sequence

```
tsk.Wait();
tsk2.Wait();
```

with

```
Task.WaitAll(tsk, tsk2);
```

The program will work the same, but the logic is cleaner and more compact.

When waiting for multiple tasks, you need to be careful about deadlocks. If two tasks are waiting on each other, then a call to **WaitAll( )** will never return. Of course, deadlock conditions are errors that you must avoid. Therefore, if a call to **WaitAll( )** does not return, consider the possibility that two or more of the tasks could be deadlocking. (A call to **Wait( )** that doesn't return could also be the result of deadlock.)

Sometimes you will want to wait until any one of a group of tasks completes. To do this, use the **WaitAny( )** method. Here is its simplest form:

public static int WaitAny(params Task[ ] *tasks*)

The tasks that you want to wait for are passed via *tasks*. The tasks can be passed either as an array of **Task** objects or separately as a list of **Task** arguments. It returns the index of the task that completes first. Various exceptions are possible.

You can try **WaitAny( )** in the previous program by substituting this call:

```
Task.WaitAny(tsk, tsk2);
```

Now, as soon as one task finishes, **Main( )** resumes and the program ends.

In addition to the forms of **Wait( )**, **WaitAll( )**, and **WaitAny( )** shown here, there are versions that let you specify a timeout period or watch for a cancellation token. (Task cancellation is described later in this chapter.)

Calling Dispose( )

The **Task** class implements the **IDisposable** interface, which specifies the **Dispose( )** method. It has this form:

public void Dispose( )

As implemented by **Task**, **Dispose( )** releases the resources used by the **Task**. In general, the resources associated with a **Task** are automatically released when the **Task** is subjected to garbage collection (or when the program terminates). However, to release those resources before then, call **Dispose( )**. This is especially important in a program in which large numbers of tasks are created and then abandoned.

It is important to understand that **Dispose( )** can be called on a task only after it has completed. Thus, you will need to use some mechanism, such as **Wait( )**, to determine that a task has completed before calling **Dispose( )**. This is why it was necessary to describe the **Wait( )** method prior to discussing **Dispose( )**. It you do try to call **Dispose( )** on a still active task, an **InvalidOperationException** will be generated.

Because all of the examples in this chapter create few tasks, are quite short, and end immediately, calls to **Dispose( )** are of essentially no benefit. (This is why it was not necessary to call **Dispose( )** in the preceding programs; they all end as soon as the tasks end, thus resulting in the disposal of the tasks.) However, so as to demonstrate its use and to avoid confusion in this regard, all subsequent examples will call **Dispose( )** explicitly when working directly with **Task** instances. However, don't be surprised if you see example code from other sources that do not. Again, if a program will be ending as soon as a task ends, then there is essentially no point is calling **Dispose( )**—aside from demonstrating its use.

Using TaskFactory to Start a Task

The preceding examples are written a bit less efficiently than they need to be because it is possible to create a task and start its execution in a single step by calling the **StartNew( )** method defined by **TaskFactory**. **TaskFactory** is a class that provides various methods that streamline the creation and management of tasks. The default **TaskFactory** can be obtained from the read-only **Factory** property provided by **Task**. Using this property, you can call any of the **TaskFactory** methods.

There are many forms of **StartNew( )**. The simplest version is shown here:

public Task StartNew(Action *action*)

Here, *action* is the entry point to the task to be executed. **StartNew( )** automatically creates a **Task** instance for *action* and then starts the task by scheduling it for execution. Thus, there is no need to call **Start( )**.

For example, assuming the preceding programs, the following call creates and starts **tsk** in one step:

```
Task tsk = Task.Factory.StartNew(MyTask);
```

After this statement executes, **MyTask** will begin executing.

Since **StartNew( )** is more efficient when a task is going to be created and then immediately started, subsequent examples will use this approach.

Use a Lambda Expression as a Task

Although there is nothing wrong with using a normal method as a task, there is a second option that is more streamlined. You can simply specify a lambda expression as the task. Recall that a lambda expression is a form of anonymous function. Thus, it can be run as a separate task. The lambda expression is especially useful when the only purpose of a method is to be a single-use task. The lambda can either constitute the entire task, or it can invoke other methods. Either way, the lambda expression approach offers a pleasing alternative to using a named method.

The following program demonstrates the use of a lambda expression as a task. It converts the **MyTask( )** code in preceding programs into a lambda expression.

```
// Use a lambda expression as a task.

using System;
using System.Threading;
using System.Threading.Tasks;

class DemoLambdaTask {

  static void Main() {

    Console.WriteLine("Main thread starting.");

    // The following uses a lambda expression to define a task.
    Task tsk = Task.Factory.StartNew( () => {
      Console.WriteLine("Task starting");

      for(int count = 0; count < 10; count++) {
        Thread.Sleep(500);
        Console.WriteLine("Task count is " + count );
      }

      Console.WriteLine("Task terminating");
    } );


    // Wait until tsk finishes.
    tsk.Wait();

    // Dispose of tsk.
    tsk.Dispose();

    Console.WriteLine("Main thread ending.");
  }
}
```

The output is shown here:

```
Main thread starting.
Task starting
Task count is 0
Task count is 1
Task count is 2
Task count is 3
Task count is 4
Task count is 5
Task count is 6
Task count is 7
Task count is 8
Task count is 9
Task terminating
Main thread ending.
```

In addition to the use of a lambda expression to describe a task, notice that **tsk.Dispose( )** is not called until after **tsk.Wait( )** returns. As explained in the previous section, **Dispose( )** can be called only on a completed task. To prove this, try putting the call to **tsk.Dispose( )** before the call to **tsk.Wait( )**. As you will see, an exception is generated.

Create a Task Continuation

One innovative, and very convenient, feature of the TPL is its ability to create a task continuation. A *continuation* is a task that automatically begins when another task finishes. One way to create a continuation is to use the **ContinueWith( )** method defined by **Task**. Its simplest form is shown here:

public Task ContinueWith(Action<Task> *continuationAction*)

Here, *continuationAction* specifies the task that will be run after the invoking task completes. This delegate has one parameter of type **Task**. Thus, this is the version of the **Action** delegate used by the method:

public delegate void Action<in T>(T *obj*)

In this case, **T** is **Task**.

The following program demonstrates a task continuation.

```
// Demonstrate a continuation.

using System;
using System.Threading;
using System.Threading.Tasks;

class ContinuationDemo {

  // A method to be run as a task.
  static void MyTask() {
    Console.WriteLine("MyTask() starting");

    for(int count = 0; count < 5; count++) {
      Thread.Sleep(500);
      Console.WriteLine("In MyTask() count is " + count );
    }

    Console.WriteLine("MyTask terminating");
  }

  // A method to be run as a continuation.
  static void ContTask(Task t) {
    Console.WriteLine("Continuation starting");

    for(int count = 0; count < 5; count++) {
      Thread.Sleep(500);
      Console.WriteLine("Continuation count is " + count );
    }
    Console.WriteLine("Continuation terminating");
  }
```

```
   static void Main() {

     Console.WriteLine("Main thread starting.");

     // Construct the first task.
     Task tsk = new Task(MyTask);

     // Now, create the continuation.
     Task taskCont = tsk.ContinueWith(ContTask);

     // Begin the task sequence.
     tsk.Start();

     // Just wait on the continuation.
     taskCont.Wait();

     tsk.Dispose();
     taskCont.Dispose();

     Console.WriteLine("Main thread ending.");
   }
}
```

The output is shown here:

```
Main thread starting.
MyTask() starting
In MyTask() count is 0
In MyTask() count is 1
In MyTask() count is 2
In MyTask() count is 3
In MyTask() count is 4
MyTask terminating
Continuation starting
Continuation count is 0
Continuation count is 1
Continuation count is 2
Continuation count is 3
Continuation count is 4
Continuation terminating
Main thread ending.
```

As the output shows, the second task did not begin until the first task completed. Also notice that it was necessary for **Main( )** to wait only on the continuation task. This is because **MyTask( )** will be finished before **ContTask** begins. Thus, there is no need to wait for **MyTask( )**, although it would not be wrong to do so.

As a point of interest, it is not uncommon to use a lambda expression as a continuation task. For example, here is another way to write the continuation used in the preceding program:

```
// Here, a lambda expression is used as the continuation.
Task taskCont = tsk.ContinueWith((first) =>
     {
        Console.WriteLine("Continuation starting");
        for(int count = 0; count < 5; count++) {
```

```
        Thread.Sleep(500);
        Console.WriteLine("Continuation count is " + count );
      }
      Console.WriteLine("Continuation terminating");
    }
);
```

Here, the parameter **first** receives the antecedent task (which is **tsk** in this case).

In addition to **ContinueWith( )** provided by **Task**, there are other methods that support task continuation provided by **TaskFactory**. These include various forms of **ContinueWhenAny( )** and **ContinueWhenAll( )**, which continue a task when any or all of the specified tasks complete, respectively.

Returning a Value from a Task

A task can return a value. This is a very useful feature for two reasons. First, it means that you can use a task to compute some result. This supports parallel computation. Second, the calling process will block until the result is ready. This means that you don't need to do any special synchronization to wait for the result.

To return a result, you will create a task by using the generic form of **Task**, which is **Task<TResult>**. Here are two of its constructors:

public Task(Func<TResult> *function*)
public Task(Func<Object, TResult> *function*, Object *state*)

Here, *function* is the delegate to be run. Notice that it is of type **Func** rather than **Action**. **Func** is used when a task returns a result. The first form creates a task that takes no arguments. The second form creates a task that takes an argument of type **Object** passed in *state*. Other constructors are also available.

As you might expect, there are also versions of **StartNew( )** provided by **TaskFactory<TResult>** that support returning a result from a task. Here are the ones that parallel the **Task** constructors just shown:

public Task<TResult> StartNew(Func<TResult> *function*)
public Task<TResult> StartNew(Func<Object,TResult> *function*, Object *state*)

In all cases, the value returned by the task is obtained from **Task**'s **Result** property, which is defined like this:

public TResult Result { get; internal set; }

Because the **set** accessor is internal, this property is effectively read-only relative to external code. The **get** accessor won't return until the result is ready. Thus, retrieving the result blocks the calling code until the result has been computed.

The following program demonstrates task return values. It creates two methods. The first is **MyTask( )**, which takes no parameters. It simply returns the **bool** value **true**. The second is **SumIt( )**, which has a single parameter (which is cast to **int**) and returns the summation of the value passed to that parameter.

```
// Return a value from a task.

using System;
```

```
using System.Threading;
using System.Threading.Tasks;

class DemoTask {

  // A trivial method that returns a result and takes no arguments.
  static bool MyTask() {
    return true;
  }

  // This method returns the summation of a positive integer
  // which is passed to it.
  static int SumIt(object v) {
    int x = (int) v;
    int sum = 0;

    for(; x > 0; x--)
      sum += x;

    return sum;
  }

  static void Main() {

    Console.WriteLine("Main thread starting.");

    // Construct the first task.
    Task<bool> tsk = Task<bool>.Factory.StartNew(MyTask);

    Console.WriteLine("After running MyTask. The result is " +
                      tsk.Result);

    // Construct the second task.
    Task<int> tsk2 = Task<int>.Factory.StartNew(SumIt, 3);

    Console.WriteLine("After running SumIt. The result is " +
                      tsk2.Result);

    tsk.Dispose();
    tsk2.Dispose();

    Console.WriteLine("Main thread ending.");
  }
}
```

The output is shown here:

```
Main thread starting.
After running MyTask. The result is True
After running SumIt. The result is 6
Main thread ending.
```

In addition to the forms of **Task<TResult>** and **StartNew<TResult>** used here, there are other forms available for use that let you specify other options.

Cancelling a Task and Using AggregateException

The .NET Framework 4.0 adds a new subsystem that provides a structured, yet highly flexible way to cancel tasks. This new mechanism is based on the *cancellation token*. Cancellation tokens are supported by the **Task** class, and through the **StartNew( )** factory method (among others).

NOTE *The new cancellation subsystem can also be used to cancel threads, which were described in the previous chapter. However, it is fully integrated into the TPL and PLINQ. For this reason, it is described here.*

In general, here is how task cancellation works. A cancellation token is obtained from a cancellation token source. This token is then passed to the task. The task must then monitor that token for a cancellation request. (This request can come only from the cancellation token source.) If a cancellation request is received, the task must end. Sometimes it is sufficient for the task to simply stop, taking no further action. Other times, the task should call **ThrowIfCancellationRequested( )** on the cancellation token. This lets the canceling code know that the task was cancelled. Now, we will look at the cancellation process in detail.

A cancellation token is an instance of **CancellationToken**, which is a structure defined in **System.Threading**. It defines several properties and methods. We will use two of them. The first is the read-only property **IsCancellationRequested**. It is shown here:

    public bool IsCancellationRequested { get; }

It returns true if cancellation has been requested on the invoking token and false otherwise. The second member that we will use is the **ThrowIfCancellationRequested( )** method. It is shown here:

    public void ThrowIfCancellationRequested( )

If the cancellation token on which it is called has received a cancellation request, then this method will throw an **OperationCanceledException**. Otherwise, it takes no action. The cancelling code can watch for this exception to confirm that cancellation did, indeed, occur. This is normally done by catching **AggregateException** and then examining the inner exception, via the **InnerException** or **InnerExceptions** properties. (**InnerExceptions** is a collection of exceptions. Collections are described in Chapter 25.)

A cancellation token is obtained from a cancellation source. This is an object of **CancellationTokenSource**, which is defined in **System.Threading**. To obtain a token, first create a **CancellationTokenSource** instance. (You can use its default constructor for this purpose.) The cancellation token associated with that source is available through the read-only **Token** property, which is shown here:

    public CancellationToken Token { get; }

This is the token that must be passed to the task that you want to be able to cancel.

To use cancellation, the task must receive a copy of the cancellation token and then monitor that token, watching for cancellation. There are three ways to watch for cancellation: polling, using a callback method, and using a wait handle. The easiest is polling, and that is the approach used here. To use polling, the task will check the **IsCancellationRequested** property of the cancellation token, described earlier. If this property is true, cancellation has been requested and the task should terminate. Polling can be quite efficient if it is done appropriately. For example, if a task contains nested loops, then checking **IsCancellationRequested** in the outer loop would often be better than checking it with each iteration of the inner loop.

To create a task that calls **ThrowIfCancellationRequested( )** when cancelled, you will often want to pass the cancellation token to both the task and the **Task** constructor, whether directly or indirectly through the **StartNew( )** method. Passing the cancellation token to the task enables a cancellation request by outside code to change the state of the task to be cancelled. Here, we will use this version of **StartNew( )**:

```
public Task StartNew(Action<Object> action, Object state,
                     CancellationToken cancellationToken)
```

In this use, the cancellation token will be passed to both *state* and *cancellationToken*. This means that the cancellation token will be passed to both the delegate that implements the task and to the **Task** instance, itself. The form of **Action** that supports this is shown here:

```
public delegate void Action<in T>(T obj)
```

In this case, **T** is **Object**. Because of this, inside the task, *obj* must be cast to **CancellationToken**.

One other point: when you are done with the token source, you should release its resources by calling **Dispose( )**.

There are various ways to determine if a task has been cancelled. The approach used here is to test the value of **IsCanceled** on the **Task** instance. If it is true, the task was cancelled.

The following program demonstrates cancellation. It uses polling to monitor the state of the cancellation token. Notice that **ThrowIfCancellationRequested( )** is called on entry into **MyTask( )**. This enables the task to be terminated if it was cancelled before it was started. Inside the loop, **IsCancellationRequested** is checked. When this property is true (which it will be after **Cancel( )** is called on the token source), a message indicating cancellation is displayed and **ThrowIfCancellationRequested( )** is called to cancel the task.

```
// A simple example of cancellation that uses polling.

using System;
using System.Threading;
using System.Threading.Tasks;

class DemoCancelTask {

  // A method to be run as a task.
  static void MyTask(Object ct) {
    CancellationToken cancelTok = (CancellationToken) ct;

    // Check if cancelled prior to starting.
    cancelTok.ThrowIfCancellationRequested();

    Console.WriteLine("MyTask() starting");

    for(int count = 0; count < 10; count++) {
      // This example uses polling to watch for cancellation.
      if(cancelTok.IsCancellationRequested) {
        Console.WriteLine("Cancellation request received.");
```

```
          cancelTok.ThrowIfCancellationRequested();
        }

        Thread.Sleep(500);
        Console.WriteLine("In MyTask(), count is " + count );
      }

      Console.WriteLine("MyTask terminating");
    }

    static void Main() {

      Console.WriteLine("Main thread starting.");

      // Create a cancellation token source.
      CancellationTokenSource cancelTokSrc = new CancellationTokenSource();

      // Start a task, passing the cancellation token to both
      // the delegate and the task.
      Task tsk = Task.Factory.StartNew(MyTask, cancelTokSrc.Token,
                                       cancelTokSrc.Token);

      // Let tsk run until cancelled.
      Thread.Sleep(2000);

      try {
        // Cancel the task.
        cancelTokSrc.Cancel();

        // Suspend Main() until tsk terminates.
        tsk.Wait();
      } catch (AggregateException exc) {
        if(tsk.IsCanceled)
          Console.WriteLine("\ntsk Cancelled\n");

        // To see the exception, un-comment this line:
        // Console.WriteLine(exc);
      } finally {
        tsk.Dispose();
        cancelTokSrc.Dispose();
      }

      Console.WriteLine("Main thread ending.");
    }
}
```

The output is shown here. Notice that the task is cancelled after 2 seconds.

```
Main thread starting.
MyTask() starting
In MyTask(), count is 0
In MyTask(), count is 1
In MyTask(), count is 2
In MyTask(), count is 3
Cancellation request received.
```

```
tsk Cancelled

Main thread ending.
```

As the output shows, **MyTask( )** was cancelled by **Main( )** after a delay of 2 seconds. Thus, **MyTask( )** executes four loop iterations. When an **AggregateException** is caught, the status of the task is checked. If it is cancelled (which it will be in this example), the cancellation of **tsk** is reported. It is important to understand that when **AggregateException** is thrown in response to a cancellation, it does not indicate an error. It simply means that the task was cancelled.

Although the preceding discussion introduces the fundamental concepts behind task cancellation and **AggregateException**, there is much more to these topics. These are areas that you will need to study in-depth if you want to create high-performance, scalable code.

Some Other Task Features

The preceding sections have described several of the concepts and fundamental techniques involved with tasks. However, there are other features that you may find useful. For example, you can create nested tasks, which are tasks created by a task, and child tasks, which are nested tasks that are closely tied to the creating task.

Although the **AggregateException** was briefly discussed in the preceding section, it has some other features that you may find useful. One is the **Flatten( )** method. It is used to convert any inner exceptions of type **AggregateException** into a single **AggregateException**. Another is the **Handle( )** method, which is used to handle an exception contained within an **AggregateException**.

When you create a task, it is possible to specify various options that affect the task's execution characteristics. This is done by specifying an instance of **TaskCreationOptions** in either the **Task** constructor or the **StartNew( )** factory method. Also, **TaskFactory** supports the **FromAsync( )** family of methods that support the Asynchronous Programming Model.

As mentioned early on in this chapter, tasks are scheduled by an instance of **TaskScheduler**. Normally, the default scheduler provided by the .NET Framework is used, but it is possible to tailor aspects of the scheduler to best fit your needs. Custom schedulers are also possible.

The Parallel Class

So far, the preceding examples have show situations in which the TPL has been used in much the same way in which **Thread** would be used, but this is just its most basic application. Significantly more sophisticated features are available. One of the most important is the **Parallel** class. It facilitates the execution of concurrent code and provides methods that streamline both task and data parallelism.

Parallel is a static class that defines the **For( )**, **ForEach( )**, and **Invoke( )** methods. Each has various forms. The **For( )** method executes a parallelized **for** loop, and the **ForEach( )** method executes a parallelized **foreach** loop. Both of these support data parallelism. **Invoke( )** supports the concurrent execution of two or more methods. Thus, it supports task parallelism. As you will see, these methods offer the advantage of providing easy ways to utilize common parallel programming techniques without the need to manage tasks or threads explicitly. The following sections examine each of these methods.

Parallelizing Tasks via Invoke( )

The **Invoke( )** method defined by **Parallel** lets you execute one or more methods by simply specifying them as arguments. If possible, it scales to utilize the available processors. Its simplest version is defined like this:

> public static void Invoke(params Action[ ] *actions*)

The methods to be executed must be compatible with the **Action** delegate that was described earlier. Recall that **Action** is declared like this:

> public delegate void Action( )

Therefore, each method passed to **Invoke( )** must have no parameters and must return **void**. Because *actions* is a **params** parameter, you can specify a variable-length argument list of methods to execute. You can also use an array of **Action**, but often the argument list is easier.

Invoke( ) will initiate execution of all of the methods that it is passed. It will then wait until all of the methods have finished. Thus, there is no need (nor ability) to call **Wait( )**, for example. **Invoke( )** handles all the details. Although there is no guarantee that the methods will execute in parallel, this is the expectation if the system supports more than one processor. Also, the order of execution, including which method starts or finishes first, cannot be specified, and may not be the same as the order as the argument list.

The following program demonstrates **Invoke( )**. It runs two methods, called **MyMeth( )** and **MyMeth2( )**, via a call to **Invoke( )**. Notice the simplicity of the process.

```
// Use Parallel.Invoke() to execute methods concurrently.

using System;
using System.Threading;
using System.Threading.Tasks;

class DemoParallel {

  // A method to be run as a task.
  static void MyMeth() {
    Console.WriteLine("MyMeth starting");

    for(int count = 0; count < 5; count++) {
      Thread.Sleep(500);
      Console.WriteLine("In MyMeth, count is " + count );
    }

    Console.WriteLine("MyMeth terminating");
  }

  // A method to be run as a task.
  static void MyMeth2() {
    Console.WriteLine("MyMeth2 starting");

    for(int count = 0; count < 5; count++) {
      Thread.Sleep(500);
      Console.WriteLine("In MyMeth2, count is " + count );
    }
```

```
      Console.WriteLine("MyMeth2 terminating");
   }

   static void Main() {

     Console.WriteLine("Main thread starting.");

     // Run two named methods.
     Parallel.Invoke(MyMeth, MyMeth2);

     Console.WriteLine("Main thread ending.");
   }
}
```

The output is shown here:

```
Main thread starting.
MyMeth starting
MyMeth2 starting
In MyMeth, count is 0
In MyMeth2, count is 0
In MyMeth, count is 1
In MyMeth2, count is 1
In MyMeth, count is 2
In MyMeth2, count is 2
In MyMeth, count is 3
In MyMeth2, count is 3
In MyMeth, count is 4
MyMeth terminating
In MyMeth2, count is 4
MyMeth2 terminating
Main thread ending.
```

There is something very important to notice in this example: **Main( )** suspends until **Invoke( )** returns. Therefore, even though **MyMeth( )** and **MyMeth2( )** are executing concurrently, **Main( )** is not. If you want the calling thread to continue execution, you can't use **Invoke( )** as shown here.

Although the previous example used named methods, this is not required when calling **Invoke( )**. Here is the same program reworked to use lambda expressions as arguments to **Invoke( )**:

```
// Use Parallel.Invoke( ) to execute methods concurrently.
// This version uses lambda expressions.

using System;
using System.Threading;
using System.Threading.Tasks;

class DemoParallel {

  static void Main() {

    Console.WriteLine("Main thread starting.");
```

```
// Run two anonymous methods specified via lambda expressions.
Parallel.Invoke( () => {
    Console.WriteLine("Expression #1 starting");

    for(int count = 0; count < 5; count++) {
      Thread.Sleep(500);
      Console.WriteLine("Expression #1 count is " + count );
    }

    Console.WriteLine("Expression #1 terminating");
  },

    () => {
      Console.WriteLine("Expression #2 starting");

      for(int count = 0; count < 5; count++) {
        Thread.Sleep(500);
        Console.WriteLine("Expression #2 count is " + count );
      }

      Console.WriteLine("Expression #2 terminating");
    }
  );

  Console.WriteLine("Main thread ending.");
  }
}
```

The output is similar to that of the previous version.

Using the For( ) Method

One way that the TPL supports data parallelism is through the **For( )** method defined by
Parallel. The are several forms of **For( )**. We will start with the simplest version, which is
shown here:

> public static ParallelLoopResult
>   For(int *fromInclusive*, int *toExclusive*, Action<int> *body*)

Here, *fromInclusive* specifies the starting value of what corresponds to the loop control
variable (also called the iteration value or index value), and *toExclusive* specifies one greater
than the ending value. Each time through the loop, the loop control variable will increase
by one. Thus, the loop will iterate from *fromInclusive* to *toExclusive* –1. The code that will be
iterated is specified by the method passed to *body*. This method must be compatible with
the **Action<int>** delegate, which is shown here:

> public delegate void Action<in T>(T *obj*)

Of course, in the case of **For( )**, **T** must be **int**. The value passed to *obj* will be the next value
of the loop control value. The method passed to *body* can be a named or anonymous method.
For( ) returns a **ParallelLoopResult** instance that describes the completion status of the loop.
For simple loops, this value can be ignored. (We will look at this value closely a bit later.)

The key point about **For( )** is that it can (when feasible) parallelize the loop code. This can, in turn, lead to performance improvement. For example, in a loop that applies a transformation to an array, the process can be broken into pieces to allow different portions of the array to be transformed simultaneously. Understand, however, that no performance boost is guaranteed because of differences in the number of available processors in different execution environments, and because parallelizing small loops may create more overhead than the time that is saved.

The following shows a simple example of **For( )**. It begins by creating an array called **data** that contains 1,000,000,000 integers. It then calls **For( )**, passing as the loop "body" a method called **MyTransform( )**. This method contains a number of statements that perform arbitrary transformations on the data array. Its purpose is to simulate an actual operation. As explained in greater detail in a moment, for data parallelism to be effective, the operation being performed must usually be non-trivial. If it isn't, then a sequential loop can be faster.

```
// Use Parallel.For() to create a data-parallel loop.

using System;
using System.Threading.Tasks;

class DemoParallelFor {
  static int[] data;

  // A method to be run as the body of a parallel loop.
  // The statements in this loop are designed to simply
  // consume some CPU time for the purposes of demonstration.
  static void MyTransform(int i) {
    data[i] = data[i] / 10;

    if(data[i] < 10000) data[i] = 0;
    if(data[i] > 10000 & data[i] < 20000) data[i] = 100;
    if(data[i] > 20000 & data[i] < 30000) data[i] = 200;
    if(data[i] > 30000) data[i] = 300;
  }

  static void Main() {

    Console.WriteLine("Main thread starting.");

    data = new int[100000000];

    // Initialize the data using a regular for loop.
    for(int i=0; i < data.Length; i++) data[i] = i;

    // A parallel For loop.
    Parallel.For(0, data.Length, MyTransform);

    Console.WriteLine("Main thread ending.");
  }
}
```

The program contains two loops. The first is a standard **for** loop that initializes **data**. The second is a parallel **For( )** loop that applies a transformation to each element in **data**. As stated, in this case, the transformation is arbitrary (being used simply for demonstration). The **For( )** automatically breaks up the calls to **MyTransform( )** so they can be run on separate portions of data in parallel. Therefore, if you run this program on a computer that has two or more available processors, the **For( )** loop can run in parallel.

It is important to understand that not all loops will be more efficient when parallelized. In general, small loops or loops that perform very simple operations are often faster as sequential rather than parallel loops. This is why the **for** loop that initializes **data** is not a parallel **For( )**. The reason that small or very simple loops might not be efficient when parallelized is because the time needed to set up the parallel tasks and the time needed to context-switch exceeds the time saved by parallelization. To prove this point, the following program creates both parallel and sequential versions of both **for** loops in the program and times each one for comparison purposes:

```
// Show timing differences between sequential and parallel for loops.

using System;
using System.Threading.Tasks;
using System.Diagnostics;

class DemoParallelFor {
  static int[] data;

  // A method to be run as the body of a parallel loop.
  // The statements in this loop are designed to simply
  // consume some CPU time for the purposes of demonstration.
  static void MyTransform(int i) {
    data[i] = data[i] / 10;

    if(data[i] < 1000) data[i] = 0;
    if(data[i] > 1000 & data[i] < 2000) data[i] = 100;
    if(data[i] > 2000 & data[i] < 3000) data[i] = 200;
    if(data[i] > 3000) data[i] = 300;
  }

  static void Main() {

    Console.WriteLine("Main thread starting.");

    // Create a Stopwatch instance to time loops.
    Stopwatch sw = new Stopwatch();

    data = new int[100000000];

    // Initialize data.
    sw.Start();

    // Parallel version of initialization loop.
    Parallel.For(0, data.Length, (i) => data[i] = i );

    sw.Stop();

    Console.WriteLine("Parallel initialization loop:   {0} secs",
                       sw.Elapsed.TotalSeconds);
```

```
   sw.Reset();

   sw.Start();

   // Sequential version of initialization loop.
   for(int i=0; i < data.Length; i++) data[i] = i;

   sw.Stop();

   Console.WriteLine("Sequential initialization loop: {0} secs",
                     sw.Elapsed.TotalSeconds);
   Console.WriteLine();

   // Perform transforms.

   sw.Start();

   // Parallel version of transformation loop.
   Parallel.For(0, data.Length, MyTransform);

   sw.Stop();

   Console.WriteLine("Parallel transform loop:   {0} secs",
                     sw.Elapsed.TotalSeconds);

   sw.Reset();

   sw.Start();

   // Sequential version of transformation loop.
   for(int i=0; i < data.Length; i++) MyTransform(i);

   sw.Stop();

   Console.WriteLine("Sequential transform loop: {0} secs",
                     sw.Elapsed.TotalSeconds);

   Console.WriteLine("Main thread ending.");
  }
}
```

The following output was produced using a dual-core processor:

```
Main thread starting.
Parallel initialization loop:   1.0537757 secs
Sequential initialization loop: 0.3457628 secs

Parallel transform loop:   4.2246675 secs
Sequential transform loop: 5.3849959 secs
Main thread ending.
```

First, notice that the parallel version of the initialization loop ran about three times slower than the sequential version. This is because (in this case) assignment takes so little time that the overhead added by parallelism exceeds the gains. Now, notice that the parallel transform loop ran faster than its sequential equivalent. In this case, the gains of parallelization more than offset the overhead added by parallelization.

NOTE *In general, you should consult Microsoft's current guidelines in regards to what types of loops make the best use of parallelization. You will also want to confirm that you are actually getting performance gains before using a parallel loop in released application code.*

There are a couple of other things to mention about the preceding program. First, notice that the parallel initialization loop uses a lambda expression to initialize data. It is shown here:

```
Parallel.For(0, data.Length, (i) => data[i] = i );
```

Here, the "body" of the loop is specified by a lambda expression. (Again, recall that a lambda expression creates an anonymous method.) Thus, there is no requirement that **For( )** be used with a named method.

The second point of interest is the use of the **Stopwatch** class to handle the loop timing. This class is in **System.Diagnostics**. To use **Stopwatch**, create an instance and then call **Start( )** to begin timing and **Stop( )** to end timing. Use **Reset( )** to reset the stopwatch. There are various ways to obtain the duration. The approach used by the program is the **Elapsed** property, which returns a **TimeSpan** object. Using the **TimeSpan** object, the seconds (including fractional seconds) are displayed by use of the **TotalSeconds** property. As this program shows, **Stopwatch** is very useful when developing parallel code.

As mentioned, the **For( )** method returns an instance of **ParallelLoopResult**. This is a structure that defines the following two properties:

public bool IsCompleted { get; }
public Nullable<long> LowestBreakIteration { get; }

IsCompleted will be true if the loop completed all requested iterations. In other words, it is true if the loop ran normally. It will be false if the loop was terminated early. **LowestBreakIteration** contains the lowest value of the loop control variable if the loop was terminated early via a call to **ParallelLoopState.Break( )**.

To have access to a **ParallelLoopState** object, you must use a form of **For( )** whose delegate takes a second parameter that receives the current loop state. Here is the simplest one:

public static ParallelLoopResult For(int *fromInclusive*, int *toExclusive*,
                                     Action<int, ParallelLoopState> *body*)

In this version, the **Action** delegate that describes the body of the loop is defined like this:

public delegate void Action<in T1, in T2>(T *arg1*, T2 *arg2*)

For use with the **For( )**, **T1** must be **int** and **T2** must be **ParallelLoopState**. Each time this delegate is called, the current loop state is passed to *arg2*.

To stop a loop early, call **Break( )** on the **ParallelLoopState** instance inside *body*. **Break( )** is defined as shown here:

public void Break( )

A call to **Break( )** requests that the parallel loop stop as soon as possible, which might be a few iterations beyond the one in which **Break( )** is called. However, all iterations prior to the one in which **Break( )** is called will still execute. Also, remember that portions of the loop might be running in parallel, so if 10 iterations have taken place, it does not necessarily mean that those 10 iterations represent the first 10 values of the loop control variable.

Breaking from a parallel **For( )** loop is often useful when data is being searched. If the desired value is found, there is no need to further execute the loop. It might also be used if invalid data is encountered during an operation.

The following program demonstrates the use of **Break( )** with a **For( )** loop. It reworks the previous example so that **MyTransform( )** now has a **ParallelLoopState** parameter and the **Break( )** method is called if a negative value is found in **data**. Inside **Main( )**, a negative value is put into the **data** array (which will cause the loop to break). The completion status of the transform loop is checked. Since the negative value in **data** will cause it to terminate early, the **IsCompleted** property will be false, and the iteration count at which the loop was terminated is displayed. (The program removes the redundant loops used by the previous version, keeping only the most efficient of each, which is the sequential initialization loop and the parallel transform loop.)

```
// Use ParallelLoopResult, ParallelLoopState, and Break()
// with a parallel For loop.

using System;
using System.Threading.Tasks;

class DemoParallelForWithLoopResult {
  static int[] data;

  // A method to be run as the body of a parallel loop.
  // The statements in this loop are designed to simply
  // consume some CPU time for the purposes of demonstration.
  static void MyTransform(int i, ParallelLoopState pls) {

    // Break out of loop if a negative value is found.
    if(data[i] < 0) pls.Break();

    data[i] = data[i] / 10;

    if(data[i] < 1000) data[i] = 0;
    if(data[i] > 1000 & data[i] < 2000) data[i] = 100;
    if(data[i] > 2000 & data[i] < 3000) data[i] = 200;
    if(data[i] > 3000) data[i] = 300;
  }

  static void Main() {

    Console.WriteLine("Main thread starting.");

    data = new int[100000000];

    // Initialize data.
```

```
       for(int i=0; i < data.Length; i++) data[i] = i;

       // Put a negative value into data.
       data[1000] = -10;

       // Parallel transform loop.
       ParallelLoopResult loopResult =
                 Parallel.For(0, data.Length, MyTransform);

       // See if the loop ran to completion.
       if(!loopResult.IsCompleted)
         Console.WriteLine("\nLoop Terminated early because a " +
                           "negative value was encountered\n" +
                           "in iteration number " +
                            loopResult.LowestBreakIteration + ".\n");

       Console.WriteLine("Main thread ending.");
     }
   }
```

Sample output is shown here:

```
Main thread starting.

Loop Terminated early because a negative value was encountered
in iteration number 1000.

Main thread ending.
```

As the output shows, the transform loop stops after 1000 iterations. This is because **Break( )**
is called inside the **MyTransform( )** method when a negative value is encountered.

In addition to the two described here, there are several additional forms of **For( )**. Some
let you specify various options. Others use **long** rather than **int** as the type of iteration
parameters. There are also forms of **For( )** that provide added flexibility, such as being able
to specify a method that is invoked when each loop thread ends.

One other point: if you want to stop a **For( )** loop and don't care if any more iterations
whatsoever are performed, use the **Stop( )** method, rather than **Break( )**.

Using the ForEach( ) Method

You can create a parallelized version of the **foreach** loop by using the **ForEach( )** method. It
has several forms. Here is its simplest form:

> public static ParallelLoopResult
>   ForEach<TSource>(IEnumerable<TSource> *source,*
>   Action<TSource> *body*)

Here, *source* specifies the collection of data over which the loop will iterate and *body*
specifies the method that will be executed with each iteration. As explained earlier in this
book, all arrays and collections (described in Chapter 25), as well as several other sources,
support **IEnumerable<T>**. The method that you pass to the *body* receives the value of or
reference to (not the index of) each element being iterated as an argument. Information
about the status of the loop is returned.

Like **For( )**, you can stop a **ForEach( )** loop early by calling **Break( )** on the **ParallelLoopState** object passed to *body* if you use this version of **ForEach( )**:

public static ParallelLoopResult
        ForEach<TSource>(IEnumerable<TSource> *source,*
               Action<TSource, ParallelLoopState> *body*)

The following program demonstrates the **ForEach( )** loop. Like the previous examples, it creates a large array of integers. It differs from the previous examples in that the method that is executed with each iteration simply displays the values of the array on the console. Normally you would not use **WriteLine( )** inside a parallelized loop because console I/O is so slow that the loop will simply be I/O bound. However, it used here to illustrate **ForEach( )**. When a negative value is encountered, the loop is stopped via a call to **Break( )**. Depending upon the precise conditions of the execution environment, you might notice that even though **Break( )** is called in one task, another task may still continue to execute a few iterations prior to the stopping point.

```
// Use ParallelLoopResult, ParallelLoopState, and Break()
// with a parallel ForEach() loop.

using System;
using System.Threading.Tasks;

class DemoParallelForWithLoopResult {
  static int[] data;

  // A method to be run as the body of a parallel loop.
  // In this version, notice that the value of an element of
  // of data is passed to v, not an index.
  static void DisplayData(int v, ParallelLoopState pls) {

    // Break out of loop if a negative value is found.
    if(v < 0) pls.Break();

    Console.WriteLine("Value: " + v);
  }

  static void Main() {

    Console.WriteLine("Main thread starting.");

    data = new int[100000000];

    // Initialize data.
    for(int i=0; i < data.Length; i++) data[i] = i;

    // Put a negative value into data.
    data[100000] = -10;

    // Use a parallel ForEach() loop to display the data.
    ParallelLoopResult loopResult =
              Parallel.ForEach(data, DisplayData);
```

```
      // See if the loop ran to completion.
      if(!loopResult.IsCompleted)
        Console.WriteLine("\nLoop Terminated early because a " +
                          "negative value was encountered\n" +
                          "in iteration number " +
                          loopResult.LowestBreakIteration + ".\n");

      Console.WriteLine("Main thread ending.");
    }
  }
```

Although the preceding code used a named method as the delegate that represented the "body" of the loop, sometimes it is more convenient to use an anonymous method. For example, here the "body" of the **ForEach( )** loop is implemented as a lambda expression:

```
// Use a parallel ForEach() loop to display the data.
ParallelLoopResult loopResult =
            Parallel.ForEach(data, (v, pls) => {
              Console.WriteLine("Value: " + v);
              if(v < 0) pls.Break();
            });
```

Exploring PLINQ

PLINQ is the parallel version of LINQ, and it is closely related to the TPL. A primary use of PLINQ is to achieve data parallelism within a query. As you will see, this is very easy to do. Like the TPL, PLINQ is a large topic with many facets. This chapter introduces the basic concepts.

ParallelEnumerable

At the foundation of PLINQ is the **ParallelEnumerable** class, which is defined in **System.Linq**. This is a static class that defines many extension methods that support parallel operations. It is, essentially, the parallel version of the standard LINQ class **Enumerable**. Many of the methods extend **ParallelQuery**. Others return **ParallelQuery**. **ParallelQuery** encapsulates a sequence that supports parallel operations. Both generic and non-generic versions are supported. We won't be working with **ParallelQuery** directly, but we will be making use of several **ParallelEnumerable** methods. The most important of these is **AsParallel( )**, described in the following section.

Parallelizing a Query with AsParallel( )

Perhaps the single most convenient feature of PLINQ is how easy it is to create a parallel query. To do this, you simply call **AsParallel( )** on the data source. **AsParallel( )** is defined by **ParallelEnumerable**, and it returns the data source encapsulated within a **ParallelQuery** instance. This enables it to support parallel query extension methods. Once this is done, the query will partition the data source and operate on each partition in parallel if possible, and if the query is likely to benefit from parallelization. (If parallelization is not possible or reasonable, the query is simply executed sequentially.) Therefore, with the addition of a single call to **AsParallel( )**, a sequential LINQ query is transformed into a parallel PLINQ query, and for simple queries, this is the only step necessary.

There are both generic and non-generic versions of **AsParallel( )**. The non-generic version and the simplest generic version are shown here:

public static ParallelQuery AsParallel(this IEnumerable *source*)
public static ParallelQuery<TSource>
                AsParallel<TSource>(this IEnumerable<TSource> *source*)

Here, **TSource** stands for the type of the elements in the sequence *source*.
Here is an example that demonstrates a simple PLINQ query:

```
// A Simple PLINQ Query.

using System;
using System.Linq;

class PLINQDemo {

  static void Main() {

    int[] data = new int[10000000];

    // Initialize the data to positive values.
    for(int i=0; i < data.Length; i++) data[i] = i;

    // Now, insert some negative values.
    data[1000] = -1;
    data[14000] = -2;
    data[15000] = -3;
    data[676000] = -4;
    data[8024540] = -5;
    data[9908000] = -6;

    // Use a PLINQ query to find the negative values.
    var negatives = from val in data.AsParallel()
                    where val < 0
                    select val;

    foreach(var v in negatives)
      Console.Write(v + " ");

    Console.WriteLine();
  }
}
```

The program begins by creating a large array of integers called **data** that contains positive values. Next, a few negative values are inserted. Then, a PLINQ query is used to return a sequence of the negative values. This query is shown here:

```
var negatives = from val in data.AsParallel()
                where val < 0
                select val;
```

In this query, **AsParallel( )** is called on **data**. This enables parallel operations on **data**, which is the data source of the query, letting multiple threads search **data** in parallel, looking for negative values. As those values are found, they are added to the output sequence. This means that the order of the output sequence may not reflect the order of the negative values within **data**. For example, here is a sample run produced on a dual-core system:

```
-5 -6 -1 -2 -3 -4
```

As you can see, the thread that searched the higher partition found –5 and –6 before the thread that searched the lower partition found –1. It is important to understand that you might see a different outcome because of differences in task load, number of available processors, and so on. The key point is that the resulting sequence will not necessarily reflect the order of the original sequence.

Using AsOrdered( )

As pointed out in the previous section, by default, the order of the resulting sequence produced by a parallel query does not necessarily reflect the order of the source sequence. Furthermore, for all practical purposes, the resulting sequence should be considered unordered. If you need to have the result reflect the order of the source, you must specifically request it by using the **AsOrdered( )** method, which is defined by **ParallelEnumerable**. Both generic and non-generic forms are defined, as shown here:

```
public static ParallelQuery AsOrdered(this ParallelQuery source)
public static ParallelQuery<TSource>
            AsOrdered<TSource>(this ParallelQuery<TSource> source)
```

Here, **TSource** stands for the type of the elements in *source*. **AsOrdered( )** can only be called on a **ParallelQuery** object because it is a **ParallelQuery** extension method.

To see the effects of using **AsOrdered( )**, substitute the following query into the program in the preceding section:

```
// Use AsOrdered() to retain the order of the result.
var negatives = from val in data.AsParallel().AsOrdered()
                where val < 0
                select val;
```

When you run the program, the order of the elements in the resulting sequence will now reflect the order of the elements in the source sequence.

Cancelling a Parallel Query

Cancelling a parallel query is similar to cancelling a task, as described earlier. Both rely on the **CancellationToken** that is obtained from a **CancellationTokenSource**. This token is passed to the query by way of the **WithCancellation( )** method. To cancel the query, call **Cancel( )** on the token source. There is one important difference, however, between cancelling a parallel query and cancelling a task. When a parallel query is cancelled, it throws an **OperationCanceledException**, rather than an **AggregateException**. However, in cases where more than one exception can be generated by the query, an **OperationCanceledException** might be combined into an **AggregateException**. Therefore, it is often best to watch for both.

The **WithCancellation( )** method is shown here:

```
public static ParallelQuery<TSource>
            WithCancellation<TSource> (
                this ParallelQuery<TSource> source,
                CancellationToken cancellationToken)
```

Here, *source* specifies the invoking query, and *cancellationToken* specifies the cancellation token. It returns a query that supports the specified cancellation token.

The following example shows how to cancel the query used in the preceding program. It sets up a separate task that sleeps for 100 milliseconds and then cancels the query. A separate task is needed because the **foreach** loop that executes the query blocks the **Main( )** method until the loop completes.

```
// Cancel a parallel query.

using System;
using System.Linq;
using System.Threading;
using System.Threading.Tasks;

class PLINQCancelDemo {

  static void Main() {
    CancellationTokenSource cancelTokSrc = new CancellationTokenSource();
    int[] data = new int[10000000];

    // Initialize the data to positive values.
    for(int i=0; i < data.Length; i++) data[i] = i;

    // Now, insert some negative values.
    data[1000] = -1;
    data[14000] = -2;
    data[15000] = -3;
    data[676000] = -4;
    data[8024540] = -5;
    data[9908000] = -6;

    // Use a PLINQ query to find the negative values.
    var negatives = from val in data.AsParallel().
                              WithCancellation(cancelTokSrc.Token)
                    where val < 0
                    select val;

    // Create a task that cancels the query after 100 milliseconds.
    Task cancelTsk = Task.Factory.StartNew( () => {
                      Thread.Sleep(100);
                      cancelTokSrc.Cancel();
                     });

    try {
      foreach(var v in negatives)
        Console.Write(v + " ");
```

```
    } catch(OperationCanceledException exc) {
      Console.WriteLine(exc.Message);
    } catch(AggregateException exc) {
      Console.WriteLine(exc);
    } finally {
      cancelTsk.Wait();
      cancelTokSrc.Dispose();
      cancelTsk.Dispose();
    }

    Console.WriteLine();

  }
}
```

The output is shown here. Because the query is cancelled prior to completion, only the exception message is displayed.

```
The query has been canceled via the token supplied to WithCancellation.
```

Other PLINQ Features

As mentioned, PLINQ is a large subsystem. Part of its size is due to the flexibility that it provides. PLINQ offers many other features that help you tailor or manage a parallel query so it best fits the demands of your situation. Here are a few examples. You can specify the maximum number of processors that will be allocated to a query by calling **WithDegreeOfParallelism( )**. You can request that a portion of a parallel query be executed sequentially by calling **AsSequential( )**. If you don't want to block the calling thread waiting for results from a **foreach** loop, you can use the **ForAll( )** method. All of these methods are defined by **ParallelEnumerable**. To override cases in which PLINQ would default to sequential execution, you can use the **WithExecutionMode( )** method, passing in **ParallelExecutionMode.ForceParallelism**.

PLINQ Efficiency Concerns

Not every query will run faster simply because it is parallelized. As explained earlier in regards to the TPL, there is overhead associated with creating and managing concurrent threads of execution. In general, if the data source is quite small and if the processing required is quite short, then adding parallelism may not increase the speed of the query. For the latest information and guidelines in this regard, consult Microsoft's current recommendations.

Collections, Enumerators, and Iterators

This chapter discusses one of the most important parts of the .NET Framework: collections. In C#, a *collection* is a group of objects. The .NET Framework contains a large number of interfaces and classes that define and implement various types of collections. Collections simplify many programming tasks because they provide off-the-shelf solutions to several common, but sometimes tedious-to-develop, data structures. For example, there are built-in collections that support dynamic arrays, linked lists, stacks, queues, and hash tables. Collections are a state-of-the-art technology that merits close attention by all C# programmers.

Originally, there were only non-generic collection classes. However, the addition of generics in C# 2.0 coincided with the addition of many new generic classes and interfaces to the .NET Framework. The inclusion of the generic collections essentially doubled the number of collection classes and interfaces. With the advent of the Task Parallel Library in .NET Framework 4.0, several new thread-safe collection classes were added that are designed for use in situations in which multiple threads access a collection. As you can surmise, the Collections API is a very large part of the .NET Framework.

Also described in this chapter are two features that relate to collections: enumerators and iterators. Both enumerators and iterators enable the contents of a class to be cycled through via a **foreach** loop.

Collections Overview

The principal benefit of collections is that they standardize the way groups of objects are handled by your programs. All collections are designed around a set of cleanly defined interfaces. Several built-in implementations of these interfaces, such as **ArrayList**, **Hashtable**, **Stack**, and **Queue**, are provided, which you can use as-is. You can also implement your own collection, but you will seldom need to.

The .NET Framework supports five general types of collections: non-generic, specialized, bit-based, generic, and concurrent. The non-generic collections implement several fundamental data structures, including a dynamic array, stack, and queue. They also include *dictionaries*, in which you can store key/value pairs. An essential point to understand about the non-generic collections is that they operate on data of type **object**. Thus, they can be used to store any type of data, and different types of data can be mixed within the same collection. Of course, because they store **object** references, they are not type-safe. The non-generic collection classes and interfaces are in **System.Collections**.

The specialized collections operate on a specific type of data or operate in a unique way. For example, there are specialized collections for strings. There are also specialized collections that use a singly linked list. The specialized collections are declared in **System.Collections.Specialized**.

The Collections API defines one bit-based collection called **BitArray**. **BitArray** supports bitwise operations on bits, such as AND and XOR. As such, it differs significantly in its capabilities from the other collections. **BitArray** is declared in **System.Collections**.

The generic collections provide generic implementations of several standard data structures, such as linked lists, stacks, queues, and dictionaries. Because these collections are generic, they are type-safe. This means that only items that are type-compatible with the type of the collection can be stored in a generic collection, thus eliminating accidental type mismatches. Generic collections are declared in **System.Collections.Generic**.

The concurrent collections support multithreaded access to a collection. These are generic collections that are defined in **System.Collections.Concurrent**.

There are also several classes in the **System.Collections.ObjectModel** namespace that support programmers who want to create their own generic collections.

Fundamental to all collections is the concept of an *enumerator*, which is supported by the non-generic interfaces **IEnumerator** and **IEnumerable**, and the generic interfaces **IEnumerator<T>** and **IEnumerable<T>**. An enumerator provides a standardized way of accessing the elements within a collection, one at a time. Thus, it *enumerates* the contents of a collection. Because each collection must implement either a generic or non-generic form of **IEnumerable**, the elements of any collection class can be accessed through the methods defined by **IEnumerator** or **IEnumerator<T>**. Therefore, with only small changes, the code that cycles through one type of collection can be used to cycle through another. As a point of interest, the **foreach** loop uses the enumerator to cycle through the contents of a collection.

A feature related to an enumerator is the *iterator*. It simplifies the process of creating classes, such as custom collections, that can be cycled through by a **foreach** loop. Iterators are also described in this chapter.

One last thing: If you are familiar with C++, then you will find it helpful to know that the collection classes are similar in spirit to the Standard Template Library (STL) classes defined by C++. What a C++ programmer calls a *container*, a C# programmer calls a *collection*. The same is true of Java. If you are familiar with Java's Collections Framework, then you will have no trouble learning to use C# collections.

Because of the differences among the five types of collections—non-generic, bit-based, specialized, generic, and concurrent—this chapter discusses each separately.

The Non-Generic Collections

The non-generic collections have been part of the .NET Framework since version 1.0. They are defined in the **System.Collections** namespace. The non-generic collections are general-purpose data structures that operate on **object** references. Thus, they can manage any type of object, but not in a type-safe manner. This is both their advantage and disadvantage. Because they operate on **object** references, you can mix various types of data within the same collection. This makes them useful in situations in which you need to manage a collection of different types of objects or when the type of objects being stored are not known in advance. However, if you intend a collection to store a specific type of object, then the non-generic collections do not have the type-safety that is found in the generic collections.

The non-generic collections are defined by a set of interfaces and the classes that implement those interfaces. Each is described by the following sections.

The Non-Generic Interfaces

System.Collections defines a number of non-generic interfaces. It is necessary to begin with the collection interfaces because they determine the functionality common to all of the non-generic collection classes. The interfaces that underpin non-generic collections are summarized in Table 25-1. The following sections examine each interface in detail.

The ICollection Interface

The **ICollection** interface is the foundation upon which all non-generic collections are built. It declares the core methods and properties that all non-generic collections will have. It also inherits the **IEnumerable** interface.

Interface	Description
ICollection	Defines the elements that all non-generic collections must have.
IComparer	Defines the **Compare( )** method that performs a comparison on objects stored in a collection.
IDictionary	Defines a collection that consists of key/value pairs.
IDictionaryEnumerator	Defines the enumerator for a collection that implements **IDictionary**.
IEnumerable	Defines the **GetEnumerator( )** method, which supplies the enumerator for a collection class.
IEnumerator	Provides methods that enable the contents of a collection to be obtained one at a time.
IEqualityComparer	Compares two objects for equality.
IHashCodeProvider	Declared obsolete. Use **IEqualityComparer** instead.
IList	Defines a collection that can be accessed via an indexer.
IStructuralComparable	Defines the **CompareTo( )** method that is used for structural comparisons.
IStructuralEquatable	Defines the **Equals( )** method that is used to determine structural (rather than reference) equality. It also defines the **GetHashCode( )** method.

TABLE 25-1 The Non-Generic Collection Interfaces

ICollection defines the following properties:

Property	Meaning
int Count { get; }	The number of items currently held in the collection.
bool IsSynchronized { get; }	Is true if the collection is synchronized and false if it is not. By default, collections are not synchronized. It is possible, though, to obtain a synchronized version of most collections.
object SyncRoot { get; }	An object upon which the collection can be synchronized.

Count is the most often used property because it contains the number of elements currently held in a collection. If **Count** is zero, then the collection is empty.

ICollection defines the following method:

void CopyTo(Array *array*, int *index*)

CopyTo( ) copies the contents of a collection to the array specified by *array*, beginning at the index specified by *index*. Thus, **CopyTo( )** provides a pathway from a collection to a standard C# array.

Because **ICollection** inherits **IEnumerable**, it also includes the sole method defined by **IEnumerable**: **GetEnumerator( )**, which is shown here:

IEnumerator GetEnumerator( )

It returns the enumerator for the collection.

Because **ICollection** implements **IEnumerable**, four extension methods are defined for it. They are **AsParallel( )**, **AsQueryable( )**, **Cast( )**, and **OfType( )**. **AsParallel( )** is declared in **System.Linq.ParallelEnumerable**. **AsQueryable( )** is declared in **System.Linq.Queryable**. Both **Cast( )** and **OfType( )** are declared in **System.Linq.Enumerable**. These methods are designed primarily to support LINQ, but may be useful in other contexts.

The IList Interface

The **IList** interface declares the behavior of a non-generic collection that allows elements to be accessed via a zero-based index. It inherits **ICollection** and **IEnumerable**. In addition to the methods defined by **ICollection** and **IEnumerable**, **IList** defines several of its own. These are summarized in Table 25-2. Several of these methods imply the modification of a collection. If the collection is read-only or of fixed size, then these methods will throw a **NotSupportedException**.

Objects are added to an **IList** collection by calling **Add( )**. Notice that **Add( )** takes an argument of type **object**. Since **object** is a base class for all types, any type of object can be stored in a non-generic collection. This includes the value types, because boxing and unboxing will automatically take place.

You can remove an element using **Remove( )** or **RemoveAt( )**. **Remove( )** removes the specified object. **RemoveAt( )** removes the object at a specified index. To empty the collection, call **Clear( )**.

You can determine whether a collection contains a specific object by calling **Contains( )**. You can obtain the index of an object by called **IndexOf( )**. You can insert an element at a specific index by calling **Insert( )**.

Method	Description
int Add(object *value*)	Adds *value* into the invoking collection. Returns the index at which the object is stored.
void Clear( )	Deletes all elements from the invoking collection.
bool Contains(object *value*)	Returns true if the invoking collection contains *value*. Returns false if *value* is not in the collection.
int IndexOf(object *value*)	Returns the index of *value* if *value* is contained within the invoking collection. If *value* is not found, –1 is returned.
void Insert(int *index*, object *value*)	Inserts *value* at the index specified by *index*. Elements at and below *index* are moved down to make room for *value*.
void Remove(object *value*)	Removes the first occurrence of *value* from the invoking collection. Elements at and below the removed element are moved up to close the gap.
void RemoveAt(int *index*)	Removes the object at the index specified by *index* from the invoking collection. Elements at and below *index* are moved up to close the gap.

TABLE 25-2   The Methods Defined by **IList**

IList defines the following properties:

bool IsFixedSize { get; }
bool IsReadOnly { get; }

If the collection is of fixed size, **IsFixedSize** is true. This means elements cannot be inserted or removed. If the collection is read-only, then **IsReadOnly** is true. This means the contents of the collection cannot be changed.

IList defines the following indexer:

object this[int *index*] { get; set; }

You will use this indexer to get or set the value of an element. However, you cannot use it to add a new element to the collection. To add an element to a list, call **Add( )**. Once it is added, you can access the element through the indexer.

The IDictionary Interface

The **IDictionary** interface defines the behavior of a non-generic collection that maps unique keys to values. A key is an object that you use to retrieve a value at a later date. Thus, a collection that implements **IDictionary** stores key/value pairs. Once the pair is stored, you can retrieve it by using its key. **IDictionary** inherits **ICollection** and **IEnumerable**. The methods declared by **IDictionary** are summarized in Table 25-3. Several methods throw an **ArgumentNullException** if an attempt is made to specify a null key and null keys are not allowed.

To add a key/value pair to an **IDictionary** collection, use **Add( )**. Notice that the key and its value are specified separately. To remove an element, specify the key of the object in a call to **Remove( )**. To empty the collection, call **Clear( )**.

Method	Description
void Add(object *key*, object *value*)	Adds the key/value pair specified by *key* and *value* to the invoking collection.
void Clear( )	Removes all key/value pairs from the invoking collection.
bool Contains(object *key*)	Returns true if the invoking collection contains *key* as a key. Otherwise, returns false.
IDictionaryEnumerator GetEnumerator( )	Returns the enumerator for the invoking collection.
void Remove(object *key*)	Removes the entry whose key equals *key*.

TABLE 25-3 The Methods Defined by **IDictionary**

You can determine whether a collection contains a specific object by calling **Contains( )** with the key of the desired item. **GetEnumerator( )** obtains an enumerator compatible with an **IDictionary** collection. This enumerator operates on key/value pairs.

IDictionary defines the following properties:

Property	Description
bool IsFixedSize { get; }	Is true if the dictionary is of fixed size.
bool IsReadOnly { get; }	Is true if the dictionary is read-only.
ICollection Keys { get; }	Obtains a collection of the keys.
ICollection Values { get; }	Obtains a collection of the values.

Notice that the keys and values contained within the collection are available as separate lists through the **Keys** and **Values** properties.

IDictionary defines the following indexer:

object this[object *key*] { get; set; }

You can use this indexer to get or set the value of an element. You can also use it to add a new element to the collection. Notice that the "index" is not actually an index, but rather the key of the item.

IEnumerable, IEnumerator, and IDictionaryEnumerator

IEnumerable is the non-generic interface that a class must implement if it is to support enumerators. As explained, all of the non-generic collection classes implement **IEnumerable** because it is inherited by **ICollection**. The sole method defined by **IEnumerable** is **GetEnumerator( )**, which is shown here:

IEnumerator GetEnumerator( )

It returns the enumerator for the collection. Also, implementing **IEnumerable** allows the contents of a collection to be obtained by a **foreach** loop.

IEnumerator is the interface that defines the functionality of an enumerator. Using its methods, you can cycle through the contents of a collection. For collections that store key/value pairs (dictionaries), **GetEnumerator( )** returns an object of type **IDictionaryEnumerator**, rather than **IEnumerator**. **IDictionaryEnumerator** inherits **IEnumerator** and adds functionality to facilitate the enumeration of dictionaries.

IEnumerator defines the methods **MoveNext( )** and **Reset( )** and the **Current** property. These methods and the techniques needed to use them are described in detail later in this chapter. Briefly, **Current** obtains the element currently being obtained. **MoveNext( )** moves to the next element. **Reset( )** restarts the enumeration from the start.

IComparer and IEqualityComparer

The **IComparer** interface defines a method called **Compare( )**, which defines the way two objects are compared. It is shown here:

int Compare(object x, object y)

It must return greater than zero if x is greater than y, less than zero if x is less than y, and zero if the two values are the same. This interface can be used to specify how the elements of a collection should be sorted.

IEqualityComparer defines these two methods:

bool Equals(object x, object y)

int GetHashCode(object *obj*)

Equals( ) must return true if x and y are equal. **GetHashCode( )** must return the hash code for *obj*.

IStructuralComparable and IStructuralEquatable

The **IStructuralComparable** and **IStructuralEquatable** interfaces were added by .NET 4.0. The **IStructuralComparable** interface defines a method called **CompareTo( )**, which defines the way two objects are structurally compared for purposes of sorting. (In other words, **CompareTo( )** compares the contents of the object, not the references.) It is shown here:

int CompareTo(object *other*, IComparer *comparer*)

It must return –1 if the invoking object precedes *other*, 1 if the invoking object follows *other*, and zero if the two values are the same for the purposes of sorting. The object passed to *comparer* provides the comparison.

IStructuralEquatable is used to determine structural equality. Thus, it compares the contents of two objects. It defines the following methods.

bool Equals(object *other*, IEqualityComparer *comparer*)
int GetHashCode(IEqualityComparer *comparer*)

Equals( ) must return true if the invoking object and *other* are equal. **GetHashCode( )** must return the hash code for the invoking object. The results of these two methods must be compatible. The object passed to *comparer* provides the comparison.

The DictionaryEntry Structure

System.Collections defines one structure type called **DictionaryEntry**. Non-generic collections that hold key/value pairs store those pairs in a **DictionaryEntry** object. This structure defines the following two properties:

public object Key { get; set; }
public object Value { get; set; }

These properties are used to access the key or value associated with an entry. You can construct a **DictionaryEntry** object by using the following constructor:

public DictionaryEntry(object *key*, object *value*)

Here, *key* is the key and *value* is the value.

The Non-Generic Collection Classes

Now that you are familiar with the non-generic collection interfaces, we can examine the standard classes that implement them. With the exception of **BitArray**, described later, the non-generic collection classes are summarized here:

Class	Description
ArrayList	A dynamic array. This is an array that can grow as needed.
Hashtable	A hash table for key/value pairs.
Queue	A first-in, first-out list.
SortedList	A sorted list of key/value pairs.
Stack	A first-in, last-out list.

The following sections examine these collection classes and illustrate their use.

ArrayList

The **ArrayList** class supports dynamic arrays, which can grow or shrink as needed. In C#, standard arrays are of a fixed length, which cannot be changed during program execution. This means you must know in advance how many elements an array will hold. But sometimes you may not know until runtime precisely how large an array you will need. To handle this situation, use **ArrayList**. An **ArrayList** is a variable-length array of object references that can dynamically increase or decrease in size. An **ArrayList** is created with an initial size. When this size is exceeded, the collection is automatically enlarged. When objects are removed, the array can be shrunk. **ArrayList** is currently in wide use in existing code. For this reason, it is examined in depth here. However, many of the same techniques that apply to **ArrayList** apply to the other collections as well, including the generic collections.

   ArrayList implements **ICollection**, **IList**, **IEnumerable**, and **ICloneable**. **ArrayList** has the constructors shown here:

    public ArrayList( )
    public ArrayList(ICollection *c*)
    public ArrayList(int *capacity*)

The first constructor builds an empty **ArrayList** with an initial capacity of zero. The second constructor builds an **ArrayList** that is initialized with the elements specified by *c* and has an initial capacity equal to the number of elements. The third constructor builds an array list that has the specified initial *capacity*. The capacity is the size of the underlying array that is used to store the elements. The capacity grows automatically as elements are added to an **ArrayList**.

   In addition to the methods defined by the interfaces that it implements, **ArrayList** defines several methods of its own. Some of the more commonly used ones are shown in

Table 25-4. An **ArrayList** can be sorted by calling **Sort( )**. Once sorted, it can be efficiently searched by **BinarySearch( )**. The contents of an **ArrayList** can be reversed by calling **Reverse( )**.

    ArrayList supports several methods that operate on a range of elements within a collection. You can insert another collection into an **ArrayList** by calling **InsertRange( )**. You can remove a range by calling **RemoveRange( )**. You can overwrite a range within an **ArrayList** with the elements of another collection by calling **SetRange( )**. You can also sort or search a range rather than the entire collection.

    By default, an **ArrayList** is not synchronized. To obtain a synchronized wrapper around a collection, call **Synchronized( )**.

Method	Description
public virtual void AddRange(ICollection *c*)	Adds the elements in *c* to the end of the invoking **ArrayList**.
public virtual int BinarySearch(object *value*)	Searches the invoking collection for the value passed in *value*. The index of the matching element is returned. If the value is not found, a negative value is returned. The invoking list must be sorted.
public virtual int BinarySearch(object *value*, IComparer *comparer*)	Searches the invoking collection for the value passed in *value* using the comparison object specified by *comparer*. The index of the matching element is returned. If the value is not found, a negative value is returned. The invoking list must be sorted.
public virtual int BinarySearch(int *index*, int *count*, object *value*, IComparer *comparer*)	Searches the invoking collection for the value passed in *value* using the comparison object specified by *comparer*. The search begins at *index* and runs for *count* elements. The index of the matching element is returned. If the value is not found, a negative value is returned. The invoking list must be sorted.
public virtual void CopyTo(Array *array*)	Copies the contents of the invoking collection to the array specified by *array*, which must be a one-dimensional array compatible with the type of the elements in the collection.
public virtual void CopyTo(Array *array*, int *arrayIndex*)	Copies the contents of the invoking collection to the array specified by *array*, beginning at *arrayIndex*. The array must be a one-dimensional array compatible with the type of the elements in the collection.
public virtual void CopyTo(int *index*, Array *array*, int *arrayIndex*, int *count*)	Copies a portion of the invoking collection, beginning at *index* and running for *count* elements, to the array specified by *array*, beginning at *arrayIndex*. *array* must be a one-dimensional array compatible with the type of the elements in the collection.
public static ArrayList FixedSize(ArrayList *list*)	Wraps *list* in a fixed-size **ArrayList** and returns the result.
public virtual ArrayList GetRange(int *index*, int *count*)	Returns a portion of the invoking **ArrayList**. The range returned begins at *index* and runs for *count* elements. The returned object refers to the same elements as the invoking object.

TABLE 25-4   Several Commonly Used Methods Defined by **ArrayList**

Method	Description
public virtual int IndexOf(object *value*)	Returns the index of the first occurrence of *value* in the invoking collection. Returns –1 if *value* is not found.
public virtual void InsertRange(int *index*, ICollection *c*)	Inserts the elements of *c* into the invoking collection, starting at the index specified by *index*.
public virtual int LastIndexOf(object *value*)	Returns the index of the last occurrence of *value* in the invoking collection. Returns –1 if *value* is not found.
public static ArrayList ReadOnly(ArrayList *list*)	Wraps *list* in a read-only **ArrayList** and returns the result.
public virtual void RemoveRange(int *index*, int *count*)	Removes *count* elements from the invoking collection, beginning at *index*.
public virtual void Reverse( )	Reverses the contents of the invoking collection.
public virtual void Reverse(int *index*, int *count*)	Reverses *count* elements of the invoking collection, beginning at *index*.
public virtual void SetRange(int *index*, ICollection *c*)	Replaces elements within the invoking collection, beginning at *index,* within those specified by *c*.
public virtual void Sort( )	Sorts the collection into ascending order.
public virtual void Sort(IComparer *comparer*)	Sorts the collection using the specified comparison object. If *comparer* is null, the default comparison for each object is used.
public virtual void Sort(int *index*, int *count*, IComparer *comparer*)	Sorts a portion of the collection using the specified comparison object. The sort begins at *index* and runs for *count* elements. If *comparer* is null, the default comparison for each object is used.
public static ArrayList Synchronized(ArrayList *list*)	Returns a synchronized version of the invoking **ArrayList**.
public virtual object[ ] ToArray( )	Returns an array that contains copies of the elements of the invoking object.
public virtual Array ToArray(Type *type*)	Returns an array that contains copies of the elements of the invoking object. The type of the elements in the array is specified by *type*.
public virtual void TrimToSize( )	Sets **Capacity** to **Count**.

TABLE 25-4   Several Commonly Used Methods Defined by **ArrayList** *(continued)*

In addition to those properties defined by the interfaces that it implements, **ArrayList** adds **Capacity**, shown here:

public virtual int Capacity { get; set; }

Capacity gets or sets the capacity of the invoking **ArrayList**. The capacity is the number of elements that can be held before the **ArrayList** must be enlarged. As mentioned, an **ArrayList** grows automatically, so it is not necessary to set the capacity manually. However, for efficiency reasons, you might want to set the capacity when you know in advance how many elements the list will contain. This prevents the overhead associated with the allocation of more memory.

Conversely, if you want to reduce the size of the array that underlies an **ArrayList**, you can set **Capacity** to a smaller value. However, this value must not be less than **Count**. Recall that **Count** is a property defined by **ICollection** that holds the number of objects currently stored in a collection. Attempting to set **Capacity** to a value less than **Count** causes an **ArgumentOutOfRangeException** to be generated. To obtain an **ArrayList** that is precisely as large as the number of items that it is currently holding, set **Capacity** equal to **Count**. You can also call **TrimToSize( )**.

The following program demonstrates **ArrayList**. It creates an **ArrayList** and then adds characters to it. The list is then displayed. Some of the elements are removed, and the list is displayed again. Next, more elements are added, forcing the capacity of the list to be increased. Finally, the contents of elements are changed.

```
// Demonstrate ArrayList.

using System;
using System.Collections;

class ArrayListDemo {
  static void Main() {
    // Create an array list.
    ArrayList al = new ArrayList();

    Console.WriteLine("Initial number of elements: " +
                       al.Count);

    Console.WriteLine();

    Console.WriteLine("Adding 6 elements");
    // Add elements to the array list
    al.Add('C');
    al.Add('A');
    al.Add('E');
    al.Add('B');
    al.Add('D');
    al.Add('F');

    Console.WriteLine("Number of elements: " +
                       al.Count);

    // Display the array list using array indexing.
    Console.Write("Current contents: ");
    for(int i=0; i < al.Count; i++)
      Console.Write(al[i] + " ");
    Console.WriteLine("\n");

    Console.WriteLine("Removing 2 elements");
    // Remove elements from the array list.
    al.Remove('F');
    al.Remove('A');
```

```
        Console.WriteLine("Number of elements: " +
                          al.Count);

        // Use foreach loop to display the list.
        Console.Write("Contents: ");
        foreach(char c in al)
          Console.Write(c + " ");
        Console.WriteLine("\n");

        Console.WriteLine("Adding 20 more elements");
        // Add enough elements to force al to grow.
        for(int i=0; i < 20; i++)
          al.Add((char)('a' + i));
        Console.WriteLine("Current capacity: " +
                          al.Capacity);
        Console.WriteLine("Number of elements after adding 20: " +
                          al.Count);
        Console.Write("Contents: ");
        foreach(char c in al)
          Console.Write(c + " ");
        Console.WriteLine("\n");

        // Change contents using array indexing.
        Console.WriteLine("Change first three elements");
        al[0] = 'X';
        al[1] = 'Y';
        al[2] = 'Z';
        Console.Write("Contents: ");
        foreach(char c in al)
          Console.Write(c + " ");
        Console.WriteLine();
    }
}
```

The output from this program is shown here:

```
Initial number of elements: 0

Adding 6 elements
Number of elements: 6
Current contents: C A E B D F

Removing 2 elements
Number of elements: 4
Contents: C E B D

Adding 20 more elements
Current capacity: 32
Number of elements after adding 20: 24
Contents: C E B D a b c d e f g h i j k l m n o p q r s t

Change first three elements
Contents: X Y Z D a b c d e f g h i j k l m n o p q r s t
```

Sorting and Searching an ArrayList   An **ArrayList** can be sorted by **Sort( )**. Once sorted, it can be efficiently searched by **BinarySearch( )**. The following program demonstrates these methods:

```
// Sort and search an ArrayList.

using System;
using System.Collections;

class SortSearchDemo {
  static void Main() {
    // Create an array list.
    ArrayList al = new ArrayList();

    // Add elements to the array list.
    al.Add(55);
    al.Add(43);
    al.Add(-4);
    al.Add(88);
    al.Add(3);
    al.Add(19);

    Console.Write("Original contents: ");
    foreach(int i in al)
      Console.Write(i + " ");
    Console.WriteLine("\n");

    // Sort
    al.Sort();

    // Use foreach loop to display the list.
    Console.Write("Contents after sorting: ");
    foreach(int i in al)
      Console.Write(i + " ");
    Console.WriteLine("\n");

    Console.WriteLine("Index of 43 is " +
                      al.BinarySearch(43));
  }
}
```

The output is shown here:

```
Original contents: 55 43 -4 88 3 19

Contents after sorting: -4 3 19 43 55 88

Index of 43 is 3
```

Although an **ArrayList** can store objects of any type within the same list, when sorting or searching a list, it is necessary for those objects to be comparable. For example, the preceding program would have generated an exception if the list had included a string. (It is possible to create custom comparison methods that would allow the comparison of strings and integers, however. Custom comparators are discussed later in this chapter.)

Obtaining an Array from an ArrayList   When working with **ArrayList**, you will sometimes want to obtain an actual array that contains the contents of the list. You can do this by calling **ToArray( )**. There are several reasons why you might want to convert a collection into an array. Here are two: You may want to obtain faster processing times for certain operations, or you might need to pass an array to a method that is not overloaded to accept a collection. Whatever the reason, converting an **ArrayList** to an array is a trivial matter, as the following program shows:

```
// Convert an ArrayList into an array.

using System;
using System.Collections;

class ArrayListToArray {
  static void Main() {
    ArrayList al = new ArrayList();

    // Add elements to the array list.
    al.Add(1);
    al.Add(2);
    al.Add(3);
    al.Add(4);

    Console.Write("Contents: ");
    foreach(int i in al)
      Console.Write(i + " ");
    Console.WriteLine();

    // Get the array.
    int[] ia = (int[]) al.ToArray(typeof(int));
    int sum = 0;

    // Sum the array.
    for(int i=0; i<ia.Length; i++)
      sum += ia[i];

    Console.WriteLine("Sum is: " + sum);
  }
}
```

The output from the program is shown here:

```
Contents: 1 2 3 4
Sum is: 10
```

The program begins by creating a collection of integers. Next, **ToArray( )** is called with the type specified as **int**. This causes an array of integers to be created. Since the return type of **ToArray( )** is **Array**, the contents of the array must still be cast to **int[ ]**. (Recall that **Array** is the base type of all C# arrays.) Finally, the values are summed.

Hashtable

Hashtable creates a collection that uses a hash table for storage. As most readers will know, a *hash table* stores information using a mechanism called *hashing*. In hashing, the informational content of a key is used to determine a unique value, called its *hash code*. The hash code is then used as the index at which the data associated with the key is stored in the table. The transformation of the key into its hash code is performed automatically—you never see the hash code itself. The advantage of hashing is that it allows the execution time of lookup, retrieve, and set operations to remain near constant, even for large sets. **Hashtable** implements the **IDictionary**, **ICollection**, **IEnumerable**, **ISerializable**, **IDeserializationCallback**, and **ICloneable** interfaces.

Hashtable defines many constructors, including these frequently used ones:

public Hashtable( )
public Hashtable(IDictionary *d*)
public Hashtable(int *capacity*)
public Hashtable(int *capacity*, float *loadFactor*)

The first form constructs a default **Hashtable**. The second form initializes the **Hashtable** by using the elements of *d*. The third form initializes the capacity of the **Hashtable** to *capacity*. The fourth form initializes both the capacity and fill ratio. The fill ratio (also called the load factor) must be between 0.1 and 1.0, and it determines how full the hash table can be before it is resized upward. Specifically, when the number of elements is greater than the capacity of the table multiplied by its fill ratio, the table is expanded. For constructors that do not take a fill ratio, 1.0 is used.

In addition to the methods defined by the interfaces that it implements, **Hashtable** also defines several methods of its own. Some commonly used ones are shown in Table 25-5. To determine if a **Hashtable** contains a key, call **ContainsKey( )**. To see if a specific value is stored, call **ContainsValue( )**. To enumerate the contents of a **Hashtable**, obtain an **IDictionaryEnumerator** by calling **GetEnumerator( )**. Recall that **IDictionaryEnumerator** is used to enumerate the contents of a collection that stores key/value pairs.

Method	Description
public virtual bool ContainsKey(object *key*)	Returns true if *key* is a key in the invoking **Hashtable**. Returns false otherwise.
public virtual bool ContainsValue(object *value*)	Returns true if *value* is a value in the invoking **Hashtable**. Returns false otherwise.
public virtual IDictionaryEnumerator GetEnumerator( )	Returns an **IDictionaryEnumerator** for the invoking **Hashtable**.
public static Hashtable Synchronized(Hashtable *table*)	Returns a synchronized version of the **Hashtable** passed in *table*.

TABLE 25-5   Several Commonly Used Methods Defined by **Hashtable**

The public properties available in **Hashtable** are those defined by the interfaces that it implements. Two especially important ones are **Keys** and **Values** because they let you obtain a collection of a **Hashtable**'s keys or values. They are specified by **IDictionary** and are shown here:

```
public virtual ICollection Keys { get; }
public virtual ICollection Values { get; }
```

Because **Hashtable** does not maintain an ordered collection, there is no specific order to the collection of keys or values obtained. **Hashtable** also has a protected property: **EqualityComparer**. Two other properties called **hcp** and **comparer** are flagged as obsolete.

Hashtable stores key/value pairs in the form of a **DictionaryEntry** structure, but most of the time, you won't be aware of it directly because the properties and methods work with keys and values individually. For example, when you add an element to a **Hashtable**, you call **Add( )**, which takes two arguments: the key and the value.

It is important to note that **Hashtable** does not guarantee the order of its elements. This is because the process of hashing does not usually lend itself to the creation of sorted tables.

Here is an example that demonstrates **Hashtable**:

```
// Demonstrate Hashtable.

using System;
using System.Collections;

class HashtableDemo {
  static void Main() {
    // Create a hash table.
    Hashtable ht = new Hashtable();

    // Add elements to the table.
    ht.Add("house", "Dwelling");
    ht.Add("car", "Means of transport");
    ht.Add("book", "Collection of printed words");
    ht.Add("apple", "Edible fruit");

    // Can also add by using the indexer.
    ht["tractor"] = "Farm implement";

    // Get a collection of the keys.
    ICollection c = ht.Keys;

    // Use the keys to obtain the values.
    foreach(string str in c)
      Console.WriteLine(str + ": " + ht[str]);
  }
}
```

The output from this program is shown here:

```
book: Collection of printed words
tractor: Farm implement
apple: Edible fruit
```

```
house: Dwelling
car: Means of transport
```

As the output shows, the key/value pairs are not stored in sorted order. Notice how the contents of the hash table **ht** were obtained and displayed. First, a collection of the keys was retrieved by the **Keys** property. Each key was then used to index **ht**, yielding the value associated with each key. Remember, the indexer defined by **IDictionary** and implemented by **Hashtable** uses a key as the index.

SortedList

SortedList creates a collection that stores key/value pairs in sorted order, based on the value of the keys. **SortedList** implements the **IDictionary**, **ICollection**, **IEnumerable**, and **ICloneable** interfaces.

SortedList has several constructors, including those shown here:

> public SortedList( )
> public SortedList(IDictionary *d*)
> public SortedList(int *initialCapacity*)
> public SortedList(IComparer *comparer*)

The first constructor builds an empty collection with an initial capacity of zero. The second constructor builds a **SortedList** that is initialized with the elements of *d* and has an initial capacity equal to the number of elements. The third constructor builds an empty **SortedList** that has the initial capacity specified by *initialCapacity*. The capacity is the size of the underlying array that is used to store the elements. The fourth form lets you specify a comparison method that will be used to compare the objects contained in the list. This form creates an empty collection with an initial capacity of zero.

The capacity of a **SortedList** grows automatically as needed when elements are added to the list. When the current capacity is exceeded, the capacity is increased. The advantage of specifying a capacity when creating a **SortedList** is that you can prevent or minimize the overhead associated with resizing the collection. Of course, it makes sense to specify an initial capacity only if you have some idea of how many elements will be stored.

In addition to the methods defined by the interfaces that it implements, **SortedList** also defines several methods of its own. Some of the most commonly used ones are shown in Table 25-6. To determine if a **SortedList** contains a key, call **ContainsKey( )**. To see if a specific value is stored, call **ContainsValue( )**. To enumerate the contents of a **SortedList**, obtain an **IDictionaryEnumerator** by calling **GetEnumerator( )**. Recall that **IDictionaryEnumerator** is used to enumerate the contents of a collection that stores key/value pairs. You can obtain a synchronized wrapper around a **SortedList** by calling **Synchronized( )**.

There are various ways to set or obtain a value or key. To obtain the value associated with a specific index, call **GetByIndex( )**. To set a value given its index, call **SetByIndex( )**. You can retrieve the key associated with a specific index by calling **GetKey( )**. To obtain a list of all the keys, use **GetKeyList( )**. To get a list of all the values, use **GetValueList( )**. You can obtain the index of a key by calling **IndexOfKey( )** and the index of a value by calling **IndexOfValue( )**. Of course, **SortedList** also supports the indexer defined by **IDictionary** that lets you set or obtain a value given its key.

The public properties available in **SortedList** are those defined by the interfaces that it implements. As is the case with **Hashtable**, two especially important properties are **Keys**

Method	Description
public virtual bool ContainsKey(object *key*)	Returns true if *key* is a key in the invoking **SortedList**. Returns false otherwise.
public virtual bool ContainsValue(object *value*)	Returns true if *value* is a value in the invoking **SortedList**. Returns false otherwise.
public virtual object GetByIndex(int *index*)	Returns the value at the index specified by *index*.
public virtual IDictionaryEnumerator GetEnumerator( )	Returns an **IDictionaryEnumerator** for the invoking **SortedList**.
public virtual object GetKey(int *index*)	Returns the value of the key at the index specified by *index*.
public virtual IList GetKeyList( )	Returns an **IList** collection of the keys in the invoking **SortedList**.
public virtual IList GetValueList( )	Returns an **IList** collection of the values in the invoking **SortedList**.
public virtual int IndexOfKey(object *key*)	Returns the index of the key specified by *key*. Returns –1 if the key is not in the list.
public virtual int IndexOfValue(object *value*)	Returns the index of the first occurrence of the value specified by *value*. Returns –1 if the value is not in the list.
public virtual void SetByIndex(int *index*, object *value*)	Sets the value at the index specified by *index* to the value passed in *value*.
public static SortedList Synchronized(SortedList *list*)	Returns a synchronized version of the **SortedList** passed in *list*.
public virtual void TrimToSize( )	Sets **Capacity** to **Count**.

TABLE 25-6   Several Commonly Used Methods Defined by **SortedList**

and **Values** because they let you obtain a read-only collection of a **SortedList**'s keys or values. They are specified by **IDictionary** and are shown here:

> public virtual ICollection Keys { get; }
> public virtual ICollection Values { get; }

The order of the keys and values reflects that of the **SortedList**.

Like **Hashtable**, a **SortedList** stores key/value pairs in the form of a **DictionaryEntry** structure, but you will usually access the keys and values individually using the methods and properties defined by **SortedList**.

The following program demonstrates **SortedList**. It reworks and expands the **Hashtable** demonstration program from the previous section, substituting **SortedList**. When you examine the output, you will see that the **SortedList** version is sorted by key.

```
// Demonstrate a SortedList.

using System;
using System.Collections;

class SLDemo {
  static void Main() {
    // Create a sorted SortedList.
    SortedList sl = new SortedList();
```

```
    // Add elements to the table
    sl.Add("house", "Dwelling");
    sl.Add("car", "Means of transport");
    sl.Add("book", "Collection of printed words");
    sl.Add("apple", "Edible fruit");

    // Can also add by using the indexer.
    sl["tractor"] = "Farm implement";

    // Get a collection of the keys.
    ICollection c = sl.Keys;

    // Use the keys to obtain the values.
    Console.WriteLine("Contents of list via indexer.");
    foreach(string str in c)
      Console.WriteLine(str + ": " + sl[str]);

    Console.WriteLine();

    // Display list using integer indexes.
    Console.WriteLine("Contents by integer indexes.");
    for(int i=0; i < sl.Count; i++)
      Console.WriteLine(sl.GetByIndex(i));

    Console.WriteLine();

    // Show integer indexes of entries.
    Console.WriteLine("Integer indexes of entries.");
    foreach(string str in c)
      Console.WriteLine(str + ": " + sl.IndexOfKey(str));
  }
}
```

The output is shown here:

```
Contents of list via indexer.
apple: Edible fruit
book: Collection of printed words
car: Means of transport
house: Dwelling
tractor: Farm implement

Contents by integer indexes.
Edible fruit
Collection of printed words
Means of transport
Dwelling
Farm implement

Integer indexes of entries.
apple: 0
book: 1
car: 2
house: 3
tractor: 4
```

Stack

As most readers know, a stack is a first-in, last-out list. To visualize a stack, imagine a stack of plates on a table. The first plate put down is the last one to be picked up. The stack is one of the most important data structures in computing. It is frequently used in system software, compilers, and AI-based backtracking routines, to name just a few examples.

The collection class that supports a stack is called **Stack**. It implements the **ICollection**, **IEnumerable**, and **ICloneable** interfaces. **Stack** is a dynamic collection that grows as needed to accommodate the elements it must store.

Stack defines the following constructors:

```
public Stack( )
public Stack(int initialCapacity)
public Stack(ICollection col)
```

The first form creates an empty stack. The second form creates an empty stack with the initial capacity specified by *initialCapacity*. The third form creates a stack that contains the elements of the collection specified by *col* and an initial capacity equal to the number of elements.

In addition to the methods defined by the interfaces that it implements, **Stack** defines the methods shown in Table 25-7. In general, here is how you use **Stack**. To put an object on the top of the stack, call **Push( )**. To remove and return the top element, call **Pop( )**. You can use **Peek( )** to return, but not remove, the top object. An **InvalidOperationException** is thrown if you call **Pop( )** or **Peek( )** when the invoking stack is empty.

Method	Description
public virtual void Clear( )	Sets **Count** to zero, which effectively clears the stack.
public virtual bool Contains(object *obj*)	Returns true if *obj* is on the invoking stack. If *obj* is not found, false is returned.
public virtual object Peek( )	Returns the element on the top of the stack, but does not remove it.
public virtual object Pop( )	Returns the element on the top of the stack, removing it in the process.
public virtual void Push(object *obj*)	Pushes *obj* onto the stack.
public static Stack Synchronized(Stack *stack*)	Returns a synchronized version of the **Stack** passed in *stack*.
public virtual object[ ] ToArray( )	Returns an array that contains copies of the elements of the invoking stack.

TABLE 25-7 The Methods Defined by **Stack**

Here is an example that creates a stack, pushes several integers onto it, and then pops them off again:

```
// Demonstrate the Stack class.

using System;
using System.Collections;

class StackDemo {
  static void ShowPush(Stack st, int a) {
    st.Push(a);
    Console.WriteLine("Push(" + a + ")");

    Console.Write("stack: ");
    foreach(int i in st)
      Console.Write(i + " ");

    Console.WriteLine();
  }

  static void ShowPop(Stack st) {
    Console.Write("Pop -> ");
    int a = (int) st.Pop();
    Console.WriteLine(a);

    Console.Write("stack: ");
    foreach(int i in st)
      Console.Write(i + " ");

    Console.WriteLine();
  }

  static void Main() {
    Stack st = new Stack();

    foreach(int i in st)
      Console.Write(i + " ");

    Console.WriteLine();

    ShowPush(st, 22);
    ShowPush(st, 65);
    ShowPush(st, 91);
    ShowPop(st);
    ShowPop(st);
    ShowPop(st);
```

```
    try {
      ShowPop(st);
    } catch (InvalidOperationException) {
      Console.WriteLine("Stack empty.");
    }
  }
}
```

Here's the output produced by the program. Notice how the exception handler for **InvalidOperationException** manages a stack underflow.

```
Push(22)
stack: 22
Push(65)
stack: 65 22
Push(91)
stack: 91 65 22
Pop -> 91
stack: 65 22
Pop -> 65
stack: 22
Pop -> 22
stack:
Pop -> Stack empty.
```

Queue

Another familiar data structure is the queue, which is a first-in, first-out list. That is, the first item put in a queue is the first item retrieved. Queues are common in real life. For example, lines at a bank or fast-food restaurant are queues. In programming, queues are used to hold such things as the currently executing processes in the system, a list of pending database transactions, or data packets received over the Internet. They are also often used in simulations.

The collection class that supports a queue is called **Queue**. It implements the **ICollection**, **IEnumerable**, and **ICloneable** interfaces. **Queue** is a dynamic collection that grows as needed to accommodate the elements it must store. When more room is needed, the size of the queue is increased by a growth factor, which, by default, is 2.0.

Queue defines the following constructors:

public Queue( )
public Queue (int *capacity*)
public Queue (int *capacity*, float *growFactor*)
public Queue (ICollection *col*)

The first form creates an empty queue with a default capacity and uses the default growth factor of 2.0. The second form creates an empty queue with the initial capacity specified by *capacity* and a growth factor of 2.0. The third form allows you to specify a growth factor in *growFactor* (which must be between 1.0 and 10.0). The fourth form creates a queue that contains the elements of the collection specified by *col*, and an initial capacity equal to the number of elements. In this form, the default growth factor of 2.0 is used.

In addition to the methods defined by the interfaces that it implements, **Queue** defines the methods shown in Table 25-8. In general, here is how you use **Queue**. To put an object in the queue, call **Enqueue( )**. To remove and return the object at the front of the queue,

Method	Description
public virtual void Clear( )	Sets **Count** to zero, which effectively clears the queue.
public virtual bool Contains(object *obj*)	Returns true if *obj* is in the invoking queue. If *obj* is not found, false is returned.
public virtual object Dequeue( )	Returns the object at the front of the invoking queue. The object is removed in the process.
public virtual void Enqueue(object *obj*)	Adds *obj* to the end of the queue.
public virtual object Peek( )	Returns the object at the front of the invoking queue, but does not remove it.
public static Queue Synchronized(Queue *queue*)	Returns a synchronized version of *queue*.
public virtual object[ ] ToArray( )	Returns an array that contains copies of the elements of the invoking queue.
public virtual void TrimToSize( )	Sets **Capacity** to **Count**.

TABLE 25-8 The Methods Defined by **Queue**

call **Dequeue( )**. You can use **Peek( )** to return, but not remove, the next object. An **InvalidOperationException** is thrown if you call **Dequeue( )** or **Peek( )** when the invoking queue is empty.

Here is an example that demonstrates **Queue**:

```
// Demonstrate the Queue class.

using System;
using System.Collections;

class QueueDemo {
  static void ShowEnq(Queue q, int a) {
    q.Enqueue(a);
    Console.WriteLine("Enqueue(" + a + ")");

    Console.Write("queue: ");
    foreach(int i in q)
      Console.Write(i + " ");

    Console.WriteLine();
  }

  static void ShowDeq(Queue q) {
    Console.Write("Dequeue -> ");
    int a = (int) q.Dequeue();
    Console.WriteLine(a);

    Console.Write("queue: ");
    foreach(int i in q)
      Console.Write(i + " ");

    Console.WriteLine();
  }
```

```
static void Main() {
  Queue q = new Queue();

  foreach(int i in q)
    Console.Write(i + " ");

  Console.WriteLine();

  ShowEnq(q, 22);
  ShowEnq(q, 65);
  ShowEnq(q, 91);
  ShowDeq(q);
  ShowDeq(q);
  ShowDeq(q);

  try {
    ShowDeq(q);
  } catch (InvalidOperationException) {
    Console.WriteLine("Queue empty.");
  }
}
}
```

The output is shown here:

```
Enqueue(22)
queue: 22
Enqueue(65)
queue: 22 65
Enqueue(91)
queue: 22 65 91
Dequeue -> 22
queue: 65 91
Dequeue -> 65
queue: 91
Dequeue -> 91
queue:
Dequeue -> Queue empty.
```

Storing Bits with BitArray

The **BitArray** class supports a collection of bits. Because it stores bits rather than objects, **BitArray** has capabilities different from those of the other collections. However, it still supports the basic collection underpinning by implementing **ICollection** and **IEnumerable**. It also implements **ICloneable**.

BitArray defines several constructors. You can construct a **BitArray** from an array of Boolean values using this constructor:

public BitArray(bool[ ] *values*)

In this case, each element of *values* becomes a bit in the collection. Thus, each bit in the collection corresponds to an element of *values*. Furthermore, the ordering of the elements of *values* and the bits in the collection are the same.

You can create a **BitArray** from an array of bytes using this constructor:

public BitArray(byte[ ] *bytes*)

Here, the bit pattern in *bytes* becomes the bits in the collection, with *bytes*[0] specifying the first 8 bits, *bytes*[1] specifying the second 8 bits, and so on. In similar fashion, you can construct a **BitArray** from an array of **int**s using this constructor:

public BitArray(int[ ] *values*)

In this case, *values*[0] specifies the first 32 bits, *values*[1] specifies the second 32 bits, and so on. You can create a **BitArray** of a specific size using this constructor:

public BitArray(int *length*)

Here, *length* specifies the number of bits. The bits in the collection are initialized to **false**. To specify a size and initial value of the bits, use the following constructor:

public BitArray(int *length*, bool *defaultValue*)

In this case, all bits in the collection will be set to the value passed in *defaultValue*. Finally, you can create a new **BitArray** from an existing one by using this constructor:

public BitArray(BitArray *bits*)

The new object will contain the same collection of bits as *bits*, but the two collections will be otherwise separate.

BitArrays can be indexed. Each index specifies an individual bit, with an index of zero indicating the low-order bit.

In addition to the methods specified by the interfaces that it implements, **BitArray** defines the methods shown in Table 25-9. Notice that **BitArray** does not supply a **Synchronized( )** method. Thus, a synchronized wrapper is not available, and the **IsSynchronized** property is always false. However, you can control access to a **BitArray** by synchronizing on the object provided by **SyncRoot**.

Method	Description
public BitArray And(BitArray *value*)	ANDs the bits of the invoking object with those specified by *value* and returns a **BitArray** that contains the result.
public bool Get(int *index*)	Returns the value of the bit at the index specified by *index*.
public BitArray Not( )	Performs a bitwise, logical NOT on the invoking collection and returns a **BitArray** that contains the result.
public BitArray Or(BitArray *value*)	ORs the bits of the invoking object with those specified by *value* and returns a **BitArray** that contains the result.
public void Set(int *index*, bool *value*)	Sets the bit at the index specified by *index* to *value*.
public void SetAll(bool *value*)	Sets all bits to *value*.
public BitArray Xor(BitArray *value*)	XORs the bits of the invoking object with those specified by *value* and returns a **BitArray** that contains the result.

TABLE 25-9   The Methods Defined by **BitArray**

To the properties specified by the interfaces that it implements, **BitArray** adds **Length**, which is shown here:

public int Length { get; set; }

Length sets or obtains the number of bits in the collection. Thus, **Length** gives the same value as does the standard **Count** property, which is defined for all collections. However, **Count** is read-only, but **Length** is not. Thus, **Length** can be used to change the size of a **BitArray**. If you shorten a **BitArray**, bits are truncated from the high-order end. If you lengthen a **BitArray**, false bits are added to the high-order end.

BitArray defines the following indexer:

public bool this[int *index*] { get; set; }

You can use this indexer to get or set the value of an element.

Here is an example that demonstrates **BitArray**:

```
// Demonstrate BitArray.

using System;
using System.Collections;

class BADemo {
  public static void ShowBits(string rem,
                              BitArray bits) {
    Console.WriteLine(rem);
    for(int i=0; i < bits.Count; i++)
      Console.Write("{0, -6} ", bits[i]);
    Console.WriteLine("\n");
  }

  static void Main() {
    BitArray ba = new BitArray(8);
    byte[] b = { 67 };
    BitArray ba2 = new BitArray(b);

    ShowBits("Original contents of ba:", ba);

    ba = ba.Not();

    ShowBits("Contents of ba after Not:", ba);

    ShowBits("Contents of ba2:", ba2);

    BitArray ba3 = ba.Xor(ba2);

    ShowBits("Result of ba XOR ba2:", ba3);
  }
}
```

The output is shown here:

```
Original contents of ba:
False  False  False  False  False  False  False  False
```

```
Contents of ba after Not:
True    True    True    True    True    True    True    True

Contents of ba2:
True    True    False   False   False   False   True    False

Result of ba XOR ba2:
False   False   True    True    True    True    False   True
```

The Specialized Collections

The .NET Framework provides some specialized collections that are optimized to work on a specific type of data or in a specific way. These non-generic collection classes are defined inside the **System.Collections.Specialized** namespace. They are synopsized in the following table:

Specialized Collection	Description
CollectionsUtil	Contains factory methods that create collections that store strings, but ignore case differences.
HybridDictionary	A collection that uses a **ListDictionary** to store key/value pairs when there are few elements in the collection. When the collection grows beyond a certain size, a **Hashtable** is automatically used to store the elements.
ListDictionary	A collection that stores key/value pairs in a linked list. It is recommended only for small collections.
NameValueCollection	A sorted collection of key/value pairs in which both the key and value are of type **string**.
OrderedDictionary	A collection of key/value pairs that can be indexed.
StringCollection	A collection optimized for storing strings.
StringDictionary	A hash table of key/value pairs in which both the key and the value are of type **string**.

System.Collections also defines three abstract base classes, **CollectionBase**, **ReadOnlyCollectionBase**, and **DictionaryBase**, which can be inherited and used as a starting point for developing custom specialized collections.

The Generic Collections

The addition of generics greatly expanded the Collections API, essentially doubling the amount of collection classes and interfaces. The generic collections are declared in the **System.Collections.Generic** namespace. In many cases, the generic collection classes are simply generic equivalents of the non-generic classes discussed earlier. However, the correspondence is not one-to-one. For example, there is a generic collection called **LinkedList** that implements a doubly linked list, but no non-generic equivalent. In some cases, parallel functionality exists between the generic and non-generic classes, but the names differ. For example, the generic version of **ArrayList** is called **List**, and the generic version of **Hashtable** is called **Dictionary**. Also, the specific contents of the various interfaces and classes contain minor reorganizations, with some functionality shifting from one interface to another, for example. However, overall, if you understand the non-generic collections, then you can easily use the generic collections.

In general, the generic collections work in the same way as the non-generic collections with the exception that a generic collection is type-safe. Thus, a generic collection can store only items that are compatible with its type argument. Therefore, if you want a collection that is capable of storing unrelated, mixed types, you should use one of the non-generic classes. However, for all cases in which a collection is storing only one type of object, then a generic collection is your best choice.

The generic collections are defined by a set of interfaces and the classes that implement those interfaces. Each is described by the following sections.

The Generic Interfaces

System.Collections.Generic defines a number of generic interfaces, all of which parallel their corresponding non-generic counterparts. The generic interfaces are summarized in Table 25-10.

The ICollection<T> Interface

The **ICollection<T>** interface defines those features that all generic collections have in common. It inherits the **IEnumerable** and **IEnumerable<T>** interfaces. **ICollection<T>** is the generic version of the non-generic **ICollection** interface. However, there are some differences between the two.

ICollection<T> defines the following properties:

int Count { get; }

bool IsReadOnly { get; }

Count contains the number of items currently held in the collection. **IsReadOnly** is true if the collection is read-only. It is false if the collection is read/write.

Interface	Description
ICollection<T>	Defines the foundational features for the generic collections.
IComparer<T>	Defines the generic **Compare( )** method that performs a comparison on objects stored in a collection.
IDictionary<TKey, TValue>	Defines a generic collection that consists of key/value pairs.
IEnumerable<T>	Defines the generic **GetEnumerator( )** method, which supplies the enumerator for a collection class.
IEnumerator<T>	Provides members that enable the contents of a collection to be obtained one at a time.
IEqualityComparer<T>	Compares two objects for equality.
IList<T>	Defines a generic collection that can be accessed via an indexer.
ISet<T>	Defines a generic collection that represents a set.

TABLE 25-10   The Generic Collection Interfaces

ICollection<T> defines the following methods. Notice it defines a few more methods than does its non-generic counterpart.

Method	Description
void Add(T *item*)	Adds *item* to the invoking collection. Throws a **NotSupportedException** if the collection is read-only.
void Clear( )	Deletes all elements from the invoking collection and sets **Count** to zero.
bool Contains(T *item*)	Returns true if the invoking collection contains the object passed in *item* and false otherwise.
void CopyTo(T[ ] *array*, int *arrayIndex*)	Copies the contents of the invoking collection to the array specified by *array*, beginning at the index specified by *arrayIndex*.
bool Remove(T *item*)	Removes the first occurrence of *item* from the invoking collection. Returns true if *item* was removed and false if it was not found in the invoking collection.

Several of these methods will throw **NotSupportedException** if the collection is read-only. Because **ICollection<T>** inherits **IEnumerable** and **IEnumerable<T>**, it also includes both the generic and non-generic forms of the method **GetEnumerator( )**.

Because **ICollection<T>** implements **IEnumerable<T>**, it supports the extension methods defined by **Enumerable**. Although the extension methods were designed mostly for LINQ, they are available for other uses, including collections.

The IList<T> Interface

The **IList<T>** interface defines the behavior of a generic collection that allows elements to be accessed via a zero-based index. It inherits **IEnumerable**, **IEnumerable<T>**, and **ICollection<T>** and is the generic version of the non-generic **IList** interface. **IList<T>** defines the methods shown in Table 25-11. Two of these methods imply the modification of a collection. If the collection is read-only or of fixed size, then the **Insert( )** and **RemoveAt( )** methods will throw a **NotSupportedException**.

IList<T> defines the following indexer:

T this[int *index*] { get; set; }

This indexer sets or gets the value of the element at the index specified by *index*.

Method	Description
int IndexOf(T *item*)	Returns the index of the first occurrence of *item* if *item* is contained within the invoking collection. If *item* is not found, –1 is returned.
void Insert(int *index*, T *item*)	Inserts *item* at the index specified by *index*.
void RemoveAt(int *index*)	Removes the object at the index specified by *index* from the invoking collection.

TABLE 25-11   The Methods Defined by **IList<T>**

The IDictionary<TKey, TValue> Interface

The **IDictionary<TKey, TValue>** interface defines the behavior of a generic collection that maps unique keys to values. That is, it defines a collection that stores key/value pairs. **IDictionary<TKey, TValue>** inherits **IEnumerable, IEnumerable<KeyValuePair<TKey, TValue>>**, and **ICollection<KeyValuePair<TKey, TValue>>** and is the generic version of the non-generic **IDictionary**. The methods declared by **IDictionary<TKey, TValue>** are summarized in Table 25-12. All throw an **ArgumentNullException** if an attempt is made to specify a null key.

IDictionary<TKey, TValue> defines the following properties:

Property	Description
ICollection Keys<TKey> { get; }	Obtains a collection of the keys.
ICollection Values<TValue> { get; }	Obtains a collection of the values.

Notice that the keys and values contained within the collection are available as separate lists through the **Keys** and **Values** properties.

IDictionary<TKey, TValue> defines the following indexer:

TValue this[TKey *key*] { get; set; }

You can use this indexer to get or set the value of an element. You can also use it to add a new element to the collection. Notice that the "index" is not actually an index, but rather the key of the item.

IEnumerable<T> and IEnumerator<T>

IEnumerable<T> and **IEnumerator<T>** are the generic equivalents of the non-generic **IEnumerable** and **IEnumerator** interfaces described earlier. They declare the same methods and properties, and work in the same way. Of course, the generic versions operate on data of the type specified by the type argument.

Method	Description
void Add(TKey *key*, TValue *value*)	Adds the key/value pair specified by *key* and *value* to the invoking collection. An **ArgumentException** is thrown if *key* is already stored in the collection.
bool ContainsKey(TKey *key*)	Returns true if the invoking collection contains *key* as a key. Otherwise, returns false.
bool Remove(TKey *key*)	Removes the entry whose key equals *key*.
bool TryGetValue(TKey *key*, out TValue *value*)	Attempts to retrieve the value associated with *key*, putting it into *value*. Returns true if successful and false otherwise. If *key* is not found, *value* is given its default value.

TABLE 25-12 The Methods Defined by **IDictionary<TKey, TValue>**

IEnumerable<T> declares the **GetEnumerator( )** method as shown here:

IEnumerator<T> GetEnumerator( )

It returns an enumerator of type **T** for the collection. Thus, it returns a type-safe enumerator.

IEnumerator<T> has the same two methods as does the non-generic **IEnumerator**: **MoveNext( )** and **Reset( )**. It also declares a generic version of the **Current** property, as shown here:

T Current { get; }

It returns a **T** reference to the next object. Thus, the generic version of **Current** is type-safe.

There is one other difference between **IEnumerator** and **IEnumerator<T>**: **IEnumerator<T>** inherits the **IDisposable** interface, but **IEnumerator** does not. **IDisposable** defines the **Dispose( )** method, which is used to free unmanaged resources.

NOTE *IEnumerable<T> also implements the non-generic IEnumerable interface. Thus, it supports the non-generic version of GetEnumerator( ). IEnumerator<T> also implements the non-generic IEnumerator interface, thus supporting the non-generic versions of Current.*

IComparer<T>
The **IComparer<T>** interface is the generic version of **IComparer** described earlier. The main difference between the two is that **IComparer<T>** is type-safe, declaring the generic version of **Compare( )** shown here:

int Compare(T x, T y)

This method compares x with y and returns greater than zero if x is greater than y, zero if the two objects are the same, and less than zero if x is less that y.

IEqualityComparer<T>
The **IEqualityComparer<T>** interface is the equivalent of its non-generic relative **IEqualityComparer**. It defines these two methods:

bool Equals(T x, T y)

int GetHashCode(T *obj*)

Equals( ) must return true if x and y are equal. **GetHashCode( )** must return the hash code for *obj*. If two objects compare as equal, then their hash codes must also be the same.

The ISet<T> Interface
The **ISet<T>** interface was added by version 4.0 of the .NET Framework. It defines the behavior of a generic collection that implements a set of unique elements. It inherits **IEnumerable**, **IEnumerable<T>**, and **ICollection<T>**. **ISet<T>** defines the set of methods shown in Table 25-13. Notice that the parameters to these methods are specified as **IEnumerable<T>**. This means you can pass something other than another **ISet<T>** as the second set. Most often, however, both arguments will be instances of **ISet<T>**.

Method	Description
void ExceptWith(IEnumerable<T> *other*)	Removes from the invoking set those elements contained in *other*.
void IntersectWith(IEnumerable<T> *other*)	After calling this method, the invoking set contains the intersection of its elements and the elements in *other*.
bool IsProperSubsetOf(IEnumerable<T> *other*)	Returns true if the invoking set is a proper subset of *other*, and false otherwise.
bool IsProperSupersetOf(IEnumerable<T> *other*)	Returns true if the invoking set is a proper superset of *other*, and false otherwise.
bool IsSubsetOf(IEnumerable<T> *other*)	Returns true if the invoking set is a subset of *other*, and false otherwise.
bool IsSupersetOf(IEnumerable<T> *other*)	Returns true if the invoking set is a superset of *other*, and false otherwise.
bool Overlaps(IEnumerable<T> *other*)	Returns true if the invoking set and *other* have at least one element in common, and false otherwise.
bool SetEquals(IEnumerable<T> *other*)	Returns true if the invoking set and *other* have all elements in common, and false otherwise. The order of the elements doesn't matter, and duplicate elements in *other* are ignored.
void SymmetricExceptWith(IEnumerable<T> *other*)	After calling this method, the invoking set will contain the symmetric difference between its elements and those in *other*.
void UnionWith(IEnumerable<T> *other*)	After calling this method, the invoking set will contain the union of its elements and those in *other*.

TABLE 25-13   The Set Operations Defined by **ISet<T>**

The KeyValuePair<TKey, TValue> Structure

System.Collections.Generic defines a structure called **KeyValuePair<TKey, TValue>**, which is used to store a key and its value. It is used by the generic collection classes that store key/value pairs, such as **Dictionary<TKey, TValue>**. This structure defines the following two properties:

```
public TKey Key { get; };
public TValue Value { get; };
```

These properties hold the key or value associated with an entry. You can construct a **KeyValuePair<TKey, TValue>** object by using the following constructor:

```
public KeyValuePair(TKey key, TValue value)
```

Here, *key* is the key and *value* is the value.

The Generic Collection Classes

As mentioned at the start of this section, the generic collection classes largely parallel their non-generic relatives, although in some cases the names have been changed. Also, some differences in organization and functionality exist. The generic collections are defined in

System.Collections.Generic. The ones described in this chapter are shown in Table 25-14. These classes form the core of the generic collections.

NOTE *System.Collections.Generic also includes the following classes:*
SynchronizedCollection<T> is a synchronized collection based on IList<T>.
SynchronizedReadOnlyCollection<T> is a read-only synchronized collection
based on IList<T>. SynchronizedKeyedCollection<K, T> is an abstract class
used as a base class by System.ServiceModel.UriSchemeKeyedCollection.
KeyedByTypeCollection<T> is a collection that uses types as keys.

The List<T> Collection

The **List<T>** class implements a generic dynamic array and is conceptually similar to the non-generic **ArrayList** class. **List<T>** implements the **ICollection, ICollection<T>, IList, IList<T>, IEnumerable**, and **IEnumerable<T>** interfaces. **List<T>** has the constructors shown here:

```
public List( )
public List(IEnumerable<T> collection)
public List(int capacity)
```

The first constructor builds an empty **List** with a default initial capacity. The second constructor builds a **List** that is initialized with the elements of the collection specified by *collection* and with an initial capacity at least equal to the number of elements. The third constructor builds an array list that has the specified initial *capacity*. The capacity is the size of the underlying array that is used to store the elements. The capacity grows automatically as elements are added to a **List<T>**. Each time the list must be enlarged, its capacity is increased.

Class	Description
Dictionary<TKey, TValue>	Stores key/value pairs. Provides functionality similar to that found in the non-generic **Hashtable** class.
HashSet<T>	Stores a set of unique values using a hash table.
LinkedList<T>	Stores elements in a doubly linked list.
List<T>	A dynamic array. Provides functionality similar to that found in the non-generic **ArrayList** class.
Queue<T>	A first-in, first-out list. Provides functionality similar to that found in the non-generic **Queue** class.
SortedDictionary<TKey, TValue>	A sorted list of key/value pairs.
SortedList<TKey, TValue>	A sorted list of key/value pairs. Provides functionality similar to that found in the non-generic **SortedList** class.
SortedSet<T>	A sorted set.
Stack<T>	A first-in, last-out list. Provides functionality similar to that found in the non-generic **Stack** class.

TABLE 25-14   The Core Generic Collection Classes

In addition to the methods defined by the interfaces that it implements, **List<T>** defines several methods of its own. A sampling is shown in Table 25-15.

Method	Description
public void AddRange(IEnumerable<T> *collection*)	Adds the elements in *collection* to the end of the invoking list.
public int BinarySearch(T *item*)	Searches the invoking collection for the value passed in *item*. The index of the matching element is returned. If the value is not found, a negative value is returned. The invoking list must be sorted.
public int BinarySearch(T *item*, IComparer<T> *comparer*)	Searches the invoking collection for the value passed in *item* using the comparison object specified by *comparer*. The index of the matching element is returned. If the value is not found, a negative value is returned. The invoking list must be sorted.
public int BinarySearch(int *index*, int *count*, T *item*, IComparer<T> *comparer*)	Searches the invoking collection for the value passed in *item* using the comparison object specified by *comparer*. The search begins at *index* and runs for *count* elements. The index of the matching element is returned. If the value is not found, a negative value is returned. The invoking list must be sorted.
public List<T> GetRange(int *index*, int *count*)	Returns a portion of the invoking list. The range returned begins at *index* and runs for *count* elements. The returned object refers to the same elements as the invoking object.
public int IndexOf(T *item*)	Returns the index of the first occurrence of *item* in the invoking collection. Returns –1 if *item* is not found.
public void InsertRange(int *index*, IEnumerable<T> *collection*)	Inserts the elements of *collection* into the invoking collection, starting at the index specified by *index*.
public int LastIndexOf(T *item*)	Returns the index of the last occurrence of *item* in the invoking collection. Returns –1 if *item* is not found.
public void RemoveRange(int *index*, int *count*)	Removes *count* elements from the invoking collection, beginning at *index*.
public void Reverse( )	Reverses the contents of the invoking collection.
public void Reverse(int *index*, int *count*)	Reverses *count* elements of the invoking collection, beginning at *index*.
public void Sort( )	Sorts the collection into ascending order.
public void Sort(IComparer<T> *comparer*)	Sorts the collection using the specified comparison object. If *comparer* is null, the default comparer for each object is used.
public void Sort(Comparison<T> *comparison*)	Sorts the collection using the specified comparison delegate.

TABLE 25-15 A Sampling of Methods Defined by **List<T>**

Method	Description

public void
    Sort(int *index*,
        int *count*,
        IComparer<T> *comparer*)
	Sorts a portion of the collection using the specified comparison object. The sort begins at *index* and runs for *count* elements. If *comparer* is null, the default comparer for each object is used.

public T[ ] ToArray( )	Returns an array that contains copies of the elements of the invoking object.
public void TrimExcess( )	Reduces the capacity of the invoking list so that it is no more than 10 percent greater than the number of elements that it currently holds.

Table 25-15 A Sampling of Methods Defined by **List<T>** *(continued)*

In addition to the properties defined by the interfaces that it implements, **List<T>** adds **Capacity**, shown here:

public int Capacity { get; set; }

Capacity gets or sets the capacity of the invoking list. The capacity is the number of elements that can be held before the list must be enlarged. Because a list grows automatically, it is not necessary to set the capacity manually. However, for efficiency reasons, you might want to set the capacity when you know in advance how many elements the list will contain. This prevents the overhead associated with the allocation of more memory.

The following indexer, defined by **IList<T>**, is implemented by **List<T>**, as shown here:

public T this[int *index*] { get; set; }

It sets or gets the value of the element at the index specified by *index*.

Here is a program that demonstrates **List<T>**. It reworks the first **ArrayList** program shown earlier in this chapter. The only changes necessary are to substitute the name **List** for **ArrayList** and to use the generic type parameters.

```
// Demonstrate List<T>.

using System;
using System.Collections.Generic;

class GenListDemo {
  static void Main() {
    // Create a list.
    List<char> lst = new List<char>();

    Console.WriteLine("Initial number of elements: " +
                      lst.Count);

    Console.WriteLine();

    Console.WriteLine("Adding 6 elements");
    // Add elements to the array list
    lst.Add('C');
    lst.Add('A');
```

```
    lst.Add('E');
    lst.Add('B');
    lst.Add('D');
    lst.Add('F');

    Console.WriteLine("Number of elements: " +
                       lst.Count);

    // Display the list using array indexing.
    Console.Write("Current contents: ");
    for(int i=0; i < lst.Count; i++)
      Console.Write(lst[i] + " ");
    Console.WriteLine("\n");

    Console.WriteLine("Removing 2 elements");
    // Remove elements from the list.
    lst.Remove('F');
    lst.Remove('A');

    Console.WriteLine("Number of elements: " +
                       lst.Count);

    // Use foreach loop to display the list.
    Console.Write("Contents: ");
    foreach(char c in lst)
      Console.Write(c + " ");
    Console.WriteLine("\n");

    Console.WriteLine("Adding 20 more elements");
    // Add enough elements to force lst to grow.
    for(int i=0; i < 20; i++)
      lst.Add((char)('a' + i));
    Console.WriteLine("Current capacity: " +
                       lst.Capacity);
    Console.WriteLine("Number of elements after adding 20: " +
                       lst.Count);
    Console.Write("Contents: ");
    foreach(char c in lst)
      Console.Write(c + " ");
    Console.WriteLine("\n");

    // Change contents using array indexing.
    Console.WriteLine("Change first three elements");
    lst[0] = 'X';
    lst[1] = 'Y';
    lst[2] = 'Z';

    Console.Write("Contents: ");
    foreach(char c in lst)
      Console.Write(c + " ");
    Console.WriteLine();
```

```
    // Because of generic type-safety,
    // the following line is illegal.
//    lst.Add(99); // Error, not a char!
  }
}
```

The output, shown here, is the same as that produced by the non-generic version of the program:

```
Initial number of elements: 0

Adding 6 elements
Number of elements: 6
Current contents: C A E B D F

Removing 2 elements
Number of elements: 4
Contents: C E B D

Adding 20 more elements
Current capacity: 32
Number of elements after adding 20: 24
Contents: C E B D a b c d e f g h i j k l m n o p q r s t

Change first three elements
Contents: X Y Z D a b c d e f g h i j k l m n o p q r s t
```

LinkedList<T>

The **LinkedList<T>** class implements a generic doubly linked list. It implements **ICollection**, **ICollection<T>**, **IEnumerable**, **IEnumerable<T>**, **ISerializable**, and **IDeserializationCallback**. (The last two interfaces support the serialization of the list.) **LinkedList<T>** defines two public constructors, shown here:

> public LinkedList( )
> public LinkedList(IEnumerable<T> *collection*)

The first creates an empty linked list. The second creates a list initialized with the elements in *collection*.

Like most linked list implementations, **LinkedList<T>** encapsulates the values stored in the list in *nodes* that contain links to the previous and next element in the list. These nodes are objects of type **LinkedListNode<T>**. **LinkedListNode<T>** provides the four properties shown here:

> public LinkedListNode<T> Next { get; }
> public LinkedListNode<T> Previous { get; }
> public LinkedList<T> List { get; }
> public T Value { get; set; }

Next and **Previous** obtain a reference to the next or previous node in the list, respectively. You can use these properties to traverse the list in either direction. A null reference is returned if no next or previous node exists. You can obtain a reference to the list itself via **List**. You can get or set the value within a node by using **Value**.

LinkedList<T> defines many methods. A sampling is shown in Table 25-16. In addition to the properties defined by the interfaces that it implements, LinkedList<T> defines these properties:

```
public LinkedListNode<T> First { get; }
public LinkedListNode<T> Last { get; }
```

First obtains the first node in the list. **Last** obtains the last node in the list.

Method	Description
public LinkedListNode<T> AddAfter(LinkedListNode<T> *node*, T *value*)	Adds a node with the value *value* to the list immediately after the node specified by *node*. The node passed in *node* must not be **null**. Returns a reference to the node containing the value *value*.
public void AddAfter(LinkedListNode<T> *node*, LinkedListNode<T> *newNode*)	Adds the node passed in *newNode* to the list immediately after the node specified by *node*. The node passed in *node* or *newNode* must not be **null**. Throws an **InvalidOperationException** if *node* is not in the list or if *newNode* is part of another list.
public LinkedListNode<T> AddBefore(LinkedListNode<T> *node*, T *value*)	Adds a node with the value *value* to the list immediately before the node specified by *node*. The node passed in *node* must not be **null**. Returns a reference to the node containing the value *value*.
public void AddBefore(LinkedListNode<T> *node*, LinkedListNode<T> *newNode*)	Adds the node passed in *newNode* to the list immediately before the node specified by *node*. The node passed in *node* or *newNode* must not be **null**. Throws an **InvalidOperationException** if *node* is not in the list or if *newNode* is part of another list.
public LinkedList<T> AddFirst(T *value*)	Adds a node with the value *value* to the start of the list. Returns a reference to the node containing the value *value*.
public void AddFirst(LinkedListNode<T> *node*)	Adds *node* to the start of the list. *node* must not be **null**. Throws an **InvalidOperationException** if *node* is part of another list.
public LinkedList<T> AddLast(T *value*)	Adds a node with the value *value* to the end of the list. Returns a reference to the node containing the value *value*.
public void AddLast(LinkedListNode<T> *node*)	Adds *node* to the end of the list. *node* must not be **null**. Throws an **InvalidOperationException** if *node* is part of another list.
public LinkedList<T> Find(T *value*)	Returns a reference to the first node in the list that has the value *value*. **null** is returned if *value* is not in the list.
public LinkedList<T> FindLast(T *value*)	Returns a reference to the last node in the list that has the value *value*. **null** is returned if *value* is not in the list.

TABLE 25-16 A Sampling of Methods Defined by **LinkedList<T>**

Method	Description
public bool Remove(T *value*)	Removes the first node in the list that has the value *value*. Returns true if the node was removed. (That is, if a node with the value *value* was in the list and it was removed.) Returns false otherwise.
public void Remove(LinkedList<T> *node*)	Removes the node that matches *node*. Throws an **InvalidOperationException** if *node* is not in the list.
public void RemoveFirst( )	Removes the first node in the list.
public void RemoveLast( )	Removes the last node in the list.

TABLE 25-16   A Sampling of Methods Defined by **LinkedList<T>** *(continued)*

Here is an example that demonstrates the **LinkedList<T>** class:

```
// Demonstrate LinkedList<T>.

using System;
using System.Collections.Generic;

class GenLinkedListDemo {
  static void Main() {
    // Create a linked list.
    LinkedList<char> ll = new LinkedList<char>();

    Console.WriteLine("Initial number of elements: " +
                      ll.Count);

    Console.WriteLine();

    Console.WriteLine("Adding 5 elements.");
    // Add elements to the linked list
    ll.AddFirst('A');
    ll.AddFirst('B');
    ll.AddFirst('C');
    ll.AddFirst('D');
    ll.AddFirst('E');

    Console.WriteLine("Number of elements: " +
                      ll.Count);

    // Display the linked list by manually walking
    // through the list.
    LinkedListNode<char> node;

    Console.Write("Display contents by following links: ");
    for(node = ll.First; node != null; node = node.Next)
      Console.Write(node.Value + " ");

    Console.WriteLine("\n");
```

```
    //Display the linked list by use of a foreach loop.
    Console.Write("Display contents with foreach loop: ");
    foreach(char ch in ll)
      Console.Write(ch + " ");

    Console.WriteLine("\n");

    // Display the list backward by manually walking
    // from last to first.
    Console.Write("Follow links backwards: ");
      for(node = ll.Last; node != null; node = node.Previous)
      Console.Write(node.Value + " ");

    Console.WriteLine("\n");

    // Remove two elements.
    Console.WriteLine("Removing 2 elements.");
    // Remove elements from the linked list.
    ll.Remove('C');
    ll.Remove('A');

    Console.WriteLine("Number of elements: " +
                      ll.Count);

    // Use foreach loop to display the modified list.
    Console.Write("Contents after deletion: ");
    foreach(char ch in ll)
      Console.Write(ch + " ");

    Console.WriteLine("\n");

    // Add three elements to the end of the list.
    ll.AddLast('X');
    ll.AddLast('Y');
    ll.AddLast('Z');

    Console.Write("Contents after addition to end: ");
    foreach(char ch in ll)
      Console.Write(ch + " ");

    Console.WriteLine("\n");
  }
}
```

Here is the output:

```
Initial number of elements: 0

Adding 5 elements.
Number of elements: 5
Display contents by following links: E D C B A

Display contents with foreach loop: E D C B A
```

```
Follow links backwards: A B C D E

Removing 2 elements.
Number of elements: 3
Contents after deletion: E D B

Contents after addition to end: E D B X Y Z
```

Perhaps the most important thing to notice in this program is that the list is traversed in both the forward and backward direction by following the links provided by the **Next** and **Previous** properties. The bidirectional property of doubly linked lists is especially important in applications such as databases in which the ability to move efficiently through the list in both directions is often necessary.

The Dictionary<TKey, TValue> Class

The **Dictionary<TKey, TValue>** class stores key/value pairs. In a dictionary, values are accessed through their keys. In this regard, it is similar to the non-generic **Hashtable** class. **Dictionary<TKey, TValue>** implements **IDictionary, IDictionary<TKey, TValue>, ICollection, ICollection<KeyValuePair<TKey, TValue>>, IEnumerable, IEnumerable<KeyValuePair<TKey, TValue>>, ISerializable**, and **IDeserializationCallback**. (The last two interfaces support the serialization of the list.) Dictionaries are dynamic, growing as needed.

Dictionary<TKey, TValue> provides many constructors. Here is a sampling:

public Dictionary( )
public Dictionary(IDictionary<TKey, TValue> *dictionary*)
public Dictionary(int *capacity*)

The first constructor creates an empty dictionary with a default capacity. The second creates a dictionary that contains the same elements as those in *dictionary*. The third lets you specify an initial capacity. If you know in advance that you will need a dictionary of a certain size, then specifying that capacity will prevent the resizing of the dictionary at runtime, which is a costly process.

Dictionary<TKey, TValue> defines several methods. Some commonly used ones are shown in Table 25-17.

Method	Description
public void Add(TKey *key*, TValue *value*)	Adds the key/value pair specified by *key* and *value* to the dictionary. If the *key* is already in the dictionary, then its value is unchanged and an **ArgumentException** is thrown. *key* must not be **null**.
public bool ContainsKey(TKey *key*)	Returns true if *key* is a key in the invoking dictionary. Returns false otherwise.
public bool ContainsValue(TValue *value*)	Returns true if *value* is a value in the invoking dictionary. Returns false otherwise.
public bool Remove(TKey *key*)	Removes *key* from the dictionary. Returns true if successful. Returns false if *key* was not in the dictionary.

TABLE 25-17   Several Commonly Used Methods Defined by **Dictionary<TKey, TValue>**

In addition to the properties defined by the interfaces that it implements, **Dictionary<TKey, TValue>** defines these properties:

Property	Description
public IEqualityComparer<TKey> Comparer { get; }	Obtains the comparer for the invoking dictionary.
public Dictionary<TKey, TValue>.KeyCollection Keys { get; }	Obtains a collection of the keys.
public Dictionary<TKey, TValue>.ValueCollection Values { get; }	Obtains a collection of the values.

Notice that the keys and values contained within the collection are available as separate lists through the **Keys** and **Values** properties. The types **Dictionary<TKey, TValue>.KeyCollection** and **Dictionary<TKey, TValue>.ValueCollection** are collections that implement both the generic and non-generic forms of **ICollection** and **IEnumerable**.

The following indexer, defined by **IDictionary<TKey, TValue>**, is implemented by **Dictionary<TKey, TValue>** as shown here:

    public TValue this[TKey *key*] { get; set; }

You can use this indexer to get or set the value of an element. You can also use it to add a new element to the collection. Notice that the "index" is not actually an index, but rather the key of the item.

When enumerating the collection, **Dictionary<TKey, TValue>** returns key/value pairs in the form of a **KeyValuePair<TKey, TValue>** structure. Recall that this structure defines the following two properties:

    public TKey Key { get; }
    public TValue Value { get; }

These properties obtain the key or value associated with an entry. However, most of the time you won't need to use **KeyValuePair<TKey, TValue>** directly because **Dictionary<TKey, TValue>** allows you to work the keys and values individually. However, when enumerating a **Dictionary<TKey, TValue>**, such as in a **foreach** loop, the objects being enumerated are **KeyValuePair**s.

In a **Dictionary<TKey, TValue>**, all keys must be unique, and a key must not change while it is in use as a key. Values need not be unique. The objects in a **Dictionary<TKey, TValue>** are not stored in sorted order.

Here is an example that demonstrates **Dictionary<TKey, TValue>**:

```
// Demonstrate the generic Dictionary<TKey, TValue> class.

using System;
using System.Collections.Generic;
```

```
class GenDictionaryDemo {
  static void Main() {
    // Create a Dictionary that holds employee
    // names and their corresponding salary.
    Dictionary<string, double> dict =
      new Dictionary<string, double>();

    // Add elements to the collection.
    dict.Add("Butler, John", 73000);
    dict.Add("Swartz, Sarah", 59000);
    dict.Add("Pyke, Thomas", 45000);
    dict.Add("Frank, Ed", 99000);

    // Get a collection of the keys (names).
    ICollection<string> c = dict.Keys;

    // Use the keys to obtain the values (salaries).
    foreach(string str in c)
      Console.WriteLine("{0}, Salary: {1:C}", str, dict[str]);
  }
}
```

Here is the output:

```
Butler, John, Salary: $73,000.00
Swartz, Sarah, Salary: $59,000.00
Pyke, Thomas, Salary: $45,000.00
Frank, Ed, Salary: $99,000.00
```

The SortedDictionary<TKey, TValue> Class

The **SortedDictionary<TKey, TValue>** class stores key/value pairs and is similar to **Dictionary<TKey, TValue>** except that it is sorted by key. **SortedDictionary<TKey, TValue>** implements **IDictionary**, **IDictionary<TKey, TValue>**, **ICollection**, **ICollection<KeyValuePair<TKey, TValue>>**, **IEnumerable**, and **IEnumerable<KeyValuePair<TKey, TValue>>**. **SortedDictionary<TKey, TValue>** provides the following constructors:

> public SortedDictionary( )
>
> public SortedDictionary(IDictionary<TKey, TValue> *dictionary*)
>
> public SortedDictionary(IComparer<TKey> *comparer*)
>
> public SortedDictionary(IDictionary<TKey, TValue> *dictionary*,
> IComparer<TKey> *comparer*)

The first constructor creates an empty dictionary. The second creates a dictionary that contains the same elements as those in *dictionary*. The third lets you specify the **IComparer** that the dictionary will use for sorting, and the fourth lets you initialize the dictionary and specify the **IComparer**.

SortedDictionary<TKey, TValue> defines several methods. A sampling is shown in Table 25-18.

Method	Description
public void Add(TKey *key*, TValue *value*)	Adds the key/value pair specified by *key* and *value* to the dictionary. If the *key* is already in the dictionary, then its value is unchanged and an **ArgumentException** is thrown. *key* must not be **null**.
public bool ContainsKey(TKey *key*)	Returns true if *key* is a key in the invoking dictionary. Returns false otherwise.
public bool ContainsValue(TValue *value*)	Returns true if *value* is a value in the invoking dictionary. Returns false otherwise.
public bool Remove(TKey *key*)	Removes *key* from the dictionary. Returns true if successful. Returns false if *key* was not in the dictionary.

TABLE 25-18   A Sampling of Methods Defined by **SortedDictionary<TKey, TValue>**

In addition to the properties defined by the interfaces that it implements, **SortedDictionary<TKey, TValue>** defines the following properties:

Property	Description
public IComparer<TKey> Comparer { get; }	Obtains the comparer for the invoking dictionary.
public SortedDictionary<TKey, TValue>.KeyCollection Keys { get; }	Obtains a collection of the keys.
public SortedDictionary<TKey, TValue>.ValueCollection Values { get; }	Obtains a collection of the values.

Notice that the keys and values contained within the collection are available as separate lists through the **Keys** and **Values** properties. The types

SortedDictionary<TKey, TValue>.KeyCollection
SortedDictionary<TKey, TValue>.ValueCollection

are collections that implement both the generic and non-generic forms of **ICollection** and **IEnumerable**.

SortedDictionary<TKey, TValue> defines the following indexer (which is specified by **IDictionary<TKey, TValue>**):

public TValue this[TKey *key*] { get; set; }

You can use this indexer to get or set the value of an element. You can also use it to add a new element to the collection. Notice that the "index" is not actually an index, but rather the key of the item.

When enumerated, **SortedDictionary<TKey, TValue>** returns key/value pairs in the form of a **KeyValuePair<TKey, TValue>** structure. Recall that this structure defines the following two properties:

```
public TKey Key { get; }
public TValue Value { get; }
```

These properties obtain the key or value associated with an entry. However, most of the time you won't need to use **KeyValuePair<TKey, TValue>** directly because **SortedDictionary<TKey, TValue>** allows you to work with the keys and values individually. However, when enumerating a **SortedDictionary<TKey, TValue>**, such as in a **foreach** loop, the objects being enumerated are **KeyValuePairs**.

In a **SortedDictionary<TKey, TValue>**, all keys must be unique, and a key must not change while it is in use as a key. Values need not be unique.

Here is an example that demonstrates **SortedDictionary<TKey, TValue>**. It reworks the **Dictionary<TKey, TValue>** example shown in the preceding section. In this version, the database of employees and salaries is sorted based on name (which is the key).

```
// Demonstrate the generic SortedDictionary<TKey, TValue> class.

using System;
using System.Collections.Generic;

class GenSortedDictionaryDemo {
  static void Main() {
    // Create a SortedDictionary that holds employee
    // names and their corresponding salary.
    SortedDictionary<string, double> dict =
      new SortedDictionary<string, double>();

    // Add elements to the collection.
    dict.Add("Butler, John", 73000);
    dict.Add("Swartz, Sarah", 59000);
    dict.Add("Pyke, Thomas", 45000);
    dict.Add("Frank, Ed", 99000);

    // Get a collection of the keys (names).
    ICollection<string> c = dict.Keys;

    // Use the keys to obtain the values (salaries).
    foreach(string str in c)
      Console.WriteLine("{0}, Salary: {1:C}", str, dict[str]);
  }
}
```

The output is shown here:

```
Butler, John, Salary: $73,000.00
Frank, Ed, Salary: $99,000.00
Pyke, Thomas, Salary: $45,000.00
Swartz, Sarah, Salary: $59,000.00
```

As you can see, the list is now sorted based on the key, which is the employee's name.

The SortedList<TKey, TValue> Class

The **SortedList<TKey, TValue>** class stores a sorted list of key/value pairs. It is the generic equivalent of the non-generic **SortedList** class. **SortedList<TKey, TValue>** implements

IDictionary, IDictionary<TKey, TValue>, ICollection, ICollection< KeyValuePair<TKey, TValue>>, IEnumerable, and **IEnumerable< KeyValuePair<TKey, TValue>>**. The size of a **SortedList<TKey, TValue>** is dynamic and will automatically grow as needed. **SortedList<TValue, TKey>** is similar to **SortedDictionary<TKey, TValue>** but has different performance characteristics. For example, a **SortedList<TKey, TValue>** uses less memory, but a **SortedDictionary<TKey, TValue>** is faster when inserting out-of-order elements.

SortedList<TKey, TValue>** provides many constructors. Here is a sampling:

```
public SortedList( )
public SortedList(IDictionary<TKey, TValue> dictionary)
public SortedList(int capacity)
public SortedList(IComparer<TKey> comparer)
```

The first constructor creates an empty list with a default capacity. The second creates a list that contains the same elements as those in *dictionary*. The third lets you specify an initial capacity. If you know in advance that you will need a list of a certain size, then specifying that capacity will prevent the resizing of the list at runtime, which is a costly process. The fourth form lets you specify a comparison method that will be used to compare the objects contained in the list.

The capacity of a **SortedList<TKey, TValue>** list grows automatically as needed when elements are added to the list. When the current capacity is exceeded, the capacity is increased. The advantage of specifying a capacity is that you can prevent or minimize the overhead associated with resizing the collection. Of course, it makes sense to specify an initial capacity only if you have some idea of how many elements will be stored.

In addition to the methods defined by the interfaces that it implements, **SortedList<TKey, TValue>** also defines several methods of its own. A sampling is shown in Table 25-19. Notice the enumerator returned by **GetEnumerator( )** enumerates the key/value pairs stored in the list as objects of type **KeyValuePair**.

In addition to the properties defined by the interfaces that it implements, **SortedList<TKey, TValue>** defines the following properties:

Property	Description
public int Capacity { get; set; }	Obtains or sets the capacity of the invoking list.
public IComparer<TKey> Comparer { get; }	Obtains the comparer for the invoking list.
public IList<TKey> Keys { get; }	Obtains a collection of the keys.
public IList<TValue> Values { get; }	Obtains a collection of the values.

SortedList<TKey, TValue> defines the following indexer (which is defined by **IDictionary<TKey, TValue>**):

```
public TValue this[TKey key] { get; set; }
```

You can use this indexer to get or set the value of an element. You can also use it to add a new element to the collection. Notice that the "index" is not actually an index, but rather the key of the item.

Method	Description
public void Add(TKey *key*, TValue *value*)	Adds the key/value pair specified by *key* and *value* to the list. If the *key* is already in the list, then its value is unchanged and an **ArgumentException** is thrown. *key* must not be **null**.
public bool ContainsKey(TKey *key*)	Returns true if *key* is a key in the invoking list. Returns false otherwise.
public bool ContainsValue(TValue *value*)	Returns true if *value* is a value in the invoking list. Returns false otherwise.
public IEnumerator<KeyValuePair<TKey, TValue>> GetEnumerator( )	Returns an enumerator for the invoking list.
public int IndexOfKey(TKey *key*)	Returns the index of the key specified by *key*. Returns –1 if the key is not in the list.
public int IndexOfValue(TValue *value*)	Returns the index of the first occurrence of the value specified by *value*. Returns –1 if the value is not in the list.
public bool Remove(TKey *key*)	Removes the key/value pair associated with *key* from the list. Returns true if successful. Returns false if *key* is not in the list.
public void RemoveAt(int *index*)	Removes the key/value pair at the index specified by *index*.
public void TrimExcess( )	Removes the excess capacity of the invoking list.

TABLE 25-19   Several Commonly Used Methods Defined by **SortedList<TKey, TValue>**

Here is an example that demonstrates **SortedList<TKey, TValue>**. It reworks the employee database example one more time. In this version, the database is stored in a **SortedList**.

```
// Demonstrate a SortedList<TKey, TValue>.

using System;
using System.Collections.Generic;

class GenSLDemo {
  static void Main() {
    // Create a SortedList for
    // employee names and salary.
    SortedList<string, double> sl =
      new SortedList<string, double>();

    // Add elements to the collection.
    sl.Add("Butler, John", 73000);
    sl.Add("Swartz, Sarah", 59000);
    sl.Add("Pyke, Thomas", 45000);
    sl.Add("Frank, Ed", 99000);
```

```
    // Get a collection of the keys.
    ICollection<string> c = sl.Keys;

    // Use the keys to obtain the values.
    foreach(string str in c)
      Console.WriteLine("{0}, Salary: {1:C}", str, sl[str]);

    Console.WriteLine();
  }
}
```

The output is shown here:

```
Butler, John, Salary: $73,000.00
Frank, Ed, Salary: $99,000.00
Pyke, Thomas, Salary: $45,000.00
Swartz, Sarah, Salary: $59,000.00
```

As the output shows, the list is sorted based on employee name, which is the key.

The Stack<T> Class

Stack<T> is the generic equivalent of the non-generic **Stack** class. **Stack<T>** supports a first-in, last-out stack. It implements the **ICollection**, **IEnumerable**, and **IEnumerable<T>** interfaces. **Stack<T>** directly implements the **Clear( )**, **Contains( )**, and **CopyTo( )** methods defined by **ICollection<T>**. (The **Add( )** and **Remove( )** methods are not supported, nor is the **IsReadOnly** property.) **Stack<T>** is a dynamic collection that grows as needed to accommodate the elements it must store. It defines the following constructors:

> public Stack( )
> public Stack(int *capacity*)
> public Stack(IEnumerable<T> *collection*)

The first form creates an empty stack with a default initial capacity. The second form creates an empty stack with the initial capacity specified by *capacity*. The third form creates a stack that contains the elements of the collection specified by *collection*.

In addition to the methods defined by the interfaces that it implements (and those methods defined by **ICollection<T>** that it implements on its own), **Stack<T>** defines the methods shown in Table 25-20. **Stack<T>** works just like its non-generic counterpart. To put an object on the top of the stack, call **Push( )**. To remove and return the top element, call **Pop( )**. You can use **Peek( )** to return, but not remove, the top object. An **InvalidOperationException** is thrown if you call **Pop( )** or **Peek( )** when the invoking stack is empty.

Method	Description
public T Peek( )	Returns the element on the top of the stack, but does not remove it.
public T Pop( )	Returns the element on the top of the stack, removing it in the process.
public void Push(T *item*)	Pushes *item* onto the stack.
public T[ ] ToArray( )	Returns an array that contains copies of the elements of the invoking stack.
public void TrimExcess( )	Removes the excess capacity of the invoking stack.

TABLE 25-20 The Methods Defined by **Stack<T>**

The following program demonstrates **Stack<T>**:

```
// Demonstrate the Stack<T> class.

using System;
using System.Collections.Generic;

class GenStackDemo {
  static void Main() {
    Stack<string> st = new Stack<string>();

    st.Push("One");
    st.Push("Two");
    st.Push("Three");
    st.Push("Four");
    st.Push("Five");

    while(st.Count > 0) {
      string str = st.Pop();
      Console.Write(str + " ");
    }

    Console.WriteLine();
  }
}
```

The output is shown here:

```
Five Four Three Two One
```

The Queue<T> Class

Queue<T> is the generic equivalent of the non-generic **Queue** class. It supports a first-in, first-out list. **Queue<T>** implements the **ICollection**, **IEnumerable**, and **IEnumerable<T>** interfaces. **Queue<T>** directly implements the **Clear( )**, **Contains( )**, and **CopyTo( )** methods defined by **ICollection<T>**. (The **Add( )** and **Remove( )** methods are not supported, nor is the **IsReadOnly** property.) **Queue<T>** is a dynamic collection that grows as needed to accommodate the elements it must store. It defines the following constructors:

> public Queue( )
> public Queue(int *capacity*)
> public Queue(IEnumerable<T> *collection*)

The first form creates an empty queue with an initial default capacity. The second form creates an empty queue with the initial capacity specified by *capacity*. The third form creates a queue that contains the elements of the collection specified by *collection*.

In addition to the methods defined by the interfaces that it implements (and those methods defined by **ICollection<T>** that it implements on its own), **Queue<T>** defines the methods shown in Table 25-21. **Queue<T>** works just like its non-generic counterpart. To put an object in the queue, call **Enqueue( )**. To remove and return the object at the front of the queue, call **Dequeue( )**. You can use **Peek( )** to return, but not remove, the next object. An **InvalidOperationException** is thrown if you call **Dequeue( )** or **Peek( )** when the invoking queue is empty.

Method	Description
public T Dequeue( )	Returns the object at the front of the invoking queue. The object is removed in the process.
public void Enqueue(T item)	Adds item to the end of the queue.
public T Peek( )	Returns the object at the front of the invoking queue, but does not remove it.
public T[ ] ToArray( )	Returns an array that contains copies of the elements of the invoking queue.
public void TrimExcess( )	Removes the excess capacity of the invoking stack.

TABLE 25-21   The Methods Defined by **Queue<T>**

Here is an example that demonstrates **Queue<T>**:

```
// Demonstrate the Queue<T> class.

using System;
using System.Collections.Generic;

class GenQueueDemo {
  static void Main() {
    Queue<double> q = new Queue<double>();

    q.Enqueue(98.6);
    q.Enqueue(212.0);
    q.Enqueue(32.0);
    q.Enqueue(3.1416);

    double sum = 0.0;
    Console.Write("Queue contents: ");
    while(q.Count > 0) {
      double val = q.Dequeue();
      Console.Write(val + " ");
      sum += val;
    }

    Console.WriteLine("\nTotal is " + sum);
  }
}
```

The output is shown here:

```
Queue contents: 98.6 212 32 3.1416
Total is 345.7416
```

HashSet<T>

HashSet<T> supports a collection that implements a set. It uses a hash table for storage.
HashSet<T> implements the **ICollection<T>**, **ISet<T>**, **IEnumerable**, **IEnumerable<T>**,
ISerializable, and **IDeserializationCallback** interfaces. **HashSet<T>** implements a set in
which all elements are unique. In other words, duplicates are not allowed. The order of the
elements is not specified. **HashSet<T>** implements the full complement of set operations
defined by **ISet<T>**, such as intersection, union, and symmetric difference. This makes

HashSet<T> the perfect choice for working with sets of objects when order does not matter. **HashSet<T>** is a dynamic collection that grows as needed to accommodate the elements it must store.

Here are four commonly used constructors defined by **HashSet<T>**:

```
public HashSet( )
public HashSet(IEnumerable<T> collection)
public HashSet(IEqualityComparer comparer)
public HashSet(IEnumerable<T> collection, IEqualityComparer comparer)
```

The first form creates an empty set. The second creates a set that contains the elements of the collection specified by *collection*. The third lets you specify the comparer. The fourth creates a set that contains the elements in the collection specified by *collection* and uses the comparer specified by *comparer*. There is also a fifth constructor that lets you initialize a set from serialized data.

Because **HashSet<T>** implements **ISet<T>**, it provides a complete assortment of set operations. Another set-related method that it provides is **RemoveWhere( )**, which removes elements that satisfy a specified predicate.

In addition to the properties defined by the interfaces that it implements, **HashSet<T>** adds **Comparer**, shown here:

```
public IEqualityComparer<T> Comparer { get; }
```

It obtains the comparer for the invoking hash set.

Here is an example that shows **HashSet<T>** in action:

```
// Demonstrate the HashSet<T> class.

using System;
using System.Collections.Generic;

class HashSetDemo {

  static void Show(string msg, HashSet<char> set) {
    Console.Write(msg);
    foreach(char ch in set)
      Console.Write(ch + " ");
    Console.WriteLine();
  }

  static void Main() {
    HashSet<char> setA = new HashSet<char>();
    HashSet<char> setB = new HashSet<char>();

    setA.Add('A');
    setA.Add('B');
    setA.Add('C');

    setB.Add('C');
    setB.Add('D');
    setB.Add('E');

    Show("Initial content of setA: ", setA);
```

```
      Show("Initial content of setB: ", setB);

      setA.SymmetricExceptWith(setB);
      Show("setA after Symmetric difference with SetB: ", setA);

      setA.UnionWith(setB);
      Show("setA after union with setB: ", setA);

      setA.ExceptWith(setB);
      Show("setA after subtracting setB: ", setA);

      Console.WriteLine();
   }
}
```

The output is shown here:

```
Initial content of setA: A B C
Initial content of setB: C D E
setA after Symmetric difference with SetB: A B D E
setA after union with setB: A B D E C
setA after subtracting setB: A B
```

SortedSet<T>

SortedSet<T> is a new collection added to the .NET Framework by version 4.0. It supports a collection that implements a sorted set. **SortedSet<T>** implements the **ISet<T>**, **ICollection**, **ICollection<T>**, **IEnumerable**, **IEnumerable<T>**, **ISerializable**, and **IDeserializationCallback** interfaces. **SortedSet<T>** implements a set in which all elements are unique. In other words, duplicates are not allowed. **SortedSet<T>** implements the full complement of set operations defined by **ISet<T>**, such as intersection, union, and symmetric difference. Because **SortedSet<T>** maintains its elements in sorted order, it is the collection of choice when working with sorted sets. **SortedSet<T>** is a dynamic collection that grows as needed to accommodate the elements it must store.

Here are four commonly used constructors defined by **SortedSet<T>**:

public SortedSet( )
public SortedSet(IEnumerable<T> *collection*)
public SortedSet(IComparer *comparer*)
public SortedSet(IEnumerable<T> *collection*, IComparer *comparer*)

The first form creates an empty set. The second creates a set that contains the elements of the collection specified by *collection*. The third lets you specify the comparer. The fourth creates a set that contains the elements in the collection specified by *collection* and uses the comparer specified by *comparer*. There is also a fifth constructor that lets you initialize a set from serialized data.

Because **SortedSet<T>** implements **ISet<T>**, it provides a compete assortment of set operations. Other set-related methods provided by **SortedSet<T>** include **GetViewBetween( )**, which returns a portion of a set in the form of a **SortedSet<T>**, **RemoveWhere( )**, which removes elements from a set that satisfy a specified predicate, and **Reverse( )**, which returns an **IEnumerable<T>** that cycles through the set in reverse order.

In addition to the properties defined by the interfaces that it implements, **SortedSet<T>** adds those shown here:

```
public IComparer<T> Comparer { get; }
public T Max { get; }
public T Min { get; }
```

Comparer obtains the comparer for the invoking set. The **Max** property obtains the largest value in the set, and **Min** obtains the smallest value.

To see an example of **SortedSet<T>** in action, simply substitute **SortedSet** for **HashSet** in the program in the preceding section.

The Concurrent Collections

The .NET Framework version 4.0 adds a new namespace called **System.Collections.Concurrent**. It contains collections that are thread-safe and designed to be used for parallel programming. This means they are safe to use in a multithreaded program in which two or more concurrently executing threads might access a collection simultaneously. The concurrent collections are shown here.

Concurrent Collection	Description
BlockingCollection<T>	Provides a wrapper for a blocking implementation of the **IProducerConsumerCollection<T>** interface.
ConcurrentBag<T>	An unordered implementation of the **IProducerConsumerCollection<T>** interface that works best when a single thread produces and consumes the information.
ConcurrentDictionary<TKey, TValue>	Stores key/value pairs. Thus, it implements a concurrent dictionary.
ConcurrentQueue<T>	Implements a concurrent queue. Implements **IProducerConsumerCollection<T>**.
ConcurrentStack<T>	Implements a concurrent stack. Implements **IProducerConsumerCollection<T>**.

Notice that several of the collections implement the **IProducerConsumerCollection** interface. This interface is also defined in **System.Collections.Concurrent**. It extends **IEnumerable**, **IEnumerable<T>**, and **ICollection**. It also specifies the **TryAdd( )** and **TryTake( )** methods that support the producer/consumer pattern. (The classic producer/ consumer pattern is characterized by two tasks. One task creates items and the other consumes them.) **TryAdd( )** attempts to add an item to the collection, and **TryTake( )** attempts to remove an item from the collection. These methods are shown here:

```
bool TryAdd(T item)
bool TryTake(out T item)
```

TryAdd( ) returns true if *item* was added to the collection, and **TryTake( )** returns true if an object was removed from the collection. If **TryTake( )** is successful, then *item* will contain the object. (**IProducerConsumerCollection** also specifies an overload to **CopyTo( )** defined by **ICollection** and **ToArray( )** that copies a collection to an array.)

The concurrent collections are often used in conjunction with the Task Parallel Library or PLINQ. Because of the specialized nature of these collections, not every class is examined in detail. However, a brief overview with examples of **BlockingCollection<T>** will be given. Once you know the basics related to **BlockingCollection<T>**, the other classes will be easy to understand.

BlockingCollection\<T> implements what is essentially a blocking queue. This means that it will automatically wait if an attempt is made to insert an item when the collection is full, and it will automatically wait if an attempt is made to remove an item if the collection is empty. Because of this, it is a perfect solution for those situations that correspond to the producer/consumer pattern. **BlockingCollection\<T>** implements the **ICollection**, **IEnumerable**, **IEnumerable\<T>**, and **IDisposable** interfaces.

BlockingCollection\<T> defines the following constructors:

```
public BlockingCollection( )
public BlockingCollection(int boundedCapacity)
public BlockingCollection(IProducerConsumerCollection<T> collection)
public BlockingCollection(IProducerConsumerCollection<T> collection,
                int boundedCapacity)
```

In the first two, the collection that is wrapped by **BlockingCollection\<T>** is an instance of **ConcurrentQueue\<T>**. In the second two, you can specify the collection that you want to underlie the **BlockingCollection\<T>**. If the *boundedCapacity* parameter is used, it will contain the maximum number of objects that the collection can hold before it blocks. If *boundedCapacity* is not specified, then the collection is unbounded.

In addition to **TryAdd( )** and **TryTake( )**, which parallel those specified by **IProducerConsumerCollection\<T>**, **BlockingCollection\<T>** defines several methods of its own. The ones we will use are shown here:

```
public void Add(T item)
public T Take( )
```

When called on an unbounded collection, **Add( )** adds *item* to the collection and then returns. When called on a bounded collection, **Add( )** will block if the collection is full. After one or more items have been removed from the collection, the item will be added and **Add( )** will return. **Take( )** removes an item from the collection and returns it. If called on an empty collection, **Take( )** will block until an item is available. (There are also versions of these methods that take a **CancellationToken**.)

Using **Add( )** and **Take( )**, you can implement a simple producer/consumer pattern, as demonstrated by the following program. It creates a producer that generates the characters A through Z and a consumer that receives them. Notice that it creates a **BlockingCollection\<T>** that has a bound of 4.

```
// A simple example of BlockingCollection.

using System;
using System.Threading.Tasks;
using System.Threading;
using System.Collections.Concurrent;

class BlockingDemo {
  static BlockingCollection<char> bc;

  // Produce the characters A to Z.
  static void Producer() {
    for(char ch = 'A'; ch <= 'Z'; ch++) {
      bc.Add(ch);
```

```
      Console.WriteLine("Producing " + ch);
    }
  }

  // Consume 26 characters.
  static void Consumer() {
    for(int i=0; i < 26; i++)
      Console.WriteLine("Consuming " + bc.Take());
  }

  static void Main() {
    // Use a blocking collection that has a bound of 4.
    bc = new BlockingCollection<char>(4);

    // Create the producer and consumer tasks.
    Task Prod = new Task(Producer);
    Task Con = new Task(Consumer);

    // Start the tasks.
    Con.Start();
    Prod.Start();

    // Wait for both to finish.
    try {
      Task.WaitAll(Con, Prod);
    } catch(AggregateException exc) {
      Console.WriteLine(exc);
    } finally {
      Con.Dispose();
      Prod.Dispose();
      bc.Dispose();
    }
  }
}
```

If you run this program, you will see a mix of producer and consumer output. Part of the reason for this is that **bc** has a bound of 4, which means that only four items can be added to **bc** before one must be taken off. As an experiment try making **bc** an unbounded collection and observe the results. In some environments, this will result in all items being produced before any are consumed. Also, try using a bound of 1. In this case, only one item at a time can be produced.

Another method that you may find helpful when working with **BlockingCollection<T>** is **CompleteAdding( )**, shown here:

   public void CompleteAdding( )

Calling this method indicates that no further items will be added to the collection. This causes the **IsAddingComplete** property to be true. If the collection is also empty, then the property **IsCompleted** is true. If **IsCompleted** is true, then calls to **Take( )** will not block.

   The **IsAddingComplete** and **IsCompleted** properties are shown here:

   public bool IsCompleted { get; }
   public bool IsAddingComplete { get; }

When a **BlockingCollection<T>** begins, these properties are false. They become true only after **CompleteAdding( )** is called.

The following program reworks the previous example so it uses **CompleteAdding( )**, **IsCompleted**, and the **TryTake( )** method:

```
// Using CompleteAdding(), IsCompleted, and TryTake().

using System;
using System.Threading.Tasks;
using System.Threading;
using System.Collections.Concurrent;

class BlockingDemo {
  static BlockingCollection<char> bc;

  // Produce the characters A to Z.
  static void Producer() {
    for(char ch = 'A'; ch <= 'Z'; ch++) {
      bc.Add(ch);
      Console.WriteLine("Producing " + ch);
    }
    bc.CompleteAdding();
  }

  // Consume characters until producer is done.
  static void Consumer() {
    char ch;

    while(!bc.IsCompleted) {
      if(bc.TryTake(out ch))
        Console.WriteLine("Consuming " + ch);
    }
  }

  static void Main() {
    // Use a blocking collection that has a bound of 4.
    bc = new BlockingCollection<char>(4);

    // Create the producer and consumer tasks.
    Task Prod = new Task(Producer);
    Task Con = new Task(Consumer);

    // Start the tasks.
    Con.Start();
    Prod.Start();

    // Wait for both to finish.
    try {
      Task.WaitAll(Con, Prod);
    } catch(AggregateException exc) {
      Console.WriteLine(exc);
    } finally {
      Con.Dispose();
```

```
      Prod.Dispose();
      bc.Dispose();
    }
  }
}
```

The output from this version will be similar to that of the previous version. The main difference between the programs is that now **Producer( )** can produce as many items as it wants. It simply calls **CompleteAdding( )** when it is finished. **Consumer( )** simply consumes items until **IsCompleted** is true.

Although the concurrent collections are somewhat specialized, being designed for concurrent programming situations, they still have much in common with the non-concurrent collections described by the preceding sections. If you are working in a parallel programming environment, you will want to make use of the concurrent collections when access by multiple threads will occur.

Storing User-Defined Classes in Collections

For the sake of simplicity, the foregoing examples have stored built-in types, such as **int**, **string**, or **char**, in a collection. Of course, collections are not limited to the storage of built-in objects. Quite the contrary. The power of collections is that they can store any type of object, including objects of classes that you create.

Let's begin with an example that uses the non-generic class **ArrayList** to store inventory information that is encapsulated by the **Inventory** class:

```
// A simple inventory example.

using System;
using System.Collections;

class Inventory {
  string name;
  double cost;
  int onhand;

  public Inventory(string n, double c, int h) {
    name = n;
    cost = c;
    onhand = h;
  }

  public override string ToString() {
    return
      String.Format("{0,-10}Cost: {1,6:C}  On hand: {2}",
                    name, cost, onhand);
  }
}

class InventoryList {
  static void Main() {
    ArrayList inv = new ArrayList();
```

```
    // Add elements to the list
    inv.Add(new Inventory("Pliers", 5.95, 3));
    inv.Add(new Inventory("Wrenches", 8.29, 2));
    inv.Add(new Inventory("Hammers", 3.50, 4));
    inv.Add(new Inventory("Drills", 19.88, 8));

    Console.WriteLine("Inventory list:");
    foreach(Inventory i in inv) {
      Console.WriteLine("   " + i);
    }
  }
}
```

The output from the program is shown here:

```
Inventory list:
   Pliers     Cost:   $5.95   On hand: 3
   Wrenches   Cost:   $8.29   On hand: 2
   Hammers    Cost:   $3.50   On hand: 4
   Drills     Cost: $19.88    On hand: 8
```

In the program, notice that no special actions were required to store objects of type **Inventory** in a collection. Because all types inherit **object**, any type of object can be stored in any non-generic collection. Thus, using a non-generic collection, it is trivially easy to store objects of classes that you create. Of course, it also means the collection is not type-safe.

To store objects of classes that you create in a type-safe collection, you must use one of the generic collection classes. For example, here is a version of the preceding program rewritten to use **List<T>**. The output is the same as before.

```
// Store Inventory Objects in a List<T> collection.

using System;
using System.Collections.Generic;

class Inventory {
  string name;
  double cost;
  int onhand;

  public Inventory(string n, double c, int h) {
    name = n;
    cost = c;
    onhand = h;
  }

  public override string ToString() {
    return
      String.Format("{0,-10}Cost: {1,6:C}  On hand: {2}",
                    name, cost, onhand);
  }
}

class TypeSafeInventoryList {
  static void Main() {
    List<Inventory> inv = new List<Inventory>();
```

```
    // Add elements to the list
    inv.Add(new Inventory("Pliers", 5.95, 3));
    inv.Add(new Inventory("Wrenches", 8.29, 2));
    inv.Add(new Inventory("Hammers", 3.50, 4));
    inv.Add(new Inventory("Drills", 19.88, 8));

    Console.WriteLine("Inventory list:");
    foreach(Inventory i in inv) {
      Console.WriteLine("   " + i);
    }
  }
}
```

In this version, notice the only real difference is the passing of the type **Inventory** as a type argument to **List<T>**. Other than that, the two programs are nearly identical. The fact that the use of a generic collection requires virtually no additional effort and adds type safety argues strongly for its use when storing a specific type of object within a collection.

In general, there is one other thing to notice about the preceding programs: Both are quite short. When you consider that each sets up a dynamic array that can store, retrieve, and process inventory information in less than 40 lines of code, the power of collections begins to become apparent. As most readers will know, if all of this functionality had to be coded by hand, the program would have been several times longer. Collections offer ready-to-use solutions to a wide variety of programming problems. You should use them whenever the situation warrants.

There is one limitation to the preceding programs that may not be immediately apparent: The collection can't be sorted. The reason for this is that neither **ArrayList** nor **List<T>** has a way to compare two **Inventory** objects. There are two ways to remedy this situation. First, **Inventory** can implement the **IComparable** interface. This interface defines how two objects of a class are compared. Second, an **IComparer** object can be specified when comparisons are required. The following sections illustrate both approaches.

Implementing IComparable

If you want to sort a collection that contains user-defined objects (or if you want to store those objects in a collection such as **SortedList**, which maintains its elements in sorted order), then the collection must know how to compare those objects. One way to do this is for the object being stored to implement the **IComparable** interface. The **IComparable** interface comes in two forms: generic and non-generic. Although the way each is used is similar, there are some small differences. Each is examined here.

Implementing IComparable for Non-Generic Collections

If you want to sort objects that are stored in a non-generic collection, then you will implement the non-generic version of **IComparable**. This version defines only one method, **CompareTo( )**, which determines how comparisons are performed. The general form of **CompareTo( )** is shown here:

   int CompareTo(object *obj)*

CompareTo( ) compares the invoking object to *obj*. To sort in ascending order, your implementation must return zero if the objects are equal, a positive value if the invoking object is greater than *obj,* and a negative value if the invoking object is less than *obj.* You can sort in descending order by reversing the outcome of the comparison. The method can throw an **ArgumentException** if the type of *obj* is not compatible for comparison with the invoking object.

Here is an example that shows how to implement **IComparable**. It adds **IComparable** to the **Inventory** class developed in the preceding section. It implements **CompareTo( )** so that it compares the **name** field, thus enabling the inventory to be sorted by name. By implementing **IComparable**, it allows a collection of **Inventory** objects to be sorted, as the program illustrates.

```
// Implement IComparable.

using System;
using System.Collections;

// Implement the non-generic IComparable interface.
class Inventory : IComparable {
  string name;
  double cost;
  int onhand;

  public Inventory(string n, double c, int h) {
    name = n;
    cost = c;
    onhand = h;
  }

  public override string ToString() {
    return
      String.Format("{0,-10}Cost: {1,6:C}  On hand: {2}",
                    name, cost, onhand);
  }

  // Implement the IComparable interface.
  public int CompareTo(object obj) {
    Inventory b;
    b = (Inventory) obj;
    return string.Compare(name, b.name, StringComparison.Ordinal);
  }
}

class IComparableDemo {
  static void Main() {
    ArrayList inv = new ArrayList();

    // Add elements to the list
    inv.Add(new Inventory("Pliers", 5.95, 3));
    inv.Add(new Inventory("Wrenches", 8.29, 2));
    inv.Add(new Inventory("Hammers", 3.50, 4));
    inv.Add(new Inventory("Drills", 19.88, 8));

    Console.WriteLine("Inventory list before sorting:");
    foreach(Inventory i in inv) {
```

```
      Console.WriteLine("    " + i);
    }
    Console.WriteLine();

    // Sort the list.
    inv.Sort();

    Console.WriteLine("Inventory list after sorting:");
    foreach(Inventory i in inv) {
      Console.WriteLine("    " + i);
    }
  }
}
```

Here is the output. Notice after the call to **Sort( )**, the inventory is sorted by name.

```
Inventory list before sorting:
    Pliers    Cost:   $5.95   On hand: 3
    Wrenches  Cost:   $8.29   On hand: 2
    Hammers   Cost:   $3.50   On hand: 4
    Drills    Cost: $19.88    On hand: 8

Inventory list after sorting:
    Drills    Cost: $19.88    On hand: 8
    Hammers   Cost:   $3.50   On hand: 4
    Pliers    Cost:   $5.95   On hand: 3
    Wrenches  Cost:   $8.29   On hand: 2
```

Implementing IComparable<T> for Generic Collections

If you want to sort objects that are stored in a generic collection, then you will implement
IComparable<T>. This version defines the generic form of **CompareTo( )** shown here:

int CompareTo(T *other)*

CompareTo( ) compares the invoking object to *other*. To sort in ascending order, your
implementation must return zero if the objects are equal, a positive value if the invoking
object is greater than *other*, and a negative value if the invoking object is less than *other*. To
sort in descending order, reverse the outcome of the comparison. When implementing
IComparable<T>, you will usually pass the type name of the implementing class as a type
argument.

The following example reworks the preceding program so that it uses **IComparable<T>**.
Notice it uses the generic **List<T>** collection rather than the non-generic **ArrayList**.

```
// Implement IComparable<T>.

using System;
using System.Collections.Generic;

// Implement the generic IComparable<T> interface.
class Inventory : IComparable<Inventory> {
  string name;
  double cost;
  int onhand;
```

```
    public Inventory(string n, double c, int h) {
      name = n;
      cost = c;
      onhand = h;
    }

    public override string ToString() {
      return
        String.Format("{0,-10}Cost: {1,6:C}  On hand: {2}",
                      name, cost, onhand);
    }

    // Implement the IComparable<T> interface.
    public int CompareTo(Inventory other) {
      return string.Compare(name, other.name, StringComparison.Ordinal);
    }
  }

class GenericIComparableDemo {
  static void Main() {
    List<Inventory> inv = new List<Inventory>();

    // Add elements to the list.
    inv.Add(new Inventory("Pliers", 5.95, 3));
    inv.Add(new Inventory("Wrenches", 8.29, 2));
    inv.Add(new Inventory("Hammers", 3.50, 4));
    inv.Add(new Inventory("Drills", 19.88, 8));

    Console.WriteLine("Inventory list before sorting:");
    foreach(Inventory i in inv) {
      Console.WriteLine("   " + i);
    }
    Console.WriteLine();

    // Sort the list.
    inv.Sort();

    Console.WriteLine("Inventory list after sorting:");
    foreach(Inventory i in inv) {
      Console.WriteLine("   " + i);
    }
  }
}
```

This program produces the same output as the previous, non-generic version.

Using an IComparer

Although implementing **IComparable** for classes that you create is often the easiest way to allow objects of those classes to be sorted, you can approach the problem in a different way by using **IComparer**. To use **IComparer**, first create a class that implements **IComparer**, and then specify an object of that class when comparisons are required.

There are two versions of **IComparer**: generic and non-generic. Although the way each is used is similar, there are some small differences, and each approach is examined here.

Using a Non-Generic IComparer

The non-generic **IComparer** defines only one method, **Compare( )**, which is shown here:

int Compare(object *x*, object *y*)

Compare( ) compares *x* to *y*. To sort in ascending order, your implementation must return zero if the objects are equal, a positive value if *x* is greater than *y*, and a negative value if *x* is less than *y*. You can sort in descending order by reversing the outcome of the comparison. The method can throw an **ArgumentException** if the objects are not compatible for comparison.

An **IComparer** can be specified when constructing a **SortedList**, when calling **ArrayList.Sort(IComparer)**, and at various other places throughout the collection classes. The main advantage of using **IComparer** is that you can sort objects of classes that do not implement **IComparable**.

The following program reworks the non-generic inventory program so that it uses an **IComparer** to sort the inventory list. It first creates a class called **CompInv** that implements **IComparer** and compares two **Inventory** objects. An object of this class is then used in a call to **Sort( )** to sort the inventory list.

```
// Use IComparer.

using System;
using System.Collections;

// Create an IComparer for Inventory objects.
class CompInv : IComparer {
  // Implement the IComparer interface.
  public int Compare(object x, object y) {
    Inventory a, b;
    a = (Inventory) x;
    b = (Inventory) y;
    return string.Compare(a.name, b.name, StringComparison.Ordinal);
  }
}

class Inventory {
  public string name;
  double cost;
  int onhand;

  public Inventory(string n, double c, int h) {
    name = n;
    cost = c;
    onhand = h;
  }

  public override string ToString() {
    return
      String.Format("{0,-10}Cost: {1,6:C}  On hand: {2}",
                    name, cost, onhand);
```

```
    }
}

class IComparerDemo {
  static void Main() {
    CompInv comp = new CompInv();
    ArrayList inv = new ArrayList();

    // Add elements to the list
    inv.Add(new Inventory("Pliers", 5.95, 3));
    inv.Add(new Inventory("Wrenches", 8.29, 2));
    inv.Add(new Inventory("Hammers", 3.50, 4));
    inv.Add(new Inventory("Drills", 19.88, 8));

    Console.WriteLine("Inventory list before sorting:");
    foreach(Inventory i in inv) {
      Console.WriteLine("   " + i);
    }
    Console.WriteLine();

    // Sort the list using an IComparer.
    inv.Sort(comp);

    Console.WriteLine("Inventory list after sorting:");
    foreach(Inventory i in inv) {
      Console.WriteLine("   " + i);
    }
  }
}
```

The output is the same as the previous version of the program.

Using a Generic IComparer<T>

The **IComparer<T>** interface is the generic version of **IComparer**. It defines the generic version of **Compare( )**, shown here:

int Compare(T *x*, T *y*)

This method compares *x* with *y* and returns greater than zero if *x* is greater than *y*, zero if the two objects are the same, and less than zero if *x* is less that *y*.

Here is a generic version of the preceding program that uses **IComparer<T>**. It produces the same output as the previous versions of the program.

```
// Use IComparer<T>.

using System;
using System.Collections.Generic;

// Create an IComparer<T> for Inventory objects.
class CompInv<T> : IComparer<T> where T : Inventory {

  // Implement the IComparer<T> interface.
  public int Compare(T x, T y) {
```

```
      return string.Compare(x.name, y.name, StringComparison.Ordinal);
  }
}

class Inventory {
  public string name;
  double cost;
  int onhand;

  public Inventory(string n, double c, int h) {
    name = n;
    cost = c;
    onhand = h;
  }

  public override string ToString() {
    return
      String.Format("{0,-10}Cost: {1,6:C}  On hand: {2}",
                    name, cost, onhand);
  }
}

class GenericIComparerDemo {
  static void Main() {
    CompInv<Inventory> comp = new CompInv<Inventory>();
    List<Inventory> inv = new List<Inventory>();

    // Add elements to the list.
    inv.Add(new Inventory("Pliers", 5.95, 3));
    inv.Add(new Inventory("Wrenches", 8.29, 2));
    inv.Add(new Inventory("Hammers", 3.50, 4));
    inv.Add(new Inventory("Drills", 19.88, 8));

    Console.WriteLine("Inventory list before sorting:");
    foreach(Inventory i in inv) {
      Console.WriteLine("   " + i);
    }
    Console.WriteLine();

    // Sort the list using an IComparer.
    inv.Sort(comp);

    Console.WriteLine("Inventory list after sorting:");
    foreach(Inventory i in inv) {
      Console.WriteLine("   " + i);
    }
  }
}
```

Using StringComparer

Although not necessary for the simple examples in this chapter, you may encounter situations when storing strings in a sorted collection, or when sorting or searching strings in a collection, in which you need to explicitly specify how those strings are compared. For example, if strings will be sorted using one cultural setting and searched under another, then explicitly specifying the comparison method may be necessary to avoid errors. A similar situation can exist when a collection uses hashing. To handle these (and other) types of situations, several of the collection class constructors and methods support an **IComparer** parameter. To explicitly specify the string comparison method, you will pass this parameter an instance of **StringComparer**.

StringComparer was described in Chapter 21, in the discussion of sorting and searching arrays. It implements the **IComparer**, **IComparer<String>**, **IEqualityComparer**, and **IEqualityComparer<String>** interfaces. Thus, an instance of **StringComparer** can be passed to an **IComparer** parameter as an argument. **StringComparer** defines several read-only properties that return an instance of **StringComparer** that supports various types of string comparisons. As described in Chapter 21, they are **CurrentCulture**, **CurrentCultureIgnoreCase**, **InvariantCulture**, **InvariantCultureIgnoreCase**, **Ordinal**, and **OrdinalIgnoreCase**. You can use these properties to explicitly specify the comparison.

For example, here is how to construct a **SortedList<TKey, TValue>** for strings that use ordinal comparisons for their keys:

```
SortedList<string, int> users =
    new SortedList<string, int>(StringComparer.Ordinal);
```

Accessing a Collection via an Enumerator

Often you will want to cycle through the elements in a collection. For example, you might want to display each element. One way to do this is to use a **foreach** loop, as the preceding examples have done. Another way is to use an enumerator. An *enumerator* is an object that implements either the non-generic **IEnumerator** or the generic **IEnumerator<T>** interface.

IEnumerator defines one property called **Current**. The non-generic version is shown here:

object Current { get; }

For **IEnumerator<T>**, **Current** is declared like this:

T Current { get; }

In both cases, **Current** obtains the current element being enumerated. Since **Current** is a read-only property, an enumerator can only be used to retrieve, but not modify, the objects in a collection.

IEnumerator defines two methods. The first is **MoveNext( )**:

bool MoveNext( )

Each call to **MoveNext( )** moves the current position of the enumerator to the next element in the collection. It returns true if the next element is available, or false if the end of the collection has been reached. Prior to the first call to **MoveNext( )**, the value of **Current** is undefined. (Conceptually, prior to the first call to **MoveNext( )**, the enumerator refers to the nonexistent element that is just before the first element. Thus, you must call **MoveNext( )** to move to the first element.)

You can reset the enumerator to the start of the collection by calling **Reset( )**, shown here:

void Reset( )

After calling **Reset( )**, enumeration will again begin at the start of the collection. Thus, you must call **MoveNext( )** before obtaining the first element.

In **IEnumerator<T>**, the methods **MoveNext( )** and **Reset( )** work in the same way.

Two other points: First, you cannot use an enumerator to change the collection that is being enumerated. Thus, enumerators are read-only relative to the collection. Second, any change to the collection under enumeration invalidates the enumerator.

Using an Enumerator

Before you can access a collection through an enumerator, you must obtain one. Each of the collection classes provides a **GetEnumerator( )** method that returns an enumerator to the start of the collection. Using this enumerator, you can access each element in the collection, one element at a time. In general, to use an enumerator to cycle through the contents of a collection, follow these steps:

1. Obtain an enumerator to the start of the collection by calling the collection's **GetEnumerator( )** method.

2. Set up a loop that makes a call to **MoveNext( )**. Have the loop iterate as long as **MoveNext( )** returns true.

3. Within the loop, obtain each element through **Current**.

Here is an example that implements these steps. It uses an **ArrayList**, but the general principles apply to any type of collection, including the generic collections.

```
// Demonstrate an enumerator.

using System;
using System.Collections;

class EnumeratorDemo {
  static void Main() {
    ArrayList list = new ArrayList(1);

    for(int i=0; i < 10; i++)
      list.Add(i);

    // Use enumerator to access list.
    IEnumerator etr = list.GetEnumerator();
    while(etr.MoveNext())
      Console.Write(etr.Current + " ");

    Console.WriteLine();

    // Re-enumerate the list.
    etr.Reset();
    while(etr.MoveNext())
      Console.Write(etr.Current + " ");

    Console.WriteLine();
  }
}
```

The output is shown here:

```
0 1 2 3 4 5 6 7 8 9
0 1 2 3 4 5 6 7 8 9
```

In general, when you need to cycle through a collection, a **foreach** loop is more convenient to use than an enumerator. However, an enumerator gives you a little extra control by allowing you to reset the enumerator at will.

Using IDictionaryEnumerator

When using a non-generic **IDictionary**, such as **Hashtable**, you will use an **IDictionaryEnumerator** instead of an **IEnumerator** when cycling through the collection. The **IDictionaryEnumerator** inherits **IEnumerator** and adds three properties. The first is

DictionaryEntry Entry { get; }

Entry obtains the next key/value pair from the enumerator in the form of a **DictionaryEntry** structure. Recall that **DictionaryEntry** defines two properties, called **Key** and **Value**, which can be used to access the key or value contained within the entry. The other two properties defined by **IDictionaryEnumerator** are shown here:

object Key { get; }
object Value { get; }

These allow you to access the key or value directly.

An **IDictionaryEnumerator** is used just like a regular enumerator, except that you will obtain the current value through the **Entry**, **Key**, or **Value** properties rather than **Current**. Thus, after obtaining an **IDictionaryEnumerator**, you must call **MoveNext( )** to obtain the first element. Continue to call **MoveNext( )** to obtain the rest of the elements in the collection. **MoveNext( )** returns false when there are no more elements.

Here is an example that enumerates the elements in a **Hashtable** through an **IDictionaryEnumerator**:

```
// Demonstrate IDictionaryEnumerator.

using System;
using System.Collections;

class IDicEnumDemo {
  static void Main() {
    // Create a hash table.
    Hashtable ht = new Hashtable();

    // Add elements to the table.
    ht.Add("Tom", "555-3456");
    ht.Add("Mary", "555-9876");
    ht.Add("Todd", "555-3452");
    ht.Add("Ken", "555-7756");

    // Demonstrate enumerator.
    IDictionaryEnumerator etr = ht.GetEnumerator();
    Console.WriteLine("Display info using Entry.");
```

```
    while(etr.MoveNext())
      Console.WriteLine(etr.Entry.Key + ": " +
                           etr.Entry.Value);

    Console.WriteLine();

    Console.WriteLine("Display info using Key and Value directly.");
    etr.Reset();
    while(etr.MoveNext())
      Console.WriteLine(etr.Key + ": " +
                           etr.Value);

  }
}
```

The output is shown here:

```
Display info using Entry.
Ken: 555-7756
Mary: 555-9876
Tom: 555-3456
Todd: 555-3452

Display info using Key and Value directly.
Ken: 555-7756
Mary: 555-9876
Tom: 555-3456
Todd: 555-3452
```

Implementing IEnumerable and IEnumerator

As mentioned earlier, normally it is easier (and better) to use a **foreach** loop to cycle through a collection than it is to explicitly use **IEnumerator** methods. However, understanding the operation of this interface is important for another reason: If you want to create a class that contains objects that can be enumerated via a **foreach** loop, then that class must implement **IEnumerator**. It must also implement **IEnumerable**. In other words, to enable an object of a class that you create to be used in a **foreach** loop, you must implement **IEnumerator** and **IEnumerable**, using either their generic or non-generic form. Fortunately, because these interfaces are so small, they are easy to implement.

Here is an example that implements the non-generic versions of **IEnumerable** and **IEnumerator** so that the contents of the array encapsulated within **MyClass** can be enumerated:

```
// Implement IEnumerable and IEnumerator.
using System;
using System.Collections;

class MyClass : IEnumerator, IEnumerable {
  char[] chrs = { 'A', 'B', 'C', 'D' };
  int idx = -1;

  // Implement IEnumerable.
```

```
    public IEnumerator GetEnumerator() {
      return this;
    }

    // The following methods implement IEnumerator.

    // Return the current object.
    public object Current {
      get {
        return chrs[idx];
      }
    }

    // Advance to the next object.
    public bool MoveNext() {
      if(idx == chrs.Length-1) {
        Reset(); // reset enumerator at the end
        return false;
      }

      idx++;
      return true;
    }

    // Reset the enumerator to the start.
    public void Reset() { idx = -1; }
}

class EnumeratorImplDemo {
  static void Main() {
    MyClass mc = new MyClass();

    // Display the contents of mc.
    foreach(char ch in mc)
      Console.Write(ch + " ");

    Console.WriteLine();

    // Display the contents of mc, again.
    foreach(char ch in mc)
      Console.Write(ch + " ");

    Console.WriteLine();
  }
}
```

Here is the output:

```
A B C D
A B C D
```

In the program, first examine **MyClass**. It encapsulates a small **char** array that contains the characters A through D. An index into this array is stored in **idx**, which is initialized to –1. **MyClass** then implements both **IEnumerator** and **IEnumerable**. **GetEnumerator( )**

returns a reference to the enumerator, which in this case is the current object. The **Current** property returns the next character in the array, which is the object at **idx**. The **MoveNext( )** method advances **idx** to the next location. It returns false if the end of the collection has been reached and true otherwise. **Reset( )** sets **idx** to –1. Recall that an enumerator is undefined until after the first call to **MoveNext( )**. Thus, in a **foreach** loop, **MoveNext( )** is automatically called before **Current**. This is why **idx** must initially be –1; it is advanced to zero when the **foreach** loop begins. A generic implementation would work in a similar fashion.

Inside **Main( )**, an object of type **MyClass** called **mc** is created and the contents of the object are twice displayed by use of a **foreach** loop.

Using Iterators

As the preceding example shows, it is not difficult to implement **IEnumerator** and **IEnumerable**. However, it can be made even easier through the use of an *iterator*. An iterator is a method, operator, or accessor that returns the members of a set of objects, one member at a time, from start to finish. For example, assuming some array that has five elements, then an iterator for that array will return those five elements, one at a time. Implementing an iterator is another way to make it possible for an object of a class to be used in a **foreach** loop.

Let's begin with an example of a simple iterator. The following program is a modified version of the preceding program that uses an iterator rather than explicitly implementing **IEnumerator** and **IEnumerable**.

```
// A simple example of an iterator.

using System;
using System.Collections;

class MyClass {
  char[] chrs = { 'A', 'B', 'C', 'D' };

  // This iterator returns the characters
  // in the chrs array.
  public IEnumerator GetEnumerator() {
    foreach(char ch in chrs)
      yield return ch;
  }
}

class ItrDemo {
  static void Main() {
    MyClass mc = new MyClass();

    foreach(char ch in mc)
      Console.Write(ch + " ");

    Console.WriteLine();
  }
}
```

The output is shown here:

```
A B C D
```

As you can see, the contents of **mc.chrs** was enumerated.

Let's examine this program carefully. First, notice that **MyClass** does not specify **IEnumerator** as an implemented interface. When creating an iterator, the compiler automatically implements this interface for you. Second, pay special attention to the **GetEnumerator( )** method, which is shown again here for your convenience:

```
// This iterator returns the characters
// in the chrs array.
public IEnumerator GetEnumerator() {
  foreach(char ch in chrs)
    yield return ch;
}
```

This is the iterator for **MyClass**. Notice that it implicitly implements the **GetEnumerator( )** method defined by **IEnumerable**. Now, look at the body of the method. It contains a **foreach** loop that returns the elements in **chrs**. It does this through the use of a **yield return** statement. The **yield return** statement returns the next object in the collection, which in this case is the next character in **chrs**. This feature enables **mc** (a **MyClass** object) to be used within the **foreach** loop inside **Main( )**.

The term **yield** is a *contextual keyword* in the C# language. This means that it has special meaning only inside an iterator block. Outside of an iterator, **yield** can be used like any other identifier.

One important point to understand is that an iterator does not need to be backed by an array or other type of collection. It simply must return the next element in a group of elements. This means the elements can be dynamically constructed using an algorithm. For example, here is a version of the previous program that returns all uppercase letters in the alphabet. Instead of using an array, it generates the letters using a **for** loop.

```
// Iterated values can be dynamically constructed.

using System;
using System.Collections;

class MyClass {
  char ch = 'A';

  // This iterator returns the letters of the alphabet.
  public IEnumerator GetEnumerator() {
    for(int i=0; i < 26; i++)
      yield return (char) (ch + i);
  }
}

class ItrDemo2 {
  static void Main() {
    MyClass mc = new MyClass();
```

```
    foreach(char ch in mc)
      Console.Write(ch + " ");

    Console.WriteLine();
  }
}
```

The output is shown here:

A B C D E F G H I J K L M N O P Q R S T U V W X Y Z

Stopping an Iterator

You can stop an iterator early by using this form of the **yield** statement:

yield break;

When this statement executes, the iterator signals that the end of the collection has been reached, which effectively stops the iterator.

The following program modifies the preceding program so that it displays only the first ten letters in the alphabet.

```
// Use yield break.

using System;
using System.Collections;

class MyClass {
  char ch = 'A';

  // This iterator returns the first 10
  // letters of the alphabet.
  public IEnumerator GetEnumerator() {
    for(int i=0; i < 26; i++) {
      if(i == 10) yield break; // stop iterator early
      yield return (char) (ch + i);
    }
  }
}

class ItrDemo3 {
  static void Main() {
    MyClass mc = new MyClass();

    foreach(char ch in mc)
      Console.Write(ch + " ");

    Console.WriteLine();
  }
}
```

The output is shown here:

A B C D E F G H I J

Using Multiple yield Directives

You can have more than one **yield** statement in an iterator. However, each **yield** must return the next element in the collection. For example, consider this program:

```
// Multiple yield statements are allowed.

using System;
using System.Collections;

class MyClass {
  // This iterator returns the letters
  // A, B, C, D, and E.
  public IEnumerator GetEnumerator() {
    yield return 'A';
    yield return 'B';
    yield return 'C';
    yield return 'D';
    yield return 'E';
  }
}

class ItrDemo5 {
  static void Main() {
    MyClass mc = new MyClass();

    foreach(char ch in mc)
      Console.Write(ch + " ");

    Console.WriteLine();
  }
}
```

The output is shown here:

```
A B C D E
```

Inside **GetEnumerator( )**, five yield statements occur. The important thing to understand is that they are executed one at a time, in order, each time another element in the collection is obtained. Thus, each time through the **foreach** loop in **Main( )**, one character is returned.

Creating a Named Iterator

Although the preceding examples have shown the easiest way to implement an iterator, there is an alternative: the named iterator. In this approach, you create a method, operator, or accessor that returns a reference to an **IEnumerable** object. Your code will use this object to supply the iterator. A named iterator is a method with the following general form:

```
public IEnumerable itr-name(param-list) {
  // ...
  yield return obj;

}
```

Here, *itr-name* is the name of the method, *param-list* specifies zero or more parameters that will be passed to the iterator method, and *obj* is the next object returned by the iterator. Once you have created a named iterator, you can use it anywhere that an iterator is needed. For example, you can use the named iterator to control a **foreach** loop.

Named iterators are very useful in some circumstances because they allow you to pass arguments to the iterator that control what elements are obtained. For example, you might pass the iterator the beginning and ending points of a range of elements to iterate. This form of iterator can also be overloaded, further adding to its flexibility. The following program illustrates two ways that a named iterator can be used to obtain elements. The first enumerates a range of elements given the endpoints. The second enumerates the elements beginning at the start of the sequence and ending at the specified stopping point.

```
// Use named iterators.

using System;
using System.Collections;

class MyClass {
  char ch = 'A';

  // This iterator returns the letters
  // of the alphabet, beginning at A and
  // stopping at the specified stopping point.
  public IEnumerable MyItr(int end) {
    for(int i=0; i < end; i++)
      yield return (char) (ch + i);
  }

  // This iterator returns the specified
  // range of letters.
  public IEnumerable MyItr(int begin, int end) {
    for(int i=begin; i < end; i++)
      yield return (char) (ch + i);
  }
}

class ItrDemo4 {
  static void Main() {
    MyClass mc = new MyClass();

    Console.WriteLine("Iterate the first 7 letters:");
    foreach(char ch in mc.MyItr(7))
      Console.Write(ch + " ");

    Console.WriteLine("\n");


    Console.WriteLine("Iterate letters from F to L:");
    foreach(char ch in mc.MyItr(5, 12))
      Console.Write(ch + " ");

    Console.WriteLine();
  }
}
```

The output is shown here:

```
Iterate the first 7 letters:
A B C D E F G

Iterate letters from F to L:
F G H I J K L
```

Creating a Generic Iterator

The preceding examples of iterators have been non-generic, but it is, of course, also possible to create generic iterators. Doing so is quite easy: Simply return an object of the generic **IEnumerator<T>** or **IEnumerable<T>** type. Here is an example that creates a generic iterator:

```
// A simple example of a generic iterator.

using System;
using System.Collections.Generic;

class MyClass<T> {
  T[] array;

  public MyClass(T[] a) {
    array = a;
  }

  // This iterator returns the characters
  // in the chrs array.
  public IEnumerator<T> GetEnumerator() {
    foreach(T obj in array)
      yield return obj;
  }
}

class GenericItrDemo {
  static void Main() {
    int[] nums = { 4, 3, 6, 4, 7, 9 };
    MyClass<int> mc = new MyClass<int>(nums);

    foreach(int x in mc)
      Console.Write(x + " ");

    Console.WriteLine();


    bool[] bVals = { true, true, false, true };
    MyClass<bool> mc2 = new MyClass<bool>(bVals);

    foreach(bool b in mc2)
      Console.Write(b + " ");

    Console.WriteLine();
  }
}
```

The output is shown here:

```
4 3 6 4 7 9
True True False True
```

In this example, the array containing the objects to be iterated is passed to **MyClass** through its constructor. The type of the array is specified as a type argument to **MyClass**. The **GetEnumerator( )** method operates on data of type **T** and returns an **IEnumerator<T>** enumerator. Thus, the iterator defined by **MyClass** can enumerate any type of data.

Collection Initializers

C# includes a feature called the *collection initializer*, which makes it easier to initialize certain collections. Instead of having to explicitly call **Add( )**, you can specify a list of initializers when a collection is created. When this is done, the compiler automatically calls **Add( )** for you, using these values. The syntax is similar to an array initialization. Here is an example. It creates a **List<char>** that is initialized with the characters C, A, E, B, D, and F.

```
List<char> lst = new List<char>() { 'C', 'A', 'E', 'B', 'D', 'F' };
```

After this statement executes, **lst.Count** will equal 6, because there are six initializers, and this **foreach** loop

```
foreach(ch in lst)
  Console.Write(ch + " ");
```

will display

```
C A E B D F
```

When using a collection such as **LinkedList<TKey, TValue>** that stores key/value pairs, you will need to supply pairs of initializers, as shown here:

```
SortedList<int, string> lst =
  new SortedList<int, string>() { {1, "One"}, {2, "Two" }, {3, "Three"} };
```

The compiler passes each group of values as arguments to **Add( )**. Thus, the first pair of initializers is translated into a call to **Add(1, "One")** by the compiler.

Because the compiler automatically calls **Add( )** to add initializers to a collection, collection initializers can be used only with collections that support a public implementation of **Add( )**. Therefore, collection initializers cannot be used with the **Stack**, **Stack<T>**, **Queue**, or **Queue<T>** collections because they don't support **Add( )**. You also can't use a collection initializer with a collection such as **LinkedList<T>**, which provides **Add( )** as an explicit interface implementation.

Networking Through the Internet Using System.Net

C# is a language designed for the modern computing environment, of which the Internet is, obviously, an important part. A main design criteria for C# was, therefore, to include those features necessary for accessing the Internet. Although earlier languages, such as C and C++, could be used to access the Internet, support server-side operations, download files, and obtain resources, the process was not as streamlined as most programmers would like. C# remedies that situation. Using standard features of C# and the .NET Framework, it is easy to "Internet-enable" your applications and write other types of Internet-based code.

Networking support is contained in several namespaces defined by the .NET Framework. The primary namespace for networking is **System.Net**. It defines a large number of high-level, easy-to-use classes that support the various types of operations common to the Internet. Several namespaces nested under **System.Net** are also provided. For example, low-level networking control through sockets is found in **System.Net.Sockets**. Mail support is found in **System.Net.Mail**. Support for secure network streams is found in **System.Net.Security**. Several other nested namespaces provide additional functionality. Another important networking-related namespace is **System.Web**. It (and its nested namespaces) supports ASP.NET-based network applications.

Although the .NET Framework offers great flexibility and many options for networking, for many applications, the functionality provided by **System.Net** is a best choice. It provides both convenience and ease-of-use. For this reason, **System.Net** is the namespace we will be using in this chapter.

The System.Net Members

System.Net is a large namespace that contains many members. It is far beyond the scope of this chapter to discuss them all or to discuss all aspects related to Internet programming. (In fact, an entire book is needed to fully cover networking in detail.) However, it is worthwhile to list the members of **System.Net** so you have an idea of what is available for your use.

The classes defined by **System.Net** are shown here:

AuthenticationManager	Authorization
Cookie	CookieCollection
CookieContainer	CookieException
CredentialCache	Dns
DnsEndPoint	DnsPermission
DnsPermissionAttribute	DownloadDataCompletedEventArgs
DownloadProgressChangedEventArgs	DownloadStringCompletedEventArgs
EndPoint	EndpointPermission
FileWebRequest	FileWebResponse
FtpWebRequest	FtpWebResponse
HttpListener	HttpListenerBasicIdentity
HttpListenerContext	HttpListenerException
HttpListenerPrefixCollection	HttpListenerRequest
HttpListenerResponse	HttpVersion
HttpWebRequest	HttpWebResponse
IPAddress	IPEndPoint
IPEndPointCollection	IPHostEntry
IrDAEndPoint	NetworkCredential
OpenReadCompletedEventArgs	OpenWriteCompletedEventArgs
ProtocolViolationException	ServicePoint
ServicePointManager	SocketAddress
SocketPermission	SocketPermissionAttribute
TransportContext	UploadDataCompletedEventArgs
UploadFileCompletedEventArgs	UploadProgressChangedEventArgs
UploadStringCompletedEventArgs	UploadValuesCompletedEventArgs
WebClient	WebException
WebHeaderCollection	WebPermission
WebPermissionAttribute	WebProxy
WebRequest	WebRequestMethods
WebRequestMethods.File	WebRequestMethods.Ftp
WebRequestMethods.Http	WebResponse
WebUtility	

System.Net defines the following interfaces:

IAuthenticationModule	ICertificatePolicy	ICredentialPolicy
ICredentials	ICredentialsByHost	IWebProxy
IWebProxyScript	IWebRequestCreate	

It defines these enumerations:

AuthenticationSchemes	DecompressionMethods	FtpStatusCode
HttpRequestHeader	HttpResponseHeader	HttpStatusCode
NetworkAccess	SecurityProtocolType	TransportType
WebExceptionStatus		

System.Net also defines several delegates.

Although **System.Net** defines many members, only a few are needed to accomplish most common Internet programming tasks. At the core of networking are the abstract classes **WebRequest** and **WebResponse**. These classes are inherited by classes that support a specific network protocol. (A *protocol* defines the rules used to send information over a network.) For example, the derived classes that support the standard HTTP protocol are **HttpWebRequest** and **HttpWebResponse**.

Even though **WebRequest** and **WebResponse** are easy to use, for some tasks, you can employ an even simpler approach based on **WebClient**. For example, if you only need to upload or download a file, then **WebClient** is often the best way to accomplish it.

Uniform Resource Identifiers

Fundamental to Internet programming is the Uniform Resource Identifier (URI). A *URI* describes the location of some resource on the network. A URI is also commonly called a *URL*, which is short for *Uniform Resource Locator*. Because Microsoft uses the term *URI* when describing the members of **System.Net**, this book will do so, too. You are no doubt familiar with URIs because you use one every time you enter an address into your Internet browser.

A URI has the following simplified general form:

Protocol:// HostName/FilePath?Query

Protocol specifies the protocol being used, such as HTTP. *HostName* identifies a specific server, such as mhprofessional.com or www.HerbSchildt.com. *FilePath* specifies the path to a specific file. If *FilePath* is not specified, the default page at the specified *HostName* is obtained. Finally, *Query* specifies information that will be sent to the server. *Query* is optional. In C#, URIs are encapsulated by the **Uri** class, which is examined later in this chapter.

Internet Access Fundamentals

The classes contained in **System.Net** support a request/response model of Internet interaction. In this approach, your program, which is the client, requests information from the server and then waits for the response. For example, as a request, your program might send to the server the URI of some website. The response that you will receive is the hypertext associated with that URI. This request/response approach is both convenient and simple to use because most of the details are handled for you.

The hierarchy of classes topped by **WebRequest** and **WebResponse** implement what Microsoft calls *pluggable protocols*. As most readers know, there are several different types of network communication protocols. The most common for Internet use is HyperText Transfer Protocol (HTTP). Another is File Transfer Protocol (FTP). When a URI is constructed, the prefix of the URI specifies the protocol. For example, http://www.HerbSchildt.com uses the prefix *http*, which specifies hypertext transfer protocol.

As mentioned earlier, **WebRequest** and **WebResponse** are abstract classes that define the general request/response operations that are common to all protocols. From them are derived concrete classes that implement specific protocols. Derived classes register themselves, using the static method **RegisterPrefix( )**, which is defined by **WebRequest**. When you create a **WebRequest** object, the protocol specified by the URI's prefix will automatically be used, if it is available. The advantage of this "pluggable" approach is that most of your code remains the same no matter what type of protocol you are using.

The .NET runtime defines the HTTP, HTTPS, file, and FTP protocols. Thus, if you specify a URI that uses the HTTP prefix, you will automatically receive the HTTP-compatible class that supports it. If you specify a URI that uses the FTP prefix, you will automatically receive the FTP-compatible class that supports it.

Because HTTP is the most commonly used protocol, it is the only one discussed in this chapter. (The same techniques, however, will apply to all supported protocols.) The classes that support HTTP are **HttpWebRequest** and **HttpWebResponse**. These classes inherit **WebRequest** and **WebResponse** and add several members of their own, which apply to the HTTP protocol.

System.Net supports both synchronous and asynchronous communication. For many Internet uses, synchronous transactions are the best choice because they are easy to use. With synchronous communications, your program sends a request and then waits until the response is received. For some types of high-performance applications, asynchronous communication is better. Using the asynchronous approach, your program can continue processing while waiting for information to be transferred. However, asynchronous communications are more difficult to implement. Furthermore, not all programs benefit from an asynchronous approach. For example, often when information is needed from the Internet, there is nothing to do until the information is received. In cases like this, the potential gains from the asynchronous approach are not realized. Because synchronous

Internet access is both easier to use and more universally applicable, it is the only type examined in this chapter.

Since **WebRequest** and **WebResponse** are at the heart of **System.Net**, they will be examined next.

WebRequest

The **WebRequest** class manages a network request. It is abstract because it does not implement a specific protocol. It does, however, define those methods and properties common to all requests. The commonly used methods defined by **WebRequest** that support synchronous communications are shown in Table 26-1. The properties defined by **WebRequest** are shown in Table 26-2. The default values for the properties are determined by derived classes. **WebRequest** defines no public constructors.

To send a request to a URI, you must first create an object of a class derived from **WebRequest** that implements the desired protocol. This can be done by calling **Create( )**, which is a **static** method defined by **WebRequest**. **Create( )** returns an object of a class that inherits **WebRequest** and implements a specific protocol.

Method	Description
public static WebRequest Create(string *requestUriString*)	Creates a **WebRequest** object for the URI specified by the string passed by *requestUriString*. The object returned will implement the protocol specified by the prefix of the URI. Thus, the object will be an instance of a class that inherits **WebRequest**. A **NotSupportedException** is thrown if the requested protocol is not available. A **UrlFormatException** is thrown if the URI format is invalid.
public static WebRequest Create(Uri *requestUri*)	Creates a **WebRequest** object for the URI specified by *requestUri*. The object returned will implement the protocol specified by the prefix of the URI. Thus, the object will be an instance of a class that inherits **WebRequest**. A **NotSupportedException** is thrown if the requested protocol is not available.
public virtual Stream GetRequestStream( )	Returns an output stream associated with the previously requested URI.
public virtual WebResponse GetResponse( )	Sends the previously created request and waits for a response. When a response is received, it is returned as a **WebResponse** object. Your program will use this object to obtain information from the specified URI.

TABLE 26-1   Commonly Used Methods Defined by **WebRequest** that Support Synchronous Communications

Property	Description
public AuthenticationLevel AuthenticationLevel(get; set; }	Obtains or sets the authentication level.
public virtual RequestCachePolicy CachePolicy { get; set; }	Obtains or sets the cache policy, which controls when a response can be obtained from the cache.
public virtual string ConnectionGroupName { get; set; }	Obtains or sets the connection group name. Connection groups are a way of creating a set of requests. They are not needed for simple Internet transactions.
public virtual long ContentLength { get; set; }	Obtains or sets the length of the content.
public virtual string ContentType { get; set; }	Obtains or sets the description of the content.
public virtual ICredentials Credentials { get; set; }	Obtains or sets credentials.
public static RequestCachePolicy DefaultCachePolicy { get; set; }	Obtains or sets the default cache policy, which controls when a request can be obtained from the cache.
public static IWebProxy DefaultWebProxy { get; set; }	Obtains or sets the default proxy.
public virtual WebHeaderCollection Headers{ get; set; }	Obtains or sets a collection of the headers.
public TokenImpersonationLevel ImpersonationLevel { get; set; }	Obtains or sets the impersonation level.
public virtual string Method { get; set; }	Obtains or sets the protocol.
public virtual bool PreAuthenticate { get; set; }	If true, authentication information is included when the request is sent. If false, authentication information is provided only when requested by the URI.
public virtual IWebProxy Proxy { get; set; }	Obtains or sets the proxy server. This applies only to environments in which a proxy server is used.
public virtual Uri RequestUri { get; }	Obtains the URI of the request.
public virtual int Timeout { get; set; }	Obtains or sets the number of milliseconds that a request will wait for a response. To wait forever, use **Timeout.Infinite**.
public virtual bool UseDefaultCredential { get; set; }	Obtains or sets a value that determines if default credentials are used for authentication. If true, the default credentials (i.e., those of the user) are used. They are not used if false.

TABLE 26-2 The Properties Defined by **WebRequest**

WebResponse

WebResponse encapsulates a response that is obtained as the result of a request. **WebResponse** is an abstract class. Inheriting classes create specific, concrete versions of it that support a protocol. A **WebResponse** object is normally obtained by calling the **GetResponse( )** method defined by **WebRequest**. This object will be an instance of a concrete class derived from

Method	Description
public virtual void Close( )	Closes the response. It also closes the response stream returned by **GetResponseStream( )**.
public virtual Stream GetResponseStream( )	Returns an input stream connected to the requested URI. Using this stream, data can be read from the URI.

TABLE 26-3   Commonly Used Methods Defined by **WebResponse**

WebResponse that implements a specific protocol. The methods defined by **WebResponse** used in this chapter are shown in Table 26-3. The properties defined by **WebResponse** are shown in Table 26-4. The values of these properties are set based on each individual response. **WebResponse** defines no public constructors.

HttpWebRequest and HttpWebResponse

The classes **HttpWebRequest** and **HttpWebResponse** inherit the **WebRequest** and **WebResponse** classes and implement the HTTP protocol. In the process, both add several properties that give you detailed information about an HTTP transaction. Some of these properties are used later in this chapter. However, for simple Internet operations, you will not often need to use these extra capabilities.

A Simple First Example

Internet access centers around **WebRequest** and **WebResponse**. Before we examine the process in detail, it will be useful to see an example that illustrates the request/response approach to Internet access. After you see these classes in action, it is easier to understand why they are organized as they are.

Property	Description
public virtual long ContentLength { get; set; }	Obtains or sets the length of the content being received. This will be –1 if the content length is not available.
public virtual string ContentType { get; set; }	Obtains or sets a description of the content.
public virtual WebHeaderCollection Headers { get; }	Obtains a collection of the headers associated with the URI.
public virtual bool IsFromCache { get; }	If the response came from the cache, this property is true. It is false if the response was delivered over the network.
public virtual bool IsMutuallyAuthenticated { get; }	If the client and server are both authenticated, then this property is true. It is false otherwise.
public virtual Uri ResponseUri { get; }	Obtains the URI that generated the response. This may differ from the one requested if the response was redirected to another URI.

TABLE 26-4   The Properties Defined by **WebResponse**

The following program performs a simple, yet very common, Internet operation. It obtains the hypertext contained at a specific website. In this case, the content of McGraw-Hill.com is obtained, but you can substitute any other website. The program displays the hypertext on the screen in chunks of 400 characters, so you can see what is being received before it scrolls off the screen.

```
// Access a website.

using System;
using System.Net;
using System.IO;

class NetDemo {
  static void Main() {
    int ch;

    // First, create a WebRequest to a URI.
    HttpWebRequest req = (HttpWebRequest)
          WebRequest.Create("http://www.McGraw-Hill.com");

    // Next, send that request and return the response.
    HttpWebResponse resp = (HttpWebResponse)
          req.GetResponse();

    // From the response, obtain an input stream.
    Stream istrm = resp.GetResponseStream();


    /* Now, read and display the html present at
       the specified URI. So you can see what is
       being displayed, the data is shown
       400 characters at a time. After each 400
       characters are displayed, you must press
       ENTER to get the next 400. */

    for(int i=1; ; i++) {
      ch =  istrm.ReadByte();
      if(ch == -1) break;
      Console.Write((char) ch);
      if((i%400)==0) {
        Console.Write("\nPress Enter.");
        Console.ReadLine();
      }
    }

    // Close the Response. This also closes istrm.
    resp.Close();
  }
}
```

The first part of the output is shown here. (Of course, over time this content will differ from that shown here.)

```
<html>
<head>
<title>Home - The McGraw-Hill Companies</title>
<meta name="keywords" content="McGraw-Hill Companies,McGraw-Hill, McGraw Hill,
Aviation Week, BusinessWeek, Standard and Poor's, Standard & Poor's,CTB/McGraw-
Hill,Glencoe/McGraw-Hill,The Grow Network/McGraw-Hill,Macmillan/McGraw-Hill,
McGraw-Hill Contemporary,McGraw-Hill Digital Learning,McGraw-Hill Professional
Development,SRA/McGraw

Press Enter.
-Hill,Wright Group/McGraw-Hill,McGraw-Hill Higher Education,McGraw-Hill/Irwin,
McGraw-Hill/Primis Custom Publishing,McGraw-Hill/Ryerson,Tata/McGraw-Hill,
McGraw-Hill Interamericana,Open University Press, Healthcare Information Group,
Platts, McGraw-Hill Construction, Information & Media Services" />
<meta name="description" content="The McGraw-Hill Companies Corporate Website." />
<meta http-equiv

Press Enter.
```

This is part of the hypertext associated with the McGraw-Hill.com website. Because the program simply displays the content character-by-character, it is not formatted as it would be by a browser; it is displayed in its raw form.

Let's examine this program line-by-line. First, notice the **System.Net** namespace is used. As explained, this is the namespace that contains the networking classes. Also notice that **System.IO** is included. This namespace is needed because the information from the website is read using a **Stream** object.

The program begins by creating a **WebRequest** object that contains the desired URI. Notice that the **Create( )** method, rather than a constructor, is used for this purpose. **Create( )** is a **static** member of **WebRequest**. Even though **WebRequest** is an abstract class, it is still possible to call a **static** method of that class. **Create( )** returns a **WebRequest** object that has the proper protocol "plugged in," based on the protocol prefix of the URI. In this case, the protocol is HTTP. Thus, **Create( )** returns an **HttpWebRequest** object. Of course, its return value must still be cast to **HttpWebRequest** when it is assigned to the **HttpWebRequest** reference called **req**. At this point, the request has been created, but not yet sent to the specified URI.

To send the request, the program calls **GetResponse( )** on the **WebRequest** object. After the request has been sent, **GetResponse( )** waits for a response. Once a response has been received, **GetResponse( )** returns a **WebResponse** object that encapsulates the response. This object is assigned to **resp**. Since, in this case, the response uses the HTTP protocol, the result is cast to **HttpWebResponse**. Among other things, the response contains a stream that can be used to read data from the URI.

Next, an input stream is obtained by calling **GetResponseStream( )** on **resp**. This is a standard **Stream** object, having all of the attributes and features of any other input stream. A reference to the stream is assigned to **istrm**. Using **istrm**, the data at the specified URI can be read in the same way that a file is read.

Next, the program reads the data from McGraw-Hill.com and displays it on the screen. Because there is a lot of information, the display pauses every 400 characters and waits for you to press ENTER. This way the first part of the information won't simply scroll off the screen. Notice that the characters are read using **ReadByte( )**. Recall that this method returns the next byte from the input stream as an **int**, which must be cast to **char**. It returns –1 when the end of the stream has been reached.

Finally, the response is closed by calling **Close( )** on **resp**. Closing the response stream automatically closes the input stream, too. It is important to close the response between each request. If you don't, it is possible to exhaust the network resources and prevent the next connection.

Before leaving this example, one other important point needs to be made: It was not actually necessary to use an **HttpWebRequest** or **HttpWebResponse** object to display the hypertext received from the server. Because the preceding program did not use any HTTP-specific features, the standard methods defined by **WebRequest** and **WebResponse** were sufficient to handle this task. Thus, the calls to **Create( )** and **GetResponse( )** could have been written like this:

```
// First, create a WebRequest to a URI.
WebRequest req =  WebRequest.Create("http://www.McGraw-Hill.com");

// Next, send that request and return the response.
WebResponse resp =  req.GetResponse();
```

In cases in which you don't need to employ a cast to a specific type of protocol implementation, it is better to use **WebRequest** and **WebResponse** because it allows protocols to be changed with no impact on your code. However, since all of the examples in this chapter will be using HTTP, and a few will be using HTTP-specific features, the programs will use **HttpWebRequest** and **HttpWebResponse**.

Handling Network Errors

Although the program in the preceding section is correct, it is not resilient. Even the simplest network error will cause it to end abruptly. Although this isn't a problem for the example programs shown in this chapter, it is something that must be avoided in real-world applications. To handle network exceptions that the program might generate, you must monitor calls to **Create( )**, **GetResponse( )**, and **GetResponseStream( )**. It is important to understand that the exceptions that can be generated depend upon the protocol being used. The following discussion describes several of the exceptions possible when using HTTP.

Exceptions Generated by Create( )

The **Create( )** method defined by **WebRequest** that is used in this chapter can generate four exceptions. If the protocol specified by the URI prefix is not supported, then **NotSupportedException** is thrown. If the URI format is invalid, **UriFormatException** is thrown. If the user does not have the proper authorization, a **System.Security.SecurityException** will be thrown. **Create( )** can also throw an **ArgumentNullException** if it is called with a null reference, but this is not an error generated by networking.

Exceptions Generated by GetReponse( )

A number of errors can occur when obtaining an HTTP response by calling **GetResponse( )**. These are represented by the following exceptions: **InvalidOperationException**, **ProtocolViolationException**, **NotSupportedException**, and **WebException**. Of these, the one of most interest is **WebException**.

WebException has two properties that relate to network errors: **Response** and **Status**. You can obtain a reference to the **WebResponse** object inside an exception handler through the **Response** property. For the HTTP protocol, this object describes the error. It is defined like this:

public WebResponse Response { get; }

When an error occurs, you can use the **Status** property of **WebException** to find out what went wrong. It is defined like this:

public WebExceptionStatus Status {get; }

WebExceptionStatus is an enumeration that contains the following values:

CacheEntryNotFound	ConnectFailure	ConnectionClosed
KeepAliveFailure	MessageLengthLimitExceeded	NameResolutionFailure
Pending	PipelineFailure	ProtocolError
ProxyNameResolutionFailure	ReceiveFailure	RequestCanceled
RequestProhibitedByCachePolicy	RequestProhibitedByProxy	SecureChannelFailure
SendFailure	ServerProtocolViolation	Success
Timeout	TrustFailure	UnknownError

Once the cause of the error has been determined, your program can take appropriate action.

Exceptions Generated by GetResponseStream( )

For the HTTP protocol, the **GetResponseStream( )** method of **WebResponse** can throw a **ProtocolViolationException**, which, in general, means that some error occurred relative to the specified protocol. As it relates to **GetResponseStream( )**, it means that no valid response stream is available. An **ObjectDisposedException** will be thrown if the response has already been disposed. Of course, an **IOException** could occur while reading the stream, depending on how input is accomplished.

Using Exception Handling

The following program adds handlers for network exceptions to the example shown earlier:

```
// Handle network exceptions.

using System;
using System.Net;
using System.IO;
```

```
class NetExcDemo {
  static void Main() {
    int ch;

    try {

      // First, create a WebRequest to a URI.
      HttpWebRequest req = (HttpWebRequest)
              WebRequest.Create("http://www.McGraw-Hill.com");

      // Next, send that request and return the response.
      HttpWebResponse resp = (HttpWebResponse)
              req.GetResponse();

      // From the response, obtain an input stream.
      Stream istrm = resp.GetResponseStream();

      /* Now, read and display the html present at
         the specified URI. So you can see what is
         being displayed, the data is shown
         400 characters at a time. After each 400
         characters are displayed, you must press
         ENTER to get the next 400. */

      for(int i=1; ; i++) {
        ch = istrm.ReadByte();
        if(ch == -1) break;
        Console.Write((char) ch);
        if((i%400)==0) {
          Console.Write("\nPress Enter.");
          Console.ReadLine();
        }
      }

      // Close the Response. This also closes istrm.
      resp.Close();

    } catch(WebException exc) {
      Console.WriteLine("Network Error: " + exc.Message +
                        "\nStatus code: " + exc.Status);
    } catch(ProtocolViolationException exc) {
      Console.WriteLine("Protocol Error: " + exc.Message);
    } catch(UriFormatException exc) {
      Console.WriteLine("URI Format Error: " + exc.Message);
    } catch(NotSupportedException exc) {
      Console.WriteLine("Unknown Protocol: " + exc.Message);
    } catch(IOException exc) {
      Console.WriteLine("I/O Error: " + exc.Message);
    } catch(System.Security.SecurityException exc) {
      Console.WriteLine("Security Exception: " + exc.Message);
    } catch(InvalidOperationException exc) {
      Console.WriteLine("Invalid Operation: " + exc.Message);
    }
  }
}
```

Now the network-based exceptions that the networking methods might generate have been caught. For example, if you change the call to **Create( )** as shown here,

```
WebRequest.Create("http://www.McGraw-Hill.com/moonrocket");
```

and then recompile and run the program, you will see this output:

```
Network Error: The remote server returned an error: (404) Not Found.
Status code: ProtocolError
```

Since the McGraw-Hill.com website does not have a directory called "moonrocket," this URI is not found, as the output confirms.

To keep the examples short and uncluttered, most of the programs in this chapter will not contain full exception handling. However, your real-world applications must.

The Uri Class

In Table 26-1, notice that **WebRequest.Create( )** has two different versions. One accepts the URI as a string. This is the version used by the preceding programs. The other takes the URI as an instance of the **Uri** class, which is defined in the **System** namespace. The **Uri** class encapsulates a URI. Using **Uri**, you can construct a URI that can be passed to **Create( )**. You can also dissect a **Uri**, obtaining its parts. Although you don't need to use **Uri** for many simple Internet operations, you may find it valuable in more sophisticated situations.

Uri defines several constructors. Two commonly used ones are shown here:

public Uri(string *uriString*)
public Uri(Uri *baseUri*, string *relativeUri*)

The first form constructs a **Uri** given a URI in string form. The second constructs a **Uri** by adding a relative URI specified by *relativeUri* to an absolute base URI specified by *baseUri*. An absolute URI defines a complete URI. A relative URI defines only the path.

Uri defines many fields, properties, and methods that help you manage URIs or that give you access to the various parts of a URI. Of particular interest are the properties shown here:

Property	Description
public string Host { get; }	Obtains the name of the server.
public string LocalPath { get; }	Obtains the local file path.
public string PathAndQuery { get; }	Obtains the absolute path and query string.
public int Port { get; }	Obtains the port number for the specified protocol. For HTTP, the port is 80.
public string Query { get; }	Obtains the query string.
public string Scheme { get; }	Obtains the protocol.

These properties are useful for breaking a URI into its constituent parts. The following program demonstrates their use:

```
// Use Uri.

using System;
using System.Net;
```

```
class UriDemo {
  static void Main() {

    Uri sample = new Uri("http://HerbSchildt.com/somefile.txt?SomeQuery");

    Console.WriteLine("Host: " + sample.Host);
    Console.WriteLine("Port: " + sample.Port);
    Console.WriteLine("Scheme: " + sample.Scheme);
    Console.WriteLine("Local Path: " + sample.LocalPath);
    Console.WriteLine("Query: " + sample.Query);
    Console.WriteLine("Path and query: " + sample.PathAndQuery);

  }
}
```

The output is shown here:

```
Host: HerbSchildt.com
Port: 80
Scheme: http
Local Path: /somefile.txt
Query: ?SomeQuery
Path and query: /somefile.txt?SomeQuery
```

Accessing Additional HTTP Response Information

When using **HttpWebResponse**, you have access to information other than the content of the specified resource. This information includes such things as the time the resource was last modified and the name of the server, and is available through various properties associated with the response. These properties, which include the six defined by **WebResponse**, are shown in Table 26-5. The following sections illustrate how to use representative samples.

Accessing the Header

You can access the header information associated with an HTTP response through the **Headers** property defined by **HttpWebResponse**. It is shown here:

public WebHeaderCollection Headers{ get; }

An HTTP header consists of pairs of names and values represented as strings. Each name/value pair is stored in a **WebHeaderCollection**. This specialized collection stores key/value pairs and can be used like any other collection. (See Chapter 25.) A **string** array of the names can be obtained from the **AllKeys** property. You can obtain the values associated with a name by calling the **GetValues( )** method. It returns an array of strings that contains the values associated with the header passed as an argument. **GetValues( )** is overloaded to accept a numeric index or the name of the header.

Property	Description
public string CharacterSet { get; }	Obtains the name of the character set being used.
public string ContentEncoding { get; }	Obtains the name of the encoding scheme.
public long ContentLength { get; }	Obtains the length of the content being received. This will be –1 if the content length is not available.
public string ContentType { get; }	Obtains a description of the content.
public CookieCollection Cookies { get; set; }	Obtains or sets a list of the cookies attached to the response.
public WebHeaderCollection Headers{ get; }	Obtains a collection of the headers attached to the response.
public bool IsFromCache { get; }	If the response came from the cache, this property is true. It is false if the response was delivered over the network.
public bool IsMutuallyAuthenticated { get; }	If the client and server are both authenticated, then this property is true. It is false otherwise.
public DateTime LastModified { get; }	Obtains the time at which the resource was last changed.
public string Method { get; }	Obtains a string that specifies the response method.
public Version ProtocolVersion { get; }	Obtains a **Version** object that describes the version of HTTP used in the transaction.
public Uri ReponseUri { get; }	Obtains the URI that generated the response. This may differ from the one requested if the response was redirected to another URI.
public string Server { get; }	Obtains a string that represents the name of the server.
public HttpStatusCode StatusCode { get; }	Obtains an **HttpStatusCode** object that describes the status of the transaction.
public string StatusDescription { get; }	Obtains a string that represents the status of the transaction in a human-readable form.

TABLE 26-5   The Properties Defined by **HttpWebResponse**

The following program displays headers associated with McGraw-Hill.com:

```
// Examine the headers.

using System;
using System.Net;

class HeaderDemo {
  static void Main() {

    // Create a WebRequest to a URI.
    HttpWebRequest req = (HttpWebRequest)
        WebRequest.Create("http://www.McGraw-Hill.com");
```

```
    // Send that request and return the response.
    HttpWebResponse resp = (HttpWebResponse)
        req.GetResponse();

    // Obtain a list of the names.
    string[] names = resp.Headers.AllKeys;

    // Display the header name/value pairs.
    Console.WriteLine("{0,-20}{1}\n", "Name", "Value");
    foreach(string n in names) {
      Console.Write("{0,-20}", n);
      foreach(string v in resp.Headers.GetValues(n))
        Console.WriteLine(v);
    }

    // Close the Response.
    resp.Close();
  }
}
```

Here is the output that was produced. (Remember, all header information is subject to change, so the precise output that you see may differ.)

```
Name                Value

Transfer-encoding   chunked
Content-Type        text/html
Date                Sun, 06 Dec 2009 20:32:06 GMT
Server              Sun-ONE-Web-Server/6.1
```

Accessing Cookies

You can gain access to the cookies associated with an HTTP response through the **Cookies** property defined by **HttpWebResponse**. Cookies contain information that is stored by a browser. They consist of name/value pairs, and they facilitate certain types of web access. The **Cookies** property is defined like this:

public CookieCollection Cookies { get; set; }

CookieCollection implements **ICollection** and **IEnumerable** and can be used like any other collection. (See Chapter 25.) It has an indexer that allows a cookie to be obtained by specifying its index or its name.

CookieCollection stores objects of type **Cookie**. **Cookie** defines several properties that give you access to the various pieces of information associated with a cookie. The two that we will use here are **Name** and **Value**, which are defined like this:

public string Name { get; set; }
public string Value { get; set; }

The name of the cookie is contained in **Name**, and its value is found in **Value**.

To obtain a list of the cookies associated with a response, you must supply a cookie container with the request. For this purpose, **HttpWebRequest** defines the property **CookieContainer**, shown here:

public CookieContainer CookieContainer { get; set; }

CookieContainer provides various fields, properties, and methods that let you store cookies. By default, this property is null. To use cookies, you must set it equal to an instance of the **CookieContainer** class. For many applications, you won't need to work with the **CookieContainer** property directly. Instead, you will use the **CookieCollection** obtained from the response. **CookieContainer** simply provides the underlying storage mechanism for the cookies.

The following program displays the names and values of the cookies associated with the URI specified on the command line. Remember, not all websites use cookies, so you might have to try a few until you find one that does.

```
/* Examine Cookies.

   To see what cookies a website uses,
   specify its name on the command line.
   For example, if you call this program
   CookieDemo, then

     CookieDemo http://msn.com

   displays the cookies associated with msn.com.
*/

using System;
using System.Net;

class CookieDemo {
  static void Main(string[] args) {

    if(args.Length != 1) {
      Console.WriteLine("Usage: CookieDemo <uri>");
      return ;
    }

    // Create a WebRequest to the specified URI.
    HttpWebRequest req = (HttpWebRequest)
          WebRequest.Create(args[0]);

    // Get an empty cookie container.
    req.CookieContainer = new CookieContainer();

    // Send the request and return the response.
    HttpWebResponse resp = (HttpWebResponse)
          req.GetResponse();

    // Display the cookies.
    Console.WriteLine("Number of cookies: " +
                      resp.Cookies.Count);
    Console.WriteLine("{0,-20}{1}", "Name", "Value");

    for(int i=0; i < resp.Cookies.Count; i++)
      Console.WriteLine("{0, -20}{1}",
                        resp.Cookies[i].Name,
                        resp.Cookies[i].Value);
```

```
      // Close the Response.
      resp.Close();
    }
}
```

Using the LastModified Property

Sometimes you will want to know when a resource was last updated. This is easy to find out when using **HttpWebResponse** because it defines the **LastModified** property. It is shown here:

public DateTime LastModified { get; }

LastModified obtains the time that the content of the resource was last modified.

The following program displays the time and date at which the URI entered on the command-line site was last updated:

```
/* Use LastModified.

   To see the date on which a website was
   last modified, enter its URI on the command
   line. For example, if you call this program
   LastModifiedDemo, then to see the date of last
   modification for HerbSchildt.com enter

     LastModifiedDemo http://www.HerbSchildt.com
*/

using System;
using System.Net;

class LastModifiedDemo {
  static void Main(string[] args) {

    if(args.Length != 1) {
      Console.WriteLine("Usage: LastModifiedDemo <uri>");
      return ;
    }

    HttpWebRequest req = (HttpWebRequest)
          WebRequest.Create(args[0]);

    HttpWebResponse resp = (HttpWebResponse)
          req.GetResponse();

    Console.WriteLine("Last modified: " + resp.LastModified);

    resp.Close();
  }
}
```

MiniCrawler: A Case Study

To show how easy **WebRequest** and **WebReponse** make Internet programming, a skeletal web crawler called MiniCrawler will be developed. A *web crawler* is a program that moves from link to link to link. Search engines use web crawlers to catalog content. MiniCrawler is, of course, far less sophisticated than those used by search engines. It starts at the URI that you specify and then reads the content at that address, looking for a link. If a link is found, it then asks if you want to go to that link, search for another link on the existing page, or quit. Although this scheme is quite simple, it does provide an interesting example of accessing the Internet using C#.

MiniCrawler has several limitations. First, only absolute links that are specified using the **href="http** hypertext command are found. Relative links are not used. Second, there is no way to go back to an earlier link. Third, it displays only the links and no surrounding content. Despite these limitations, the skeleton is fully functional, and you will have no trouble enhancing MiniCrawler to perform other tasks. In fact, adding features to MiniCrawler is a good way to learn more about the networking classes and networking in general.

Here is the entire code for MiniCrawler:

```
/* MiniCrawler: A skeletal Web crawler.

   Usage:
     To start crawling, specify a starting
     URI on the command line. For example,
     to start at McGraw-Hill.com use this
     command line:

       MiniCrawler http://McGraw-Hill.com

*/

using System;
using System.Net;
using System.IO;

class MiniCrawler {

  // Find a link in a content string.
  static string FindLink(string htmlstr,
                         ref int startloc) {
    int i;
    int start, end;
    string uri = null;

    i = htmlstr.IndexOf("href=\"http", startloc,
                        StringComparison.OrdinalIgnoreCase);
    if(i != -1) {
      start = htmlstr.IndexOf('"', i) + 1;
```

```
      end = htmlstr.IndexOf('"', start);
      uri = htmlstr.Substring(start, end-start);
      startloc = end;
    }

    return uri;
  }

  static void Main(string[] args) {
    string link = null;
    string str;
    string answer;

    int curloc; // holds current location in response

    if(args.Length != 1) {
      Console.WriteLine("Usage: MiniCrawler <uri>");
      return ;
    }

    string uristr = args[0]; // holds current URI

    HttpWebResponse resp = null;

    try {

      do {
        Console.WriteLine("Linking to " + uristr);

        // Create a WebRequest to the specified URI.
        HttpWebRequest req = (HttpWebRequest)
             WebRequest.Create(uristr);

        uristr = null; // disallow further use of this URI

        // Send that request and return the response.
        resp = (HttpWebResponse) req.GetResponse();

        // From the response, obtain an input stream.
        Stream istrm = resp.GetResponseStream();

        // Wrap the input stream in a StreamReader.
        StreamReader rdr = new StreamReader(istrm);

        // Read in the entire page.
        str = rdr.ReadToEnd();

        curloc = 0;

        do {
          // Find the next URI to link to.
          link = FindLink(str, ref curloc);

          if(link != null) {
            Console.WriteLine("Link found: " + link);
```

```
        Console.Write("Link, More, Quit?");
        answer = Console.ReadLine();

        if(string.Equals(answer, "L",
           StringComparison.OrdinalIgnoreCase)) {
          uristr = string.Copy(link);
          break;
        } else if(string.Equals(answer, "Q",
                  StringComparison.OrdinalIgnoreCase)) {
          break;
        } else if(string.Equals(answer, "M",
                  StringComparison.OrdinalIgnoreCase)) {
          Console.WriteLine("Searching for another link.");
        }
      } else {
        Console.WriteLine("No link found.");
        break;
      }

    } while(link.Length > 0);

    // Close the Response.
    if(resp != null) resp.Close();
  } while(uristr != null);

} catch(WebException exc) {
  Console.WriteLine("Network Error: " + exc.Message +
                    "\nStatus code: " + exc.Status);
} catch(ProtocolViolationException exc) {
  Console.WriteLine("Protocol Error: " + exc.Message);
} catch(UriFormatException exc) {
  Console.WriteLine("URI Format Error: " + exc.Message);
} catch(NotSupportedException exc) {
  Console.WriteLine("Unknown Protocol: " + exc.Message);
} catch(IOException exc) {
  Console.WriteLine("I/O Error: " + exc.Message);
} finally {
  if(resp != null) resp.Close();
}

Console.WriteLine("Terminating MiniCrawler.");
  }
}
```

Here is a short sample session that begins crawling at McGraw-Hill.com. (Remember, the precise output will vary over time as content changes.)

```
Linking to http://mcgraw-hill.com
Link found: http://sti.mcgraw-hill.com:9000/cgi-bin/query?mss=search&pg=aq
Link, More, Quit? M
Searching for another link.
Link found: http://investor.mcgraw-hill.com/phoenix.zhtml?c=96562&p=irol-irhome
Link, More, Quit? L
Linking to http://investor.mcgraw-hill.com/phoenix.zhtml?c=96562&p=irol-irhome
Link found: http://www.mcgraw-hill.com/index.html
```

```
Link, More, Quit? L
Linking to http://www.mcgraw-hill.com/index.html
Link found: http://sti.mcgraw-hill.com:9000/cgi-bin/query?mss=search&pg=aq
Link, More, Quit? Q
Terminating MiniCrawler.
```

Let's take a close look at how MiniCrawler works. The URI at which MiniCrawler begins is specified on the command line. In **Main( )**, this URI is stored in the string called **uristr**. A request is created to this URI and then **uristr** is set to null, which indicates that this URI has already been used. Next, the request is sent and the response is obtained. The content is then read by wrapping the stream returned by **GetResponseStream( )** inside a **StreamReader** and then calling **ReadToEnd( )**, which returns the entire contents of the stream as a string.

Using the content, the program then searches for a link. It does this by calling **FindLink( )**, which is a **static** method also defined by **MiniCrawler**. **FindLink( )** is called with the content string and the starting location at which to begin searching. The parameters that receive these values are **htmlstr** and **startloc**, respectively. Notice that **startloc** is a **ref** parameter. **FindLink( )** looks for a substring that matches **href="http**, which indicates a link. If a match is found, the URI is copied to **uri**, and the value of **startloc** is updated to the end of the link. Because **startloc** is a **ref** parameter, this causes its corresponding argument to be updated in **Main( )**, enabling the next search to begin where the previous one left off. Finally, **uri** is returned. Since **uri** was initialized to null, if no match is found, a null reference is returned, which indicates failure.

Back in **Main( )**, if the link returned by **FindLink( )** is not null, the link is displayed, and the user is asked what to do. The user can go to that link by pressing L, search the existing content for another link by pressing M, or quit the program by pressing Q. If the user presses L, the link is followed and the content of the link is obtained. The new content is then searched for a link. This process continues until all potential links are exhausted.

You might find it interesting to increase the power of MiniCrawler. For example, you might try adding the ability to follow relative links. (This is not hard to do.) You might try completely automating the crawler by having it go to each link that it finds without user interaction. That is, starting at an initial page, have it go to the first link it finds. Then, in the new page, have it go to the first link and so on. Once a dead-end is reached, have it backtrack one level, find the next link, and then resume linking. To accomplish this scheme, you will need to use a stack to hold the URIs and the current location of the search within a URI. One way to do this is to use a **Stack** collection. As an extra challenge, try creating tree-like output that displays the links.

Using WebClient

Before concluding this chapter, a brief discussion of **WebClient** is warranted. As mentioned near the start of this chapter, if your application only needs to upload or download data to or from the Internet, then you can use **WebClient** instead of **WebRequest** and **WebResponse**. The advantage to **WebClient** is that it handles many of the details for you.

WebClient defines one constructor, shown here:

public WebClient( )

WebClient defines the properties shown in Table 26-6. **WebClient** defines a large number of methods that support both synchronous and asynchronous communication. Because asynchronous communication is beyond the scope of this chapter, only those methods that support synchronous requests are shown in Table 26-7. All methods throw a **WebException** if an error occurs during transmission.

Property	Description
public string BaseAddress { get; set; }	Obtains or sets the base address of the desired URI. If this property is set, then relative addresses specified by the **WebClient** methods will be relative to the base address.
public RequestCachePolicy CachePolicy { get; set; }	Obtains or sets the policy that determines when the cache is used.
public ICredentials Credentials { get; set; }	Obtains or sets authentication information. This property is null by default.
public Encoding Encoding { get; set; }	Obtains or sets the character encoding used while transferring strings.
public WebHeaderCollection Headers{ get; set; }	Obtains or sets the collection of the request headers.
public bool IsBusy(get; }	If the request is still transferring information, this property is true. It is false otherwise.
public IWebProxy Proxy { get; set; }	Obtains or sets the proxy.
public NameValueCollection QueryString { get; set; }	Obtains or sets a query string consisting of name/value pairs that can be attached to a request. The query string is separated from the URI by a **?**. If more than one name/value pair exists, then an **&** separates each pair.
public WebHeaderCollection ResponseHeaders{ get; }	Obtains a collection of the response headers.
public bool UseDefaultCredentials { get; set; }	Obtains or sets a value that determines if default credentials are used for authentication. If true, the default credentials (i.e., those of the user) are used. They are not used if false.

TABLE 26-6   The Properties Defined by **WebClient**

Method	Description
public byte[ ] DownloadData(string *address*)	Downloads the information at the URI specified by *address* and returns the result in an array of bytes.
public byte[ ] DownloadData(Uri *address*)	Downloads the information at the URI specified by *address* and returns the result in an array of bytes.
public void DownloadFile(string *address*, string *fileName*)	Downloads the information at the URI specified by *address* and stores the result in the file specified by *fileName*.
public void DownloadFile(Uri *address*, string *fileName*)	Downloads the information at the URI specified by *address* and stores the result in the file specified by *fileName*.
public string DownloadString(string *address*)	Downloads the information at the URI specified by *address* and returns the result as a **string**.
public string DownloadString(Uri *address*)	Downloads the information at the URI specified by *address* and returns the result as a **string**.
public Stream OpenRead(string *address*)	Returns an input stream from which the information at the URI specified by *address* can be read. This stream must be closed after reading is completed.
public Stream OpenRead(Uri *address*)	Returns an input stream from which the information at the URI specified by *address* can be read. This stream must be closed after reading is completed.
public Stream OpenWrite(string *address*)	Returns an output stream to which information can be written to the URI specified by *address*. This stream must be closed after writing is completed.
public Stream OpenWrite(Uri *address*)	Returns an output stream to which information can be written to the URI specified by *address*. This stream must be closed after writing is completed.
public Stream OpenWrite(string *address*, string *method*)	Returns an output stream to which information can be written to the URI specified by *address*. This stream must be closed after writing is completed. The string passed in *method* specifies how the information will be written.
public Stream OpenWrite(Uri *address*, string *method*)	Returns an output stream to which information can be written to the URI specified by *address*. This stream must be closed after writing is completed. The string passed in *method* specifies how the information will be written.
public byte[ ] UploadData(string *address*, byte[ ] *data*)	Writes the information specified by *data* to the URI specified by *address*. The response is returned.
public byte[ ] UploadData(Uri *address*, byte[ ] *data*)	Writes the information specified by *data* to the URI specified by *address*. The response is returned.
public byte[ ] UploadData(string *address*, string *method*, byte[ ] *data*)	Writes the information specified by *data* to the URI specified by *address*. The response is returned. The string passed in *method* specifies how the information will be written.

TABLE 26-7   The Synchronous Methods Defined by **WebClient**

Method	Description
public byte[ ] UploadData(Uri *address*, string *method*, byte[ ] *data*)	Writes the information specified by *data* to the URI specified by *address*. The response is returned. The string passed in *method* specifies how the information will be written.
public byte[ ] UploadFile(string *address*, string *fileName*)	Writes the information in the file specified by *fileName* to the URI specified by *address*. The response is returned.
public byte[ ] UploadFile(Uri *address*, string *fileName*)	Writes the information in the file specified by *fileName* to the URI specified by *address*. The response is returned.
public byte[ ] UploadFile(string *address*, string *method*, string *fileName*)	Writes the information in the file specified by *fileName* to the URI specified by *address*. The response is returned. The string passed in *method* specifies how the information will be written.
public byte[ ] UploadFile(Uri *address*, string *method*, string *fileName*)	Writes the information in the file specified by *fileName* to the URI specified by *address*. The response is returned. The string passed in *method* specifies how the information will be written.
public string UploadString(string *address*, string *data*)	Writes *data* to the URI specified by *address*. The response is returned.
public string UploadString(Uri *address*, string *data*)	Writes *data* to the URI specified by *address*. The response is returned.
public string UploadString(string *address*, string *method*, string *data*)	Writes *data* to the URI specified by *address*. The response is returned. The string passed in *method* specifies how the information will be written.
public string UploadString(Uri *address*, string *method*, string *data*)	Writes *data* to the URI specified by *address*. The response is returned. The string passed in *method* specifies how the information will be written.
public byte[ ] UploadValues(string *address*, NameValueCollection *data*)	Writes the values in the collection specified by *data* to the URI specified by *address*. The response is returned.
public byte[ ] UploadValues(Uri *address*, NameValueCollection *data*)	Writes the values in the collection specified by *data* to the URI specified by *address*. The response is returned.
public byte[ ] UploadValues(string *address*, string *method*, NameValueCollection *data*)	Writes the values in the collection specified by *data* to the URI specified by *address*. The response is returned. The string passed in *method* specifies how the information will be written.
public byte[ ] UploadValues(Uri *address*, string *method*, NameValueCollection *data*)	Writes the values in the collection specified by *data* to the URI specified by *address*. The response is returned. The string passed in *method* specifies how the information will be written.

TABLE 26-7   The Synchronous Methods Defined by **WebClient** *(continued)*

The following program demonstrates how to use **WebClient** to download data into a file:

```
// Use WebClient to download information into a file.

using System;
using System.Net;
using System.IO;

class WebClientDemo {
  static void Main() {
    WebClient user = new WebClient();
    string uri = "http://www.McGraw-Hill.com";
    string fname = "data.txt";

    try {
      Console.WriteLine("Downloading data from " +
                        uri + " to " + fname);
      user.DownloadFile(uri, fname);
    } catch (WebException exc) {
      Console.WriteLine(exc);
    }

    user.Dispose();

    Console.WriteLine("Download complete.");
  }
}
```

This program downloads the information at McGrawHill.com and puts it into a file called **data.txt**. Notice how few lines of code are involved. By changing the string specified by **uri**, you can download information from any URI, including specific files.

Although **WebRequest** and **WebResponse** give you greater control and access to more information, **WebClient** is all that many applications will need. It is particularly useful when all you need to do is download information from the Web. For example, you might use **WebClient** to allow an application to obtain documentation updates.

Documentation Comment Quick Reference

C# supports three types of comments. The first two are // and /* */. The third type is based on XML tags and is called a *documentation comment*. (The term *XML comment* is also commonly used.) A single-line documentation comment begins with ///. A multiline documentation comment begins with /** and ends with */.

Documentation comments precede the declaration of such things as classes, namespaces, methods, properties, and events. Using documentation comments, you can embed information about your program into the program itself. When you compile the program, you can have the documentation comments placed into an XML file. Documentation comments can also be utilized by the IntelliSense feature of Visual Studio.

The XML Comment Tags

C# supports the XML documentation tags shown in Table A-1. Most of the XML comment tags are readily understandable, and they work like all other XML tags with which most programmers are already familiar. However, the **<list>** tag is more complicated than the others. A list contains two components: a list header and list items. The general form of a list header is shown here:

```
<listheader>
  <term> name </term>
  <description> text </description>
</listheader>
```

Here, *text* describes *name*. For a table, *text* is not used. The general form of a list item is shown next:

```
<item>
  <term> item-name </term>
  <description> text </description>
</item>
```

Here, *text* describes *item-name*. For bulleted or numbered lists or tables, *item-name* is not used. There can be multiple **<item>** entries.

Tag	Description
<c> *code* </c>	Specifies the text specified by *code* as program code.
<code> *code* </code>	Specifies multiple lines of text specified by *code* as program code.
<example> *explanation* </example>	The text associated with e*xplanation* describes a code example.
<exception cref = "*name*"> *explanation* </exception>	Describes an exception. The exception is specified by *name*.
<include file = '*fname*' path = '*path* [@*tagName* = "*tagID* "]' />	Specifies a file that contains the XML comments for the current file. The file is specified by *fname*. The path to the tag, the tag name, and the tag ID are specified by *path*, *tagName*, and *tagID*, respectively.
<list type = "*type*""> *list-header* *list-items* </list>	Specifies a list. The type of the list is specified by *type*, which must be either bullet, number, or table.
<para> *text* </para>	Specifies a paragraph of text within another tag.
<param name = '*param-name*'> *explanation* </param>	Documents the parameter specified by *param-name*. The text associated with e*xplanation* describes the parameter.
<paramref name = "*param-name*" />	Specifies that *param-name* is a parameter name.
<permission cref = "*identifier*"> *explanation* </permission>	Describes the permission setting associated with the class members specified by *identifier*. The text associated with e*xplanation* describes the permission settings.
<remarks> *explanation* </remarks>	The text specified by *explanation* is a general commentary often used to describe a type, such as a class or structure.
<returns> *explanation* </returns>	The text specified by *explanation* documents the return value of a method.
<see cref = "*identifier*" />	Declares a link to another element specified by *identifier*.
<seealso cref = "*identifier*" />	Declares a "see also" link to *identifier*.
<summary> *explanation* </summary>	The text specified by *explanation* is a general commentary often used to describe a method or other class member.
<typeparam name = "*param-name*"> *explanation* </typeparam>	Documents the type parameter specified by *param-name*. The text associated with e*xplanation* describes the type parameter.
<typeparamref name = "*param-name*"/>	Specifies that *param-name* is the name of a type parameter.

TABLE A-1 The XML Comment Tags

Compiling Documentation Comments

To produce an XML file that contains the documentation comments, specify the **/doc** option. For example, to compile a file called **DocTest.cs** that contains XML comments, use this command line:

```
csc DocTest.cs /doc:DocTest.xml
```

To create an XML output file when using the Visual Studio IDE, you must activate the Properties page. Next, select Build. Then, check the XML Documentation File box and specify the name of the XML file.

An XML Documentation Example

Here is an example that demonstrates several documentation comments. It uses both the multiline and the single-line forms. As a point of interest, many programmers use a series of single-line documentation comments rather than a multiline comment even when a comment spans several lines. (Several of the comments in this example use this approach.) The advantage is that it clearly identifies each line in a longer documentation comment as being part of a documentation comment. This is, of course, a stylistic issue, but it is common practice.

```
// A documentation comment example.

using System;

/** <remark>
 This is an example of multiline XML documentation.
 The Test class demonstrates several tags.
</remark>
*/

class Test {
  /// <summary>
  /// Main is where execution begins.
  /// </summary>
  static void Main() {
    int sum;

    sum = Summation(5);
    Console.WriteLine("Summation of " + 5 + " is " + sum);
  }

  /// <summary>
  /// Summation returns the summation of its argument.
  /// <param name = "val">
  /// The value to be summed is passed in val.
  /// </param>
  /// <see cref="int"> </see>
  /// <returns>
  /// The summation is returned as an int value.
  /// </returns>
  /// </summary>
  static int Summation(int val) {
    int result = 0;

    for(int i=1; i <= val; i++)
      result += i;

    return result;
  }
}
```

Assuming the preceding program is called **XmlTest.cs**, the following line will compile the program and produce a file called **XmlTest.xml** that contains the comments:

```
csc XmlTest.cs /doc:XmlTest.xml
```

After compiling, the following XML file is produced:

```xml
<?xml version="1.0"?>
<doc>
    <assembly>
        <name>DocTest</name>
    </assembly>
    <members>
        <member name="T:Test">
            <remark>
             This is an example of multiline XML documentation.
             The Test class demonstrates several tags.
            </remark>
        </member>
        <member name="M:Test.Main">
            <summary>
            Main is where execution begins.
            </summary>
        </member>
        <member name="M:Test.Summation(System.Int32)">
            <summary>
            Summation returns the summation of its argument.
            <param name="val">
            The value to be summed is passed in val.
            </param>
            <see cref="T:System.Int32"> </see>
            <returns>
            The summation is returned as an int value.
            </returns>
            </summary>
        </member>
    </members>
</doc>
```

Notice that each documented element is given a unique identifier. These identifiers can be used by other programs that use the XML documentation.

Index